ORIGEN:
CONTRA CELSUM

ORIGEN:
CONTRA CELSUM

TRANSLATED
WITH AN INTRODUCTION & NOTES
BY

HENRY CHADWICK

CAMBRIDGE UNIVERSITY PRESS

CAMBRIDGE

LONDON NEW YORK NEW ROCHELLE
MELBOURNE SYDNEY

PUBLISHED BY THE PRESS SYNDICATE OF THE UNIVERSITY OF CAMBRIDGE
The Pitt Building, Trumpington Street, Cambridge, United Kingdom

CAMBRIDGE UNIVERSITY PRESS
The Edinburgh Building, Cambridge CB2 2RU, UK
40 West 20th Street, New York NY 10011- 4211, USA
477 Williamstown Road, Port Melbourne, VIC 3207, Australia
Ruiz de Alarcón 13, 28014 Madrid, Spain
Dock House, The Waterfront, Cape Town 8001, South Africa

http://www.cambridge.org

First published 1953
Reprinted with corrections 1965
First paperback edition 1980

A catalogue record for this book is available from the British Library

ISBN 0 521 05866 x hardback
ISBN 0 521 29576 9 paperback

Transferred to digital printing 2003

PREFATORY NOTE TO THE 1965 REPRINT

The reprinting of this book gives a necessarily restricted opportunity for small changes. There are rare additions in the commentary. Three books published since 1953 call for special mention. The first is Jean Scherer's fine edition of the seventh century papyrus from Tura, *Extraits des Livres I et II du Contre Celse d'Origène d'après le papyrus no. 88747 de Musée du Caire* (Institut français d'archéologie orientale, Bibliothèque d'étude, XXVIII, 1956). The papyrus shows that the Vatican manuscript has suffered minor losses here and there, and that the biblical quotations are better preserved in the Philocalia tradition; but it gives good ground for general confidence in the tradition represented by the Vatican text. The places where the translation is affected by the improved text that the papyrus makes possible are extremely rare. In *J.T.S.* new series viii (1957), pp. 322–326, I have discussed and attempted to meet some of the arguments advanced by Professor Scherer about the authority of the corrections in the Vatican manuscript.

Secondly the achievement of Celsus as a whole has been admirably treated by Carl Andresen, *Logos und Nomos: Die Polemik des Kelsos wider das Christentum* (Arbeiten zur Kirchengeschichte, 30, 1955). Although reserved towards some of his language about Celsus' philosophy of history or 'Geschichtssystematik', I think there is probability in his thesis that Celsus has Justin in mind and is formulating a rejoinder to his proposals for a marriage between Christianity and Platonism and a divorce between the best Greek philosophy and the old polytheistic tradition. It is in any event a masterly study.

Thirdly, on a point of detail, one complex passage about the knowledge of God (VII, 43–44) has been illuminated by Fr. A.-J. Festugière in the fourth volume of his *magnum opus*, *La Révélation d'Hermès Trismégiste*, IV *Le Dieu inconnu et la gnose* (1954).

On particular questions, however, enlargement of the commentary has not been possible. Occasionally, citations from Celsus are more clearly marked. Attention may be drawn to the obscure passage in II, 6–7 where Origen meets the charges (*a*) that Jesus kept the Jewish Law, and (*b*) that he was 'arrogant, deceitful and profane'. I now think that everything becomes clear if Celsus had put the question, 'If Jesus' intention was to abolish the Mosaic Law, why did he observe it? It was deceitful to keep it if he wanted to do away with it, and arrogant and profane to treat in this way the sacred and ancient traditions of the Jewish people.' Origen leaves out more of Celsus' text than may appear at first sight, but it is sometimes possible to conjecture with probability at the lost words or ideas.

The bibliography remains unaltered. On Origen's work as a whole the best bibliography for work up to 1958 is given by H. Crouzel, *Origène et la 'Connaissance Mystique'* (1959). Fr. Crouzel has occasion to treat parts of the *contra Celsum* both there and in his more recent *Origène et la Philosophie* (1961). H.C.

CHRIST CHURCH
OXFORD
September 1964

POSTSCRIPT (1979)

In this third printing of a work first published more than 25 years ago I have introduced minor changes affecting both translation and notes, the more important being in I, 10–11; II, 78; VIII, 75. Among a number of weighty contributions to the study of Origen's work, special mention must be made of Marcel Borret's full edition and annotated translation in the series Sources Chrétiennes, in five volumes (1967–76). The variant readings of the Tura papyrus are recorded in his apparatus criticus. A forthcoming study of the text is announced by Pierre Nautin in his important revision of the biography of Origen (*Origène, sa vie et son œuvre,* 1977). A full critical bibliography of Origen has been published by Henri Crouzel (The Hague, 1971). I have discussed the broad intellectual and religious context of Celsus and Origen in *Early Christian Thought and the Classical Tradition* (Oxford, 1966).

H.C.

CONTENTS

INTRODUCTION

I. PHILOSOPHICAL BACKGROUND

There are perhaps few works of the early Christian Church which compare in interest or in importance with that which is here translated. The *contra Celsum* stands out as the culmination of the whole apologetic movement of the second and third centuries. The apostolic church had not included among its members many wise or many mighty, and as Christianity spread it was natural enough that some attempts should be made to make this Oriental faith, which had not the merit of great antiquity behind it, into a creed which could be found acceptable by thinking minds. The Apologists have in view two closely related objects. They hope to assure the Roman authorities that Christians are not a pernicious and unpatriotic minority group with seditious tendencies and immoral rites; and they want to present Christianity to the educated classes as something intellectually respectable. In the work of Origen it is primarily the latter desire which is uppermost. What he gives us in the *contra Celsum* is not merely a refutation point by point of a remarkably well-informed opponent. The apology also helps us to see both the arguments which Origen would have used when engaged in disputation with learned pagans at Alexandria or Caesarea, and the way in which he himself in his own mind could be satisfied that Christianity was not an irrational credulity but a profound philosophy.

Origen stands upon the shoulders of his predecessors who made his achievement a possibility. Although he never mentions him, he owed much to Clement; even if it cannot now be taken as certain that Origen was his pupil,[1] nevertheless he had certainly read his works and absorbed his point of view. He is considerably indebted to such predecessors as Justin, Tatian, Theophilus, and Athenagoras, not for detailed arguments, but for having so to speak constructed a platform for his own apologetic. All of them had taken over the traditional apologetic for Judaism which had been developed in the hellenistic synagogue. From this they took the contention that Moses and the prophets could be proved to be earlier than the Greek philosophers and poets, and therefore must have been the source of their learning,[2] so that all the mysteries of Greek philosophy are therefore to be found expressed, even if obscurely, in the Pentateuch;

---

[1] Cf. J. Munck, *Untersuchungen über Klemens von Alexandria (Forschungen zur Kirchen- und Geistesgeschichte* 2, Stuttgart, 1933), pp. 224–9.

[2] Cf. *c. Cels.* IV, 39; VI, 19.

from the same source they could borrow the defence of an absolute monotheism over against the pagan arguments by which polytheism was
rationalized. All this in turn became part of the regular stock-in-trade
of the Christian Apologist as much as it had been that of his Jewish
predecessor.

To no less an extent were the Apologists indebted to the debates
between the various schools of Greek philosophy in the hellenistic period.
The Stoics had undertaken the defence and rationalization of the traditional religion: oracles and the practice of divination were indeed a necessary
corollary of the existence of divine providence; the Homeric gods and the
whole pantheon could be so discreetly allegorized as to make it possible
for a philosophical mind to continue to worship according to the tradition
of his fathers without the disturbance of an undue number of mental
reservations. On the other hand the Academy, the successors of Plato,
who had made such offensive comments on the morality of the Homeric
gods and had even gone so far as to expel the ancient poet from his ideal
state, developed almost into a professional opposition to all Stoic doctrines
and, in particular, to the Stoic defence of the traditional cultus. The
Academy, especially as led by the brilliant debater Carneades in the middle
of the second century B.C., the force of whose destructive criticisms is
apparent from Cicero's writings, thus built up an arsenal of argument
against the cultus of the anthropomorphic and immoral deities of Homer
and the poets; and upon this arsenal both Jewish and Christian Apologists
were not slow to draw. The arguments become quite stereotyped in the
tradition: for example, the Cretans say that they have the tomb of Zeus—
how then can Zeus be a god if he is dead? The Egyptians worship animals,
cats, crocodiles, monkeys, and indeed a whole divine menagerie; could
anything be more degrading or absurd? These and many other such
arguments are preserved in the Academic polemic contained in Cicero's
work *On the Nature of the Gods* and in Lucian of Samosata, and they
reappear with unfailing constancy in one apologist after another. They
recur in Origen.

In truth, the Stoa and the Academy had provided arguments and
counter-arguments on a wide range of subjects, with the result that we
frequently find that where Celsus shows affinity with the Academy,
Origen has only to fall back on the traditional refutation provided by the
Stoics, and vice versa. If Celsus takes one side in the debate, Origen will
usually take the other. An example of this occurs at the end of the fourth
book where Celsus ridicules as naïve the Christian belief that the people
of God are the aim and centre of the creation and that the world was made
for them; Celsus develops here a long attack on the view that the world

exists for the sake of man any more than for the irrational animals. His arguments are almost certainly lifted straight out of some tractate deriving from the Academic tradition which contained a polemic against the Stoic doctrine that the animals exist for the sake of mankind. Origen's reply is simply based on the traditional Stoic answer to the Academy.[1]

Partly in consequence of this continual reference to the debates of the hellenistic philosophical schools the *contra Celsum* is of high interest not merely to the historian of the Christian Church, but also to the student of hellenistic philosophy. In respect of some Stoic doctrines it has been observed that they are first made intelligible by Origen's comments thereon.[2] He is well read in the works of Chrysippus and is particularly interested in the arguments about providence, and about fate and free will. He drew freely on the traditional theodicy used by the Stoics to defend their doctrine of *pronoia*.[3] Like several other contemporary Platonists his philosophical affinities are mainly with the eclectic type of Platonism which emerges in the later hellenistic period, a type of thought which felt itself to stand fundamentally in the Platonic tradition in its theology and *Weltanschauung*, but which, partly unconsciously, absorbed much of the Stoic conception of ethics and of providence. Even such Platonists of the second century A.D. as Plutarch, Atticus, and Calvisius Taurus, who are concerned to purify Platonism from the dilution and perversion resulting from fusion with Aristotelian and Stoic doctrines, are indebted to the Stoa in spite of themselves.

Popular philosophy under the Empire was in fact thoroughly impregnated with Stoicism, and the essential concern of the school with ethical problems enabled the Church to come to terms with it to a remarkable degree. So it is that Tertullian in his famous phrase can speak of *Seneca saepe noster*. Platonic metaphysics were the peculiar study of the few, of an intellectual aristocracy, while there was an immediate popular appeal about the simple ethical exhortations of Epictetus' discourses, as Origen himself tells us (*c. Cels.* VI, 2). The philosopher of the period was not expected to concern himself with an abstract and detached search for metaphysical truth, but rather with practical ethical questions; his vocation is that of a missionary; he is a physician of souls, whose ideal for himself and his fellow-men is summed up in the Platonic phrase 'likeness to God as far as possible' (*Theaet.* 176B). For Origen in particular, the Stoics made a considerable contribution to his theology by their defence of the doctrine of providence. The Epicureans admittedly believed in gods,

[1] Cf. my remarks in *J.T.S.* XLVIII (Jan. 1947), at pp. 36f.
[2] Cf. H. von Arnim, *Stoicorum Veterum Fragmenta*, 1 (1905), Praef. pp. xlvif.
[3] Cf. Karl Gronau, *Das Theodizeeproblem in der altchristlichen Auffassung* (1922).

beings in human form compounded of atoms, dwelling in the spaces
between the worlds, who discussed Epicurean philosophy in a language
very like Greek; but these gods took no interest whatever in earthly
affairs. The Peripatetics only believed in a limited sphere of divine
providence and denied that it operated at all in the region below the moon.
As against these the Stoics firmly asserted the reality of providence. To
those who asked hard questions about the reasons for the suffering of the
righteous and the prosperity of the wicked, or why the best people are
killed in wars,[1] the Stoic affirmed his faith in the ultimate purpose of the
divine *pronoia* immanent in the cosmos. Even things in nature apparently
useless or worse all had their place. When Chrysippus was asked, 'What
is the use of bugs?' he could reply that 'They prevent us from sleeping too
long.'[2] And if suffering were caused to individuals, yet it was possible to
believe that providence cares for the whole and must put that before the
well-being of the individual person (cf. IV, 70).

To deal thoroughly with Origen's debt to the philosophical background
would demand much extended discussion which would be out of place in
this introduction; but so much may be said to make the controversy with
Celsus appear in its historical setting. In the *contra Celsum* Origen does
not merely vindicate the character of Jesus and the credibility of the
Christian tradition; he also shows that Christians can be so far from being
irrational and credulous illiterates such as Celsus thinks them to be that
they may know more about Greek philosophy than the pagan Celsus
himself, and can make intelligent use of it to interpret the doctrines of the
Church. In the range of his learning he towers above his pagan adversary,
handling the traditional arguments of Academy and Stoa with masterly
ease and fluency. He saw clearly how the principles involved in these
debates could be used to illuminate the discussion of Christian theology.
So, for example, his well-known criticisms of the traditional Church
doctrine of the resurrection of the flesh are in fact nothing more than
a slight modification of the arguments used by the Academy against the
anthropomorphism of the Epicurean notion of the gods.[3] And even his
famous illustration, which passed through numerous ecclesiastical writers
down the centuries (even to appear in Luther's ninety-five theses), comparing the unity of the divine and human natures in Christ to the unity of
red-hot iron in the fire where the iron and the fire become indistinguishable
from one another, was borrowed from Chrysippus himself who used it to
explain the way in which the soul permeated the body in every part.[4] It is

[1] Cf. Epicurus in Lactantius, *Div. Inst.* III, 17, 8 (= *frag.* 370 Usener).
[2] Plutarch, *Moralia*, 1044D.   [3] I have argued this in *H.T.R.* XLI (1948), pp. 83–102.
[4] Cf. *J.T.S. loc. cit.* pp. 39–40; also *J.T.S.* (n.s.), II (1951), at pp. 160ff.

worth noting also that the idea which has been described as his most notable contribution to Christian theology, the concept of the eternal generation of the Son and the formulation of the famous phrase which was to play so prominent a part in the Arian controversy—οὐκ ἦν ποτὲ ὅτε οὐκ ἦν—was but an adaptation of the language and argument used by contemporary Platonists in discussing the problem of the eternity of the cosmos.[1]

Such illustrations of Origen's method help to make clear his historical significance. In spite of his apparent opposition to philosophy as identified with paganism and the polytheistic tradition, his whole position is informed by a philosophical approach, the influence of which on his mind he himself was perhaps inclined to underestimate. Recent studies have laid emphasis on the religious and mystical side of Origen,[2] as opposed to the intellectualist and philosophical aspect. That Origen was a 'mystic' is perhaps doubtful; but that his whole attitude was fundamentally religious is no doubt true. This explains why in the preface of the *contra Celsum* he feels it necessary to apologise to his readers for undertaking such a rational defence at all, and tells Ambrose his patron that he regards it as unnecessary to argue the matter. The *contra Celsum*, in fact, brings into prominence one side of Origen's work and shows him diverted from his central task of Biblical exegesis and textual criticism into the line of apologetic. It seems that the subsequent influence of the work on the Church was not very great; what the Church absorbed from Origen was felt primarily in the sphere of Biblical interpretation and in the profound influence of his ideals of the spiritual life upon later monasticism. But in the history of the intellectual struggle between the old and the new religion the *contra Celsum* is of the first importance, comparable only with Augustine's *City of God*. For whereas to Celsus writing about seventy years earlier the majority of Christians seemed to be stupid and uneducated fools, if they were not knaves, with Origen Christians and pagans met intellectually on equal terms.

[1] See Hal Koch, *Pronoia und Paideusis: Studien über Origenes und sein Verhältnis zum Platonismus* (Berlin and Leipzig, 1932), pp. 259–61.

[2] W. Völker, *Das Vollkommenheitsideal des Origenes* (Tübingen, 1931), criticized by Koch, *op. cit.* pp. 330 ff.; A. Lieske, *Die Theologie der Logos-Mystik bei Origenes* (Münster, 1938); J. Daniélou, *Origène* (Paris, 1948); H. de Lubac, *Histoire et Esprit: L'Intelligence de l'Écriture d'après Origène* (Paris, 1950); F. Bertrand, *Mystique de Jésus chez Origène* (Paris, 1951); J. Lebreton, 'La source et le caractère de la mystique d'Origène', in *Anal. Boll.* LXVII (1949), pp. 55–62.

II. DATE OF THE CONTRA CELSUM

All discussion of the date of Origen's work must begin from the statement
of Eusebius (*H.E.* VI, 36, 2) that during the reign of Philip the Arabian
(A.D. 244–9) when Origen was over sixty years of age (i.e. after 245) 'he
wrote the eight treatises in reply to the work of Celsus the Epicurean
entitled *The True Doctrine*'. Eusebius puts this in the same period as the
great commentary on St Matthew and that on the twelve minor prophets.

The internal evidence is coherent with this notice in Eusebius, and
points to a date earlier than the outbreak of the Decian persecution. First,
Origen says that the Church has been enjoying a long period of peace
(III, 15 ad init.), and that, because the deaths of the martyrs defeat the
power of the evil daemons, the daemons have not been too keen to return
to the struggle, so that until they forget the suffering which they have
brought on themselves the world will probably remain at peace with the
Church (VIII, 44 ad init.; cf. VIII, 70, Koetschau II, 287, 10). During this
long period of peace the Church has expanded and increased to become
a vast multitude (VII, 26).

Secondly, in the course of the work Origen refers to his commentaries
on the Bible, such as his commentary on Genesis (IV, 37, 39; VI, 49, 51, 60),
an early work written mainly in his Alexandrian period; his commentaries
on Isaiah, Ezekiel, and some of the minor prophets (VII, 11) which fall in
the period between 238 and 244;[1] and his commentary on the Epistle to
the Romans (V, 47; VIII, 65) which was probably composed during the
period 244–7.[2] These references again substantiate the information offered
by Eusebius.

Thirdly, in III, 15 Origen says that although the Church has had peace
for a long time, nevertheless 'it is probable that the freedom of believers
from anxiety for their lives will come to an end when again those who
attack Christianity in every possible way regard the multitude of believers
as responsible for the revolt which is so strong at this moment, because
they are not being persecuted by the governors as they were formerly'.
In the year 248 the Arabian emperor was faced with three usurpers in the
Empire. The Pannonian armies set up Pacatianus as a rival emperor;
on the borders of Cappadocia and Syria there appeared Jotapianus
as a claimant, and in Syria itself Uranius Antoninus.[3] It is at least

---

[1] Cf. A. von Harnack, *Geschichte der altchristlichen Litteratur bis Eusebius*, II (*Die Chronologie*), ii, p. 34.

[2] The commentary is often dated exactly in 246, but the evidence is quite insufficient.

[3] Cf. W. Ensslin in *Camb. Anc. Hist.* XII (1939), p. 92; M. Rostovtzeff in *Berytus*, VIII, fasc. 1 (1943), at p. 31; A. T. Olmstead in *Class. Philol.* XXXVII (1942), pp. 261 f.

a probability that Origen has this in mind when he refers to ἡ ἐπὶ τοσοῦτο νῦν στάσις. Evidently contemporary pagans were saying that the trouble was caused by the fact that nothing was being done to persecute the Christians. It is well known that public calamities were usually put to the account of the Christians, as Tertullian complains in a famous passage (*Apol.* XL, 1–2) 'quod existiment omnis publicae cladis, omnis popularis incommodi primordio [a primordio, *Waltzing*] temporum Christianos esse in causa. Si Tiberis ascendit in moenia, si Nilus non ascendit in rura, si caelum stetit, si terra movit, si fames, si lues, statim "Christianos ad leonem".' The persecution in Asia Minor under Maximinus Thrax in 235 was a direct consequence of severe earthquakes in Cappadocia and Pontus according to the testimony of Firmilian of Caesarea (in Cyprian, *Ep.* LXXV, 10). And Origen refers elsewhere to this common pagan attitude.[1]

It has been suggested[2] that the occasion of Origen's work was the celebration of Rome's millennium in 247–8, a reminder to all citizens of the Empire that the greatness of Rome had depended on the goodwill of the gods who had been propitious. If the *contra Celsum* was Origen's reply to these celebrations, then the work can be dated precisely to 248. But there is no reference to this anywhere in the work, and no reliance can be put on this argument. In any event it is not certain that the celebrations were the cause of the Decian persecution. The occasion of this seems not to have been the restoration of the *pax deorum* so much as the result of Decius' demand for sacrifice as an act of loyalty to the emperor and of his attempt by this means to achieve some unity in the Empire in face of the tremendous crisis of the time.[3] It is difficult to say what effect the millennium had on the public mind, and whether this effect extended much into the provinces. Harnack rejects Neumann's attempt to date the *contra Celsum* in 248 exactly, and prefers to leave the question open within the period from 246 to 248,[4] but he is perhaps inclined to underestimate the evidence of III, 15 (quoted above) which suggests that Origen is writing on the eve of a persecution, the imminence of which is already apparent to those with eyes to see.[5]

---

[1] Origen, *in Matt. Comm. Ser.* 39. Cf. note on III, 15.

[2] K. J. Neumann, *Der römische Staat und die allgemeine Kirche bis auf Diocletian*, I (1890), p. 273.

[3] Cf. A. Alföldi, 'Zu den Christenverfolgungen in der Mitte des 3. Jahrhunderts', in *Klio*, XXXI (1938), pp. 323–48. He summarizes his view in *Camb. Anc. Hist.* XII (1939), pp. 202 ff. Cf. N. H. Baynes in *ibid.* pp. 656f.

[4] *Op. cit.* II, p. 35 n. 4, p. 51 n. 6.

[5] In the Commentary on St Matthew (XIII, 23), written about the same time as the *contra Celsum* (Eus. *H.E.* VI, 36, 2), Origen observes that the daemons are furious because they are now deprived of Sacrifices. Evidently anti-Christian feeling was rising.

III. CELSUS' THEOLOGY

Celsus begins his assault upon Christianity by observing that, because the Church is a secret society, it is an illegal body which ought not to exist. The Christian associations violate the common law. What, then, are the characteristics of this powerful secret society with its firm coherence in face of common dangers? 'The doctrine was originally barbarian.' That in the eyes of a Greek is something to be placed on the debit side for a start. Celsus' respect for the Platonic tradition (*Epinomis*, 987 E) leads him to admit that the barbarians have indeed discovered sound doctrines; the pre-eminence of the Greeks lies in the fact that they have interpreted them philosophically and understood them better.

Nevertheless, the barbarian nations are of theological importance to Celsus. 'There is an ancient doctrine which has existed from the beginning, which has always been maintained by the wisest nations and cities and wise men' (I, 14). This ancient tradition has been handed down among the Egyptians, Assyrians, Indians, Persians, Odrysians, Samothracians, Eleusinians, and Hyperboreans.[1] Among the wise men are included 'inspired theologians' such as Linus, Musaeus, and Orpheus,[2] together with Pherecydes, Zoroaster, and Pythagoras.

But what does Celsus conceive as being the content of this ancient tradition which, in his view, the Christians have abandoned and corrupted?

Some seventy years or so before Celsus' time the travelling philosopher and orator, Dio of Prusa, speaks in his Olympic oration of the way in which men first attained their knowledge of the gods, as follows:

Now concerning the nature of the gods in general, and especially that of the ruler of the universe, first and foremost an idea regarding him and a conception of him common to the whole human race, to the Greeks and to the barbarians alike, a conception that is inevitable and innate in every creature endowed with reason, arising in the course of nature without the aid of human teacher and free from the deceit of any expounding priest, has made its way, and it rendered

---

[1] For the popular hellenistic notion that races living in remote places or dating from remote antiquity were extremely pious, cf. the remarks of A. Dieterich, *Nekyia* (1893), pp. 35 f.; W. L. Knox, *Some Hellenistic Elements in Primitive Christianity* (1944), p. 16 n. 3. Numenius (ap. Eus. *P.E.* IX, 7, 411 c) similarly holds that the tradition of Plato and Pythagoras is in concord with the traditions of the famous nations (τὰ ἔθνη τὰ εὐδοκιμοῦντα), the Brahmans, Jews, Magi, and Egyptians. Cf. H. C. Puech, 'Numénius d'Apamée et les théologies orientales au IIe siècle', in *Mélanges Bidez* (1934), pp. 745–78. For the appeal to barbarian cosmogonies, cf. A. D. Nock in *Journ. Rom. Stud.* XXVII (1937), p. 111, quoting Damascius. The interest in Persian and Indian philosophy which Ammonius Saccas aroused in Plotinus led him to join Gordian's army against Persia (Porphyry, *Vita Plot.* III).

[2] For the importance of these cf. Plato, *Apol.* 41 A. For Celsus' appeal to their authority, VI, 42, 80; VII, 28, 45, 58. Musaeus and Linus were said to have been the first to be inspired by the gods: Cosmas Hieros., *ad Carm. S. Greg. Theol.* 64, 243 (Migne, *P.G.* XXXVIII, 496).

manifest God's kinship with man and furnished many evidences of the truth, which did not suffer the earliest and most ancient men to doze and grow indifferent to them.[1]

Here is a notion of the way men first acquired knowledge of God which admittedly is more coloured by Stoicism than the theology found in Celsus. But it throws some light on what Celsus thought he meant by an 'ancient doctrine which has existed from the beginning'. In the theology of the hellenistic age it has become possible to harmonize a continued acceptance of the old polytheism with a kind of monotheism. The one God was felt to be manifested in different forms in nature—in water, air, earth, and fire, said the Stoics. The Platonic tradition since the time of Xenocrates in the latter part of the fourth century B.C. had thought of the popular gods as intermediate between the supreme God and man. They were 'daemons'. It was not a long step to affirm that in the local deities of each nation there were to be found subordinate administrators of the one supreme God. Such a conception underlies Celsus' declaration that 'it makes no difference whether we call Zeus the Most High, or Zen, or Adonai, or Sabaoth, or Amoun like the Egyptians, or Papaeus like the Scythians' (v, 45). 'The gods are one nature, but many names', remarks Celsus' contemporary, the Platonizing sophist Maximus of Tyre; it is only from ignorance that we give God different names in accordance with the various benefits he confers on us. The ocean is one, but has various parts, such as the Aegean or the Ionian sea. So also the good is one, and it is only through lack of insight and of knowledge that we divide it up.[2]

'The one doctrine upon which all the world is united', says the same Maximus in another discourse, 'is that one God is king of all and father, and that there are many gods, sons of God, who rule together with God. This is believed by both the Greek and the barbarian.'[3]

For such a theology monotheism and polytheism are not mutually exclusive. And so the philosophers have come to provide a method of rationalizing cultus offered to any number of deities. All such worship is offered ultimately to the one supreme God; but it reaches him by being offered through his subordinates, the local deities. In the short tractate

---

[1] Dio Chrysostom, *Orat.* xii, 27 (trans. J. W. Cohoon, Loeb Class. Libr.); cf. *ibid.* 39 for ἡ ἔμφυτος ἅπασιν ἀνθρώποις ἐπίνοια...παρὰ πᾶσι τοῖς ἔθνεσιν ἀρξαμένη καὶ διαμένουσα. Similarly Clement, *Protr.* xxv, 3 ἦν δέ τις ἔμφυτος ἀρχαία πρὸς οὐρανὸν ἀνθρώποις κοινωνία.

[2] Max. Tyr. xxxix, 5. Cf. Dio Chrys. xxxi, 11 'Some say that Apollo, Helios, and Dionysus are the same god, as indeed you also think; and many maintain that all the gods are simply one particular force and power so that it makes no difference whether one worships this one or that one.'

[3] *Idem* ii, 5. Cf. Plotinus, v, 8, 9–10.

Concerning the World,[1] which became included in the Aristotelian corpus (its indebtedness to Posidonius has been much canvassed), we find an interesting attempt by a philosopher strongly influenced by later Stoicism to combine a belief in a transcendent supreme Deity with belief in numerous subordinate powers. The writer feels that it is unseemly for the supreme King of the universe to be involved in the petty details of its administration.

It is therefore better, even as it is more seemly and befitting God, to suppose that the power which is stablished in the heavens is the cause of permanence even in those things which are furthest removed from it—in a word, in all things—rather than to hold that it passed forth and travels to and fro to places which become and befit it not, and personally administers the affairs of this earth. For indeed, to superintend any and every operation does not become even the rulers among mankind—the chief, for example, of an army or a city, or the head of a household, if it were necessary to bind up a sack of bedding or perform any other somewhat menial task, such as in the days of the Great King [of Persia] would not be performed by any ordinary slave.

The writer continues by developing at length his comparison of God with the Persian Great King. Every department of State had its appointed head with a hierarchy of subordinates below him.

All the Empire of Asia, bounded on the west by the Hellespont and on the east by the Indus, was apportioned according to races among generals and satraps and subject-princes of the Great King; and there were couriers and watchmen and messengers and superintendents of signal-fires. So effective was the organization, in particular the system of signal-fires, which formed a chain of beacons from the furthest bounds of the empire to Susa and Ecbatana, that the king received the same day the news of all that was happening in Asia.

If, therefore, the dignity of Xerxes and Darius was so great as this, must not the majesty of the supreme God be even greater?

If it was beneath the dignity of Xerxes to appear himself to administer all things and to carry out his own wishes and superintend the government of his kingdom, such functions would be still less becoming for God.

God, the writer suggests, is like a marionette-showman.[2] He has only to pull a single string, and the chain of consequences duly follows.

The comparison of God with the Great King of Persia could be used on the other side of the theological controversy. Philo, the learned Jew of Alexandria, has an interesting polemic against the pagan worship offered to beings subordinate to God.

---

[1] In what follows I am indebted to the evidence assembled by E. Peterson, *Der Monotheismus als politisches Problem* (1935). I have used E. S. Forster's translation of the *De Mundo* (1914).

[2] For this figure cf. Synesius, *de Providentia*, IX (Migne, *P.G.* LXVI, 1228 B), and J. H. Waszink's commentary on Tertullian, *de Anima*, VI, 3 (pp. 136–7).

Just as anyone who rendered to the subordinate satraps the honours due to the Great King would have seemed to reach the heights not only of unwisdom but of foolhardiness, by bestowing on servants what belonged to their master, in the same way anyone who pays the same tribute to the creatures as to their Maker may be assured that he is the most senseless and unjust of men in that he gives equal measure to those who are not equal, though he does not thereby honour the meaner many but deposes the superior.[1]

Even by the time of Philo, therefore, it was evidently common enough to justify polytheistic practice by pleading that the local deities are as it were God's provincial administrators and governors. In the second century A.D. the notion is widespread. In the orations of the neurotic valetudinarian Aelius Aristides, we learn that Zeus appoints administrators for the various regions of the world, like governors and satraps—οἶον ὕπαρχοί τινες καὶ σατράπαι.[2] It is on this basis that Celsus develops his argument for polytheism. 'The satrap and subordinate governor or officer or procurator of the Persian or Roman emperor, and, furthermore, even those who hold lesser positions or responsibilities or offices, could do much harm if they were slighted. Would the satraps and ministers both in the air and on the earth do but little harm if they were insulted?'[3]

Accordingly, for monotheism Celsus has little to say. The origins of monotheism, he thinks, are that 'Moses heard of this doctrine which was current among the wise nations and distinguished men and acquired a name for divine power' (I, 21). As all pagans knew, Moses was an expert magician. And so, 'the goatherds and shepherds who followed Moses as their leader were deluded by clumsy deceits into thinking that there was only one God called the Most High, or Adonai, or the Heavenly One, or Sabaoth, or however they like to call this world; and they acknowledged nothing more' (I, 23–4). The Christians are even worse. They reject the worship of daemons and quote the saying of Jesus, 'No man can serve two masters.' But this for Celsus is 'a rebellious utterance of people who wall themselves off and break away from the rest of mankind' (VIII, 2). What is more, the fantastic respect shown by the Christians for this Jew who was crucified a few years back shows just how seriously they take all their talk about serving only one master. 'If these men worshipped no other God but one, perhaps they would have had a valid argument against the others. But in fact they worship to an

---

[1] Philo, de Decal. 61 (trans. F. H. Colson).

[2] Aelius Aristides, Orat. XLIII, 18 (Keil II, 343, 26).

[3] Celsus in VIII, 35. For further material, Cumont, Les Religions orientales dans le paganisme romain (4th ed. 1929), p. 299 n. 21, and to the references there given add Prudentius, Apotheosis, 186 ff.; Maximus of Madaura in Augustine, Ep. XVI (C.S.E.L. XXXIV, 37 ff.).

extravagant degree this man who appeared recently, and yet think it is not inconsistent with monotheism if they also worship his servant' (VIII, 12).

Celsus' respect for tradition and the custom of antiquity comes out in several passages. For the Jews he shares all the contempt and hostility which was characteristic of the age. But one thing could be said in their favour. Even if they had abandoned the belief in many gods and only worshipped their own God as if he were the only one, at any rate they did worship in accordance with the customs of their fathers. 'Their worship may be very peculiar, but is at least traditional' (V, 25). Each nation ought to observe its own traditions of worship, whatever they may be. For they accord with the wish of the daemon in charge of the nation. *Cuius regio eius religio.*[1] 'The practices done by each nation are right when they are done in the way that pleases the overseers; and it is impious to abandon the customs which have existed in each locality from the beginning.' The Jews are thus not entirely without defence. But not so the Christians. 'I will ask them where they have come from, or who is the author of their traditional laws. Nobody, they will say' (V, 33). The Christians have no authority for their doctrine, which is a perversion and caricature of the ancient tradition (V, 65).

That the Christians have corrupted ancient tradition is a leading theme in Celsus' book.[2] Christian notions of hell misunderstand the ancient beliefs about judgment beneath the earth (III, 16). Their ethical teaching is borrowed from other philosophers (I, 4). Their idea of humility grossly misunderstands the teaching of Plato (*Laws*, 715 E), and Jesus' saying that it is hard for a rich man to enter into the kingdom of God corrupts the doctrine of Plato, *Laws*, 743 A (VI, 15–16). Again the idea of 'the kingdom of God' is taken from the Platonic saying 'God is King of all' (*Epist.* 312 E); the belief that God is in heaven misunderstands *Phaedrus*, 247 B (VI, 18–20). The Christian belief in seven heavens is frankly plagiarized from the Mithraic mysteries (VI, 21 ff.). The fantastic notion of Satan is a misunderstanding of 'the divine enigmas', hinted at in ancient writers like Heraclitus, Pherecydes, and Homer, and symbolized in the myths of the Titans, of Osiris and Typhon, and in the festival of the Panathenaia (VI, 42–3). Even the title 'Son of God' which they give to Jesus is taken from the ancient manner of referring to the world as God's

---

[1] The Jewish idea that each nation is under an angel is used by Origen in V, 30 ff. For discussion, cf. E. Peterson, 'Das Problem des Nationalismus im alten Christentum', in *Theol. Zeits.* VII (1951), pp. 81–91; J. Daniélou, 'Les sources juives de la doctrine des anges des nations chez Origène', in *Rech. de science religieuse* XXXVIII (1951), pp. 132–7. For Clement of Alexandria, cf. *Strom.* VII, 6, 4. Also Iamblichus, *de Myst.* V, 24–5.

[2] This has been admirably emphasized by A. Wifstrand, 'Die wahre Lehre des Kelsos' in *Bull. Soc. Roy. Lund* (1941–2), pp. 391–431.

child (VI, 47). Their belief in heaven as a place of bliss is only taken from the ancient belief in the Islands of the Blest or the Elysian Fields (VII, 28). Their teaching about non-resistance to evil plagiarizes Plato's *Crito*, 49 B–E (VII, 58). Their refusal to tolerate images and temples and altars is derived from the Scythians, Libyans, and Persians, if it is not a misunderstanding of an obscure saying of Heraclitus (VII, 62). If they say that God is a spirit, even that is simply borrowed from the Stoics (VI, 71).

It is this ancient tradition which is for Celsus *The True Doctrine*, ἀληθὴς λόγος as he entitles his work. The title itself has a strongly Platonic ring. In support of the view that it is Platonizing, Bader refers to Plato, *Epist*. VII, 342 A, which Celsus quotes in VI, 9.[1] Wifstrand is able to quote a still more likely source in *Meno*, 81 A, where Socrates says: ἀκήκοα γὰρ ἀνδρῶν τε καὶ γυναικῶν σοφῶν περὶ τὰ θεῖα πράγματα. – Meno: τίνα λόγον λεγόντων; – Socrates: ἀληθῆ, ἔμοιγε δοκεῖν, καὶ καλόν. Socrates goes on to speak of the content of this 'true doctrine', which concerns the immortality of the soul.[2]

Accordingly Celsus believes that there is a true doctrine, of the greatest antiquity, held by the most ancient and pious races and the wisest of men. It has been perverted or misunderstood first by the Jews, and then by the Christians, who are only an offshoot from an already corrupt stem, Judaism.

It is necessary to keep this belief in mind when reading Celsus' work if a true historical perspective is to be kept. Although he says many sarcastic things about Christianity, it is not fair to think of him as merely destructive. He is no cold, ridiculing rationalist like Lucian for whom 'Christianity is only one more futility to add to the interminable list of human insanities'.[3] It is clear from the last section of Celsus' polemic that he is in truth deeply concerned about this fanatical new movement that is taking people away from the worship of the old gods and is undermining the structure and stability of society. Let the Christians return to take their stand upon the old paths and abandon this newly invented absurdity of worshipping a Jew recently crucified in disgraceful circumstances. Let them return to the old polytheism, to the customs of their fathers.[4] Christianity is a dangerous modern innovation, and if it is not

[1] Bader, *Der Alethes Logos des Kelsos*, pp. 2–3.
[2] Wifstrand, 'Kelsos', p. 399. Wifstrand also compares *Laws*, 757 A; *Tim*. 20 D; *Epin*. 992 C; *Phaedr*. 270 C; *Laws*, 783 A. (We may add *Epin*. 977 D.)
[3] P. de Labriolle, *La Réaction païenne*, p. 108.
[4] Celsus' high estimate of oracles is significant (VII, 2; VIII, 45). Although the oracles at Delphi and elsewhere had been much neglected in the first century B.C. and the first century A.D., there was a revival in the first half of the second century A.D. under Trajan and Hadrian. Cf. Cumont, *Religions orientales* (1929), p. 285 n. 2.

checked it will be a disaster for the Roman Empire. The Christians are not pulling their weight; they ought to take their share of civic responsibility, hold public office, fight in the army, and support the Emperor in his struggle to maintain the peace of the Empire.[1]

In short, Celsus is no second-century Voltaire. That is a title perhaps appropriate to Lucian, but not to Celsus, who had he been writing his book in the twentieth century might well have entitled his work 'A Recall to Religion'.

IV. THE RECONSTRUCTION OF CELSUS' TEXT

Much—perhaps too much—energy has been expended upon the attempt to reconstruct Celsus' text. Origen's method of quoting his opponent sentence by sentence, paragraph by paragraph, has ensured that a substantial part of the work is preserved in its original wording. Concerning how much has been lost estimates have varied. Neumann thought that a tenth had been altogether omitted by Origen, but that for three-quarters the actual words have been faithfully preserved.[2] Neumann himself projected a reconstruction of the work, but it was never published. An attempt to reproduce Celsus' words in the Greek text[3] was made by Otto Glöckner in Lietzmann's *Kleine Texte*, 151 (1924).[4] However, this little book has now been superseded by the more competent work of Robert Bader, *Der ἀληθὴς λόγος des Kelsos* (Tübinger Beiträge zur Altertumswissenschaft 33, Stuttgart-Berlin, 1940).

Bader takes a less sanguine view than Glöckner of the possibility of reconstructing Celsus' text, and in a long and carefully argued introduction shows that Origen omits and abbreviates more freely than one might be led to suppose from a superficial reading.[5] There are some passages where it is clear from Origen's explicit statements that he has omitted or abbreviated matter. For example, II, 32 where Origen refuses to discuss the charge that Jesus was a sorcerer on the ground that it is only a repeti-

[1] It is worth noting that no appeal to the Christians to be patriotic occurs in Porphyry, the next and most formidable pagan critic of Christianity, not, at least, in any of the surviving fragments. By the time of Porphyry in the latter part of the third century the Christian attitude has begun to change. In any event, Porphyry and the neo-Platonist opponents of Christianity were scarcely in a position to criticize the Church on this ground.

[2] K. J. Neumann, art. 'Celsus' in Herzog-Hauck, *Realencycl. f. prot. Theol. u. Kirche* (3rd ed.), III, p. 773.

[3] Keim, *Celsus' Wahres Wort* (1873), gives only a German version, no Greek text. An earlier attempt to reconstruct the Greek was published by Jachmann in 1836.

[4] On the inadequacies of this book, see Kurt Schmidt in *Gnomon*, III (1927), pp. 117–25. The text is taken from Glöckner's dissertation for his Münster doctorate, which has not been published, and exists (or at least existed) only in manuscript. I have only known this work through the occasional quotations from it given in Bader's notes.

[5] Cf. II, 20 where Origen says that he wishes to comply with Ambrose's request that he will answer even the most futile arguments.

tion of what has already been answered; II, 79 ('he says nothing else worth mentioning'); VI, 22 ('it seemed to me that to quote Celsus' words here would be absurd'); VI, 26 ('we leave on one side what Celsus has said on this question as superfluous and irrelevant'). Similar evidence of omissions occurs at III, 64; VI, 17, 50, 74; VII, 27, 32.

Bader adds other passages where a close inspection reveals evidence of the same process. Thus I, 34 where Origen says that Celsus 'has quoted several things from the gospel according to Matthew, such as the star that arose at the birth of Jesus and other miracles'. We hear more of the star, nothing of the other miracles. Also there are several places where Origen's words convey the impression of providing what can scarcely be more than a bare summary of Celsus' words (e.g. II, 7, 34, 40–2; III, 73; IV, 20). He complains of Celsus' repetitions and says he will not trouble to refute them a second time (II, 70). Occasionally an indication is given when Origen refers back to previous remarks made by Celsus which in fact he has not quoted before at all (IV, 79, 97). V, 20 shows that somewhere Celsus compared Jesus with Zeno of Citium, the founder of the Stoic school, to the disadvantage of the former; but the passage is nowhere quoted.[1] The information Celsus provides about the Ophites (VI, 27) is sadly truncated. In VI, 73 Origen remarks that Celsus 'claims to have learnt about things indifferent'; no sentence on this subject occurs in any quotation given elsewhere. Celsus' remarks about the martyrs are entirely passed over (VIII, 48). Origen comments (I, 32) that Celsus often refers to Pythagoras, Plato, and Empedocles; yet Empedocles is only mentioned once (VIII, 53).[2]

For the fact that it is possible to reconstruct what remains of Celsus' work in some sort of order we have to thank Origen's decision to change his method after he had begun to compose his reply. He informs us explicitly of this decision in his preface which he prefixed after he had completed the first twenty-seven chapters of the first book.

I decided to put this preface at the beginning after I had composed the reply to everything up to the point where Celsus puts the attack against Jesus into the mouth of the Jew [cf. I, 28 ff.]. . . . The preface may serve as my apology for the fact that I wrote the beginning of my answer to Celsus on one plan, but after the first part followed a different one. At first I contemplated making notes on the main points and giving brief answers to them, and then putting the work into definite shape. But afterwards the material itself suggested to me that I would save time if I were to be content with the points which I had answered in this way at the beginning, and in what followed to combat in detail Celsus' charges against us to the best of our ability.

[1] This is pointed out by Labriolle, *La Réaction païenne*, p. 117 n.
[2] For all this, see Bader's introduction, pp. 10–24.

Accordingly the fragments from Celsus which occur in I, 1–27 cannot necessarily be taken to have occurred at the beginning of Celsus' book. And some of the matter there answered is in fact quoted again later in the work when Origen comes to the place in Celsus' text. Thus Wifstrand[1] has observed that I, 17 refers to Celsus' criticisms of the Mosaic cosmogony and of Christians who tried to interpret it allegorically; these criticisms Origen quotes in IV, 48 f. In I, 24 the first sentence quoted from Celsus evidently came near the beginning of his book. But the second, to the effect that 'it makes no difference whether one calls the supreme God by the name used among the Greeks, or by that, for example, used among the Indians, or by that among the Egyptians', is only a summary of what Origen quotes more fully in V, 41.

V. THE IDENTITY AND DATE OF CELSUS

The identity of Celsus was a matter of uncertainty even to Origen himself. He knows that Celsus 'has already been dead a long time' (Praef. 4), but is not sure who he was. 'We have heard', he says, 'that there were two Epicurean philosophers called Celsus, the earlier one a contemporary of Nero, while the other lived in Hadrian's time and later' (I, 8). If our Celsus can be identified with either of these two, he must be identified with the second. At any rate, Origen takes his opponent, though with some hesitation, to be an Epicurean.

We know of a Celsus who was an Epicurean, flourishing in the latter half of the second century, from other sources. Lucian of Samosata dedicated to him his amusing pamphlet *Alexander the False Prophet*, and from Lucian's language it appears that his friend was an Epicurean (cf. 25, 43 and 61); Lucian's friend was also the author of a book attacking magicians (*ibid.* 21: κατὰ μάγων). This last work is mentioned by Origen (I, 68): 'You see how by these words he gives his assent, as it were, to the reality of magic. I do not know whether he is the same as the man who wrote several books against magic.' It was probably the same writer with whom Galen had some correspondence.[2]

Some scholars have maintained that Origen was right, and that the author of the attack on Christianity is to be identified with Lucian's Epicurean friend. The most persuasive statement of this view is to be found in the work of Theodor Keim, *Celsus' Wahres Wort* (Zürich, 1873), pp. 275–93, whose arguments convinced Harnack among others.[3] This

---

[1] 'Kelsos', pp. 393–5.
[2] Galen, *de Libris Propriis*, 16 (*Scripta minora*, ed. I. Müller, II, p. 124), mentions 'a letter to Celsus the Epicurean'.
[3] A. von Harnack, *Chronologie*, I (1897), pp. 314–15.

identification is open to the serious objection that it is perfectly clear from almost every page of the *contra Celsum* that Celsus is far from being in any sense an Epicurean. His philosophy is that of Middle Platonism, and with Epicureanism he betrays no affinities at all. Keim tries to evade this difficulty by arguing that the friend of Lucian was not 'a full-blooded Epicurean', and could even have been an eclectic Platonist like the Celsus of Origen; he argues that the characteristics of Lucian's friend and Origen's opponent are strikingly similar; Lucian writes of his friend's 'wisdom, love of truth, gentleness, moderation, tranquillity of life, and courtesy' (*Alex.* 61). According to Keim, 'one must be almost blind not to recognize our Celsus in the description of the character of Lucian's Celsus' (p. 287). Again, both men are hostile to sorcerers. Lucian's friendship with the Epicurean is significant; cannot one picture Origen's opponent arm in arm with the Samosatene? Furthermore, Lucian's friend lived under Commodus about A.D. 180, and Origen's opponent probably wrote about 177–80 (see below). They lived about the same time, and even in the same place. It is therefore probable that they are one and the same person.

But as against Keim's view there are strong considerations on the other side. In the first place, his arguments that Lucian's friend was not a whole-hearted Epicurean read uncomfortably like special pleading when the text of Lucian is fairly considered. For example, at the end of his *Alexander* (61) Lucian says that he has written the tract not only to please his friend, but also to vindicate Epicurus, 'which you will like also' (ὅπερ καὶ σοὶ ἥδιον, Ἐπικούρῳ τιμωρῶν). Earlier (47) he tells Celsus that Alexander burnt the Κύριαι Δόξαι of Epicurus, 'which, as you know, is the finest of his books'. Similarly, he says that Alexander, being a sorcerer and an enemy of the truth, was naturally hostile to Epicurus, 'who perceived the nature of things and alone understood the truth'; with the Platonists, Stoics, and Pythagoreans, however, he was on excellent terms (25). The natural interpretation of these passages is that Celsus, the friend to whom Lucian was writing, was himself an avowed Epicurean.

In the second place, if Origen's opponent really could be identified with Lucian's Epicurean friend, we should expect to find some traces, at least, of this philosophy in the quotations which Origen gives. But Origen's Celsus at no point shows any signs of holding any Epicurean opinions whatever. Origen admits as much himself when he remarks: 'From *other* writings he is found to be an Epicurean' (1, 8). Evidently he could find no support for this view in the work before him. Possibly Origen was led to suppose that his opponent was given to Epicureanism by Ambrose, his friend and patron, who sent the work to him with a request for a refutation. Perhaps also Origen himself concluded that so bitter an attack on

Christianity could only be the work of an atheist. It is a plausible suggestion that, although Origen eventually realized that Celsus was a Platonist, he accused him of Epicureanism partly to discredit him in the eyes of his readers. As Dr W. R. Inge has observed, '"Epicurean" was then a term of abuse, like Fascist or Bolshevik now.'[1] But it is significant that Origen's references to Celsus' alleged philosophy become more and more hesitant, and cease entirely after the beginning of the fifth book (the last reference is v, 3). In the early part of his reply Origen attempts to make out that Celsus is a secret Epicurean who is disguising his real belief (cf. III, 22, 35, 80) to avoid discrediting his polemic. But his hesitancy increases; in IV, 54 he thinks it possible that Celsus may have been converted from his Epicureanism, or that his opponent is another writer of the same name. Ultimately, Origen recognizes that his opponent is a 'Platonizing' philosopher (IV, 83), and notes that Celsus often speaks of Plato in terms of profound respect (VI, 47).

Celsus' philosophy is that of an eclectic Platonist. His affinities are with the Middle Platonists like Albinus. It is, accordingly, inconceivable that he can be identified with a well-known Epicurean. The name was common enough at this period; Keim himself reckons that he could count two dozen men named Celsus in the first three centuries (*op. cit.* p. 276). We must therefore conclude that we know nothing of Origen's opponent except what can be inferred from the text of Origen himself.[2]

For the determination of Celsus' date the significant passages are as follows: (*a*) in VIII, 69 Celsus writes that the Christians are hunted out and liable to the death penalty: ὑμῶν δὲ κἄν πλανᾶταί τις ἔτι λανθάνων, ἀλλὰ 3ητεῖται πρὸς θανάτου δίκην. This seems clearly to point to a time of active persecution, and is connected by Keim (p. 271) and Neumann (p. 58 n. 1) with the persecution at Lyon and Vienne in 177 which followed the rescript of Marcus Aurelius; (*b*) in VIII, 71 Celsus writes: 'It is quite intolerable of you to say that, if those who reign over us now were persuaded by you and were taken prisoner, you would persuade those who reign after them...', etc. The phrase οἱ νῦν βασιλεύοντες points to the conclusion that at the time of writing there was more than one emperor, and may refer to the joint *imperium* of Marcus Aurelius with Verus (161–9) or to that of Marcus Aurelius with Commodus (177–80).

[1] 'Origen', p. 3 (in *Proceedings of the British Academy*, XXXII, Annual Lecture on a Master Mind, dated 20 March 1946).
[2] In IV, 36 Origen writes ironically: 'Celsus the Epicurean, if, at least, he is the one who also composed two other books against the Christians...'. Neumann (in Pauly-Wissowa, III, 1885) thinks the two other books are to be identified with the *True Doctrine* and the second treatise projected by Celsus (VIII, 76).

The latter period is adopted by Neumann; Keim (p. 273) would even date the work precisely in 178.[1]

This view, however, was criticized by Lightfoot.[2] He points out that once the identification of Origen's opponent with Lucian's friend is discarded, we have no direct clue to the date. He admits that in VIII, 71 οἱ νῦν βασιλεύοντες might be evidential if it stood alone. But elsewhere Celsus uses the singular (e.g. VIII, 73), and in VIII, 68 quotes the well-known verse from the *Iliad*—'let there be one king'—to urge Christians to obey the emperor. 'Could any language more unfortunate be conceived, if at this very time there were two Augusti? Why should he, when he was expressly enforcing the duty of loyalty to two emperors, quote as authoritative a passage which declares emphatically that there ought only to be one?' Lightfoot accordingly concludes that Celsus could not have written later than 161 when Marcus Aurelius and Verus were joint-emperors, and that the phrase 'those who now reign over us' in VIII, 71 is to be taken generically, and so does not imply more than one emperor at the time of writing. Thus Justin (*Apol.* 1, 14, 17) can speak of Pius, Marcus, and Lucius as βασιλεῖς although there was then only one emperor. Therefore, Lightfoot 'provisionally' assigned Celsus' work to the reign of Antoninus Pius.

Neumann argued against Lightfoot that his interpretation was ruled out by the νῦν. More cogent is the consideration that the Homeric verse was a stock quotation; and the sharing of the *imperium* was not held to affect in any way the *monarchia* of the emperor.[3] The quotation is not such strong evidence as Lightfoot assumes.

A position intermediate between that of Lightfoot and that of Neumann is taken by F. X. Funk.[4] He agrees with both that Lucian's friend cannot be Origen's opponent. But he questions the view of Neumann and Keim that there was a widespread persecution of the Church throughout the Empire in 177, appealing to the words of Eusebius (*H.E.* v. praef. 1) that the persecution occurred 'in some parts of the world'. The martyrs at Lyon and Vienne would then be victims of a local and sporadic outbreak, not of a general and universal proscription of Christianity. On the other hand, he thinks it difficult to put Celsus' work as early as Antoninus Pius. The developed state of heresy reflected in the remarks about the Gnostic sects points to a slightly later date. Irenaeus (*adv. Haer.* 1, 25, 6, Harvey,

[1] Aubé, *Hist. des pers. de l'église*, II (1878), pp. 172 ff., dates the work 176–80.
[2] J. B. Lightfoot, *The Apostolic Fathers*, pt. II (2nd ed. 1889), I, pp. 530–1.
[3] See Peterson, *Monotheismus*, pp. 13, 119, and *passim*.
[4] 'Die Zeit des wahren Wortes von Celsus', in *Kirchengeschichtliche Abhandlungen und Untersuchungen*, II (1899), pp. 152–61. This paper is a revision of his article in *Theol. Quartalschr.* LXVIII (1886), pp. 302–15.

I, 210) tells us that the foundress of the Marcellinian sect, mentioned by Celsus in v, 54, came to Rome in the time of bishop Anicetus, that is, at the earliest in 154. Celsus' appeal to the Christians to support the emperor and fight in the army lest the Empire be overrun by barbarians (VIII, 68, 71, 73, 75) suggests that he is writing in the late sixties or more probably the seventies, about the time of the wars of Marcus Aurelius with the Parthians, Quadi, and Marcomanni. Accordingly, he would leave the date open between 161 and 185, within which period a date between 170 and 185 is more probable than the early part of Marcus' reign.

The weakness in Funk's argument against Keim and Neumann is his belittling of the evidence for widespread persecution in 177. The evidence is not confined to Eusebius' statement in the preface to the fifth book of his *Church History* that it occurred 'in some parts of the world'. In the fourth book he seems to assign the death of Polycarp to the same persecution (*H.E.* IV, 15) and recently Professor Henri Grégoire has argued that this date should be accepted.[1] If there was severe persecution in Asia Minor, it is intelligible that the Gallic churches should write to encourage their brethren in Asia and Phrygia (Eus. *H.E.* v, 1, 3) who were enduring similar distresses. It is possible that the martyrs of Pergamum, Carpus, Papylus, and Agathonice, also suffered at this time.[2]

On balance, therefore, probability lies with the view that Celsus' date is to be assigned to the period 177–80.

The place of origin of Celsus' work is even more uncertain. Celsus is excellently informed about the Gnostic sects. Many of these flourished at Rome, which was the scene of the most acute conflict between orthodoxy and heresy in the second century. It is an attractive conjecture that Celsus wrote in Rome (Keim, pp. 274 f.), and his patriotic appeal at the end of book VIII might lend support to the view that he lived in the imperial capital. On the other hand, Celsus is interested in Egyptian lore (III, 17, 19; VIII, 58),[3] and quotes the opinion of a certain Dionysius, an Egyptian musician, in VI, 41. In II, 31 he seems to betray knowledge of the Logos-theology of Hellenistic Judaism (see note *ad loc.*). These latter considera-

---

[1] 'La Véritable Date du Martyre de S. Polycarpe (23 février 177) et le corpus Polycarpianum', in *Anal. Boll.* LXIX (1951), pp. 1–38. For a statement of the arguments in favour of 155 or 156, see Lightfoot, *op. cit.* I, pp. 646–715, 727. Grégoire is severely criticized by W. Telfer in *J.T.S.* n.s. III (1952), pp. 79–83.

[2] Cf. H. Delehaye, *Les Passions des Martyrs et les genres littéraires* (1921), pp. 136 f., and in *Anal. Boll.* LVIII (1940), pp. 142 ff.; Grégoire, *loc. cit.* p. 3.

[3] Celsus' remarks in III, 17 are a literary commonplace (see note there) and are *not* evidential. This is ignored by E. C. Butler, in *J.T.S.* XXII (1921), p. 143.

tions may suggest Alexandria as his home.[1] We may also add to the considerations in favour of Alexandria, that Origen is not infrequently incensed that Celsus confuses the tenets of orthodox Christianity with beliefs held by Gnostic sects.[2] At Rome the Christian community appears to have been very conscious of the dividing line between heresy and orthodoxy. At Alexandria, on the other hand, such little evidence as there is rather suggests that the dividing line was not precisely delineated.[3] Celsus' confusion is therefore more intelligible if he is writing at Alexandria. Moreover, in VI, 22 Celsus describes the Mithraic mystery of the ladder with seven gates, corresponding to the seven planets, and explains it by means of 'musical theories'. This indicates that Celsus explains the peculiar order of the planets in the Mithraic list (i.e. that of the days of the week) by neo-Pythagorean doctrines of the harmony of the spheres and of the tetrachord. There is other evidence that the neo-Pythagorean sect was interested in the beliefs of the Persian magi.[4] This suggests that Celsus may have met with the sect in Rome or Alexandria where it flourished.

VI. MANUSCRIPTS, EDITIONS AND TRANSLATIONS

For the text we are dependent upon two lines of tradition. The first is the direct tradition represented by the Vatican manuscript, Vatic. Gr. 386 (= A), of the thirteenth century, which contains the complete work. All other manuscripts of the *contra Celsum* are derived from this.[5] The second is the indirect tradition represented by the manuscripts of the *Philocalia*, the anthology of passages from Origen's works compiled by St Basil and St Gregory in the fourth century. This contains extracts of

---

[1] Neumann, article 'Celsus', in P.-W., III (1899), 1885, thinks Celsus' home was in the East. Cf. VII, 3, 9.

[2] Cf. V, 61–5; VI, 24 ff.; VII, 25; VIII, 15.

[3] The evidence is set out by W. Bauer, *Rechtgläubigkeit und Ketzerei im ältesten Christentum (Beitr. z. hist. Theol.* X, 1934), pp. 49–64.

[4] Cumont, in *Rev. de l'hist. des Relig.* CIII (1931), p. 90 n. 2, remarks that Lydus, treating of the days of the week (*de Mens.* II, 4, 6), cites as authorities Zoroaster and Hystaspes, but the chapter is full of speculations on numbers, which suggests that Lydus knew about the Oriental sages through some neo-Pythagorean intermediary. Furthermore, Nicomachus of Gerasa, the Pythagorean of the first century, also appeals to Zoroaster and Ostanes when speaking of planetary spheres (in Iamblichus, *Theol. arithm.* p. 56 Falco). Cumont (p. 55 n. 4) thinks it must have been through some neo-Pythagorean work that Celsus knew of the Persian theology.

[5] Koetschau originally thought that Codex Parisinus Suppl. Gr. 616 (= P), dated 1339, is independent of A: *Die Textüberlieferung der Bücher des Origenes gegen Celsus* (Texte und Untersuchungen VI, 1, Leipzig, 1889). But he became convinced that P is a copy of A by the arguments of J. A. Robinson (*Journal of Philology*, XVIII (1890), pp. 288–96). See Robinson's introduction to his edition of the *Philocalia* (Cambridge, 1893), pp. ix, xxviii; Neumann in Koetschau's introduction to his edition of the *contra Celsum*, pp. lix–lxvi.

varying length from books I–VII. The manuscripts of the *Philocalia* are generally earlier. The two earliest are Venice 47, of the eleventh century, and the Patmos manuscript of the tenth century.

It is now necessary to add that the direct tradition has been strengthened by a recent papyrus find in Egypt. In 1941 there was found at Tura, a few miles south of Cairo, a considerable theological library. The papyri date from the sixth century, and include the minutes of a disputation between Origen and a bishop Heraclides whose Trinitarian orthodoxy was suspect,[1] and parts of the first two books of the *contra Celsum*. The text of the latter is proved to derive from the same line of tradition as the Vatican manuscript by the fact that at the end of the first book it has exactly the same subscription as is found in A: μετεβλήθη καὶ ἀντεβλήθη ἐξ ἀντιγράφων τῶν αὐτοῦ ὠριγένους βιβλίων—'it was copied from and compared with copies of the books of Origen himself'. When this papyrus text is published, it will no doubt throw light on some obscure places.

The *contra Celsum* was first printed by David Hoeschel, and published at Augsburg in 1605. This text was reprinted by William Spencer, Fellow of Trinity College, Cambridge, and published by the University Press in 1658 (2nd ed. 1677). A better edition was produced by the Benedictine C. Delarue (Paris, 1733), reprinted in volumes XVIII–XX of the convenient edition of Lommatzsch (Berlin, 1845–6), and also in Migne's *Patrologia Graeca* (XI, 1857).

The standard text today is that undertaken by the late Dr Paul Koetschau for the Berlin Academy corpus.[2] This edition was based on the critical investigation of the manuscript tradition carried out by Armitage Robinson, Neumann, and Koetschau himself. Its foundation is the text of A, of which Koetschau collated books I–III, Neumann books IV–VIII. I have been able to check the collations by means of photostats of the manuscript.[3]

Koetschau's text had no sooner appeared than it was met by a bitter and hasty review from the pen of P. Wendland in the *Göttingische gelehrte Anzeigen* for 1899 (pp. 276–304). Wendland's chief complaint was that

---

[1] At the time of writing (1953) this is the only part of the find published: *Entretien d'Origène avec Héraclide et les évêques ses collègues sur le Père, le Fils, et l'Âme*, ed. J. Scherer (Publications de la Société Fouad I de Papyrologie, Textes et Documents, IX, Cairo, 1949). For reports on the find, see O. Guéraud in *Rev. d'Hist. des Religions*, 131 (Jan. 1946), pp. 85–108; H. C. Puech in *Comptes Rendus de l'Acad. des Inscr.* (1946), pp. 367–9; E. Klostermann in *Theol. Lit.-Zeit.* (Oct. 1947), pp. 203–8. Further discussion in B. Capelle, 'L'Entretien d'Origène avec Héraclide', in *Journ. Eccl. Hist.* II (1951), pp. 143–57; H. C. Puech, 'Les nouveaux écrits d'Origène et de Didyme découverts à Toura', in *Revue d'histoire et de philosophie religieuses*, XXXI (1951), pp. 293–329.

[2] *Die griechischen christlichen Schriftsteller der ersten drei Jahrhunderte*, Bde II–III (1899).

[3] I am indebted to the Managers of the Hort Memorial Fund for having made such an investigation possible, and to the Prefect of the Vatican Library for his good offices.

Koetschau had preferred the authority of the Vatican manuscript to that of the *Philocalia* tradition. Wendland also contributed numerous conjectural emendations, some of which are as brilliant as others are unreasonable. To this attack Koetschau attempted a reply in his *Kritische Bemerkungen ɀu meiner Ausgabe von Origenes*, in turn reviewed by Wendland in the same periodical (pp. 613–22). The bitter feeling that informs this controversy makes it unedifying reading.[1]

An attempt to clarify the question was made by Franz Anton Winter in a dissertation of great diligence and carefulness.[2] The conclusion reached by Winter is that the *Philocalia* text is superior to that of the direct tradition. Koetschau, although convinced by Winter's argument in several particular instances, remained unconvinced on the general question. In 1926–7 he produced a translation in the series *Bibliothek der Kirchenväter*, edited by Bardenhewer, Weyman, and Zellinger.[3] In the introduction (p. xv) he had occasion to refer to the controversy, and remarked that 'even by Winter the controversy does not seem to me to have been finally decided yet'.

It is noteworthy, however, that in several places Koetschau came to accept in his translation suggestions made by Wendland which he had scornfully rejected in his *Kritische Bemerkungen*. And the necessity of providing an intelligible interpretation of his own text led him to make over four hundred changes, roughly two for every three pages of the Greek text. Several of these changes I have accepted in the present translation.

Recently a valuable list of suggested emendations has been made by Professor Albert Wifstrand, of Lund.[4] The majority of these I have accepted.

In revising the present translation I have found it useful to refer to my predecessors in this task. The French translation by Élie Bouhéreau (*Traité d'Origène contre Celse*, Amsterdam, 1700) remains valuable not only for the appended notes containing several conjectural emendations

[1] Koetschau's edition received favourable notice from other scholars, and Wendland's criticisms did not carry the day. Cf. P. M. Barnard in *J.T.S.* 1 (1900), pp. 455–61; A. Jülicher in *Theol. Lit.-Zeit.* (1899), cols. 599–606.
[2] *Über den Wert der direkten und indirekten Überlieferung von Origenes Büchern contra Celsum* (Programm Burghausen, 1902/3 and 1903/4). It appears that the only copy of this work in England is that possessed by the Bodleian Library, Oxford. I am indebted to the Curators for having made the book available for me to read at Cambridge.
[3] Bde LII–III, Munich, 1926–7.
[4] See his 'Eikota' IV, in *Bull. Soc. Roy. Lund* (1938/9), pp. 9–40, and 'Die Wahre Lehre des Kelsos', *ibid.* (1941/2), pp. 391–431, reviewed by O. Stählin in *Philologische Wochenschrift* for 10 June 1944, cols. 124–6. Reference may also be made here to Wifstrand's review of R. Bader's reconstruction of Celsus in *Theol. Lit.-Zeit.* (1941), nr. 11/12; Stählin reviews Bader in *Philol. Woch.* (1942), pp. 1–7.

but also for the interpretation of some difficult passages. In Delarue's edition there is printed by the side of the Greek text a Latin translation by Vincent Thuillier. The first German translation is that of J. L. Mosheim, *Acht Bücher von der Wahrheit der christlichen Religion wider den Weltweisen Celsus* (Hamburg, 1745). It is also translated by Rohm in Thalhofer's *Bibliothek der Kirchenväter* (Kempten, 1874). The German translation which I have found most useful is that of Koetschau himself, already mentioned.

The first English translation was produced in the eighteenth century, and only includes the first two books.[1] The standard of accuracy is not high. The first complete translation into English was that made by F. Crombie and W. H. Cairns for the *Ante-Nicene Christian Library* (vols. x and xxiii, Edinburgh, 1869–72). This is a serviceable translation, based on the Delarue text; it provides little or nothing by way of explanatory notes.

The text used as the basis of the present translation is that of Koetschau. All variations from his text are noted. Occasionally, in the textual notes, references to the *contra Celsum* give not only the book and chapter but also in brackets the page and line in Koetschau. References to other works of Origen are to the Berlin Corpus edition where this is available. Where it is not, I have used Lommatzsch.

Irenaeus is quoted by Massuet's divisions, often with the volume and page of Harvey. Philo is cited by the sections of Cohn-Wendland, Maximus Tyrius from Hobein.

References to the Old Testament are to the Septuagint, and follow the edition of Swete.

For passages where the Synoptic Gospels are parallel usually the Matthaean reference only is given.

[1] *Origen against Celsus, Translated from the Original into English* by James Bellamy, Gent. London, Printed by B. Mills and sold by J. Robinson, at the Golden Lyon in St Paul's Church-Yard (n.d. *c.* 1712). The preface of this work is lively reading, but the translation of insufficient accuracy.

ABBREVIATIONS

The *Realencyclopädie* of Pauly-Wissowa-Kroll is commonly abbreviated as P.-W. H. von Arnim's *Stoicorum Veterum Fragmenta* is cited as *S.V.F.*

In textual notes the following abbreviations are used:

K.tr. = Koetschau's German translation	Bo. = Bouhéreau
We. = Wendland	Del. = Delarue
Wi. = Winter	Ba. = Bader
Wif. = Wifstrand	Rob. = Robinson

MANUSCRIPTS

A = Vaticanus graecus 386, saec. xiii

M = Venetus Marcianus 45, saec. xiv

P = Parisinus suppl. graecus 616, a. 1339

V = Venetus Marcianus 44, saec. xiv

Φ = Consensus of *Philocalia* manuscripts

BIBLIOGRAPHY

(Items marked with an asterisk have been inaccessible, but are included for information)

ALFÖLDI, A. Zu den Christenverfolgungen in der Mitte des 3. Jahrhunderts. *Klio*, XXXI, 1938, pp. 323–48.

AMANDRY, P. *La Mantique apollinienne à Delphes*. Paris, 1950.

AUBÉ, B. *Histoire des persécutions de l'église*, II. Paris, 1878.

BADER, R. *Der Alethes Logos des Kelsos*. (Tübinger Beiträge zur Altertumswissenschaft, Heft 33.) Stuttgart-Berlin, 1940.

*BAIL, P. *Die philosophische Fundamentierung von Celsus' Angriffen wider das Christentum*. Diss. Erlangen, 1921.

BALTHASAR, H. VON. Le Mystérion d'Origène. *Recherches de science religieuse*, XXVI, 1936, pp. 513–62.

BARDY, G. Les traditions juives dans l'œuvre d'Origène. *Revue Biblique*, XXXIV, 1925, pp. 217–52.

—— Origène et la magie. *Recherches de science religieuse*, XVIII, 1928, pp. 126 ff.

—— Origène et l'aristotélisme. *Mélanges Glotz*, Paris, 1932, I, pp. 75 ff.

—— Aux origines de l'école d'Alexandrie. *Recherches de science religieuse*, XXVII, 1937, pp. 65 ff.

—— Pour l'histoire de l'école d'Alexandrie. *Vivre et Penser*, 2e série, Paris, 1942, pp. 80–109.

—— *Origène*. (Les Moralistes chrétiens.) Paris, 2nd ed. 1931.

BARNARD, P. M. Review of Koetschau's edition of the *contra Celsum* in *Journal of Theological Studies*, I, 1900, pp. 455–61.

BAUER, W. *Das Leben Jesu im Zeitalter der neutestamentlichen Apokryphen*. Tübingen, 1909.

—— *Rechtgläubigkeit und Ketzerei im ältesten Christentum* (Beiträge zur historischen Theologie, 10). Tübingen, 1934.

BENZ, E. Der gekreuzigte Gerechte bei Plato, im Neuen Testament, und in der alten Kirche. *Abhandlungen der Akademie der Wissenschaften und der Literatur*, Geistes- und Sozialwissenschaftlichen Klasse, Mainz, 1950, no. 12.

—— Indische Einflüsse auf die frühchristliche Theologie. *Ibid*. 1951, no. 3.

BERTRAND, F. *Mystique de Jésus chez Origène*. Paris, 1951.

BEUTLER, R. Article, 'Numenios v. Apamea', in Pauly-Wissowa, *Realencyclopädie*, Suppl. VII, 1940, cols. 664–78.

BEVAN, E. R. *Holy Images*. London, 1940.

BIDEZ, J. and CUMONT, F. *Les Mages hellénisés*. Paris, 1938.

BIGG, C. *The Christian Platonists of Alexandria*. Oxford, 2nd ed. 1913.

BONNER, C. *Studies in Magical Amulets, chiefly Graeco-Egyptian*. (University of Michigan Studies, Humanistic Series, 49.) Ann Arbor, 1950.

*BORDES, G. *L'Apologétique d'Origène d'après le contre Celse*. Thèse, Paris, 1900.

BORNKAMM, G. *Mythos und Legende in den Thomas-Akten*. Göttingen, 1933.

BOUSSET, W. Die Himmelreise der Seele. *Archiv für Religionswissenschaft*, IV, 1901, pp. 136–69, 229–73.

—— *Hauptprobleme der Gnosis*. Göttingen, 1907.

BUTTERWORTH, G. W. *Origen on First Principles*. London, 1936.

CADIOU, R. *Introduction au système d'Origène*. Paris, 1932.

CADIOU, R. *La Jeunesse d'Origène*. Paris, 1935.

—— Dictionnaires antiques dans l'œuvre d'Origène. *Revue des études grecques*, XLV, 1932, pp. 271 ff.

CATAUDELLA, Q. Tracce della sofistica nella polemica celso-origeniana. *Rendiconti del R. Istituto Lombard. di sc. e lettere*, XXX, 3, 1937, pp. 186–201 [on Antiphon in c. Cels. IV, 25].

—— Celso e gli apologeti cristiani. *Nuovo Didaskaleion*, I, 1947, pp. 28–34.

*—— Celso e l'epicureismo. *Annuale della scuola normale superiore di Pisa*, 1943, pp. 1–23.

CHADWICK, H. Origen, Celsus, and the Stoa. *Journal of Theological Studies*, XLVIII, 1947, 34–49.

—— Origen, Celsus, and the Resurrection of the Body. *Harvard Theological Review*, XLI, 1948, pp. 83–102.

COOK, A. B. *Zeus*. Cambridge, 1914–40.

CUMONT, F. *Textes et Monuments figurés relatifs aux Mystères de Mithra*. Brussels, 1894–1900.

—— *Les Mystères de Mithra*. Brussels, 3rd ed. 1913.

—— *Les Religions orientales dans le paganisme romain*. Paris, 4th ed. 1929.

—— La fin du monde selon les mages occidentaux. *Revue de l'histoire des religions*, CIII, 1931, pp. 29–96.

—— *Lux Perpetua*. Paris, 1949.

DANIÉLOU, J. *Origène*. Paris, 1948.

—— Origène et Maxime de Tyr. *Recherches de science religieuse*, XXXIV, 1947, pp. 359–61.

—— L'Unité des deux Testaments dans l'œuvre d'Origène. *Revue des sciences religieuses*, XXII, 1948, pp. 27–56.

—— Les sources juives de la doctrine des anges des nations chez Origène. *Recherches de science religieuse*, XXXVIII, 1951, pp. 132–7.

DENIS, M. J. *De la Philosophie d'Origène*. Paris, 1884.

DOELGER, F. J. *Antike und Christentum*, I–VI, Münster, 1929–50.

DRAESEKE, J. Das Johannesevangelium bei Celsus. *Neue kirchliche Zeitschrift*, IX, 1898, pp. 139–55.

*FABRE, E. *Celse et le Discours véritable*. Thèse, Geneva, 1878.

FAYE, E. DE. *Origène, sa vie, son œuvre, sa pensée*. (Bibliothèque de l'école des hautes études, sciences religieuses, 37, 43, 44.) Paris, 1923–8.

—— *Gnostiques et gnosticisme*. Paris, 2nd ed. 1925.

—— *Origen and his work*. Trans. Fred Rothwell. London, 1926.

FESTUGIÈRE, A. J. *La Révélation d'Hermès Trismégiste*: I, *L'Astrologie et les sciences occultes*. Paris, 2nd ed. 1950. II, *Le Dieu Cosmique*. Paris, 2nd ed. 1949.

FUNK, F. X. Die Zeit des wahren Wortes von Celsus, in his *Kirchengeschichtliche Abhandlungen und Untersuchungen*, II, 1899, pp. 152–61.

GEFFCKEN, J. *Zwei griechische Apologeten*. Leipzig, 1907.

—— *Der Ausgang des griechisch-römischen Heidentums*. Heidelberg, 1920–9.

GLÖCKNER, O. *Celsi Alethes Logos*. (Kleine Texte 151.) Bonn, 1924.

—— Die Gottes- und Weltanschauung des Kelsos. *Philologus*, LXXXII, 1926–7, pp. 329–52.

GLOVER, T. R. *The Conflict of Religions in the Early Roman Empire*. London, 1909.

GRONAU, K. *Poseidonios und die jüdisch-christliche Genesisexegese*. Leipzig-Berlin, 1914.

—— *Das Theodizeeproblem in der altchristlichen Auffassung*. Tübingen, 1922.

GUÉRAUD, O. Note préliminaire sur les papyrus d'Origène découverts à Toura. *Revue de l'histoire des religions*, CXXXI, 1946, pp. 85–108.

BIBLIOGRAPHY

GUTHRIE, K. S. *Numenius of Apamea.* Grantwood, New Jersey, 1917.

GUTHRIE, W. K. C. *Orpheus and Greek Religion.* London, 1935.

—— *The Greeks and their Gods.* London, 1950.

HARNACK, A. VON. *Geschichte der altchristlichen Litteratur bis Eusebius.* I. Die Überlieferung, II. Die Chronologie. Leipzig, 1893–1904.

—— *Lehrbuch der Dogmengeschichte.* Tübingen, 4th ed. 1909.

—— *Der kirchengeschichtliche Ertrag der exegetischen Arbeiten des Origenes.* Texte und Untersuchungen, XLII, Leipzig, 1919.

—— *Marcion, das Evangelium vom fremden Gott.* Leipzig, 2nd ed. 1924.

—— *Die Mission und Ausbreitung des Christentums.* Leipzig, 4th ed. 1924.

HEINE, O. Ueber Celsus' Alethes Logos. In *Philologische Abhandlungen Martin Hertz dargebracht* (1888), pp. 197–214.

HILGENFELD, A. *Die Ketzergeschichte des Urchristentums.* Leipzig, 1884.

HOPFNER, T. Das Diagramm der Ophiten. In *Charisteria Alois Rzach dargebracht.* Reichenberg, 1930.

INGE, W. R. *The Philosophy of Plotinus.* London, 3rd ed. 1929.

—— Origen. *Proceedings of the British Academy,* XXXII (1946).

*JACHMANN. *De Celso philosopho disputatur et fragmenta libri quem contra Christianos edidit colliguntur.* Programm Königsberg, 1836.

JORDAN, H. Celsus, die älteste umfassende Kritik des Christentums. In W. Laible, *Moderne Irrtümer im Spiegel der Geschichte,* Leipzig, 1912, pp. 1–31.

JUELICHER, A. Review of Koetschau's edition of the *contra Celsum* in *Theologische Literaturzeitung,* 1899, cols. 599–606.

JUSTER, J. *Les Juifs dans l'empire romain.* Paris, 1914.

KARPP, H. *Probleme altchristlicher Anthropologie.* (Beiträge zur Förderung christlicher Theologie 44, Heft 3.) Gütersloh, 1950.

KLOSTERMANN, E. Origeniana. In *Neutestamentliche Studien G. Heinrici dargebracht,* Leipzig, 1914, pp. 245–51.

—— Ueberkommene Definitionen im Werke des Origenes. *Zeitschrift für die neutestamentliche Wissenschaft,* XXXVII, 1938, pp. 54–61.

—— Formen der exegetischen Arbeiten des Origenes. *Theologische Literaturzeitung,* 1947, cols. 203–8.

KNOX, W. L. Jewish Liturgical Exorcism. *Harvard Theological Review,* XXXI, 1938, pp. 191–203.

—— Origen's Conception of the Resurrection Body. *Journal of Theological Studies,* XXXIX, 1938, pp. 247–8.

—— *St Paul and the Church of the Gentiles.* Cambridge, 1939.

—— *Some Hellenistic Elements in Primitive Christianity.* London, 1944.

KOCH, HAL. *Pronoia und Paideusis: Studien über Origenes und sein Verhältnis zum Platonismus.* Berlin and Leipzig, 1932.

—— Article, 'Origenes', in Pauly-Wissowa, *Realencyclopädie,* XVIII, 1 (1939).

KOETSCHAU, P. Die Gliederung des Alethes Logos des Celsus. *Jahrbücher für protestantische Theologie,* XVIII, 1892, pp. 604–32.

—— *Die Textüberlieferung der Bücher des Origenes gegen Celsum.* (Texte und Untersuchungen, VI, 1.) Leipzig, 1889.

—— *Origenes Werke,* I–II. Leipzig, 1899.

—— *Kritische Bemerkungen zu meiner Ausgabe von Origenes, Exhortatio, contra Celsum, de Oratione.* Leipzig, 1899.

KOETSCHAU, P. Bibelcitate bei Origenes. *Zeitschrift für wissenschaftliche Theologie*, XLIII, 1900, pp. 321–78.

—— *Des Origenes ausgewählte Schriften aus dem Griechischen übersetzt.* (Bibliothek der Kirchenväter 48, 52, 53.) Munich, n.d. [1926–7].

LABRIOLLE, P. DE. *La Réaction païenne.* Paris, 1934.

LAGRANGE, F. *La Raison et la Foi, ou étude sur la controverse entre Celse et Origène.* Thèse, Paris, 1856.

LEEMANS, E. A. *Studie over den wijsgeer Numenius van Apamea met uitgave der fragmenten.* (Académie Royale de Belgique, Classe des Lettres, Mémoires 2ᵉ série, tome XXXVII, fasc. 2.) Brussels, 1937.

LEISEGANG, H. *Die Gnosis.* 3rd ed. Stuttgart, 1941.

LIESKE, A. *Die Theologie der Logos-Mystik bei Origenes.* (Münsterische Beiträge zur Theologie, Heft 22.) 1938.

LIGHTFOOT, J. B. *The Apostolic Fathers*, Part II (2nd ed. London, 1899), vol. I.

LODS, M. Étude sur les sources juives de la polémique de Celse contre les chrétiens. *Revue d'histoire et de philosophie religieuses*, XXI, 1941, pp. 1–31.

LOESCHE, G. Haben die späteren neuplatonischen Polemiker gegen das Christentum das Werk des Celsus benutzt? *Zeitschrift für wissenschaftliche Theologie*, XXVII, 1884, pp. 257–302.

LUBAC, H. DE. *Histoire et Esprit: L'intelligence de l'écriture d'après Origène.* Paris, 1950.

MIURA-STANGE, A. *Celsus und Origenes: das Gemeinsame ihrer Weltanschauung.* (Beiheft z. Zeitschrift für die neutestamentliche Wissenschaft, 4.) Giessen, 1926.

MOLLAND, E. *The Conception of the Gospel in the Alexandrian Theology.* Oslo, 1938.

MOSHEIM, J. L. *Acht Bücher von der Wahrheit der christlichen Religion wider den Weltweisen Celsus.* Hamburg, 1745.

MUELLER, F. M. Die wahre Geschichte des Celsus. *Deutsche Rundschau*, LXXXIV, 1895, pp. 79–97.

MUTH, J. F. S. *Der Kampf des heidnischen Philosophen Celsus gegen das Christentum.* Mainz, 1899.

NESTLE, W. Die Haupteinwände des antiken Denkens gegen das Christentum. *Archiv für Religionswissenschaft*, XXXVII, 1941, pp. 51–100.

NEUMANN, K. J. Articles on Celsus in Pauly-Wissowa, *Realencyclopädie* and in Herzog-Hauck, *Realencyclopädie für protestantische Theologie und Kirche.*

—— *Der römische Staat und die allgemeine Kirche bis auf Diocletian*, I. Leipzig, 1890.

NILSSON, M. P. *Greek Piety.* Oxford, 1948.

—— *Geschichte der griechischen Religion*, II. Munich, 1950.

—— Sophia-Prunikos. *Eranos*, XLV, 1947, pp. 169–72.

—— Die Religion in den griechischen Zauberpapyri. *Bulletin de la Société royale des lettres de Lund*, 1947–8.

NOCK, A. D. *Sallustius concerning the gods and the universe.* Cambridge, 1926.

—— *Conversion.* Oxford, 1933.

—— Conversion and Adolescence. *Pisciculi für F. J. Dölger* (Antike und Christentum, Ergänzungsband). Münster, 1939.

—— Article, 'Bekehrung', in Klauser's *Reallexikon für Antike und Christentum* II, cols. 105–18. Stuttgart, 1951.

PARKE, H. W. *A History of the Delphic Oracle.* Oxford, 1939.

PATRICK, J. *The Apology of Origen in reply to Celsus.* Edinburgh and London, 1892.

PÉLAGAUD, É. *Un conservateur au second siècle: étude sur Celse et la première escarmouche entre la philosophie antique et le christianisme naissant.* Lyon, 1878.

BIBLIOGRAPHY

PETERSON, E. *Der Monotheismus als politisches Problem*. Leipzig, 1935.

—— 'Das Problem des Nationalismus im alten Christentum', in *Theologische Zeitschrift*, VII, 1951, pp. 81–91.

PHILIPPI, F. A. *De Celsi adversarii christianorum philosophandi genere*. Berlin, 1836.

POHLENZ, M. *Vom Zorne Gottes*. (Forschungen zur Religion und Literatur des Alten und Neuen Testaments 12.) Göttingen, 1909.

—— Klemens von Alexandreia und sein hellenisches Christentum. *Göttingen Nachrichten* 1943, phil.-hist. Klasse, Heft 3.

—— *Die Stoa*. Göttingen, 1948.

PREUSCHEN, E. Review of Koetschau's edition of the *contra Celsum* in *Berliner philologische Wochenschrift*, 1899, cols. 1185 ff.

—— Bibelcitate bei Origenes. *Zeitschrift für die neutestamentliche Wissenschaft*, IV, 1905, pp. 67–74.

PUECH, H. C. La mystique d'Origène. *Revue d'histoire et de philosophie religieuses*, XIII, 1933, pp. 508–36.

—— Numénius d'Apamée et les théologies orientales au IIe siècle. In *Mélanges Bidez*, II, (Brussels, 1934), pp. 745–78.

—— Les nouveaux écrits d'Origène et de Didyme découverts à Toura. *Revue d'histoire et de philosophie religieuses*, XXXI, 1951, pp. 293–329.

QUISPEL, G. *Gnosis als Weltreligion*. Zürich, 1951.

REDEPENNING, E. R. *Origenes, eine Darstellung seines Lebens und seiner Lehre*. Bonn, 1841.

REINHARDT, K. Poseidonios über Ursprung und Entartung. *Orient und Antike*, VI, 1925.

ROBINSON, J. A. On the text of Origen against Celsus. *Journal of Philology*, XVIII, 1890, pp. 288–96.

ROHDE, E. *Psyche*. Trans. W. B. Hillis. London, 1925.

ROUGIER, L. *Celse ou le conflit de la civilisation antique et du Christianisme primitif*. Paris, 1925.

SCHERER, J. *Entretien d'Origène avec Héraclide et les évêques ses collègues sur le Père, le Fils, et l'Âme*. (Publications de la société Fouad I de Papyrologie, Textes et Documents, IX.) Cairo, 1949.

SCHMIDT, C. In *Philotesia P. Kleinert dargebracht* (Berlin, 1907), pp. 317 ff.

SCHMIDT, K. Review of Glöckner's reconstruction of Celsus in *Gnomon*, III, 1927, pp. 117–25.

—— De Celsi libro qui inscribitur Alethes Logos quaestiones ad philosophiam pertinentes. *Jahrbuch der philosophischen Fakultät in Göttingen*, 1922, II, pp. 69–74. (Summary of his dissertation.)

SCHOEPS, H. J. *Theologie und Geschichte des Judenchristentums*. Tübingen, 1949.

*SCHROEDER, H. O. *Der Alethes Logos des Celsus*. Untersuchungen zum Werk und seinem Verfasser mit einer Wiederherstellung des griechischen Textes und Kommentar. Giessen, 1939. [Only a summary of the dissertation printed.]

SCHUERER, E. *Geschichte des jüdischen Volkes im Zeitalter Jesu Christi*. 4th ed. 1901.

SIMON, M. *Verus Israel*. Paris, 1948.

STÄHLIN, O. Reviews of R. Bader and A. Wifstrand in *Philologische Wochenschrift*, 1942, cols. 1–7, and 1944, cols. 124–6.

STEIN, E. De Celso Platonico Philonis Alexandrini imitatore. *Eos*, XXXIV, 1932–3, pp. 205 ff.

STRACK, H. L. *Jesus, die Häretiker und die Christen*. 1910.

THEDINGA, J. F. *De Numenio philosopho Platonico*. Bonn, 1875.

TURNER, W. Celsus, the Voltaire of the second century. *Irish Theological Quarterly*, III, 1908, pp. 137–50.

*VÖLKER, W. Die Kritik des Celsus am Leben Jesu und die Korrekturen der Gnostiker. *Theologische Blätter*, 1926, pp. 25–39.

—— *Das Bild vom nichtgnostischen Christentum bei Celsus*. Halle, 1928.

—— *Das Vollkommenheitsideal des Origenes*. (Beiträge zur historischen Theologie 7.) Tübingen, 1931.

WALTZING, J. P. Le crime rituel reproché aux chrétiens du IIe siècle. *Académie royale de Belgique, Bulletins de la Classe des Lettres*, 1925, pp. 205–39.

WALZER, R. *Galen on Jews and Christians*. Oxford, 1949.

WASZINK, J. H. *Tertulliani de Anima*. Amsterdam, 1947.

WENDLAND, P. *Philos Schrift über die Vorsehung*. Berlin, 1892.

—— Reviews of Koetschau's edition of the *contra Celsum* and his *Kritische Bemerkungen* in *Göttingische gelehrte Anzeigen*, 1899, pp. 276–304, 613–22.

—— *Die hellenistisch-römische Kultur*. 3rd ed. Leipzig, 1912.

WHALE, J. S. Great Attacks on Christianity: Celsus. *Expository Times*, XLII, 1930–1, pp. 119–24.

WHITTAKER, T. *Apollonius of Tyana and other essays*. Cambridge, 1906.

WIFSTRAND, A. Eikota IV. *Bulletin de la Société royale des lettres de Lund*, 1938–9, II.

—— Die wahre Lehre des Kelsos. *Ibid.* 1941–2, V.

—— Review of R. Bader in *Theologische Literaturzeitung*, 1941, cols. 334–5.

WILLIAMS, A. L. *Adversus Judaeos*. Cambridge, 1935.

WINTER, F. A. *Über den Wert der direkten und indirekten Überlieferung von Origenes Büchern contra Celsum*. Programm Burghausen, 1902–3 and 1903–4.

WITT, R. E. *Albinus and the History of Middle Platonism*. Cambridge, 1937.

WOLFSON, H. A. *Philo*. Cambridge, Mass. 1947.

ZELLER, E. *Die Philosophie der Griechen*. 6th ed. Leipzig, 1920.

CONTRA CELSUM

PREFACE

1. Our Saviour and Lord Jesus Christ was silent[1] when false witnesses spoke against him, and answered nothing[2] when he was accused; he was convinced that all his life and actions among the Jews were better than any speech in refutation of the false witness and superior to any words that he might say in reply to the accusations. And, God-loving Ambrose, I do not know why you wanted me to write an answer to Celsus' false accusations in his book against the Christians and the faith of the churches. It is as though there was not in the mere facts a clear refutation better than any written reply, which dispels the false charges and deprives the accusations of any plausibility and force. Concerning the silence of Jesus when false witnesses spoke against him, it is enough here to quote Matthew's version; for Mark's words amount to the same thing. The text of Matthew reads as follows:[3] 'The high priest and the sanhedrin sought for false witness against Jesus, that they might put him to death; and they found it not, though many false witnesses came. But afterward there came two who said, This man said, I am able to destroy the temple of God and to build it up again in three days. And the high priest stood up and said to him, Answerest thou nothing to what they witness against thee? But Jesus kept silence.' Moreover, of the fact that he did not reply when accused it is written as follows:[4] 'And Jesus stood before the governor; and he questioned him saying, Art thou the king of the Jews? And Jesus said to him, Thou sayest. And when he was accused by the chief priests and elders he answered nothing. Then said Pilate unto him, Dost thou not hear how many things they witness against thee? And he answered him not a word, so that the governor marvelled greatly.'

2. It might well cause amazement among those with moderate intellectual powers that a man who was accused and charged falsely did not defend himself and prove himself not guilty of any of the charges, although he could have done so by expatiating on the fine quality of his life and showing that his miracles were done by God, to give the judge an opportunity of giving his case a more favourable judgment. This he did not do, but despised and nobly ignored his accusers. That the judge would have released Jesus without hesitation if he had made any defence is clear from what is written about him where he said: 'Which of the two do you wish me to release to you, Barabbas or Jesus who is called Christ?' and, as the

---

[1] Matt. xxvi. 59–63; Mark xiv. 55–61.
[2] Matt. xxvii. 12–14; Mark xv. 3–5; Luke xxiii. 9.
[3] Matt. xxvi. 59–63.   [4] Matt. xxvii. 11–14.

3

scripture goes on to say: 'For he knew that for envy they delivered him.'[1]
Now Jesus is always being falsely accused, and there is never a time when
he is not being accused so long as there is evil among men. He is still
silent in face of this and does not answer with his voice; but he makes his
defence in the lives of his genuine disciples, for their lives cry out the real
facts and defeat all false charges, refuting and overthrowing the slanders
and accusations.

3. I would therefore go so far as to say that the defence which you ask
me to compose will weaken the force of the defence that is in the mere
facts, and detract from the power of Jesus which is manifest to those who
are not quite stupid. Nevertheless, that we may not appear to shirk the task
which you have set us, we have tried our best to reply to each particular
point in Celsus' book and to refute it as it seemed fitting to us, although
his arguments cannot shake the faith of any true Christian. God forbid
that there should be found anyone who, after receiving such love of
God as that which is in Christ Jesus, has been shaken in his purpose by
the words of Celsus or one of his sort. For when Paul gave a list of
the countless things which usually tend to separate men from the love of
Christ and the love of God which is in Christ Jesus, to all of which the
love that is in him is superior, he did not include argument in the number.
Notice what he says first: 'Who shall separate us from the love of Christ?
Shall tribulation, or anguish, or persecution, or famine, or nakedness, or
peril, or sword? As it is written, For thy sake we are killed all the day long;
we were accounted as sheep for the slaughter. But in all these things we
are more than conquerors through him that loved us.' And secondly, when
setting forth another list of things which naturally tend to separate people
who are unstable in their religion, he says: 'For I am persuaded that neither
death nor life, nor angels, nor principalities, nor things present, nor things
to come, nor powers, nor height, nor depth, nor any other creature, shall
be able to separate us from the love of God which is in Christ Jesus our
Lord.'[2]

4. We in truth might well be proud if tribulation and the things
following it in this first list do not separate us. But not so for Paul and
the apostles, and anyone like them; it is because he was far above such
things that he said: 'In all these things we are more than conquerors through
him that loved us.' That is greater than just conquering. But if even
apostles may be proud that they are not being separated from the love
of God which is in Christ Jesus our Lord, they would boast on the ground
that 'neither death, nor life, nor angels, nor principalities', nor any of
those that follow, can separate them 'from the love of God which is in

[1] Matt. xxvii. 17–18.   [2] Rom. viii. 35–9.

Christ Jesus our Lord'. Accordingly I have no sympathy with anyone who had faith in Christ such that it could be shaken by Celsus (who is no longer living the common life among men but has already been dead a long time), or by any plausibility of argument. I do not know in what category I ought to reckon one who needs written arguments in books to restore and confirm him in his faith after it has been shaken by the accusations brought by Celsus against the Christians. But nevertheless, since among the multitude of people supposed to believe some people of this kind might be found, who may be shaken and disturbed by the writings of Celsus, and who may be restored by the reply to them if what is said is of a character that is destructive of Celsus' arguments and clarifies the truth, we decided to yield to your demand and to compose a treatise in reply to that which you sent us. But I do not think that any of those who have made even slight progress in philosophy will agree that it is *The True Doctrine* as Celsus has entitled it.

5. Now Paul perceived that there are impressive doctrines in Greek philosophy which are convincing to most people, but which present as truth what is untrue, and says of them: 'Take heed lest there shall be anyone that makes spoil of you through his philosophy and vain deceit, after the tradition of men, after the elements of the world, and not after Christ.'[1] Seeing that there was some greatness apparent in the theories of the wisdom of the world, he said that the theories of the philosophers were 'after the elements of the world'. But no intelligent man would say that Celsus' writings were 'after the elements of the world'. Those ideas which have some deceit about them Paul calls 'vain deceit', perhaps in antithesis to deceit that is not vain. Jeremiah had this in mind when he dared to say to God: 'O Lord, thou hast deceived me, and I was deceived; thou wast stronger than I and didst prevail.'[2] But Celsus' arguments appear to me to have no deceit at all, not even vain deceit such as that in the opinions of those who have established philosophical schools and have[3] received exceptional mental ability in that respect. And just as no one would call an elementary blunder in geometrical propositions a fallacy, or would even put it on record for the sake of the training derived from these exercises, so what is to be called vain deceit 'after[4] the tradition of men, after the elements of the world', ought to resemble the ideas of those who have founded philosophical sects.

6. I decided to put this preface at the beginning after I had composed the reply to everything up to the point where Celsus puts the attack against Jesus into the mouth of the Jew.[5] I did this so that the reader of

[1] Col. ii. 8.   [2] Jer. xx. 7.   [3] Om. τῶν with K. tr.
[4] Read κατὰ παράδοσιν with Wi.   [5] I, 28 ff.

my replies to Celsus may start with it and see that this book is not written at all for true Christians, but either for those entirely without experience of faith in Christ, or for those whom the apostle calls 'weak in faith'; for he says this: 'Him that is weak in faith receive ye.'[1] The preface may serve as my apology for the fact that I wrote the beginning of my answer to Celsus on one plan but after the first part followed a different one. At first I contemplated making notes on the main points and giving brief answers to them, and then putting the work into definite shape. But afterwards the material itself suggested to me that I would save time if I were to be content with the points which I had answered in this way at the beginning, and in what followed to combat in detail Celsus' charges against us to the best of our ability. We therefore ask indulgence for the part at the beginning following the preface. If; however, you are not impressed also by the effectiveness of the answers after that, then I ask pardon likewise for those and refer you, if you still want a written reply, to people wiser[2] than myself, who can refute by words and books Celsus' charges against us. Yet better is the man who, even if he meets with Celsus' book, has no need of any answer to it at all, but pays no attention to anything in his book, which is despised with good reason even by the ordinary believer in Christ on account of the Spirit which is in him.

[1] Rom. xiv. 1.   [2] Om. δυνατούς with Bo.

BOOK I

1. Celsus' first main point in his desire to attack Christianity is that the Christians secretly make associations with one another contrary to the laws, because *societies which are public are allowed by the laws, but secret societies are illegal.* And wishing to slander the so-called *love (agape)*[1] *which Christians have for one another,* he says that *it exists because of the common danger and is more powerful than any oath.*[2] As he talks much of *the common law* saying that *the associations of the Christians violate this,* I have to make this reply. Suppose that a man were living among the Scythians whose laws are contrary to the divine law, who had no opportunity to go elsewhere and was compelled to live among them; such a man for the sake of the[3] true law, though illegal among the Scythians, would rightly form associations with like-minded people contrary to the laws of the Scythians. So, at the bar of truth, the laws of the nations such as those about images and the godless polytheism are laws of the Scythians or, if possible, more impious than theirs. Therefore it is not wrong to form associations against the laws for the sake of truth. For just as it would be right for people to form associations secretly to kill a tyrant who had seized control of their city, so too, since the devil, as Christians call him, and falsehood reign as tyrants, Christians form associations against the devil contrary to his laws, in order to save others whom they might be able to persuade to abandon the law which is like that of the Scythians and of a tyrant.[4]

2. Next he says that *the doctrine* (obviously meaning Judaism with which Christianity is connected) *was originally barbarian.* Having an open mind he does not reproach the gospel for its barbarian origin, but praises *the barbarians* for being *capable of discovering doctrines*; but he adds to this that *the Greeks are better able to judge the value of what the barbarians have discovered, and to establish the doctrines and put them into practice by virtue.*[5] Taking up the words he has used this is our reply in respect of the fundamental truths of Christianity. A man coming to the gospel from Greek

---

[1] That ἀγάπη probably means brotherly love and not the love-feast is shown by πρὸς ἀλλήλους. Cf. Völker, *Das Bild*, pp. 44–5. For danger as uniting the Christians, cf. III, 14. For illegal Societies, cf. *Dig.* XLVII, 22; Pliny, *Ep. ad Tr.* XCVI, 7.

[2] Perhaps read ὑπὲρ ὅρκια, cf. Homer, *Il.* III, 299; IV, 67.

[3] Read τὸν with A.

[4] For the contrast between the law of nature and the existing codes, cf. v, 37. It is worth noting that Origen is apparently the first to justify the right to resist tyranny by appealing to natural law. Cf. VIII, 65.

[5] Cf. [Plato], *Epinomis*, 987 E: 'We may take it that whatever the Greeks take from the barbarians, they turn it to something better'; Celsus in VI, 1.

7

conceptions and training would not only *judge* that it[1] was true, but would also *put* it *into practice* and so prove it to be correct; and he would complete what seemed to be lacking judged by the criterion of a Greek proof, thus establishing the truth of Christianity. Moreover, we have to say this, that the gospel has a proof which is peculiar to itself, and which is more divine than a Greek proof based on dialectical argument. This more divine demonstration the apostle calls a 'demonstration of the Spirit and of power'[2]—of spirit because of the prophecies and especially those which refer to Christ, which are capable of convincing anyone who reads them; of power because of the prodigious miracles which may be proved to have happened by this argument among many others, that traces of them still remain among those who live according to the will of the Logos.[3]

3. After this he says that *Christians perform their rites and teach their doctrines in secret*, and *they do this with good reason to escape the death penalty that hangs over them.* He compares the *danger* to *the risks encountered for the sake of philosophy as by Socrates.* He could also have added 'as by Pythagoras and other philosophers'. I reply to this that in Socrates' case the Athenians at once regretted what they had done,[4] and cherished no grievance against him or against Pythagoras; at any rate, the Pythagoreans have for a long time established their schools in the part of Italy which has been called Magna Graecia. But in the case of the Christians the Roman Senate, the contemporary emperors, the army, the people, and the relatives of believers fought against the gospel and would have hindered it; and it would have been defeated by the combined force of so many unless it had overcome and risen above the opposition by divine power, so that it has conquered the whole world that was conspiring against it.

4. Let us see also how he thinks he can criticize our *ethical teaching* on the grounds that it *is commonplace and in comparison with the other philosophers contains no teaching that is impressive or new.*[5] I have to reply to this that for people who affirm the righteous judgment of God, it would have been impossible to believe in the penalty inflicted for sins unless in accordance with the universal ideas all men had a sound conception of moral principles.[6] There is therefore nothing amazing about it if the same

---

[1] Read αὐτὸν with K. tr.   [2] I Cor. ii. 4.

[3] Cf. I, 46; II, 8; VII, 8.

[4] Diog. Laert. II, 43; Maximus Tyr. III, 2e.

[5] Cf. Celsus in II, 5; Tert. *Apol.* XLVI, 2 'Eadem, inquit, et philosophi monent atque profitentur, innocentiam, iustitiam, patientiam, sobrietatem, pudicitiam.'

[6] Origen appeals in reply to the Stoic doctrine of κοιναὶ ἔννοιαι implanted in every man by nature; cf., for example, Cicero, *de Legibus*, I, 6, 18; Philo, *Quod Omnis Prob.* 46.

God has implanted in the souls of all men the truths which He taught through the prophets and the Saviour; He did this that every man might be without excuse at the divine judgment, having the requirement of the law written in his heart.[1] The Bible hinted at this in what Greeks regard as a myth when it made God write the commandments with His own finger and give them to Moses.[2] The sin of the people who made the calf shattered them,[3] which is as if he said, the flood of evil swept them away. But when Moses had cut a stone God wrote them a second time[4] and gave them again, which is as if the prophetic word was preparing the soul after the first sin for a second writing of God.

5. In giving an account of the attitude to idolatry as characteristic of Christians he even supports that view, saying: *Because of this they would not regard as gods those that are made with hands, since it is irrational that things should be gods which are made by craftsmen of the lowest kind who are morally wicked. For often they have been made by bad men.*[5] Later, when he wants to make out that the idea is commonplace and that it was not discovered first by Christianity, he quotes the saying of Heraclitus which says: '*Those who approach lifeless things as gods act like a man who holds conversation with houses.*'[6] I would reply in this instance also, as in that of the other ethical principles, that moral ideas have been implanted in men, and that it was from these that Heraclitus and any other Greek or barbarian conceived the notion of maintaining this doctrine. He also quotes *the Persians* as *holding this view*, adducing *Herodotus as authority for this.*[7] We will also add that Zeno of Citium says in his *Republic*: 'There will be no need to build temples; for nothing ought to be thought sacred, or of great value, and holy, which is the work of builders and artisans.'[8] Obviously therefore, in respect of this doctrine also, the knowledge of what is right conduct was written by God in the hearts of men.

6. After this, impelled by some unknown power, Celsus says: *Christians get the power which they seem to possess by pronouncing the names of certain daemons and incantations,*[9] hinting I suppose at those who subdue daemons by enchantments and drive them out. But he seems blatantly to misrepresent the gospel. For they do not *get the power which they seem to possess* by

---

[1] Rom. ii. 15.   [2] Exod. xxxi. 18.
[3] Exod. xxxii. 19.   [4] Exod. xxxiv. 1.
[5] For an attack on the character of image-makers, cf. Clem. Al. *Protr.* IV, 53; Origen in III, 76 below.
[6] Heraclitus, *frag.* B 5 Diels, quoted below in VII, 62, 65; Clem. Al. *Protr.* IV, 50, 4.
[7] Herodotus I, 131.
[8] *S.V.F.* I, 265. Koetschau (trans.) wants to emend the text on the basis of Clem. Al. *Strom.* v, 76, and Plutarch, *Mor.* 1034B; but Origen may be quoting from memory.
[9] For this charge, cf. Celsus in VI, 40; VIII, 37; *Passio S. Perpetuae* 16.

any *incantations* but by the name of Jesus with the recital of the histories about him.[1] For when these are pronounced they have often made daemons to be driven out of men, and especially when those who utter them speak with real sincerity and genuine belief. In fact the name of Jesus is so powerful against the daemons that sometimes it is effective even when pronounced by bad men. Jesus taught this when he said: 'Many shall say to me in that day, In thy name we have cast out daemons and performed miracles.'[2] I do not know whether Celsus intentionally and wickedly overlooked this, or if he was ignorant of it. However he next attacks the Saviour also, saying that *it was by magic that he was able to do the miracles which he appeared to have done; and because he foresaw that others too would get to know the same formulas and do the same thing, and boast that they did so by God's power, Jesus expelled them from his society.*[3] He makes the accusation against him that *if he was right in driving them out, although he was guilty of the same himself, he is a bad man; but if he is not a bad man for having done this, neither are they bad who acted as he did.* But, on the contrary, even if it seems impossible to prove how Jesus did these things, it is clear that Christians make no use of spells, but only of the name of Jesus with other words which are believed to be effective, taken from the divine scripture.[4]

7. Then since he often calls our doctrine *secret*, in this point also I must refute him. For almost the whole world has come to know the preaching of Christians better than the opinions of philosophers. Who has not heard of Jesus' birth from a virgin, and of his crucifixion, and of his resurrection in which many have believed, and of the proclamation of the judgment which punishes sinners according to their deserts and pronounces the righteous worthy of reward? Moreover, the mystery of the resurrection, because it has not been understood, is a byword and a laughing-stock with the unbelievers. In view of this it is quite absurd to say that *the doctrine is secret.* The existence of certain doctrines, which are beyond those which are exoteric and do not reach the multitude, is not a peculiarity of Christian doctrine only, but is shared by the philosophers. For they had some doctrines which were exoteric and some esoteric. Some hearers of

---

[1] The ἱστορία was probably some such phrase as 'crucified under Pontius Pilate'. Cf. III, 24; Justin, *Apol.* II, 6; *Dial.* 30 and 76; Irenaeus, *adv. Haer.* II, 32, 4 (Harvey I, 375); *Epideixis*, 97. Cf. R. H. Connolly, *J.T.S.* XXV (1924), p. 346 n.; J. Kroll, *Gott u. Hölle* (1932), p. 128 n. 1. But narratives from the gospels are found used as spells in the magical papyri.

[2] Matt. vii. 22.

[3] Bader suggests that ἀπελαύνει τῆς ἑαυτοῦ πολιτείας may allude to Plato's expulsion of Homer and the poets from his Republic.

[4] For the superior potency of scriptural names and phrases cf. Origen, *Hom. in Iesu Nave*, XX, 1 (*Philocalia*, 12); Athanasius, *Ep. ad Marcellinum* 33 (*P.G.* XXVII, 45).

Pythagoras only learnt of the master's 'ipse dixit';[1] but others were taught in secret doctrines which could not deservedly reach ears that were uninitiated and not yet purified. None of the mysteries in any place, in Greece and in barbarian lands, has been attacked for being secret. Therefore Celsus has no reason to attack the secrecy of Christianity and has no accurate understanding of it.

8. He appears shrewd in approving somehow of the actions of those who witness for Christianity to the point of death, saying: *And I do not mean that a man who embraces a good doctrine, if he is about to run into danger from men because of it, ought to renounce the doctrine, or pretend that he had renounced it, or come to deny it.* He condemns people who hold Christian opinions but pretend that they do not do so or deny them, saying that a man who holds the doctrine ought not to pretend that he had renounced it or come to deny it. But I may prove that Celsus contradicts himself. For from other writings he is found to be an Epicurean. But here because he appears to have more reasonable grounds for criticising Christianity if he does not confess the opinions of Epicurus, he pretends that *there is something in man superior to the earthly part, which is related to God.* He says that *those in whom this part is healthy* (that is, the soul) *always long*[2] *for him to whom it is related* (he means God), *and they desire to hear something of him and to be reminded about him.* See now the corruption of his soul; for although just now he said that *the man who embraces a good doctrine,* even *if he is about to run into danger from men because of it,* ought not *to renounce the doctrine, or pretend that he had renounced it, or come to deny it,* yet he himself falls into doing quite the opposite. He knew that if he admitted he was an Epicurean, he would not be worthy of credit in his criticisms of those who in some way introduce a doctrine of providence and who set a God over the universe. But we have heard that there were two Epicureans called Celsus, the earlier one a contemporary of Nero, while our Celsus lived in Hadrian's time and later.[3]

---

[1] This was proverbial. Cf. Philo, *Quaest. in Gen.* I, 99; Clem. Al. *Strom.* II, 24, 3; Cicero, *de Nat. Deor.* I, 5, 10; Quintilian, *Inst. Orat.* II, 1, 27; Schol. Aristoph. *Nub.* 195; Diog. Laert. VIII, 46; Julian, 452C; Jerome, *Praef. in Ep. ad Galat.* (Migne, *P.L.* XXVI, 331C); Greg. Nyss. *c. Eunom.* I, 225 (i. 87 Jaeger). Cf. below, IV, 9.
For the Pythagorean practice, Porphyry, *Vita Pyth.* 37; Clem. Al. *Strom.* V, 59, 1; Aulus Gellius, I, 9, 3 ff.

[2] Read ἐφίενται with Guiet. For the idea cf. Celsus in VIII, 63; for the soul's affinity with God, Plato, *Timaeus*, 90A; Porphyry, *ad Marcellam*, 16 (Nauck 284, 25 f.): μόνη γὰρ ἀρετὴ τὴν ψυχὴν ἄνω ἕλκει καὶ πρὸς τὸ συγγενές. Iamblichus, *de Myst.* I, 15 (Parthey 46, 14) where the divine element in us is roused by prayer and ἐφίεται τοῦ ὁμοίου διαφερόντως καὶ συνάπτεται πρὸς αὐτοτελειότητα.

[3] See the Introduction, p. xxiv *supra.*

9. After this he urges us to *follow reason and a rational guide in accepting doctrines* on the ground that *anyone who believes people without so doing is certain to be deceived.*[1] And he compares those who believe without rational thought to the *begging priests of Cybele and soothsayers, and to worshippers of Mithras and Sabazius, and whatever else one might meet, apparitions of Hecate or of some other daemon or daemons.*[2] *For just as among them scoundrels frequently take advantage of the lack of education of gullible people and lead them wherever they wish, so also,* he says, *this happens among the Christians.* He says that *some do not even want to give or to receive a reason for what they believe,* and use such expressions as '*Do not ask questions; just believe*', and '*Thy faith will save thee*'.[3] And he affirms that they say: '*The wisdom in the world is an evil, and foolishness a good thing.*' My answer to this is that if every man could abandon the business of life and devote his time to philosophy, no other course ought to be followed but this alone. For in Christianity, if I make no vulgar boasting, there will be found to be no less profound study of the writings that are believed; we explain the obscure utterances of the prophets, and the parables in the gospels, and innumerable other events or laws which have a symbolical meaning. However, if this is impossible, since, partly owing to the necessities of life and partly owing to human weakness, very few people are enthusiastic about rational thought, what better way of helping the multitude could be found other than that given to the nations by Jesus?

Moreover, concerning the multitude of believers who have renounced the great flood of evil in which they formerly used to wallow, we ask this question—is it better that those who believe without thought should somehow have been made reformed characters and be helped by the belief that they are punished for sin and rewarded for good works, or that we should not allow them to be converted with simple faith until they might devote themselves to the study of rational arguments? For obviously all but a very few would fail to obtain the help which they have derived from simple belief, but would remain living a very evil life. Therefore whatever other proof there may be that a doctrine so beneficial to mankind could not have come to human life apart from divine providence this consideration must also be enumerated with the rest. A religious man will not suppose that even a physician concerned with bodies, who restores many people to

---

[1] For philosophy as the only safe guide Bader compares Plutarch, *de Is. et Os.* 67–8 (378).

[2] Cf. Lobeck, *Aglaophamus*, pp. 120 f.; Plutarch, *de Superstitione*, 3 (166A). For the begging priests cf. A. D. Nock, *Conversion* (1933), pp. 82f.

[3] Cf. Galen's remark: 'If I had in mind people who taught their pupils in the same way as the followers of Moses and Christ teach theirs—for they order them to accept everything on faith—I should not have given you a definition' (R. Walzer, *Galen on Jews and Christians* (1949), pp. 15, 48–56). Celsus in VI, 11–12.

health, comes to live a mong cities and nations without divine providence;[1] for no benefit comes to mankind without God's action. If a man who has healed the bodies of many or improved their condition does not cure people without divine providence, how much more must that be true of him who cured, converted, and improved the souls of many, and attached them to the supreme God, and taught them to refer every action to the standard of His pleasure, and to avoid anything that is displeasing to Him, down to the most insignificant of words or deeds or even of casual thoughts?

10. As this matter of faith is so much talked of, I have to reply that we accept it as useful for the multitude, and that we admittedly teach those who cannot abandon everything and pursue a study of rational argument to believe without thinking out their reasons. But, even if they do not admit it, in practice others do the same. What man who is urged to study philosophy and throws himself into some school of philosophers at random or because he has met a philosopher of that school, comes to do this for any reason except that he has faith that this school is better? He does not wait to hear the arguments of all the philosophers and of the different schools, and the refutation of one and the proof of another, when in this way he chooses to be a Stoic, or a Platonist, or a Peripatetic, or an Epicurean, or a follower of some such philosophical school. Even though they do not want to admit it, it is by an unreasoning impulse that people come to the practice of, say, Stoicism and abandon the rest; or Platonism, because they despise the others as of lesser significance;[2] or Peripateticism, because it corresponds best to human needs and sensibly admits the value of the good things of human life more than other systems. And some, who at their first encounter were alarmed at the argument about providence based on the earthly circumstances of bad and good men,[3] have too hastily concluded that providence does not exist, and have adopted the opinion of Epicurus and Celsus.

[1] Cf. 1, 26 below; Dio Chrys. Orat. xxxii, 14.
[2] Read τοὺς λοιπούς, ἢ τὸν Πλατωνικόν, ὑπερφρονήσαντες ὡς ταπεινοτέρων τῶν ἄλλων, ἢ τὸν...κτλ. with codex B of Φ, Wendland, Winter, and K. tr.
[3] Cf., for example, Sextus Empiricus, P.H. 1, 32: 'When anyone argues that providence exists from the order of the heavenly bodies, we oppose him with the argument that frequently the good suffer evil while the wicked prosper, and by this reasoning we conclude that providence does not exist.' For the argument of this chapter, cf. Galen, de Ordine Libr. Suor. 1 (xix, 50 Kühn): 'People admire this or that particular physician or philosopher without proper study of their subject and without a training in scientific demonstration, with the help of which they would be able to distinguish between false and true arguments; some do this because their fathers, others because their teachers, others because their friends were either empirics or dogmatics or methodics, or simply because a representative of a particular school was admired in their native city. The same applies to the philosophical schools: different people have for different reasons become Platonists, Aristotelians, Stoics, or Epicureans' (trans. Walzer, op. cit., pp. 19f.); Greg. Thaum. Paneg. xiii, 154 ff.

11. If, as my argument has shown, belief is inevitable in following a particular individual among those who have founded sects among the Greeks or the barbarians, why should we not far more believe in the supreme God and in him who teaches that we ought to worship Him alone, but to pay no attention to the rest, either as being non-existent, or, if they do exist, as being worthy of honour but certainly not of worship and adoration? In respect of these matters a man who not only believes, but also uses reason in considering these questions, will declare the proofs that suggest themselves to him which he may discover as the result of an exhaustive inquiry. Why is it not more reasonable, seeing that all human acts depend on faith, to believe in God rather than in them? Who goes on a voyage, or marries, or begets children, or casts seeds into the ground, unless he believes that things will turn out for the better, although it is possible that the opposite may happen—as it sometimes does?[1] But nevertheless the faith that things will turn out for the better and as they wish makes all men take risks, even where the result is not certain and where things might turn out differently. Now if it is hope and the faith that the future will be better which maintain life in every action where the result is uncertain, is it not more reasonable for a man to trust in God than in the outcome of a sea voyage or of seed sown in the earth or of marriage to a wife or any other human activity? For he puts his faith in the God who created all these things, and in him who with exceptional greatness of mind and divine magnanimity ventured to commend this doctrine to people in all parts of the world, and who incurred great risks and a death supposed to be disgraceful, which he endured for the sake of mankind; and he taught those who were persuaded to obey his teaching at the beginning boldly to travel everywhere in the world for the salvation of men through all dangers and continual expectation of death.

12. Then Celsus goes on to speak in these very words: *If they would be willing to answer my questions, which I do not put as one who is trying to understand their beliefs (for I know them all), all would be well. But if they will not consent but say, as they usually do, 'Do not ask questions', and so on, then it will be necessary to teach them,*[2] he says, *the nature of the doctrines which they affirm, and the source from which they came . . .* etc. In reply to his claim, *For I know them all*, which he very boastfully dared to make, I have to say that if he had read the prophets especially, which are full of

---

[1] Cf. Philo, *de Praem. et Poen.* 11 ἐλπίς, ἡ πηγὴ τῶν βίων; Maximus Tyr. I, 5; XXIX, 3; Theophilus, *ad Autol.* I, 8; Arnobius, II, 8. Origen's four examples, sailing, sowing seeds, marrying, and begetting children, are commonplace, and go back to Clitomachus, leader of the New Academy. Cf. Cicero, *Lucullus*, 109, and the remarks of R. M. Grant in *H.T.R.* XLIII (1950), p. 182.

[2] Taking αὐτούς as object of διδάξαι, cf. Wifstrand, *Wahre Lehre*, p. 402.

admitted obscurities and of sayings of which the meaning is not clear to the multitude, and if he had read the parables of the gospels and the rest of the Bible, the law, the history of the Jews, and the utterances of the apostles, and if he had read with an open mind and a desire to enter into the meaning of the words, he would not have boasted in this way nor have said: *For I know them all*. Not even we, who have spent much time in the study of these books, would say, 'I know them all'. For we have a love for the truth.[1] None of us would say, 'I know all the doctrines of Epicurus', or would be so bold as to assert that he knew all the doctrines of Plato, since there are so many different interpretations even among those who expound them. Who is so bold as to say, 'I know all the Stoic or all the Peripatetic doctrines'? But perhaps after hearing the claim *I know them all* from some vulgar blockheads who were unaware of their own ignorance, he imagined that after he had been taught by such teachers he knew everything. He seems to me to have done something of this sort: he is like a man who went to stay in Egypt, where the Egyptian wise men who have studied their traditional writings give profound philosophical interpretations of what they regard as divine, while the common people hear certain myths of which they are proud, although they do not understand the meaning; and he imagined that he knew all the doctrines of the Egyptians after learning from their common people without having had conversation with any of the priests or having learnt from any of them the secret teachings of the Egyptians. What I have said about the Egyptian wise men and common people can also be seen in the case of the Persians; among them there are mysteries which are explained rationally by the learned men among them, but which are taken in their external significance by rather superficial minds and by the common people among them. The same may be said of the Syrians and Indians, and of all who have both myths and interpretative writings.

13. Celsus asserted that many Christians say *Wisdom in this life is evil, but foolishness is good*. My reply is that he misrepresents Christianity, since he has not quoted the actual words as they are in Paul, which read as follows: 'If any man among you think himself to be wise, let him become foolish in this world that he may become wise; for the wisdom of this world is foolishness with God.'[2] The apostle does not say simply: Wisdom is foolishness with God, but 'the wisdom of this world'. And again he does not just say simply, 'If any among you seem to be wise, let him become foolish', but 'let him become foolish in this world that he may become wise'. Accordingly we give the name 'the wisdom of this world'

---

[1] The phrase occurs also in III, 16; *Ep. ad Africanum*, 6 (XVII, 28 Lomm.).
[2] I Cor. iii. 18–19.

to all philosophy that holds wrong opinions, which according to the
scriptures is being brought to nought.¹ We do not call foolishness a good
thing without qualification, but only when anyone becomes foolish to this
world. It is as if we were to say that Platonism, in believing in the immortality of the soul and what is said about its reincarnation, accepted foolishness because the Stoics ridicule belief in these doctrines, and because the
Peripatetics talk of the Platonic ideas as 'twitterings',² and because the
Epicureans accuse of superstition people who introduce providence and
set a God over the universe. Moreover, it is in harmony with scripture to
say that it is far better to accept doctrines with reason and wisdom than
with mere faith. That it was only in certain circumstances that the Logos
wanted the latter, so that he might not allow mankind to be entirely
without help, is shown by Paul, the genuine disciple of Jesus, when he
said: 'For since in the wisdom of God the world knew not God through
wisdom, it pleased God by the foolishness of preaching to save them that
believe.'³ Obviously these words mean that men ought to have known
God in the wisdom of God. But since this did not happen, as an alternative
measure it pleased God to save them that believe not simply by foolishness,
but by foolishness in so far as that applies to preaching. For it is manifest
that the preaching of Jesus Christ as crucified is the foolishness of preaching.
Since he understood this Paul says: 'But we preach Christ crucified, to the
Jews a stumbling-block, to the heathen foolishness, but to those who are
called, both Jews and Greeks, Christ the power of God and the wisdom
of God.'⁴

14. Thinking that *between many of the nations there is an affinity* in that
they hold the same doctrine, Celsus names all the nations which he supposes
to have held this doctrine originally. But for some unknown reason he
misrepresents the Jews alone, and does not include their race in the list
with the others; nor does he say of them either that they *took part in labours*
equal to theirs and *had the same notions* or that they *held similar doctrines
in many respects*. It is therefore worth while asking him why ever he
believed in barbarian and Greek stories about the antiquity of the people
whom he mentioned, while it is only this nation whose histories he regards
as untrue. If all historians gave an honest account of their respective
nations, why are we to disbelieve the prophets of the Jews alone? If *Moses
and the prophets wrote much about their own people which is biased in favour
of their own doctrine*, why may we not say as much of the compositions of
the other nations also? Or are *the Egyptians* reliable authorities when in
their histories they speak evil of the Jews? And when the Jews say the same

¹ I Cor. ii. 6.   ² Aristotle, *Anal. Post.* 1, 22 (83 a 33). Cf. 11, 12, below.
³ I Cor. i. 21.   ⁴ I Cor. i. 23–4.

about the Egyptians, recording that they suffered much wrongfully and saying that for this reason they were punished by God, are they lying? Moreover, this may be said not only of the Egyptians; for we shall find a connexion between the Assyrians and the Jews, and that this is recorded in the Assyrian antiquities. So also the historians of the Jews (to avoid appearing to beg the question[1] I do not use the word 'prophets') wrote that the Assyrians were their enemies. See then the wilfulness of the man who believes some particular nations to be *wise* while he condemns others as *utterly stupid*. Hear Celsus' words: *There is an ancient doctrine which has existed from the beginning, which has always been maintained by the wisest nations and cities and wise men*. And he would not speak of the Jews as being *a very wise nation* on a par with *the Egyptians, Assyrians, Indians, Persians, Odrysians, Samothracians, and Eleusinians*.

15. How much better than Celsus is Numenius the Pythagorean,[2] a man who showed himself in many works to be very learned and who by studying several doctrines made from many sources a synthesis of those which seemed to him to be true. In the first book of his work on *The Good* where he speaks of the nations that believe God to be incorporeal, he also included the Jews among them, and did not hesitate to quote the sayings of the prophets in his book and to give them an allegorical interpretation. It is said also that Hermippus in his first book on 'Lawgivers' related that Pythagoras brought his philosophy to the Greeks from the Jews.[3] Moreover, a book about the Jews is attributed to Hecataeus the historian, in which the wisdom of the nation is emphasized even more strongly—so much so that Herennius Philo in his treatise about the Jews even doubts in the first place whether it is a genuine work of the historian, and says in the second place that if it is authentic, he had probably been carried away by the Jews' powers of persuasion and accepted their doctrine.[4]

[1] Read perhaps προλαμβάνειν λέγων with K. tr.
[2] *Frag.* ıxa Thedinga; *frag.* 9b Leemans. Numenius was probably a contemporary of Marcus Aurelius. For his syncretism, cf. Eus. *P.E.* ıx, 7, 411c, who quotes the passage to which Origen probably refers. See E. des Places, *Numénius: Fragments* (Paris, 1973), and Introd. p. xvi.   [3] Cf. Josephus, *c. Apion.* ı, 22, 163–5 and 183 ff.
[4] Read αὐτῶν τῷ λόγῳ with Bo. Herennius Philo of Byblus in Phoenicia lived approximately A.D. 50–130, but exact dating is not possible. Cf. Gudemann in P.-W. vııı, 650 ff. He wrote a 'Phoenician history', part of which was devoted to the Jews; an extract is given by Eus. *P.E.* ı, 10, 42, 40b. Hecataeus of Abdera or Teos was a contemporary of Alexander the Great who wrote a book on Egypt in which he mentioned the Jews (Diod. Sic. xl, 3). His remarks were sufficiently kind to lead Jewish apologists to appeal to his work (Ep. Arist. 31) in answering the pagan question, Why, if the Jews were so ancient, were they not mentioned by Greek historians? (cf. Celsus in ıv, 31). But Josephus (*c. Apion.* ı, 22, 183) knows of a special treatise on the Jews by him, and also one about Abraham (*Antiq.* ı, 7, 159). The latter is certainly, and the former probably, a Jewish forgery. The doubts of Herennius Philo appear well founded. See further v. Radinger in P.-W. vıı, 2765 f. who refers to the relevant literature.

16. I am surprised that Celsus numbers the *Odrysians, Samothracians, Eleusinians, and Hyperboreans* among the *most ancient and wise nations,* and yet does not reckon the Jews worth including with the wise or the ancient. For there are many treatises in circulation among the Egyptians, Phoenicians, and Greeks which testify to their antiquity, but I have thought it superfluous to quote them here. For anyone interested can read what has been written by Flavius Josephus in two books on the antiquity of the Jews,[1] where he produces a considerable collection of writers who testify to the antiquity of the Jews. There is also in circulation the 'Address to the Greeks' of Tatian the younger, who with great learning quotes historians who have written about the antiquity of the Jews and of Moses. Therefore Celsus seems to have said these things not because they are true but out of mere perversity, with a view to impugning the origin of Christianity which depended on the Jews. He says, moreover, that *the Galactophagi of Homer,*[2] *the Druids of the Gauls,*[3] *and the Getae are very wise and ancient nations, who believe doctrines akin to those of the Jews.* I do not know whether their writings are extant; but it is only the Hebrews that he rejects, as far as he can, in respect of both antiquity and wisdom.

Again, when he makes a list of *ancient and wise men who were of service to their contemporaries and to posterity by their writings,* he rejects Moses from the list of wise men. Linus, whom Celsus puts first of those that he names, is not credited with laws or writings that have converted and healed nations; whereas a whole nation, scattered throughout the whole world, has the laws of Moses. Consider then whether he did not exclude Moses from the list of wise men out of downright wickedness. For he says that *Linus, Musaeus, Orpheus, Pherecydes, Zoroaster the Persian,*[4] *and Pythagoras understood these doctrines, and their opinions were put down in books and are preserved to this day.*

17. He intentionally omitted to mention the myth about the supposed gods describing them as possessing human passions, which was composed for the most part by Orpheus;[5] [17] but later when he criticizes the Mosaic history he finds fault with those who interpret it figuratively and allegorically. But it could be said to this most worthy fellow who entitles his book *The True Doctrine*: Why, my good sir, are you so proud that the gods encountered such misfortunes as your wise poets and philosophers record, that they even indulged in sexual immorality, fought against their fathers,

---

[1] Commonly called *contra Apionem.*   [2] *Iliad,* XIII, 6.
[3] On the Druids, cf. A. S. Pease on Cicero, *de Divin.* I, 41, 90.
[4] For Zoroastrian books, cf. J. Bidez and F. Cumont, *Les Mages hellénisés* (1938), I, p. 85, who collect references.
[5] Putting a comma after Ὀρφέως with Wifstrand, to make the sentence run on. The beginning of the chapter has been changed accordingly.

and cut off their private parts, and that history has recorded that they dared to commit such crimes and suffered such indignities? On the other hand, when Moses says nothing of this kind about God, or even about the holy angels, and relates stories about men which are far less offensive (for no one in Moses' writings went so far as to do what Kronos did to Uranus or what Zeus did to his father, or to behave like 'the father of gods and men'[1] when[2] he had sexual intercourse with his daughter), do you think that those to whom he gave laws were led astray and deceived? It seems to me that Celsus is doing much the same as Thrasymachus in Plato who would not leave it to Socrates to answer the question about justice as he liked, but said: 'See that you do not say that justice is what is convenient, nor what is necessary, nor anything like that.'[3] So when Celsus attacks, as he thinks, the Mosaic history and finds fault with *those who treat it allegorically*, although at the same time he gives them some credit for being *the more reasonable*,[4] by the form of his criticism as it were he hinders[5] (as he intends to do) those who are able to explain in reply how matters really stand.

18. We might challenge him to a comparison of our respective books and say: Come, sir, examine the poems of Linus, Musaeus, and Orpheus, and the writings of Pherecydes, side by side with the laws of Moses, comparing histories with histories, moral precepts with laws and commandments; and see which are more able to transform instantly those who hear them, and which of them would do harm to the hearer. Notice also that the men in your list of writers pay little attention to those who would read them without any deeper understanding; they wrote down *their own philosophy*, as you call it, only for people able to interpret figuratively and allegorically. But in his five books Moses acted like a distinguished orator who pays attention to outward form and everywhere keeps carefully the concealed meaning of his words. To the multitude of the Jews under his legislation he provided no occasions for them to come to any harm in their moral behaviour, and yet he did not produce a work which gave no opportunities for deeper study for the few who are able to read with more understanding, and who are capable of searching out his meaning. It seems that not even the books of your wise men are still extant, although they would have been preserved if the readers had felt them to be beneficial; but the writings of Moses have moved many even of those alien to Jewish culture to believe, as the writings claim, that the God who first made these laws and gave them to Moses was the Creator of the world. For it was

---

[1] Cf. Homer, *Il.* 1, 544, etc.
[3] Plato, *Rep.* 336 C, D.
[5] Read κωλύει with Guiet.

[2] Read ὅτε with We.
[4] Cf. IV, 38 below.

fitting that the Creator of the whole world who appointed laws for the whole world should have given a power to the words that was able to overcome men everywhere. I am saying this without raising as yet any question about Jesus, but still treating of Moses who was far inferior to the Lord, to show that, as my argument will prove, he was far superior to your wise poets and philosophers.

19. After this, secretly wishing to attack the Mosaic cosmogony which indicates that the world is not yet ten thousand years old but is much less than this, Celsus agrees with those who say that the world is uncreated, although he hides his real intention. For in saying that *there have been many conflagrations from all eternity and many floods, and that the deluge which lately happened in the time of Deucalion was the most recent*, he clearly suggests to those able to understand him that he thinks the world is uncreated. But let this man who attacks the faith of the Christians tell us by what sort of arguments he was forced to accept the doctrine that *there have been many conflagrations and many floods, and that more recent than all others is the flood in the time of Deucalion and the conflagration in the time of Phaethon*. If he adduces the dialogues of Plato[1] as authority for these, we would say to him that we are free to believe that in the pure and pious soul of Moses, who rose above all that is created, and united himself to the Creator of the universe, there dwelt a divine spirit which showed the truth about God far clearer than Plato and the wise men among the Greeks and barbarians. If he asks us for our reasons for believing this, let him first give a defence of the views which he has set forth without furnishing any proof, and then we will argue for the truth of our doctrines.

20. Nevertheless unintentionally Celsus fell into testifying that the world is quite recent and not yet ten thousand years old when he said: *The Greeks thought these things ancient since they did not perceive or possess records of earlier events on account of the floods and conflagrations.*[2] Let us suppose that Celsus has been taught the myth about the conflagrations and floods by *the Egyptians*,[3] who in his opinion are *very wise*—traces of whose wisdom exist in the irrational animals which they worship and in interpretations which show that this sort of worship of God is reasonable and rather recondite and mysterious. If, to make their doctrine about the animals respectable, the Egyptians introduce theological interpretations, they are wise; but if a man who has accepted the Jewish law and lawgiver

---

[1] *Timaeus*, 22 c, d. On the development of this doctrine see the fundamental discussion in W. L. Knox, *St Paul and the Church of the Gentiles* (1939), pp. 1–8. For Celsus' view of the eternity of the world, cf. IV, 79.

[2] Plato, *Timaeus*, 23 A, B.

[3] In Plato, *Timaeus*, 22, the myth of the world catastrophes is put into the mouth of an Egyptian priest. For Celsus' praise of Egyptian wisdom, cf. I, 14; VI, 80.

refers everything to the only God, the Creator of the universe, he is
regarded by Celsus and people like him as inferior to one who brings God
down to the level not only of rational and mortal beings but even to that
of irrational animals. This view is even worse than the myth of transmigration, that the soul falls from the vaults of heaven and descends as far
as irrational animals, not merely the tame but even those which are very
wild.[1] And if the Egyptians relate this mythology, they are believed to
be concealing philosophy in obscurities and mysteries; but if Moses wrote
for a whole nation and left them histories and laws, his words are considered
to be empty myths not even capable of being interpreted allegorically.[2]
[21] For so Celsus and the Epicureans think.

21. *Accordingly*, he says, *Moses heard of this doctrine which was current
among the wise nations and distinguished men and acquired a name for divine
power.*[3] My reply to this is that supposing we grant to him that Moses
heard an older doctrine and passed this on to the Hebrews, if he heard
a doctrine that was untrue and neither wise nor holy, and if he accepted it
and passed it on to the Hebrews, he is open to criticism. But if, as you say,
he accepted wise and true doctrines and educated his own people by them,
what did he do deserving of criticism? I wish that Epicurus and Aristotle,
who is less irreverent about providence, and the Stoics who maintain that
God is a material substance, had heard of this doctrine, that the world
might not be filled with a doctrine that abolishes providence, or limits it,
or introduces a corruptible first principle which is corporeal. According
to this last view, of the Stoics, even God is a material substance, and they
are not ashamed to say that He is capable of change and complete alteration and transformation,[4] and in general liable to corruption if there is
anyone to corrupt Him; as there is nothing which can do so He is fortunate
enough not to be corrupted. But the doctrine of Jews and Christians which
preserves the unchangeable and unalterable nature of God has been
regarded as irreverent, since it is not in agreement with those who hold
impious opinions about God. For in prayers to God the scripture says:
'Thou art the same.'[5] And God is believed to have said 'I change
not'.[6]

22. After this, though he does not attack the circumcision of the
private parts which is the custom of the Jews, Celsus says that *it came from*

---

[1] Plato, *Phaedrus*, 246 B–D.   [2] See IV, 48–51.
[3] The abilities of Moses as a magician were well known to the Greeks and Romans.
Cf. Pliny, *N.H.* xxx, 11; Apuleius, *Apol.* 90. For his wisdom, cf. Strabo, xvi, 11, 35
(pp. 760 f.). J. G. Gager, *Moses in Greco-Roman Paganism* (Nashville, 1972).
[4] The usual doxographic school formula. Cf. III, 75 (Koetschau, I, 267, 4); *Comm. in
Joann.* XIII, 21. Cf. also my remarks in *J.T.S.* XLVIII (1947), p. 35.
[5] Ps. ci. 8.   [6] Mal. iii. 6.

the Egyptians.[1] He believed the Egyptians rather than Moses, who says that Abraham was first among men to be circumcised. Now Moses is not the only one who records the name of Abraham and says that he was related to God; for many also of those who chant incantations for daemons use among their formulas 'the God of Abraham'; they do this on account of the name and the familiarity between God and this righteous man. It is for this reason that they employ the expression 'the God of Abraham' although they do not know who Abraham is. The same may be said of Isaac and Jacob and Israel; although these names are generally known to be Hebrew they have been inserted in formulas in many places by the Egyptians who claim to produce some magical effect.[2] However, it is not my task here to explain the meaning of circumcision which began with Abraham and was stopped by Jesus as he did not wish his disciples to do the same. For it is not now the right time to explain his teaching on this matter, but rather to endeavour to destroy the accusation brought by Celsus against the doctrine of the Jews; for he thinks he will more easily prove Christianity to be untrue if he can show its falsehood by attacking its origin in Judaism.

23. Celsus next says: *The goatherds and shepherds who followed Moses as their leader were deluded by clumsy deceits into thinking that there was only one God.*[3] Let him show how, since it was, as he thinks, *without any rational cause* that *these goatherds and shepherds abandoned the worship of many gods*, he is able to commend the large number of gods among the Greeks or the other barbarian deities. Let him prove the existence and reality of Mnemosyne who gave birth to the Muses by Zeus, or of Themis the mother of the Hours; or let him prove that the ever naked Graces could really have existed. However, he will not be able to show from the facts that the inventions of the Greeks, which seem to be personified abstractions, are gods. Why are the Greek myths about the gods more true than, say, those of the Egyptians who in their language know nothing of Mnemosyne mother of the nine Muses, nor of Themis mother of the Hours, nor Eurynome mother of the Graces, nor the names of the others? How much more certain and superior to all these fantasies is it to be persuaded by the visible universe that the world is well ordered and to worship the one Maker of that which is itself one! For the world possesses unity throughout its whole self and therefore cannot have been made by many makers. Nor can it be held together by many souls which move the

---

[1] Cf. Celsus in v, 41; he follows Herodotus, II, 104 (cf. II, 36). Egyptian circumcision is also mentioned by Origen, *Hom. in Jerem.* v, 14; Philo, *de Sp. Leg.* I, 2. Further material and discussion in Reitzenstein, *Zwei religionsgeschichtliche Fragen* (1901), pp. 1–46.
[2] Similarly IV, 33–4; V, 45. Cf. Justin, *Dial.* 85.   [3] Cf. Celsus in v, 41.

whole heaven.[1] For one soul is enough, which bears up the whole fixed sphere from east to west, and comprehends within itself all that the world needs and that is not complete in itself. All things are parts of the world; but God is not part of the whole. For God may not be incomplete as the part is incomplete. And probably a deeper inquiry could show that, strictly speaking, just as God is not a part, so also He is not the whole, since the whole is made up of parts.[2] And reason does not demand that we should accept the view that the supreme God is made up of parts, each one of which cannot do what the other parts can.

24. After this he says: *The goatherds and shepherds thought that there was one God called the Most High, or Adonai, or the Heavenly One, or Sabaoth, or however they like to call this world;*[3] *and they acknowledged nothing more.* Later he says that *it makes no difference whether one calls the supreme God*[4] *by the name used among the Greeks, or by that, for example, used among the Indians, or by that among the Egyptians.* My answer to this is that a profound and obscure question is raised by this subject, that concerning the nature of names. The problem is whether, as Aristotle thinks, names were given by arbitrary determination;[5] or, as the Stoics hold, by nature, the first utterances being imitations of the things described and becoming their names (in accordance with which they introduce certain etymological principles);[6] or whether, as Epicurus teaches (his view not being the same as that held by the Stoics), names were given by nature, the first men having burst out with certain sounds descriptive of the objects.[7] Now if by a special study we could show the nature of powerful names, some of which are used by the Egyptian wise men, or the learned men among the Persian magi, or the Brahmans, or Samanaeans among the Indian philosophers, and so on according to each nation, and if we could establish that so-called magic is not, as the followers of Epicurus and

[1] For the unity of the world, cf. Plotinus, VI, 5, 9.

[2] The Stoics held that the whole of anything was not to be identified simply with the sum of its parts. Cf. the references collected in *J.T.S.* XLVIII (1947), pp. 44–5.

[3] A reminiscence of Plato, *Timaeus*, 28 B (cf. *Epinomis*, 977 B; *Laws*, 821 A). Seneca says that Jupiter may be called the world, *N.Q.* II, 45, 3 'vis illum [sc. Iovem] vocare mundum; non falleris, ipse enim est hoc quod vides totum, partibus suis inditus, et se sustinens et sua.' Cf. Macrobius, *Sat.* I, 18, 15.

[4] Reading ἐν τοῖς ἑξῆς with Φ, and omitting Δία with Wifstrand. Origen summarizes the passage of Celsus he quotes in V, 41.

[5] Aristotle, *de Interpr.* 2 (16 a 27). The question is discussed also in V, 45 below; *Exh. Mart.* 46; Clem. Al. *Strom.* I, 143, 6; Plato, *Cratylus*; and in the Middle Platonist Albinus, *Epit.* 6. Cf. Pohlenz, *Die Stoa* (1948), II, p. 24.

[6] For Stoic etymologies, cf. the criticisms in Cicero, *de Nat. Deor.* III, 24, 62; Diogenianus *ap.* Eus. *P.E.* VI, 8, 8, 263 C, D. Varro discusses agricultural terms in this way (*de Re Rustica*, I, 48, 2 ff.). Cf. Dio Chrys. *Orat.* XII, 28.

[7] Epicurus, *frag.* 334 Usener; cf. his *Ep. ad Herodotum* in Diog. Laert. X, 75, and Lucretius, V, 1028 ff. Diogenes of Oenoanda, *frag.* 10 col. III.

Aristotle think, utterly incoherent, but, as the experts in these things prove, is a consistent system, which has principles known to very few; then we would say that the name Sabaoth, and Adonai, and all the other names that have been handed down[1] by the Hebrews with great reverence, are not concerned with ordinary created things, but with a certain mysterious divine science that is related to the Creator of the universe. It is for this reason that when these names are pronounced in a particular sequence which is natural to them,[2] they can be employed for certain purposes; and so also with other names in use in Egyptian which invoke certain daemons who have power only to do certain particular things; and other names in Persian which invoke other powers, and so on with each nation. So also the names of the daemons upon earth, which have possession of different localities, will be found to be related to the languages used in each respective locality and nation. A man, then, who has grasped a more profound understanding of these matters, even if only to a small extent, will take care to apply names correctly in their respective connexions, some in one case, some in another; lest he should be like those who mistakenly apply the name God to lifeless matter, or degrade the name of goodness from the first cause or from virtue and beauty to the level of blind wealth and to the harmony of flesh and blood and bones that exists when we are in good health and vigour, and to supposed nobility of birth.[3]

25. Perhaps also it is no less dangerous for a man to degrade the name of God or that of goodness to things to which these names ought not to be applied, than it is for a man to change names the nature of which is in accordance with a certain mysterious principle, and to apply the names of what is bad to what is good and of what is good to what is bad. Moreover, I say nothing of the fact that with the name of Zeus one at once associates the son of Kronos and Rhea, and husband of Hera, and brother of Poseidon, and father of Athena and Artemis, and the one who had sexual intercourse with his daughter Persephone. Or that with Apollo one associates the son of Leto and Zeus, the brother of Artemis and half-brother of Hermes.[4] Nor do I mention all the other names in the writings of Celsus' wise men, the authors of his doctrines, and the ancient theologians of the Greeks. Is it not absurd to hold that while it is right to call him Zeus, yet Kronos

---

[1] Read παραδεδομένα with Φ. [2] Read συμφυοῦς with Φ.

[3] Origen is using the Stoic argument that the προηγμένα, 'the preferred things' (i.e. relative values), such as wealth, birth, and health, do not belong to what is strictly good. Cf. the remarks on this passage by O. Rieth, 'Grundbegriffe der stoischen Ethik', *Problemata*, Heft IX (1933) at p. 175. 'Blind wealth' was proverbial; Plato, *Laws*, 631 c.

[4] Origen similarly attacks the morality of the Homeric gods in IV, 48. It was part of the traditional Academic polemic; cf., for example, Lucian, *de Sacrificiis*, 5; see Introduction, p. x.

was not his father, nor Rhea his mother?[1] The case is similar with the other so-called gods. But this criticism does not in any way apply to people who give the name Sabaoth to God in accordance with a certain mysterious principle, or the name Adonai, or any of the other names.

If anyone is capable of understanding philosophically the mysterious significance of names, he would find much also about the titles of the angels of God. One of these is called Michael, another Gabriel, and another Raphael, and they are named after their activities which they execute in the whole world in accordance with the will of the God of the universe.[2] The name of our Jesus is also connected with the same philosophy of names; for it has already been clearly seen to have expelled countless daemons from souls and bodies, and to have had great effect on those people from whom they were expelled.

On the subject of names I have to say further that experts in the use of charms relate that a man who pronounces a given spell in its native language can bring about the effect that the spell is claimed to do. But if the same spell is translated into any other language whatever, it can be seen to be weak and ineffective.[3] Thus it is not the significance of the things which the words describe that has a certain power to do this or that, but it is the qualities and characteristics of the sounds. By considerations of this kind we would in this way defend the fact that Christians strive to the point of death to avoid calling God Zeus or naming him in any other language. For either they use the ordinary name 'God' without qualification, or with the addition of the words 'the Creator of the universe, the Maker of heaven and earth, who sent down to the human race such and such wise men'. And when the name 'God' is linked with the names of these men a miraculous effect is produced among men.[4]

Much more might be said on the subject of names to those who think that it makes no difference how they are used. And if Plato is admired for his words in the *Philebus*, 'My reverence, Protarchus, for the names of the

---

[1] The Stoics distinguished between the Zeus of mythology and the Zeus of philosophy who was the guiding mind of the universe; cf. Seneca, *N.Q.* II, 45, 1 'Ne hoc quidem crediderunt, Iovem, qualem in Capitolio et in ceteris aedibus colimus, mittere manu fulmina, sed eumdem, quem nos, Iovem intellegunt, rectorem custodemque universi, animum ac spiritum mundi, operis huius dominum et artificem, cui nomen omne convenit.' Lactantius, *Div. Inst.* I, 11, 37; Augustine, *de Civ. Dei* v, 8 *ad fin.*; Plutarch, *Mor.* 379 D; Macrobius, *Sat.* I, 18, 15.

[2] Cf. *de Princ.* I, 8, 1; *Hom. in Iesu Nave*, XXIII, 4; *Hom. in Num.* XIV, 2.

[3] So also v, 45 below; cf. Celsus in VIII, 37; Iamblichus, *de Myst.* VII, 5; W. Kroll, *Oracula Chaldaica*, p. 58: ὀνόματα βάρβαρα μήποτ' ἀλλάξῃς. It was a principle of the later Neoplatonic theurgy; see E. R. Dodds in *Journ. Rom. Stud.* XXXVII (1947), at p. 63. The prologue to Sirach, quoted by A. D. Nock on *Corp. Herm.* XVI, 1, is different in its reference. Cf. also Xenophon Ephes. I, 5, 7.

[4] Cf. IV, 33–4.

gods is profound',[1] when Philebus had called pleasure a god in his discussion with Socrates, why should we not give even more approval to the Christians for their carefulness not to apply any of the names used in mythologies to the Creator of the universe? But that is enough on this point for the present.

26. Let us see how Celsus, who professes to know everything, misrepresents the Jews when he says that *they worship angels and are addicted to sorcery of which Moses was their teacher.*[2] As he professes to know the books of Christians and Jews let him declare where in Moses' writings he found the lawgiver enjoining them to worship angels. How also can there be sorcery among people who accepted the law of Moses if they have read the commandment: 'Ye shall not cleave to enchanters to be polluted by them'?[3] He next promises to *teach* us *how the Jews fell into error through ignorance and were deceived.* If he had found ignorance about Jesus Christ among the Jews because they did not give heed to the prophecies about him, he really would have *taught how the Jews fell into error.* But actually he had no desire to suggest this, and he suspects that the Jews are in error about things which are not errors at all.

After Celsus has promised that *later* he *will teach about the Jewish doctrines*, he first discusses our Saviour as *the founder* of the community through which we are Christians, saying that *a very few years ago*[4] he *taught this doctrine and was considered by the Christians to be son of God.* Concerning the point that he lived a few years ago, we will say this. Could it have happened apart from God's providence that in so few years Jesus, desiring to spread his teaching and message, has been able to do so much that in many parts of the contemporary world a large number of Greeks and barbarians, wise and stupid, have been so disposed towards his doctrine that they fight for Christianity to the point of death to avoid abjuring him, which no one is related to have done for any other doctrine? I do not wish to flatter Christianity, but rather to examine the facts carefully. And I would say that not even those who heal many sick bodies can attain their object of restoring health to the body without God's help.[5] But if any man were able to deliver souls from the flood of evil and from

---

[1] *Philebus*, 12C, quoted again in IV, 48. It seems to have been a proof-text in discussing this subject; cf. Julian, *Or.* VII, 237A. In *Didascalia Apost.* 21 recitations of pagan poetry are forbidden to avoid naming pagan gods.

[2] For Jewish angel-worship, cf. Col. ii. 18; Preaching of Peter *ap.* Clem. Al. *Strom.* VI, 41, 2 and Origen, *Comm. in Joann.* XIII, 17; Aristides, *Apol.* 14 (Syriac); Celsus in V, 6 below. These texts are taken to refer to Jewish sects by H. J. Schoeps, *Theol. u. Gesch. d. Judenchristentums* (1949), p. 82 n. 1.

[3] Lev. xix. 31.

[4] For the novelty of Christianity, cf. Celsus in II, 4; VI, 10; VIII, 12.

[5] Cf. I, 9 above, and for the theme, Clement, *Protr.* CX, 1.

licentiousness and wrongdoing and from despising God, and were to give
as a proof of this work one hundred reformed characters (supposing this
to be the number for the purposes of argument), could one reasonably say
that it was without divine help that this man had implanted in the hundred men a doctrine capable of delivering them from evils of such
magnitude? If a man who considers these things with an open mind would
agree that no good thing happens among men apart from God's providence, how much more may he boldly declare as much of Jesus, when he
compares the former lives of many converts to his message with their
subsequent behaviour and considers in what a depth of licentiousness and
of injustice and covetousness each of them was before they were *deceived*,
as Celsus and those who think the same as he say, *and accepted a doctrine
harmful*, so they say, *to the life of mankind?* For he may see how from the
time when they accepted the word they have become more reasonable and
reverent and stable, so that some of them through a desire for a higher
chastity and for a purer worship of God do not even indulge in the sexual
pleasures that are allowed by the law.

27. Anyone who examines the facts will see that Jesus ventured to do
things beyond the power of human nature and that what he ventured to
do he accomplished. From the beginning every one opposed the spread
of his doctrine over the whole world, the emperors in each period, the chief
generals under them, and all governors, so to speak, who had been
entrusted with any power at all, and furthermore, the rulers in each city,
the soldiers, and the people. Yet it conquered, since as the word of God it
could not be prevented; and as it was stronger than all those adversaries
it overcame all Greece and the most part of the barbarian countries, and
converted innumerable souls to follow its worship of God. However, it
was inevitable that in the great number of people overcome by the word,
because[1] there are many more *vulgar and illiterate* people than those who
have been trained in rational thinking, the former class should far out-
number the more intelligent. But as Celsus did not want to recognize this
fact, he thinks that the love to mankind shown by the word, which even
extends to every soul from the rising of the sun,[2] is *vulgar*, and that *it is
successful only among the uneducated because of its vulgarity and utter
illiteracy.* Yet not even Celsus asserts that only vulgar people have been
converted by the gospel to follow the religion of Jesus; for he admits that
*among them there are some moderate, reasonable, and intelligent people who
readily interpret allegorically.*

28. He also introduces an imaginary character, somehow imitating
a child having his first lessons with an orator, and brings in a Jew who

---

¹ Read ὡς with Bo. (K. tr. and Bader suggest ὅσῳ).   ² Cf. Rev. vii. 2; xvi. 12.

addresses childish remarks to Jesus and says nothing worthy of a philosopher's grey hairs. This too let us examine to the best of our ability and prove that he has failed to keep the character entirely consistent with that of a Jew in his remarks. After this[1] he represents the Jew as having a conversation with Jesus himself and refuting him on many charges, as he thinks: first, because *he fabricated the story of his birth from a virgin*; and he reproaches him because *he came from a Jewish village and from a poor country woman who earned her living by spinning.* He says that *she was driven out by her husband, who was a carpenter by trade, as she was convicted of adultery.* Then he says that *after she had been driven out by her husband and while she was wandering about in a disgraceful way she secretly gave birth to Jesus.* And he says that *because he was poor he hired himself out as a workman in Egypt, and there tried his hand at certain magical powers on which the Egyptians pride themselves; he returned full of conceit because of these powers, and on account of them gave himself the title of God.*[2] In my judgment, however (and I cannot allow anything said by unbelievers to pass unexamined, but study the fundamental principles), all these things are in harmony with the fact that Jesus was worthy of the proclamation that he is son of God.

29. Among men noble birth, honourable and distinguished parents, an upbringing at the hands of wealthy people who are able to spend money on the education of their son, and a great and famous native country, are things which help to make a man famous and distinguished and get his name well known. But when a man whose circumstances are entirely contrary to this is able to rise above the hindrances to him and to become well known, and to impress those who hear him so that he becomes eminent and famous throughout the whole world so that people alter their tone about him, should we not admire at once such a nature for being noble, for tackling great difficulties, and for possessing remarkable boldness?

If one were also to inquire further into the circumstances of such a man, how could one help trying to find out how a man, brought up in meanness and poverty, who had no general education and had learnt no arguments and doctrines by which he could have become a persuasive speaker to crowds and a popular leader and have won over many hearers, could devote himself to teaching new doctrines and introduce to mankind a doctrine which did away with the customs of the Jews while reverencing their

---

[1] Origen probably wrote the first sentence of this chapter before the Preface to the whole work, and then forgot what he had already dictated and made a fresh start.

[2] For the charge that Jesus did his miracles by magic, cf. the rabbinic references in Strack-Billerbeck, *Kommentar z. N.T. aus Talmud u. Midrasch*, 1, p. 631. For Egyptian magic, Lucian, *Philopseudes*, 31.

prophets, and which abolished the laws of the Greeks particularly in respect of the worship of God? How could such a man, brought up in this way, who had received no serious instruction from men (as even those who speak evil of him admit), say such noble utterances about the judgment of God, about the punishments for wickedness, and rewards for goodness, that not only rustic and illiterate people were converted by his words, but also a considerable number of the more intelligent, whose vision could penetrate the veil of apparently quite simple expressions, which conceals within itself, as one might say, a more mysterious interpretation?

The Seriphian in Plato[1] reproached Themistocles after he had become famous for his generalship, saying that he had not won his fame by his own character, but from the good luck to have had the most famous city in all Greece as his home. From Themistocles, who was open-minded and saw that his home had also contributed to his fame, he received the answer: 'I would never have been so famous if I had been a Seriphian, nor would you have been a Themistocles if you had had the good luck to be an Athenian.' But our Jesus, who is reproached for having *come from a village*, and that not a Greek one, who did not belong to any nation prominent in public opinion, and who is maligned as the son of *a poor woman who earned her living by spinning* and as having left his home country *on account of poverty* and *hired himself out as a workman in Egypt*, was not just a Seriphian, to take the illustration I have quoted, who came from the least and most insignificant island, but was a Seriphian of the very lowest class, if I may say so. Yet he has been able to shake the whole human world, not only more than Themistocles the Athenian, but even more than Pythagoras and Plato and any other wise men or emperors or generals in any part of the world.

30. Who, therefore, that does not give merely a cursory study to the nature of the facts, would not be amazed at a man who overcame and was able to rise above all the factors that tended to discredit him, and in his reputation to surpass all the distinguished men that have ever lived? It is uncommon for people who are eminent among men to have the ability to acquire fame for several things[2] at once. One has been admired and become famous for wisdom, another for generalship, and some barbarians for miraculous powers in incantations, and some for one talent, some for another; they have not been admired and become eminent for several abilities at the same time. Yet Jesus, in addition to his other abilities, is

---

[1] *Republic*, 329 E. The story is repeated by Cicero, *de Senectute*, III, 8; Plutarch, *Vita Themist.* XVIII, 3; *Mor.* 185 C. It first appears in a different setting in Herodotus, VIII, 125.

[2] Read πλειόνων with V and K. tr.

admired for his wisdom, for his miracles, and for his leadership. For he
persuaded some to join him in abandoning the laws, not like a tyrant, nor
like a robber who incites his followers against men, nor like a rich man who
provides support for those who come over to his side, nor like any who by
common consent are regarded as blameworthy. He did this as a teacher of
the doctrine about the God of the universe, of the worship offered to Him
and of every moral action which is able to bring the man whose life follows
his teaching into relationship with the supreme God. To Themistocles or
any of the other eminent men nothing happened to militate against their
fame; but in the case of Jesus, besides the points I have mentioned which
have sufficient influence to hide a man's character in ignominy even if he
were a most noble person, his death by crucifixion which seems to be
disgraceful was enough to take away even such reputation as he had already
gained, and to make those who had been deluded (as people who do not
agree with his teaching think) abandon their delusion and condemn the
man who had deceived them.

31. In addition to this, if, as people who malign Jesus say, his disciples
did not see him after he rose from the dead and were not convinced that
there was something divine about him, one might wonder how it came
about that they were not afraid to suffer the same fate as their master and
met danger boldly, and that they left their homes to obey Jesus' will by
teaching the doctrines which he gave to them. I think that a man who
examines the facts[1] with an open mind would say that these men would
not have given themselves up to a precarious existence for the sake of
Jesus' teaching unless they had some deep conviction which he implanted
in them when he taught them that they should not only live according to
his precepts but should also influence others—and should do so in spite of
the fact that destruction, as far as human life is concerned, clearly awaited
anyone who ventured to introduce new opinions in all places and to all
people, and who would not keep up friendship with any man who
continued to hold his former opinions and habits. Did the disciples of
Jesus fail to see this?[2] They dared not only to show to the Jews from the
sayings of the prophets that he was the one to whom the prophets referred,
but also showed to the other nations that he who was crucified quite
recently accepted this death willingly for the human race, like those who
have died for their country to check epidemics of plague, or famines, or
stormy seas. For it is probable that in the nature of things there are
certain mysterious causes which are hard for the multitude to understand,
which are responsible for the fact that one righteous man dying voluntarily
for the community may avert the activities of evil daemons by expiation,

[1] Read ⟨τὰ⟩ πράγματα with Winter.   [2] Read ἑώρων ⟨ταῦτα⟩ with K. tr.

since it is they who bring about plagues, or famines, or stormy seas, or anything similar.[1]

Let people therefore who do not want to believe that Jesus died on a cross for men, tell us whether they would not accept the many Greek and barbarian stories about some who have died for the community to destroy evils that had taken hold of cities and nations. Or do they think that, while these stories are historically true, yet there is nothing plausible about this man (as people suppose him to be) to suggest that he died to destroy a great daemon, in fact the ruler of daemons, who held in subjection all the souls of men that have come to earth? As the disciples of Jesus saw this and much more besides, which they probably learnt from Jesus in secret, and as they were also filled with a certain power, since it was not just a virgin imagined by a poet[2] who gave them 'strength and courage' but the true understanding and wisdom of God, they sought eagerly that they might become 'well-known among all men', not only among all the Argives, but even among all the Greeks and barbarians also, and that 'they might carry away a good report'.

32. Let us return, however, to the words put into the mouth of the Jew, where *the mother of Jesus* is described as having been *turned out by the carpenter who was betrothed to her, as she had been convicted of adultery and had a child by a certain soldier named Panthera.*[3] Let us consider

---

[1] Cf. VIII, 31 below; Plutarch, *Mor.* 417 D, E; *Corp. Herm.* XVI, 10, with Festugière's note *ad loc.*; Augustine, *de Civ. Dei*, X, 21.

[2] Not Pallas Athene, who inspired the men in Homer, *Il.* v, 1–3, quoted in the next few lines.

[3] The title Jesus ben Panthera is not uncommon in the Talmud. The material is collected in H. L. Strack, *Jesus die Häretiker u. die Christen* (1910). Cf. *Tosephta Hullin*, II, 22–3 'A story of Rabbi Eleazar ben Dama who was bitten by a snake. Jacob of Kephar Sama came to heal him in the name of Jesus ben Panthera, but R. Ishmael would not let him. He said to him: You may not do that, ben Dama. He replied to R. Ishmael: I will prove to you that he can heal me. But he had not yet completed the proof before he died. Then said R. Ishmael: Blessed art thou, ben Dama, that thou hast gone from here into peace and not pulled down the wall of the wise; for if ever the wall of the wise is pulled down, final punishment comes upon him, as it is written...' (Eccles. x. 8). Eusebius, *Ecl. Proph.* III, 10, commenting on Hos. v. 14: ἐγώ εἰμι ὡς πάνθηρ τῷ Ἐφραίμ (cf. xiii. 7), says: 'The text may be quoted against those of the circumcision who slanderously and abusively assert that our Lord and Saviour Jesus Christ was born of Panthera....' Epiphanius, *Panar.* LXXVIII, 7, 5: 'This Joseph was brother of Clopas, and was son of Jacob, surnamed Panther; both of them were sons of him who was surnamed Panther' (Zahn, *Forsch. z. Gesch. d. N.T. Kanons*, VI (1900), p. 267, thinks Hegesippus the source here; cf. Eus. *H.E.* III, 11). According to Andrew, Archbishop of Crete in the eighth century, Panther was an ancestor of Mary (Migne, *P.G.* XCVII, 916, followed by John Damasc. *de Fide Orthod.* IV, 14); cf. also the ninth-century monk Epiphanius (*P.G.* CXX, 190) referring to a lost work of Cyril of Jerusalem. Strack (p. 21*) thinks that Joseph's father may have had this surname; he rejects the view that it is a corruption of *pornos*. Deissmann, 'Der Name Panthera', in *Orient. Stud. f. Nöldeke* (1906), pp. 871 ff., shows that the name was common at this period, especially as a surname of Roman soldiers. L. Patterson, in *J.T.S.* XIX (1917), pp. 79–80, thinks that some Jewish controversialist seized on the name perhaps because of its similarity to *parthenos*.

whether those who fabricated the myth that the virgin and Panthera committed adultery and that the carpenter turned her out, were not blind when they concocted all this to get rid of the miraculous conception by the Holy Spirit. For on account of its highly miraculous character they could have falsified the story in other ways without, as it were, unintentionally admitting that Jesus was not born of an ordinary marriage. It was inevitable that those who did not accept the miraculous birth of Jesus would have invented some lie. But the fact that they did not do this convincingly, but kept as part of the story that the virgin did not conceive Jesus by Joseph, makes the lie obvious to people who can see through fictitious stories and show them up. Is it reasonable that a man who ventured to do such great things for mankind in order that, so far as in him lay, all Greeks and barbarians in expectation of the divine judgment might turn from evil and act in every respect acceptably to the Creator of the universe, should have had, not a miraculous birth, but a birth more illegitimate and disgraceful than any? As addressing Greeks and Celsus in particular who, whether he holds Plato's doctrines or not, nevertheless quotes them, I would ask this question. Would He who sends souls down into human bodies compel a man to undergo a birth more shameful than any, and not even have brought him into human life by legitimate marriage, when he was to do such great deeds and to teach so many people and to convert many from the flood of evil? Or is it more reasonable (and I say this now following Pythagoras, Plato, and Empedocles, whom Celsus often mentions) that there are certain secret principles by which each soul that enters a body does so in accordance with its merits and former character? It is therefore probable that this soul, which lived a more useful life on earth than many men (to avoid appearing to beg the question by saying 'all' men), needed a body which was not only distinguished among human bodies, but was also superior to all others.[1]

33. Suppose it is true that a certain soul which in accordance with certain mysterious principles does not deserve to be in the body of a completely irrational being, yet is not worthy to be in that of a purely rational being, puts on a monstrous body so that reason cannot be fully developed in one born in this way, whose head is out of proportion to the rest of the body and is far too small; and suppose that another soul receives a body of such a kind that it is slightly more rational than the former instance, and another still more so, the nature of the body being more or less opposed to the apprehension of reason. Why then should there not be a certain soul that takes a body which is entirely miraculous, which has something in common with men in order to be able to live with

[1] Cf. Celsus in VI, 75.

them, but which also has something out of the ordinary, in order that the
soul may remain uncontaminated by sin? Suppose that the views of the
physiognomists are granted, of Zopyrus, Loxus, or Polemon,[1] or anyone
else who wrote about these matters and professed to possess some
remarkable knowledge, that all bodies conform to the habits of their
souls; then for the soul that was to live a miraculous life on earth and to do
great things, a body was necessary, not, as Celsus thinks, produced by the
adultery of Panthera and a virgin (for the offspring of such impure
intercourse must rather have been some stupid man who would harm men
by teaching licentiousness, unrighteousness, and other evils, and not
a teacher of self-control, righteousness and the other virtues), [34] but,
as the prophets foretold, the offspring of a virgin who according to the
promised sign should give birth to a child whose name was significant of
his work, showing that at his birth God would be with men.

34. It appears to me that it would have been appropriate to the words
he has put into the mouth of the Jew to have quoted the prophecy of
Isaiah which says that Emmanuel shall be born of a virgin. Celsus,
however, did not quote this, either because he did not know it, though
he professes to know everything, or if he had read it, because he wilfully
said nothing of it to avoid appearing unintentionally to support the
doctrine which is opposed to his purpose. The passage reads as follows:
'And the Lord spake again to Ahaz saying, Ask thee a sign of the Lord thy
God, either in the depth or in the height. And Ahaz said, I will not ask,
neither will I tempt the Lord. And he said, Hear ye now, ye house of
David, is it a small thing to you to strive with men? How also do you
strive with the Lord? Therefore shall the Lord give you a sign. Behold
a virgin shall conceive in her womb and bring forth a son, and thou shalt
call his name Emmanuel', which is interpreted 'God with us'.[2] That it
was out of wickedness that Celsus did not quote the prophecy is made
clear to me from the fact that although he has quoted several things from
the gospel according to Matthew, such as *the star that arose at the birth of
Jesus* and other miracles, yet he has not even mentioned this at all. But if

---

[1] Zopyrus was probably the subject of the dialogue *Zopyrus* by Phaedo (Diog.
Laert. II, 105; Suidas, *s.v.*). For the story of how he pronounced upon the stupidity and
loose morals of Socrates after study of his physiognomy see Cicero, *de Fato*, v, 10; *Tusc.
Disp.* IV, 37, 80; Alexander of Aphrodisias, *de Fato*, 6; Maximus Tyrius, xxv, 3c; Pseudo-
Plutarch, περὶ ἀσκήσεως (German translation of Syriac in *Rh. Mus.* XXVII (1872), p. 527);
Schol. Persius, *Sat.* IV, 24; Cassian, *Coll.* XIII, 5.
Loxus is dated in the third century B.C. by R. Förster, 'De Loxi physiognomonia', in
Rh. Mus. XLIII (1888), pp. 505-11. Loxus and Polemo were both sources used by the
anonymous writer edited by Förster, *Scriptores Physiognomonici Graeci et Latini*, II, pp. 3 ff.
Cf. further J. Schmidt in P.-W. xx (1941), 1064-74.
[2] Isa. vii. 10-14; Matt. i. 23.

a Jew should ingeniously explain it away by saying that it is not written 'Behold a virgin' but, instead of that, 'behold a young woman', we should say to him that the word Aalma, which the Septuagint translated by 'parthenos' (virgin) and others[1] by 'neanis' (young woman), also occurs, so they say, in Deuteronomy applied to a virgin. The passage reads as follows: 'If a girl that is a virgin is betrothed to a man, and a man find her in a city and lie with her, ye shall bring both out to the gate of the city and stone them with stones that they die, the young woman because she did not cry out in the city, and the man because he disgraced his neighbour's wife.' And after that: 'If a man finds a girl that is betrothed in the country and the man force her and lie with her, ye shall kill only the man that lay with her, and ye shall do nothing to the young woman; there is no sin worthy of death in the young woman.'[2]

35. However, lest we appear to depend on a Hebrew word[3] to explain to people, who do not understand whether to accept it or not, that the prophet said that this man would be born of a virgin (concerning whose birth it was said 'God with us'), let us explain the affirmation from the passage itself. The Lord, according to the scripture, said to Ahaz: 'Ask thee a sign from the Lord thy God, either in the depth or in the height.' And then the sign that is given is this: 'Behold a virgin shall conceive and bear a son.' What sort of a sign would it be if a young woman not a virgin bore a son?[4] And which would be more appropriate as the mother of Emmanuel, that is 'God with us', a woman who had had intercourse with a man and conceived by female passion, or a woman who was still chaste and pure and a virgin?[5] It is surely fitting that the latter should give birth to a child at whose birth it is said 'God with us'. If, however, he explains this away by saying that Ahaz was addressed in the words 'ask thee a sign of the Lord thy God', we will say: Who was born in Ahaz's time whose birth is referred to in the words 'Emmanuel, which is God with us'? For if no one is to be found, obviously the words to Ahaz were addressed to the house of David, because according to the scripture our Saviour was 'of the seed of David according to the flesh'.[6] Furthermore, this sign is said to be 'in the depth or in the height', since 'this is he who descended and who ascended far above all heavens that he might fill all

[1] Aquila and Theodotion; cf. Irenaeus, *adv. Haer.* III, 21, 1 (Harvey, I, 110). For the difficulty cf. Justin, *Dial.* 43; 67; *Dial. Athan. et Zacch.* 32 (ed. F. C. Conybeare, *Anecdota Oxon.* (1898), p. 22).
[2] Deut. xxii. 23–6. The Masoretic text does not support Origen. The argument recurs in Basil the Great, *Hom. in sanctam Chr. gener.* 4 (Migne, *P.G.* XXXI, 1468 A).
[3] For a similar apology for basing exposition on the Hebrew, cf. *Hom. in Num.* XXVII, 13.
[4] For this argument, cf. Justin, *Dial.* 84; Tertullian, *adv. Jud.* 9; *adv. Marc.* III, 13.
[5] Cf. Origen's remarks on the Pythian priestess in VII, 5.
[6] Rom. i. 3.

things'.[1] I say these things as speaking to a Jew who believes the prophecy. But perhaps Celsus or any who agree with him will tell us with what kind of mental apprehension the prophet speaks about the future, whether in this instance or in the others recorded in the prophecies. Has he fore-knowledge of the future or not? If he has, then the prophets possessed divine inspiration. If he has not, let Celsus account for the mind of a man who ventures to speak about the future and is admired for his prophecy among the Jews.

36. Since we have just mentioned the question of the prophets, what we are about to bring forward will be of value not only to Jews, who believe that the prophets spoke by divine inspiration, but also to those Greeks who have an open mind. We will say to them that it will be admitted that the Jews had to have prophets, if they were to be kept obedient to the legislation which had been given to them, and were to believe in the Creator according to the traditions they had received, and were not to have any opportunities, as far as the law could forbid it, of apostatising to heathen polytheism. We will show that this was necessary in this way. 'The nations', as it is written in this very law of the Jews, 'will listen to omens and divination'; but to the Jewish people it is said: 'But the Lord thy God did not grant this to thee.' After this the scripture continues: 'A prophet shall the Lord thy God raise up unto thee out of thy brethren.'[2] While, therefore, the heathen were using divination, whether by omens or auguries or by birds or by ventriloquists, or even by those who profess to divine by means of sacrifices or Chaldean astrologers, all of these things were forbidden to the Jews. But if the Jews had had no knowledge of the future to console them, they would have been led by the insatiable desire of man to know the future, would have despised their own prophets for having nothing divine about them, and would not have accepted any prophet after Moses nor recorded their words. But of their own accord they would have turned to heathen divination and oracles, or even attempted to establish something of the kind among themselves. Conse-quently, there is nothing inappropriate about the fact that the prophets among them uttered predictions even about everyday matters for the consolation of those who wanted that kind of thing. Thus Samuel prophesied even about lost asses,[3] and so occurred the affair recorded in the third book of the Kingdoms about the king's sick son.[4] Otherwise, how could those who maintained the commandments of the law of the Jews have rebuked anyone who wanted to obtain an oracle from the idols? Thus Elijah is found rebuking Ahaziah and saying: 'Is it because there is

[1] Eph. iv. 10.   [2] Deut. xviii. 14–15. Cf. Philo, *de Spec. Leg.* I, 64.
[3] I Sam. (I Regn.) ix. 20.   [4] I Kings (III Regn.) xiv. 1–18.

no God in Israel that you go to seek out a fly, the god of Ekron, in the Baal?'[1]

37. I think that it has been fairly substantiated not only that our Saviour was to be born of a virgin, but also that there were prophets among the Jews who did not merely make general pronouncements about the future, such as those about Christ and about the kingdoms of the world, and the future destiny of Israel, and that the Gentiles would believe in the Saviour, and many other utterances about him. They also made particular predictions, as for instance of the way in which the lost asses of Kish were to be found, and of the illness which the son of the king of Israel suffered, or any other story of this sort.

To Greeks, however, who disbelieve in the virgin birth of Jesus I have to say that the Creator showed in the birth of various animals that what He did in the case of one animal, He could do, if He wished, also with others and even with men themselves. Among the animals there are certain females that have no intercourse with the male, as writers on animals say of vultures;[2] this creature preserves the continuation of the species without any copulation. Why, therefore, is it incredible that if God wished to send some divine teacher to mankind He should have made the organism of him that was to be born come into being in a different way instead of using a generative principle[3] derived from the sexual intercourse of men and women? Moreover, according to the Greeks themselves not all men were born from a man and a woman. For if the world was created as even many Greeks think,[4] the first men must have come into existence without sexual intercourse, but from the earth instead, generative principles having existed in the earth. But I think this more incredible than that Jesus should have been born half like other men. And in addressing Greeks it is not out of place to quote Greek stories, lest we should appear to be the only people to have related this incredible story. For some have thought fit (not in respect of any ancient stories and heroic tales but of people born quite recently) to record as though it were possible that when Plato was born of Amphictione Ariston was prevented from having sexual intercourse with her until she had brought forth the child which she had by Apollo.[5] But these stories are really myths, which have led

[1] II Kings (IV Regn.) i. 3.

[2] Cf. Tertullian, *adv. Val.* 10; Plutarch, *Mor.* 286c; and many other references in D'Arcy Thompson, *Glossary of Greek Birds* (2nd ed. 1936), p. 83.

[3] On Origen's use of the Stoic theory of heredity, cf. my remarks in *J.T.S.* XLVIII (1947), p. 44.
The text of this sentence is unsatisfactory. Read perhaps ἀντὶ ⟨τοῦ διὰ⟩ σπερματικοῦ λόγου τοῦ ἐκ μίξεως τῶν ἀρρένων ταῖς γυναιξὶ ποιῆσαι, κτλ. Koetschau brackets ποιῆσαι.

[4] As the Stoics (*S.V.F.* II, 739). For the background of this controversy see Critolaus' criticisms ap. Philo, *de Aetern. Mundi*, 55 ff.   [5] Cf. VI, 8 below.

people to invent such a tale about a man because they regarded him as having superior wisdom and power to the multitude, and as having received the original composition of his body from better and more divine seed, thinking that this was appropriate for men with superhuman powers. But when Celsus has introduced the Jew as disputing with Jesus and pouring ridicule on the pretence, as he thinks, of his birth from a virgin, and as quoting the Greek myths about *Danae* and *Melanippe* and *Auge* and *Antiope*, I have to reply that these words would be appropriate to a vulgar buffoon and not to a man who takes his professed task seriously.

38. Moreover, although he took the story of Jesus' departure to Egypt from the narrative in the gospel according to Matthew, he did not believe all the miracles connected with it, nor that an angel directed this, nor that Jesus' departure from Judaea and sojourn in Egypt had some hidden meaning. He made up another tale. For although he somehow accepts the incredible miracles which Jesus did, by which he persuaded the multitude to follow him as Christ, yet he wants to attack them as though they were done by magic and not by divine power. He says: *He was brought up in secret and hired himself out as a workman in Egypt, and after having tried his hand at certain magical powers he returned from there, and on account of those powers gave himself the title of God.* I do not know why a magician should have taken the trouble to teach a doctrine which persuades every man to do every action as before God who judges each man for all his works, and to instil this conviction[1] in his disciples whom he intended to use as the ministers of his teaching. Did they persuade their hearers because they had been taught to do miracles in this way, or did they not do any miracles? It is quite irrational to maintain that they did no miracles at all, but that, although they had believed without any adequate reasons comparable to the dialectical wisdom of the Greeks, they devoted themselves to teaching a new doctrine to any whom they might visit. What inspired them with confidence to teach the doctrine and to put forward new ideas? On the other hand, if they did perform miracles, is it plausible to suggest that they were magicians, when they risked their lives in great dangers for a teaching which forbids magic?

39. I do not think it worth while to combat an argument which he does not put forward seriously, but only as mockery: *Then was the mother of Jesus beautiful? And because she was beautiful did God have sexual intercourse with her, although by nature He cannot love a corruptible body? It*[2] *is not likely that God would have fallen in love with her since she was neither*

---

[1] Read διατιθέναι with K. tr.

[2] Perhaps read καίτοι for ἢ ὅτι with K. tr. and Bader. But ὅτι may well be pleonastic in force here; cf. the instances collected by A. Wifstrand in *Eranos*, XLIII (1945), pp. 342–6.

wealthy nor of royal birth; for nobody knew her, not even her neighbours. It is just ridicule also when he says: *When she was hated by the carpenter and turned out, neither divine power[1] nor the gift of persuasion saved her. Therefore,* he says, *these things have nothing to do with the kingdom of God.[2]* What is the difference between this and vulgar abuse at street corners, and the talk of people who say nothing worth serious attention?

40. After this he takes the story from the gospel according to Matthew and perhaps also from the other gospels, about the descent of the dove upon the Saviour when he was baptized by John, and wants to attack the story as a fiction. But after he has pulled to pieces, as he thought, the story of our Saviour's birth from a virgin, he does not quote the next events in order. For passion and hatred have no orderly method, and people who are in a rage and have some personal hostility say whatever comes into their heads when they attack those whom they hate, since they are prevented by their passion from stating their accusations carefully and in order. If he had been careful about the order, he would have taken the gospel and, having set out to criticise it, would have brought his objections against the first story first, and then the second, and so on with the rest. But in fact after the birth from the virgin Celsus, who professed to know everything, goes on to criticize our story about the appearance of the Holy Spirit in the form of a dove at the Baptism; then after this he attacks the prophecy about our Saviour's advent, and after that runs back to what is recorded after the birth of Jesus, the story about the star and the magi who came from the east to worship the child. And if you were to look yourself, you would find many muddled statements of Celsus throughout his book; so by this those who know how to preserve and to look for order may prove that he was very arrogant and boastful when he entitled his book *The True Doctrine*, a title used by none of the distinguished philosophers. Plato says that a sensible man will not be confident about such obscure questions.[3] And Chrysippus, who always gave an account of the reasons which influenced him, refers us to people whom we might find to give a better explanation than himself. Celsus, therefore, is wiser than both these men and the other Greeks; it was consistent with his assertion that he knows everything when he entitled his book *The True Doctrine*.

41. Lest we should appear to pass over his points intentionally for lack of an answer, we decided to refute each of his objections to the best of our ability, with a view not to the natural order and sequence of subjects but to the order of the objections written in his book. Let us, then, see what

---

[1] Celsus is thinking of the angel of Matt. i. 21 (Bader).
[2] Celsus uses the N.T. phrase also in III, 59; VI, 17; VIII, 11.   [3] *Phaedo*, 114C.

he says when attacking the story of the physical appearance, as it were, of the Holy Spirit seen by the Saviour in the form of a dove. His Jew continues by saying this to him whom we confess to be our Lord Jesus: *When*, he says, *you were bathing near John, you say that you saw what appeared to be a bird fly towards you out of the air.* His Jew then asks: *What trustworthy witness saw this apparition, or who heard a voice from heaven adopting you as son of God? There is no proof except for your word and the evidence which you may produce of one of the men who were punished with you.*

42. Before we begin the defence, we must say that an attempt to substantiate almost any story as historical fact, even if it is true, and to produce complete certainty[1] about it, is one of the most difficult tasks and in some cases is impossible. Suppose, for example, that someone says the Trojan war never happened,[2] in particular because it is bound up with the impossible story about a certain Achilles having had Thetis, a sea-goddess, as his mother, and Peleus, a man, as his father, or that Sarpedon was son of Zeus, or Ascalaphus and Ialmenus of Ares, or Aeneas of Aphrodite. How could we substantiate this, especially as we are embarrassed by the fictitious stories which for some unknown reason are bound up with the opinion, which everyone believes, that there really was a war in Troy between the Greeks and the Trojans? Suppose also that someone does not believe the story about Oedipus and Jocasta, and Eteocles and Poly-neices, the sons of them both, because the half-maiden Sphinx[3] has been mixed up with it. How could we prove the historicity of a story like this? So also in the case of the Epigoni, even if there is nothing incredible involved in the story, or in that of the return of the Heraclidae, or innumer-able other instances. Anyone who reads the stories with a fair mind, who wants to keep himself from being deceived by them, will decide what he will accept and what he will interpret allegorically, searching out the meaning of the authors who wrote such fictitious stories, and what he will disbelieve as having been written to gratify certain people. We have said this by way of introduction to the whole question of the narrative about Jesus in the gospels, not in order to invite people with intelligence to mere irrational faith, but with a desire to show that readers need an open mind

---

[1] Direct apprehension, καταληπτικὴ φαντασία, is a fundamental idea in Stoic epistemo-logy; it is an impression on the mind of such a kind that no doubt can be entertained as to its truth. Cf. VIII, 53 below; Sextus Emp. *adv. Math.* VII, 227; Pohlenz, *Die Stoa*, I, pp. 60 f.

[2] Exactly the same argument appears in Dio Chrysostom, *Orat.* 11 *passim*. Perhaps it goes back to Eratosthenes; cf. the polemic of Strabo, I, 2, 7 ff. (pp. 18–19).

[3] Euripides, *Phoenissae*, 1023. Cf. Roscher, *Lexikon d. griech. u. röm. Mythologie*, IV, 1364–5.

and considerable study, and, if I may say so, need to enter into the mind of the writers to find out with what spiritual meaning each event was recorded.

43. In the first place, we would say that if the man who disbelieves in the story of the appearance of the Holy Spirit in the form of a dove had been recorded to be an Epicurean, or a follower of Democritus or a Peripatetic, the criticism might have had some force, since it would have been consistent with the imaginary character. The most intelligent Celsus, however, did not see that he has put words of this nature into the mouth of a Jew, who believes greater and more miraculous accounts in the prophetic scriptures than the story about the form of the dove. For one might say to the Jew, who does not believe in the *apparition* and thinks he can charge it with being fictitious: How, good sir, are you going to prove that the Lord God said to Adam, or Eve, or Cain, or Noah, or Abraham or Isaac, or Jacob, the words which according to the Bible he said to these men? And to compare this story with another, I would say to the Jew: Your Ezekiel wrote these words: 'The heavens were opened, and I saw a vision of God.' After explaining the vision he continues: 'This is the vision of the likeness of the glory of the Lord. And he spoke to me.'[1] If the stories recorded of Jesus are untrue, since, as you suppose, we are unable to show beyond doubt that these things are true which were seen or heard by him alone and, as you appear to have noticed, also by one of those who were punished,[2] would we not be even more justified in saying that Ezekiel was telling monstrous stories when he said that 'the heavens were opened' and so on? Moreover, if Isaiah affirms, 'I saw the Lord of Sabaoth sitting on a throne high and lifted up; and the Seraphim stood round about it, with six wings on one and six wings on the other'[3] etc., how can you prove that he really did see this? For you, my good Jew, have believed that these things were free from error and that it was by divine inspiration not only that they were seen by the prophet, but also that they were described verbally and in writing. Whom are we more justified in believing when he asserts that the heavens were opened to him and that he heard a voice or saw 'the Lord of Sabaoth sitting upon a throne high and lifted up'? Should we believe Isaiah and Ezekiel or Jesus? No work of theirs is to be found of comparable importance; whereas the goodness of Jesus towards men was not confined to the period of the incarnation only, but even to this day the power of Jesus brings about conversion and moral reformation in those who believe in God through him. That this happens by his power is clearly proved by the fact that, as he himself said, and as experience proves, so great is the harvest of people gathered in and

[1] Ezek. i. 1; i. 28; ii. 1.   [2] John i. 32.   [3] Isa. vi. 1–2.

collected into the threshing-floors of God, which are churches, that there are not labourers to reap the harvest of souls.[1]

44. I say this to the Jew, not because as a Christian I disbelieve Ezekiel and Isaiah, but to put him to shame by quoting the writers whom we both believe, that Jesus is far more deserving of belief than they when he says that he saw such a vision, and, as is probable, when he told his disciples of the vision which he saw and the voice which he heard. Some one else might say, however, that not all those who recorded the accounts of the form of the dove and the voice from heaven heard Jesus describing these things; but the Spirit that taught Moses the history before his time, beginning from the cosmogony down to the history of Abraham his father, also taught the writers of the gospel about this miracle which occurred at the time of Jesus' baptism. A man who has been adorned with the spiritual gift called 'the word of wisdom'[2] will also explain the reason for the opening of the heavens and the form of the dove, and why the Holy Spirit did not appear to Jesus in the form of any other living being but this. But the argument does not demand that we explain this now. For it is our object to prove Celsus wrong in attributing to a Jew disbelief expressed in such words as these, when the event concerned has more historical probability than the stories which he has believed.

45. I remember that once in a discussion with some Jews,[3] who were alleged to be wise, when many people were present to judge what was said, I used the following argument. Tell me, sirs: there have been two men who have come to visit the human race of whom supernatural miracles have been recorded; I mean Moses, your lawgiver, who wrote about himself, and Jesus who left no book about himself but had the testimony of his disciples in the gospels. Is it not absurd to believe that Moses spoke the truth, in spite of the fact that the Egyptians malign him as a sorcerer who appeared to do his miracles by means of trickery, while disbelieving Jesus, since you accuse him? Both of them have the testimony of nations; the Jews bear witness to Moses, while the Christians, without denying that Moses was a prophet, prove from his prophecy the truth about Jesus, and accept as true the miraculous stories about him that have been recorded by his disciples. But if you demand that we give a reason for believing in Jesus, first give yours for believing in Moses, since he lived before Jesus, and then we will give ours about him after that. If you shirk and avoid giving the proofs about Moses, for the moment we will do as

[1] Matt. ix. 37–8; Luke x. 2.   [2] I Cor. xii. 8.
[3] For Origen's disputes with Rabbis, cf. I, 55; II, 31; *Sel. in Ps.* XI, 352 (ed. Lommatzsch); G. F. Moore, *Judaism*, I (1927), p. 165. For the importance of these disputes as leading to the composition of the *Hexapla*, cf. P. E. Kahle, *The Cairo Geniza* (1947), p. 159.

you do and offer no argument. Admit, none the less, that you have no proof about Moses, and listen to the evidence about Jesus from the law and the prophets. Indeed, what is startling is that it is the evidence about Jesus in the law and the prophets which is used to prove that Moses and the prophets really were prophets of God.

46. The law and the prophets are filled with accounts as miraculous as that recorded of Jesus at the baptism about the dove and the voice from heaven. But I think that the miracles performed by Jesus are evidence that the Holy Spirit was seen then in the form of a dove, although Celsus attacks them by saying that he learnt how to do them among the Egyptians. And I will not mention these only, but also, as is reasonable, those which were done by Jesus' apostles. For without miracles and wonders they would not have persuaded those who heard new doctrines and new teachings to leave their traditional religion and to accept the apostles' teachings at the risk of their lives. Traces of that Holy Spirit who appeared in the form of a dove are still preserved among Christians.[1] They charm daemons away and perform many cures and perceive certain things about the future according to the will of the Logos. Even if Celsus, or the Jew that he introduced, ridicule what I am about to say, nevertheless it shall be said that many have come to Christianity as it were in spite of themselves, some spirit having turned their mind suddenly from hating the gospel to dying for it by means of a vision by day or by night. We have known many instances like this. But if we were to commit them to writing, although we were eyewitnesses present at the time, we would bring upon ourselves downright mockery from the unbelievers, who would think that we were inventing the stories ourselves like those whom they suspect of having invented such tales. But as God is witness of our good conscience, we want to lend support to the divine teaching not by any false reports, but by definite facts of various kinds.

Since, however, it is a Jew who raises difficulties in the story of the Holy Spirit's descent in the form of a dove to Jesus, I would say to him: My good man, who is the speaker in Isaiah that says 'And now the Lord sent me and his spirit'? In this text although it is doubtful whether it means that the Father and the Holy Spirit sent Jesus or that the Father sent Christ and the Holy Spirit, it is the second interpretation which is right.[2] After the Saviour had been sent, then the Holy Spirit was sent, in order that the prophet's saying might be fulfilled; and, as it was necessary that the fulfilment of the prophecy should also be made known

---

[1] Put a comma after σῴζεται for full stop, with Wifstrand.

[2] Isa. xlviii. 16, so interpreted also in *Comm. in Matt.* XIII, 18, but not so in *Comm. in Joann.* II, 11 (6).

to posterity, for this reason the disciples of Jesus recorded what had happened.

47. I would like to have told Celsus, when he represented the Jew as in some way accepting John as a baptist in baptizing Jesus, that a man who lived not long after John and Jesus recorded that John was a baptist who baptized for the remission of sins. For Josephus in the eighteenth book of the Jewish antiquities bears witness that John was a baptist and promised purification to people who were baptized.[1] The same author, although he did not believe in Jesus as Christ, sought for the cause of the fall of Jerusalem and the destruction of the temple. He ought to have said that the plot against Jesus was the reason why these catastrophes came upon the people, because they had killed the prophesied Christ; however, although unconscious of it, he is not far from the truth when he says that these disasters befell the Jews to avenge James the Just, who was a brother of 'Jesus the so-called Christ', since they had killed him who was a very righteous man.[2] This is the James whom Paul, the true disciple of Jesus, says that he saw,[3] describing him as the Lord's brother, not referring so much to their blood-relationship or common upbringing as to his moral life and understanding. If therefore he says that the destruction of Jerusalem happened because of James, would it not be more reasonable to say that this happened on account of Jesus the Christ? His divinity is testified by great numbers of churches, which consist of men converted from the flood of sins and who are dependent on the Creator and refer every decision to His pleasure.

48. Even if the Jew can offer no defence of Ezekiel and Isaiah, as we have compared the account of the opening of the heavens to Jesus and of the voice which he heard with the similar accounts recorded in Ezekiel and in Isaiah, or in any other prophet also, we at least will establish the argument to the best of our ability by saying this. All who accept the doctrine of providence are obviously agreed in believing that in dreams

---

[1] *Antiq.* XVIII, 5, 2 (116–19).

[2] Cf. II, 13. Origen also quotes this as from Josephus in *Comm. in Matt.* x, 17. But it does not occur in any extant MS. of the *Antiquities* at the relevant place (*Antiq.* XX, 9, 1 (200–1)) or elsewhere. Eusebius, *H.E.* II, 23, 20, quotes the sentence in *oratio recta*; Lawlor and Oulton (*ad loc.*) think Eusebius is independent of Origen, and suggest a common source, perhaps a collection of extracts. Eusebius' debt to Origen is vast enough to make this improbable, and his verbatim quotation corresponds exactly to Origen's words here with only such alterations as are necessary to turn it from *oratio obliqua*.
The passage may be a Christian interpolation in the text of Josephus: cf. E. Schürer, *Geschichte des jüdischen Volkes im Zeitalter Jesu Christi* (4th ed. 1901), I, p. 581; C. Martin in *Revue Belge de philologie et d'histoire*, XX (1941), at p. 421, n. 1. H. St J. Thackeray (*Josephus the Man and the Historian* (1929), pp. 134 f.) thinks Origen confused Josephus with Hegesippus who gives a Christian account of the death of James (ap. Euseb. *H.E.* II, 23) which ends: 'And immediately Vespasian besieged them.'   [3] Gal. i. 19.

many people form images in their minds,[1] some of divine things, others being announcements of future events in life, whether clear or mysterious. Why then is it strange to suppose that the force which forms an impression on the mind in a dream can also do so in the daytime for the benefit of the man on whom the impression is made, or for those who will hear about it from him? Just as we receive an impression in a dream that we hear and that our sense of hearing has been physically affected, and that we see with our eyes, although these impressions are not experienced by our bodily eyes or made by any vibration in our ears, but are only in our mind;[2] so also there is nothing extraordinary in such things having happened to the prophets when, as the Bible says, they saw certain marvellous visions, or heard utterances of the Lord, or saw the heavens opened. For I do not imagine that the visible heaven was opened, or its physical form divided, for Ezekiel to record such an experience. Perhaps therefore the intelligent reader of the gospels ought to give a similar interpretation also in respect of the Saviour, even if this opinion may cause offence to the simple-minded, who in their extreme *naïveté* move the world and rend the vast, solid mass of the entire heaven.

Anyone who looks into this subject more deeply will say that there is, as the scripture calls it, a certain generic divine sense which only the man who is blessed finds on this earth. Thus Solomon says: 'Thou shalt find a divine sense.'[3] There are many forms of this sense: a sight which can see things superior to corporeal beings, the cherubim or seraphim being obvious instances, and a hearing which can receive impressions of sounds that have no objective existence in the air, and a taste which feeds on living bread that has come down from heaven and gives life to the world.[4] So also there is a sense of smell which smells spiritual things, as Paul speaks of 'a sweet savour of Christ unto God',[5] and a sense of touch in accordance with which John says that he has handled with his hands 'of the Word of life'.[6] The blessed prophets found this divine sense, and their vision and hearing were spiritual; in a similar way they tasted and smelt, so to speak, with a sense which was not sensible. And they touched the Word by faith so that an emanation came from him to them which healed them. In this way they saw what they record that they saw, and they heard what they

---

[1] Tertullian remarks that the majority of mankind 'ex visionibus deum discunt' (*de Anima* XLVII, 2; cf. Waszink's note, p. 504). For the Christian evaluation of dreams, cf. Cumont, *Lux perpetua*, p. 92 'L'oniromancie est le seul mode païen de divination que l'Église n'ait pas répudié.' For Constantine and the fourth century, cf. A. Alföldi, *The Conversion of Constantine and Pagan Rome* (1948), pp. 125 f.

[2] Plutarch, *Mor.* 588 D, similarly discusses the 'inner voice' heard by Socrates.

[3] Prov. ii. 5, not as LXX, but so in Clem. Al. *Strom.* 1, 27, 2, and often in Origen.

[4] John vi. 33.   [5] II Cor. ii. 15.   [6] I John i. 1.

say they heard, and their experience was similar when, as they recorded, they ate the roll of a book which was given to them.[1] So also Isaac smelled the scent of his son's spiritual garments, and after the spiritual blessing said: 'Behold the smell of my son is as the smell of a full field which the Lord blessed.'[2] In the same way as in these instances Jesus touched the leper[3] spiritually rather than sensibly, to heal him, as I think, in two ways, delivering him not only, as the multitude take it, from sensible leprosy by sensible touch, but also from another leprosy by his truly divine touch. Similarly, 'John bore witness saying, I have seen the Spirit descending as a dove from heaven, and it abode upon him. And I knew him not, but he who sent me to baptize in water said to me, Upon whom you see the Spirit descending and abiding on him, this is he who baptizes with the Holy Spirit. And I have seen and borne witness that this is the Son of God.'[4] It was to Jesus that the heavens were opened; and at that time no one but John is recorded to have seen the heavens opened. But the Saviour foretells that the heavens will open in this way to his disciples and says that they too will see this come to pass, in the words: 'Verily, verily, I say unto you, you shall see the heavens opened and the angels of God ascending and descending upon the Son of man.'[5] So also Paul was caught up to the third heaven, having seen it opened before, since he was a disciple of Jesus. But it is not now the right moment to explain why Paul says: 'Whether in the body I cannot tell, whether out of the body I cannot tell; God knoweth.'[6]

Furthermore, I will add to my discussion the point made by Celsus when he thinks that Jesus himself spoke about the opening of the heavens and the descent of the Holy Spirit upon him in the form of a dove by the Jordan. The Bible does not actually show that he said he saw this. And this most worthy fellow did not perceive that it is not consistent with the character of him who said to his disciples at the vision on the mountain, 'Tell the vision to no man, until the Son of Man rise from the dead',[7] that he should have told his disciples of what was seen and heard by John at the Jordan. We may also notice that it was a habit of Jesus everywhere to avoid speaking about himself. That is why he said: 'If I speak of myself, my witness is not true.'[8] And since he avoided speaking about himself, and wanted to show that he was Christ rather by his deeds than by his talk, on this account the Jews say to him: 'If thou art the Christ tell us plainly.'[9] As, however, it is a Jew in Celsus' attack who speaks to Jesus about the Holy Spirit's coming in the form of a dove, saying: *There is no proof*

---

[1] Ezek. ii. 9–iii. 3.   [2] Gen. xxvii. 27.   [3] Matt. viii. 3.
[4] John i. 32–4.   [5] John i. 51.   [6] II Cor. xii. 2.
[7] Matt. xvii. 9.   [8] John v. 31.   [9] John x. 24.

except for your word and the evidence which you may produce of one of the men who were punished with you, we have to inform him that these words also which he has put into the Jew's mouth are inappropriate to his character. For the Jews do not connect John with Jesus, nor the punishment of John with that of Jesus. Therefore here too, he who boasted that he knew everything is convicted of not having known what words to attribute to the Jew in his address to Jesus.

49. After this for some unknown reason he intentionally evades the strongest argument confirming Jesus' authority, that he was prophesied by the prophets of the Jews, Moses and those after him and even before him. I think that he does this because he is unable to reply to the argument. For neither the Jews nor any of the sects are unwilling to admit that the Messiah[1] has been prophesied. But perhaps he did not even know the prophecies about Jesus. If he had understood what Christians affirm, that there were many prophets who foretold the advent of the Saviour, he would not have put into the mouth of the Jew statements which would be more appropriate to a Samaritan or a Sadducee. A Jew introduced as an imaginary character would not have said: *But my prophet said once in Jerusalem that God's son would come to judge* the holy and to punish the unrighteous. It is not only one prophet[2] that prophesied about Jesus. And even if the Samaritans and Sadducees, who accept only the books of Moses, say that the Messiah has been prophesied in those books, yet even so the prophecy was not spoken in Jerusalem, which in Moses' time had not yet been mentioned. I wish that all opponents of the gospel were in such ignorance not merely of the facts but even of the mere text of scripture, and would attack Christianity in such a way that their argument would not even possess cheap plausibility such as can make people who are unstable, and who believe for a time,[3] fall away not from their faith, but from their little faith. And a Jew would not confess that a certain *prophet said that God's son would come*. What they do say is that the Christ of God will come. Frequently in fact they press us with questions on this very title of the son of God, saying that there is no such person, and that the prophets do not mention him. Now we do not say that no son of God has been mentioned in prophecy,[4] but we do affirm that it does not suit the character of the Jew, who would not confess anything of the kind, when he attributes to him the words: *My prophet said once in Jerusalem that God's son would come.*

50. As if it was not he alone of whom the prophets foretold that he would *judge the holy and punish the unrighteous*, and as if nothing was foretold concerning his birthplace or the passion which he would suffer at the

---

[1] Read χριστὸν with M² edd. K. tr.
[2] Cf. II, 4, 79.
[3] Luke viii 13; Mark iv. 17.
[4] Read πεπροφήτευται with K. tr.

hands of the Jews, or his resurrection, or the wonderful miracles which he would perform, he says: *Why should you be the subject of these prophecies rather than the thousands of others who lived after the prophecy was uttered?* For some unknown reason he wants to ascribe to others the possibility that they may be supposed to have been referred to by the prophecies, and says: *Some people in ecstasy and others who go about begging say that they are sons of God*[1] *who have come from above.* But we have not observed that these things are admitted to have occurred among the Jews. Accordingly I may say first that many prophets foretold in all kinds of ways the things concerning Christ, some in riddles and others by allegories or some other way, while some even use literal expressions. Later, i.. the words attributed to the Jew when he is addressing believers from his own people, he says that *the prophecies that are applied to this man can be referred to other events as well,*[2] which he says with a cunning and wicked purpose; accordingly we will select a few prophecies out of many more, in respect of which I challenge anyone who likes to offer a cogent argument to overthrow them, which is able to turn away from the faith even intelligent believers.[3]

51. Concerning his birthplace it was said that 'the ruler shall come from Bethlehem' in the following words: 'And thou Bethlehem, house of Ephrata, art least of the thousands that are in Judah; out of thee shall come to me the one who is to be the ruler in Israel, and his outgoings are from the beginning from eternal days.'[4] This prophecy would not fit any of those who are in ecstasy and go about begging and saying that they have come from above, as Celsus' Jew says, unless it is quite clear that the man was born in Bethlehem, or as some one else might say, came from Bethlehem to rule the people. If anyone wants further proof to convince him that Jesus was born in Bethlehem besides the prophecy of Micah and the story recorded in the gospels by Jesus' disciples, he may observe that, in agreement with the story in the gospel about his birth, the cave[5] at Bethlehem is shown where he was born and the manger in the cave where he was wrapped in swaddling-clothes. What is shown there is famous in these parts even among people alien to the faith, since it was in this cave

---

[1] Read υἱοὶ θεοῦ with Wifstrand. Cf. vii, 9.　　　[2] Cf. Celsus in ii, 28.

[3] Read ⟨καὶ τοὺς⟩ ἐντρεχῶς with K. tr.　　　[4] Mic. v. 2.

[5] The cave is mentioned by Justin, *Dial.* 78 (cf. also 70), and in the *Protevangelium* of James, 18 ff. (M. R. James, *Apocr. N.T.* p. 46), a work known to Origen (*Comm. in Matt.* x, 17). Cf. Eus. *D.E.* iii, 2, 97c; vii, 2, 343b; *V.C.* iii, 42 f.; Epiphanius, *Panarion*, li, 9, 6; Jerome, *Ep.* lviii, 3; cxlvii, 4; Philoxenus of Mabbug, *de Trin. et Incarn.* 3 (p. 186, Vaschalde). The cave was shown to pilgrims in the sixth century, according to the itinerary of Antoninus of Placentia (*C.S.E.L.* xxxix, 178). For discussion of this tradition see W. Bauer, *Das Leben Jesu im Zeitalter der neutestamentlichen Apokryphen* (1909), pp. 61–8, who gives further references. The only manuscript of the gospels to mention the cave is the oldest Armenian version; cf. E. Preuschen in *Z.N.T.W.* iii (1902), pp. 359 f.

that the Jesus who is worshipped and admired by Christians was born. And I believe that before the advent of Christ the chief priests and scribes of the people taught that the Christ would be born in Bethlehem on account of the distinct and clear character of the prophecy. This interpretation even reached the multitude of the Jews. This explains why Herod is recorded to have inquired of the chief priests and scribes of the people and to have heard from them that Christ would be born in Bethlehem of Judaea 'whence David was'. Furthermore, in John's gospel it is stated that the Jews said Christ would be born in Bethlehem 'whence David was'.[1] But after the advent of Christ people busied themselves with destroying the idea that his birth had been prophesied from early times, and took away such teaching from the people. Their action was akin to that of those who won over the soldiers of the guard at the tomb who were eyewitnesses of his resurrection from the dead and reported it, and persuaded them by giving them money[2] and saying to them: 'Say that his disciples stole him by night while we slept. And if this come to the governor's ears we will persuade him and rid you of care.'[3]

52. Quarrelling and prejudice are troublesome in that they make men disregard even obvious facts, preventing them from giving up doctrines to which they have somehow become accustomed, which colour and mould their soul.[4] Indeed a man would more readily give up his habits in other respects, even if he finds it hard to tear himself away from them, than in the case of his religious opinions. Nevertheless, men of fixed habits do not easily abandon even what is not connected with religion. Thus people who have become biased in favour of particular homes, or cities, or villages, or familiar friends, are not readily willing to abandon them. This was the reason why many of the Jews at the time disregarded the obvious fulfilments of the prophecies and the wonders which Jesus performed and the sufferings he is recorded to have endured. That something of this sort has been the natural experience of men, will be clear to those who observe that people who have once become prejudiced in favour even of the most shameful and futile traditions of their fathers and fellow-citizens, are not easily changed. For instance, one would not quickly persuade an Egyptian to despise what he had received from his fathers, so as not to regard as god any irrational animals or to guard himself even on pain of death from tasting the flesh of an animal of this kind.[5] Although we have gone into detail, then, in examining at length this matter of

---

[1] John vii. 42.
[2] The MS. text is corrupt. Read perhaps with K. tr. τοῦτ' ἀπαγγέλλοντας ⟨τῷ ἀργύρια δοῦναι καὶ⟩ εἰρηκέναι κτλ.
[3] Matt. xxviii. 13–14.   [4] For the idea, cf. Seneca, *Ep.* LXXI, 31.   [5] Cf. III, 36.

Bethlehem and the prophecy about it, we think it was necessary to do this in reply to those who would say that, if the prophecies of Jesus possessed by the Jews were so clear, why then, when he came, did they not accept his teaching and change to the superior doctrines which Jesus had shown to them? But let no one bring a reproach of this kind against any of us who believe, perceiving that impressive reasons for faith in Jesus are brought forward by those who have learnt to give an account of them.

53. If a second prophecy is also needed which seems to us to refer clearly to Jesus, we will quote that written by Moses very many years before the advent of Jesus, when he tells how Jacob, departing this life, prophesied to each of his sons and said to Judah among other things: 'The ruler will not depart from Judah nor a leader from his loins, until the things which are laid up for him come.'[1] Anyone reading this prophecy, which in reality is far earlier than Moses although an unbeliever might suppose it was spoken by Moses, would be amazed at the way in which Moses was able to foretell that the kings of the Jews, who have among them twelve tribes, would be born of the tribe of Judah and would rule the people. That is why the whole people are called Jews, being named after the chief tribe. And in the second place, the man who reads the prophecy with an open mind would be amazed at the way in which, after saying that the rulers and leaders of the people would come from the tribe of Judah, he also fixes the time when the rule itself is to come to an end, when he says that 'the ruler shall not depart from Judah nor a leader from his loins until that which is laid up for him come, and he shall be the expectation of nations'. The Christ of God, for whom are the things which are laid up, has come, the ruler of whom the promises of God speak.[2] He was obviously the only one among all his predecessors and, I would make bold to say, among posterity as well who was the expectation of nations. People from all nations have believed in God through him, and in accordance with Isaiah's saying nations have put their hope in his name, when he said: 'In his name shall the Gentiles trust.' And to those in prison, since 'each man is bound by the cords of his own sins',[3] Jesus also said 'Come forth', and those in ignorance he commanded to come to the light. These prophecies read as follows: 'And I have given thee for a covenant of the nations to establish the earth and to inherit the heritage of the wilderness, so that you may say to them that are in prison, Come forth, and to them that are in darkness, Show yourselves.' And by his advent we can see in the simple-minded believers throughout the world the fulfilment of the words: 'And they shall feed in all the paths and on all the beaten tracks shall be their pasture.'[4]

[1] Gen. xlix. 10.   [2] Cf. Justin, *Dial.* 120.   [3] Prov. v. 22.   [4] Isa. xlix. 8–9.

54. Since Celsus, who professes to know everything about the gospel, reproaches the Saviour for his passion, saying that *he was not helped by his Father, nor was he able to help himself,* I have to affirm that his passion was prophesied with the reason for it, which was that it was a benefit to men that he should die for them and endure the stripe to which he was condemned. It was also foretold that the people of the Gentiles would 'take notice of him', although the prophets have not lived among them. And it was said that he shall be seen with a form dishonourable as men regard it. The passage reads as follows:

Behold, my servant shall have understanding, and shall be exalted and glorified and raised very high. Just as many will be astonished at thee (so inglorious will thy form be among men, and thy glory among men), even so many nations shall be amazed at him and kings shall shut their mouths; because those to whom he was not proclaimed shall see him and those who have not heard shall take notice of him. Lord, who has believed our report? And to whom was the arm of the Lord revealed? We proclaimed as a child before him, as a root in a thirsty land; there is no form nor glory in him. And we saw him, and he had not form or beauty, but his form was dishonourable and deserted more than any other man; being a man in calamity who had learnt how to bear sickness; because his face was turned away, he was dishonoured and not considered. This man bears our sins and suffers pain for us, and we considered him to be in trouble and in calamity and affliction. But he was wounded for our transgressions, and he was made sick for our iniquities; the chastisement of our peace was upon him; by his stripe we were healed. All we like sheep went astray, a man went astray in his path; and the Lord delivered him for our sins, and because of his affliction he opens not his mouth. As a sheep he was led to the slaughter, and as a lamb before his shearer is dumb, so he opens not his mouth. In his humiliation his judgment was taken away; who shall explain his generation? Because his life is taken away from the earth, because of the iniquities of my people he was led to death.[1]

55. I remember that once in a discussion with some whom the Jews regard as learned[2] I used these prophecies. At this the Jew said that these prophecies referred to the whole people as though of a single individual, since they were scattered in the dispersion and smitten, that as a result of the scattering of the Jews among the other nations many might become proselytes. In this way he explained the text: 'Thy form shall be inglorious among men'; and 'those to whom he was not proclaimed shall see him'; and 'being a man in calamity'. I then adduced many arguments in the disputation which proved that there is no good reason for referring these prophecies about one individual to the whole people. And I asked which person could be referred to in the text: 'This man bears our sins and suffers

[1] Isa. lii. 13–liii. 8.   [2] I.e. Rabbis. Cf. note on I, 45, p. 41.

pain for us' and 'but he was wounded for our transgressions, and he was made sick for our iniquities'; and I asked which person fitted the words 'by his stripe we were healed'. Obviously those who say this were once in their sins, and were healed by the passion of the Saviour, whether they were of the Jewish people or of the Gentiles; the prophet foresaw this and put these words into their mouths by inspiration of the Holy Spirit. But we seemed to put him in the greatest difficulty with the words 'because of the iniquities of my people he was led to death'. If according to them the people are the subject of the prophecy, why is this man said to have been led to death because of the iniquities of the people of God, if he is not different from the people of God? Who is this if not Jesus Christ, by whose stripe we who believe in him were healed, when he put off the principalities and powers among us, and made a show of them openly on the cross?[1] However, it is appropriate to a different occasion to explain each point in the prophecy and to study each detail. Although this point has received an extended treatment, I think it has been necessary on account of the passage which we have quoted from Celsus' Jew.

56. Celsus and his Jew, and all who have not believed in Jesus, have failed to notice that the prophecies speak of two advents of Christ. In the first he is subject to human passions and deeper humiliation, in order that by being with men Christ might teach the way that leads to God and might leave no one living this life among men an opportunity of defending themselves on the ground that they were ignorant of the judgment to come. In the second he is coming in glory and in divinity alone, without any human passions bound up with his divine nature. To quote all these prophecies would be too long. It is enough at this moment to quote that from the forty-fourth Psalm, which among other things is entitled 'a song for the beloved', where Christ is clearly addressed as God in the words: 'The grace in thy lips was poured forth; therefore God blessed thee for ever. Gird thy sword on thy thigh, O mighty one, in thy beauty and thy fairness, and exert thyself and ride on and rule for the sake of truth and meekness and righteousness, and thy right hand shall guide thee wonderfully. Thine arrows are sharpened, O mighty one, the peoples will fall under thee; they go into the heart of the king's enemies.' And note carefully what follows, where he is called God. For the scripture says: 'Thy throne, O God, is for ever and ever, a sceptre of equity is the sceptre of thy kingdom. Thou hast loved righteousness and hated iniquity; therefore God, even thy God, hath anointed thee with the oil of gladness above thy fellows.'[2] Notice that the prophet addresses a God whose throne is for ever and ever, and that a sceptre of equity is the sceptre of his kingdom;

[1] Col. ii. 15.   [2] Ps. xliv. 3–8.

he says that this God has been anointed by a God who is his God, and that he has been anointed because he loved righteousness and hated iniquity more than his fellows. I remember putting the Jew who was thought to be wise into great difficulties with this passage. He did not know what to make of it, and answered in a way consistent with his Judaism by saying that the words were addressed to the God of the universe when it said 'thy throne, O God, is for ever and ever, a sceptre of equity is the sceptre of thy kingdom'; but the Messiah was addressed in the words 'thou hast loved righteousness and hated iniquity; therefore God, even thy God, hath anointed thee' etc.

57. Again, his Jew says to the Saviour: *If you say that every man has become a son of God by divine providence, what is the difference between you and anyone else?*[1] We would reply to him that every man, who, as Paul expresses it, no longer has fear as his schoolmaster but chooses what is good for its own sake, is a son of God. But Jesus is far, far superior to every one who for his virtue is called a son of God, since he is as it were the source and origin[2] of such virtues. Paul's words read as follows: 'For you did not receive the spirit of slavery again to fear, but you received the spirit of adoption, whereby we cry Abba, Father.'[3] *But some thousands,*[4] so Celsus' Jew says, *will refute Jesus by asserting that the prophecies which were applied to him were spoken of them.* We do not know whether Celsus knew of some who came to this life and wanted to emulate Jesus and to give themselves the title of sons of God, or a power of God.[5] But since we study the subject honestly, we would say that among the Jews there was one Theudas before the birth of Jesus, who said that he was some great one; after his death those deceived by him were scattered. And after him 'in the days of the enrolment', when it seems that Jesus was born, one Judas of Galilee drew away to himself many from the people of the Jews, as though he were some wise man and an introducer of new doctrines; but when he also paid the penalty by death, his teaching perished and remained among a very few insignificant people.[6] After the time of Jesus Dositheus the Samaritan[7] also wanted to persuade the Samaritans that he was the Christ prophesied by Moses, and he appeared to have won over some folk to his teaching. But we may reasonably quote the very wise saying of

---

[1] This may mean: 'If you say that every man who is born according to divine providence is a son of God...' (so, for example, Keim). Harnack (*D.G.* 1, 4th ed. p. 212) thinks Celsus shows knowledge of controversy about the uniqueness of Jesus' sonship.

[2] The phrase ultimately comes from Plato, *Phaedrus*, 245 C. Cf. IV, 53; IV, 44; VIII, 17; *de Orat.* XXII, 3; in Philo, *de Mut. Nom.* 58, God is 'the source and origin of all graces'. Cf. *de Sp. Leg.* II, 156.

[3] Rom. viii. 14–15.

[4] K. tr. wants to emend τινὲς δὲ καὶ ἐλέγξουσιν, ⟨ἢ⟩ ὥς φησιν ὁ παρὰ Κέλσῳ Ἰουδαῖος μυρίοι, τὸν Ἰησοῦν κτλ. This is rightly rejected by Bader.

[5] Acts viii. 10. [6] Acts v. 36–7. [7] See note on VI, 11.

Gamaliel, recorded in the Acts of the Apostles, to show that these men had
nothing to do with the promise, and were neither sons of God nor His
powers, whereas Jesus the Christ was truly God's son. Gamaliel there
says: 'If this counsel or this doctrine be of men, it will be overthrown',
even as theirs perished when they died; 'but if it be of God, you will not
be able to overthrow this man's teaching, lest haply you be found to be
fighting against God'.[1] Simon the Samaritan magician also wanted to
draw away some folk by magic, and he succeeded in his deception at the
time. But now of all the Simonians in the world it is not possible, I believe,
to find thirty,[2] and perhaps I have exaggerated the number. There are very
few in Palestine, while in the rest of the world he is nowhere mentioned,
though his ambition was to spread his fame throughout it. Where his name
is mentioned, it comes from the Acts of the Apostles, and the only people
who speak of him are Christians, while the facts manifestly witnessed that
there was nothing divine about Simon.

58. After this instead of the magi of the gospel Celsus' Jew speaks of
Chaldaeans,[3] saying that *according to the account of Jesus they were moved to
come to his birth to worship him as God although he was still an infant; and
they informed Herod the tetrarch*[4] *of this: but he sent men to kill those born just
at that time, thinking that he would destroy him also with them, lest somehow,
after he had lived for the time sufficient for him to grow up, he should become
king.* See here the blunder of the man who does not distinguish magi from
Chaldaeans, and fails to notice their different professions, and who on
this account corrupts what is written in the gospel. For some unknown
reason he has omitted to mention that which influenced the magi, and does
not say that it was a star seen by them in the east according to the Biblical
record.[5] Let us see then what may be our reply to this. We think that the
star which appeared in the east was a new star[6] and not like any of the
ordinary ones, neither of those in the fixed sphere nor of those in the
lower spheres, but it is to be classed with the comets which occasionally
occur, or meteors, or bearded or jar-shaped stars, or any other such name
by which the Greeks may like to describe their different forms.[7] We
establish this point as follows.

[1] Acts v. 38–9.   [2] Origen confuses Simon with Dositheus; see note on VI, 11.
[3] For the identification of Magi and Chaldaeans, cf. J. Bidez and F. Cumont, *Les Mages
hellénisés* (1938), I, pp. 33–6.
[4] Celsus confuses Herod the tetrarch (Luke iii. 1) with Herod the Great, his father
(Matt. ii. 1–3).   [5] But cf. Celsus in I, 34 above.
[6] Cf. *Comm. in Joann.* I, 26 (24). For its newness cf. Clement, *Exc. Theod.* LXXIV, 2;
Ignatius, *Ephes.* 19.
[7] The phrase is borrowed by Eusebius, *D.E.* IX, 1, 420A. For the comet in the ancient
world, cf. Gundel in P.-W. XI (1922), 1143–93. On the names of comets, cf. A. Rehm, in
SB. bay. Ak. d. Wiss. (1921), I, p. 31 n. 1.

59. It has been observed that at great events and the most far-reaching changes of history stars of this kind appear which are significant of changes of dynasties, or wars, or whatever may happen among men which has the effect of shaking earthly affairs. We have read in the book on comets by Chaeremon the Stoic how comets have sometimes appeared even when good events were about to happen, and he gives an account of these.[1] If then a comet, as it is called, or some similar star appears at new dynasties or other great events on earth, why is it amazing that a star should have appeared at the birth of a man who was to introduce new ideas among the human race and to bring a doctrine not only to Jews but also to Greeks and to many barbarian nations as well? I would say, however, that there is no prophecy about comets in circulation, saying that such and such a comet would appear with a particular dynasty or at particular times; but the star which appeared at the birth of Jesus was prophesied by Balaam, as Moses recorded, when he said: 'A star shall appear out of Jacob, and a man shall rise up out of Israel.'[2] If then it will be necessary also to examine what the scriptures say about the magi at the birth of Jesus and the star which appeared, we would give the following explanation of it, addressing some remarks to Greeks and others to Jews.

60. To Greeks I say this. Magi are in communion with daemons and by their formulas invoke them for the ends which they desire; and they succeed in these practices so long as nothing more divine and potent than the daemons and the spell that invokes them appears or is pronounced. But if anything more divine were to appear, the powers of the daemons would be destroyed, since they would be unable to withstand the light of the divine power. Accordingly, it is probable that at the birth of Jesus when, as Luke records and as I believe, 'a multitude of the heavenly host praised God and said, Glory to God in the highest, and on earth peace, goodwill among men',[3] the effect of this was that the daemons lost their strength and became weak; their sorcery was confuted and their power overthrown; they were not only overthrown by the angels who visited the earthly region on account of the birth of Jesus, but also by the soul of Jesus and the divine power in him. Accordingly, when the magi wanted

---

[1] Chaeremon was tutor of Nero (Suidas, *s.v.* Ἀλέξανδρος Αἰγαῖος). The fragments are collected by H.-R. Schwyzer, *Chairemon* (*Klass.-Philol. Studien* hrsg. E. Bickel u. C. Jensen, Heft IV), 1932. The usual ancient opinion about comets was that they were a sign of impending disaster. Only very rarely is a comet taken as a good sign. Comets appeared in A.D. 54 and 60 (Gundel in P.-W. XI, 1188), and that of 60 apparently aroused expectations of Nero's death. Seneca (*N.Q.* VII, 17, 2) says of it: 'qui sub Nerone Caesare apparuit et cometis detraxit infamiam'. Cf. *ibid.* VII, 21, 3 'quem (cometam) nos Neronis principatu laetissimo vidimus'. Schwyzer (pp. 61–3) argues that as Tacitus and Suetonius regard this comet as an evil sign, Seneca and Chaeremon are deliberately flattering Nero.

[2] Num. xxiv. 17.   [3] Luke ii. 13–14.

to perform their usual practices, which they had previously effected by certain charms and trickery, they tried to find out the reason why they no longer worked, concluding that it was an important one. Seeing a sign from God in heaven they wished to see what was indicated by it. I think that they had the prophecies of Balaam recorded by Moses,[1] who was also an expert in this kind of thing. They found there the prophecy of the star and the words: 'I will show to him, but not now; I call him blessed, though he is not at hand.'[2] And they guessed that the man foretold as coming with the star had arrived; and as they had already found that he was superior to all daemons and the beings that usually appeared to them and caused certain magical effects, they wanted to worship him. They therefore came to Judaea, because they were convinced that some king had been born and[3] because they knew where he would be born, but without understanding over what kingdom he would rule. They brought gifts which they offered to him who was, so to speak, a combination of God and mortal man. These gifts were symbols, the gold being offered as to a king, the myrrh for one who would die, and the frankincense to God;[4] they offered them when they learnt his birth-place. Since, however, the Saviour of the human race was God and superior to the angels who help man, an angel rewarded the piety of the magi in worshipping[5] Jesus by warning them not to go to Herod but to return to their own country by another route.

61. It is not remarkable that Herod plotted against the child, even though Celsus' Jew would not believe that this really happened. For wickedness is a blind force and, imagining itself stronger than destiny, desires to overcome it. Herod was in this state. He believed that the king of the Jews had been born, and yet gave his assent to an action which was inconsistent with this belief. He did not see that either he is a king and will reign in any event, or that he will not reign and that it would be futile to kill him. Accordingly, in his desire to kill him he was subject to conflicting judgments[6] on account of his wickedness, and was impelled by the blind and evil devil, who from the very beginning conspired against the

---

[1] Cf. *Hom. in Num.* XIII, 7 'Si enim prophetiae eius a Moyse sacris insertae sunt voluminibus, quanto magis descriptae sunt ab his, qui habitabant tunc Mesopotamiam, apud quos magnificus habebatur Balaam quosque artis eius constat fuisse discipulos?...Haec scripta habebant magi apud semet ipsos et ideo, quando natus est Jesus, agnoverunt stellam et intellexerunt adimpleri prophetiam...'. Balaam could be identified with Zoroaster; cf. Bidez and Cumont, *Les Mages hellénisés*, I, pp. 47–8. Basil the Great thinks Balaam was a magus (*Hom. in sanctam Christi gener.*, Migne, P.G. XXXI, 1469 A).

[2] Num. xxiv. 17.   [3] Read καὶ for ἣ with Wendland and Wifstrand.

[4] Cf. Irenaeus, *adv. Haer.* III, 9, 2 (Harvey II, 32); Clem. Al. *Paed.* II, 63, 5. For later writers, cf. W. Theiler, *Die chaldäischen Orakel u. d. Hymnen d. Synesios* (1942), p. 38.

[5] Read ἐπὶ τῷ with K. tr.   [6] Cf. the discussion of Judas in II, 11.

Saviour, as he had an idea that Jesus was and would be some great person. Therefore an angel that kept an eye on the course of events, even if Celsus does not believe it, warned Joseph to depart with the boy and his mother to Egypt. But Herod destroyed all the children in Bethlehem and its neighbourhood, intending to include in the massacre him who was born king of the Jews. He did not see the sleepless power which guards people worthy to be protected and preserved for the salvation of men.[1] Among these Jesus was first, being greater than all others in honour and in all pre-eminence. He was to be king, not in the way that Herod supposed, but because it was fitting that God should give him a kingdom for the benefit of those under his rule, since he would bestow no moderate and indifferent benefit, so to speak, upon his subjects, but by truly divine laws would educate them and lead them on. Jesus also knew this, and denied that he was a king in the sense the multitude expected. He taught that his kingdom had a special character, saying: 'If my kingdom were of this world, then would my servants fight that I should not be delivered to the Jews; but now is my kingdom not of this world.'[2] If Celsus had seen these things, he would not have said: *If Herod did this in order that when you were grown up you might not reign instead of him, why then when you had grown up did you not become king, but, though son of God, go about begging so disgracefully, cowering from fear, and wandering up and down in destitution?* But it is not disgraceful carefully to avoid running straight into dangers,[3] not from fear of death but for the sake of bringing help to others by continuing to live, until the time came when it was expedient for him who had assumed human nature to die a human death which brought a certain benefit to mankind. This is obvious to anyone who has understood that Jesus died for men; on this subject we have spoken as well as we could in the previous arguments.

62. After this, not even knowing the number of the apostles, he says: *Jesus collected round him ten or eleven infamous men, the most wicked tax-collectors and sailors,*[4] *and with these fled hither and thither, collecting a means of livelihood in a disgraceful and importunate way.* Let us now deal with this as well as we can. It is obvious to readers of the gospels, which Celsus does not appear even to have read, that Jesus chose twelve apostles, of whom only Matthew was a *tax-collector.* Those whom he muddles together as *sailors* are probably James and John, since they left the ship and their father Zebedee and followed Jesus. For Peter and his brother Andrew, who earned the necessities of life with a fishing-net, are to be reckoned not

---

[1] For Origen's view of guardian angels, cf. VIII, 27 and 34 ff.; *Comm. in Matt.* XIII, 5; *Hom. in Luc.* 12 (after Hermas, *Mand.* VI, 2).
[2] John xviii. 36.   [3] Cf. VIII, 44.   [4] Cf. Celsus in II, 46.

among sailors, but, as the Bible says, among fishermen. I grant that the Leves also who followed Jesus was a tax-collector; but he was not of the number of the apostles, except according to one of the copies of the gospel according to Mark. But we do not know what were the trades by which the others earned their living before they became disciples of Jesus.

I also affirm in reply to this that to people who can study the question about Jesus' apostles intelligently and reasonably it will appear that these men taught Christianity and succeeded in bringing many to obey the word of God by divine power. For in them there was no power of speaking or of giving an ordered narrative by the standards of Greek dialectical or rhetorical arts which convinced their hearers. It seems to me that if Jesus had chosen some men who were wise in the eyes of the multitude, and who were capable of thinking and speaking acceptably to crowds, and if he had used them as the means of propagating his teaching, he might on very good grounds have been suspected of making use of a method similar to that of philosophers who are leaders of some particular sect.[1] The truth of the claim that his teaching is divine would no longer have been self-evident, in that the gospel and the preaching were in persuasive words of the wisdom that consists in literary style and composition. And the faith, like the faith of the philosophers of this world in their doctrines, would have been in the wisdom of men, and not in the power of God. If anyone saw fisherfolk and tax-collectors *who had not had even a primary education* (as the gospel records of them—and Celsus did believe them in this respect, that they were right about the disciples' lack of learning), and who with great courage not only spoke to Jews about faith in Jesus but also preached him among the other nations with success, would he not try to find out the source of their persuasive power? For it is not that which is popularly supposed to be power. Who would not say that Jesus had fulfilled the saying, 'Come follow me, and I will make you fishers of men',[2] by a certain divine power in his apostles? Paul also, after showing this as we have said above, says: 'And my word and my preaching were not in persuasive words of man's wisdom, but in demonstration of the spirit and of power, that our faith may not be in the wisdom of men but in the power of God.'[3] According to what is said in the prophets when proclaiming with foreknowledge the preaching of the gospel, 'the Lord gave the word to the preachers of the gospel with great power, the king of the powers of the beloved',[4] so that the prophecy was fulfilled which says 'his word will run quickly'.[5] And we see that the sound of the apostles of Jesus has 'gone out into all the earth, and their words unto the ends of the

---

[1] Cf. III, 39; Tertullian, *de Anima*, 3.   [2] Matt. iv. 19.   [3] I Cor. ii. 4–5.
[4] Ps. lxvii. 12–13.   [5] Ps. cxlvii. 4.

world'.[1] On account of this those who hear the word proclaimed with power are filled with power, which they show forth by their sincerity and life and by the fact that they fight to the death for the truth.[2] But there are some empty people who, although they may profess to believe in God through Jesus, have no divine power and only appear to be converted to the Word of God.

Although I mentioned above a saying spoken by the Saviour in the gospels, nevertheless I will also quote it now as it is relevant; for it shows both the foreknowledge of our Saviour about the preaching of the gospel, which is obviously divine, and the strength of the Word which without teachers conquers those who believe by the divine power of its persuasion. Jesus says: 'The harvest is plenteous, but the labourers are few; pray therefore that the Lord of the harvest will send forth labourers into his harvest.'[3]

63. Since Celsus says that the apostles of Jesus were *infamous men*, and calls them *the most wicked tax-collectors and sailors*, we will say about this point also that he seems to believe the scriptures whenever he wants to do so in order to criticize Christianity, and seems to disbelieve the gospels when he wishes to avoid accepting the obviously divine character proclaimed in those very books. If he saw the honest purpose of the writers to be shown by the fact that they recorded discreditable things, he ought also to believe them where divine things are concerned. It is indeed written in the general epistle of Barnabas, from where Celsus perhaps took his statement that the apostles were *infamous* and *most wicked*, that Jesus 'chose his own apostles, who were sinners above all others'.[4] And in the gospel according to Luke Peter says to Jesus: 'Depart from me, for I am a sinful man, O Lord.'[5] Moreover, Paul says in the Epistle to Timothy, even though he himself had later become an apostle of Jesus, 'this is a faithful saying, that Christ Jesus came into the world to save sinners, of whom I am chief'.[6] For some unknown reason he forgot or did not think of saying anything about Paul, who after Jesus established the churches in Christ. He probably saw that he would have to explain the history of Paul, how he persecuted the church of God and fought bitterly against the believers, so that he even wanted to deliver to death Jesus' disciples, but afterwards was so profoundly converted that from Jerusalem to Illyricum he had fully preached the gospel of Christ, being ambitious to preach so as not to build on another man's foundation, but in places where the gospel of God in Christ was not even preached at all.[7] Why then is it outrageous

---

[1] Ps. xviii. 5; Rom. x. 18.
[3] Matt. ix. 37–8; cf. 1, 43 above.
[5] Luke v. 8.   [6] I Tim. 1. 15.
[2] Sirach iv. 28.
[4] *Ep. Barn.* v. 9.
[7] Rom. xv. 19–21.

if Jesus, wanting to show mankind the extent of his ability to heal souls, chose *infamous* and *most wicked men*, and led them on so far that they were an example of the purest moral character to those who were converted by them to the gospel of Christ?

64. If we were going to reproach people whose lives have changed on the ground of their past, we could well attack Phaedo the philosopher, since, as the story goes, Socrates led him out from a house of ill-fame to study philosophy. Furthermore, we would reproach philosophy for the licentiousness of Polemo, Xenocrates' successor.[1] In these instances philosophy should be approved on the ground that its doctrine in those who persuaded them had the power to change men from such evils although they had previously been gripped by them. Among the Greeks there was but one Phaedo (I do not know of a second) and but one Polemo, who changed from a licentious and most depraved life to study philosophy; but among the followers of Jesus there were not only the twelve while he was on earth, but also there continues to be a much larger number who having become a band of self-controlled men say of their past life: 'For we also were previously foolish, disobedient, deceived, serving divers lusts and pleasures, living in malice and envy, hateful, hating one another. But when the kindness of God our Saviour appeared and his love towards man', we became people of such character as we are now, 'through the washing of regeneration and renewing of the Spirit, which he poured out upon us'.[2] For God 'sent forth his word and healed them and delivered them out of their distresses',[3] as he who prophesied in the psalms taught us. I would also add this to what I have said, that Chrysippus in his book on the cure of the passions, with the aim of suppressing the passions of human souls, tries to cure those already gripped by the passions by telling them to follow the teaching of the different sects, although he makes no pretence of deciding how far any particular doctrine is true. He says that 'if pleasure is an ultimate value, men should try to heal their passions assuming this to be correct; and supposing that there are three kinds of good, it is just as true to say that people who are entangled with their passions ought to be delivered from them by following this principle'.[4] The critics of

---

[1] Cf. III, 67 below. For Phaedo, cf. Diog. Laert. II, 105; Aulus Gellius, II, 18; Suidas, *s.v.*; Lactantius, *Div. Inst.* III, 25, 15; Macrobius, *Sat.* I, 11, 41. For Polemo, cf. Diog. Laert. IV, 16; Epictetus, *Diss.* III, 1, 14; Horace, *Sat.* II, 3, 253–7; Plutarch, *Mor.* 71E; Lucian, *Bis Accus.* 16–17; Valerius Max. VI, 9, 1; Cosmas Hieros., *Ad Carm. S. Greg.* 119, 792 (*P.G.* XXXVIII, 579); Ambrose, *de Elia et Ieiunio* XII, 45 (*P.L.* XIV, 712); Augustine, *c. Jul. Pelag.* I, 4, 12; I, 7, 35. On the theme of conversion to philosophy, see A. D. Nock, *Conversion* (1933), pp. 164–86, and 'Conversion and Adolescence', in *Pisciculi, Studien zur Religion u. Kultur des Altertums F. J. Dölger dargeboten*, (Münster, 1939) = *Antike und Christentum*, Ergänzungsband, I, pp. 165–77.
[2] Tit. iii. 3–6.   [3] Ps. cvi. 20.   [4] Cf. VIII, 51.

Christianity do not see in how many people the passions are suppressed and in how many the flood of evil is restrained, and in how many wild habits are tamed by reason of the gospel. They ought to have confessed their gratitude to the gospel when they observe its services to the community,[1] and borne testimony to it that, even if it may not be true, at any rate it is of advantage to the human race.

65. Jesus taught his disciples not to be rash, saying to them: 'If they persecute you in this city flee to another; and if they persecute you in that, flee again to yet another.'[2] And he gave them an example of his teaching by his tranquil life; he was careful not to meet dangers unnecessarily or at the wrong time or for no good reason. This again Celsus wickedly misrepresents when his Jew says to Jesus: *You fled hither and thither with your disciples.* We may remark that the story told of Aristotle resembles the slander which the Jew has made against Jesus and his disciples. When Aristotle saw that the court of justice was about to be gathered together against him on the charge of impiety on account of certain doctrines of his philosophy which the Athenians considered to be impious, he went away from Athens and set up his school in Chalcis, defending himself to his pupils by saying: 'Let us depart from Athens, lest we give the Athenians an occasion for becoming guilty a second time as in the case of Socrates, and lest once again they treat philosophy irreverently.'[3] According to Celsus *Jesus went about with his disciples collecting their livelihood in a disgraceful and importunate way.* Let him declare where he got his idea of disgraceful and importunate beggary. For in the gospels certain women who had been healed from their ailments, among whom was Susanna, provided the disciples with meals out of their own substance.[4] But what philosopher who was devoted to the benefit of his pupils did not receive from them money for his needs? Or was it proper and right for them to do this, whereas when Jesus' disciples do it, they are accused by Celsus of *collecting their means of livelihood in a disgraceful and importunate way?*

66. After these remarks the Jew of Celsus next says to Jesus: *Why also when you were still an infant did you have to be taken away to Egypt lest you should be murdered? It is not likely that a god would be afraid of death. But an angel came from heaven, commanding you and your family to escape, lest by being left behind you should die. And could not the great God, who had already sent two angels on your account, guard you, His own son, at that very place?* In these words Celsus thinks that there was nothing divine about

[1] Read αὐτοὺς ἐντυχόντας τῷ κοινωνικῷ with Φ.   [2] Matt. x. 23.
[3] Cf. Aelian, *Var. Hist.* III, 36; Ps.-Ammonius, *Vita Arist.* p. 11, ed. Didot; Diog. Laert. v, 5; Seneca, *de Otio*, VIII, 1.
[4] Luke viii. 2–3.

the human body and soul of Jesus, and even suggests that his body had
characteristics such as those mentioned by the Homeric myths. At any
rate, he mocks the blood of Jesus which was poured forth on the cross,
and says it was not

Ichor such as flows in the veins of the blessed gods.[1]

But we believe Jesus himself when he says of the divinity in him: 'I am
the way, the truth, and the life',[2] or any other similar saying: and again
when he says this, meaning that he was in a human body: 'But now you
seek to kill me, a man who told you the truth.'[3] So we say that he was
a sort of composite being. And as he had come into human life to live as
a man, it was right for him to take care not to run into danger of his life
at the wrong time. Thus he had to be taken away by those who brought
him up, who were directed by an angel of God, who warned them the
first time in the words: 'Joseph, son of David, do not fear to take Mary
thy wife; for that which is conceived in her is of the Holy Spirit';[4] and
on the second occasion in the words: 'Rise, take the child and his mother
and flee to Egypt, and be there until I tell you; for Herod intends to seek
the child to destroy him.'[5] Here the Biblical record seems to me to be not
in the least incredible. In both passages of scripture the angel is said to
have told these things to Joseph in a dream; and that it should be indicated
to certain people in a dream that they ought to do certain things is an
experience which happens to many others also, whether an angel or any
other agent brings the suggestion before the soul. Why therefore is it
absurd that once he had become incarnate he was cared for even in his
human life with a view to avoiding dangers, not because it was impossible
that it should happen in any other way, but because all possible ways and
means ought to be carefully used for the safety of Jesus? It was better that
the child Jesus should avoid the plot of Herod and depart with those who
were bringing him up to Egypt until the death of the man who had designs
against him, than that the providence guarding Jesus should hinder the
free will of Herod in his desire to kill the child, or that what the poet calls
'the helmet of Hades'[6] or anything similar should have been put round
Jesus, or that providence should have smitten those who came to kill him
like the people in Sodom.[7] The highly miraculous character and increased
publicity of the help given to him would not have helped his object, which

[1] Homer, *Il.* v, 340. See II, 36 below.   [2] John xiv. 6.
[3] John viii. 40.   [4] Matt. i. 20.
[5] Matt. ii. 13. Whether Origen rightly identifies the 'two angels' of Celsus is doubtful.
Bader thinks Celsus had in mind those of Luke i. 26–38 and ii. 9–14.
[6] Homer, *Il.* v, 845. It made the wearer invisible.
[7] With blindness (Gen. xix. 11).

was to teach, as a man to whom God bore witness, that within the visible man he possessed something more divine; this was the part to which the title 'son of God' is properly applied, the divine Logos, the power and wisdom of God, the so-called Christ. This, however, is not the right time to explain the composite nature and of what elements the incarnate Jesus consisted, since this is, so to speak, a matter for private investigation by believers.

67. After this Celsus' Jew, as though he were some Greek that loved learning and had been educated to Greek literature, says: *The old myths that attributed a divine birth to Perseus and Amphion and Aeacus and Minos (we do not believe even them) are nevertheless evidence of their great and truly wonderful works for mankind, so that they do not appear lacking in plausibility; but as for you, what have you done in word or deed that is fine or wonderful? You showed nothing to us, although they challenged you in the temple to produce some obvious token that you were the son of God.*[1] To this my answer is as follows. Let the Greeks show to us a work of any one of those enumerated above which has been of outstanding benefit to human life, and has had influence upon posterity, and which is of such importance as to lend probability to the legend about them which asserts that they were born of a divine birth. But they can show nothing about the men whom he mentions which is nearly as important as the works which Jesus showed, unless perhaps the Greeks would refer us to myths and to their stories, and wish us to believe them without rational thought while disbelieving the story of Jesus which has the support of much evidence. We affirm that the whole human world has evidence of the work of Jesus since in it dwell the churches of God which consist of people converted through Jesus from countless evils. Moreover, the name of Jesus still takes away mental distractions from men, and daemons and diseases as well, and implants a wonderful meekness and tranquillity of character, and a love to mankind and a kindness and gentleness, in those who have not feigned to be Christians on account of their need of the necessities of life or some other want,[2] but have genuinely accepted the gospel about God and Christ and the judgment to come.

68. After this, suspecting that the great works done by Jesus would be pointed out, of which, although there is much to say, we have only said a little, Celsus pretends to grant that the scriptures may be true when they speak of *cures or resurrection or a few loaves feeding many people, from which many fragments were left over, or any other monstrous tales,* as he thinks, *related by the disciples.* And he goes on to say: *Come, let us believe that these miracles really were done by you.* Then he at once puts them on a level with *the works of sorcerers who profess to do wonderful miracles, and the*

[1] John x. 23–4.   [2] Cf. Lucian, *de Morte Peregrini* 12 f.

accomplishments of those who are taught by the Egyptians, who for a few obols make known[1] their sacred lore in the middle of the market-place and drive daemons out of men and blow away diseases and invoke the souls of heroes, displaying expensive banquets and dining-tables and cakes and dishes which are non-existent, and who make things move as though they were alive although they are not really so, but only appear as such in the imagination. And he says: *Since these men do these wonders, ought we to think them sons of God? Or ought we to say that they are the practices of wicked men possessed by an evil daemon?*

You see how by these words he gives his assent, as it were, to the reality of magic. I do not know whether he is the same as the man who wrote several books against magic.[2] But because it happens to be to his advantage for his purpose he compares the stories about Jesus with tales of magic. They might have been comparable if Jesus had done his miracles, like magicians, merely to show his own powers. But in fact no sorcerer uses his tricks to call the spectators to moral reformation; nor does he educate by the fear of God people who were astounded by what they saw, nor does he attempt to persuade the onlookers to live as men who will be judged by God. Sorcerers do none of these things, since they have neither the ability nor even the will to do so. Nor do they even want to have anything to do with reforming men, seeing that they themselves are filled with the most shameful and infamous sins. Is it not likely that one who used the miracles that he performed to call those who saw the happenings to moral reformation, would have shown himself as an example of the best life, not only to his genuine disciples but also to the rest? Jesus did this in order that his disciples might give themselves up to teaching men according to the will of God, and that the others, who have been taught as much[3] by his doctrine as by his moral life and miracles the right way to live, might do every action by referring to the pleasure of the supreme God. If the life of Jesus was of this character, how could anyone reasonably compare him with the behaviour of sorcerers and fail to believe that according to God's promise[4] he was God who had appeared in a human body for the benefit of our race?

69. After this he muddles Christianity with the view of some sect as though Christians shared their opinions and applies his objections to all

[1] Read ἀποδιδομένων with Wendland. For magicians in the market-places, cf. III, 50 below; Apuleius, *Metam.* I, 4 where a juggler swallowed a sharp sword and then *exiguae stipis* ate a spear with the point downwards by the Painted Porch in Athens. Maximus of Tyre XIII, 3 c (Hobein, 160, 19) speaks of some who in their conception of oracles are like people who δυοῖν ὀβολοῖν τῷ προστυχόντι ἀποθεσπίζουσιν.

[2] See Introduction, p. xxiv.

[3] Read οὐ πλέον with A³ K. tr.   [4] Read τοῦ ⟨θεοῦ⟩ with Guiet.

people converted by the divine word, saying *a god would not have had a body such as yours*. But we say to this that at his advent into this life, as he was born of a woman, he assumed a body which was human and capable of dying a human death. For this reason, in addition to other things, we say that he was also a great wrestler, because his human body was tempted in all points like all other men, and yet was no longer like sinful men in that it was entirely without sin.[1] For it appears clear to us that 'he did no sin neither was guile found in his mouth',[2] and God delivered him up, who knew no sin,[3] as a pure offering for all those who had sinned. Celsus then says: *The body of a god would not have been born as you, Jesus, were born.* Yet he perceived that if he had been born as the Bible says, his body could somehow have been more divine than that of the multitude[4] and in some sense the body of God. Moreover, he disbelieves the stories recorded about his conception by the Holy Spirit, and believes that his father was a certain Panthera who corrupted the virgin. That is why he said that *the body of a god would not have been born as you were born*. But on these matters we have spoken at length in the earlier part of the book.[5]

70. He says that *the body of a god would also not eat such food*,[6] as though able to show from the gospels both that he ate and what kind of food he ate. However, supposing that he can do this, he might mention that he ate the passover with the disciples, holding that he did not merely say 'with desire I have desired to eat this passover with you', but also actually ate it. He might also mention that when he was thirsty he drank at Jacob's well.[7] What has this to do with what we say about his body? He evidently seems to have eaten some fish after his resurrection.[8] But in our view he assumed a body because he was born of a woman. Furthermore, he says: *The body of a god does not use a voice of that kind, nor that method of persuasion.* This also is a worthless and quite insignificant objection. We will answer him by saying that the Pythian and Didymean Apollo, believed by the Greeks to be a god, makes use of *a voice of that kind* in the Pythian priestess or the prophetess at Miletus. Yet among the Greeks no criticism is founded on this that the Pythian or Didymean Apollo, or any other such Greek god that is established in one particular place, is not a god. But how much superior to this was it for God to make use of a voice which effected conviction in those who heard in some indescribable way, because it was proclaimed with power.

71. Then this man who is, so to speak, *hated by God* for his impiety and *wicked* doctrines, hurls abuse at Jesus and says: *These were the actions of*

---

[1] Heb. iv. 15.   [2] Isa. liii. 5.   [3] II Cor. v. 21.
[4] Read παρὰ τοὺς πολλούς with Guiet, K. tr.   [5] I, 32 above.
[6] Cf. VII, 13 below.   [7] John iv. 6–7.   [8] John xxi. 13.

one hated by God and of a wicked sorcerer. If the words used and the real facts are strictly examined, however, it will be seen to be impossible that a man should be hated by God, since God 'loves all that exists and hates nothing that he has made; for he made nothing in hatred'.[1] If certain passages in the prophets do say that kind of thing, they are to be explained by this general principle, that the Bible uses words of God as if he possessed human passions. However, why need I make any reply to a man who, in arguments which he professes to be honest, thinks it right to make use of invective and abuse against Jesus, as if he were a wicked man and a sorcerer? This is the action, not of a man who is arguing seriously, but of one who suffers from a vulgar and unphilosophical mind. He ought to state the facts and study them with an open mind, making such observations upon them as occur to him to the best of his ability.

But as Celsus' Jew has with these words closed his remarks to Jesus, here too will we bring to a conclusion the first book of our reply to him. If God grants the truth that destroys lying words in accordance with the prayer which says 'destroy them in thy truth',[2] we will begin in the following book with the second appearance of his Jew, where he is made to address his next remarks to those who have been won over by Jesus.

---

[1] Wisd. of Sol. xi. 24.   [2] Ps. liii. 7.

BOOK II

1. In the first book of our reply to Celsus' book, *The True Doctrine*, as he entitled it, we ended with the remarks addressed to Jesus which he put into the mouth of the Jew, as the book had reached sufficient dimensions. We propose to write this book in reply to the charges brought by him against those of the Jewish people who have believed in Jesus. It is this very point to which we first call attention: why, when Celsus had once decided to introduce an imaginary character, did he not represent the Jew as addressing Gentile instead of Jewish believers? If his argument were written against us, it might have seemed very convincing. But perhaps this fellow, who professes to know everything, did not see what would be appropriately attributed to an imaginary character.

Notice, then, what he says to Jewish believers. He says that *deluded by Jesus, they have left the law of their fathers, and have been quite ludicrously deceived, and have deserted to another name and another life.*[1] He failed to notice that Jewish believers in Jesus have not left the law of their fathers.[2] For they live according to it, and are named from the poverty of their interpretation of the law. The Jews call a poor man Ebion, and those Jews who have accepted Jesus as the Christ are called Ebionites.[3] Moreover, Peter seems to have kept the customs of the Mosaic law for a long time, as he had not yet learnt from Jesus to ascend from the letter of the law to its spiritual interpretation. This we learn from the Acts of the Apostles. For on the day after the angel of God was seen by Cornelius, enjoining him to send to Joppa to Simon surnamed Peter;

> Peter went up to the upper room about the ninth hour, and he became hungry and desired to eat. But while they made ready, he fell into a trance, and beheld the heaven opened and a certain vessel descending, as it were a great sheet, let down by four corners to the earth, wherein were all manner of fourfooted beasts and creeping things of the earth and fowls of heaven. And there came

---

[1] Bader compares Tertullian, *ad Nat.* I, 10 'divortium ab institutis maiorum'. Lactantius, *de M.P.* 34 'Christiani, qui parentum suorum reliquerant sectam.'

[2] But cf. Celsus in v, 61.

[3] For Ebionites, cf. v, 61 below; for their rejection of the Pauline epistles, v, 65. For their Christology, *Comm. in Matt.* XVI, 12, where Origen derives their name from the 'poverty of their faith in Jesus'. Similarly *de Princ.* IV, 3, 8 where 'they are named after the poverty of their mind'. Other allusions in Origen's works are *Comm. in Matt.* XI, 12; *Comm. in ep. ad Titum* (Lommatzsch, v, 286); *Hom. in Jerem.* XIX, 12. The primary source for the history of the sect is Irenaeus, *adv. Haer.* I, 26, 2 (Harvey, I, 212). For recent discussions see M. Simon, *Verus Israel* (1948), pp. 277 ff.; H. J. Schoeps, *Theol. u. Gesch. d. Judenchristentums* (1949).

a voice to him, Rise, Peter; kill and eat. But Peter said, Not so, Lord; for I have never eaten anything that is common and unclean. And a voice came to him a second time, What God has cleansed, make not thou common.[1]

See here how Peter is shown to be still keeping the Jewish customs about clean and unclean things. And from what follows it is clear that he needed a vision so that he would share the doctrines of the faith with Cornelius, who was not an Israelite according to the flesh, and those with him, because he was still a Jew and was still living according to the traditions of the Jews, despising those outside Judaism. And in the epistle to the Galatians Paul shows that Peter, still fearing the Jews, ceased to eat with the Gentiles; for when James came to him, 'he separated himself' from the Gentiles, 'fearing those of the circumcision'; and the other Jews and Barnabas did the same as he.[2]

It was appropriate that those sent to the circumcision should not abandon Jewish customs, when 'they who seemed to be pillars gave to Paul and Barnabas the right hand of fellowship',[3] and agreed that they would go to the circumcision that the latter might preach to the Gentiles. But why do I say that those preaching to the circumcision drew back and separated themselves from the Gentiles, when even Paul himself became a Jew to the Jews that he might gain the Jews?[4] For this reason, as it is written in the Acts of the Apostles, he even brought an offering to the altar, that he might[5] persuade the Jews that he was not an apostate from the law.[5] If Celsus had known all this, he would not have represented the Jew as saying to converts from Judaism: *What was wrong with you, citizens, that you left the law of our fathers, and, being deluded by that man whom we were addressing just now, were quite ludicrously deceived and have deserted us for another name and another life?*

2. As we have just mentioned the passage about Peter and those who taught Christianity to people of the circumcision, I do not think it out of place to quote a certain utterance of Jesus from John's gospel, and to explain it. It is written that he said: 'I have still many things to say to you, but you cannot bear them now; but when he, the Spirit of truth, is come, he shall guide you into all the truth; for he will not speak of himself but whatsoever he hears he shall speak.'[6] The question in this passage is what were the many things which Jesus had to say to his disciples, which at that time they were not able to bear. This is my view. Perhaps because the apostles were Jews and had been brought up in the literal interpretation of the Mosaic law, he had to tell them what was the true law, and of what

---

[1] Acts x. 9–15.   [2] Gal. ii. 12.   [3] Gal. ii. 9.
[4] I Cor. ix. 20.   [5] Acts xxi. 26.   [6] John xvi. 12–13.

heavenly things the Jewish worship was a pattern and shadow,[1] and what were the good things to come[2] of which a shadow was provided by the law about meat and drink and feasts and new moons and sabbaths.[3] These were the 'many things' which he had to tell them. But he saw that it is very difficult to eradicate from a soul doctrines with which he was almost born and was brought up until he reached man's estate, and which persuade those who accept them that they are divine and that to overthrow them is impious. He perceived that it is hard to prove that they are 'dung' and 'loss'[4] compared with the pre-eminence of the knowledge that is according to Christ, that is the truth, so that those who heard would have been convinced. He therefore put it off until a more suitable time after his passion and resurrection. Moreover, it was really the wrong moment to bring help to people as yet unable to accept it, because possibly it might have destroyed the impression of Jesus which they had already gained, that he was Christ and Son of the living God.[5] Consider then whether it does not command respect as a sensible interpretation if we take in this sense the words 'I have still many things to say to you, but you cannot bear them now'. By 'many things' he means the method of explanation and exegesis of the law according to the spiritual sense, and somehow the disciples could not bear them because they had been born and brought up among the Jews.

I think also that it was because those ceremonies were a type, while the ultimate reality was that which the Holy Spirit was to teach them, that he said: 'When he, the Spirit of truth, is come, he shall guide you into all the truth.'[6] This is as if he had said 'into all the truth of the matters of which you had the types, although you thought that by them you were offering true worship to God'. According to Jesus' promise the Spirit of truth came to Peter and, referring to the quadrupeds and creeping things of the earth and birds of heaven, said to him: 'Rise, Peter; kill and eat.' He came to him when he was still held by superstition, for he even said to the divine voice, 'Not so, Lord, for I have never eaten anything that is common and unclean.' And He taught the doctrine about true and spiritual meats when He said: 'What God has cleansed, make not thou common.' After that vision the Spirit of truth who was leading Peter into all the truth told him the many things which he could not bear when Jesus was still with him according to the flesh. However, another time will be more suitable for explaining the way to interpret the Mosaic law.

3. It is, however, my present task to refute Celsus' ignorance when his Jew says to the *citizens* and Israelites who have believed in Jesus: *What*

---

[1] Heb. viii. 5.   [2] Heb. x. 1.   [3] Col. ii. 16.
[4] Phil. iii. 8.   [5] Matt. xvi. 16.   [6] John xvi. 13.

was wrong with you that you left the law of our fathers? But in what way
have they left the law of their fathers who rebuke people who do not hear
it, and say: 'Tell me, you who read the law, do you not hear the law? For
it is written that Abraham had two sons' and so on as far as the words
'which things are an allegory'[1] and the next verses? In what way have
they left the law of their fathers who are always calling to mind the words
of their ancestors and saying: 'Does not the law say this also? For it is
written in the law of Moses, Thou shalt not muzzle the ox that is treading
out the corn. Is it for oxen that God cares? Or does he say this altogether
for our sake? Yes, for our sake it was written'[2] and so on? Moreover,
Celsus' Jew makes these assertions because he is muddled, although he
could have said with greater plausibility: Some of you have left these
customs because you follow interpretations and allegories; others interpret spiritually, as you profess to do, but observe the customs of your
fathers just as much as before; while others do not even give interpretations, but want both to accept Jesus as the one prophesied and to observe
the law of Moses according to the traditional customs, thinking that they
possess in the letter the whole meaning of the Spirit. Furthermore, how
could Celsus have got a clear idea of this matter, seeing that later he has
even mentioned godless heresies which are entirely alien to Jesus, and
others that have abandoned the Creator, and did not see that there are
also Israelites who believe in Jesus who have not left the law of their
fathers? But he had no intention of examining the whole question with
a desire to find out the truth, so that if he found anything of value he might
accept it; he wrote this merely out of hostility, being fully determined to
pull everything to pieces the moment he heard it.

4. His Jew then says to believers from the Jewish people: *Quite
recently, when we punished this fellow who cheated you, you abandoned the
law of our fathers.* But we have shown that he has no accurate knowledge
of what he is discussing. After this he seems to me to possess shrewdness
when he says: *Or why do you take your origin from our religion, and then,
as if you are progressing in knowledge, despise these things, although you
cannot name any other origin for your doctrine than our law?* It is true that
for Christians the introduction to the faith is based on the religion of Moses
and the prophetic writings. And after the introduction the next stage of
progress for beginners consists in the interpretation and exegesis of these.
They seek the mystery 'according to revelation', which has been kept in
silence through times eternal, but now is manifested by the prophetic
utterances and by the appearing of our Lord Jesus Christ.[3] It is not true,

---

[1] Gal. iv. 21–4.   [2] I Cor. ix. 8–10.
[3] Rom. xvi. 25–6.

as you say,[1] that as if progressing in knowledge they despise what is written in the law, but they accord it greater honour by showing what a depth of wise and mysterious doctrines is contained by those writings. The Jews, on the other hand, have not looked deeply into them, but read them superficially and only as stories.

Why is it absurd that the law is the origin of our doctrine, that is, the gospel? Even our Lord himself says to those who do not believe in him: 'If you had believed Moses, you would have believed me; for he wrote of me. But if you do not believe his writings, how will you believe my words?'[2] Furthermore, one of the evangelists, Mark, says: 'The beginning of the gospel of Jesus Christ, as it is written in Isaiah the prophet, Behold I send my messenger before thy face, who shall prepare thy way before thee',[3] showing that the beginning of the gospel is connected with the Jewish writings. Why therefore does Celsus' Jew speak against us and say: *For if there was anyone who proclaimed to you that the son of God would come down to men, it was our prophet, the prophet of our God?* But what sort of objection is it to Christianity that *John who baptized Jesus was a Jew?* It does not follow that, since he was a Jew, every believer, whether he comes to the gospel from the Gentiles or from the Jews, must keep the law of Moses literally.

5. After this, even though Celsus repeats himself about John, saying now for the second time that *as an offender he was punished by the Jews,*[4] nevertheless I will not repeat the defence as I am content with what I have said. Then his Jew disparages as stale stuff *the doctrine of the resurrection of the dead and of God's judgment giving reward to the righteous but fire to the unrighteous.* He thinks he can overthrow Christianity by saying that in these matters *Christians teach nothing new.*[5] My answer to him is that our Jesus, seeing that the Jews were doing nothing worthy of the teaching in the prophets, taught by a parable that 'the kingdom of God would be taken away from them' and given to the people of the Gentiles.[6] For this reason it is possible to see that in reality all the doctrines of the Jews living now are myths and trash (for they have not the light of the knowledge of the scriptures), whereas the Christian doctrines are true, and are able to lift and raise up the soul and mind of man and convince him that he has a certain citizenship, not like the earthly Jews, somewhere down here on earth, but in heaven.[7] This is obvious to people who contemplate the greatness of the ideas of the law and the prophets, and who are capable of showing them to others.

---

[1] Read οὐδέ, ὡς λέγεται, οἱ ... with K. tr.   [2] John v. 46–7.
[3] Mark i. 1–2.   [4] Cf. II, 4, above.   [5] Cf. I, 4, above.
[6] Matt. xxi. 43.   [7] Phil. iii. 20.

6. Supposing also that *Jesus kept all the Jewish customs, and even took part in their sacrifices*; why does this lend support to the view that *we ought not to believe in him as Son of God?* Jesus is Son of the God who gave the law and the prophets; and we of the church do not leave this out.[1] But, while we have avoided the mythologies of the Jews, yet we are made wise and are educated by mystical contemplation of the law and the prophets. The prophets also do not limit the meaning of their sayings to the obvious history and to the text and letter of the law. For in one place, when about to recount supposed history, they say: 'I will open my mouth in parables, I will utter dark sayings of old.'[2] And in another place, when praying about the law because it is obscure and in need of God to make it intelligible, they say in prayer: 'Open my eyes, and I will understand thy wonders out of thy law.'[3]

7. I challenge anyone to show where there can be found even a suggestion of a saying uttered by Jesus from *arrogance*. How was he arrogant when he says: 'Learn of me, for I am meek and lowly of heart, and you shall find rest for your souls'?[4] Or how was he arrogant who, during supper, took off his clothes among his disciples and, girding himself with a towel, poured water into a basin and washed the feet of each one; and he rebuked the one who was unwilling to offer his feet to be washed, saying: 'If I do not wash you, you have no part with me'?[5] Or how was he arrogant who said: 'And I have lived in the midst of you not as the man who sits at meat, but as the man who serves'?[6] I challenge anyone to prove what *lies* he told; and let him give an account of great and small lies, that he may prove that *Jesus told great lies.* Celsus can also be refuted in another way. Just as one lie is not more untrue than any other lie, and is not a lie in any greater degree, so a truth is not more true than any other truth or in a greater degree.[7] And let Celsus' Jew in particular tell us what were the *profane* actions of Jesus. Was it profane to abandon physical circumcision, and a literal sabbath and literal feasts, literal new moons,[8] and clean and unclean things, and rather to turn the mind to the true and spiritual law, worthy of God? In this respect the ambassador for Christ[9] knows how to become a Jew to the Jews that he may gain Jews, and to those under the law as one under the law, that he may gain those under the law.[10]

8. He says that *many others of the same type as Jesus have appeared to people who are willing to be deceived.* Let Celsus' Jew show us not *many*, nor

---

[1] For anti-Marcionite polemic, cf. VII, 25 below.   [2] Ps. lxxvii. 2.
[3] Ps. cxviii. 18.   [4] Matt. xi. 29.   [5] John xiii. 1 ff.   [6] Luke xxii. 27.
[7] This is Stoic doctrine, that there is an absolute distinction, without any relative degrees, between virtue and vice, truth and error. Cf. my remarks in *J.T.S.* XLVIII (1947), p. 39.
[8] Col. ii. 16.   [9] II Cor. v. 20.   [10] I Cor. ix. 20.

even a few, but just one man of the same type as Jesus, who by the power within him introduced a system and doctrines which benefited the life of mankind and converted men from the flood of sins. He remarks that *this charge is brought against the Jews by believers in Christ, that they have not believed in Jesus as God.* On this matter also we made our reply above,[1] showing both in what way we regard him as God, and also in what sense we speak of him as man. *But how,* says he, *would we despise him when he came, when we declare plainly to all men that the one who will punish the unrighteous will come from God?* This is very foolish, and I do not think it is reasonable to reply to it. It is as if someone were to say: How should we who have taught self-control have done anything licentious? Or how could we who maintain righteousness have been unrighteous? For just as that kind of thing is to be found among men, so was it according to human nature that the people who affirmed that they believed the prophets which speak of the coming of Christ, disbelieved him when he did come according to the prophecies.

If we may add another reason as well, we will say that the prophets foretold even this very thing. At any rate, Isaiah clearly says: 'By hearing you shall hear, and shall not understand; and seeing you shall see and shall not perceive. For this people's heart is waxed gross',[2] etc. And let anyone tell us why it was prophesied to the Jews that, although they heard and saw, they would not understand what was said, nor would see in the right way what was to be seen. Yet indeed, it is obvious that although they saw Jesus, they did not know who he was, and although they heard him they did not comprehend the divinity within him from his sayings, so that God's care of the Jews was transferred to those Gentiles who believe in him.[3] Accordingly, it may be observed that after Jesus' advent the Jews have been entirely forsaken and possess nothing of those things which from antiquity they have regarded as sacred, and have not even any vestige of divine power among them. They no longer have any prophets or wonders, though traces of these are to be found to a considerable extent among Christians. Indeed, some works are even greater;[4] and if our word may be trusted, we also have seen them. Celsus' Jew says: *Why should we have despised the one whom we proclaimed beforehand? Or was it that we might be punished more than others?* The answer to this may be that on account of their disbelief in Jesus and all their other insults to him the Jews not only will suffer at the judgment which is believed to be coming, but also have already suffered *more than others.* What nation but the Jews alone has been banished from its own capital city and the native

---

[1] Cf. 1, 67, 69, above.   [2] Isa. vi. 9–10.
[3] Matt. xxi. 43.   [4] John xiv. 12.

place of its ancestral worship? They suffered this because they were very ignoble people; and although they committed many sins they did not suffer for them any comparable calamities to those caused by what they had dared to do against our Jesus.

9. After this the Jew says: *How could we regard him as God when in other matters, as people perceived, he did not manifest anything which he professed to do, and when we had convicted him, condemned him and decided that he should be punished, was caught hiding himself and escaping most disgracefully, and indeed was betrayed by those whom he called disciples? And yet,* says the Jew, *if he was God he could not run away nor be led away under arrest, and least of all could he, who was regarded as Saviour, and Son of the greatest God, and an angel, be deserted and betrayed by his associates who had privately shared everything with him and had been under him as their teacher.* To this we will reply that not even we suppose that the body of Jesus, which could then be seen and perceived by the senses, was God. And why do I say the body? For not even his soul was God; for he said of it: 'My soul is exceeding sorrowful even unto death.'[1] However, according to the doctrine of the Jews it is believed to be God who says: 'I am the Lord, the God of all flesh.'[2] And, 'Before me there was no other God, and after me there will be none.'[3] He was using the soul and body of the prophet as an instrument. According to the Greeks, it is believed to be a god who is speaking and being heard through the Pythian priestess, who says

> But I know the number of the sand and the measure of the sea,
> And I understand the dumb and I hear him that speaketh not.[4]

Similarly in our opinion it was the divine Logos and Son of the God of the universe that spoke in Jesus, saying: 'I am the way, the truth, and the life', and 'I am the door', and 'I am the living bread that came down from heaven',[5] and any other such saying.

Therefore, we bring the charge against the Jews that they have not believed in Jesus as God, because he had been everywhere witnessed by the prophets as being a great power and a God like the God and Father of the universe. We say that it was to him that the Father gave the command in the Mosaic story of creation, when He said, 'Let there be light', and 'Let there be a firmament', and all the other things which God commanded to come into being. To him also He said, 'Let us make man according to our image and likeness.'[6] And when the Logos was commanded, he made everything that the Father enjoined him. We say this, not as our own

---

[1] Matt. xxvi. 38.   [2] Jer. xxxix. 27.   [3] Isa. xliii. 10.
[4] Herodotus, I, 47.   [5] John xiv. 6; x. 7; vi. 51.   [6] Gen. i. 3, 6, 26.

original contribution, but because we believe the prophecies current among the Jews, in which it is said of God and creation as follows, in these very words: 'He spake and they were made, He commanded and they were created.'¹ If God commanded, and the creation was made, who, in harmony with the spirit of the prophecy, could be the one who was capable of fulfilling a command of such magnitude from the Father, except, if I may so say, he who was the living Logos and truth? It is clear from many points that even the Gospels realize that he, who said in Jesus, 'I am the way, the truth, and the life', was not circumscribed, as though the Logos did not exist anywhere outside the soul and body of Jesus.² We will set out a few of these as follows. John the Baptist, prophesying that the Son of God would presently stand among them, not existing in a particular body and soul only but also extending to every place, said of him, 'There stands one in the midst of you whom you know not, coming after me.'³ If, therefore, he thought that the Son of God was only in the place where Jesus' body was visible, how could he have said, 'There stands one in the midst of you whom you know not'? Jesus himself also raises the thoughts of those learning from him to greater conceptions of the Son of God when he says: 'Where two or three are gathered together in my name, there am I in the midst.'⁴ Such is also the meaning of his promise to his disciples when he said: 'And lo, I am with you always until the end of the world.'⁵

When we say this, we do not separate the Son of God from Jesus. For after the incarnation the soul and body of Jesus became very closely united with the Logos of God. According to Paul's teaching 'he who is joined to the Lord is one spirit',⁶ and every one who has understood what it means to be joined to the Lord and has actually been joined to him is one spirit with the Lord. If so, then how much more is it true that in a superior and more divine way that which was at one time a composite being in relation to the Logos of God is one with Him? Jesus, in fact, showed himself among the Jews to be 'the power of God'⁷ by the miracles that he did, although they have been suspected of sorcery by Celsus, while the Jews at the time, who from some unknown source had learnt about Beelzebul, suspected that he expelled daemons by Beelzebul, the prince of daemons.⁸ These quite absurd assertions our Saviour refuted with the argument that the kingdom of evil had not yet come to an end. This will be clear to any who read the gospel intelligently. It is not the right time to explain it now.

¹ Ps. xxxii. 9; cxlviii. 5.
² For this difficulty of the particularity of the Incarnation, cf. IV, 5, 12; V, 12.
³ John i. 26–7. This is Origen's standing exegesis of this text.
⁴ Matt. xviii. 20.   ⁵ Matt. xxviii. 20.   ⁶ I Cor. vi. 17.
⁷ Cf. I Cor. i. 18, 24.   ⁸ Matt. xii. 24.

10. I challenge Celsus to show and prove also what Jesus promised but did not perform. He will not be able to do so, especially since he thinks that he can produce his charges against Jesus or against us out of stories which he has misunderstood or even from his reading of the gospels, or from Jewish tales. Moreover, since the Jew says again that *we convicted him and condemned him and decided that he should be punished*, let any show us how they who were trying to produce false witness against him convicted him, unless perhaps the great charge against Jesus was that which the accusers brought—'this man said, I am able to destroy the temple of God and in three days to raise it up again'.[1] But he was speaking of 'the temple of his body'.[2] They did not know how to interpret the meaning of his words, and thought that his saying concerned the stone temple, which was held in honour by the Jews more than the one which they ought to have held in honour, the true temple of God, the Logos, the wisdom, and the truth. And let anyone tell us how Jesus *hid most disgracefully and fled*. Let anyone point out anything deserving of reproach.

Furthermore, as he also says that *he was caught*, I would reply that, if to be caught means that it was against his will, then Jesus was not caught; for at the right time, he did not prevent himself from falling into the hands of men, as being the 'lamb of God', that he might 'bear away the sin of the world'.[3] 'Knowing therefore all that was coming upon him he went out and said to them, Whom do you seek? And they answered, Jesus of Nazareth. And he said to them, I am he. And Judas also who betrayed him was standing with them. When therefore he said unto them, I am he, they went backward and fell to the ground. Again therefore he asked them, Whom do you seek? And they said again, Jesus of Nazareth. Jesus answered them, I told you that I am he; if therefore you seek me, let these go their way.'[4] Moreover, to the man who wanted to come to his aid, and struck the servant of the high-priest and cut off his ear, he said: 'Put up your sword into its place; for all they that take the sword shall perish with the sword. Or do you think that I cannot now beseech my Father, and he will send me here more than twelve legions of angels? How then should the scriptures be fulfilled, that thus it must be?'[5] If anyone thinks that this is invented by the writers of the gospels, is it not more likely that the statements of people who speak out of hostility and hatred to Jesus and to the Christians are inventions? Whereas, would not those be true which are made by men who prove the sincerity of their attitude to Jesus by enduring anything whatever on account of his words? How could Jesus' disciples have received such great patience and determination to the point

[1] Matt. xxvi. 61.   [2] John ii. 20.   [3] John i. 29.
[4] John xviii. 4–8.   [5] Matt. xxvi. 52–4.

of death if they had been prepared to invent fictitious stories about their master? To people with an open mind it is quite clear that they were convinced of the truth of what they recorded from the fact that they endured such persecutions for the sake of him whom they believed to be Son of God.

II. Then, that he was *betrayed by those whom he called disciples* Celsus' Jew learnt from the gospels, although he called the one man Judas *many disciples* to make the charge seem more effective. But he did not investigate thoroughly all that the scripture says of Judas. He had fallen into conflicting and contradictory judgments[1] about his master. He was neither whole-heartedly against him, nor did he whole-heartedly preserve the respect of a pupil to his teacher. 'For he that betrayed him gave a sign' to the crowd which came to arrest Jesus, saying, 'whomsoever I kiss, it is he; take him'.[2] He preserved some reverence for him; for had he not kept that he would have betrayed him boldly without a pretence of a kiss. Concerning Judas' motive this will[3] persuade every one that besides the covetous and wicked motive that led him to betray Jesus, he had an element side by side with it in his soul, which had a vestige of some remnant of decency, so to speak, implanted in him by the words of Jesus.[4] For it is written that 'when Judas who betrayed him saw that he was condemned, he repented and brought back the thirty pieces of silver to the chief priests and elders, saying, I have sinned in that I have betrayed innocent blood. But they said, What is that to us? See thou to it. And he cast down the silver pieces into the temple and departed, and he went away and hanged himself.'[5] Although Judas was covetous of money and used to steal the money that was thrown into the bag for the poor, as he repented and brought back the thirty pieces of silver to the chief priests and elders, it is clear that the teachings of Jesus had been able to put into him some capacity for repentance, and were not utterly despised or abominated by the traitor. Furthermore, the confession 'I have betrayed innocent blood' was the utterance of a man admitting that he had sinned. See how he was overcome by such agonising remorse when he repented of his sins that he could no longer bear even to live, but after casting the pieces of silver into the temple departed, and went away and hanged himself. By condemning

---

[1] Cf. I, 61, of Herod.   [2] Matt. xxvi. 48.

[3] Omit οὐ, and read as statement, not question, with O. Stählin, *Philol. Wochenschrift* (1944), 124.

[4] For Origen's denial of the total depravity of Judas, see *Comm. ser. in Matt.* 117 (ed. Lommatzsch, v, 23); *Comm. in Joann.* XXXII, 19 (12); *Comm. in ep. ad Rom.* IX, 41. It seems that Judas was used by the Gnostics in their polemic to prove that some are totally depraved by nature. Cf. also IV, 25, 83, below; and *de Princ.* IV, 4, 9–10; *ibid.* I, 8, 3 'ne diabolus quidem ipse incapax fuit boni...'; Seneca, *de Benef.* VII, 19, 5–6.

[5] Matt. xxvii. 3–5.

himself he showed what effect the teaching of Jesus could have even on
a sinner like Judas, the thief and traitor, who could not utterly despise
what he had learnt from Jesus. Or will Celsus and his friends say that the
statements are fictitious which indicate that Judas' apostasy was not
complete, even after what he had dared to do against his master, and that
the only truth in what they say is that one of the disciples betrayed him?
And will they exaggerate the record by saying that he also betrayed him
whole-heartedly? But it is not convincing to treat every statement in
a hostile spirit, and to believe some things but to disbelieve others in the
same documents.

If we may produce an argument about Judas which will put him out
of countenance, we will say that in the book of Psalms the whole of the
108th contains the prophecy about Judas, which begins thus: 'O God,
hold not thy peace at my praise, because the mouth of a sinner and the
mouth of a deceiver have been opened against me.' It is prophesied here
both that Judas separated himself from the number of the apostles by his
sin, and that another was chosen in his place; this is made clear by the
words 'And his office let another take'.[1] Supposing, however, that he had
been betrayed by one of his disciples who was in a worse state of mind than
Judas, who as it were cast away all the doctrines which he had heard from
Jesus, why would this strengthen an accusation against Jesus or Christianity? And how does this prove the gospel to be false? We made our
reply to Celsus' next objections in the arguments above when we showed
that Jesus was not *caught* in flight, but willingly gave himself up for us all.
It follows from this that if he was *arrested*, he was arrested with his own
consent, teaching us to accept such ill-treatment for the sake of religion
without objecting.

12. This objection also seems to me to be puerile: *No good general who
led many thousands was ever betrayed, nor was any wicked robber-chieftain,
who was captain of very bad men, while he appeared to bring some advantage
to his associates. But he, who was betrayed by those under his authority,
neither ruled like a good general; nor, when he had deceived his disciples, did
he even inspire in the men so deceived that goodwill, if I may call it that,
which robbers feel towards their chieftain.* One might find several stories
about generals who were betrayed by intimate friends and of robber-
chieftains captured because their men did not keep the agreements with
them. But supposing that no general or robber-chieftain has been betrayed,
why is any support given to the charge against Jesus by the fact that one
of his disciples became his betrayer? Since Celsus shows off philosophy,
we might ask him if perhaps it was an objection to Plato that after listening

[1] Ps. cviii. 1–2, 8; cf. Acts i. 15–26.

to his teaching for twenty years Aristotle deserted him,[1] and criticized his
doctrine of the immortality of the soul, and called the Platonic Ideas
'twitterings'?[2] We might raise yet another question and say this: Was
Plato no longer competent in dialectic or able to substantiate his views,
since Aristotle deserted him, and is this a reason why the doctrines of
Plato should be false? Or is it possible that if Plato was right, as Platonic
philosophers would say, Aristotle became wicked and ungrateful to his
teacher? Chrysippus also in many passages in his writings appears to
attack Cleanthes, putting forward new ideas contrary to the doctrines of
the latter, even though he became his teacher when he was still a young
man and was beginning to study philosophy. And yet Aristotle is said to
have been Plato's disciple for twenty years, and Chrysippus also to have
studied with Cleanthes for quite a long time; whereas Judas did not even
spend three years with Jesus.[3] From the biographies of the philosophers
one might find many examples of this sort similar to the desertion of
Judas which Celsus makes a ground for accusation against Jesus. The
Pythagoreans built cenotaphs to those who, after turning to philosophy,
slid back into an uncultured life.[4] But this is no reason for supposing
that Pythagoras and his disciples were incompetent in argument and
reasoning.

13. After this Celsus' Jew says: *Although I could say much about what
happened to Jesus which is true, and nothing like the account which has been
written by the disciples of Jesus, I leave that out intentionally.* What are these
true stories which are not like those recorded in the gospels, which Celsus'
Jew leaves out? Or is he pretending by a veneer of rhetorical cleverness
that he could say something which could impress the hearer as true and
constitute an obvious charge against Jesus and his teaching, whereas in
fact he could produce nothing from any source but the gospels?

He accuses the disciples of having *invented the statement that Jesus
foreknew and foretold all that happened to him.* But we will establish that this
also is true, even if Celsus will not admit it, from many other prophetic
utterances of the Saviour in which he foretold what happened to Christians
even of later generations. Who indeed would not wonder at the prediction
'You will be brought before governors and kings for my sake for a

[1] Cf. Diog. Laert. v, 9; Dion. Halic. *Ep. ad Ammaeum* i, 5 (728).
[2] See I, 13 and note.
[3] For the length of Jesus' ministry, cf. *Comm. ser. in Matt.* 40.
[4] Cf. III, 51, below. This seems to allude to the story of the expulsion from the Pythagorean society of Hipparchus because he declared in plain language the doctrines of the
school. The story is found in the forged letter of Lysis to Hipparchus given by Iamblichus,
V. Pythag. 75, and quoted by Diog. Laert. VIII, 42 and Clem. Al. *Strom.* v, 57, 2–3. Cf. also
Lycurgus, *in Leocratem* 117; and for discussion of the letter of Lysis, A. Delatte in *Revue de
Philologie*, XXXV (1911), pp. 255–75.

testimony to them and to the Gentiles',[1] and at any other prophecy that his disciples would be persecuted? What other doctrine of those that have been held by men has caused its adherents to be punished? If there were any other instance, one of Jesus' critics might say that because he saw that impious or false doctrines would be attacked, he thought that it would bring him honour if he made an apparent prediction about this. But if any ought to be led before governors and kings for their doctrines, who deserve to be so treated more than Epicureans who entirely deny providence and also the Peripatetics who say that prayers and sacrifices to God have no effect?[2]

But someone may say that Samaritans are also persecuted for their religion. Our answer to him would be as follows. They are put to death on account of circumcision as Sicarii,[3] on the ground that they are mutilating themselves contrary to the established laws and are doing what is allowed to Jews alone. A judge is never to be heard asking whether a Sicarius who strives to live in accordance with the principles of his supposed religion will be let off if he changes his mind, while if he persists he will be led away to death.[4] The mere evidence of the circumcision is enough to condemn to death a man who has been circumcised. But in accordance with the words of their Saviour when he said, 'You shall be brought before governors and kings for my sake', Christians alone are allowed by the judges even at their last gasp to renounce Christianity and to sacrifice according to the common customs, and after taking their oath to dwell at home and live without danger.

Consider whether there is not great authority in his saying: 'Whosoever will confess me before men, him will I confess before my Father who is in heaven; and whosoever will deny me before men',[5] etc. Come with me, and imagine Jesus as he says this; and notice that what he prophesies has not yet taken place. Perhaps you would disbelieve him and say that he talks nonsense here (for what he says will not come to pass); or perhaps

---

[1] Matt. x. 18.   [2] Cf. de Oratione, v, 1.

[3] Read ὡς Σικάριοι with E. Schürer, Geschichte des jüdischen Volkes im Zeitalter Jesu Christi, ed. 4, I (1901), p. 678 n. 83. According to the Lex Cornelia de sicariis et veneficis, castration was forbidden. Although under Hadrian after the Jewish revolt circumcision, which was equated with it, was prohibited, this was withdrawn under Antoninus Pius who decreed that it should be allowed, though only to Jews. Cf. Digest, XLVIII, 8, 8, 11 (from Modestinus) 'Circumcidere Iudaeis filios suos tantum rescripto divi Pii permittitur: in non eiusdem religionis qui hoc fecerit, castrantis poena irrogatur.' There is no allusion here to the Sicarii or Zealots of the Jewish revolt. Origen means that the Samaritans are not punished for their religion, but for their circumcision under the Lex Cornelia de sicariis. See further J. Juster, Les Juifs dans l'Empire romain, I (Paris, 1914), pp. 263–71; M. Simon, Verus Israel, pp. 131 f. This explains Origen's remark in Comm. in Matt. XVII, 29 that the Samaritans 'strive to the point of death for the law of Moses and circumcision'.

[4] For persecution of the Samaritans for circumcision, cf. Comm. in Matt. XVII, 30.

[5] Matt. x. 32 f.

you would doubt whether to give assent to his words, and say: If these predictions are fulfilled and the teaching of Jesus' words is proved correct by the fact that governors and kings attempt to kill those who confess Jesus, then we may believe that he said these things because he had received great authority from God with a view to implanting this doctrine among mankind and was convinced that he would be successful. Who would not be amazed if he imagines him teaching at that time and saying: 'This gospel shall be preached in all the world for a testimony to them and to the Gentiles',[1] and if he considers that, just as he said, the gospel of Jesus Christ has been preached in all creation under heaven,[2] 'to Greeks and barbarians, to wise and foolish'?[3] For the word that is spoken with power has overcome men of all sorts; and it is impossible to see any race of men which has avoided accepting the teaching of Jesus.[4]

As for Celsus' Jew who disbelieves that Jesus *foreknew all that happened to him*, let him consider that while Jerusalem was still standing and all the Jewish worship was going on in it, Jesus foretold what was to happen to it through the Romans. For surely they will not say that Jesus' own pupils and hearers handed down the teaching of the gospels without writing it down, and that they left their disciples without their reminiscences of Jesus in writing. In them it is written: 'And when you see Jerusalem compassed with armies, then know that her desolation is at hand.'[5] At that time there were no armies at all round Jerusalem, compassing it about and surrounding and besieging it. The siege began when Nero was still emperor, and continued until the rule of Vespasian. His son, Titus, captured Jerusalem, so Josephus says, on account of James the Just, the brother of Jesus the so-called Christ,[6] though in reality it was on account of Jesus the Christ of God.

14. Celsus of course, by accepting it or allowing it as a possibility that he foreknew what would happen to him, could seem to disparage these predictions, as he has done with the miracles, by saying that they were done by sorcery. He could have said that many have known what was to happen to them from oracles by using birds of omen, or auguries, or sacrifices, or astrology. But he did not want to agree to the latter view, as this would be to go too far, and although he has accepted the fact that he

---

[1] Matt. xxiv. 14.   [2] Read ἐν ⟨πάσῃ κτίσει⟩ τῇ ὑπὸ τὸν οὐρανόν, as Col. i. 23.
[3] Rom. i. 14.
[4] Contrast *Comm. ser. in Matt.* 39 'non ergo fertur praedicatum esse evangelium apud omnes Aethiopas, maxime apud eos qui sunt ultra flumen, sed nec apud Seras nec apud Ariacin nec...audierant Christianitatis sermonem. quid autem dicamus de Britannis aut Germanis qui sunt circa Oceanum, vel apud barbaros Dacos et Sarmatas et Scythas, quorum plurimi nondum audierunt evangelii verbum, audituri sunt autem in ipsa saeculi consummatione?'
[5] Luke xxi. 20.   [6] Cf. I, 47, above.

performed the miracles somehow he seems to have attacked them on the charge of sorcery. However, Phlegon in the thirteenth or fourteenth book, I think, of his Chronicle even grants to Christ foreknowledge of certain future events, although he was muddled and said that some things which really happened to Peter happened to Jesus; and he testified that it turned out in accordance with what Jesus had said. But even he by his remarks about foreknowledge unintentionally, as it were, affirmed that the word of the authors of our doctrines was not lacking in divine power.[1]

15. Celsus says: *As the disciples of Jesus were unable to conceal the self-evident fact, they conceived this idea of saying that he foreknew everything.* He did not pay attention, nor did he want to pay attention, to the honest intentions of the writers, who affirmed both that Jesus predicted to his disciples, 'All of you shall be offended this night',[2] and that this proved to be correct when they were offended, and that he also prophesied to Peter, 'Before the cock crow thou shalt deny me thrice',[3] and that Peter denied three times. If they were not honest, but, as Celsus thinks, were composing fictitious stories, they would not have recorded Peter's denial or that Jesus' disciples were offended. But even if these events did take place, who could have made it a charge against Christianity that they did turn out in this way? In fact, these matters probably ought not to have been mentioned by men who wanted to teach the readers of the gospels to despise death in order to confess Christianity. But seeing that the word would conquer men by its power, they even put down these stories, which for some unknown reason will not harm people who read them, and will not give them any excuse for denial.

16. He makes the very silly statement that *the disciples recorded such things about Jesus to excuse the events of his life.* He says: *It is as if someone, while saying that a certain man is righteous, shows him to be doing wrong, and, while saying that he is holy, shows him to be a murderer, and, while saying that he is immortal, shows him to be dead, and then to all this adds that he had predicted it.* His instance is manifestly irrelevant, since it is in no way unreasonable that the man who was to be the moral ideal living among men as an example of how they ought to live[4] should have undertaken to show how they ought to die for the sake of religion, apart from the consideration that his death for men was a benefit to the whole world, as we showed in the previous book.[5] Then he thinks that the whole confession

---

[1] Phlegon was a freedman of Hadrian. His Chronicle was regarded as a very dull work by Photius (*Bibl.* 97). For extant fragments see Jacoby, *Fr. gr. Hist.* IIB (1929), p. 1159. Cf. also II, 33 and 59, below; *Comm. ser. in Matt.* 40 and 134; Eusebius, *Chronic.* p. 174, ed. Helm. See, further, E. Frank in P.-W. xx (1941), 261–4.

[2] Matt. xxvi. 31.   [3] Matt. xxvi. 34.
[4] Perhaps a reminiscence of Plato, *Gorgias*, 507D.   [5] Cf. I, 54–5, above.

of the sufferings of Jesus strengthens rather than weakens his criticism. He did not see how profound was Paul's philosophy about this, and how much was spoken by the prophets. He failed to notice also that some heretics have said that Jesus suffered these agonies in appearance only and not in reality. If he had known he would not have said this: *For you do not even say that he seemed to the impious men to endure these sufferings although he did not really do so; but on the contrary, you admit that he did suffer.* The reason why we do not admit that he suffered only in appearance is that his resurrection also may not be false but a reality. For if he really died, then if he did rise again, his resurrection was real; but if he only appeared to die, then he did not really rise again.

As the unbelievers mock at the resurrection of Jesus Christ, we will quote Plato who says that Er the son of Armenius rose again from the funeral pyre after twelve days and gave an account of his adventures in Hades.[1] And, as I am addressing unbelievers, it will not be at all irrelevant to mention here Heraclides' story about the lifeless woman.[2] Several people are recorded to have returned even from their tombs, not only on the same day, but even on the day after. Why then is it amazing if he who performed many miracles of a superhuman nature and so manifest in character that those who cannot disregard the fact that they happened malign them by putting them on a level with sorceries, also had something extraordinary about his death so that, if he so wished, his soul might leave his body and, after performing certain services[3] without it, might return to it again when it wished? Jesus is recorded by John to have uttered a saying to this effect in the words: 'No man takes my soul from me, but I lay it down of myself. I have power to lay it down and I have power to take it again.'[4] Perhaps it was on this account that he soon departed from the body that he might keep it intact and that his legs might not be broken like those of the robbers crucified with him. 'For the soldiers broke the legs of the first and of the other man who was crucified with him; but when they came to Jesus and saw that he was dead, they did not break his legs.'[5]

Accordingly we make this reply to the following remarks: *What trustworthy evidence is there that he made these predictions?* and, *How can a dead man be immortal?* Anyone who is interested may realize that it is not the dead man that is immortal, but he who rose from the dead. Not

[1] *Republic*, 614–21.
[2] Heraclides of Pontus (fourth century B.C.) related that Empedocles preserved a woman without breathing for thirty days. Cf. Diog. Laert. VIII, 60–1, 67; Pliny, *N.H.* VII, 175, where the period is said to have been seven days; Galen, *de Locis Affectis* VI, 5 (Kühn, VIII, 414 f.); Suidas, *s.v.* ἄπνους. Cf. Dodds, *The Greeks and the Irrational*, p. 145.
[3] A reference to the descent to Hades.
[4] John x. 18. Cf. III, 32, below; *Comm. in Joann.* XIX, 16 (4).
[5] John xix. 32–3.

only was the dead man not immortal, but even Jesus, who was a composite being, was not immortal before his death since he was going to die. No one who is going to die at some future date is immortal, but he becomes immortal when he will no longer die. 'And Christ being raised from the dead dies no more; death has no more dominion over him',[1] even if people who have not the capacity to understand what this means may not be willing to accept it.

17. This too is very stupid: *Who, whether god or daemon, or sensible man, if he foreknew that such things would happen to him, would not avoid them if at least he could do so, instead of meeting with just the events which he had foreseen?* At any rate, Socrates knew that if he drank the hemlock he would die, and, if he had yielded to Crito's persuasion, he could have escaped the guard and avoided suffering any of this; but he chose the course that seemed to him reasonable, thinking that it was better for him to die in accordance with the principles of his philosophy than to live in contradiction to them.[2] Furthermore, Leonidas the Spartan general, though he knew that presently he was to die with the men at Thermopylae, did not concern himself to live in disgrace, but said to the men with him, 'Let us eat breakfast, for we shall dine in Hades'.[3] People interested in collecting such stories will find several instances like this. Why also is it amazing if, although Jesus knew the things which would happen, he did not avoid them, but met with just the events which he had foreseen? For when his disciple Paul also heard what would happen to him when he went up to Jerusalem, he went to face the dangers and rebuked those who were in tears round him and were hindering him from going up to Jerusalem.[4] And many of our contemporaries who have known that if they confessed Christianity they would die, while if they denied they would be set free and regain their possessions, have despised life and willingly chosen death for the sake of religion.

18. After this Celsus' Jew makes yet another silly remark: *If he foretold both the one who was to betray him and the one who was to deny him, why did they not fear him as God, so that the one did not betray him nor the other deny him?* In fact this most intelligent Celsus did not see here the contradiction; if, as God, he had foreknowledge and his foreknowledge could not have been wrong, it was impossible that the one whom he foreknew to be his future betrayer should not have done so, and that the one whom he had declared to be about to deny him should not have done so. If it had been possible for the one not to betray him and for the other not to

---

[1] Rom. vi. 9.   [2] Plato, *Crito*, 44–6.
[3] A well-known anecdote; cf. Cicero, *Tusc. Disp.* I, 42, 101; Diodorus Sic. II, 9, 4; Seneca, *Ep.* LXXXII, 21; Plutarch, *Mor.* 225 D, 306 D.
[4] Acts xxi. 12–14.

deny him, because they would have learnt their lesson beforehand and so
would not have betrayed and denied him, then he would no longer have
been correct in saying that the one would betray him and the other deny
him. For if he foreknew the man who would betray him, then he saw the
wickedness which caused him to do it, which was not at all destroyed by
his foreknowledge. And again, if he perceived who would deny him, he
foretold that he would do so because he saw the weakness which caused
his denial; but the weakness would not have been destroyed all at once
merely by his foreknowledge. How then can he say this: *But they
betrayed and denied him without any respect for him?* For it has been shown[1]
in the case of the traitor that it is untrue that he betrayed him without any
respect for his master; and no less is this clear of the one who denied,
since after the denial 'he went out and wept bitterly'.[2]

19. This also is superficial: *Furthermore, if people conspire against a man
and he perceives it, then if he predicts it to the conspirators they turn back and
are on their guard.* For many people have conspired against men who have
perceived that there was a plot against them. He next as it were brings his
argument to a conclusion by saying: *These things certainly did not happen
because they were foretold, for that is impossible; but since they did happen,
the assertion that he predicted them is proved to be false. For it would be
utterly inconceivable that those who had already heard that Jesus knew their
intentions would still have betrayed and denied him.* But if the first part of
his argument has been overthrown, then the conclusion also falls that
since these events were foretold, they did not happen. We maintain that
they did happen, as it was possible, and that since they happened it is
shown to be true that he foretold them; for the truth about the future is
decided by actual events. Consequently it is false when Celsus says as
follows, that *the assertion that he predicted them is proved to be false.* And
this is a futile remark: *For it is quite inconceivable that those who had already
heard that Jesus knew their intentions would still have betrayed and denied him.*

20. Let us see what he says after this: *If he foretold these events as being
a god,* he says, *then what he foretold must assuredly have come to pass.*[3]
*A god, therefore, led his own disciples and prophets with whom he used to eat
and drink so far astray that they became impious and wicked. But a god
above all ought to have done good to all men, in particular to those who have
lived with him. A man who had shared meals with another would not further
plot against him. Would one who had eaten a banquet with a god have become
a conspirator against him? And what is more outrageous still, God himself*

---

[1] Cf. II, 11, above.   [2] Matt. xxvi. 75.
[3] Cf. Marcion's criticism of the Fall narrative of Genesis (in Jerome, *adv. Pelag.* III, 6;
Vallarsi, II, 787–8): 'If God foreknew the fall of Adam, He is responsible; if He did not
foreknow it, He is not God.'

conspired against those who ate with him, by making them traitors and impious men. As you want me to meet even those attempts at argument on Celsus' part which seem to me worthless, we will reply even to this as follows. Celsus thinks that if something has been predicted by some sort of foreknowledge, then it takes place because it was predicted. But we do not grant this. We say that the man who made the prediction was not the cause of the future event, because he foretold that it would happen; but we hold that the future event, which would have taken place even if it had not been prophesied, constitutes the cause of its prediction by the one with foreknowledge.[1] And all this is present in the foreknowledge of the prophet; if it is possible for a particular event to happen and possible for it not to happen, either of these alternatives may come to pass. We do not maintain that the one who has foreknowledge takes away the possibility of an event happening or not happening,[2] saying something of this sort: This will assuredly happen, and it is impossible for it to turn out otherwise. This holds good for all foreknowledge about matters controlled by free will, whether we are dealing with the divine scriptures or with Greek stories. And in fact what is called by logicians an idle argument, which is a sophism, would not even be regarded as fallacious by Celsus (so mean is his ability), although by the standards of sound logic it is a sophism.

To make this point clear, I will quote from the Scripture the prophecies about Judas or the foreknowledge of our Saviour that he would betray him; and from Greek stories I will quote the oracle to Laius, allowing for the moment that it is true, since its historicity does not affect the argument. The Saviour is represented as speaking about Judas in the 108th Psalm which begins like this: 'O God, hold not thy peace at my praise, because the mouth of a sinner and the mouth of the deceitful man have been opened against me.'[3] By carefully studying what is written in the Psalm you will discover that, as the Psalmist foreknew that Judas would betray the Saviour, so also he implies that he was responsible for the betrayal and deserved the curses uttered in the prophecy on account of his wickedness. For he says that he is to suffer these things 'because he remembered not to show mercy, but persecuted the poor and needy man'.[4] It follows that he could have remembered to show mercy, and might not have persecuted the man whom he did persecute; but, although he could have done so, he did not, but betrayed him so that he deserved the curses against him in the prophecy. Moreover, addressing Greeks we will use the utterance to Laius which goes as follows, whether these are the actual words of the

---

[1] Cf. *Comm. in Genes.* 3 (Lommatzsch, VIII, 21) = Eus. *P.E.* VI, 11, 287D = *Philocalia*, XXIII, 8.
[2] This is a Stoic argument, severely criticized by Alexander of Aphrodisias, *de Fato*, 10. Cf. *S.V.F.* II, 959 ff.   [3] Ps. cviii. 1–2.   [4] Ps. cviii. 16.

oracle, or words to the same effect composed by the tragedian. This is
what was said to him by the one who had foreknowledge of the future:

> Beget no children against the will of the gods,
> For if thou dost produce a child, thy offspring shall slay thee,
> And thy whole house shall pass through bloodshed.[1]

Here too, then, it is clearly shown that it was possible for Laius not to
beget children, for the oracle would not give him an impossible command;
yet it was also possible for him to have children; neither of these alternatives was necessarily determined. But the result of his failure to avoid
having children was that he suffered in consequence the disasters related
in the tragedy about Oedipus and Jocasta and their sons.

The so-called 'idle' argument,[2] which is a sophism, is as follows. It is
addressed, let us suppose, to a sick man, and by sophistical reasoning
dissuades him from having a physician to restore him to health. The
argument runs like this. If it is fated that you recover from the illness, you
will recover whether you call in a physician or not; moreover, if it is fated
that you will not recover from the illness, you will not recover, whether
you call in the physician or not; either it is fated that you will recover from
the illness, or it is fated that you will not do so; therefore it is futile to call
in a physician. With this argument, however, some such argument as this
may cleverly be compared. If it is fated that you beget a child, whether
you have sexual intercourse with a woman or whether you do not, you
will beget a child; but if it is fated that you will not beget a child, whether
you have intercourse with a woman or not, you will not beget a child;
either it is fated that you will beget a child, or that you will not do so;
therefore it is futile to have intercourse with a woman. For just as, in this
instance, it is not futile to have intercourse with a woman, since it is
inconceivable and impossible for a man to have children if he has no such
intercourse, so also if recovery from illness comes by medical treatment,
it is necessary to employ a physician, and it is wrong to say 'it is futile for
you to call in a physician'. We have set forth all these arguments on
account of the opinion put forward by the most intelligent Celsus, who
says: *He foretold these events as being a god, and what he foretold must
assuredly have come to pass.* If by *assuredly* he means 'necessarily', we will
not grant that to him; for it was also possible for it not to happen. But if
by *assuredly* he means simply that 'it will come to pass' (and nothing

[1] Euripides, *Phoenissae*, 18–20, a stock example since Chrysippus. For references, cf.
J.T.S. XLVIII (1947), p. 46 n. 2.
[2] For this argument see Cicero, *de Fato*, XII, 28 ff.; cf. Ps.-Plutarch, *de Fato* XI, 574E.
The argument was originally anti-Stoic; it could only be refuted if free will were admitted;
cf. Zeller, *Philos. d. Gr.* III, ed. 4, I, p. 171 n. 1. The Stoic reply lies behind Seneca, *N.Q.*
II, 38, 4.

prevents that from being true, even if it is possible for it not to happen), then my position is in no way affected.[1] For it does not follow from the fact that Jesus correctly predicted the actions of the traitor and of the one who denied him, that he was responsible for their impiety and wicked conduct. He saw his evil state of mind, since according to our scriptures 'he knew what was in man',[2] and perceived what he would venture to do as a result of his love of money and lack of the firm loyalty which he ought to have had towards his master; and so among many other things he said: 'He that dipped his hand with me in the dish, that man will betray me.'[3]

21. Notice also the shallowness and outright lying of Celsus when he says this sort of thing, declaring that *one who had shared meals with a man would not plot against him; and if he would not plot against a man,* a fortiori *one who had eaten a banquet with a god would not have become a conspirator against him.* Who does not know that many men who have shared the salt of hospitality have conspired against their associates? The history of Greeks and barbarians is full of such examples; in fact, the Parian poet, the inventor of the iambus,[4] reproaches Lycambes for breaking covenants sworn by the salt of hospitality, when he says to him:

> But thou hast forsaken a great oath
> By the salt of hospitality.

Further instances could be quoted by people who are interested in literary scholarship, who have devoted themselves wholly to it and have abandoned studies which are more necessary for practical conduct; they could show how many[5] men who have shared meals with certain people have conspired against them.

22. Then, as though gathering up his argument with watertight proofs and inferences, he says: *And what is still more outrageous, God himself conspired against those who ate with him by making them traitors and impious men.* He would not be able to show how Jesus either conspired or made his disciples traitors and impious men, except by some inference, as he might suppose it, which even an uneducated man could very easily refute.

23. After this he says that *if these things had been decreed for him and if he was punished in obedience to his Father, it is obvious that since he was a god and acted intentionally, what was done of deliberate purpose was neither painful nor grievous to him.* He did not see that he immediately contradicts his own statement. For if he granted that he was punished, since these things had been decreed for him, and that he gave himself up in obedience to his Father, it is clear that he really was punished, and that it was not

---

[1] Cf. *Philocalia*, XXIII, 8.　　　[2] John ii. 25.　　　[3] Matt. xxvi. 23.
[4] Archilochus, *frag.* 96 Bergk.
[5] Read ὅσοι with A³, K. tr. Cf. Dio Chrys. LXXIV, passim.

possible for him not to suffer pain from the torments inflicted upon him by
his executioners. For pain is an experience outside the control of the will.
If the sufferings inflicted were neither *painful* nor *grievous* to him because
he suffered *intentionally*, why did Celsus grant that he was punished? He
did not see that once he had assumed his body by birth he had assumed
that which in its nature is capable of feeling pain and the grievous agonies
which befall those who live in bodies, understanding the word 'grievous'
as not including what is under the control of the will. Accordingly, just
as he *intentionally* assumed a body whose nature was not at all different
from human flesh, so he assumed with the body also its pains and griefs.
He was not lord of these so that he felt no pain; this was in the power of the
men who were disposed to inflict the pains and griefs upon him. We have
previously answered this difficulty in what we said earlier,[1] that if he had
not been willing to fall into the hands of men he would not have come.
Yet he did come, since he wanted to do so, for the reason which we have
stated above,[2] that his death for men would benefit the whole world.

24. After this he wants to argue that the things that happened to Jesus
were *painful* and *grievous*, and that it was impossible for him to prevent
them being so, even if he had desired, saying: *Why then does he utter loud
laments and wailings, and pray that he may avoid the fear of death, saying
something like this, ' O Father, if this cup could pass by me'?* Here, too,
notice the wickedness of Celsus. For he did not accept the honesty of the
writers of the gospels who could have been silent on these matters which
Celsus regards as a ground for criticism; yet they did not remain silent for
several reasons which at a suitable time might be given by someone
explaining the gospel. But he attacks the words of the gospels by
exaggerating and quoting the text incorrectly. No statement is to be
found that Jesus *uttered wailings*. And he alters the original text ' Father,
if it be possible, let this cup pass from me';[3] and he does not quote the
saying which at once shows Jesus' piety towards his Father and his
greatness of soul; this is recorded after the previous saying, and reads as
follows: 'Nevertheless, not as I will but as thou wilt.' He pretends also
not to have read of the willing obedience of Jesus to the will of his Father
concerning the sufferings to which he was condemned, which is made
clear by the words: 'If this cannot pass from me except I drink it, thy will
be done.'[4] He behaves rather like those impious people who understand
the divine scriptures wickedly and 'speak unrighteousness in the height'.[5]
They seem to have heard the words 'I will kill' and often reproach us with
it, while they do not also remember 'I will make to live'.[6] The whole

---

[1] Cf. II, 10, above.   [2] Cf. I, 54–5, above.   [3] Matt. xxvi. 39.
[4] Matt. xxvi. 42.   [5] Ps. lxxii. 8.   [6] Deut. xxxii. 39.

saying shows that people who are living in open wickedness and whose actions are evil are put to death by God, and a better life is implanted in them, even that which God may give to those who have died to sin. So also they take the saying 'I will smite', but they do not go on to see 'and I will heal'.[1] It is rather like what is said[2] by a physician[3] who has cut open bodies and inflicted painful wounds in order to cut out of them the things which are harmful and hinder good health; he does not leave off with the pains and the incision, but by his cure he restores the body to the health that is intended for it. Furthermore, they have not heeded the whole of the utterance 'for he makes sore and binds up again', but only the words 'he makes sore'.[4] So also Celsus' Jew quotes the text 'O Father, would that this cup could pass from me', but he does not go on to the words which follow, which prove that Jesus was ready and courageous in face of his suffering. However, at the present we postpone the discussion of these problems which require a long explanation which would appropriately be given with the help of God's wisdom to those whom Paul called perfect, when he said: 'But we speak wisdom among those who are perfect.'[5] We only make brief mention of the points which are helpful for our present purpose.

25. We were saying in the previous arguments that some utterances of Jesus belong to the firstborn of all creation with him, such as 'I am the way, the truth, and the life',[6] and sayings of this character; while others belong to the supposedly human Jesus,[7] such as this: 'But now you seek to kill me, a man that has told you the truth which I heard from the Father.'[8] Now in this instance he is speaking in his humanity both of the weakness of the human flesh and the willingness of the spirit. He refers to the weakness in the words 'Father, if it be possible, let this cup pass from me', and to the willingness of the spirit in 'Nevertheless not as I will, but as thou wilt'. If we may also pay attention to the order of what is said, notice that the first utterance which is made, as one might say, in the weakness of the flesh occurs only once, whereas the second which is spoken in the willingness of the spirit occurs several times. For there is but one instance of the words 'Father, if it be possible, let this cup pass from me', whereas there are a number of occurrences of the latter, as 'Not as I will but as thou wilt',

---

[1] Deut. xxxii. 39.   [2] Read ⟨τῷ⟩ λεγομένῳ with K. tr.

[3] The figure is usual in Origen to explain threats and punishments, and in this connexion goes back to Plato, *Gorgias*, 480c. The polemic about Deut. xxxii. 39 is anti-Marcionite; cf. *Hom. in Luc.* 16; *Comm. in Matt.* xv, 11; *Hom. in Jerem.* 1, 16; and for Marcion, Tert. *adv. Marc.* IV, 1.

[4] Job v. 18.   [5] I Cor. ii. 6.   [6] John xiv. 6; cf. II, 9 above.

[7] The Greek phrase is common in Origen; for references, cf. *Harv. Theol. Rev.* XLI (1948), p. 100 n. 30.

[8] John viii. 40.

and 'My Father, if this cannot pass from me except I drink it, thy will be done'. It is also to be noted that he did not merely say, 'Let this cup pass from me'. The saying as a whole was spoken with piety and reverence: 'Father, if it be possible, let this cup pass from me.' I am aware that there is also an explanation of the passage to this effect: the Saviour saw what disasters would befall the people and Jerusalem to avenge the acts which the Jews had dared to commit against him, and it was simply because of his love to them, and because he did not want the people to suffer what they were to suffer, that he said: 'Father, if it be possible, let this cup pass from me.' It is as if he said: Since as a consequence of my drinking this cup of punishment a whole nation will be deserted by thee, I pray that, if it be possible, this cup may pass from me, that thy portion which has dared to attack me may not be utterly deserted by thee.[1] Furthermore, if as Celsus says nothing painful or grievous happened to Jesus at this time, how would posterity be able to follow Jesus as a pattern of the way to endure religious persecution, if he did not really suffer human agonies but only appeared to do so?

26. Moreover, Celsus' Jew charges the disciples of Jesus with having invented these stories, saying: *Although you lied you were not able to conceal plausibly your fictitious tales.* My reply to this would be that the way to conceal tales of this sort was easy—not to have recorded them at all. For if the gospels had not included them who could have reproached us because Jesus said such things during his incarnation? Celsus did not understand that it was impossible for the same men both to be deceived into thinking that Jesus was God and the prophesied Christ, and to have invented tales about him, when they obviously would have known that the tales were untrue. Either therefore they did not invent them, but really did hold these beliefs and recorded the narratives without any deception, or they lied in their writings and did not in fact hold these beliefs, and were not deceived into regarding him as God.

27. After this he says that *some believers, as though from a drinking bout, go so far as to oppose themselves and alter the original text of the gospel three or four or several times over, and they change its character to enable them to deny difficulties in face of criticism.*[2] I do not know of people who have altered the gospel apart from the Marcionites and Valentinians, and I think

---

[1] For this interpretation, cf. *Comm. ser. in Matt.* 92.

[2] Celsus' meaning is uncertain. He may mean the different gospels, *three or four* being a reference to the canonical four (it is just conceivable that the phrase shows knowledge of those who rejected St John), and *several* to the apocryphal gospels. It is not likely that Celsus has in mind the different manuscript readings. Origen, however, may well be right, in view of Celsus' knowledge of Marcion, in taking him to refer to Marcion's alteration of the text.

also the followers of Lucan.[1] But this statement is not a criticism of Christianity, but only of those who have dared lightly to falsify the gospels. And just as it is no criticism of philosophy that there are the sophists or the Epicureans or the Peripatetics, or any others who hold false doctrines, so those who alter the gospels and introduce heresies foreign to the meaning of Jesus' teaching do not give ground for any criticism of genuine Christianity.[2]

28. As after this Celsus' Jew also reproaches Christians for *quoting prophets who proclaimed beforehand the facts of Jesus' life,* we will say this in addition to what we have already said earlier on this subject.[3] If, as he says, he *has consideration for men,*[4] he ought to have quoted the prophecies and, while admitting their plausible characteristics, to have set forth such a refutation of our use of the prophecies as might seem fitting to him. For then he would not have seemed to jump to such an important conclusion after a few minor remarks. This is particularly true when he says that *the prophecies could be applied to thousands of others far more plausibly than to Jesus.* In fact, he ought to have carefully stated his reply to this strong argument of the Christians since it is a very powerful one, and to have explained from each prophecy how it could be applied to others more plausibly than to Jesus.[5] He did not even perceive that, even if an opponent of the Christians could say this with any plausibility at all, it might perhaps have had some force if it had come from those who do not accept the writings of the prophets. But in this instance Celsus has put into the mouth of a Jew what no Jew would have said. For a Jew would not agree that the prophecies could be applied to thousands far more plausibly than to Jesus; he would set out the explanation of each prophecy as it appears to him, and would try to state his reply to the interpretation of the Christians; and although he would not produce any convincing argument at all, yet he would try to do so.

29. We have already said above[6] that it was prophesied that Christ would have two advents to the human race. For this reason we have no need to reply to this remark attributed to the Jew: *The prophets say that the one who will come will be a great prince, lord of the whole earth and of all nations and armies.* But it is just like a Jew, I think, and consistent with their bitterness, when he reviles Jesus without giving even any plausible[7]

---

[1] Lucan was an independent teacher within the Marcionite church; cf. Hippolytus, *Ref.* VII, 11; VII, 37, 2; Tertullian, *de Carn. Res.* 2; Ps.-Tert. *adv. omn. Haer.* 6. See Harnack, *Marcion* (2nd ed. 1924), pp. 401* ff.

[2] For the argument, cf. III, 12; V, 61.   [3] I, 49–57, above.

[4] Celsus must have used some phrase about sparing his readers as an excuse for omitting instances.

[5] Cf. Celsus in I, 50, 57.   [6] I, 56.

[7] Read πιθανῆς with Bo., K. tr.

argument, saying: *But they did not proclaim a pestilent fellow like him.*
Indeed, neither the Jews nor Celsus nor anyone else could establish by
argument that he was a pestilent fellow who converted so many men from
the flood of evil to live according to nature practising self-control and the
other virtues.

30. Celsus also threw out this remark: *But no one gives a proof of a god
or son of a god by such signs and false stories, nor by such disreputable evidence.*
He ought to have quoted the false stories and refuted them, and to have
shown by argument the disreputable evidence, so that if a Christian
appeared to say anything convincing, he might attempt to combat it and
to overthrow the statement. Now that which he says ought to have
happened[1] to Jesus actually did happen, because Jesus was a great person;
but he did not want to see that this was so, as the self-evident nature of
the facts about Jesus proves. *For,* he says, *as the sun which illuminates
everything else first shows itself, so ought the Son of God to have done.* We
would maintain that he actually did this. For 'righteousness arose in his
days and abundance of peace'[2] began with his birth; God was preparing
the nations for his teaching, that they might be under one Roman emperor,
so that the unfriendly attitude of the nations to one another, caused by the
existence of a large number of kingdoms, might not make it more
difficult for Jesus' apostles to do what he commanded them when he said,
'Go and teach all nations'.[3] It is quite clear that Jesus was born during the
reign of Augustus, the one who reduced to uniformity, so to speak, the
many kingdoms on earth so that he had a single empire. It would have
hindered Jesus' teaching from being spread through the whole world if
there had been many kingdoms, not only for the reasons just stated, but
also because men everywhere would have been compelled to do military
service and to fight in defence of their own land. This used to happen
before the times of Augustus and even earlier still when a war was
necessary, such as that between the Peloponnesians and the Athenians,
and similarly in the case of the other nations which fought one another.
Accordingly, how could this teaching, which preaches peace and does
not even allow men to take vengeance on their enemies, have had any
success unless the international situation had everywhere been changed
and a milder spirit prevailed at the advent of Jesus?

31. After this he accuses Christians of *sophistry when they say that the
Son of God is the very Logos himself,* and actually thinks he can substantiate

---

[1] K. tr. reads εἶπε ⟨χρῆναι ἀπαντᾶν⟩ περί. The correction is perhaps unnecessary.

[2] Ps. lxxi. 7. For the connexion of the *pax Romana* and the gospel, see Melito *ap.* Eus.
H.E. IV, 26, 7; Hippolytus, *Comm. in Dan.* IV, 9. For discussion of these passages and of the
development in Eusebius, cf. E. Peterson, *Monotheismus*, pp. 66 ff.

[3] Matt. xxviii. 19.

the accusation by saying that *although we proclaim the Son of God to be Logos we do not bring forward as evidence a pure and holy Logos, but a man who was arrested most disgracefully and crucified.* On this point also I spoke briefly in the earlier arguments in answer to Celsus' criticisms, when I proved that the firstborn of all creation assumed a body and a human soul, and that God gave command about the vast things in the world and they were created, and that he who received the command was the divine Logos.[1] Since it is a Jew who says this in Celsus' book, we will quote, not inappropriately, 'He sent forth his word and healed them, and delivered them from their distresses',[2] a text which we have also mentioned above. But although I have met with many Jews who were alleged to be wise, I have not heard any who approved of the opinion that the Son of God is the Logos, as Celsus has said when he attributes this to the Jew, representing him as saying: *Now if the Logos in your view is Son of God, we too approve of that.*[3]

32. We have said earlier[4] that Jesus could not have been either a *boaster* or a *sorcerer*. It is therefore not necessary to recapitulate what we have said lest in answering the repetitions of Celsus we also should come to repeat ourselves. In criticizing the genealogy he does not mention at all the discrepancy between the genealogies which is a problem discussed even among Christians, and which some bring forward as a charge against them.[5] For Celsus, who is really the one who is a boaster since he professes to know all the beliefs of Christians, did not know how to raise difficulties in the Bible in an intelligent way. But he says *the men who compiled the genealogy boldly said that Jesus was descended from the first man and from the kings of the Jews.* He thinks he makes a fine point in saying that *the carpenter's wife would not have been ignorant of it had she had such a distinguished ancestry.* But how is this relevant to the argument? Suppose that she was not in ignorance of it. Why does that affect the point in question? Suppose that she was in ignorance. Why, just because she was ignorant of it, should it be untrue that she was descended from the first man, and that her descent went back to the rulers of the Jews? Or does Celsus think that the poorer people must have been descended entirely from poor parents, or kings from kings? I think it is pointless to spend labour on this argument, since it is obvious that in our time too some poorer than Mary

---

[1] II, 9, above.   [2] Ps. cvi. 20, quoted in I, 64.

[3] This passage shows that Celsus is aware of the Logos-theology of Hellenistic Judaism. For the Logos as Son of God cf. Philo, *de Agric.* 51; *de Conf. Ling.* 146. Origen is thinking of Palestinian Rabbis, as in I, 49, above.

[4] II, 7, above.

[5] Cf. Africanus *ap.* Eus. *H.E.* I, 7; Origen, *Hom. in Luc.* 28; Julian, *adv. Galilaeos*, p. 212, ed. Neumann (253 E).

have ancestors who were rich and famous, and that leaders of nations and emperors have had a most undistinguished origin.

33. *Moreover,* he says, *what fine action did Jesus do like a god? Did he despise men's opposition and laugh and mock at the disaster that befell him?* In reply to this question, if we were able to substantiate at all the *fine action* of Jesus and the miracle which happened at the time when the disasters befell him, what source could we use other than the gospels? They say that 'the earth was shaken and the rocks rent and the tombs opened',[1] and that 'the veil of the temple was rent from top to bottom', and that there was 'darkness' in the daytime because there was an eclipse of the sun.[2] However, if Celsus believes the gospels in places which, he thinks, will provide an opportunity of attacking Jesus[3] and the Christians, but disbelieves them when they prove the divinity in Jesus, we will say to him: My good man, either disbelieve the gospels entirely and do not think of using them as affording ground for accusation, or believe them all, and admire the incarnate Logos of God who wished to do good to the whole human race. The *fine action* of Jesus consists in this, that to this day people whom God wills are cured by his name. And concerning the eclipse in the time of Tiberius Caesar, during whose reign Jesus appears to have been crucified, and about the great earthquakes that happened at that time, Phlegon has also made a record in the thirteenth or fourteenth book, I think, of his Chronicles.[4]

34. Celsus' Jew, while mocking Jesus as he thinks, is described as having some knowledge of *the remark of Bacchus in Euripides:*

The god himself will set me free whenever I wish it.[5]

Jews are not at all well read in Greek literature. But supposing that some Jew had become so well read as this, why then was Jesus not able to set himself free because he did not do so when bound? Suppose that he believed the stories from my scriptures that Peter also was bound in prison, and when the angels loosed his chains he went out, and that Paul, though bound with Silas at Philippi in Macedonia, was set free by divine power when also the prison gates were opened.[6] But probably Celsus ridicules these stories, or has not even read them at all; for he would very likely say about it that certain sorcerers also loose chains and open doors by

---

[1] Mark xv. 38; Matt. xxvii. 51. [2] Luke xxiii. 44-5.

[3] Read ('Ιησοῦ) καὶ with Bo., K. tr.

[4] See note on II, 14 above. [5] Euripides, *Bacchae*, 498.

[6] Acts xii. 6-9; xvi. 24-6. See K. Lake's note in *The Beginnings of Christianity,* IV (1933), pp. 196 f. For magic rings and spells to loose chains and open doors, cf. Lucian, *Navig.* 42; Arnobius I, 43; and for quotations from magical papyri, J. Kroll, *Gott und Hölle* (1932), p. 483 n. 5. For the theme see O. Weinreich, *Gebet u. Wunder* (1929).

spells, so that he would put the stories told of sorcerers on a level with those in our books.

But the one who condemned him did not even suffer any such fate as that of Pentheus by going mad or being torn in pieces,[1] he says. He did not see that it was not so much Pilate who condemned him, since 'he knew that for envy the Jews had given him up',[2] as the Jewish people. This nation has been condemned by God and *torn in pieces*, and scattered over all the earth, a fate more terrible than the rending suffered by Pentheus. Why also did he intentionally omit the story of Pilate's wife, who was so moved by a dream she had seen that she sent to her husband and said: 'Have thou nothing to do with that righteous man; for I have suffered many things this day in a dream because of him'?[3]

And again, Celsus says nothing of the facts which point to the divinity of Jesus and reproaches him on the ground of what is written in the Gospel about Jesus, mentioning *those who mocked him and put a purple robe round him and the crown of thorns and the reed in his hand.*[4] Where, Celsus, did you learn this except from the Gospels? You regarded these things as deserving reproach; but those who recorded them did not suppose that you and your sort would ridicule them. They supposed that others would take him, who died willingly for religion, as an example of the way to despise people who laugh and mock at it. Rather therefore admire their truthfulness and the spirit[5] of him who willingly suffered these things for mankind, and endured them with all forbearance and longsuffering. For it is not recorded that *he lamented* or that in consequence of his condemnation he either thought[6] or uttered anything ignoble.

35. Then he says: *Why, if not before, does he not at any rate now show forth something divine, and deliver himself from this shame, and take his revenge on those who insult both him and his Father?* To this I reply that much the same can also be said to the Greeks who believe in providence and accept the reality of divine signs: why indeed does not God punish people who insult the deity and deny providence? For if the Greeks will answer this difficulty, then we too will give a similar or even better reply. There was, however, a divine sign from heaven in the eclipse of the sun

---

[1] In the *Bacchae* Dionysus stands bound before Pentheus, who does not believe he is a god, and warns him that the divinity within him can set him free when he wishes; later Pentheus is torn to pieces as a punishment for his impiety in refusing to honour Dionysus as a god. Celsus' point is that if Jesus really had been a god he could have delivered himself (like Dionysus), and his judge (like Pentheus) would have come to a bad end. Cf. Celsus in VIII, 41.

[2] Matt. xxvii. 18. [3] Matt. xxvii. 19. [4] Cf. Matt. xxvii. 28–9.

[5] Something is missing in the Greek here; perhaps read with K. tr. ὑπομείναντος ⟨τὸ γενναῖον⟩.

[6] Read ἐνόησεν with K. tr.

and other miracles, showing that the crucified man possessed something divine and was superior to ordinary men.

36. Then Celsus says: *What does he say while his body is being crucified? Was his blood like*

Ichor such as flows in the veins of the blessed gods?[1]

He is merely mocking. But we will show from the Gospels which were written seriously, even if Celsus will not accept them, that it was not the mythical ichor of Homer which poured out of his body. After he had already died 'one of the soldiers pierced his side with a spear, and there came out blood and water. And he who saw bore witness and his witness is true, and he knows that he is speaking the truth.'[2] In other dead bodies the blood coagulates and pure water does not flow forth; yet in Jesus' dead body the miracle was that even after his body was dead water and blood poured forth from his sides. But as for Celsus, who gets accusations against Jews and Christians out of the gospel and does not even interpret the text properly, and says nothing of the facts which show the divinity of Jesus, if he is willing to attend to the divine signs, let him read the gospels and see that when 'the centurion and those with him guarding Jesus saw the earthquake and the portents that happened, they were very frightened, and said, This man was the son of God'.[3]

37. After this the Jew,[4] who takes out of the gospel texts which, he thinks, provide opportunity for criticism, reproaches Jesus with *the vinegar and the gall,* saying that *he rushed greedily to drink and did not bear his thirst patiently as even an ordinary man often bears it.* The explanation of this is to be found by a particular[5] allegorical interpretation; but here it is necessary[6] only to give an ordinary answer to his criticism—that prophets predicted this very thing. It is written in the sixty-eighth Psalm, as though Christ were speaking: 'And they gave gall for my meat, and for my thirst they gave me vinegar to drink.'[7] Let the Jews tell us now who is this who says these words in the prophets, and let them mention some historical character who received gall for his meat and was given vinegar to drink. Or supposing that they even went so far as to say that the Christ, whose coming they think is in the future, will be the one in question here, our answer will be: What is there against the view that the

---

[1] Cf. I, 66. Celsus has in mind the common story that Alexander the Great, when wounded, pointed to his blood and said, 'This is not ichor...' etc. For this story, cf. Aristobulus *ap.* Athenaeus, VI, 251 A; Plutarch, *Alex.* 28; *Mor.* 180 E; 341 B; Dio Chrysostom, LXIV, 21; Diogenes Laertius, IX, 60; a variant in Q. Curtius VIII, 10, 29, and Seneca, *Ep.* LIX, 12. For its historicity, see W. W. Tarn, *Alexander the Great* (1948), II, p. 358 n. 5.

[2] John xix. 34–5.

[3] Matt. xxvii. 54.

[4] Read ὁ ⟨'Ιουδαῖος⟩ with K. tr.

[5] Read ἰδίας with Bo., K. tr.

[6] Read δέοιτο with K. tr.

[7] Ps. lxviii. 22.

prophecy has already been fulfilled? The very fact that this was spoken a long time beforehand, taken together with the other cases of prophetic foreknowledge, is enough to influence the man who examines the whole question with an open mind to accept Jesus as the prophesied Christ and Son of God.

38. After this the Jew further says to us: *Do you, who are such great believers, criticize us because we do not regard this man as a god nor agree with you that he endured these sufferings for the benefit of mankind, in order that we also may despise punishments?*[1] To this also we will reply that we criticize the Jews, who have been brought up in the law and the prophets who proclaimed Christ beforehand, on the ground that they neither refute the arguments we bring against them which prove that Jesus was the Christ, furnishing this refutation as a defence of their unbelief, nor believe in Jesus as the prophesied Christ even though they do not refute these arguments. Jesus clearly showed among those who were his disciples even after the time of his incarnation that *he endured these sufferings for the benefit of mankind.* For it was not his purpose at his first advent to judge men's deeds even before he had taught them and given them an example of the life that they ought to live, nor did he come to punish the wicked and to save the good. He intended to sow the seed of his word by miracles and by a certain divine power among the whole human race, even as the prophets showed. Moreover, we criticize them since they did not believe him who showed forth the power within him,[2] but said that he cast daemons out of the souls of men by Beelzebul the prince of daemons.[3] We criticize them because they attack his love to man, although he did not overlook either a city or even a village of Judaea, that he might proclaim the kingdom of God everywhere. For they misrepresent him as a vagabond, and they accuse him of being an outcast who roamed about with his body disgracefully unkempt.[4] But it is not disgraceful to endure such hardships for the benefit of those in all places who are able to understand him.

39. How is it anything but a downright lie when Celsus' Jew asserts that *as long as he lived he convinced nobody, not even his own disciples, and was punished and endured such shame?* What roused against him the envy of the chief priests, elders, and scribes of the Jews except the crowds, who were persuaded to follow him even into the deserts? They were won over not only by his well-reasoned arguments (for he always expressed himself in language appropriate to his hearers), but also by the fact that by his miracles he impressed those who did not believe the sequence of his

---

[1] Cf. Celsus in II, 73; VI, 42.   [2] Read ἐνυπάρχουσαν.
[3] Matt. xii. 24; ix. 34.   [4] Cf. I, 61, 69, above.

argument. How is it anything but a downright lie that he did not even convince his own disciples? Although they showed some degree of human cowardice at the time (for they were not yet steeled to being brave), yet they certainly did not give up the conclusion to which they had come that he was the Christ. For after his denial Peter perceived how deeply he had sinned, and 'he went out and wept bitterly';[1] and although the others lost heart at the disasters which befell him, yet they still admired him, and were encouraged by his appearing to them so that their belief that he was Son of God was still greater and firmer than before.

40. Celsus is also a bad philosopher when he imagines that Jesus' message of salvation and moral purity was not sufficient to prove his superiority among men.[2] He supposes that he should have acted in a way contrary to the character of the role which he had assumed, and although he had assumed mortality, *should not have died;* or, if he had to die, at least he should not have died a death which could become an example to men: for they would know even from that very deed how to die for the sake of religion, and to be bold in maintaining it in face of those who have been perverted in their ideas of piety and impiety, and who think that pious people are the most impious. Such people imagine that the most pious people are those who hold wrong ideas about God and attribute the pure conception of Him to anything rather than to God Himself; this is especially true when they even set out to destroy those who have wholeheartedly given themselves up to the point of death because of their clear vision of the one supreme God.

41: Celsus further criticizes Jesus by words put into the mouth of the Jew, saying that *he did not show himself to be pure from all evils.* Let Celsus' learned Jew tell us from what kind of evils Jesus failed to show himself pure. If he means that he was not pure from evils, taking the word in the strict sense,[3] let him give a clear proof of an evil deed done by him. But if he considers as evils poverty, and a cross, and the conspiracy of wicked men, obviously he would say that evil also befell Socrates, who would not have been able to prove that he was pure from all evils. Furthermore, even the common people among the Greeks know how numerous is the band of poor philosophers among them who have intentionally accepted poverty. For they have the recorded stories about Democritus who allowed his estate to become a pasture for sheep, and about Crates who set himself free by giving to the Thebans the money which he realized by selling all his

---

[1] Matt. xxvi. 75.

[2] Here and in what follows Origen is paraphrasing and interpreting a sentence of Celsus, the wording of which cannot be recovered. Cf. Bader, p. 74.

[3] The Stoics said that strictly speaking the only evil was moral evil. Cf. vi, 54–5, below. For their argument from Socrates' death, Philo, *de Provid.* ii, 24; Plutarch, *Mor.* 1051 c.

possessions.[1] Moreover, Diogenes used to live in a tub on account of his abject poverty.[2] Yet no person even of mean intelligence thinks that on this account Diogenes was subject to evils.

42. Moreover, as Celsus wants to make out that *Jesus was also not free from blame*, let him show who among those who assented to his doctrine recorded anything really blameworthy about Jesus; or if he does not base his criticism that he was blameworthy on what they wrote, let him show his source of information for the statement that he *was not free from blame*. Jesus inspired confidence in his promises by the teaching which he gave to his adherents. And we are always seeing the events being fulfilled of which he spoke before they happened, that the Gospel would be preached in all the world, and that his disciples would go to all nations to proclaim his word, and furthermore that they would be brought before governors and kings for no other reason than that of his teaching.[3] Thus we are full of admiration for him and our faith in him is strengthened every day. But I do not know by what greater and clearer facts Celsus wants Jesus to confirm the truth of the predictions. Perhaps, as it seems, he did not understand the doctrine that Jesus was a man, and did not want him to have any human experience, nor to become a noble example to men to show how to bear calamities. This seems to Celsus to be just lamentable and reprehensible, since he regards pain as the greatest evil and pleasure as the greatest good, although this view is accepted by no philosopher among those who believe in providence and admit that courage, bravery, and noble-mindedness are virtues. So Jesus did not cause difficulties for the Christian faith by the sufferings which he endured, but rather strengthened its cause among those who are willing to accept courage as a virtue, and among those who were taught by him that the truly blessed life in the proper sense of the word is not upon this earth, but in the world to come,[4] as he calls it, and that life in what is called 'this present world'[5] is a calamity, or the first and greatest struggle of the soul.

43. After this he says to us: *You will not say of him, I presume, that having failed to convince men on earth he travelled to Hades to convince them there.* Even if he dislikes it, we maintain this, that when he was in the body he convinced not merely a few, but so many that the multitude of those persuaded by him led to the conspiracy against him; and that when he

---

[1] These are stock examples; Cicero, *Tusc. Disp.* v, 38, 114; Philo, *de Vita Cont.* II, 14; Clement, *Quis Dives*, XI, 4; Lactantius, *D.I.* III, 23, etc. For Crates cf. VI, 28 below; Origen, *Comm. in Matt.* XV, 15; Diog. Laert. VI, 87; Apuleius, *Florida*, XIV. They are commonplace instances in the Academic-Stoic arguments about providence and the suffering of the righteous; cf. Philo, *de Prov.* II, 13.

[2] Diog. Laert. VI, 23.   [3] Mark xiii. 10; Matt. xxviii. 19; x. 18. Cf. II, 13, above.

[4] Matt. xii. 32.   [5] Gal. i. 4.

became a soul unclothed by a body he conversed with souls unclothed by
bodies, converting also those of them who were willing to accept him,
or those who, for reasons which he himself knew, he saw to be ready to
do so.[1]

44. After this for some unknown reason he makes a very silly remark:
*If you think that you provide a true defence by discovering absurd justifications
for those doctrines[2] in which you have been ridiculously deceived, why may we
not think that everyone else as well who has been condemned and come to an
unfortunate end is an angel greater and more divine than Jesus?* That it is
absolutely obvious that Jesus' recorded sufferings have no similarity to
those of men who have met with an unfortunate end on account of sorcery
or some other such charge is self-evident to anyone. For no one could
suggest that it is the work of sorcerers to convert souls from the multitude
of sins among mankind and from the flood of evil.

Celsus' Jew also compares him with robbers saying that *anyone with
similar shamelessness could say even of a robber and murderer who had been
punished that he, forsooth, was not a robber but a god; for he foretold to his
robber-gang that he would suffer the sort of things that he did in fact suffer.*
First, it would be said in reply that it is not because he foretold that he
would suffer these things that we hold these views about Jesus, as for
instance when we boldly declare that he has come down to us from God.
Secondly, we also say that these things described in the Gospels were
somehow foretold, since God was 'numbered with the transgressors'[3] by
the transgressors themselves. For they desired rather that a robber who
had been cast into prison for sedition and murder should be released and
that Jesus should be crucified; and they crucified him between two robbers.
Moreover, Jesus in the person of his genuine disciples and witnesses for
the truth is always being crucified with robbers and suffers the same
condemnation among men as they do. And we say that if there is any
similarity at all between robbers and these men, who accept every kind of
outrage and death for their devotion towards the Creator that they may
preserve it pure and untarnished as Jesus taught them, then obviously it
is also legitimate for Celsus to compare Jesus with robbers, as he was the
originator of this teaching. It was not right either for Jesus, who was dying
for the common good of mankind, to be put to death, or for these men
who endure these sufferings for their piety, and who of all men are the
only people to be treated as criminals simply because of the method of
worshipping God which has seemed right to them. And it was an impious
act that men plotted against Jesus.

[1] Cf. Clem. Al. *Strom.* VI, 64, 4.   [2] Read ἐφ' οἷς with Bo.
[3] Mark xv. 28 (Isa. liii. 12).

45. Notice also the shallowness of the argument about those who were Jesus' disciples at the time, when he says: *When those who were living with him at the time, who heard him speak and were taught by him, saw that he was being punished and was dying, they did not die with him, or for his sake, nor were they persuaded to despise punishments. But they even denied that they were disciples. Yet now you die with him.* Here, so that he may criticize Christianity, he believes that the sin recorded in the Gospels took place, which was committed when the disciples were still beginners and immature. But he is silent about their reform after the sin when they were bold in face of the Jews and suffered countless distresses at their hands and finally died for Jesus' teaching. He did not want to pay attention to Jesus' prediction to Peter, 'When you are old, you will stretch out your hands' and so on, to which the Bible adds: 'Now he said this, signifying by what death he should glorify God.'[1] Nor would he observe that James the brother of John, an apostle who was the brother of an apostle, was killed with the sword by Herod on account of the word of Christ. Nor would he see how many things Peter and the other apostles did, being bold in the word,[2] and how after they had been beaten they went out from the presence of the Sanhedrin rejoicing that they were counted worthy to be put to shame for his name,[3] even surpassing many stories told by the Greeks about the courage and bravery of the philosophers. From the beginning, therefore, this doctrine of Jesus had great influence upon his hearers, teaching them to despise the life led by the multitude, and to seek earnestly to live a life like that of God.

46. Is it anything but lying when Celsus' Jew says: *When he was alive he won over only ten sailors and tax-collectors of the most abominable character,[4] and not even all of these?* It is clear that even the Jews would admit that he did not win over only ten men, nor even only a hundred or a thousand. But on one occasion he won over five thousand all at once, and on another four thousand;[5] and he won them over so effectively that they even followed him into the deserts which alone had room for gathering in one place the multitude of those who believed in God through Jesus; and there he displayed not only his words but his deeds. By repeating himself Celsus compels us to do the same as he, since we are anxious to avoid the suspicion that we are passing over any criticism which he makes. On the point in question, the next thing which he says in his book is this: *Is it not utterly ludicrous that when he was alive himself he convinced nobody; but now that he is dead, those who wish to do so convince multitudes?* To be in keeping with the facts he ought to say that after his death the

---

[1] John xxi. 18–19.   [2] Cf. Acts iv. 13.   [3] Acts v. 41.
[4] Cf. Celsus in I, 62.   [5] Matt. xiv. 21; xv. 38.

multitudes were convinced not just by those who wished to do so, but by those who wished and had the power to do so. But how much more reasonable is it to say that while he lived this life he convinced a far greater number both by his powerful teaching and by his actions?

47. He invents out of his own head what he asserts to be our answer to his question when he says: *What argument led you to regard this man as Son of God?* He has made us reply that *we were led by this argument, because we know that his punishment was meant to destroy the father of evil.* But we were led to this belief by thousands of other reasons, a very few of which we set out above, and, God willing, will further set out, not only when composing a reply to *The True Doctrine,* as Celsus considers it, but also in countless other places. Also, as though we maintained that *we regard him as Son of God because he was punished,* he says: *What then? Have not many others also been punished and that no less disgracefully?* Here Celsus behaves like the lowest class of the enemies of the faith, who even think that it follows from the story about the crucifixion of Jesus that we worship anyone who has been crucified.

48. Many times already[1] when Celsus has been unable to disregard the miracles which Jesus is recorded to have done he has misrepresented them as sorceries; and often we have replied to his arguments to the best of our ability. But here he says that this is the reply, as it were, which we make, that we *regarded him as Son of God for this reason, because he healed the lame and the blind.* And he goes on to say: *He raised the dead also,[2] so you say.* That he healed the lame and the blind, for which reason we regard him as Christ and Son of God, is clear to us from what was also written in the prophecies: 'Then shall the eyes of the blind be opened, and the ears of the deaf shall hear. Then shall the lame man leap as a hart.'[3] That he really did raise the dead, and that this is not a fiction of the writers of the Gospels, is proved by the consideration that if it was a fiction, many would have been recorded to have been raised up, including people who had already been a long time in their tombs. But since it is not a fiction, those of whom this is recorded may easily be enumerated. There was the daughter of the ruler of the synagogue (of whom for some unknown reason he said 'she is not dead but is asleep',[4] saying something about her which did not apply to all who died), and the only son of the widow, on whom he had compassion and raised him up, and made the bearers of the corpse stand still; thirdly, there was Lazarus, who was four days in the tomb.[5]

We will further say on this subject to people with an open mind, and

---

[1] Cf. Celsus in I, 6, 68, 71; II, 32.
[2] Perhaps read ⟨καὶ⟩ νεκρούς with Glöckner, Bader.   [3] Isa. xxxv. 5–6.
[4] Luke viii. 52.   [5] Luke vii. 11–17; John xi. 38–44.

particularly to the Jew, that just as 'there were many lepers in the days of
Elisha the prophet, and none of them was cleansed except Naaman the
Syrian', and as 'there were many widows in the days of Elijah the
prophet, and Elijah was not sent to any of them except to one at Zarephath
in Sidonia'[1] (for in accordance with a certain divine decision she had been
considered worthy of the miracles of the loaves of bread performed by
the prophet):[2] so also there were many dead men in the days of Jesus, but
only those rose again whom the Logos knew to be suitable for resurrection, not only that what was done by the Lord might be symbolic of
certain truths, but also that there and then he might lead many to the
wonderful teaching of the gospel. And I might say that according to the
promise of Jesus[3] the disciples have done even greater works than the
physical miracles which Jesus did. For the eyes of people blind in soul
are always being opened, and the ears of those who were deaf to any talk
of virtue eagerly hear about God and the blessed life with Him; and many
too who were lame in the feet of their inner man, as the Bible calls it, but
have now been healed by the Logos, do not just leap, but 'leap as a hart',[4]
an animal hostile to serpents and superior to all the poison of vipers. In
fact, these lame people who have been healed receive from Jesus power to
walk on their feet, where before they were lame, over all the serpents and
scorpions of evil, and in general over all the power of the enemy,[5] and in
their walk they do nothing wrong; for they have even become superior to
all evil and the poison of daemons.

49. Jesus does not warn his disciples not to pay attention to sorcerers
in general and those who profess to perform wonders by some such method
(for his disciples did not need this warning). But he does warn them off
any who give themselves the title of the Christ of God and attempt by
certain suggestions to turn Jesus' disciples towards themselves, when he
says in one place: 'At that time if any say to you, Lo there is Christ, or
here, believe him not. For there shall arise false Christs and false prophets,
who will show you signs and great wonders, so as to lead astray, if possible,
even the elect. Behold, I have told you beforehand. If therefore they say
unto you, Behold he is in the wilderness, go not forth; Behold, he is in
the inner chambers, believe it not. For as the lightning comes forth from
the east, and is seen even unto the west, so shall the coming of the Son of

---

[1] Luke iv. 27, 25–6.   [2] I Kings (III Regn.), xvii. 11–16.   [3] John xiv. 12.
[4] Isa. xxxv. 6. Cf. Origen, *Comm. in Matt.* xi, 18; *Hom. in Jerem.* xviii, 9; *Hom. in Cant.*
ii, 11. For the story about the way in which stags kill snakes, see Pliny, *N.H.* viii, 118;
xxviii, 149–50; Aelian, *N.A.* ii, 9; Plutarch, *Mor.* 976d; Xenophon ap. Cassianus Bassus,
Geoponica xix, 5, 3; Tertullian, *de Pallio* 3; Tatian 18; Cosmas Hieros., *Ad carm. S. Greg.*
(*P.G.* xxxviii, 633).
[5] Luke x. 19.

man be.' And in another place he says: 'Many will say to me in that day, Lord, Lord, did we not eat in thy name and drink in thy name and in thy name cast out daemons, and do many miracles? And I will say to them, Depart from me, because you are workers of iniquity.'[1] Celsus wants to put the wonders of Jesus on a level with human sorcery and says in these very words: *O light and truth, with his own voice he explicitly confesses, as even you have recorded, that there will come among you others also who employ similar miracles, wicked men and sorcerers, and he names one Satan as devising this: so that not even he denies that these wonders have nothing divine about them, but are works of wicked men. Nevertheless, being compelled by the truth, he both reveals the deeds of others and proves his own to be wrong. Is it not a miserable argument to infer from the same works that he is a god while they are sorcerers? Why should we conclude from these works that the others were any more wicked than this fellow, taking the witness of Jesus himself? In fact, even he admitted that these works were not produced by any divine nature, but were the signs of certain cheats and wicked men.* Consider now whether Celsus is not clearly convicted of wickedly misrepresenting the faith, since Jesus said one thing about those who would perform signs and wonders, where Celsus' Jew said another. Moreover, if Jesus simply told his disciples to beware of those who profess to do wonders, but did not mention what title they would give themselves, perhaps his suspicion might have had possible grounds. But since the men of whom Jesus wants us to beware profess to be the Christ, which sorcerers do not do, and what is more, since he says[2] that certain people who live evil lives will do miracles and cast daemons out of men in the name of Jesus, then, if I may say so, sorcery and any suspicion of it is entirely ruled out by[3] the passage in question. But the divine power of Jesus and that of his disciples is suggested by the fact that it was possible for someone to use his name and in some unknown way being influenced by a certain power to pretend that he was the Christ, and to appear to perform much the same miracles as Christ, and for others to do in the name of Christ much the same, as it were, as his true disciples.

50. In the Second Epistle to the Thessalonians, Paul also makes it clear how one day there will be revealed 'the man of sin, the son of destruction, who opposes and exalts himself against all that is called God and is worshipped, so that he sits in the temple of God, setting himself forth as God'. And again he says to the Thessalonians: 'And now you know that which restrains, to the end that he may be revealed in his own season. For the mystery of iniquity is already at work, only until he that now restrains is

---

[1] Matt. xxiv. 23–7; vii. 22–3.   [2] Matt. vii. 22.
[3] Read ⟨διὰ⟩ τῶν with Wifstrand.

taken out of the way; and then shall the lawless one be revealed, whom the
Lord Jesus shall slay with the breath of his mouth and bring to nought by
the manifestation of his coming; even he whose coming is according to
the working of Satan with all power and signs and lying wonders, and
with all deceit of unrighteousness among them that are perishing.' And
he gives the reason why the lawless one is allowed to live, saying:
'Because they received not the love of the truth that they might be saved.
And for this cause God sends them a working of error, that they should
believe a lie, that they all might be judged who believed not the truth but
had pleasure in unrighteousness.'[1]

Let anyone tell us if anything in the gospel or in the apostle's writings
could afford occasion for a suspicion that sorcery was being set forth in
the passage. And anyone interested can also take the prophecy about
Antichrist from Daniel.[2] Now Celsus falsely represents Jesus' words,
since he did not say that *there will come others who employ similar miracles,
wicked men and sorcerers*, while Celsus asserts that he did say this. Just as
the power of the Egyptian spells was not like the virtue in the miracle done
by Moses, for the conclusion showed up the wonders of the Egyptians to
have been produced by trickery, while those of Moses were divine;[3] so
also the wonders of the Antichrists and those who pretend to do miracles
like the signs and wonders of Jesus' disciples are said to be 'lying',
prevailing 'by all deceit of unrighteousness among them that are perishing';
whereas the wonders of Christ and his disciples bore fruit not in deceit but
in the salvation of souls. For who can reasonably say that the higher life,
which restricts evil actions so that they decrease every day, is produced by
deceit?

51. Celsus was aware of the statement of the Bible when he made Jesus
say that *one Satan will devise this*. But he begs the question by saying that
*Jesus did not deny that these wonders have nothing divine about them, but are
works of wicked men*. He puts together in one category things which really
fall into two different categories. Just as a wolf is not of the same species
as a dog, even if it seems to have some similarity in the shape of its body
and its bark, and just as a wild pigeon is not the same as a tame one; so
also what is accomplished by God's power is nothing like what is done by
sorcery.

Moreover, we will say this in reply to Celsus' wicked words: Are those
miracles done through sorcery and wicked daemons, while no miracle at
all is accomplished by the divine and blessed nature of God? And does the
life of mankind put up with the worse and have no room at all for the
better? This also seems to me to be a general principle that where

_____
[1] II Thess. ii. 1–12.   [2] Dan. vii. 23–6.   [3] Exod. vii. 8–12.

something bad is pretending to be of the same kind as something good, then there must be something good which is its opposite.[1] So also it is true of miracles done[2] by sorcery that there must necessarily be miracles in human life which are wrought by divine action. It follows from the same principle either that he should deny both kinds, and say that neither exists, or that he should take one, and in particular the bad kind, and admit that the good exists also. If anyone holds that wonders produced by sorcery are real, but does not hold this view of those done by divine power, he seems to me to be much like the man who holds that sophisms and plausible arguments are real, although they fail to be true and only pretend to establish realities, but that truth and dialectical argument which has no place for sophisms have nowhere any practical reality among men.

If we once agree that it is a corollary from the existence of magic and sorcery, wrought by evil daemons who are enchanted by elaborate spells and obey men who are sorcerers, that wonders done by divine power must also exist among men, then why should we not also examine carefully people who profess to do miracles, and see whether their lives and moral characters, and the results of their miracles, harm men or effect moral reformation? We should know in this way who serves daemons and causes such effects by means of certain spells and enchantments, and who has been on pure and holy ground[3] before God in his own soul and spirit (and I think also in his body), and has received a certain divine spirit, and performs such wonders for the benefit of mankind and in order to exhort men to believe in the true God. If we may once ask, without being carried off our feet by the miracles, who does these wonders from a good motive and who from a bad, so that we neither speak evil of them all, nor admire and accept them all as divine, will it not be self-evident from what happened in the case of Moses and Jesus, since whole nations owed their origin to their miracles, that these men did by divine power what they are said to have done in the Bible? Wickedness and trickery would not have gathered together a whole nation, which has risen not only above images and statues set up by men, but also above all created nature, and ascends to the uncreated power of the God of the universe.

52. As it is a Jew who is saying these things in Celsus' book, we would say to him: As for you, sir, why do you believe to be divine the miracles which according to your scriptures were wrought by God through Moses; and why do you try to argue against those who misrepresent them as

---

[1] It was a commonplace that opposites imply one another; cf. Philo, *de Aetern. Mundi*, 104. The Stoics used this in their theodicy to explain the existence of evil; it was an inevitable necessity if there was to be any good. Cf. Chrysippus ap. Aulus Gellius VII, 1 (*S.V.F.* II, 1169); Plutarch, *Mor.* 1065 B (*ibid.* 1181).

[2] Read ἐπιτελουμένων with K. tr.   [3] Cf. Exod. vii. 8 ff.

though they were done by sorcery like those performed by the Egyptian wise men? For when you say that the miracles of Jesus, which you admit to have occurred, were not divine, you follow the example of the Egyptians who criticize your opinion of Moses.[1] For if the outcome, which was that a whole nation owed its origin to the wonders of Moses, shows the indubitable fact that it was God who caused the miracles of Moses, why should not this argument be even more cogent in the case of Jesus, since he did a greater work than that of Moses? Moses took those of the nation who, being Abraham's seed, observed the rite of circumcision according to tradition, and were actively enthusiastic for the customs of Abraham, and led them out of Egypt, appointing laws for them which you have believed to be divine. But Jesus made a greater venture when he introduced the life according to the gospel into that already existing with its ancestral ethical codes and traditional way of life which conformed to the established laws. And just as the signs which Moses is recorded to have done were needed in order that Moses might be believed not only by the elders but also by the people; so would not Jesus also need such miracles in order that he might be believed by those among the people who had learned to ask for signs and wonders? For because in comparison with the wonders of Moses Jesus' miracles were superior and more divine, they could turn men away from Jewish legends and their human traditions, and could make them accept him who taught and performed these miracles as being greater than the prophets. Was he not greater than the prophets when he was proclaimed by them as the Christ and Saviour of mankind?

53. All that Celsus' Jew says to believers in Jesus can be applied equally well to the criticism of Moses, so that we could say either that the sorcery of Jesus is no different from that of Moses or that it is much about the same thing, since as far as the words of Celsus' Jew go both could be subject to the same objections. For instance, Celsus' Jew says about Christ: *O light and truth, with his own voice Jesus explicitly confesses, as even you have recorded, that there will come among you others also who employ similar miracles, wicked men and sorcerers.* But concerning Moses, anyone who disbelieves his wonders, whether an Egyptian or anyone else, might say to the Jew: O light and truth, with his own voice Moses explicitly confesses, as even you have recorded, that there will come among you others who employ similar miracles, wicked men and sorcerers. For it is written in your law: 'If there arise among you a prophet or a dreamer of dreams, and he give you a sign or a wonder, and the sign or wonder come to pass, of which he spoke unto you, saying, Let us go and follow other gods which you have not known, and let us worship them, you shall not

---

[1] K. tr. proposes κατά σε ⟨σοφούς⟩ but the text is better as it stands.

hear the words of that prophet or the dreamer of that dream',[1] and so on. If he who misrepresents the words of Jesus says that *he names one Satan as devising these things*, the man who applies this to Moses would say that he names a dreaming prophet who devises these things. And as Celsus' Jew says of Jesus that *not even he himself denied that these wonders have nothing divine about them, but are works of wicked men*, so also the one who does not believe the wonders of Moses would say to him the words which he has just said and make the same point: Not even Moses himself denies that these things have nothing divine about them, but are works of wicked men. Here again he would do the same: Nevertheless, being compelled by the truth, Moses both reveals the deeds of others and refutes his own. And when the Jew says this, *Is it not a miserable argument to infer from the same works that he is a god while they are sorcerers?* one might say to him on account of the words of Moses we have quoted: Is it not a miserable argument to infer from the same works that he is a prophet of God and his servant, while they are sorcerers?

Celsus spends still more time on this subject, and after the comparisons which I have quoted goes on to say: *Why should we conclude from these works that the others were any more wicked than this fellow, taking the witness of Jesus himself?* We also will add this to what we have said: Why from these works should we conclude that the people whom Moses forbade you to believe when they displayed signs and wonders were any more wicked than Moses, on the grounds that he used to attack others for their signs and wonders? Celsus says even more on this subject, to appear to augment his argument, saying: *In fact, even he admitted that these works were not produced by any divine nature, but were the signs of certain cheats and wicked men.* Who is the person here? You, Jew, assert that Jesus admitted this. But the man who attacks you as subject to the same criticisms would apply the word 'he' to Moses.

54. After this Celsus' Jew (to keep the part given to the Jew from the beginning) in the address to his fellow-citizens who believe says to us, forsooth: *What led you to believe, except that he foretold that after his death he would rise again?* This also would apply to Moses, like the previous instances. We would say to him: What led you to believe, except that he wrote about his own death in these words: 'And there Moses, the servant of the Lord, died in the land of Moab by the word of the Lord; and they buried him in the land of Moab near the house of Phogor; and no man knows his sepulchre to this day'?[2] Just as the Jew attacks Jesus because he foretold that after his death he would rise again, the man who says similar things about Moses could reply to his remark that Moses (for

---

[1] Deut. xiii. 1–3.   [2] Deut. xxxiv. 5–6.

Deuteronomy is written by him) recorded that 'no man knows his sepulchre to this day', boasting and exalting even his own tomb as unknown to mankind.

55. After this the Jew says to his fellow-citizens who believe in Jesus: *Come now, let us believe your view that he actually said this. How many others produce wonders like this to convince simple hearers whom they exploit by deceit? They say that Zamolxis, the slave of Pythagoras, also did this among the Scythians,¹ and Pythagoras himself in Italy,² and Rhampsinitus in Egypt. The last-named played dice with Demeter in Hades and returned bearing a gift from her, a golden napkin.³ Moreover, they say that Orpheus did this among the Odrysians,⁴ and Protesilaus in Thessaly,⁵ and Heracles at Taenarum, and Theseus.⁶ But we must examine this question whether anyone who really died ever rose again with the same body. Or do you think that the stories of these others really are the legends which they appear to be, and yet that the ending of your tragedy is to be regarded as noble and convincing— his cry from the cross when he expired, and the earthquake and the darkness? While he was alive he did not help himself, but after death he rose again and showed the marks of his punishment and how his hands had been pierced. But who saw this? A hysterical female, as you say, and perhaps some other one⁷ of those who were deluded by the same sorcery, who either dreamt in a certain state of mind and through wishful thinking had a hallucination due to some mistaken notion (an experience which has happened to thousands), or, which is more likely, wanted to impress the others by telling this fantastic tale, and so by this cock-and-bull story to provide a chance for other beggars.*

As it is a Jew who says this, we will reply in defence of our Jesus as though our opponent really were a Jew, by making a further application of his argument to Moses, and will say to him: How many others produce wonders like these which Moses did, to convince simple hearers whom they exploit by deceit? The ability to quote the prodigious stories of Zamolxis and Pythagoras would be more appropriate for a man who disbelieves Moses than for a Jew who has no great interest in Greek stories. And it would be more plausible for an Egyptian, who does not believe the miracles of Moses, to quote the instance of Rhampsinitus; for he would

¹ According to Herodotus (IV, 95) Zamolxis hid in a cave and after four years reappeared to the Thracians, saying he had risen again. Cf. Lucian, *Deorum concilium*, 9.
² The story is told by Hermippus ap. Diog. Laert. VIII, 41. Cf. Rohde, *Psyche* (E.T.), pp. 600 f.; Waszink on Tert. *de Anima*, 28.
³ Celsus quotes Herodotus, II, 122.
⁴ For references to Orpheus in the underworld cf. J. G. Frazer on Apollodorus, *Bibl.* I, 3, 2 (14–15); discussion in Guthrie, *Orpheus and Greek Religion* (1935), pp. 29 ff.
⁵ Apollodorus, *Epit.* III, 30–1.
⁶ For Heracles' rescue of Theseus from Hades, cf. Frazer on Apollodorus, *Bibl.* II, 5, 12.
⁷ Possibly a reference to Peter.

say that the story that he descended to Hades and played dice with Demeter and carried off a golden napkin from her, showing it as a sign of what had happened in Hades, and that he had returned from there, was far more convincing than that of Moses when he writes that he entered 'the darkness where God was',[1] and that he alone drew nearer to God than the rest. For he wrote as follows: 'And Moses alone shall come near unto God, but the others shall not come near.'[2] Accordingly, we who are disciples of Jesus will say to the Jew when he says this: Defend yourself now, you who attack us for our faith in Jesus, and say what you would reply to the Egyptian and the Greeks[3] if the charges which you have brought against our Jesus had first been brought against Moses. And even if you strive energetically to defend Moses, seeing that the narratives about him are also capable of a striking and clear vindication, in your defence of Moses you will in spite of yourself establish that Jesus is more divine than Moses.

56. Celsus' Jew says that the heroic stories about the men alleged to have descended to Hades and returned from there are fantastic tales, and thinks that the heroes disappeared for a time and took themselves off secretly from the sight of all men, and after that showed themselves as though they had returned from Hades (for this seems to be his view of the story of Orpheus among the Odrysians, and of Protesilaus in Thessaly, and of Heracles at Taenarum, and also of Theseus). Let us prove, then, that the history of Jesus' resurrection from the dead cannot be compared with such tales. Each of the heroes whom he mentions with their respective places could, if he wished, have taken himself off secretly from the sight of all men and then decided to return again to the men whom he had left. But since Jesus was crucified before all the Jews and his body put to death in the sight of their people, how can he say that this is a similar invention like the story of those heroes who are related to have descended to Hades and returned from there? In our opinion perhaps something of the following kind might be said in defence of the crucifixion of Jesus, especially on account of the stories about the heroes who are thought to have forced their way down to Hades. Suppose that Jesus had died an unknown death, so that when he died the Jewish people did not know it. If then after this he had really risen from the dead, what he suspects of being true of the heroes might possibly be said of him. In addition, therefore, to other causes for the crucifixion of Jesus perhaps this also might be an additional reason why his death on the cross was a public event, that no one may be able to say that he deliberately retired out of sight of men, and that although he appeared to die he did not really do so,

[1] Exod. xx. 21.   [2] Exod. xxiv. 2.
[3] With Wifstrand put a comma after λέγε and delete colon before τί.

110

but, when he wanted to, again reappeared and told the portentous tale that he had risen from the dead. But I think that the clear and certain proof is the argument from the behaviour of the disciples, who devoted themselves to a teaching which involved risking their lives. If they had invented the story that Jesus had risen from the dead, they would not have taught this with such spirit, in addition to the fact that in accordance with this[1] they not only prepared others to despise death but above all despised it themselves.

57. Consider the utter blindness of Celsus' Jew when he holds that it is impossible for anyone to rise again from the dead with the same body, saying: *But we must examine this question whether anyone who really died ever rose again with the same body.* No Jew would ever have said this, since he believes what is written in the third and fourth books of the Kingdoms about the young boys, one of whom was raised by Elijah and the other by Elisha.[2] I think it was just for this reason that Jesus did not come to live among any other nation but the Jews, because they had become used to miracles, so that, by comparing their beliefs in earlier miracles with those reported to have been done by Jesus, they might accept the view that he was superior to all of them, since greater miracles happened in his case and more wonderful things were performed by him.

58. After the Greek stories which the Jew quoted about those who, as it were, told cock-and-bull stories and alleged[3] that they had risen from the dead, he says to Jewish believers in Jesus: *Or do you think that the stories of these others really are the legends which they appear to be, and yet that the ending of your tragedy is to be regarded as noble and convincing—his cry from the cross when he expired?* We would reply to the Jew: The myths which you have quoted we regard as such; but we certainly do not consider as legends the stories in our Bible which we and you share in common, which not only you but we also hold in reverence. For this reason we believe that the authors who wrote in scripture about people who rose from the dead were not telling cock-and-bull stories, and we believe that Jesus actually rose again as he foretold and as the prophets predicted. But Jesus' resurrection from the dead was more remarkable than the former instances, because the prophets Elijah and Elisha raised them up, whereas he was raised up not by any of the prophets, but by his Father in heaven. Consequently his resurrection had greater effects than theirs. For what important benefit has come to the world from the fact that the boys were raised up by Elijah and Elisha comparable to that brought about by

---

[1] For καὶ αὐτοὶ read with K. tr. κατὰ τοῦτο.
[2] I Kings (III Regn.) xvii. 21–2; II Kings (IV Regn.) iv. 34–5.
[3] K. tr. brackets the second περὶ τῶν ὡς, but I think it better to read περὶ ἑαυτῶν ὡς.

the preaching of the resurrection of Jesus when it is believed by divine power?

59. He thinks that *the earthquake and the darkness* are a fantastic tale. We defended these as well as we could earlier, quoting Phlegon who related that these events happened at the time of the Saviour's passion.[1] He also thinks that *while he was alive he did not help himself,* but *after death Jesus rose again and showed the marks of his punishment and how his hands had been pierced.* We put the question to him, what does he mean by the phrase *he did not help himself?* If he means in relation to virtue, we would affirm that he certainly did help himself. For he neither uttered nor did anything wrong, but in truth 'was led as a sheep to the slaughter, just as a lamb before the shearer is dumb', and the Gospel testifies that 'so he opened not his mouth'.[2] But if he takes the phrase *he did not help himself* to refer to things indifferent and corporeal, we reply that we proved from the Gospels that of his own free will he underwent this. Then after this he refers to the words of the gospel saying that he showed the marks of his punishment after he had risen from the dead and how his hands had been pierced. And he asks: *Who saw this?* He attacks the story in the Bible that Mary Magdalene saw him saying: *A hysterical female, as you say.* And because she is not the only one recorded to have seen the risen Jesus, and as there are others as well, Celsus' Jew attacks these narratives too saying *and perhaps some other one of those who were deluded by the same sorcery.*

60. Then as though this could have happened (I mean that someone should have such a vivid vision of a dead man as to suppose that he were alive) he continues like an Epicurean, saying that someone *dreamt in a certain state of mind or through wishful thinking had a hallucination due to some mistaken notion (an experience,* he says, *which has happened to thousands),* and so came to tell this story. Even if this seems to have been very cleverly expressed, nevertheless it serves to confirm the essential doctrine that the souls of dead men have a real existence, and that the man who has accepted the doctrine of the immortality of the soul, or at any rate of its survival, does not believe in an illusion. Thus in his dialogue on the soul Plato says that 'shadowy apparitions' of men already dead have appeared to some people round tombs.[3] The apparitions round about the tombs[4] of dead men are caused by the fact that the soul is subsisting in what is called the luminous body.[5] Celsus, however, refuses to believe

---

[1] Cf. II, 14, 33.   [2] Isa. liii. 7; Matt. xxvi. 62–3; xxvii. 12, 14.
[3] *Phaedo,* 81 D; cf. VII, 5, below.   [4] Read μνημεῖα with K. tr.
[5] For the development of this idea in later Platonism see E. R. Dodds' discussion in his edition of Proclus, *The Elements of Theology* (1933), pp. 313–21; for Origen, cf. my remarks in *Harv. Theol. Rev.* XLI (1948), pp. 99 f.

this, and wants to make out that certain people were day-dreaming, and
through wishful thinking had a hallucination due to some mistaken notion.
His view would not be unreasonable if the visions had occurred by night.
But his idea of a vision in the daytime is not convincing when the people
were in no way mentally unbalanced and were not suffering from delirium
or melancholy. Because Celsus foresaw this objection he said that the
woman was hysterical; but there is no evidence of this in the scriptural
account which was the source upon which he drew for his criticism.

61. *After his death,* Celsus thinks, *Jesus used to produce only a mental
impression of the wounds he received on the cross, and did not really appear
wounded in this way.* But according to the account in the gospel, of which
Celsus believes the parts he wants to believe where it helps his criticisms,
while he disbelieves the other parts, Jesus called to himself one of the
disciples who did not believe and thought the miracle to be impossible. For
he accepted the statement of the woman that she had seen him, as it was
not impossible that the soul of a dead man should have been seen; but he
did not yet think it was true that he had been raised in a body exactly like
that which he had had before. On this account he said: 'Unless I see, I will
not believe', and even went on to say: 'Unless I thrust my hand into the
print of the nails and touch his side, I will not believe.'[1] This was said by
Thomas because he thought that it was possible for the physical eyes to
see the body of the soul in a form in every respect like its former shape,

and often
> In stature and beautiful eyes and voice,
>
> Having the same garments about the skin.[2]

But Jesus called Thomas to him and said: 'Reach hither your finger and
see my hands; and reach hither your hand and put it into my side; and
be not faithless but believing.'[3]

62. That this, the greatest of all miracles, should really have happened
fitted in with all the prophecies about him, one of which I will quote here,
and with what he had done and with what befell him. For it was foretold
by the prophet, putting words into the mouth of Jesus: 'My flesh shall rest
in hope; and thou wilt not leave my soul in Hades, and wilt not suffer thy
holy one to see corruption.'[4] But at the time of his resurrection he was,
as it were, in a sort of intermediate state between the solidity of the body
as it was before his passion and the condition of a soul uncovered by any
body. This explains why 'when his disciples and Thomas with them were
gathered together, Jesus came after the doors had been shut and stood in

[1] John xx. 25.
[2] Origen quotes Homer, *Il.* xxiii, 66–7, where Patroclus' ghost appears to Achilles. The
point is that while Thomas believed in ghosts, he did not believe in a physical resurrection.
[3] John xx. 27.   [4] Ps. xv. 9–10.

the midst, and said, Peace be unto you. Then he said to Thomas, Reach hither your finger',¹ and so on. And in Luke's gospel, when Simon and Cleopas were talking to one another about all that had happened to them, Jesus drew near to them and 'went with them; and their eyes were holden that they should not know him; and he said unto them, What communications are these which you have with one another, as you walk? And when their eyes were opened, and they knew him', then the scripture says in these very words: 'and he vanished out of their sight'.² Thus even if Celsus wants to put the appearances of Jesus and the experience of those who saw him after his resurrection on a level with other imagined appearances and people subject to such visions, yet to any who examine the facts sensibly and with an open mind they will appear even more miraculous.

63. After this Celsus speaks evil of the biblical story in a way that cannot be lightly passed over, when he says that *if Jesus really wanted to show forth divine power, he ought to have appeared to the very men who treated him despitefully and to the man who condemned him and to everyone everywhere.* It is true that according to the gospel he seems to us not to have appeared after the resurrection in the same way that he appeared before it when he was in public and before everyone. Although in the Acts it is written, 'He was seen for forty days and proclaimed to his disciples the things concerning the kingdom of God',³ yet in the gospels it is not said that he was with them all the time, but that on one occasion he appeared in the midst, after the doors had been shut, for eight days,⁴ and on another occasion he appeared under similar conditions. Paul also in the closing section of the First Epistle to the Corinthians implies that he was not seen publicly just as he had been in the period before his passion, when he writes these words: 'For I delivered unto you first of all that which I also received, how that Christ died for our sins according to the scriptures, and that he appeared to Cephas, then to the twelve; then he appeared to above five hundred brethren at once, of whom the greater part remain until now, but some are fallen asleep. Then he appeared to James, then to all the apostles. And last of all, as to one born out of due time, he appeared to me also.'⁵ I suspect that this passage contains certain great and wonderful truths, the understanding of which is beyond the merit not only of the multitude of believers but even of those quite advanced. They would make clear the reason why after he rose from the dead he did not appear in the same way as he did during the previous period. I will select a few out of many points, considering the character of the treatise

¹ John xx. 26–7.   ² Luke xxiv. 14–17, 31.   ³ Acts i. 3.
⁴ John xx. 26.   ⁵ I Cor. xv. 3, 5–8.

which is written in reply to an attack upon the Christians and their faith; and see whether we are able to make a reasonable impression on people who will listen to our defence.

64. Although Jesus was one, he had several aspects;[1] and to those who saw him he did not appear alike to all. That he had many aspects is clear from the saying, 'I am the way, the truth, and the life', and 'I am the bread', and 'I am the door',[2] and countless other such sayings. Moreover, that his appearance was not just the same to those who saw him, but varied according to their individual capacity, will be clear to people who carefully consider why, when about to be transfigured on the high mountain, he did not take all the apostles, but only Peter, James, and John. For they alone had the capacity to see his glory at that time, and were able also to perceive Moses and Elijah when they appeared in glory, and to hear them conversing together, and the voice from heaven out of the cloud. I think that at the time before he ascended the mountain when his disciples alone came to him and he taught them the beatitudes, even here when he was somewhere lower down the mountain, when it was late and he healed those brought to him, delivering them from all illness and disease, he did not appear the same to those who were ill and needed his healing as he did to those who were able to ascend the mountain with him and were in good health. Furthermore he privately explained to his disciples the parables which had been spoken to the crowds outside with the meaning concealed; just as those who heard the explanation of the parables had a greater capacity to hear than those who heard the parables without any explanations, so also was this the case with their vision, certainly with that of their souls and I think also of their bodies. And it is clear that he did not always appear the same from the remark of Judas when about to betray him. For he said to the crowd that came with him, as though they did not know him, 'Whomsoever I kiss, it is he'.[3] I think that the Saviour himself also makes this point clear by the words, 'I was daily with you in the temple teaching, and you laid no hand upon me'.[4] Accordingly, as we hold that Jesus was such a wonderful person, not only as to the divinity within him which was hidden from the multitude, but also as to his body which was transfigured when he wished and before whom he wished, we affirm that everyone had the capacity to see Jesus only when he had not 'put off the principalities and powers'[5] and had not yet died to sin; but after he had put off principalities and powers, all those who formerly saw him could not look upon

---

[1] Origen works out this idea in the first book of the *Commentary on St John*; for discussion of it, cf. C. Bigg, *The Christian Platonists of Alexandria* (2nd ed. 1913), pp. 209 ff.; VI, 77 and note.

[2] John xiv. 6; vi. 35; x. 9.   [3] Matt. xxvi. 48.

[4] Matt. xxvi. 55.   [5] Col. ii. 15.

him, as he no longer had anything about him that could be seen by the multitude. For this reason it was out of consideration for them that he did not appear to all after rising from the dead.

65. And why do I say 'to all'? For not even with the apostles themselves and the disciples was he always present or always apparent, because they were unable to receive his divinity without some periods of relief. After he had accomplished the work of his incarnation his divinity was more brilliant. Cephas, that is Peter, who was as it were the firstfruits of the apostles, was able to see this, and after him the twelve, Matthias having been appointed in place of Judas; and after them he appeared to more[1] than five hundred brethren at once; then he appeared to James, then to all the apostles as distinct from the twelve (probably the seventy); and last of all to Paul who, as one born out of due time, knew in what sense he meant the words, 'To me who am less than the least of all saints was this grace given.'[2] Probably the phrase 'less than the least' is equivalent to 'one born out of due time'. Therefore, as one would not easily find fault with Jesus because he did not take all the apostles up the high mountain, but only the three mentioned above, where he was to be transfigured and to show the brightness of his garments and the glory of Moses and Elijah conversing with him, so also in this instance one could not reasonably criticize the words of the apostles because they represent Jesus as having appeared after the resurrection not to all men but only to those whom he perceived to have obtained eyes which had the capacity to see his resurrection.

I think that the following saying about Jesus is helpful for the justification of the views put forward here: 'For to this end Christ died and rose again, that he might be Lord both of the dead and the living.'[3] Notice here that Jesus died that he might be Lord of the dead, and rose again that he might be Lord not only of the dead but also of the living. The apostle means by the dead of whom Christ is Lord the people enumerated as follows in the First Epistle to the Corinthians: 'For the trumpet shall sound, and the dead shall rise incorruptible.'[4] And by the living he means those who will be changed, who are not the same as the dead who will be raised. The passage referring to these comes just after the words 'the dead shall rise first' and reads thus: 'And we shall be changed.' Furthermore, in the First Epistle to the Thessalonians he makes the same distinction in different words, saying that there are two classes, those who are asleep and those who are alive. He says: 'But we would not have you ignorant, brethren, concerning them that fall asleep; that you sorrow not even as the rest who have no hope. For if we believe that Jesus died and rose

---

[1] Read ἐκείνους ⟨ὤφθη ἐπάνω⟩ with K. tr. [2] I Cor. xv. 5–8.
[3] Rom. xiv. 9. [4] I Cor. xv. 52.

again, even so those who are fallen asleep in Jesus will God bring with him. For this we say unto you by the word of the Lord, that we that are alive, that are left unto the coming of the Lord, shall in no way precede those who are fallen asleep.'[1] We set forth the explanation that seemed right to us on this subject in the commentary which we composed on the First Epistle to the Thessalonians.

66. Do not be surprised if the crowds who have believed in Jesus do not all see his resurrection, since Paul, writing to the Corinthians who were incapable of receiving greater truths, says: 'And I determined to know nothing among you save Jesus Christ and him crucified.'[2] To the same effect is the following sentence: 'For you were not yet able to bear it; and not even now are you able, for you are still carnal.'[3] Accordingly, the scripture, in which all is done by divine appointment, recorded that before his passion Jesus appeared quite generally to the crowds, although even this he did not do all the time; but that after his passion he no longer appeared in the same way, but with deliberate care measured out to each individual that which was right. Just as it is recorded that God appeared to Abraham or to one of the saints,[4] and that this appearing was not happening all the time but only at intervals, and just as He did not appear to all, so also I think that the Son of God appeared in much the same way to the apostles as God appeared to the saints in the Old Testament.

67. We have replied to the best of our ability in a treatise of this character to the criticism that *if Jesus really wanted to show forth divine power, he ought to have appeared to the very men who treated him despitefully, and to the man who condemned him and to everyone everywhere.* It would not have been right for him to have appeared to the man who condemned him and to those who treated him despitefully. For Jesus had consideration both for the one who condemned him and for those who treated him despitefully, lest they should be smitten with blindness as the men of Sodom were smitten when they conspired in lust for the beauty of the angels lodged at Lot's house. This incident is referred to in the words: 'But the men put forth their hand, and they brought Lot into the house to them, and shut the door; and they smote the men that were at the door with blindness, both small and great, so that they were exhausted in their search for the door.'[5] Jesus, then, wanted to show forth his divine power to each of those able to see it, and according to the measure of his individual capacity. In fact, perhaps he avoided appearing simply because he was considering the mean abilities of people who had not the capacity to see him.

---

[1] I Thess. iv. 13–15.   [2] I Cor. ii. 2 (Origen's standing exegesis of this text).
[3] I Cor. iii. 2–3.   [4] Cf. Gen. xii. 7; xlviii. 3.   [5] Gen. xix. 10–11.

This was a futile argument of Celsus: *For he no longer feared any man after he died and, as you say, was a god; and he was not sent at all with the intention that he might be hid.* For when he was sent into the world he did not merely make himself known; he also concealed himself.[1] For his whole nature was not known even to the people who knew him, but some part of him escaped them; and to some he was entirely unknown. But he opened the gates of light to them that were in darkness and were sons of night, and to those who devoted themselves to becoming sons of the day and the light.[2] And our Lord and Saviour came as a good physician among men laden with sins, rather than to the righteous.

68. Let us see the way in which Celsus' Jew continues: *But if he really was so great he ought, in order to display his divinity, to have disappeared suddenly from the cross.*[3] This seems to me to be like the argument of people who oppose belief in providence and describe things as other than they are in fact, and say 'it would be better if the world were such as we have described'. For where their ideas are possible, they are refuted by the fact that they make the world worse, as far as they and their description can do so; on the other hand, where they do not seem to be representing it as worse than it really is, they are proved to be desiring things which are intrinsically impossible; so that in either case they are ridiculous. In this instance also that it was not an impossibility for the divine nature that Jesus should disappear whenever he wished, is both obvious in itself and clear also from the Scripture about him—clear at least to those who do not believe some parts of the Bible in order to attack the faith, while regarding other parts as fictitious. For it is written in Luke's gospel that after the resurrection Jesus took bread and blessed and broke it, and gave it to Simon and Cleopas; and when they took the bread, 'their eyes were opened and they knew him; and he vanished out of their sight'.[4]

69. We want to show that it was not to the greater advantage of the whole purpose of the incarnation that he should have suddenly disappeared physically from the cross. The truth of the events recorded to have happened to Jesus cannot be fully seen in the mere text and historical narrative; for each event to those who read the Bible more intelligently is clearly a symbol of something as well. Thus in this way his crucifixion contains the truth indicated by the words 'I am crucified with Christ',[5] and by the sense of the words 'But God forbid that I should glory save in

[1] In Origen's view the incarnation concealed God as much as it revealed Him; cf. II, 72; IV, 15, 19.   [2] Cf. I Thess. v. 5.
[3] Cf. Philostratus' story that Apollonius of Tyana vanished before Domitian (*Vita Apollonii*, VIII, 5); Porphyry asks why Jesus did not vanish like Apollonius (*frag.* 63 Harnack).
[4] Luke xxiv. 30–1; for Simon, cf. II, 68; *Comm. in Joann.* I, 5, 8.   [5] Gal. ii. 20.

the cross of my Lord Jesus Christ, by whom the world is crucified unto
me and I unto the world.'[1] His death was necessary because 'in that he
died, he died unto sin once', and because the righteous man says that he is
'being conformed unto his death', and 'for if we die with him, we shall also
live with him'.[2] So also his burial extends to those who are conformed to
his death and crucified with him and dying with him, as Paul also says: 'For
we are buried together with him by baptism',[3] and we have risen together
with him.

We will explain the meaning of his burial and the tomb and the man
who buried him at a more suitable time at length in other writings where
it is our primary purpose to discuss these matters. At the moment,
however, it is enough to mention the linen cloth in which the pure body
of Jesus had to be wrapped up, and the new tomb which Joseph had hewn
out in the rock 'where never man had yet lain', or as John says 'in which
no man had yet been put'.[4] Notice also whether the agreement of the
three evangelists is not impressive when they take the trouble to record
that the tomb was hewn or cut out[5] in the rock, so that the man who
examines the words of the Bible might see some point worthy of comment
both on these matters and also on the newness of the tomb, which Matthew
and John mention, or on the fact that according to Luke and John no dead
man had lain there.[6] For he who was unlike other dead men, but showed
even as a corpse signs of life in the water and the blood,[7] ought as a new
dead man, so to speak, to be in a new and clean tomb. Thus, just as his birth
was purer than all other births in that he was born not of sexual intercourse
but of a virgin, so also his burial had the purity which was symbolically
shown by the fact that his body was put away in a newly made tomb; this
was not built of unhewn stones without any natural unity, but consisted
of one rock all of one piece which was cut and hewn.

However, the explanation of these points, which ascends from the
events recorded to have happened to the truths which they signified,
would be set forth at greater length and with a more spiritual interpretation at a more suitable time, when giving an account of such matters in
a volume primarily concerned with the subject. The text would be literally
interpreted in this way by saying that it was consistent with his determination to be hanged on a cross that he also kept to the results of his decision,
so that as he had been killed as a man and had died as a man, he might also
be buried as a man. But even supposing that it had been written in the
Gospels that he disappeared suddenly from the cross, Celsus and the

[1] Gal. vi. 14.   [2] Rom. vi. 10; Phil. iii. 10; II Tim. ii. 11.
[3] Rom. vi. 4.   [4] Matt. xxvii. 59–60; Luke xxiii. 53; John xix. 41.
[5] Matt. xxvii. 60; Luke xxiii. 53.
[6] Matt. xxvii. 60; John xix. 41; Luke xxiii. 53.   [7] Cf. II, 36, above.

unbelievers would have pulled it to pieces, and would have accused him as follows: Why did he disappear after arriving at the cross, when he did not do this before his passion? If they have learnt from the Gospels that *he did not suddenly disappear from the cross* and think that they can bring an accusation against the Bible because the writers did not invent (as they suppose) the story that he suddenly disappeared from the cross but told the truth, is it not reasonable to believe them also in their account of his resurrection, and that he appeared when he so desired, as when the doors had been shut and he stood in the midst of the disciples, and when having given bread to two of his friends he suddenly vanished out of their sight after saying some words to them?

70. What source had Celsus' Jew for the assertion that *Jesus hid himself?* For he says of Jesus: *But what messenger that has been sent ever hid himself when he ought to be delivering the message that he had been commanded to proclaim?* He did not hide himself, since he said to those who sought to arrest him: 'I was daily in the temple teaching openly, and you laid no hold on me.'[1] To the next objection of Celsus, which is a repetition, we have answered once and will be content with what we have already said.[2] For we replied earlier to this: *At the time when he was disbelieved while in the body, he preached without restraint to all; but when he would establish a strong faith after rising from the dead, he appeared secretly to just one woman and to those of his own confraternity.* But it is not true that he appeared to just one woman. In Matthew's gospel it is written that 'late on the sabbath day as it began to dawn toward the first day of the week, came Mary Magdalene and the other Mary to see the sepulchre; and behold there was a great earthquake; for an angel of the Lord descended from heaven and came and rolled away the stone'. And a little later Matthew says: 'And behold, Jesus met them' (clearly meaning the Marys just mentioned) 'saying, All hail; and they came and took hold of his feet and worshipped him.'[3] We also replied to this, *When he was being punished he was seen by all; but by only one person after he rose again*, when we answered the objection that he was not seen by everyone. However, we will also say here that his human characteristics were visible to all, while the divine characteristics could not be seen by all (I do not mean his characteristics as they are related to other things, but in respect of their difference from them). Notice also how Celsus at once contradicts himself. At least, although he said just now that *he appeared secretly to one woman and to his own confraternity*, he immediately goes on to say: *When he was punished he was seen by all, but by only one person after he rose again; whereas the opposite ought to have happened.* Let us hear why he thinks the

---

[1] Matt. xxvi. 55.   [2] Cf. II, 63–7.   [3] Matt. xxviii. 1–2, 9.

opposite ought to have happened, instead of his being seen by all when he was being punished, and by only one person after he rose again. As far as his words go, he wanted something both impossible and irrational, that while being punished he should have been seen by only one person and after rising again by all. Or how else will you explain the words *Whereas the opposite ought to have happened?*

71. Jesus taught us *who it was that sent him* in the words 'No man has known the Father save the Son', and in this, 'No man has seen God at any time; the only begotten God who is in the bosom of the Father, he has declared him.'[1] He revealed to his true disciples the nature of God and told them about His characteristics. We find traces of these in the scriptures and make them the starting-points of our theology. In one place we hear, 'God is light and in him is no darkness at all'; and in another place, 'God is spirit, and they that worship him must worship him in spirit and in truth.'[2] Furthermore, *the reasons why the Father sent him* are innumerable. Anyone interested may learn of these, partly from what the prophets proclaimed about him beforehand, and partly from the evangelists; and he would also learn much from the apostles and in particular from Paul. Moreover, Jesus enlightens the pious but punishes sinners, which Celsus did not see when he wrote: *And he will enlighten the pious while he will have mercy on sinners whether they repent or not.*

72. After this he says: *If he wanted to be unnoticed, why was the voice from heaven heard, proclaiming him as Son of God? Yet if he did not want to be unnoticed why was he punished or why did he die?* He thinks that by these words he can convict the scriptures about him of discrepancy, not seeing that neither did he want everything about himself known to anyone and everyone, nor that everything about him should be unnoticed. The voice from heaven proclaiming him as Son of God, which said, 'This is my beloved Son in whom I am well pleased',[3] is not recorded to have been heard by the crowds, as Celsus' Jew imagined. Furthermore, the voice out of the cloud on the very high mountain was heard only by the men who went up with him.[4] For the divine voice is such that it is heard only by those whom the speaker wishes to hear it. I have not yet mentioned that the utterance of God which is mentioned in scripture is certainly not vibrated air, or a concussion of air, or any other definition given in the text-books on sound,[5] because it is heard by a superior sense, more divine

---

[1] Matt. xi. 27; John i. 18.   [2] I John i. 5; John iv. 24.
[3] Matt. iii. 17.   [4] Matt. xvii. 5.
[5] Similarly VI, 62; Philo, *Quod Deus sit Immut.* 83. For the definitions, cf. Plato, *Timaeus,* 67B; Aristotle, *de Anima,* II, 8 (420b 5 ff.); *Probl.* XI, 23, 51 (901b 16; 904b 27); Plutarch, *Mor.* 390B; Diog. Laert. VII, 55; Diels, *Dox. Gr.* 407a, 21; 500, 14; 515, 8; 516, 8; 525, 17; Aulus Gellius V, 15, 6–8; Clem. Al. *Strom.* VI, 57, 4; Lactantius, *Opif.* xv, 1; Augustine, *de Civ. Dei,* XI, 2.

than physical hearing. And since when God speaks He does not want His voice to be audible to all, a man who has superior hearing hears God, whereas a man who has become hard of hearing in his soul does not perceive that God is speaking. I say this on account of his question: *Why was the voice from heaven heard, proclaiming him as Son of God?* But in reply to the objection, *if he did not want to be unnoticed, why was he punished and why did he die?* we said enough in our lengthy discussion above about his suffering.

73. After this Celsus' Jew draws a conclusion which does not follow at all. For it does not follow from the fact that *he wanted to teach us even to despise death by the punishments which he suffered* that *after his resurrection from the dead he ought to have called all men clearly to the light and taught them why he came down.* For he called all men to the light earlier when he said: 'Come unto me all that travail and are heavy laden, and I will give you rest.'[1] And the reason why he came down is recorded in the extensive discourses in the beatitudes and the sermon that followed them, in parables and in the addresses to the scribes and Pharisees. The greatness of his teaching is indicated[2] in John's gospel, for he shows that the eloquence of Jesus consisted not in words but in facts. And it is clear from the Gospels that 'his word was with power', at which they even marvelled.[3]

74. To all this Celsus' Jew adds: *However, these objections come from your own writings, and we need no other witness; for you provide your own refutation.* We have proved that whether Celsus' Jew has been addressing Jesus or us he has talked a lot of nonsense against our writings, the gospels. But I do not think that he has given any evidence that we provide our own refutation; he has merely stated his opinion. His Jew goes on after this: *O most high and heavenly one,*[4] *what God that comes among men is completely disbelieved?* I reply to him that according to the law of Moses God is recorded to have been most clearly present with the Hebrews not only by the signs and wonders in Egypt, and, what is more, by the way through the Red Sea and the pillar of fire and the cloud of light, but also when the Decalogue was proclaimed to the whole nation. Yet He was disbelieved by the people who knew Him. For if they had believed Him whom they had seen and heard, they would not have prepared a calf, nor have 'changed their glory into the likeness of a calf that eats hay'.[5] Nor would they have said to one another about the calf, 'These are thy gods, Israel, which led thee out of the land of Egypt.'[6] Consider also whether it

---

[1] Matt. xi. 28.
[2] Read ἐκτέθειται with K. tr.
[3] Luke iv. 32.
[4] Cf. Celsus in I, 24.
[5] Ps. cv. 20.
[6] Exod. xxxii. 4, 9.

is not characteristic of the same people that in spite of such great wonders and manifestations of God even in early times they should have disbelieved throughout the period in the wilderness, as it is written in the law of the Jews, and that at the time of the miraculous advent of Jesus they should not have been convinced by his words, which were spoken with authority, and by the miracles which he did in the sight of all the people.

75. In fact, I think that this is enough for anyone who wants an explanation of the Jews' disbelief in Jesus, that it was consistent with the behaviour of the people from the beginning as described in scripture. When Celsus' Jew says: *What God that comes among men is disbelieved, and that when he appears*[1] *to those who were waiting for him? Or why ever is he not recognized by people who had been long expecting him?* I would reply to him, Are you, sirs, prepared to reply to our questions? Which miracles seem to you to be greater in your estimation, those in Egypt and in the wilderness, or those which we say Jesus has done among you? If the former are in your judgment greater than the latter, does not that show at once that it is characteristic of the people who disbelieved the greater miracles that they should also despise the lesser? I assume that this is the view you take of the miracles of Jesus of which we are speaking. But if Jesus' miracles are said to be equal to those recorded of Moses, what an extraordinary thing is this that the people[2] should in both cases disbelieve in the beginning of God's covenants? For it was when the Mosaic law was first given that your sins of unbelief[3] are recorded to have been committed. And according to our belief it was Jesus who first gave the second law and covenant. You testify by the fact that you disbelieve in Jesus that you are sons of those in the wilderness who disbelieved the manifestations of God. Our Saviour's words will also be applied to you who have disbelieved him: 'So you are witnesses and consent to the works of your fathers.'[4] In you also is the prophecy fulfilled which says, 'Your life shall be hung before your eyes, and you will not believe your life':[5] for you did not believe the life that came to dwell among mankind.

76. In the remarks put into the mouth of the Jew Celsus was incapable of finding criticisms such as he could attribute to him in his argument which could not be brought against the Jew himself from the law and the prophets. For he finds fault with Jesus, saying of him that *he utters threats and empty abuse whenever he says, Woe unto you, and, I declare unto you.*[6] *For in these words he openly admits his inability to carry conviction, which no god, nor even a sensible man, would fail to do.* Consider whether this does

[1] H. Herter (ap. Bader, p. 82) suggests ἐπιφαινόμενος.
[2] Read λαῷ ⟨τῷ⟩ with K. tr.
[3] Omit καὶ τῶν ἁμαρτανόντων with K. tr.   [4] Matt. xxiii. 31; Luke xi. 48.
[5] Deut. xxviii. 66.   [6] Cf. Matt. xxiii. 13–29; xi. 22–5.

not come right back on the Jew. In the law and the prophets God threatens
and utters abuse whenever He speaks, in terms no less minatory than the
woes in the gospels. Such sayings occur in Isaiah, as follows: 'Woe unto
them that join house to house and lay field to field'; and 'Woe unto them
that rise up early in the morning and follow strong drink'; and 'Woe unto
them that draw iniquity after them as with a long rope'; and 'Woe unto
them that are mighty among you to drink wine.'[1] You would also find
countless other examples. Are not these much the same as the threats, as
he calls them: 'Woe unto the sinful nation, a people laden with iniquity,
an evil seed, iniquitous sons',[2] and so on? Such terrible threats follow this
that they are no less minatory in tone than those which he says Jesus
uttered. Is it not a threat, and indeed a terrible one, which says: 'Your
land shall be deserted, your cities burned with fire. As for your country
strangers shall consume it before you, and it shall be desolated, overthrown
by strange people'?[3] Are they not threats also which are uttered to the
people in Ezekiel, where the Lord is speaking to the prophet, 'You dwell
in the midst of scorpions'?[4] If, Celsus, this had dawned on you, would you
have made the Jew say of Jesus that *he utters threats and empty abuse
whenever he says, Woe unto you, and, I declare unto you?* Do you not see
that the criticisms which your Jew makes of Jesus could be brought
against him in respect of God? For it is obvious that we find God in the
prophets open to similar accusations, as the Jew thinks them, on the
ground that He is *unable to carry conviction.*

Furthermore, I would say on this subject to people who think that
Celsus' Jew scores a good point against Jesus, that there are a large number
of curses written in Leviticus and Deuteronomy. If the Jew were to
defend them and support the scripture, we would give our defence, either
by a similar argument or an even better one, of what he regards as *abuse
and threats* uttered by Jesus. Moreover, where the Mosaic law is concerned
we are better able to give a defence than the Jew, in that we have been
taught by Jesus to understand the law more intelligently. Furthermore, if
the Jew perceives the meaning of the prophetic sayings, he will be able to
show[5] that God does not *utter empty threats and abuse* when he says *Woe*
and, *I declare unto you*, and will show how God says such things in order
to convert men, although Celsus thinks that *not even a sensible man* would
have done that. But Christians, who hold that it is the same God who
spoke in the prophets and in the Lord, will prove the reasonableness of
what Celsus regards as *threats* and of what he calls *abuse.*

[1] Isa. v. 8, 11, 18, 20, 22.   [2] Isa. i. 4.
[3] Isa. i. 7.   [4] Ezek. ii. 6.
[5] Read παραστῆσαι with Del., We., and τό with Bo., We.

I will address a few remarks on this subject to Celsus, who professes to be a philosopher and also to know our beliefs: If, sir, Hermes says to Odysseus in Homer,

> Unhappy man, why are you going alone through the hills?[1]

are you content to defend this by saying that the Homeric Hermes says such things to Odysseus with the intention of warning him? For to flatter and compliment is the part of the Sirens, with whom there is

> A heap of bones all around,

and who say,

> Come hither, famous Odysseus, great glory of the Achaeans.[2]

On the other hand, if my prophets and Jesus himself with a view to the conversion of their hearers utter the word *Woe* and the *abuse*, as you regard it, is there in the use of such words no accommodation to the capacity of the hearers, and does he not apply such a warning to them as a healing medicine? Perhaps, however, you want God, or him who shares in the divine nature, in addressing mankind to consider only His real nature and what is worthy of Himself, and no more to consider what is suitable for proclamation to men who are under the care and guidance of His Logos, and what may be appropriately addressed to each individual according to his fundamental character. Moreover, is not his remark ludicrous that Jesus was *unable to carry conviction?* For it applies just as much not only to the Jew who has a lot of sayings like these in the prophets, but also the Greeks. Among the latter none of those who have made a great reputation for their wisdom has been able to carry conviction with those who conspired against him, or with his judges or accusers, so that they cease from evil and follow the path to virtue by philosophy.

77. After this his Jew says, obviously as though[3] his remark were consistent with the doctrine of the Jews: *We hope, it is true, to be resurrected in the body and to have everlasting life, and that he who is sent to us will be a pattern and leader of this by showing that it is not impossible for God to raise someone up again with his body.* We are not aware that a Jew would say that the expected Christ would show in himself an example of the resurrection; but suppose that he does, and that he would both think and say this. And when he says that he has *quoted to us from our own books* we would answer him: Sir, you may have read those books by which you suppose that you can accuse us, but did you study in detail the resurrection

---

[1] Homer, *Od.* x, 281. Hermes warns Odysseus of the wiles of Circe.
[2] Homer, *Od.* xii, 45, 184.
[3] Origen's reply suggests that here we should read ⟨ὡς⟩ κατά.

of Jesus and understand that he is firstborn from the dead?'[1] Or, just because you are unwilling to believe it, was nothing said about this? However, as Celsus' Jew continues by allowing the resurrection of bodies, I do not think that it is now a good opportunity to discuss this matter in detail with one who both believes and says that there is a resurrection of bodies, whether he has a clear conception of this doctrine and is able to give a good explanation of it, or whether he cannot and merely gives his assent to the doctrine with a superficial understanding of it.

Such, then, may be our reply to Celsus' Jew. After this he says: *Where is he then, that we may see and believe?* We would reply, *Where is he* now who spoke by the prophets and did wonders, *that we may see and believe* that you are the 'portion' of God?[2] Or are you allowed to give a defence of the fact that God is not always appearing to the Hebrew race, while we are not granted the same right in the case of Jesus? For he once both rose again and convinced his disciples about his resurrection, and convinced them to such an extent that they show to all men by their sufferings that they are looking for eternal life and for the resurrection which has been exemplified before them in word and deed, and that they deride all the troubles of life.

78. After this the Jew says: *Or was his purpose in coming down that we might disbelieve?* My reply to this is as follows: He did not come with the aim of bringing about the unbelief of the Jews, but by his foreknowledge he foretold that this would happen and used the unbelief of the Jews to call the Gentiles. For by their sin 'salvation is come to the Gentiles',[3] of whom Christ said in the prophets, 'A people that I have not known shall serve me; to the hearing of the ear they were obedient'; and 'I was found by them who sought me not, I appeared for those who asked not for me.'[4] It is clear that the Jews received their punishment in this life after having treated Jesus as they did. Let the Jews answer us when their critics[5] say: 'The providence of God and His loving care are indeed amazing to you, seeing that you are liable to punishment, and have been deprived even of Jerusalem and of the so-called sanctuary and most solemn worship.' But whatever they say in defence of God's providence, we will give a stronger and better argument by affirming that God's providence has been amazing in that He has made use of the sin of the Jews to call the people of the Gentiles into the kingdom of God by Jesus, although they were strangers to the covenants and were not included in the promises.[6] This also was foretold by the prophets, that through the sins of the Hebrew

[1] Cf. Col. i. 18; Rev. i. 5.
[2] Israel is God's portion, Deut. xxxii. 9. Read ἐστὲ with Bo.   [3] Rom. xi 11.
[4] II Sam. xxii. 44-5; Isa. lxv. 1.   [5] Read ἡμῖν ἐὰν ⟨οἱ⟩.   [6] Cf. Eph. ii. 12.

people God would choose out, not one nation, but picked men from all places, and that after choosing 'the foolish things of this world'[1] He would make the 'foolish nation' to inherit the divine words, the kingdom of God being taken from one and given to the other. At present it is enough to quote out of several prophecies the one from the song in Deuteronomy about the calling of the Gentiles, where the Lord is speaking. It reads as follows: 'For they have moved me to jealousy with those that are no gods, they have provoked me to anger with their idols; and I will move them to jealousy with those which are not a people, I will provoke them to anger with a foolish nation.'[2]

79. The Jew then concludes all this by saying about Jesus: *However, he was a mere man, and of such a character as the truth itself makes obvious and as reason shows.* If he was a mere man, I do not know how he ventured to spread his religion and teaching in all the world, and was able to do what he desired without God's help and to rise above all the people opposing the spread of his teaching—kings, governors, the Roman Senate, rulers everywhere, and the common people.[3] How is it possible for a natural man with nothing more than that about him to convert such a vast multitude? It would not be remarkable if only some of the intelligent people were converted. But there are also some of the most irrational people and those most subject to their passions, who on account of their lack of reason are changed to a more self-controlled life with greater difficulty. However, as Christ was the power of God and the wisdom of the Father,[4] on this account he accomplished this, and is still doing so, even if neither Jews nor Greeks are willing to accept him because they disbelieve his word.

We, therefore, will not cease to believe in God in the way Jesus Christ has taught us, and to desire the conversion of people who are blind where religion is concerned, even if those who are in reality blind themselves abuse us as though we were blind, and if those, whether Jews or Greeks, who themselves beguile people who agree with them, attack us as though we beguiled men. Indeed it is fine beguiling which aims to make men become controlled instead of licentious or at least making progress in self-control, and righteous instead of unrighteous or making progress in that direction, and sensible instead of stupid or on the road to good sense; instead of being cowardly, mean, and unmanly, men become brave and bold; and they show this particularly in their struggles for piety towards the God who created all things. Accordingly, Jesus Christ came after being proclaimed beforehand, not just by one prophet, but by all. This too was

---

[1] I Cor. i. 27.　　　　　　　　　　　　[2] Deut. xxxii. 21.
[3] Wif. reads δήμων, perhaps rightly.　　[4] I Cor. i. 24.

the result of Celsus' ignorance, that he put into the Jew's mouth that *one prophet* had foretold the Christ.[1]

Celsus' Jew has been introduced as saying these things as if, indeed, they were consistent with his own law. And since he has just about ended his argument, and says nothing else worth mentioning, I also will end at this point the second book of my reply to his treatise. If God grants it, and if the power of Christ dwells in my soul, I will try in the third book to deal with the next objections in Celsus' attack.

[1] Cf. I, 49; II, 4.

BOOK III

1. In the first of our replies to the book which Celsus composed against us, which he boastfully entitled *The True Doctrine*, to the best of our ability, as you commanded, most Christian Ambrose, we dealt with his preface and the subsequent arguments,[1] testing each objection, and we ended with the fictitious harangue which his Jew addressed to Jesus. In the second we did our best to answer all the similar remarks which his Jew addressed to us who believe in God through Christ. We now begin the third book, in which it is our object to contest the points which he makes in his own person. He says now that *Christians and Jews quarrel with one another very foolishly,* and that *our wrangle with one another about Christ is no different from that called in the proverb a fight about the shadow of an ass.*[2] And he thinks *there is nothing worthy of attention in the dispute of Jews and Christians with one another, since they both believe that by divine inspiration a certain saviour was prophesied to be coming to dwell among mankind; but they do not agree as to whether the one prophesied has come or not.* For we Christians have believed that Jesus is the one who has come in accordance with the prophecies; whereas most of the Jews are so far from believing in him that those of that time conspired against Jesus, and those of our own time are delighted by what the Jews dared to do against him then, and accuse Jesus of having used some sort of sorcery to pretend that perhaps he was the one whom the prophecies proclaimed as the coming one, traditionally called Christ by the Jews.

2. Let Celsus and people who agree with his criticisms of us tell us whether it seems like the shadow of an ass that the prophets of the Jews foretold the birthplace of him who would be ruler of those who live good lives and are called God's portion,[3] and that a virgin should conceive Emmanuel, that signs and wonders of a certain kind would be done by the prophesied Christ, that his word would run so swiftly that the voice of his apostles would go forth into all the earth; and that they predicted the sufferings that he would endure after his condemnation by the Jews, and how he would rise again.[4] Did the prophets merely say whatever occurred to them without any conviction to impel them not only to say these things but also to consider them worth writing down? And[5] was it without any

---

[1] Read ⟨τὰ⟩ ἑξῆς.
[2] Proverbial for a dispute about nothing; cf. Plato, *Phaedrus*, 260 c; Dio Chrys. xxxiv, 48; etc.
[3] Deut. xxxii. 9.
[4] Mic. v. 2; Isa. vii. 14; Ps. cxlvii. 4; xviii. 5; Isa. liii. 5; Ps. xv. 10.
[5] Read ὅρά γε with K. tr.

conviction that the mighty race of the Jews, who had in olden times taken the land as their own home, called some men prophets while they rejected others as false prophets? Was it nothing to them that they were led to include with the books of Moses believed to be sacred the utterances of men of a later age who were regarded as prophets? Can those who accuse Jews and Christians of foolishness explain to us how the Jewish nation could have held together if nobody among them could proclaim the future and possessed foreknowledge? And how was it that, while the surrounding nations believed that they received oracles and divination from the beings regarded by them as gods, each one according to its ancestral traditions, yet the Jews alone, who had been taught to despise all the beings considered among the nations to be gods on the ground that they are not gods but daemons (since their prophets said, 'All the gods of the nations are daemons'),[1] had no one who professed to be a prophet and could dissuade people who wanted to know the future from a desire to go off to the daemons of other nations? Consider therefore whether it is not necessary that a whole nation which is taught to despise the gods of other nations should have had plenty of prophets, who made it quite obvious that their prophetic power was superior and far better than the oracles everywhere else.

3. Again, if miracles have occurred everywhere or in many places, as even Celsus thinks, quoting later[2] the instances of *Asclepius who did good and foretold the future to whole cities which were dedicated to him such as Tricca, Epidaurus, Cos, and Pergamum,* and of *Aristeas the Proconnesian, a certain Clazomenian, and Cleomedes the Astypalean,* yet are we to suppose that among the Jews alone, who say that they are dedicated to the God of the universe, there was no sign or wonder to strengthen and confirm their faith in the Creator of the universe and their hope of another and a better life? How is such a thing possible? For they would at once have changed to the worship of the daemons who uttered oracles and wrought cures, and would have deserted the God who in theory was believed to help them, but who gave no practical manifestation of Himself at all. But since this did not occur, and they endured countless sufferings to avoid renouncing Judaism and their law, as at the time when they suffered in Assyria, and in Persia, and under Antiochus, is it not proved by probability to those who disbelieve in the miraculous histories and prophecies that these things are not inventions, but that a divine spirit dwelling in the pure souls of the prophets, who underwent any trouble for the sake of virtue, impelled them to prophesy some things for their contemporaries and others for posterity, and above all to prophesy concerning *a certain saviour who would come to dwell among mankind?*

[1] Ps. xcv. 5.   [2] Cf. III, 22, 24, 26.

4. If this is the case, how can it be true that Jews and Christians *wrangle with one another about the shadow of an ass* when from the prophecies in which they both believe they examine the question whether the prophesied Christ has come, or whether he has not come at all and is still being awaited? Even supposing that it were granted to Celsus that the one whom the prophets proclaimed was not Jesus, even so it is just as true that the dispute about the meaning of the prophetic scriptures is not one about the shadow of an ass. We seek to have clear evidence about the person proclaimed beforehand, and to find out what kind of person was prophesied, what he is to do, and, if possible, when also he will come. We said earlier that Jesus was the prophesied Christ and quoted a few out of several prophecies on this point.[1] Accordingly, neither Jews nor Christians make any mistake in believing that the prophets spoke by divine inspiration, although they are wrong in holding the mistaken opinion that the prophesied Christ is still awaited, whose identity and origin have been proclaimed in accordance with the true meaning of the prophets.

5. In his next remarks Celsus imagines that *the Jews were Egyptian by race, and left Egypt after revolting against the Egyptian community and despising the religious customs of Egypt.*[2] He says that *what they did to the Egyptians they suffered in turn through those who followed Jesus and believed him to be the Christ; in both instances a revolt against the community led to the introduction of new ideas.* Notice what Celsus has done here. The ancient Egyptians much ill-treated the Hebrew race who came to live in Egypt on account of a famine that had overtaken Judaea; and as men who had wronged strangers and suppliants they suffered the punishment which by divine providence the whole nation had to bear, since they had conspired against the whole nation who were their guests, although they had done the Egyptians no harm. After they had been smitten with plagues by God they reluctantly and grudgingly[3] let those whom they had wrongly enslaved go where they liked. Accordingly, because they are selfish and give honour to any of their own kin in preference to more righteous strangers, there is no accusation which they have failed to bring against Moses and the Hebrews. For although they do not entirely deny the wonderful miracles done by Moses, they allege that they were done by sorcery and not by divine power. But Moses was not a sorcerer but a pious man, dedicated to the God of the universe; and partaking of a divine spirit, he gave laws to the Hebrews as God prompted him, and recorded events as they actually happened.

[1] Cf. I, 51, 53–4.
[2] Celsus uses here current anti-Jewish propaganda; cf. Apion ap. Jos. *c. Ap.* II, 3, 28; Strabo, XVI, 11, 35–6 (p. 761), and ap. Jos. *Antiq.* XIV, 7, 2, 118.
[3] Read καὶ μετὰ πολὺ with Wif.

6. Celsus was not impartial in his examination of the facts which are interpreted in one way by the Egyptians and in another by the Hebrews, but was prejudiced as though by Egyptian spells. Although they had wronged their guests he believed them to be speaking the truth, while he said that the Hebrews, who were the wronged party, had revolted and left Egypt. He failed to see that it was impossible for such a seditious multitude of Egyptians, who originated as the result of a revolt, to have become a nation at the very moment of their rebellion and to have changed their language, so that people who hitherto had been speaking Egyptian suddenly spoke Hebrew and nothing else.[1] But for the purposes of argument suppose that they did leave Egypt and even hated the language in which they had been brought up; how then is it that after this they did not speak the language of the Syrians or Phoenicians, but composed Hebrew which is different from both of these? My argument aims at proving the falsehood of the assertion that *certain people who were Egyptian by race revolted against the Egyptians and left Egypt, and came to Palestine where they inhabited the part now called Judaea.* For the Hebrews had their traditional language before they went down to Egypt, and Hebrew letters were different from those of the Egyptians; Moses used them when he wrote the five books which the Jews believe to be sacred.

7. Just as it is false that the Hebrews, being Egyptians, originated from a revolt, it is equally false that others who were Jews revolted at the time of Jesus against the Jewish community and followed Jesus. Celsus and people who think as he does will not be able to show any sign of a revolt. If a revolt had been the cause of the Christians existing as a separate group (and they originated from the Jews for whom it was lawful to take up arms in defence of their families and to serve in the wars), the lawgiver of the Christians would not have forbidden entirely the taking of human life. He taught that it was never right for his disciples to go so far against a man, even if he should be very wicked; for he did not consider it compatible with his inspired legislation to allow the taking of human life in any form at all. Moreover, if Christians had originated from a revolt, they would not have submitted to laws which were so gentle, which caused them to be killed 'as sheep',[2] and made them unable ever to defend themselves against their persecutors.[3] However, a more profound study of this question enables us to say of the people who came out of the land of Egypt, that it would be amazing if the whole people had taken up

---

[1] Cf. Gregory of Nyssa, *c. Eunomium* II, 256 (Jaeger, i, 288): 'Some of those who have carefully studied the scriptures say that the Hebrew language is not ancient like the others, but that along with the other miracles which happened to the Israelites this also occurred, that this language was suddenly improvised by the nation after leaving Egypt.'

[2] Ps. xliii. 23 (Rom. viii. 36).   [3] On this section see p. 512.

Hebrew all at once, as though the language had come down from heaven. So also one of their prophets said: 'In their going out of the land of Egypt he heard a language which he did not know.'[1]

8. In this way also we may establish that those who came out of Egypt with Moses were not Egyptians. If they had been Egyptians, their names must have been Egyptian, because in each language names are of the same type as the vernacular. But it is obvious that they were not Egyptians from the fact that the names are Hebrew (for the Bible is full of Hebrew names even of those in Egypt who gave such names to their sons). If so, then clearly the assertion of the Egyptians is false that those who were driven out of Egypt with Moses were Egyptians; and it is perfectly clear that they were descended from Hebrew stock according to the history recorded by Moses, and that they spoke their own language which they also employed to give names to their sons. Concerning the Christians, on the other hand, we say that they have been taught not to defend themselves against their enemies; and because they have kept the laws which command gentleness and love to man, on this account they have received from God[2] that which they could not have succeeded in doing if they had been given the right to make war, even though they may have been quite able to do so. He always fought for them and from time to time stopped the opponents of the Christians and the people who wanted to kill them. For a few, whose number could be easily enumerated, have died occasionally for the sake of the Christian religion by way of reminder to men that when they see a few striving for piety they may become more steadfast and may despise death. But God prevented their whole race from being annihilated because He wanted it to be established and the whole world to be filled by this most pious teaching of salvation. And again, that the weaker men might recover from anxiety about death, God's providence has cared for believers; for by His will alone He has dispersed all the opposition to them, so that kings and local governors and the common people were unable to be too violently inflamed against them. This is my reply to Celsus' assertion that a revolt was the origin of the establishment of the Jews in ancient times, and later of the existence of the Christians.

9. As in what follows he lies blatantly, come, let us quote his words: *If all men wanted to be Christians, the Christians would no longer want them.* That this is a lie is obvious from the fact that as far as they are able Christians leave no stone unturned to spread the faith in all parts of the world. Some, in fact, have done the work of going round not only cities but even villages and country cottages to make others also pious towards God.

[1] Ps. lxxx. 6.   [2] After ἤνυσαν read comma for colon with We., K. tr.

One could not say that they did this for the sake of wealth, since sometimes they do not even accept money for the necessities of life, and if ever they are compelled to do so by want in this respect, they are content with what is necessary and no more, even if several people are willing to share with them and to give them more than they need. I admit that at the present time perhaps, when on account of the multitude of people coming to the faith even rich men and persons in positions of honour, and ladies of refinement and high birth, favourably regard adherents of the faith, one might venture to say that some become leaders of the Christian teaching for the sake of a little prestige.[1] Yet at the beginning when there was great risk attached particularly to teachers, no such suspicion could be reasonably entertained. Even now, however, the disgrace among the rest of society is greater than the supposed reputation among fellow-believers, and this does not exist in every case. It is therefore a blatant lie that *if all men wanted to be Christians, the Christians would no longer want them.*

10. Consider also what he asserts to be evidence for this: *When they were beginning,* he says, *they were few and were of one mind; but since they have spread to become a multitude, they are divided and rent asunder, and each wants to have his own party. For they wanted this from the beginning.* It is clear that in comparison with the multitudes later the Christians were few when they began; yet they were not so few when all things are considered. For the point which aroused envy against Jesus and provoked the Jews to conspire against him was the multitude of people who followed him into the wilderness; four and five thousand men used to follow him, not counting women and children. There was such a charm in Jesus' words that not only men wanted to follow him into the deserts but women too, disregarding[2] their feminine weakness and outward propriety in following the teacher into the wilderness; and children, who are usually quite unmoved, went after him with their fathers and mothers, either because they were following their parents, or perhaps even because they were led on by his divinity so that some divine seed might be implanted in them. But even if we allow that they were few at the beginning, why does this support his assertion that Christians would not want to make all men believe the gospel?

11. He also says that *they were of one mind,* not seeing even here that from the outset there were disagreements among the believers about the interpretation of the books regarded as divine. At least, when the apostles were preaching and the eyewitnesses of Jesus were teaching his precepts,

[1] Cf. III, 30, below.
[2] The text of A (ὑποτεμνομένας) is impossible; the above translation reads ὑπομεμνημένας with Bo., Del., K. tr. Possibly Origen wrote ὑποτιμωμένας, 'not alleging as an excuse' (so F. J. A. Hort, ap. Selwyn in *Journal of Philology*, v (1874), p. 250).

no minor dispute in the Church took place among the Jewish believers
about those of the Gentiles who were converted to the faith; the question
was whether they ought to keep the Jewish customs, or if the burden of
clean and unclean meats ought to be taken away so that it would not be
a load upon those Gentiles who abandoned their traditional customs and
believed in Jesus.[1] Furthermore, in the Epistles of Paul, who was contemporary with those who had seen Jesus, there are some statements to be
found which concern certain disputes about the resurrection, and about
the view that it had already occurred, and about the question whether the
day of the Lord was already present or not.[2] Moreover, the words
'Turning away from the profane babblings and oppositions of the knowledge which is falsely so-called, which some have professed and made
shipwreck concerning the faith',[3] show that from the beginning there
were certain varieties of interpretation, although there were not yet, as
Celsus thinks, many who believed.

12. Then as though it was a criticism of the gospel he reproaches us
for the sects within Christianity, saying: *But since they have spread to
become a multitude, they are divided and rent asunder, and each wants to have
his own party.* He says that *they are divided again by becoming too numerous,
and condemn one another; they only have one thing still in common, so to
speak, if indeed they have that—the name. And, in spite of all this, this alone
are they ashamed to desert; in other respects, they are at sixes and sevens.* To
this we will reply that any teaching which has had a serious origin, and
is beneficial to life, has caused different sects.[4] For since medicine is
beneficial and essential to mankind, and there are many problems in it as
to the method of curing bodies, on this account several sects in medicine
are admittedly found among the Greeks, and, I believe, also among the
barbarians such as profess to practise medicine. And again, since philosophy which professes to possess the truth and knowledge of realities
instructs us how we ought to live and tries to teach what is beneficial to
our race, and since the problems discussed allow of considerable diversity
of opinion, on this account very many sects indeed have come into existence,
some of which are well known, while others are not. Moreover, there
was in Judaism a factor which caused sects to begin, which was the variety
of the interpretations of the writings of Moses and the sayings of the
prophets. So then, since Christianity appeared to men as something worthy

[1] Acts x. 14; xi. 8; xv. 28.   [2] I Cor. xv. 12 ff.; II Tim. ii. 18; I Thess. v. 2.
[3] I Tim. vi. 20–1; i. 19.
[4] For the argument, cf. II, 27; v, 61; Clem. Al. *Strom.* VII, 89 ff.; Isid. Pelus. *Ep.* IV, 55
(*P.G.* LXXVIII, 1105). The background is probably the Sceptic contention that because on
all serious questions philosophers disagree one can only suspend judgment; Sextus Emp.
P.H. I, 165; Philo, *de Ebrietate* 198 ff. (Aenesidemus).

of serious attention, not only to people of the lower classes as Celsus thinks, but also to many scholars among the Greeks, sects inevitably came to exist, not at all on account of factions and love of strife, but because several learned men made a serious attempt to understand the doctrines of Christianity. The result of this was that they interpreted differently the scriptures universally believed to be divine, and sects arose named after those who, although they admired the origin of the word, were impelled by certain reasons which convinced them to disagree with one another. But the sects in medicine would be no good reason for avoiding it; nor would anyone who was endeavouring to act rightly hate philosophy, alleging the existence of many sects as an excuse for his hatred of it. Similarly, the sacred books of Moses and of the prophets ought not to be despised because of the sects among the Jews.

13. If this argument is logical, why may we not make a similar reply concerning the sects among the Christians. It seems to me that Paul's words on this subject are quite admirable: 'For there must also be heresies among you, that they which are approved may be made manifest among you.'[1] The man who is qualified in medicine is he who is trained in the various sects and who after examining the several schools of thought with an open mind chooses the best; and a man who is well advanced in philosophy is he who by having known about several schools of thought is trained in them and follows the doctrine which has convinced him. So also I would say that a man who looks carefully into the sects of Judaism and Christianity becomes a very wise Christian. Anyone who criticizes Christianity on account of the sects might also criticise the teaching of Socrates; for from his instruction many schools have come into being, whose adherents do not hold the same opinions. Furthermore, one might criticize Plato for his doctrines on the ground that Aristotle left his instruction and introduced new ideas; we mentioned this above.[2] But I think that Celsus has come to know of certain heresies which do not share with us even the name of Jesus. Probably he got wind of the so-called Ophites and Cainites, or some other such doctrine which has entirely abandoned Jesus. But this is irrelevant to a criticism of the doctrine of Christians.

14. After this he says: *Their agreement is quite amazing—the more so as it may be proved to rest on no trustworthy foundation. However, they have a trustworthy foundation for their unity in revolt and the advantage which it brings and in the fear of outsiders. These are factors which strengthen their faith.* We will reply to this that our agreement is based on such an important foundation, or rather not on a foundation but on a divine action, that

[1] I Cor. xi. 19.   [2] II, 12.

its origin was God who taught men by the prophets to wait for the advent of Christ who would save men. In so far as this is not really refuted, even if it may seem to be refuted by the unbelievers, so much the more is the doctrine established as the doctrine of God, and Jesus is proved to be Son of God both before and after his incarnation. But I affirm that even after his incarnation he is always found to be most divine in character by people who have very sharp eyes in their soul, and to have truly descended to us from God, and not to have owed his origin or development to human sagacity but to God's manifestation; for it was He who by varied wisdom and various miracles established Judaism in the first place, and later Christianity. However, Celsus' idea that a revolt and the advantage which it brings were the originating cause is also refuted by the fact that the gospel reforms and improves so many people.

15. That not even the fear of outsiders maintains our unity is clear from the fact that by the will of God this has ceased for a long time now. It is, however, probable that the freedom of believers from anxiety for their lives will come to an end when again those who attack Christianity in every possible way regard the multitude of believers as responsible for the rebellion which is so strong at this moment,[1] thinking that it is because they are not being persecuted by the governors as they used to be. But we have learned from Christianity neither to slack off in time of peace and to give ourselves to relaxation, nor when persecuted by the world to lose heart and to give up the love of the God of the universe in Jesus Christ. We clearly show the sacred character of our origin, and do not *conceal* it, as Celsus thinks, since even in people only just converted we inculcate a scorn of idols and all images, and in addition to this raise their thoughts from serving created things in the place of God and lift them up to the Creator of the universe. We openly set forth him who was foretold, both on the ground of the prophecies about him (and there are many of them) and from the tested traditions handed on by those able to receive them intelligently, namely the gospels and utterances of the apostles.

16. Let anyone who likes show what sort of *miscellaneous ideas* we *use to persuade men to follow us*, or what *terrors* we *invent*, as Celsus writes, though he gives no proof. Perhaps, however, Celsus wants to give the name *invented terrors* to the doctrine that God is a Judge and that men are judged for all their deeds, although it can be supported on various grounds, partly from the Bible and partly from rational probability. And yet towards the end (for we have a love for the truth) Celsus says: *God forbid*

---

[1] See Introduction, p. xiv. For the pagan view that Christians were the cause of catastrophes, see Origen, *Comm. ser. in Matt.* 39; Melito ap. Eus. *H.E.* IV, 26; Tertullian, *Apol.* 40; Arnobius, I, 4; Augustine, *de Civ. Dei*, II, 3; and for the Christian view that they are caused by an excessive number of bad Christians, Salvian, *de Gubernatione Dei*.

that they or I or any other man should do away with the doctrine that the unrighteous will be punished and that the righteous will be deemed worthy of rewards. If, then, you except[1] the doctrine of punishment, what terrors do we invent that we may persuade men to follow us? Furthermore, he says that *with these we combine misunderstandings of the ancient tradition,*[2] *and we overwhelm*[3] *men beforehand by playing flutes and music like the priests of Cybele who with their clamour stupefy the people whom they wish to excite into a frenzy.* We reply to him: What sort of ancient tradition is it of which we have misunderstandings? Whether he means the Greek tradition which taught the existence of law-courts under the earth, or the Jewish which among other things prophesied about the life following this one, he would not be able to prove that we have misunderstood the truth, and that we live according to doctrines of this nature—not, at any rate, those of us who endeavour to believe rationally.

17. He wants to put the doctrines of our faith on a level with the religion of the Egyptians: *Confronting the man who approaches their shrines the Egyptians have magnificent precincts, a sacred close, a fine great entrance, wonderful temples, splendid tents all around, and very superstitious and mysterious rites. But when he enters and goes inside he sees a cat being worshipped, or a monkey, or a crocodile, or a goat, or a dog.*[4] But what do we possess which is comparable to the Egyptians' devices to impress people who approach their shrines, and what that is comparable to the irrational animals which are worshipped inside after passing the splendid gateway? Are we to think[5] that the prophecies and the supreme God and the condemnations of images are in his opinion objects of worship, and that Jesus Christ crucified is comparable to an irrational animal that is worshipped? If this is his meaning (I do not think he would say anything else), we will answer that above[6] we argued at length about the things which happened to Jesus to prove that even the disasters, as they seem from a human point of view, which befell him brought benefit to the universe and salvation to the world.

[1] Read ἀφέλῃς with H. Herter, *Theol. Literaturzeitung*, LXIX, col. 73 (March 1944). If ἀνέλῃς is kept, read ἐὰν ⟨μή⟩ with Wif.: 'if you do not deny...'. For Celsus' belief in punishment, cf. VIII, 48–9.

[2] Cf. Plato, *Laws* 716c, D; *Ep.* VII, 335 A 'We ought always to believe truly in the ancient and sacred doctrines (τοῖς παλαιοῖς τε καὶ ἱεροῖς λόγοις) which declare to us that the soul is immortal and has judges and pays the greatest penalties whenever a soul is released from the body.'

[3] Read perhaps προκατέχομεν. For threats of torment in the mystery-religions, cf. Celsus in IV, 10.

[4] Celsus uses a literary commonplace about Egyptian religion; cf. Lucian, *Imagines*, 11; Clem. Al. *Paed.* III, 4; Palladius, *Dialogus de Vita S. Joannis Chrysostomi*, IV, p. 27 (ed. Coleman-Norton).

[5] Read ⟨νοεῖν⟩ ἐστι with Wif.

[6] I, 54, 61; II, 16, 23.

18. Then concerning the practices of the Egyptians who use fine words even about irrational animals and affirm that they are certain symbols of God, or whatever name their so-called prophets care to give them, he says that *they produce an impression on people who have learnt these matters that they have not been initiated in vain.* But concerning the truths in our teachings which are shown to those who are learned in Christian doctrine by reason of the spiritual gift, as Paul calls it, which consists in the word of wisdom through the spirit and in the word of knowledge according to the spirit,[1] Celsus seems to me not even to have grasped the first idea. I base my opinion not only on what he says here, but also on his later criticism of the Christian system, when he says that *they drive away every intelligent man from arguing about this faith, and invite only the stupid and low-class folk.* We shall consider this at the right time when we come to the passage.[2]

19. Moreover, he says that we *mock the Egyptians[3] although they show many profound mysteries and teach that such worship is respect to invisible ideas and not, as most people think, to ephemeral animals; and he says that we are silly since we introduce in our explanation about Jesus nothing more worthy of attention than the goats and dogs of the Egyptians.* To this we will reply: My good man, you commend the Egyptians with good reason for showing *many mysteries which are not evil,* and *obscure explanations* about their animals; but you do not act as you should do in criticizing us, since you are convinced that we say nothing except all that is irrational and vulgar, when in accordance with the wisdom of the word we discuss in detail with those who are perfect in Christianity the doctrines about Jesus. Paul teaches that such people are capable of understanding the wisdom in Christianity when he says: 'But we speak wisdom among the perfect; yet a wisdom not of this world, nor of the rulers of this world who are coming to nought. But we speak God's wisdom in a mystery, even the wisdom which has been hidden, which God foreordained before the worlds unto our glory, which none of the rulers of this world knew.'[4]

20. We say to people who agree with Celsus: Did Paul have no idea of any superior wisdom when he professed to speak 'wisdom among the perfect'? He would say, in his reckless way, that though Paul professed this claim he knew nothing of wisdom; we would reply to him as follows: First, understand clearly the epistles of the man who says this, and look

---

[1] I Cor. xii. 8.   [2] Cf. III, 44, 50, 55, 74.

[3] Mockery at Egyptian animal-worship is common in the Apologists; see the vast list of references in J. B. Lightfoot, *The Apostolic Fathers*, part II, vol. II, pp. 510 ff. For Egyptian rationalization, cf. Porphyry, *de Abstinentia* IV, 9. The argument was part of the Academic-Sceptic polemic against traditional religion (e.g. Sextus Emp. *P.H.* III, 219) which was taken over by the Jews (e.g. Jos. *c. Ap.* II, 7, 81; Aristeas, 138) and so passed to the Christians.

[4] I Cor. ii. 6–8.

carefully into the meaning of each word in them, for example, in the Epistles to the Ephesians, the Colossians, the Thessalonians, the Philippians, and the Romans; then show both that you have understood Paul's words, and that you can show some to be *silly* or foolish. If he devotes himself to attentive reading, I know well that either he will admire the mind of the man who uses an ordinary vocabulary to contemplate great truths, or, if he does not do that, will himself appear ludicrous, whether he explains what he has understood of the man's meaning, or attempts to oppose and refute what he imagined he had understood.

21. I have not yet mentioned also the careful study of everything written in the gospels. Each saying possesses a great meaning, hard to perceive[1] not only for the multitude but even for some of the intelligent, together with a most profound interpretation of the parables. Jesus spoke these to the people outside, and kept their explanation for those who had advanced beyond exoteric understanding and who came to him privately 'in the house'.[2] Celsus would be amazed if he understood what meaning there is in the fact that some are said to be outside and others 'in the house'. Again, who would not be astounded if he could see the changes of Jesus when he ascends the mountain to preach certain doctrines or to do certain things or for his transfiguration, while down below he heals the weak who are not able to ascend where his disciples follow him?[3] But now it is not the right time to discuss here the truths of the gospels which really are solemn[4] and divine, or the mind of Christ,[5] that is of wisdom and of the Logos, in Paul. However, this is enough in reply to the unphilosophical mockery of Celsus, who likens the inner mysterious doctrines of the Church of God to the Egyptians' cats or monkeys or crocodiles or goats or dogs.

22. Celsus, the coarse fellow, does not omit any kind of mockery and ridicule of us in his argument against us, and mentions *the Dioscuri, Heracles, Asclepius, and Dionysus,*[6] men who were believed by the Greeks to have become gods. He says that we *do not tolerate the opinion that they are gods because they were human in the first place,*[7] *even though they performed many noble acts on behalf of mankind; yet we say that after Jesus died he appeared to his own confraternity.*[8] He also accuses us of saying that *he appeared even then only as a phantom.* We would answer to this that

---

[1] Cf. Heb. v. 11.   [2] Matt. xiii. 36.   [3] See II, 64 f.
[4] Celsus' word in III, 19.   [5] I Cor. ii. 16.
[6] These are stock instances in the Apologists' polemic (e.g. Clem. Al. *Protr.* 30; Minucius Felix XXIII, 7) derived from the old Sceptic arguments. Cf. J. Geffcken, *Zwei griechische Apologeten*, pp. 225 f., on Athenagoras, *Leg.* 29.
[7] Read καὶ πρῶτον with Bo., Bader. K. tr. suggests καὶ τρωτοί.
[8] Cf. Celsus in II, 70.

Celsus was clever in that he neither showed clearly that he does not reverence them as gods (for he had an eye to the opinion of those who would read his book, who would suspect him of atheism if[1] he were to put forward his true opinion), nor again did he pretend that he himself thought they were gods; for we could have given an answer to either of these opinions.

Let us, then, say this to those who do not regard them as gods. Is it the case that these men do not exist at all, but that their souls were destroyed, as is held by some who think that the human soul is suddenly destroyed at death?[2] Or, following the opinion of those who say that the soul continues to exist or is immortal, do these men continue to exist, or are they immortal?[3] And in the latter case are they not gods but heroes? Or are they not heroes but simple souls? If you do not think that they exist, we shall have to establish the doctrine of the soul which to us is of primary importance. But if they do exist, even so we shall have to state the proof[4] for the doctrine of immortality, not only on the ground of what has been well said by the Greeks on this subject, but also in accordance with the divine teachings. And we will show that these men could not have joined the number of the gods when they departed from this life to live in a better country and region, by quoting the stories told of them, in which much licentiousness on the part of Heracles is recorded, and we read of his effeminate bondage to Omphale,[5] and the tale of Asclepius who was killed by their Zeus with a thunderbolt.[6] We will also mention the story of the Dioscuri that they often die

> At one time living on alternate days, while at another
> They die; but they have been given honour equal to the gods.[7]

How, then, can[8] any one of these reasonably be regarded as a god or hero?

23. We will prove the truth about our Jesus from the prophecies and after that compare his history with theirs, and show that there is no suspicion of licentiousness in his case. Not even those who took counsel against him and sought false witness against him found any plausible excuse for bringing a false accusation of licentiousness. Furthermore, his death was caused by men's conspiracy, and had no resemblance to Asclepius' death by a thunderbolt. And what respect is commanded by the frenzied Dionysus, clad in feminine clothing, so that he should be

---

[1] Read εἰ τὰ with Del., We.
[2] The Epicureans held that the soul ceased to exist at death.
[3] The Stoics believed in the survival of the soul, the Platonists in its immortality. Cf. III, 80.   [4] Read ἀποδεικτέον with Bo., K. tr.
[5] For Heracles and Omphale, see J. G. Frazer on Apollodorus, *Bibl.* II, 6, 3 (131–2).
[6] Zeus killed Asclepius because of his success as a physician; cf. Frazer on Apollodorus III, 10, 4 (122).   [7] Homer, *Od.* XI, 303–4.
[8] Read οἷόν τε with Selwyn (*Journal of Philology*, V (1874), p. 249) and K. tr.

worshipped as a god? If, however, those who compose a defence of these
stories take refuge in allegories, we must examine the allegories one by
one to see if they are sound and if men who were rent asunder by Titans[1]
and cast down from the heavenly throne[2] can have any real existence, and
be worthy of reverence and worship. But when our Jesus (to use Celsus'
phrase) *appeared to his own confraternity*, he really did appear, and Celsus
brings a false charge against Christianity when he says that he appeared
as a *phantom*. However, let the stories about them be examined side by
side with that of Jesus. Does Celsus want to make out that their stories
are true, while these of Jesus are inventions, although they were recorded
by people who were eyewitnesses, and showed in practice their clear
apprehension of the one whom they saw, and proved their sincerity by
the persecutions which they willingly suffered for his doctrine? Who that
wants to do all in accordance with right reason would give irrational
assent to their stories, while with Jesus he rushes on to disbelieve his
history without examining the question?

24. Again, when it is said of Asclepius that *a great multitude of men,
both of Greeks and barbarians, confess that they have often seen and still do see
not just a phantom, but Asclepius himself healing men and doing good and
predicting the future*,[3] Celsus asks us to believe it; he would not criticize
believers in Jesus if we were to believe in these testimonies. But when we
accept the testimony of the disciples who both saw the wonders of Jesus
and show clearly their good conscience, since we see their unqualified
goodness, in so far as it is possible to see conscience from writings, we are
called by Celsus *silly people*. He cannot show that there is, as he says, *an
untold number of men, Greeks and barbarians, who believe in Asclepius*. If he
considers this impressive, we produce clear evidence that there is an untold
number of both Greeks and barbarians who believe in Jesus. Some
display evidence of having received some miraculous power because of
this faith, shown in the people whom they cure; upon those who need
healing they use no other invocation than that of the supreme God and of
the name of Jesus together with the history about him.[4] By these we also
have seen many delivered from serious ailments, and from mental distraction and madness, and countless other diseases, which neither men nor
daemons had cured.

[1] I.e. Dionysus.   [2] I.e. Asclepius.
[3] Cf. Celsus in VII, 35. This is conventional language, e.g. Diodorus Sic. I, 25, 3–5, of
Isis. For similar language of Asclepius, cf. J. Geffcken, *Der Ausgang des griechisch-
römischen Heidentums* (1920), pp. 7, 249 nn. 36–9, referring to Maximus Tyr. IX, 7 (Hobein,
p. 110): 'I saw Asclepius himself, it was not a dream.' For Asclepius' healing miracles, cf. R.
Herzog, *Die Wunderheilungen von Epidauros* (1931). For discussion of the comparison
between Jesus and Asclepius, see Dölger in *Antike und Christentum*, VI, 4 (1950), pp. 250–7.
[4] See note on I, 6.

25. However, supposing I grant that a daemon called Asclepius possesses the power of healing and cures bodies, I would say to people who admire this or *Apollo's power of divination*, that if the cure of bodies is a thing indifferent and a gift which happens to be given not only to good men but to bad, and if the foreknowledge of the future is a thing indifferent also (for the man who has foreknowledge does not necessarily manifest goodness),[1] show me then how those who perform cures or who possess foreknowledge are not bad at all, but are proved to be good in every way and not far from being regarded as gods. But they will not be able to prove that those who perform cures or possess foreknowledge are good, since many who are not worthy even to live are said to have been healed; and no wise doctor would have consented to cure those who live in immorality.

In the utterances of the Pythian oracle you may find some injunctions which are unreasonable, two of which I will quote now.[2] The oracle commanded that Cleomedes (the boxer, I think) should be given honours equal to the gods,[3] perhaps because it perceived something sacred about his boxing. But it gave neither Pythagoras nor Socrates the honours which the boxer received. Furthermore, it called Archilochus 'servant of the Muses',[4] although he was a man who displayed his poetic gifts in the lowest and most licentious subjects and showed that his habits were immoral and impure;[5] and inasmuch as he was servant of the Muses, who are regarded as goddesses, it called him pious. But I do not know if even an uneducated man would call anyone pious who was not adorned with all moderation and virtue, and if any decent man would say the sort of things which the improper iambics of Archilochus contain. If it is shown to be self-evident that there is nothing divine about the healing of Asclepius and the divination of Apollo, how could anyone reasonably worship them as pure gods, allowing for the purposes of argument that they have this power? Worst of all, the oracular spirit, Apollo, free from any earthly body, passes into the so-called prophetess seated at the Pythian cave through her genitals.[6] But we hold no such opinion about

---

[1] Cf. IV, 96; VII, 5. Celsus must have said something about Delphi.
[2] Origen here follows the Epicurean polemic against oracles. The instances he gives, Cleomedes and Archilochus, occur together in the same type of polemic in Oenomaus (second century A.D.), quoted by Eus. *P.E.* v, 33–4. Cf. Socrates, *H.E.* III, 23, 57.
[3] See III, 33.
[4] When the man who had killed Archilochus in battle went to the temple at Delphi, he was sent away by the oracle because he had killed the servant of the Muses; Dio Chrysostom XXXIII, 12; Galen, *Protrept.* 9; Plutarch, *Mor.* 560E; Aristides, *Or.* 46 (II, 380 Dindorf); Libanius, *Or.* I, 74; Suidas *s.v.* 'Archilochus'. Cf. Parke, *History of the Delphic Oracle*, pp. 406f.
[5] The moral tone of Archilochus' poetry is criticized also in Plutarch, *Mor.* 520B; Clem. Al. *Strom.* I. 1; Eus. *P.E.* v, 32, 227A. He was forbidden reading for priests of the Julianic revival (Julian 300D). Cf. Max. Tyr. XVIII, 9.   [6] Cf. VII, 3.

Jesus and his power; the body born of a virgin consisted of human substance, capable of suffering wounds and death like other men.

26. Let us see what Celsus says next. He quotes from histories
miracles which in themselves seem incredible but which are not disbelieved
by him; at least, his words give no hint of disbelief. First we may take the
story about Aristeas the Proconnesian, saying this of him: *Then as for
Aristeas the Proconnesian who both vanished so miraculously from men and
again clearly appeared, and a long time afterwards visited many parts of the
world and related amazing tales, so that Apollo even commanded the Metapontines to regard Aristeas as a god, nobody still thinks him a god.* He seems to
have taken the story from Pindar and Herodotus.[1] It is enough here to
quote the text of Herodotus from the fourth book of the Histories, which
gives the following account of him:

And I have mentioned the origin of Aristeas who said this. I will give
a story which I heard about him in Proconnesus and Cyzicus. For they say that
Aristeas was by birth inferior to none of the citizens; and as he entered a fuller's
shop in Proconnesus he died; and that the fuller shut up his workshop and went
to tell the dead man's relations. But when the story had already spread throughout the city that Aristeas was dead, a man from Cyzicus, who had come from
the city of Artake, came into controversy with those who told the story; he
said that he had met him coming to Cyzicus, and had had conversation. And
he vehemently argued, while the dead man's relations went to the fuller's shop
with means to take him away. But when the house was opened Aristeas was
not to be seen, neither living nor dead. Seven years later, he appeared in
Proconnesus to write these verses which the Greeks now call Arimaspian, and
after doing so disappeared a second time. This then is the account given by
these cities; and I know that these things happened to the Metapontines in Italy
two hundred and forty years after the second disappearance of Aristeas, as
I found by comparison in Proconnesus and Metapontium. Now the Metapontines say that Aristeas himself appeared in their country and commanded
them to build an altar to Apollo, and to place by it a statue inscribed with the
name of Aristeas the Proconnesian; for he said that theirs was the only country
in Italy to which Apollo had come, and he who followed him was now Aristeas;
but at the time when he followed the god, he was a crow.[2] And after saying this
he vanished; but the Metapontines say that they sent to Delphi to ask the god
what this apparition of the man meant. The Pythian oracle commanded them
to obey the apparition, and, if they obeyed it, it would be to their advantage.
And after receiving this reply they acted accordingly. Even now a statue
inscribed with the name of Aristeas stands beside the image of Apollo, and round
it there are laurels; and the image is set up in the market-place. Let so much be
said here of Aristeas.

[1] Pindar, *frag.* 284, ed. Bowra; Herodotus, IV, 14–15. Cf. Max. Tyr. X, 2; XXXVIII, 3.
[2] For the crow as sacred to Apollo, cf. Aelian, *N.A.* I, 48; Porphyry, *de Abst.* III, 5.

27. I may reply to this story about Aristeas that if Celsus had quoted it as a story and indicated that he did not accept it as true, we would have met his argument in another way. But since he says that he vanished miraculously and again clearly appeared, and visited many parts of the world and related amazing tales, and, furthermore, gives his personal approval of the oracle of Apollo commanding the Metapontines to regard Aristeas as a god, we will make the following reply[1] to him. If you suspect the miracles recorded of Jesus by his disciples of being entirely fictitious, and if you criticize people who believe them, why do you not regard this as an incredible tale or as an invention? And why do you accuse others of believing irrationally in the miracles of Jesus while you appear to believe such stories as these, without adducing any proof of them, or any evidence that they really happened? Do you think that Herodotus and Pindar tell no lies? While, as for those who have trained themselves to die for the teachings of Jesus and have left writings about their beliefs to posterity, can it be a matter of inventions, as you think, and myths and incredible tales, which leads these people to fight so vigorously that life is precarious and death violent? Take an unbiased view of the story about Aristeas, and of that related about Jesus, and consider whether, in view of the result in the lives of those who have been helped to reform their moral character and to become devoted to the supreme God, we should not say that it is right to believe that the events related of Jesus could not have happened apart from divine providence, while this cannot be said of Aristeas the Proconnesian.

28. Why providence should want to enable Aristeas to do these miracles, and why, if providence wants to benefit the human race, these great wonders, as you suppose them, should be displayed, are questions to which you can provide no answer.[2] But in our case, when we tell the stories about Jesus, we give a powerful defence to show why they happened. We argue that God wanted to establish the doctrine spoken by Jesus which brought salvation to men; and it was strengthened by the apostles who were, so to speak, foundations of the building of Christianity which he was beginning to build, and it is increasing even in recent times, when many cures are done in the name of Jesus and there are other manifestations of considerable significance.

Moreover, what sort of a god is the Apollo who commands the Metapontines to regard Aristeas as a god? With what intention did he do this? And what benefit does he confer on the Metapontines as a result of the honour paid to Aristeas as a god, if they reckon as a god the one who

---

[1] Read ⟨οὕτως κατασκευάσομεν τὸν⟩ λόγον with K. tr.

[2] Read comma before οὐκ with We.

a short time before was a man? It seems to you also to be worth while mentioning Apollo's commendation of Aristeas, though we regard him as a daemon who obtained the reward of 'drink-offering and burnt-offering'.[1] But are you not moved by the commendations of the supreme God and of His holy angels, uttered through prophets not after Jesus' life but before he came to live among men, so that you admire both the prophets who received divine inspiration and the one of whom they prophesied? It so happened that his advent to this life was proclaimed many years beforehand by several men in such a way that the whole Jewish race was hanging on the expectation of him whom they hoped would come, and came to dispute with one another after Jesus' advent; a large number of them confessed him to be Christ and believed him to be the one prophesied; but those who did not believe despised the meekness of those who, on account of Jesus' teaching, did not want even a trivial disturbance, and they ventured to inflict on Jesus such sufferings as his disciples have truthfully and honestly recorded, without secretly omitting from the amazing history of him what in the eyes of most people brings shame on the doctrine of the Christians.

Both Jesus himself and his disciples did not want people who came to them to believe only in his divine nature and miracles, as though he did not share in human nature and had not assumed the human flesh which lusts against the Spirit;[2] but as a result of their faith they also saw the power that descended into human nature and human limitations, and which assumed a human soul and body, combined with the divine characteristics, to bring salvation to believers. For Christians see that with Jesus human and divine nature began to be woven together, so that by fellowship with divinity human nature might become divine, not only in Jesus, but also in all those who believe and go on to undertake the life which Jesus taught, the life which leads everyone who lives according to Jesus' commandments to friendship with God and fellowship with Jesus.

29. According to Celsus, Apollo wanted the Metapontines to regard Aristeas as a god. But, as the Metapontines thought that the obvious fact that Aristeas was a man, and perhaps not a good one, was more important than the oracle which pronounced him to be a god, or worthy of divine honours, on this account they were not willing to obey Apollo, and thus

---

[1] Homer, *Il.* IV, 49; IX, 500; XXIV, 70. The idea that daemons feed on sacrifices is universal at this time; cf. the Pythagorean quoted in VII, 6; Celsus in VIII, 60; Porphyry, *de Abst.* II, 42; Philo, *de Decal.* 74; Oenomaus ap. Eus. *P.E.* V, 21, 5, 213 B; etc. According to Origen, *Comm. in Matt.* XIII, 23, the evil powers are furious with Jesus' teaching because it robs them of their sacrifices. Cf. Geffcken, *Zwei griechische Apologeten*, pp. 220 f.; E. R. Bevan, *Holy Images*, p. 91.
[2] Gal. v. 17.

146

no one thinks Aristeas a god. But of Jesus we would say that since it was expedient for the human race to accept him as Son of God, as God come in a human soul and body, and since this did not seem to benefit the gluttony of the daemons who love bodies, and suppose that they are gods, for this reason the daemons on earth, who are thought to be gods by people who have not been educated in the matter of daemons, and those who serve them, wanted to prevent the spread of Jesus' teaching. They saw the 'drink-offerings and burnt-offerings', in which they greedily delighted, being taken away by the success of Jesus' teaching. But God, who sent Jesus, destroyed the whole conspiracy of daemons, and everywhere in the world in order that men might be converted and reformed He made the gospel of Jesus to be successful, and caused churches to exist in opposition to the assemblies of superstitious, licentious, and unrighteous men. For such is the character of the crowds who everywhere constitute the assemblies of the cities. And the Churches of God which have been taught by Christ, when compared with the assemblies of the people where they live, are 'as lights in the world'.[1] Who would not admit that even the less satisfactory members of the Church and those who are far inferior when compared with the better members are far superior to the assemblies of the people?

30. The Church of God, say, at Athens is meek and quiet, since it desires to please God. But the assembly of the Athenians is riotous and in no way comparable to the Church of God there. You may say the same of the Church of God at Corinth and the assembly of the people of the Corinthians, and of the Church of God, say, at Alexandria and the assembly of the people of Alexandria. If the man who hears this has an open mind, and examines the facts with a desire to find out the truth, he will be amazed at the one who both planned and had the power to carry into effect the establishment of the Churches of God in all places, living beside the assemblies of the people in each city. And so also, if you compare the council of the Church of God with the council in each city, you will find that[2] some councillors of the Church are worthy to hold office in a city which is God's, if there is such a city anywhere in the universe.[3] But the councillors in every city do not show in their moral character anything worthy of their pre-eminent authority by which they

---

[1] Phil. ii. 15. Throughout this passage the play on the double meaning of *ecclesia*, as the secular assembly and as the Church, cannot be reproduced in translation.

[2] Read ἃν ⟨ὅτι⟩ with K. tr.

[3] Harnack (*Mission u. Ausbr.* 4th ed. 1924, p. 548) takes this to mean that if a city existed which was wholly Christian, some bishops would be worthy to be magistrates in it. Comparison with VIII, 74, however, suggests that Origen has in mind the Parable of the Pounds (Luke xix. 12 ff.), and that the city which is God's is heaven.

appear to be superior to the citizens. So also, compare the ruler of the Church in each city with the ruler of the citizens, and you will understand how even in those councillors and rulers of the Church of God who fail badly, and live in idleness compared with those who are more active,[1] nevertheless we find that, broadly speaking, there is superior progress towards the virtues surpassing the character of those who are councillors and rulers in the cities.

31. If this is so, is it not reasonable to think that in Jesus, who was able to accomplish such great results, the divine element was exceptional, and that there was none whatever in Aristeas the Proconnesian, even though Apollo may want us to regard him as a god, nor in any of those whom Celsus enumerates? He says: *No one thinks Abaris the Hyperborean to be a god, though he had such power that he was carried along by an arrow.*[2] With what intention did the divinity which empowered Abaris the Hyperborean to be carried along by an arrow bestow on him such a gift? So that[3] the human race might receive some benefit? Or did Abaris himself derive any advantage from being carried along by an arrow? For the purposes of argument, I am assuming that this story is not in any way fictitious, but that this happened through the operation of a daemon. However, if my Jesus is said to be 'received up in glory',[4] I perceive God's care for man; God caused this to happen that He might commend the Master to those who saw this, so that they might fight not for human learning, but for divine teaching, and with all their power devote themselves to the supreme God and do everything to please Him, in order that at the divine judgment they may receive according to their deserts a reward for what they have done in this life, whether good or bad.

32. After this Celsus also speaks of *the Clazomenian*, adding to what he says of him: *Do they not say that his soul often left his body and wandered*

---

[1] Read εὐτονωτέρους with We., K. tr. Origen can be scathing about bishops; III, 9, above; *Comm. in Matt.* XVI, 25 and esp. 8 'In many so-called Churches, especially those in large cities, one can see rulers of the people of God who do not allow anyone, sometimes not even the noblest of Jesus' disciples, to speak with them on equal terms.' Here Origen speaks from experience.

[2] In Herodotus IV, 36 Abaris carried an arrow over the whole world without eating. Later writers made the arrow carry Abaris; he figured much in late Pythagorean legends. Cf. Porphyry, *Vita Pythag.* 28–9: Abaris was priest among the Hyperboreans; Pythagoras showed him his golden thigh; Apollo gave him an arrow on which he was carried over rivers, seas, and untravelled places. Similarly Iamblichus, *Vita Pythag.* XIX, 91; probable allusion in Julian 269D; Gregory Naz. *Orat.* XLIII, 21; *Ep.* 2 (*P.G.* XXXVI, 524B; XXXVII, 24A); Libanius, *Ep.* CXLIII, 3; Cosmas Hieros., *Ad carm. S. Greg.* LXIV, 274 (*P.G.* XXXVIII, 509). Discussion in E. Rohde, *Psyche* (E.T., 1925), pp. 327–8, who also refers to Himerius, *Orat.* XXV, 2, 4; Nonnus, *Dionys.* XI, 132–3; Procopius of Gaza, *Ep.* 36 (Rohde, wrongly, 96) (*P.G.* LXXXVII, 2748C). Cf. also Lucian, *Philops.* 13 ff.

[3] Read ἵνα τί and in the next line ⟨ἀπὸ τοῦ⟩ ὀϊστῷ with We., K. tr.

[4] I Tim. iii. 16.

about in a bodiless state? Yet men do not think that even he was a god.[1] I will
reply to this that probably certain daemons arranged for this story to be
written (I do not believe that they also arranged for it to happen), so that
the prophecies about Jesus and his sayings might either be attacked as if
they were inventions like these stories, or arouse no admiration on the
ground that they were no more remarkable than other tales. My Jesus
said of his own soul that it was not separated from his body by the
compulsion of men, but through the miraculous power given to him also
in this respect, saying: 'No man takes my soul from me, but I lay it down
of myself. I have power to lay it down, and I have power to take it again.'[2]
As he had the power to lay it down, this he did when he said: 'Father, why
hast thou forsaken me? And crying with a loud voice, he gave up the
ghost.'[3] This forestalled the executioners of those who were being
crucified, for they break the legs of people who are crucified with the
intention that they may not suffer further punishment.[4] He took his soul
again when he manifested himself among his disciples; he foretold this in
their presence when he said to the Jews who did not believe him: 'Destroy
this temple and in three days I will raise it up.' Now 'this he said of the
temple of his body'.[5] And the prophets foretold this by this prophecy
among many others: 'Furthermore, my flesh shall rest in hope; for thou
wilt not leave my soul in Hades, neither wilt thou suffer thine holy one to
see corruption.'[6]

33. To show that he has read many Greek stories, Celsus also quotes
that about *Cleomedes the Astypalean*. He relates that *he got into a chest and
after shutting himself inside was not to be found in it;*[7] but by some miraculous

---

[1] Read comma after ἄνθρωποι with K. tr. Hermotimus of Clazomenae told his wife that
in sleep his soul left his body; she told his enemies who burnt him while he was asleep; the
Clazomenians made amends by dedicating a temple to him, to which no woman was
admitted. The story is given by Apollonius, *Mirabilia*, 3 (prob. from Theopompus:
Rohde, *Rhein. Mus.* XXVI, 1871, p. 558); Pliny, *N.H.* VII, 174; Lucian, *Muscae encomium* 7;
Tertullian, *de Anima* 44. Plutarch, *Mor.* 592 C, D, calls him Hermodorus (as Proclus,
in Remp. II, 113, 23–5, ed. Kroll, which shows that in Plut. it is not a mere 'copyist's
error'; cf. Rohde, *Psyche*, E.T. p. 331). J. H. Waszink, 'Traces of Aristotle's lost dialogues
in Tertullian', in *Vigiliae Christianae*, I (1947), pp. 137–49, argues that Theopompus took
the story from the lost 'Eudemus' of Aristotle. In any event, all Celsus' instances are stock
miracle-stories which often occur together in similar groups elsewhere, e.g. Plutarch,
Romulus, 28 (Aristeas, Cleomedes); Pliny, *N.H.* VII, 174–6 (Hermotimus, Aristeas,
Epimenides, Heraclides' lifeless woman—cf. II, 16, above); Clem. Al. *Strom.* I, 133, 2
(Abaris, Aristeas, Epimenides); Proclus, *in Remp.* II, 113, 23–5 (Aristeas, Hermodorus,
Epimenides). For the theme, K. Kerényi, *Die griechisch-orientalische Romanliteratur* (1927),
p. 39; E. R. Dodds, *The Greeks and the Irrational* (1951), pp. 140 ff.
[2] John x. 18; cf. II, 16, above.   [3] Matt. xxvii. 46, 50.   [4] John xix. 31–4.
[5] John ii. 19, 21.   [6] Ps. xv. 9–10.
[7] Read comma after ἔνδον with Wif. Cleomedes killed his boxing opponent at the
Olympic festival, 486 B.C. Being disqualified he went mad, returned to Astypalea, and
pulled down the roof of a school upon the children within. Stoned by the townsfolk, he

*providence he had vanished from it when people broke the chest in pieces to
arrest him.* Even if this tale is not[1] the invention which it seems to be, it
cannot be compared with the stories of Jesus. For in Celsus' examples no
evidence of the divinity attributed to them is to be found in the life of the
men, whereas the evidences of Jesus' divinity are the Churches of people
who have been helped, the prophecies spoken about him, the cures which
are done in his name, the knowledge and wisdom in Christ, and reason
which is to be found in those who know how to advance beyond mere
faith, and how to search out the meaning of the divine scriptures. Jesus
commanded this when he said 'search the scriptures', and that was what
Paul meant when he taught that we must 'know how we ought to answer
each one'. Moreover, another said: 'Being always ready to give answer
to every man that asks you concerning the faith that is in you.'[2] But if
Celsus wants to believe that the story is not an invention, let him inform
us with what intention the superhuman power made him vanish from the
chest by some miraculous providence. If he will show that there was some
important purpose, and that it would have been worthy of God to bestow
such a gift upon Cleomedes, we will decide what we ought to say to him.
But if he is at a loss how to say even anything plausible on this point
(obviously because there is no argument to be found), then we will either
support[3] the opinion of those who do not believe the story and will
criticize it as untrue, or we will say that the disappearance[4] of the Astypalean
was effected by some daemon by methods similar to those employed when
sorcerers deceive the eyes of spectators. Celsus, however, thinks that
there was *an oracle* which *declared that he had vanished from the chest by
some miraculous providence.*

34. I think that these were the only stories that Celsus knew. But so
that he may appear deliberately to omit other stories of the same sort, he
says: *And one might give many other examples of this character.* Suppose
that this is so, and that there are many other such examples; they have done
no good to mankind; and what action done by them could be found
comparable[5] with the work of Jesus and the miraculous stories about him,
of which we have spoken at length?

fled to a chest in the sanctuary of Athena; when the chest was broken open, he had vanished.
The people inquired at Delphi, and the priestess replied, 'Last of the heroes is Cleomedes
the Astypalean; honour him with sacrifices as no longer mortal.' The story is told by
Plutarch, *Romulus* 28; Pausanias VI, 9, 6–8; Oenomaus ap. Eus. *P.E.* v, 34, 2, 230B, C.
Cf. III, 25, above; Rohde, *Psyche*, E.T. pp. 129 f.; Parke, *History of the Delphic Oracle*
pp. 362 f. A. Wifstrand, *Bull. Soc. Roy. Lund* (1941–2), p. 416, acutely points out that the
poetic ἔκτοθι and hexameter ending δαιμονίᾳ τινὶ μοίρᾳ are the remnant of the oracular
utterance.   [1] Read μὴ for μέν, with Del.
[2] John v. 39; Col. iv. 6; I Pet. iii. 15.   [3] Read συμβαλοῦμεν with Wif.
[4] Read ⟨τὰ⟩ περὶ with K. tr.   [5] Read εἰκαστὸν with K. tr.

After this he thinks that *because we worship the man who was arrested and died, we behave like the Getae who reverence Zamolxis, and the Cilicians who worship Mopsus, the Acarnanians Amphilochus, the Thebans Amphiaraus, and the Lebadians Trophonius.*[1] Here also we will prove that it is not reasonable that he should liken us to the people he mentions. For they built temples and images to the persons he has enumerated; whereas we take away from the deity worship by any such means (we think this more appropriate to daemons who in some unknown way are localized in a particular place, which they either seize on their own initiative or inhabit, as it were,[2] because they have been brought there by certain rites and magical spells). We admire Jesus who changed our thoughts from considering all objects of sense, not only everything corruptible but also what will be corrupted,[3] and who led us to honour the supreme God with upright conduct and prayers. And we offer these prayers to Him through him who is, as it were, midway[4] between uncreated nature and that of all created things; and he brings to us the benefits of the Father, while as our high priest he conveys our prayers to the supreme God.

35. Why he says this I do not know; but I would like to reply to him by putting to him some such pertinent questions as the following. Are these names which you enumerate of no significance, and is there no power in Lebadia possessed by Trophonius, nor in Thebes at the shrine of Amphiaraus, nor in Acarnania at that of Amphilochus, nor in Cilicia at that of Mopsus? Or is there a power in these places, perhaps a daemon, or a hero, or even a god, who performs wonders beyond human ability? If he says that there is nothing different about these oracles, and that there is neither a daemon nor a god there, then at any rate now let him admit his own opinion and confess that he is an Epicurean and does not hold the same views as the Greeks, and that he neither recognizes the existence of daemons nor worships the gods as the Greeks do. That will prove that there is no force in his argument from the oracles which he quoted as though he believed them to be real, and from those which he mentions later. But if he maintains that the persons he has mentioned were daemons, or heroes, or even gods, let him observe that in saying this he has proved the very thing he did not want to accept, that Jesus was a person of this nature. For Jesus has been able to show to a considerable number of men

---

[1] See Rohde, *Psyche*, E.T., pp. 89 ff.; VII, 35, below. For such lists of oracles, cf. J. H. Waszink's commentary on Tertullian, *de Anima* 46 (p. 497); and for Zamolxis, A. B. Cook, *Zeus*, II, pp. 226 f.; Dodds, *op. cit.* p. 166.

[2] Read ὡσπερεί with K.

[3] The language reflects the Platonic view that although the cosmos is corruptible, by divine providence it will not in fact be corrupted. Cf. IV, 61.

[4] Read perhaps αὐτῷ διὰ τοῦ ὡς μεταξύ. In Philo, *Q.R.D.H.* 206, the Logos is neither uncreated like God nor created like us, but midway.

that he came from God to visit the human race. If once he accepts this, consider whether he will not be forced to say that Jesus was more powerful than these beings with whom Celsus reckons him. At any rate, none of them prevents honours from being given to others; but Jesus, being convinced that he was more powerful than all of them, forbade the bestowing of favours on them, on the ground that they are wicked daemons who have taken possession of places on earth because they are unable to attain to the purer and more divine region far removed from the grossness of the earth and the countless evils in it.

36. After this he even thinks that *the honour which we give to Jesus is no different from that paid to Hadrian's favourite* (that is to say, the boy Antinous)[1] by the inhabitants of Antinoopolis in Egypt. He said this, as we may prove, merely out of hostility. What is there in common between the noble life of our Jesus and the life of the favourite of Hadrian who did not even keep the man from a morbid lust for women? Against Jesus not even those who brought countless accusations and told enormous lies against him were able to accuse him of having had the slightest contact with the least licentiousness. Furthermore, if the worship of Antinous were to be examined honestly and impartially, it would probably be found that it is owing to Egyptian magic and spells that he appears to do miracles in Antinoopolis even after his death. This is related to have been done in other temples by Egyptians and those expert in such matters. They set up in particular places daemons with the power to utter oracles or to heal, who often even inflict pain on people who appear to have transgressed some rule about impure food, or about touching a dead man's body, that they may be able[2] to frighten the uneducated masses. Such is the character also of him who is thought to be a god in Antinoopolis in Egypt. His virtues were invented by people who live by cheating; but others who are deceived by the daemon established there, and others convicted by their weak conscience, imagine that they pay a penalty inflicted by the god Antinous. And such is the character of the mysteries they celebrate and of their supposed oracles. The case of Jesus is very different from this. No sorcerers came together to oblige some king who commanded them to come or to obey the order of a governor, thinking

[1] Bader rightly ends the parenthesis after μειρακίου. Antinous was drowned in the Nile, A.D. 130; Hadrian founded Antinoopolis in memory of him, and he was formally deified. Coins with his portrait were issued in 134. Cf. C. T. Seltman in *Hesperia* 17 (1948) at pp. 80 ff. Cf. Celsus in v, 63 for the immoral cult, a common argument in the Apologists; Hegesippus ap. Eus. *H.E.* IV, 8, 2; Justin, *Apol.* I, 29; Tatian, 10; Athenagoras, *Leg.* 30; Theophilus, III, 8; *Or. Sib.* VIII, 57; Clem. Al. *Protr.* 49; Origen in VIII, 9, below; Tertullian, *Apol.* XIII, 9; Athanasius, *c. Gent.* 9; Prudentius, *c. Symm.* I, 271 ff.

[2] Read ἔχοιεν with K. tr., and in the next line ἐστι καὶ ⟨ὁ⟩ ἐν with K. tr., Wif. For the connexion of magic with the cult of Antinous cf. Dio Cassius LXIX, 11

that they would make him a god.[1] But the Creator of the universe
Himself, by means of the persuasive power of His miraculous utterances,
showed Jesus to be worthy of honour, not only to the men who were
willing to welcome him, but also to daemons and other invisible powers;
to the present day these appear either to fear the name of Jesus as superior
to them, or to accept him in reverence as their lawful ruler. For if the
commendation had not been given by God, the daemons would not have
yielded and departed from men against whom they were fighting at the
mere pronouncement of his name.

37. Egyptians who have been taught to worship Antinous will tolerate
it if you compare him with Apollo or Zeus, because they are proud that
he should be reckoned with them. And it is obvious that Celsus lies when
he says this: *And if you compare him[2] with Apollo or Zeus, they will not
tolerate it.* But Christians have learnt that their eternal life consists in
knowing that only true supreme God, and Jesus Christ whom He sent.[3]
They have learnt that 'all the gods of the heathen'[4] are gluttonous daemons,
who wander around sacrifices and blood and the portion taken from the
sacrifices, and deceive those who have not fled for refuge to the supreme
God. They understand that the divine and holy angels of God are of
a nature and character other than that of all the daemons on earth,[5] and
that these are known to a very few who make an intelligent and careful
study of this subject. That is why they will not tolerate it if you compare
Jesus with Apollo or Zeus or any of those beings that are worshipped with
burnt-offering and blood and sacrifices. There are some who because of
their great simplicity do not know how to explain their actions, although
it is with good reason that they observe the traditions which they have
received. But there are others who explain their actions with arguments
which may not be lightly regarded but which are profound and, as a Greek
might say, esoteric and mysterious. They believe a profound doctrine
about God and about those beings who through the only-begotten divine
Logos have been so honoured by God that they participate in the divine
nature, and for this reason are also granted the name.[6] There is also
a profound doctrine about the divine angels and the opponents of the
truth who have been deceived, and who because of this call themselves[7]
gods, or angels of God, or good daemons, or heroes who come into being

---

[1] See Numenius in v, 38; viii, 61.

[2] In the original text of Celsus αὐτῷ must have referred to Jesus; Origen takes it here to
mean Antinous.

[3] John xvii. 3.   [4] Ps. xcv. 5.

[5] Cf. v, 5, below.

[6] In Ps. lxxxi God 'stands in the assembly of the gods'. Origen takes this to mean the
angels.

[7] Read ἑαυτούς with K. tr.

through the transformation of a good human soul.[1] Such Christians will also argue that, just as in philosophy many may think that they are in the right, either because they have fallaciously deceived themselves by plausible arguments, or because they have unthinkingly believed in notions suggested and discovered by others, so also there are some among the bodiless souls and angels and daemons who have been led by plausibilities to call themselves gods. But it was because of these doctrines which men have not been able to discover exactly and perfectly that it was not considered safe for a man to entrust himself to any being as a god, except only to Jesus Christ who rules over all like an arbiter. For he both perceived these very profound truths and passed them on to a few.

38. A belief in Antinous or any other like him, either among the Egyptians or among the Greeks, is, so to speak, a matter of ill fortune. But it seems that faith in Jesus may be either the result of good fortune or the conclusion of a rigorous examination of the evidence. For with the multitude it seems to be the result of good fortune, while it is only with very few people that it is the conclusion of a rigorous examination of the evidence. Although I say that a particular faith is a matter of good fortune, to use the popular word, even in this case I refer the question to God who knows the causes of the experiences assigned to each one who comes to live the life of men. Moreover, the Greeks will say that even among people supposed to be very clever, in many instances it is good luck which is responsible, because, for example, they have had particular teachers or have happened to fall in with the better type, although there are also teachers of the opposite opinions, and because they have been educated among people of the better classes. Many people have been brought up in such circumstances that they have not been allowed to receive even a suggestion of better things; but even from their earliest years they have always been either in the position of favourite to licentious men or masters, or in some other unfortunate condition which prevents their soul from looking to higher things.[2] Probably the causes of these inequalities lie entirely in the sphere of providence, and it is not easy for men to come upon their explanation. I thought that I would discuss this question by way of parenthesis because of his remark: *Such is the effect of the faith which has prejudiced their minds.* He ought to have said that differences of belief among men are caused by differences of upbringing, so that some

[1] Cf. III, 80; Diog. Laert. VII, 151; Philo, *de Plant.* 14. See Rohde, *Psyche*, E.T., pp. 527 ff.
[2] The inequalities of life are a problem to which Origen often refers; the argument was used polemically by the Gnostics (Origen, *de Princ.* II, 9, 5). The difficulty was important in the contemporary debates on providence; cf. *de Princ.* II, 9, 3; Clem. *Hom.* XIX, 23 = *Recog.* IX, 5, 7.

are more, others less fortunate in this respect. And from this he ought to
have gone on to say that even with the more intelligent people it is
so-called good luck and so-called bad luck which help towards making
them appear to belong to the intelligentsia and enable them to have
rational grounds for their beliefs in many cases. However, that is enough
said on this subject.

39. Celsus' next remark must now be considered, where he says that
our faith has prejudiced our souls and makes us hold this belief about Jesus.
It is true that our faith makes us hold this belief; but consider whether our
faith does not of itself prove that it is laudable. For we entrust ourselves
to the supreme God, confessing our gratitude to him who guided us to
this faith and saying that without God's power he could not have ventured
upon or accomplished so great an undertaking. We also believe in the
honest purpose of the authors of the gospels, inferring this from their
piety and the good conscience which they indicate in their writings. For
they have nothing in them that is spurious, cheating, invented, and wicked.
We are convinced that men who had not learnt the technique taught by
the pernicious sophistry of the Greeks, which has great plausibility and
cleverness, and who knew nothing of the rhetoric prevalent in the law-
courts, could not have invented stories in such a way that their writings
were capable in themselves of bringing a man to believe and to live a life
in conformity with his faith. I think it was for this reason that Jesus chose
to employ such men to teach his doctrine, that there might be no possible
suspicion of plausible sophisms,[1] but that to those able to understand, the
innocence of the writers' purpose, which if I may say so was very naïve,
might be obviously manifest; and that they might see that the writers were
considered worthy to be endowed with divine power, which accomplished
far more than seems to be achieved by involved verbosity and stylish
constructions, and by a logical argument divided into distinct sections
and worked out with Greek technical skill.

40. Consider whether the doctrines of our faith are not in complete
accord with the universal notions when they change the opinions of
people who give a fair hearing to what we say. For even if the perverted
idea, supported by much instruction, has been able to implant in the
multitude the conception that images are gods and that objects made of
gold, silver, ivory, and stone, are worthy of worship, nevertheless the
universal notion[2] demands that we do not think of God as corruptible
matter at all, nor that He is honoured when men make images of Him in
lifeless material objects, as though they were made 'in his image'[3] or

---

[1] Cf. I, 62.   [2] Cf. Zeno as quoted in I, 5, above.
[3] Gen. i. 26. For justification of images, cf. Celsus in VII, 62.

were symbols of Him. That is why Christians forthwith say of images that 'they are not gods',[1] and maintain that created objects such as these are not comparable with the Creator, and are worth little beside the supreme God who created, holds together, and governs the universe. And the rational soul, which at once recognizes that which is, so to speak, akin to it, discards the images which it has hitherto thought to be gods, and assumes its natural affection for the Creator; because of this affection for Him it also accepts the one who first showed these truths to all nations by the disciples whom he trained, and whom he sent out with divine power and authority to preach the message about God and His kingdom.

41. He attacks us, as he has done I do not know how many times already, by saying of Jesus that *we think him a god though he was born of a mortal body, and in this think that we act piously.* It is superfluous to speak further on this subject, for we discussed it at length above. Nevertheless, let our critics know that he, whom we think and have believed to be God and Son of God from the beginning, is the very Logos and wisdom and truth itself. We affirm that his mortal body and the human soul in him received the greatest elevation not only by communion but by union and inter-mingling, so that by sharing in His divinity he was transformed into God. If anyone should take offence because we say this even of his body, let him consider what is asserted by the Greeks about matter, that properly speaking it is without qualities, but is clothed with qualities such as the Creator wishes to give it, and that often it puts aside its former qualities and receives better and different ones. If this is right, why is it remarkable that by the providence of God's will the mortal quality of Jesus' body should have been changed into an ethereal and divine quality?[2]

42. Celsus does not talk like a man skilled in argument when he compares the human flesh of Jesus to *gold, silver, and stone,*[3] saying that *his flesh was more corruptible than these.* For strictly speaking neither is one incorruptible thing more incorruptible than any other incorruptible thing, nor is any one corruptible thing more corruptible than another.[4] But supposing that there are degrees of corruptibility, nevertheless we would say that if it is possible for the matter underlying all qualities to possess varying qualities, why is it impossible for the flesh of Jesus to have changed qualities, and to become of such a character as flesh would need to be, if it is to live in aether and the realms above it, where it no longer

[1] Acts xix. 26.
[2] Cf. my remarks in *Harv. Theol. Rev.* XLI (1948), at p. 101; and in *J.T.S.*, n.s. II (1951) at p. 163.
[3] The material out of which images are made. Bader thinks Celsus has in mind the saying of Heraclitus, quoted in VII, 62 (I, 5).
[4] Cf. the Stoic argument in II, 7.

has the properties belonging to carnal weakness and those which Celsus calls *abominable?* This word also would not have been used by a philosopher. For what is properly speaking abominable is of the nature of evil. But the nature of the body is not abominable; for in itself bodily nature is not involved in evil which is the originating cause of what is abominable.[1]

Then because he suspected what would be our reply to him, he says about the change of his body: *But when he had put off this flesh, perhaps he became a god? Then why not rather Asclepius, Dionysus, and Heracles?* We will answer: What work as great as his has been done by Asclepius, Dionysus, and Heracles? Can they support their claim to be gods by proving that there are people who have been reformed in morals and have become better as a result of their life and teaching? Let us read the numerous stories about them and see whether they were free from licentiousness, or unrighteousness, or folly, or cowardice. If nothing of the kind were to be found in them, Celsus' argument, which puts Jesus on a level with those he has mentioned, would be strong. But if it is clear that, although some good things are related of them, they are recorded to have done countless things contrary to right reason, why would it be more reasonable if you were to say of them any more than of Jesus that they became gods when they had put off their mortal body?

43. After this he says of us that *we ridicule those who worship Zeus because his tomb is shown in Crete,*[2] *without knowing how and why the Cretans do this; none the less we worship one who rose from his tomb.* Notice that he here defends the Cretans' account of Zeus and their story about his tomb by hinting that there are hidden allegorical meanings which, it is said, the myth of Zeus was invented to convey. He criticizes us because we confess that our Jesus was buried; but we maintain that he also rose from the tomb; the Cretans do not go on to relate that of Zeus. However, since he seems to believe in the story about the tomb of Zeus in Crete when he says *without knowing how and why the Cretans do this,* we will say that Callimachus the Cyrenaean, who had read a vast number of poems and almost every Greek history, knows of no allegorical interpretation of the story

---

[1] Origen adopts the Stoic view that the body is morally neutral. Cf. IV, 66. Origen parts company with the Platonic tradition here. See Hal Koch, *Pronoia und Paideusis,* pp. 101 f.

[2] This is evidence that Celsus had read Christian apologists. It was an argument drawn from the old Academic polemic; cf. Cicero, *de Nat. Deor.* III, 21, 53; Lucian, *de Sacr.* 10. It is very common in the Apologists: Tatian 27; Athenagoras 30; Theophilus I, 10; Clem. Al. *Protr.* XXXVII, 4; Tertullian, *Apol.* XXV, 7; Minucius, XXI, 8; *Clem. Recog.* X, 23; Arnobius, IV, 14; Athanasius, *c. Gent.* 10. See the exhaustive collection of references in A. B. Cook, *Zeus* II, pp. 940–3; III, p. 1173; cf. I, pp. 157–63. Also Guthrie, *The Greeks and their Gods* (1950), pp. 50 f.

of Zeus and his tomb. Accordingly, in the hymn which he wrote to Zeus he attacks the Cretans, saying:

> The Cretans are always liars: indeed, a tomb for thee, O King,
> The Cretans have devised. But thou didst not die, for thou ever livest.[1]

Although he said 'But thou didst not die, for thou ever livest', and denied the existence of the tomb of Zeus in Crete, he relates that Zeus experienced what is the beginning of death. For the origin of death is earthly birth.[2] He speaks as follows:[3]

> Rhea gave birth to thee among the Parrhasians after her marriage.

Since he denied that Zeus was born in Crete because of the story of his tomb, he ought to have seen that he who was born in Arcadia must also have died. About this Callimachus speaks thus:[4]

> Zeus, some say that thou wast born in Ida's mountains;
> Zeus, others say that thou wast born in Arcadia.
> Which, Father, have lied? The Cretans are always liars

and so on. Celsus has led us to mention this by treating Jesus unfairly; for he accepts the Scriptures when they say that he died and was buried, but thinks that it is a fiction when they also say that he rose from the dead, and disbelieves in spite of the fact that countless prophets foretold this very thing, and that there are many evidences of his appearing after death.

44. Then after this Celsus quotes what is entirely contrary to Jesus' teaching, and is maintained only by a few people who are supposed to be Christians, not, as he thinks, by *the more intelligent*, but by the most ignorant. He says: *Their injunctions are like this.* ' *Let no one educated, no one wise, no one sensible draw near. For these abilities are thought by us to be evils. But as for anyone ignorant, anyone stupid, anyone uneducated, anyone who is a child, let him come boldly.' By the fact that they themselves admit that these people are worthy of their God, they show that they want and are able to convince only the foolish, dishonourable and stupid, and only slaves, women, and little children.* This is our reply to this. Suppose that, in spite of the fact that Jesus teaches self-control, saying, 'Whosoever looks upon a woman to lust after her has already committed adultery with her in his heart',[5] some one were to see a few out of the large number of supposed Christians who were living licentiously. He would quite rightly accuse them of living contrary to Jesus' teaching. But it would be most irrational if he were to apply to Christianity the charge against them. So also, if anyone should find that there are Christians who do less than nothing to

---

[1] Callimachus, *Hymn to Zeus*, 8–9. Cf. Titus i. 12.
[2] A philosophical axiom: Seneca, *ad Polybium de Consol.* 1, 1 'Quicquid coepit et desinit'; Philo, *de Aetern. Mundi* 27; *Qu. in Gen.* I, 10; *de Decal.* 58; Clem. Al. *Strom.* III, 45, 3.
[3] Callimachus 10.   [4] *Ibid.* 6–8.   [5] Matt. v. 28.

encourage men to be wise, his criticism ought to be directed against those who are content with their own ignorance and who, although they do not say the words which Celsus has attributed to them (for not even they speak so shamelessly, though some may be unlettered and ignorant), say things which are much less strong in discouraging people from practising wisdom.

45. That the gospel wants us to be wise I may show both from the ancient Jewish scriptures, which we also use, and equally from those written after the time of Jesus which are believed in the Churches to be divine. In the fiftieth Psalm David is described as saying in prayer to God: 'Thou hast shown to me the obscure and hidden secrets of thy wisdom.'[1] And anyone who reads the Psalms will find the book full of many wise doctrines. Moreover, when Solomon asked for wisdom he was approved.[2] And it is possible to see traces of his wisdom in his books where he expresses profound thoughts in terse phrases. You will find in them many eulogies of wisdom and exhortations about the necessity of taking up wisdom. In fact, Solomon was so wise that the Queen of Sheba heard his name and the name of the Lord, and came to try him with hard questions. And she 'spoke to him all that was in her heart. And Solomon told her all her questions; there was no question overlooked by the king which he did not tell her. And the Queen of Sheba saw all Solomon's wisdom' and his property. 'And she was beside herself. And she said to the king, The report is true which I heard in my land about thee and about thy wisdom; and I did not believe them that told me until the time that I came, and my eyes have seen it. And behold, they did not tell me the half. Thou hast surpassed in wisdom and goodness all the rumour that I heard.'[3] It is written about the same man: 'And the Lord gave Solomon understanding and very great wisdom and largeness of heart as the sand that is beside the sea. And Solomon's wisdom excelled far above the understanding of the ancients and all the wise men of Egypt. And he was wiser than all men; and he was wiser than Gethan the Ezrahite, and Emad and Chalcadi and Arada, sons of Mad; and he was famous in all the surrounding nations. And Solomon spoke three thousand parables, and his songs were five thousand. And he spoke of trees from the cedar that is in Lebanon even unto the hyssop that springs out of the wall. He spoke also of fishes and beasts. And all nations came to hear the wisdom of Solomon, even from all the kings of the earth who heard of his wisdom.'[4] And the gospel so desires wise men among believers that, in order to exercise the understanding of the hearers, it has expressed certain truths in enigmatic forms,

[1] Ps. l. 8.
[2] II Chron. i. 10–11.
[3] I Kings (III Regn.) x. 1–7.
[4] I Kings (III Regn.) iv. 25–30.

and some in the so-called dark sayings, some by parables, and others by problems. In fact, one of the prophets, Hosea, says at the end of his utterances: 'Who is wise and will understand these things? Or who is prudent and will know them?'[1] And Daniel and those imprisoned with him were so advanced in learning what was practised by the king's wise men in Babylon that they were shown to be ten times better than any of them.[2] It is also said in Ezekiel to the ruler of Tyre who was proud of his wisdom: 'Art thou wiser than Daniel? Every secret was not shown to thee.'[3]

46. If you also come to the books written after the time of Jesus you will find that the crowds of believers hear the parables outside, as they were worthy only of exoteric teaching. But the disciples privately learnt the explanation of the parables. For 'privately to his own disciples Jesus expounded all things',[4] honouring above the crowds those who were deemed worthy of his wisdom. And he promises to send to those who believe in him wise men and scribes, saying: 'Behold I will send to you wise men and scribes, and some of them you will kill and crucify.'[5] Moreover, Paul in the list of spiritual gifts given by God puts first the gift of wisdom, and second, as inferior to that, the word of knowledge, and third, even lower I think, faith. And as he values reason above miraculous workings, on this account he puts 'workings of miracles' and 'gifts of healing' in a lower place than the intellectual gifts.[6] In the Acts of the Apostles Stephen testified to Moses' scholarship, no doubt basing his statement on ancient documents which have not come to the notice of the multitude. For he says: 'And Moses was educated in all the wisdom of the Egyptians.'[7] This explains why it was suspected that in his wonders he did not produce the miracles in the way that he professed, through God's power, but by means of Egyptian spells because he was wise in these matters. The king suspected him of this and called the Egyptian magicians and wise men and sorcerers who were proved to be nothing in comparison with the wisdom in Moses which surpassed all the wisdom of the Egyptians.[8]

47. However, it is probably the words written by Paul in the first Epistle to the Corinthians,[9] where he is addressing Greeks who prided themselves on Greek wisdom, which have led some people to imagine that the Gospel does not want wise men. But let the man who imagines this understand that the passage is an attack upon bad men, saying that they are not wise concerning intelligible, invisible, and eternal things, but only interest themselves in things of sense, and that because they put every-

---

[1] Hos. xiv. 10. [2] Dan. i. 20. [3] Ezek. xxviii. 3.
[4] Mark iv. 34. [5] Matt. xxiii. 34. [6] I Cor. xii. 8–10.
[7] Acts vii. 22. [8] Exod. vii. 11. [9] I Cor. i. 18 ff.

thing into this last category, they become wise men of the world. So also, since there are many doctrines, those systems which regard material and corporeal things as fundamental and assert that all ultimate realities are corporeal, and which deny that there is anything beyond them, either what is called invisible or what is termed incorporeal, are, he says, the wisdom of this world, which is being brought to nought and made foolish as being the wisdom of this age. But when he speaks of the wisdom of God, he means those doctrines which change the soul from the things of this earth to be concerned with the blessedness with God and with what is called His kingdom, and which teach men to despise as transitory all sensible and visible things, to seek earnestly the invisible and to look on things that are unseen.[1] Being a lover of the truth Paul says of certain wise men among the Greeks, referring to the doctrines in which they are right, that 'though they knew God, they glorified him not as God, neither were thankful'. He testifies to the fact that they knew God. But he also says that they did not achieve this without God's help when he wrote: 'For God manifested it unto them.' And he hints, I think, at those who ascend to intelligible things when he writes that 'the invisible things of God from the creation of the world are clearly seen, being perceived through the things that are made, even his everlasting power and divinity, that they might be without excuse, because that knowing God they glorified him not as God neither were thankful'.[2]

48. Perhaps also some were led to suppose that no educated or wise or sensible man is converted because of the words, 'But you see your calling, brethren, how that not many wise men after the flesh, not many mighty, not many noble are called; but God chose the foolish things of the world, that he might put to shame those who are wise; and God chose the base things, and the things that are despised, and the things that are not, that he might bring to nought the things that are, that no flesh should glory in his presence.'[3] To one who thinks this we would say that Paul's words are not 'no wise man after the flesh', but 'not many wise men after the flesh'. And clearly, when Paul describes the character of those who are called bishops and portrays what sort of a man a bishop ought to be, he appoints that he should be a teacher, saying that he must be 'able also to refute the adversaries', that by his wisdom he may restrain those who speak vainly and deceive souls. Just as he prefers for the episcopate a man once married rather than one twice married, and a man unblameable rather than blameable, and a sober man rather than one not of this character, and a prudent man rather than one imprudent, and an orderly man rather than one even slightly disorderly; so he wishes that the man who is to obtain

---

[1] II Cor. iv. 18.　　　[2] Rom. i. 19–21.　　　[3] I Cor. i. 26–9.

preferment to the episcopate should be a teacher and capable of 'refuting the adversaries'.[1] How, then, is it reasonable for Celsus to criticize us as though we asserted, *Let no one educated, no one wise, no one sensible draw near?* On the contrary, let the educated, wise and sensible man come if he wishes, and none the less let anyone ignorant, stupid, uneducated, and childish, come as well. For the word promises to heal even such people if they come, and makes all men *worthy of God.*

49. It is a lie that those who teach the divine word want to *convince only the foolish, dishonourable, and stupid, and only slaves, women, and little children.* Not only does the gospel call these that it may make them better, but it also calls people much superior to them. For Christ is the Saviour of all men and specially of believers,[2] whether intelligent or simple-minded; and he is a propitiation to the Father for our sins, 'but not for our sins only, but also for those of the whole world'.[3] It is, therefore, super-fluous after this to desire us to reply to the following question of Celsus: *In any event, why is it bad to have been educated and to have studied the best doctrines, and both to be and to appear intelligent?* To have been truly educated is certainly not a bad thing. For education is the way to virtue. But not even *the wise men of the Greeks* would say that those who hold mistaken doctrines may be reckoned among the educated. And again, who would not admit that it is a good thing to have studied the best doctrines? But what doctrines shall we call the best other than those which are true and which exhort men to virtue? Furthermore, it is an excellent thing to be intelligent, but not merely to appear so, as Celsus says. In fact, to have been educated, and to have studied the best doctrines, and to be intelligent, does not hinder us from knowing God, but helps us. To say this is more appropriate for us than for Celsus, particularly if he is proved to be an Epicurean.

50. Let us see what he says next: *Moreover, we see that those who display their trickery in the market-places and go about begging would never enter a gathering of intelligent men, nor would they dare to reveal their noble beliefs*[4] *in their presence; but whenever they see adolescent boys and a crowd of slaves and a company of fools they push themselves in and show off.* Notice here also how he falsely accuses us when he likens us to people who display their *trickery* in the market-places and go about begging. What *trickery* do we display? Or what do we do that resembles these folk? For we, by readings of the Bible and explanations of the readings, encourage men to be pious towards the God of the universe and the virtues that share

[1] Titus i. 9-11; cf. I Tim. iii. 2.   [2] I Tim. iv. 10.
[3] I John ii. 1-2.
[4] K. tr. (prob. rightly) reads καλὰ τολμήσαντας with Pat.

piety's throne;[1] whereas we discourage people from despising the Deity and from all action contrary to right reason. Even philosophers would desire to gather so many to hear their words of exhortation to goodness. In particular, some of the Cynics have done this, conversing in public with any whom they meet.[2] Will people assert, then, that these philosophers who do not gather together the so-called educated, but call men from the street-corners to gather round and listen, are like those who display their *trickery* in the market-places and go about begging? Yet neither Celsus nor anyone of the same opinions finds fault with men who from philanthropic motives, as it seems to them, address their teaching even to the common people.

51. If the Cynics are not criticized for doing this, let us consider whether Christians do not exhort the masses to be good even better than they do. For philosophers who converse in public do not select their hearers, but anyone interested stops to listen. But as far as they can, Christians previously examine the souls of those who want to hear them, and test[3] them individually beforehand; when before entering the community the hearers seem to have devoted themselves sufficiently to the desire to live a good life, then they introduce them. They privately appoint one class consisting of recent beginners who are receiving elementary instruction and have not yet received the sign that they have been purified, and another class of those who, as far as they are able, make it their set purpose to desire nothing other than those things of which Christians approve. Among the latter class some are appointed to inquire into the lives and conduct of those who want to join the community in order that they may prevent those who indulge in trickery from coming to their common gathering; those who do not do this they whole-heartedly receive, and make them better every day. They follow a similar method also with those who fall into sin, and especially with the licentious, whom they drive out of the community—yet in Celsus' opinion they are like those who display trickery in the market-places! The distinguished school of the Pythagoreans built cenotaphs to those who turned back from their philosophy, reckoning that they had died.[4] But Christians mourn as dead men those who have been overcome by licentiousness or some outrageous sin because they have perished and died to God. They admit them some time later as though they had risen from the dead provided that they show a real conversion, though their period of probation is

---

[1] For the phrase, cf. Philo, *Leg. Alleg.* III, 247.
[2] For the similarity between Christian and Cynic preachers cf. Aelius Aristides, *Orat.* 46 (Dindorf, II, 394 f.), discussed by P. de Labriolle, *La Réaction païenne* (1934), pp. 79–87.
[3] Read προετάσαντες with Rob.   [4] See II, 12.

longer than that required of those who are joining the community for the first time. But they do not select those who have fallen after their conversion to Christianity for any office or administration in the Church of God,[1] as it is called.

52. Notice that Celsus says after this: *We see those who display their trickery in the market-places and go about begging*. Is not this a manifest lie and an irrelevant comparison? Celsus says that these people to whom he likens us, the men who display their *trickery* in the market-places and go about begging, *would never enter a gathering of intelligent men, nor would they dare to reveal their noble beliefs[2] in their presence; but whenever they see adolescent boys and a crowd of slaves and a company of fools, then they push themselves in and show off.* Here he is simply pouring abuse on us like the women on street corners, whose only object is to speak evil of one another. For we do everything in our power to see that our gathering consists of intelligent men, and we do dare to bring forward in the common discourse at the time of our gathering our most noble and divine beliefs when we have an intelligent audience. But we conceal and pass over the more profound truths whenever we see that the meeting consists of simple-minded folk who are in need of teaching which is figuratively called milk.

53. When Paul was writing to the Corinthians who were Greeks and had not yet been purified in their habits, he wrote: 'I have fed you with milk, not meat; for you were not yet able to bear it; nay, not even now are you able; for you are still carnal. For whereas there is among you jealousy and strife, are you not carnal and walk after the manner of men?'[3] The same writer, knowing that some truths are the food of a more perfect soul, but that other truths given to beginners are comparable to the milk of babes, says: 'And you have become such as have need of milk, and not solid food. For every one that partakes of milk is without experience of the word of righteousness; for he is a babe. But solid food is for perfect men, who by reason of use have their senses exercised to discern good and evil.'[4] Accordingly, would people who think that these sayings are right suppose that the noble beliefs of Christianity would never be mentioned at a gathering of intelligent men, but that whenever they see adolescent boys and a crowd of slaves and a company of fools, they publicly proclaim the divine and sacred doctrines, and show off about them to people like that? It is clear, however, to anyone who examines the whole purpose of our writings that Celsus was irritated against the Christian race like the vulgar mob and told these lies without looking into the matter.

---

[1] For exclusion of the lapsed from the clergy, cf. Cyprian, *Ep.* LXVII, 6; LXXII, 2; Peter of Alexandria, *Ep. Canon.* 10 (M. J. Routh, *Reliquiae Sacrae*, 2nd ed. 1846, IV, p. 35).

[2] Read καλὰ τολμᾶν with *Philocalia*, K. tr.

[3] I Cor. iii. 2–3.				[4] Heb. v. 12–14.

54. We confess that we do want to educate all men with the Word of God, even if Celsus does not wish to believe it, so that we may impart even to adolescent boys the encouragement appropriate to them and may teach slaves how they may obtain a free mind and receive noble birth from the Logos. Those among us who give a competent account of Christianity affirm that they are 'debtors to Greeks and barbarians, to wise and to unwise'.[1] For they do not deny that they ought to cure the souls even of the unwise, that as far as possible they may put away ignorance and earnestly seek more understanding; they hear the words of Solomon, 'O ye fools, be of an understanding heart', and 'Whoever among you is most stupid, let him incline to me, and I, wisdom who speak, exhort those lacking in sense.' 'Come, eat my bread and drink my wine which I mixed for you; leave folly that you may live and reform understanding in knowledge.'[2] I might also say this in reply to Celsus' argument as it is to the point. Do not philosophers call adolescent boys to hear them? And do they not exhort youths to abandon a very evil life for better things? Do they not want slaves to study philosophy? Or shall we criticize philosophers for encouraging slaves to pursue virtue, as Pythagoras did to Zamolxis, and Zeno to Persaeus, and those who recently encouraged Epictetus to be a philosopher? Or are you, Greeks, to be allowed to call adolescent boys and slaves and stupid men to study philosophy, while if we do this our action does not arise from love to our fellow-men, although we desire to heal every rational soul by the medical treatment of the Logos and to reconcile them to God, the Creator of all things? However, this is enough in reply to Celsus' attacks which are abuse rather than serious criticism.

55. Since he is so pleased with his abusive objections against us that he adds more of them, let us quote them and see whether it is the Christians or Celsus who are disgraced by what he says. He asserts: *In private houses also we see wool-workers, cobblers, laundry-workers, and the most illiterate and bucolic yokels, who would not dare to say anything at all in front of their elders and more intelligent masters. But whenever they get hold of children in private and some stupid women with them, they let out some astounding statements as, for example, that they must not pay any attention to their father and school-teachers, but must obey them; they say that these talk nonsense and have no understanding, and that in reality they neither know nor are able to do anything good, but are taken up with mere empty chatter. But they alone, they say, know the right way to live, and if the children would believe them, they would become happy and make[3] their home happy as well. And if just as they are speaking they see one of the school-teachers coming, or*

---

[1] Rom. i. 14.   [2] Prov. viii. 5; ix. 16 (4); ix. 5–6.
[3] Read ἀποφαίνειν with Bo., We.

some intelligent person, or even the father himself, the more cautious of them
flee in all directions; but the more reckless urge the children on to rebel. They
whisper to them that in the presence of their father and their schoolmasters
they do not feel able to explain anything to the children, since they do not want
to have anything to do with the silly and obtuse teachers who are totally
corrupted and far gone in wickedness and who inflict punishment on the children.
But, if they like, they should leave father and their schoolmasters, and go
along with the women and little children who are their playfellows to the
wooldresser's shop,[1] or to the cobbler's or the washerwoman's shop, that they
may learn perfection. And by saying this they persuade them.

56. See here also how he ridicules our teachers of the gospel who try
to elevate the soul in every way to the Creator of the universe, and who
show how men ought to despise all that is sensible and temporary and
visible, and who urge them to do all they can to attain to fellowship with
God and contemplation of intelligible and invisible things, and to reach
the blessed life with God and the friends of God. He compares them to
wool-workers in houses, cobblers, laundry-workers, and the most obtuse
yokels, as if they called children quite in infancy and women to evil
practices, telling them to leave their father and teachers and to follow
them. But let Celsus show us what prudent father or what teachers who
teach noble doctrines we have made children and women to leave. And
let him consider the women and children before and after their conversion
to our faith, to see whether the doctrines which they used to hear are better
than ours. Let him tell us how we make women and children leave noble
and sound teaching, and call them to wicked practices. But he will not be
able to prove anything of the kind against us. On the contrary, we deliver
women from licentiousness and from perversion caused by their associates,[2]
and from all mania for theatres and dancing, and from superstition; while
we make boys self-controlled when they come to the age of puberty and
burn with desires for sexual pleasure, showing them not only the disgrace
of their sins, but also what a state these pleasures produce in the souls of
bad men, and what penalties they will suffer and how they will be punished.

57. What teachers are said by us to talk nonsense and to have no
understanding, whom Celsus defends as men who teach excellent doctrines? Perhaps he thinks that those who call men to superstition and to
reverence licentious goddesses are fine teachers of women, and do not
talk nonsense, and also that the men are not lacking in understanding who
lead young men astray and bring them to all the wild excesses which we
know they do in many places. We, however, do all in our power to call

---

[1] For this translation, cf. W. den Boer in *Vigiliae Christianae*, IV (1950), pp. 61-4.
[2] Stoic language: cf. *J.T.S.* XLVIII (1947), p. 44.

students of philosophical doctrines to our worship of God and to show them its extraordinary purity. Celsus suggested in his remarks that we do not do this, but call only the stupid. We would say to him: If you were accusing us of drawing away from philosophy those who have been previously interested in it, you would not be speaking the truth, though your argument might have some plausibility. But here you say that we draw our converts away from good teachers. Show that these teachers are different from the teachers of philosophy or those who have laboured[1] to impart useful knowledge. However, he will not be able to show anything of the kind. We proclaim boldly, and not secretly, that those who live according to the word of God and look at everything from His point of view, and do every action whatsoever as in God's sight, will be blessed. Are these, then, the teachings of wool-workers, cobblers, laundry-workers, and the most illiterate yokels? No. And he will not be able to show that they are.

58. Those who in Celsus' opinion are similar to wool-workers in houses, and also like cobblers and laundry-workers and the most illiterate yokels, will not feel able, he says, to say anything in the presence of the children's father or schoolmasters, and cannot explain anything to them. To this we would reply: What kind of a father do you mean, sir, and what kind of teacher? If you mean one who approves of virtue and turns away from evil and welcomes that which is good, take notice that we would be very bold in telling our doctrines to his children, since we would be approved of by such a judge. If, on the other hand, we are silent before a father who has become notoriously opposed to virtue and goodness, and before men who teach doctrines contrary to sound reason, this is no charge against us, and it is not reasonable that you should make it so. In fact, although you yourself would pass on the mysteries of philosophy to young men and boys even if their father regarded philosophy as a fruitless and futile study, you would not teach them to the boys in the presence of their wicked fathers. You would want to give separate treatment to those you were encouraging to study philosophy if they were sons of bad parents, and would watch for opportunities of teaching the doctrines of philosophy to the young men. And we will say the same of teachers. If we turn them away from teachers who instruct them in the improprieties of the Comedy and the licentious writers of iambics, and in all else which neither improves the speaker nor benefits the hearers, and who do not know[2] how to interpret poems philosophically and to choose in each case those which contribute to the welfare of the young, then we are doing something which

---

[1] Read πεπονημένους with K. tr.
[2] Read εἰδότων with K. tr., agreeing with the previous διδασκάλων.

we are not ashamed to confess. But if you were to show me teachers who
give preparatory teaching in philosophy and train people in philosophical
study, I would not dissuade young men from listening to these; but after
they had first been trained in a general education and in philosophical
thought I would try to lead them on to the exalted height, unknown to
the multitude, of the profoundest doctrines of the Christians, who discourse about the greatest and most advanced truths, proving and showing
that this philosophy was taught by the prophets of God and the apostles
of Jesus.

59. Then after this Celsus realizes that he has abused us too bitterly,
and continues as if he were excusing himself: *And that I am not criticizing
them any more bitterly than the truth compels me, anyone may see also from
this. Those who summon people to the other mysteries make this preliminary
proclamation: Whosoever has pure hands and a wise tongue. And again,
others say: Whosoever is pure from all defilement, and whose soul knows
nothing of evil, and who has lived well and righteously. Such are the preliminary exhortations of those who promise purification from sins. But let us
hear what folk these Christians call. Whosoever is a sinner, they say,
whosoever is unwise, whosoever is a child, and, in a word, whosoever is
a wretch, the kingdom of God will receive him.*[1] *Do you not say that a sinner
is he who is dishonest, a thief, a burglar, a poisoner, a sacrilegious fellow, and
a grave-robber? What others would a robber invite and call?* We reply to this
that it is not the same thing to call men who are sick in their souls to be
cured, as it is to call healthy men to a knowledge and understanding of
deeper spiritual truths. We consider both of these. At the beginning
when we call men to be cured we encourage sinners to come and hear
words which teach them not to sin, and the unwise to hear words which
will implant in them understanding, and children to advance to a manly
character, and those, who are in a word wretches, to happiness, or, to use
a more appropriate word, to blessedness.[2] But when some of those who
have been thus encouraged make progress and show that they have been
purified by the Logos, and do all in their power to live better lives, then
we call them to our mysteries. 'For we speak wisdom among the perfect.'[3]

60. As we teach that 'into a malicious soul wisdom shall not enter, nor
dwell in the body that is subject to sin',[4] we say: Let anyone come to us
who has *pure hands* and so lifts up holy hands[5] to God, and who because

---

[1] Cf. Julian, 239C; 336A, B. On the moral standards required of would-be initiates in the
Eleusinian mysteries, cf. Cumont, *Lux perpetua*, pp. 240 f., who remarks that originally no
moral requirement was made. Later purity was demanded, as Celsus' words here show.
[2] *Eudaimonia* does not occur in Biblical Greek.
[3] I Cor. ii. 6.   [4] Wisd. of Sol. i. 4.
[5] I Tim. ii. 8.

he offers sublime and heavenly sacrifices can say, 'The lifting up of my
hands is an evening sacrifice.'[1] And anyone who has *a wise tongue*
because he studies the law of the Lord day and night, and has his senses
exercised by reason of use to discern good and evil,[2] should not fear to go
on to solid, rational food, which is suited to athletes of piety and every
virtue. And since the grace of God is with all who love in incorruptness[3]
the teacher of the doctrines of immortality, let anyone who is pure not
only *from all defilement,* but also from what are regarded as minor sins, be
boldly initiated into the mysteries of the religion of Jesus which are
delivered only to the holy and pure. Celsus' priest says: *Anyone whose
soul knows nothing of evil,* let him come. But according to Jesus' teaching
the one who leads to God initiates who have been purified in soul will say:
Anyone whose soul has for a long time known nothing of evil, and especially
since he came to be healed by the Logos, let him hear even those doctrines
which were privately revealed by Jesus to his genuine disciples. Accordingly, in his contrast between the exhortations of those who initiate men
among the Greeks and those who teach the doctrines of Jesus, he does not
know the difference between calling bad men to be cured and calling those
already pure to more mystical doctrines.

61. It is not, therefore, to mysteries and to share in wisdom 'hidden in
a mystery which God foreordained before the ages to the glory'[4] of his
saints that we call the dishonest man, the thief, burglar, poisoner, sacrilegious fellow, grave-robber, and any others whom Celsus might name
for rhetorical effect, but it is for healing. There are some characteristics in
the divine nature of the Logos which help to cure those who are sick, of
whom the Logos says: 'They who are strong need no physician, but they
who are sick.'[5] But there are others which show to those who are pure in
soul and body 'the revelation of the mystery which has been kept in silence
through times eternal, but is now manifested, both by the prophetic scriptures and by the appearance of our Lord Jesus Christ';[6] which is made
clear to each one of the perfect, and illuminates the mind so that it grasps
the true knowledge of reality. It is merely a rhetorical accusation against
us when, after giving a list of the most repulsive men, he continues: *What
others would a robber invite and call?* We will reply to this that a robber
calls such men in order to use their wickedness against men whom he wants
to murder and rob. But even if a Christian does call those whom the
robber would call, he does so with a different motive, that he may bind up

---

[1] Ps. cxl. 2.
[2] Ps. i. 2; Heb. v. 14.
[3] Eph. vi. 24.
[4] I Cor. ii. 7.
[5] Matt. ix. 12. For the Christology here, cf. II, 64, above.
[6] Rom. xvi. 25–6; II Tim. i. 10.

their wounds by the gospel,[1] and pour medicines of the gospels upon the soul festering with evils, like the wine, olive-oil and emollient, and the other medicinal aids which relieve the soul.

62. Then he misrepresents the exhortations which have been said and written to persuade people who live evil lives to pursue virtue, which call them to repentance and to reform their souls, asserting that we *say that God has been sent to sinners.* When he says this, it is as if he criticized certain people for saying that a physician was sent by a very philanthropic king for the sake of the sick folk in his city. The divine Logos was sent as a physician to sinners, but to those already pure and no longer sinning as a teacher of divine mysteries. But Celsus was not able to see this distinction (for he did not want to find the truth) and says: *But why was he not sent to those without sin? What evil is it not to have sinned?* We answer to this that, if by *those without sin* he means those who no longer sin, Jesus our Saviour was sent to them also, but not as a physician. If, however, by *those without sin* he means those who have never sinned (for his words do not state his precise meaning), we will say that it is impossible for a man to be without sin in this sense.[2] But when we say this we except the supposedly human Jesus,[3] who did no sin.[4] Celsus speaks out of mere malice against us, as if we asserted that *God will receive the unrighteous man if, conscious of his wickedness, he humbles himself; but as for the righteous man, though he may look up to Him with virtue from the beginning, God will not receive him.* We say that it is impossible for any man to look up to God with virtue from the beginning. For of necessity evil must exist among men from the first, as Paul says: 'But when the commandment came sin revived and I died.'[5] Furthermore, we do not teach that in order that the unrighteous man may be accepted by God it is enough for him to humble himself, conscious of his wickedness. It is only if after condemning himself for his past life he walks humbly for the past and orderly for the future, that God will accept him.

63. Then he does not understand the meaning of the words 'Every one that exalts himself shall be humbled',[6] nor did he learn even from Plato that the noble and good man walks humble and orderly.[7] He did not know also that we say, 'Humble yourselves therefore under the mighty hand of God, that he may exalt you in due time.'[8] For he says that *men who are appointed to preside over legal proceedings stop people who lament over their misdeeds from uttering piteous wails,[9] that their judgment may not be affected*

---

[1] Cf. Luke x. 34.   [2] Cf. IV, 96; Origen, *Comm. in Matt.* XIII, 23.
[3] For the phrase, cf. II, 25.   [4] I Pet. ii. 22.   [5] Rom. vii. 9–10.
[6] Luke xiv. 11; xviii. 14.   [7] Plato, *Laws*, 716A.   [8] I Pet. v. 6.
[9] 'Piteous wails': Plato, *Phaedrus* 267C. Celsus' language is Stoic; cf. *J.T.S.* XLVIII (1947), p. 47.

*by feelings of mercy, but should rather be based on the truth. But perhaps God
does not judge on consideration of the truth, but is influenced by flattery.*
What sort of flattery and what piteous wailing is to be found in the divine
scriptures? The sinner says in his prayer to God: 'I acknowledged my sin
and I did not hide my iniquity; I said, I will confess my iniquity to the
Lord',[1] and so on. But could he show that such a confession has not the
power to bring about the conversion of sinners when they humble themselves under God in their prayers? Confused by his hasty criticisms he
contradicts himself. In one place he appears to recognize that a man may
be righteous and without sin if he looks up to God with virtue from the
beginning, while in another he accepts the view which we hold when we
ask: 'What man is perfectly righteous? Or who is without sin?'[2] For as
if accepting this he says: *It is probably true that it is somehow natural for
the human race to sin.* Then as though all people are not called by the
Logos, he says: *Therefore, he ought to have called all men in general if, in
fact, all men commit sin.* But we showed earlier that Jesus said 'Come unto
me all you who labour and are heavy laden, and I will give you rest.'[3]
Accordingly, all men who labour and are heavy laden because of their
sinful nature are called to the rest of the Logos of God. For 'God sent
forth his word and healed them and delivered them from their distresses'.[4]

64. He asks *Why on earth this preference for sinners?* and continues in
the same vein; we reply that it is not true without qualification that
a sinner is preferred before one who is not a sinner. But sometimes
a sinner who realizes his own sin, and on this account comes to repentance
and walks humbly for his sins, is preferred before one who is thought to
be less of a sinner, and who does not think himself to be a sinner, but is
conceited on account of certain superior qualities of which he thinks he is
conscious, and on which he prides himself. This is made clear to those
who are willing to read the gospels with an open mind by the parable
about the publican who said, 'Be merciful to me a sinner', and about the
Pharisee who boasted with a wicked pride, saying, 'I thank thee that I am
not as other men are, extortionate, unjust, adulterers, or even as this
publican.' After quoting the words uttered by both Jesus went on to say:
'This man went down to his house justified rather than the other; for every
one that exalts himself shall be abased, and every one that humbles himself
shall be exalted.'[5] Therefore, we do not *blaspheme God* or *tell lies* when we
teach everyone and anyone to realize the smallness of man in comparison
with the greatness of God, and to ask Him always for the needs of our
nature, since He alone is able to complete our deficiencies.

[1] Ps. xxxi. 5.   [2] Job xv. 14; xxv. 4.   [3] Matt. xi. 28; cf. II, 73.
[4] Ps. cvi. 20.   [5] Luke xviii. 13; xi, 14.

65. He thinks that *we say such things to encourage sinners because we are unable to convert anyone really good and righteous, and that this is the reason why we open our doors to the most impious and abominable men.* If anyone were to consider our people as a whole with an open mind, we could show him more who have turned from a not very wicked life than who have turned from most abominable sins. Moreover, those who are conscious of living better lives, who long that the doctrines preached about the change for a better life brought by God may be true, are naturally more ready to accept what is said than people who have lived very wicked lives, who by their conscience itself are hindered from believing the truth that they will be punished by the Judge of all with a punishment which will be appropriate to anyone who has committed such great sins, and which will be inflicted with good reason by the Judge of all. Sometimes when even utterly abominable people are willing to believe in the doctrine of punishment on account of the hope which repentance offers,[1] they are hindered by the habit of sinning because they have been, as it were, dyed deep in evil[2] and are no longer able to forsake it easily to live a life that is ordered and which follows the principles of right reason. Even Celsus understood this when for some unknown reason he later says this: *And yet I suppose it is obvious to every one that no one could entirely change people who sin by nature and habit, not even by punishment, much less by mercy; for it is very hard to change a nature completely; but those without sin take part in a better life.*

66. But even here Celsus seems to me to be quite wrong, since he does not allow the possibility of a complete change with people who have sinned *by nature* and who do this out of *habit*, and thinks that they are not even to be healed *by punishment*. It seems clear that all men have a natural tendency to sin, and that some not only have a natural tendency, but sin also by habit. But it is not true that all men are incapable of a complete change. For we learn both from every sect of philosophy and from the divine word that there are people who have undergone so great a change that they have manifested[3] an example of the best life. Some say this of Heracles and Odysseus among the heroes, and of Socrates among those of a later age, and Musonius among those who have lived quite recently.[4] Therefore, Celsus does not only lie against us when he says *I suppose it is obvious to every one that people who sin by nature and habit* would not be led

---

[1] The passage should so be read with Wif., omitting the marginal gloss which K. includes in the text, and placing a comma not before διά but after ἐλπίδα.

[2] Cf. I, 52.

[3] Read ἐκκεῖσθαι with Wif.

[4] For an account of Musonius, see M. P. Charlesworth, *Five Men* (1936), pp. 33–61; C. E. Lutz in *Yale Classical Studies*, X (1947), pp. 3–147.

entirely to change for the better by anyone, *not even by punishment;* he is also opposed to eminent philosophers who have not denied the possibility that men may attain to virtue.

Although he does not show exactly what he meant, nevertheless even if we give him the benefit of the doubt we will prove that his argument is not sound. For he says, *No one could entirely change people who sin by nature and habit, not even by punishment;* and we have refuted him as well as we could on what is the apparent sense of his statement.

67. But probably he wanted to indicate that no one could entirely change, even by punishment, people who not only have a natural tendency to sins of this sort which are committed by the most abominable men, but are also gripped by habit. This also is proved false by the stories of certain philosophers. For who would not reckon among the most abominable men a man who somehow endured obedience to a master who put him in a house of ill-fame, so that he should receive anyone who desired to dishonour him? Such is the story told of Phaedo. And who would not say that he was one of the most repulsive men who with a flute-girl and profligate fellow-revellers burst in upon the school of the venerable Xenocrates to insult a man whom his associates admired?[1] But nevertheless reason was strong enough to convert even these men, and to make them advance so far in philosophy that Phaedo was adjudged by Plato as worthy to expound Socrates' discourse on immortality and to describe his courage in prison, when he gave no thought to the hemlock but fearlessly and with complete calm in his soul talked of important and profound questions, which even people who are quite ordered in mind and are undisturbed by any difficult circumstance are scarcely able to follow. And Polemo instead of being a drunkard became very temperate, and succeeded to the school of Xenocrates who was famous for his moral earnestness. Celsus, then, does not speak the truth when he says: *No one could entirely change people who sin by nature and habit, even by punishment.*

68. However, it is not at all remarkable that order, arrangement, and style of philosophical doctrines should have caused such effects in those I have mentioned, and in others[2] who have lived evil lives. But when we consider that the doctrines which Celsus calls *vulgar*[3] have been filled with power as though they were spells, and when we see that the words[4] turn multitudes all at once from being licentious to living the most tranquil life, and from being unrighteous to nobility of character, and from being cowards or effeminate to such bravery that they even despise death for the

---

[1] See 1, 64, above.   [2] Read ἄλλους with Bo., K. tr.
[3] Cf. III, 73.
[4] Wif. brackets τοὺς λόγους, perhaps rightly.

sake of the piety which they believe to be right,[1] are we not justified in
admiring the power in the message? For the word of those who proclaimed
these doctrines at the beginning and laboured to establish Churches of
God, and their preaching also, did not possess a persuasion such as that of
those who profess the wisdom of Plato or one of the philosophers, who
were but men and had nothing beyond human nature about them. The
demonstration in Jesus' apostles was given by God and convinced men by
spirit and power.[2] For this reason their word ran very quickly[3] and sharply,
or rather God's Word which was working through them to change many
of those who sin by nature and by habit. Those whom a man could not
change even by punishment, the Word transformed, shaping and moulding
them according to His will.

69. Celsus is consistent with what he has already said when he
continues: *It is very difficult to change a man's nature completely.* We
affirm that every rational soul is of the same nature, and deny that any
wicked nature has been made by the Creator of the universe; but we think
that many men have become evil by upbringing and by perversion and by
environment,[4] so that in some people evil has even become second nature.
We are convinced that for the divine Logos to change evil which has
become second nature is not only not impossible, but is not even very
difficult, if only a man admits that he must trust himself to the supreme
God and do every action by reference to His good pleasure. With God it
is not true that

In equal honour are both bad and good,

nor do

The idle man and he who has laboured much perish alike.[5]

And if for some it is very hard to change, we must say that the cause lies
in their will, which refuses to accept the fact that the supreme God is to
each man a righteous Judge of every past action done in this life. Determination and application can achieve much even with problems which
appear very difficult, and, if I may exaggerate, which are all but impossible.
Men have made it their aim to walk on a tight-rope stretched across the
middle of the theatre in mid-air, and to carry very heavy objects; if it has
been possible for human nature to achieve this with application and practice, is it impossible for a nature which has desired to live virtuously to do
so, even if formerly it was very bad?[6] Moreover, consider whether the

[1] Omit ἐν. In the next line K. tr. would read αὐτῷ ⟨τῷ λόγῳ⟩ which is better Greek
and good sense; perhaps we should read αὐτοῖς, but the singular may be influenced by
what follows.   [2] Cf. I Cor. ii. 4.   [3] Ps. cxlvii. 4.
   [4] Stoic language: cf. III, 57, above.   [5] Homer, *Il.* IX, 319–20.
   [6] A Stoic illustration, used to make the same point by Seneca, *de Ira* II, 12, 5;
Musonius Rufus, p. 30 (ed. Hense); Epictetus III, 12, 2; Chrysostom, *Hom. de Statuis*,
XIX, 4 (13); *Hom. in Matt.* XXI, 3.

man who asserts that it is impossible is not finding fault with the nature of the Creator of the rational being rather than with the creature, as if He had made human nature capable of doing very difficult things which are quite unprofitable, but incapable of attaining its own blessedness. But this is a sufficient reply to his remark that *it is very hard to change a nature completely.*

Next he says that *those without sin take part in a better life.* He does not make clear whom he holds to be without sin, whether he means those who have never sinned from the beginning, or those who have not sinned since their conversion. It is impossible for men not to have sinned *from* the beginning; but on rare occasions some are to be found who have not sinned since their conversion, who achieve this because they have turned to the saving word. But at the time when they came to the word they were not like this. For without the word, the perfect word indeed, it is impossible for any man to become sinless.

70. Then he answers us as though we asserted that *God will be able to do everything.* He does not consider what we mean by this, and in what sense we use the word 'everything' here, and in what way He is *able.* It is not necessary to discuss this now, for not even he objected to this view, although it was possible for him to have done so with plausible arguments. Perhaps, however, he did not understand the persuasive argument which could be brought against this opinion; or, if he did understand it, he may have perceived the reply to the objections. In our opinion God is able to do everything which He can do without abandoning His position as God, and as good, and as wise. But Celsus talks like one who did not understand in what sense God can do everything, when he says, *He will not want to do anything unrighteous,* and when he allows that *He could even do what is unrighteous, but does not wish to do so.* We, however, maintain that just as that which is naturally sweet, by the very fact of its sweetness, cannot make anything bitter because it only has the power to sweeten,[1] and as nothing which naturally illuminates can darken anything because it is light, so also God can do nothing wrong. For the power to do wrong contradicts His divinity and all His divine power.[2] If there is anything in existence which can do wrong and which has a natural tendency to do so, the reason why it can do wrong is that in its nature there is nothing at all which excludes this possibility.

---

[1] This peculiar sense of αἰτία is common in Origen; emendation is unnecessary. Wif. reads οὐσίαν. The illustration itself is Stoic: Diog. Laert. VII, 103 'Just as it is the property of heat to warm and not to cool, so also is it that of good to benefit, not to do harm.' Cf. Clem. Al. *Strom.* I, 86, 3; VI, 159, 4; Philo, *Leg. Alleg.* I, 5; Athenagoras, *Leg.* 24; Tertullian, *adv. Hermog.* 13. It goes back to Plato, *Rep.* 335 D.

[2] On divine omnipotence, cf. Celsus in V, 14; Origen in V, 23; *de Princ.* II, 9, 1; IV, 4, 8; *Comm. ser. in Matt.* 95. See R. M. Grant, *Miracle and Natural Law* (1952), pp. 127 ff.

71. After this he assumes to be our opinion what is not admitted by intelligent believers, although perhaps it may be held by some unintelligent folk, saying that *God, like those who are subject to feelings of pity, is subject to compassion for people who lament and relieves bad men, while He casts out good men who have done nothing of that kind, which is very unfair.*[1] We believe that God does not relieve any bad man who has not yet been led to pursue virtue, nor does He have mercy, to use the word in its usual sense, on anyone who laments because He is influenced by his lamentation; but on the ground of repentance God will accept even those who change from the worst life,[2] if they severely condemn themselves for their past sins, so that for this they mourn, as it were, and lament for themselves as people who have perished because of their past misdeeds, and if they show evidence of a repentance worthy of the name. For virtue grants forgiveness to men like this, and comes to dwell in their souls after it has cast out the evil which previously used to grip them. But even if it were not virtue, but only a genuine progress which the soul had achieved, even this is enough, in proportion to the degree of progress, to cast out and to remove the flood of evil, so that it almost[3] ceases to exist any longer in the soul.

72. Then he makes this remark, put into the mouth of a teacher of our doctrine: *For the wise turn away from what we say, since they are led astray and hindered by wisdom.* We will reply to this that, whether wisdom is knowledge of things divine and human and of their causes,[4] or, as the divine word defines it, 'a breath of the power of God, and a pure influence of the glory of the Almighty', and 'the brightness of the everlasting light and unspotted mirror of the power of God and image of his goodness',[5] nobody wise would be turned away from what is said by a Christian who has a competent knowledge of Christian doctrine, nor would he be led astray or hindered by it. For it is not true wisdom which leads astray, but ignorance; and the only sure realities in the world are knowledge and truth which are derived from wisdom.[6] But if you would deny this definition of wisdom, and call wise a man who forms any doctrine whatever on the basis of certain sophisms, we will say that the sort of man who possesses what you call wisdom is in truth turned away from the words of God since he is led astray by plausible fallacies and sophisms and is hindered by them. According to our scriptures 'knowledge of wickedness is not wisdom';[7] as it is, if I may use the phrase, 'knowledge of wickedness'

---

[1] Cf. Celsus in III, 63. With Origen's apology for the word 'mercy', which to the Stoics was a vice and not a virtue, cf. Clem. Al. *Strom.* IV, 38, 1: see my remarks in *J.T.S.* XLVIII (1947), p. 47.

[2] Omit comma after θεός.

[3] Read ἐγγύς που with Wif.

[4] The standard Stoic definition.

[5] Wisd. of Sol. vii. 25–6.

[6] For the language, cf. Plato, *Rep.* 508E.

[7] Sirach xix. 22.

which is possessed by those who hold false opinions and have been deceived by petty sophisms, on this account in such people I would call it ignorance rather than wisdom.

73. After this he again pours abuse on the man who teaches Christian doctrine and asserts of him that he expounds *ludicrous opinions*. But he does not clearly show what he asserts to be ludicrous. He merely abuses us, saying that *no intelligent man believes the doctrine, since he is vexed*[1] *by the multitude of people who are converted by it.* Here he behaves like a man who says that, on account of the multitude of uneducated people who live according to the laws, no intelligent man obeys Solon, for example, or Lycurgus, or Zaleucus, or one of the other lawgivers. This argument is particularly strong if he admits that an intelligent man is one who lives virtuously. Just as in these instances the lawgivers did what they thought would be beneficial when they surrounded the people with particular directions and laws, so also because God gives laws by Jesus to men everywhere, He leads even the unintelligent since such people can be led on to what is better. As we have explained above, God knew this when He said by Moses: 'They have moved me to jealousy with that which is no god, they have provoked me to anger with their idols; and I will move them to jealousy with those which are not a people, I will provoke them to anger with a foolish nation.'[2] Paul also knew this when he said: 'God chose the foolish things of the world that he might put to shame the wise',[3] using the word 'wise' in a loose sense to mean those who seem to have made progress in learning, although they have fallen away to atheistic polytheism. For 'professing themselves to be wise, they became fools, and changed the glory of the incorruptible God for the likeness of an image of corruptible man, and of birds, and of fourfooted beasts, and of creeping things'.[4]

74. He criticizes *the teacher* also for *seeking the stupid*. We would say to him, Whom do you call stupid? Strictly speaking, every bad man is stupid.[5] If, then, you call bad men stupid, in leading men to study philosophy would you seek to lead bad men or good? You cannot do so to the good; for they have already become philosophers. What of the bad then? But if you lead bad men, then you lead stupid men. If you also seek to bring many people like this to philosophy, then you also are *seeking the stupid*. But I, although I do seek the so-called stupid, follow the method[6] of a philanthropic physician who seeks the sick that he may bring relief

---

[1] Read περισπώμενον with Bo., Del. Cf. Bader, p. 8.
[2] Deut. xxxii. 31, quoted in II, 78, above.
[3] I Cor. i. 27.   [4] Rom. i. 22–3.
[5] Stoic doctrine. Cf. H. v. Arnim, *S.V.F.* III, 657 ff.
[6] Read ὁμοιόν τι and in the next line προσαγάγῃ with *Philocalia*.

to them and strengthen them. But if by 'stupid' you mean those who are not clever but very superstitious, I answer you that I do all in my power to improve even these, but I certainly do not want the assembly of Christians to consist of these. I seek rather the cleverer and sharper minds because they are able to understand the explanation of problems and of the hidden truths set forth in the law, the prophets, and the gospels. You despised these as if they contained nothing of importance; but you did not examine their meaning, or attempt to enter into the purpose of the writers.

75. After this he also says that *the man who teaches the doctrines of Christianity is like a man who promises to restore bodies to health, but turns his patients away from attending to expert physicians because his lack of training would be shown up by them.*[1] We will answer to this: Who are the physicians from whom, you say, we turn away the uneducated? For you do not recognize that we attempt to convert philosophers to Christianity, in order that you may regard as physicians those philosophers from whom we turn away those whom we call to the divine word. Either he makes no reply since he cannot call them physicians, or he has to take refuge in finding them among the vulgar who even indulge in vulgar chatter about polytheistic worship and anything else of which uneducated people talk. In either case his answer will prove that there is no force in his objection that our teacher turns men away from expert physicians.

Supposing that we were to turn away from the philosophy of Epicurus and from the supposed physicians who follow his opinions, people who are deceived by them, would we not act most reasonably in keeping them away from a dangerous disease, for which Celsus' physicians are responsible, which denies providence and maintains that pleasure is the highest good? Let us grant, also, that we turn those whom we convert to our doctrine away from other physicians who are philosophers, such as the Peripatetics who deny that providence has any care for us and that there is any relationship between God and man. Are we not pious to train and cure those who have been persuaded to follow us, urging them to devote themselves to the supreme God, and when we deliver those who believe us from serious wounds caused by the doctrines of so-called philosophers? Let us grant, again, that we turn away others from Stoic physicians because they think that God is corruptible, and affirm that His essence is a material substance, which is entirely changeable and subject to alteration and transformation, and believe that at some times everything is destroyed and God alone left.[2] Why should we not deliver those who believe us

[1] Read ἐλέγχεσθαι ⟨ἀν⟩ with K. tr.
[2] For these doxographic formulas, cf. I, 21.

from such evil doctrines, and lead them to the pious doctrine which teaches them to devote themselves to the Creator, and to admire the author of the teaching of the Christians, who out of his very great love to man converts men to God and has arranged for his teaching to be spread abroad for the instruction of the souls of all mankind? It may be true, also, that we cure those who have suffered harm caused by the foolish doctrine of re-incarnation, taught by the physicians who degrade the rational nature sometimes to an entirely irrational animal, sometimes even to that which is incapable of perception.[1] Do we not train those who believe in the Gospel to be better in their souls? Christian doctrine does not teach that unconsciousness or loss of reason will be inflicted on a bad man as a punishment, but shows that troubles and punishments are applied by God to bad men as medicines to convert them. This is the view of intelligent Christians, though they accommodate themselves to the more simple-minded in the way that fathers do with very young children.

We do not *take refuge with silly and foolish yokels, saying to them, Run away from physicians.* Nor do we say *See that none of you ever obtains knowledge,* nor that *knowledge is a bad thing.* Nor are we so crazy as to say that *knowledge takes away from men the health of their soul.* Further, we would not say that anyone ever *perished by wisdom,* and we do not say *attend to me,* even if we are *teaching.* But we do say, Attend to the God of the universe, and to Jesus the teacher of the doctrines about Him. And none of us is so boastful as to say to pupils what Celsus has put into the mouth of *the teacher,* that *I alone will save you.* See, therefore, what lies he tells against us. Nor do we say that genuine *physicians destroy those whom they profess to cure.*

76. He also has a second illustration to bring against us, saying that our *teacher acts like a drunkard who enters a party of drunkards and accuses sober people of being drunk.* Let him show from the Bible, taking Paul for example, that Jesus' apostle was drunk and that his words were not sober, or from John's writings that his ideas do not breathe a spirit which shows him to be temperate and free from the drunkenness of evil. Therefore, no one who is self-controlled and teaches Christian doctrine is drunk; and when Celsus says this he is pouring abuse on us in an unphilosophical manner. Let Celsus tell us which sober men are accused by us when we expound the doctrines of Christianity; for in our opinion all people are drunk who address lifeless objects as gods. And why do I say 'drunk'? For rather are they demented to rush eagerly to the temples and to worship

---

[1] Plato held that human souls could become re-incarnate in animals; metempsychosis into plants, though not stated by Plato himself, was held by later Platonists such as Plotinus (e.g. *Enn.* III, 4, 2).

images or animals as gods. And no less insane than these are people who think that things made by labourers and sometimes by very wicked men are made to the honour of true gods.[1]

77. After this he asserts that *the teacher is like a man with ophthalmia*, and that the learners are like *men with ophthalmia*, and he says that *the teacher in the presence of people suffering from ophthalmia accuses men with sharp eyes of having defective eyesight.* In our view, however, who are the people who cannot see? Are they not those[2] who cannot look up from the vast size of the things in the world and from the beauty of the creatures, and perceive that they ought to worship and admire and reverence only the Maker of these things, and that it is not fitting to reverence any of the objects made by men and used to the honour of the gods, whether this worship is associated with the divine Creator or not? For it is the act of people blind in understanding to compare the Infinite, which surpasses in excellence all created nature, with objects which are in no way comparable. Therefore, we do not say that people with sharp eyesight suffer from ophthalmia or are defective; but we do maintain that those who in ignorance of God give themselves to the temples, the images, and so-called sacred months, have been blinded in mind, and especially when they live in impiety and licentiousness, not even seeking to do anything honourable at all, but doing everything of which they ought to be ashamed.

78. After this, though he has brought such grave charges against us, he wants to make it look as if he could speak still further, but passes these over. His words are as follows: *These are the accusations which I bring, and there are others like them (for I will not recount every one); and I affirm that they offend and insult God, that they may lead wicked men away with vain hopes and persuade them to despise good men,[3] saying that if they keep away from them it will be better for them.* Our reply to this would be based on the evidence[4] of those who are converted to Christianity which shows that it is not wicked men who are persuaded by this gospel so much as the more simple-minded and (as the multitude would say) the unsophisticated. For these men try to devote themselves to the Christian religion out of fear of the threatened punishments; so successfully are they overcome by the gospel that by fear of what are called in the Bible everlasting punishments they despise every torture devised by men against them and death with countless agonies. No sensible person would say that this was the behaviour of people with wicked motives. How could people with a wicked motive practise chastity and self-control, or generosity and social

[1] Cf. 1, 5.
[2] Read with Wif. τίνες οὖν, εἴποιμεν ⟨ἂν⟩, οἱ καθ᾽ ἡμᾶς, omitting Ἕλληνες as a gloss.
[3] In Celsus κρειττόνων is masculine; Origen takes it as neuter in the next chapter.
[4] Read ἐναργείας with We., K. tr.

service? Not even the fear of God, which the Word uses as beneficial for
the masses to exhort those who are not yet able to see what ought to be
chosen for its own sake to choose it as the supreme good, even surpassing all that it is said to be, is able to have any effect upon a man who
wilfully lives in wickedness.[1]

79. If anyone imagines that in this respect with the majority of those
who believe the gospel there is more superstition than wickedness, and
finds fault with our doctrine for making them superstitious, we would say
to him that, just as one of the lawgivers[2] replied to the man who asked if he
had given the citizens the best laws that he had not given them absolutely
the best, but the best that they were able to receive, so also the author of
Christian doctrine could speak as follows: 'I gave the multitude the best
laws and teaching that they were able to receive for their moral improvement, threatening sinners with pains and punishments which are not false
but real,[3] and which are necessarily inflicted for the correction of those who
resist, even though they do not understand at all the intention of the one
who inflicts the punishment on the object of the pains; for this is beneficial
in intention, and is expressed sometimes in accordance with the truth, and
sometimes in a veiled form when that it is expedient.' But, broadly
speaking, those who set forth the doctrines of Christianity do not *lead
away wicked men*, nor do they *insult God*. For we say of God both what is
true and what seems to the multitude to be clear, although it is not clear to
them in the way that it is to the few who endeavour to understand Christian doctrines philosophically.

80. Celsus says that Christians are led away with *vain hopes*, and
attacks the doctrine of the blessed life and of fellowship with God.
We answer him thus. My good man, the implication of your attack is
that both the Pythagoreans and the Platonists are led away with vain hopes
in believing the doctrine that the soul can ascend to the vault of heaven and
in the region above the heavens gaze on the things seen by the blessed
spectators.[4] By what you say, Celsus, those also who believe in the
survival of the soul and who live so that they may become heroes and enjoy
the company of the gods, are led away with vain hopes.[5] And probably
also those who have been convinced that the mind from without[6] is

---

[1] The text is restored by Wif. Read ἐπαγγελίαν, οὐδ' οὗτος τῷ κατὰ....
[2] The story is told of Solon by Plutarch (*Solon*, 15).
[3] Contrast IV, 19 where such threats are 'more false than true'.
[4] Cf. Plato, *Phaedrus*, 247, 250.
[5] For the Stoic conception of heroes, cf. III, 37.
[6] Aristotle, *de Gen. Anim.* II, 3 (736b 5 ff.); cf. *Placita*, IV, 5, 11 (Diels, *Dox. Gr.* 392); Alex. Aphrod. *de Anima Libri Mantissa*, 108, 19 ff. Bruns. The text should read ὡς ἀθανάτου καὶ μόνου διεξαγωγὴν after Rohde, *Psyche*, E. T., p. 511 (though his correction διαγωγὴν is quite unnecessary). So also We., K. tr.

immortal and will alone have life after death, would be said by Celsus to be led away with vain hopes. Let him, therefore, no longer conceal the sect to which he belongs, but admit that he is an Epicurean. And let him argue in opposition to the opinions held by Greeks and barbarians, which are not to be lightly passed over, concerning the immortality of the soul, or its survival, or the immortality of the mind. Let him show that these doctrines deceive with vain hopes those who accept them, while those of his own philosophy are free from vain hopes, and either that they win men with good hopes, or, which is more appropriate in his case, that they produce no hope at all, because they affirm that the soul is completely destroyed at the moment of death. Perhaps, however, Celsus and the Epicureans would deny that it is a vain hope concerning pleasure, which to them is the highest good and is their end in life, 'a healthy condition of the body and the sure confidence in this',[1] which is the ideal of Epicurus.

81. Do not suppose that it is not consistent with Christian doctrine when in my reply to Celsus I accepted the opinions of those philosophers who have affirmed the immortality or the survival of the soul. We have some ideas in common with them. But at a more suitable time we will show that the blessed future life will be for those alone who have accepted the religion of Jesus, and who reverence the Creator of the universe with a pure and untainted worship, uncontaminated by anything created. Let anyone who likes show what sort of *good* things we persuade people to despise; let him consider what we think to be the blessed end with God in Christ, who is the Logos, wisdom, and every virtue, which will be the experience of those who have lived purely and unblameably, and have recovered their undivided and unbroken love for the God of the universe, and which will be bestowed by God's gift, in contrast with the end as it is conceived by each philosophical sect among the Greeks or barbarians, or in the proclamation of some mystery-religion. Let him show that the end as it is conceived by one of these others is superior to the end as we understand it, and that their conception is fitting because it is true, whereas the blessedness in which we believe could not appropriately be given by God even to people who have lived a good life; let him prove that this hope was not declared by a divine Spirit which filled the souls of the pure prophets. And let anyone who likes show that the teaching which all agree to be merely human is better than that proved to be divine and proclaimed by divine inspiration. What also are the *good* things which we teach people to avoid[2] on the ground that *it will be better for them*? For

---

[1] Epicurus, *frag.* 68 Usener.
[2] Read ἀπεχομένους with Bo., Del., We., K. tr.

without boasting it is self-evident that nothing better could be conceived than to entrust oneself to the supreme God and to be dedicated to a doctrine which teaches us to leave everything created and leads us to the supreme God through the animate and living Logos, who is both living wisdom and Son of God.

However, as with these remarks the third volume of our reply to Celsus' treatise has reached adequate dimensions, we shall end the argument at this point, and in what follows will combat Celsus' next objections.

BOOK IV

1. In the three preceding books we have set out in detail the arguments that occurred to us in reply to Celsus' treatise; and now, holy Ambrose, after prayer to God through Christ we are undertaking a fourth book in reply to his next objections. May words be given to us, like those which are described in Jeremiah, where the Lord said to the prophet: 'Behold, I have put my words in thy mouth as fire. Behold, I have this day set thee over nations and kingdoms, to root out and to destroy, to abolish and to pull down, to build up and to plant.'[1] For now we also need words to root out ideas contrary to the truth from every soul which has been distressed by Celsus' treatise or by opinions like his. And we also need ideas to destroy buildings of all false opinions and the arguments[2] in Celsus' treatise which are like the building of those who said: 'Come let us build ourselves a city and a tower, of which the top shall reach to heaven.'[3] Furthermore, we need wisdom to pull down every proud thought that exalts itself against the knowledge of God[4] and Celsus' proud boasting which exalts itself against us. Then, since we must not stop with rooting out and destroying the things just mentioned, but in place of the things rooted out must plant a planting which is of God's husbandry,[5] and in place of what is destroyed must construct a building of God and a temple of God's glory, we must therefore pray to the Lord who bestowed the gifts described in Jeremiah, that He may give words also to us which build up the doctrines of Christ and plant the spiritual law and the prophetic words corresponding to it.

Our main task now is to reply to what Celsus says immediately after the remarks we have quoted, to show that the prophecies about Christ were true. For Celsus opposes both Jews and Christians at once: the Jews who deny that Christ has come, but hope that he will do so; and the Christians who affirm that Jesus was the prophesied Christ. This is what he says.

2. *The assertion made both by some of the Christians and by the Jews, the former saying that some God or son of God has come down to the earth as judge of mankind, the latter saying that he will come, is most shameful, and no lengthy argument is required to refute it.* He seems to speak accurately when he says of the Jews that it is not merely some but all of them who think that some person will come down to the earth; whereas of the Christians he says that only some of them say that he has come down. He

[1] Jer. i. 9–10.   [2] Read ⟨τὰ⟩ τῆς with Bo., K. tr.   [3] Gen. xi. 4.
[4] II Cor. x. 5.   [5] I Cor. iii. 9.

shows that he is aware of those who argue from the Jewish scriptures that
the advent of Christ has already taken place, and seems to know that there
are certain sects which deny that Christ Jesus is the person prophesied.[1]
Above[2] we have already discussed as well as we could the fact that the
prophecies referred to Jesus; and for this reason we do not repeat the
numerous arguments which could be adduced on the subject to avoid any
repetition. But notice that if he wanted with any show of logical argument
to refute the belief in the prophecies, whether the coming of Christ is
regarded as in the future or in the past, he ought to have quoted the
prophecies used by Christians and Jews in disputing with one another.
In this way he would at least have seemed to dissuade those who are led
astray, as he thinks, by the plausible argument from accepting the
prophecies and from believing on this ground that Jesus was really the
Christ. But in fact, whether because he is unable to reply to the prophecies
about Christ, or because he does not even know at all what the prophecies
about him are, he quotes not a single passage from the prophets, even
though there are thousands about Christ; and he thinks he can criticize the
prophecies without giving any example of what he would call their plausible
argument. In any event, he does not know that the Jews certainly do not
say that the Christ who will come down is God or Son of God, as we also
said earlier.[3]

3. After saying that according to us Christ has come down, but that
according to the Jews his coming as judge is still in the future, he thinks
he can attack this opinion as being most shameful and as requiring no
lengthy refutation. [3] He goes on to say: *What is the purpose of such
a descent on the part of God?* He fails to see that in our view the purpose
of the descent was in the first place to convert those whom the Gospel
calls 'the lost sheep of the house of Israel',[4] and in the second place,
because of their unbelief, to take away from the former Jewish husbandmen what is called 'the kingdom of God' and to give it to 'other husbandmen', the Christians, who will render to God the fruits of the kingdom of
God in due season,[5] each of their actions being a fruit of the kingdom.

We have selected a few points out of much that we could say in reply to
Celsus' question when he asks: *What is the purpose of such a descent on the
part of God?* But Celsus is inventing out of his own head notions held
neither by Jews nor by us when he says: *Was it in order to learn what was
going on among men?*[6] None of us says that Christ comes to this life in order
to learn what is going on among men. Then, as if some people would say

[1] Cf. I, 49. For Marcion's view that the Jewish Messiah was quite different from Jesus
Christ cf. Tertullian, *adv. Marc.* IV, 6; Harnack, *Marcion* (ed. 2), p. 117.
[2] I, 49–57; II, 28–30.   [3] I, 49.   [4] Matt. x. 6; xv. 24.
[5] Matt. xxi. 43, 41.   [6] Cf. *Clem. Hom.* III, 39, on Gen. xviii. 21.

that this was the reason, he makes the rejoinder to his own question: *Does not he know everything?* Then, as if we answer that he does know, he again raises a fresh objection, saying: *If, then, he does know, why does he not correct men, and why can he not do this by divine power?* All these questions are foolish. For by His Word God is always correcting those who listen to what He says. In each generation His Word descends into holy souls and makes them friends of God and prophets.[1] And by the advent of Christ he corrects through the Christian gospel not the unwilling but those who choose the higher life which is pleasing to God.

I do not know what sort of correction Celsus would have liked when he raised another question, saying: *Was he then unable to correct men merely by divine power, without sending some one specially endowed for the purpose?* Did he want God to appear to men in visions and to use this means of correction in order to take away evil altogether and to implant virtue? Some one else might ask whether this is consistent with nature and intrinsically possible. But we would say: we may allow that this is possible; but what about free will? And what of the merit attaching to acceptance of the truth and of the blame in refusing what is false? Furthermore, if we allow for the moment that this is not only possible but also appropriate, would one not be even more justified in asking a similar question of Celsus? Viz.: Was it impossible for God by divine power even to make men needing correction good and perfect there and then so that evil should not exist at all? These arguments may carry away uneducated and unintelligent folk, but certainly not the man who analyses the nature of the problem. For if you take away the element of free will from virtue, you also destroy its essence. A complete discussion of this subject is needed, though the Greeks have said much about it in their writings on providence. They would never say what Celsus has asserted when he asks: *If he knew, why did he not correct men? And why could he not do this by divine power?* We too have discussed these questions in many places to the best of our ability,[2] and the divine scriptures have shown the truth to those able to understand them.

4. Accordingly, the objection which Celsus brings against us and the Jews may be addressed to him also: My good man, does the supreme God know what is going on among men, or does He not? If you think that God and providence exist, as your treatise suggests, then He must know. But if He does know, why does He not correct men? Or have we to explain why He knows but does not correct, while you (as you do not appear from your treatise to be an Epicurean at all, but pretend to believe in providence) may not fairly be asked why the God who knows all that goes on among men

---

[1] Wisd. of Sol. vii. 27.   [2] Cf. I, 57; II, 35, 78; III, 28; *de Princ.* III, 1.

does not correct them and also deliver all men from evil by divine power?
But we are not ashamed to say that He is continually sending people to
correct men; for it is because God has given them that there are among
men doctrines calling them to live the highest life. Now among the
ministers of God there are many differences, and there are few who wholly
and purely set forth the doctrines of the truth and bring about complete
moral reformation. Moses and the prophets were men of this character.
But greater than all these was the reformation brought about by Jesus, who
did not want to cure only those in one corner[1] of the world, but as far as
possible to heal people everywhere. For he came as 'saviour of all men'.[2]

5. After this the most estimable Celsus for some unknown reason
brings up the objection against us that we affirm that *God Himself will come
down to men.* And he thinks it follows from this that *He leaves his throne.*
He does not understand the power of God, and that 'the Spirit of the Lord
has filled the world, and that which holds all things together has knowledge
of every voice'.[3] Nor is he able to understand the words, 'Do not I fill
heaven and earth, saith the Lord?'[4] Nor does he see that according to the
Christian doctrine in Him we all 'live and move and have our being',[5] as
Paul also taught in his public speech to the Athenians. Even, then, if the
God of the universe descends with Jesus into human life by His power,
and even if the Word who 'was in the beginning with God', who was
himself God,[6] comes to us, He does not go away from where He was, nor
does He leave His throne, as though one place were deprived of him, and
another which previously did not possess him were filled. The power and
divinity of God come to dwell among men through the man whom God
wills to choose and in whom He finds room without any changing from
one place to another or leaving His former place empty and filling another.
Even supposing that we do say that He leaves one place and fills another,
we would not mean this in a spatial sense.[7] We would say that the soul of the
bad man who is deluged with evil is deserted by God, and would maintain
that the soul of the man who desires to live virtuously, or has even made
some progress, or is even already living virtuously, is filled by or shares in
a divine spirit. Therefore, it is not necessary for the descent of Christ or
the movement of God towards men that He should forsake an exalted
throne and change things on earth, as Celsus thinks when he says: *For if
you changed any one quite insignificant thing on earth, you would upset and
destroy everything.* But if one may say that certain things change by the

---

[1] Cf. Celsus in IV, 23, 36; VI, 78.   [2] I Tim. iv. 10.
[3] Wisd. of Sol. i. 7.   [4] Jer. xxiii. 24.
[5] Acts xvii. 28.   [6] John i. 1–2.
[7] Cf. IV, 12; V, 12. Aristobulus ap. Eus. *P.E.* VIII, 10, 15, 377D; Philo, *de Post. Caini,* 6,
30; Justin, *Dial.* 127; Clem. Al. *Strom.* VII, 5, 5.

presence of God's power and the advent of the Word to man, we will not
hesitate to affirm that anyone who has received the coming of the Word of
God into his own soul changes from bad to good, from licentiousness to
self-control, and from superstition to piety.

6. If you want us to meet even the most ludicrous arguments of Celsus,
listen to him when he says: *Furthermore, if God was unknown among men
and on this account thought Himself to be underrated, would he want to make
Himself known, and try out both those who believe Him and those who do not,
just like men who have just come into wealth and show off? It is, indeed, a strong
and very mortal ambition which they attribute to God.* We say that God,
being unknown by bad men, wanted to make Himself known, not because
He thought Himself to be underrated, but because the knowledge of Him
delivers from misfortune the man who knows Him. Furthermore, it is
not with any desire to *try out those who believe Him and those who do not*
that He either dwells in certain people Himself by a mysterious divine
power, or sends His Christ. He does so with the motive of delivering
from all misfortune those who believe and comprehend His divinity, and
in order that those who disbelieve may no longer have any occasion for
excusing themselves on the ground that the reason why they do not
believe is that they have not heard and been taught. By what argument,
then, can he show that it follows from our opinion that God is like *men
who have come into wealth and show off?* God does not want to show off
to us when He wants us to understand and think about His excellence.
But, from a desire to implant in us the blessedness which comes to our
souls as a result of knowing Him, He is concerned to enable us to obtain
friendship with Him through Christ and the constant indwelling of the
Word. The Christian doctrine, therefore, attributes no *mortal ambition*
to God.

7. For some unknown reason, after talking the futile nonsense which
we have just quoted, he afterwards affirms that *God does not need to be
known for His own sake, but He wants to give us knowledge of Himself for our
salvation, in order that those who accept it may become good and be saved, but
that those who do not accept it may be proved to be wicked and punished.* After
this affirmation he raises a new objection saying *Is it only now after such
a long age that God has remembered to judge the life of men? Did he not care
before?*[1] We will reply to this that God has at no time not desired to *judge
the life of men,* but He has always cared for the reformation of the rational
being and given opportunities of virtue. For in each generation the wisdom
of God, entering into souls which she finds to be holy, makes them friends
of God and prophets.[2] In fact, in the sacred books you could find holy

[1] Cf. Celsus in vi, 78.   [2] Wisd. of Sol. vii. 27.

men in each generation who were receptive of the divine Spirit, and who devoted all their powers to converting their contemporaries.

8. It is not surprising that there have been prophets in certain generations, who on account of their more active and zealous life surpassed other prophets in their reception of divine inspiration, some of whom were their contemporaries while others lived earlier and later than they. So also it is not surprising that it has happened at a certain time that some special person has visited the human race, who was pre-eminent beyond those who lived before or even after him. The explanation of this has something rather mysterious and profound about it, the understanding of which is quite beyond the capacity of the common people. To explain these matters, and to reply to Celsus' question about Christ's advent *Is it only now after such a long age that God has remembered to judge the human race? Did He not care before?* it is necessary to touch on the subject of divisions, and to explain why 'when the most High divided the nations, as he scattered the sons of Adam, he set the boundaries of the nations according to the number of the angels of God; and the Lord's portion was Jacob his people, Israel the lot of his inheritance'.[1] And it will be necessary in each case to give the reason for the birth of a man into a particular region as the subject of the one who has been assigned that region, and how it is reasonable that 'the Lord's portion was Jacob his people, Israel the lot of his inheritance'. We must explain why formerly 'the Lord's portion was Jacob his people, Israel the lot of his inheritance', whereas concerning the later dispensation the Father said to the Saviour, 'Ask of me and I will give thee the heathen for thine inheritance, and the bounds of the earth for thy possession.'[2] For there are logical and consistent reasons for the different ways in which providence cares for human souls which cannot be expressed or explained in detail.

9. Accordingly, even if Celsus will not admit it, after many prophets who were reformers of the old Israel, Christ came as reformer of the whole world. He did not need to punish men by the method of the earlier dispensation, with whips and bonds and tortures. For when 'the sower went forth to sow',[3] his teaching was enough to sow the word everywhere. But if there will be a certain fixed time when the world will be brought to the end which it must necessarily have if it had any beginning,[4] and if it is true that there will be a certain appointed end of the world and after that a righteous Judgment of all men, then anyone who constructs a Christian philosophy will need to argue the truth of his doctrines with proofs of all kinds, taken both from the divine scriptures and from rational arguments.

---

[1] Deut. xxxii. 8–9. Cf. v, 25–30, below.   [2] Ps. ii. 8.   [3] Matt. xiii. 3.
[4] Axiomatic in discussions of the destructibility of the world; cf. Philo, *de Aetern.* 27.

The simple-minded masses, however, who cannot comprehend the complex theology of the wisdom of God, must trust themselves to God and to the Saviour of our race, and be content simply with the *ipse dixit*[1] of Jesus rather than with anything beyond this.

10. After this again Celsus as usual produces no argument or proof at all, and as though we babbled about God impiously and impurely says: *It is quite clear that they babble about God impiously and impurely.* And he thinks that we do this *to arouse the amazement of the uneducated people,* and that we *do not speak the truth about the punishments* which are necessary *for those who have sinned.* For this reason he compares us to *those in the Bacchic mysteries who introduce phantoms and terrors.*[2] Now concerning the Bacchic mysteries it is for the Greeks to say whether there is a convincing interpretation of them, or if there is nothing of the kind; and Celsus and his associates may listen to them. But we defend our teaching by saying that we are concerned with the improvement of the human race, whether we use threats of punishments which, we have been persuaded, are necessary for the whole world, and probably also not unbeneficial to those who will suffer them, or whether we use promises of what is in store for those who have lived good lives, which include promises of the blessed life after death in the kingdom of God for those worthy to be under His rule.

11. After this he wants to make out that we have nothing either remarkable or original to say about a *flood or conflagration,*[3] and furthermore that it is because we have *misunderstood what is said by the Greeks or barbarians about these matters* that we have believed the accounts of them in our scriptures. This is what he says: *This idea occurred to them because they misunderstood the doctrine of the Greeks and barbarians, namely, that after cycles of long periods and after returns and conjunctions of stars there are conflagrations and floods, and that after the last flood in the time of Deucalion the cycle demands a conflagration in accordance with the alternating succession of the universe. This was responsible for their mistaken opinion that God will come down and bring fire like a torturer.* We will reply to this that for some unknown reason, although Celsus has read widely and shows that he knows many stories, he failed to give attention to the antiquity of Moses, who is related by certain Greek writers to have lived in the time of Inachus the son of Phoroneus.[4] He is also admitted by Egyptians to be

[1] Cf. i, 7.
[2] For threats of torment in the mystery-religions, cf. Celsus in iii, 16; viii, 48. Discussion in Cumont, *Lux perpetua,* pp. 219 ff.
[3] See Celsus in i, 19; iv, 41.
[4] Inachus was father, not son, of Phoroneus according to the usual story. Origen's memory probably failed him. Moses is said to be Inachus' contemporary by Ptolemy, priest of Mendes (Tatian, 38); Apion ap. Africanus ap. Eus. *P.E.* x, 10, 16, 490B; Tertullian, *Apol.* 19; Clem. Al. *Strom.* i, 101, 5; Ps.-Justin, *Cohort.* 9; Eus. *Chronic.* (p. 7, ed. Helm).

of great antiquity, and also by those who compiled Phoenician history. Anyone interested may read the two books of Flavius Josephus on the Antiquity of the Jews,[1] that he may know how Moses was more ancient than those who said that at long intervals of time there are floods and conflagrations in the world. Celsus maintains that these men were misunderstood by Jews and Christians who, because they did not understand the doctrine about the conflagration, said that *God will come down and bring fire like a torturer*.

12. It is not the right time to say whether or not there are cycles, and floods or conflagrations in each cycle, and whether this doctrine is mentioned in the Bible, as in these words of Solomon among many others: 'What is it that has been? That very thing which shall be. And what is that which has been made? That very thing which shall be made',[2] and so on. It is enough merely to remark that Moses and some of the prophets, being men of great antiquity, did not receive from others the idea of the world-conflagration. The truth is rather, if we may pay regard to the matter of their dates, that others misunderstood them and failed to reproduce accurately what they said, and invented the notion that identical occurrences happen periodically, which are indistinguishable[3] from one another in both their essential[4] and their incidental characteristics. But we do not attribute either the flood or the conflagration to any cycles and periodical conjunctions of the stars. We maintain that the cause of these events is the excessive torrent of evil which is purged by a flood or conflagration. If the words of the prophets speak of God as coming down, we take this in a symbolical sense; for He says: 'Do not I fill heaven and earth? saith the Lord.'[5] God comes down from His own greatness and majesty when He cares for the affairs of men, and particularly of bad men. Just as people commonly say that teachers come down to the level of children, and wise men or advanced students to those only recently led to study philosophy, without meaning that they make a physical descent; so, if anywhere in the divine scriptures God is said to 'come down', it is to be understood in a similar sense to that of the common usage. The same is true also of 'going up'.

13. As Celsus says in mockery that we say God comes down bringing fire like a torturer, and compels us to examine profound problems at an inappropriate time, we will make a few observations sufficient for our

---

[1] Josephus, *c. Apionem*, 1, 13, 70 ff., quotes Egyptian and Phoenician writers on this point. Cf. Tatian, 37–8; Theophilus, *ad Autol.* III, 21–2.

[2] Eccles. i. 9. Origen's exegesis of this text (*de Princ.* III, 5, 3) aroused the wrath of Jerome (*Ep.* CXXIV, 9) and Augustine (*de Civ. Dei* XII, 13).

[3] Stoic doctrine; cf. IV, 68; V, 20.   [4] Read ἰδίως with A (We., K. tr.).

[5] Jer. xxiii. 24.

hearers to get an outline of an answer which deals with Celsus' mockery against us, and then turn to what follows. The divine Word says that 'our God is a consuming fire',[1] and that He 'draws forth rivers of fire before him',[2] and also that He enters 'like fire of a smelting-furnace, and like a cleaner's herb',[3] that He may mould His people. When, therefore, He is said to be a consuming fire, we inquire what is fit to be consumed by God; and we say that as fire God consumes evil and the actions resulting from it, which are figuratively described as 'wood, hay, and stubble'. At any rate, the bad man is said to build upon the spiritual foundation already laid 'wood, hay, and stubble'.[4] If anyone could show that the writer meant something different, and could prove that the bad man literally builds wood, hay, and stubble, then clearly the fire also is to be taken as material and sensible. But if, on the contrary, the works of the bad man are allegorically called wood, hay, and stubble, does it not become self-evident[5] what kind of fire is used to consume this sort of wood? For he says: 'The fire itself shall prove each man's work, of what sort it is. If any man's work shall abide which he has built thereon, he shall receive a reward; if any man's work shall be burned, he shall suffer loss.'[6] What sort of work could here be said to be burned except every action which results from evil? Therefore, 'our God is a consuming fire' in the sense in which we have interpreted this. So also He enters 'like the fire of a smelting-furnace' to mould the rational nature which has been filled by the lead of evil and other impure substances which adulterate the soul's golden or silver nature, so to speak. In this sense also 'rivers of fire' are said to be before God, since He makes the evil which has permeated the whole soul to disappear. But this is a sufficient reply to Celsus' assertion: *This was responsible for their mistaken opinion that God will come down and bring fire like a torturer.*

14. Let us see also what great claims[7] Celsus makes next when he talks as follows. *Furthermore,* he says, *let us take up the argument again with further proofs. I have nothing new to say, but only ancient doctrines.*[8] *God is good and beautiful and happy, and exists in the most beautiful state. If then He comes down to men, He must undergo change, a change from good to bad, from beautiful to shameful, from happiness to misfortune, and from what is best to what is most wicked. Who would choose a change like this? It is the nature only[9] of a mortal being to undergo change and remoulding, whereas it is*

---

[1] Deut. iv. 24; ix. 3; Heb. xii. 29.   [2] Dan. vii. 10.
[3] Mal. iii. 2.   [4] I Cor. iii. 12.
[5] Read προσπίπτει with M¹, K. tr.   [6] I Cor. iii. 13–15.
[7] Read ἐπαγγελίας with Selwyn, We.
[8] What follows is Platonic (*Rep.* 381B, C; *Phaedrus,* 246D).
[9] Read καὶ μόνῳ δὴ with K. tr.

the nature of an immortal being to remain the same without alteration.
Accordingly, God could not be capable of undergoing this change. I think that
I made[1] the necessary reply to this when I discussed what is called in the
Bible God's descent to human affairs. In this respect it is not that *He must*
undergo change, as Celsus thinks we say; nor must He turn *from good to bad,*
or from beautiful to shameful, or from happiness to misfortune, or from what
is best to what is most wicked. While remaining unchanged in essence, He
comes down in His providence and care over human affairs. We show
that the divine scriptures also say that God is not subject to change in the
words 'But thou art the same', and 'I change not'.[2] But the gods of
Epicurus, who are compounded of atoms and, in so far as they are compounded, are liable to dissolution, are at pains to throw off the atoms
which may cause their destruction.[3] Furthermore, the God of the Stoics,
in that He is corporeal, at one time when the conflagration occurs consists
entirely of mind, while at another time, when the new world-order comes,
He becomes a part of it. Not even they have been able to perceive clearly
the true conception of God's nature, as being entirely incorruptible,
simple, uncompounded, and indivisible.

15. He who came down to men was originally 'in the form of God'
and because of his love to men 'emptied himself'[4] that men might be able
to receive him. But he underwent no change from good to bad; for 'he
did no sin';[5] nor from beautiful to shameful, for 'he knew no sin'.[6] Nor
did he pass from happiness to misfortune; although 'he humbled himself',[7]
nevertheless he was happy, even when he humbled himself in the way
expedient for our race. Moreover, he underwent no change from what is
best to what is most wicked; for in what way is goodness and love to man
most wicked? It is relevant to observe that a physician also, who 'sees
terrible things and touches unpleasant wounds'[8] in order to heal the sick,
does not pass[9] from good to bad, or from beautiful to shameful, or from
happiness to misfortune, although the physician who sees the terrible
things and touches the unpleasant wounds does not wholly avoid the
possibility that he may fall into the same plight. But he who heals the
wounds of our souls through the divine Word within him was incapable
of any evil. If the immortal divine Word assumes both a human body and
a human soul, and by so doing appears to Celsus to be subject to change

---

[1] Read λελέχθαι with We., K. tr.   [2] Ps. ci. 28; Mal. iii 6.
[3] Cf. my remarks in *Harv. Theol. Rev.* XLI (1948), p. 92 n. 15.
[4] Phil. ii. 6–7.   [5] I Pet. ii. 22.
[6] II Cor. v. 21.   [7] Phil. ii. 8.
[8] Origen quotes Hippocrates, *De Flatibus* 1, a hackneyed quotation; cf. Origen, *Hom. in*
Jerem. XIV, 1; Eusebius, *H.E.* X, 4, 11; Lucian, *Bis Accus.* 1; Plutarch, *Mor.* 291 C.
[9] Read ⟨οὐκ⟩ ἔρχεσθαι, καίτοι . . . .

and remoulding, let him learn that the Word remains Word in essence. He suffers nothing of the experience of the body or the soul. But sometimes he comes down to the level of him who is unable to look upon the radiance and brilliance[1] of the Deity, and becomes as it were flesh, and is spoken of in physical terms, until he who has accepted him in this form is gradually lifted up by the Word and can look even upon, so to speak, his absolute form.

16. There are, as it were, different forms of the Word. For the Word appears to each of those who are led to know him in a form corresponding to the state of the individual, whether he is a beginner, or has made a little progress, or is considerably advanced, or has nearly attained to virtue already, or has in fact attained it. For this reason it is not true, as Celsus and those like him would say, that our God was transformed when he went up a high mountain and showed his other form, which was far superior to that which was seen by the people down below, who were unable to follow him to the high place. For the people down below had not eyes capable of seeing the transfiguration of the Word into something wonderful and more divine. They were hardly able to receive him as he was, so that it was said of him by those not able to see his higher nature, 'We saw him, and he had no form or beauty, but his form was dishonourable, deserted more than the sons of men.'[2] Let this, then, be our reply to the opinion assumed by Celsus: that he failed to understand the 'changes' (to use the word common in ordinary literature) or transfigurations[3] of Jesus, and the fact that he had both immortal and mortal nature.

17. Surely these narratives, particularly when properly understood, will appear more impressive than that of Dionysus, that he was deceived by the Titans so that he left the throne of Zeus and was torn in pieces by them, that after this he was put together again and was, as it were, restored to life, and went up to heaven?[4] Or are the Greeks allowed to explain and allegorize this story as referring to the soul, while against us

---

[1] Verbal allusion to Plato, *Rep.* 518 A. Cf. VI, 17.   [2] Isa. liii. 2–3.

[3] μεταβολή is common, μεταμόρφωσις late and rare.

[4] For this Orphic myth, cf. Rohde, *Psyche* (E.T.), pp. 340 f.; A. B. Cook, *Zeus*, II, pp. 1030–2; Guthrie, *Orpheus and Greek Religion* (1935), pp. 107 ff. Zeus' enemies, the Titans, won the confidence of the child Dionysus, son of Zeus and Persephone, by giving him toys; they lured him away from the royal throne, and tore him in pieces. Accounts vary concerning what became of the pieces. According to one story the Titans ate them; Zeus destroyed them, and of their ashes sprang the human race, which thus possesses a divine and a wicked element. But others (e.g. Clem. Al. *Protr.* 17) say that Zeus gave the fragments to Apollo for burial. In this passage Origen seems to know of a tradition that the pieces were put together again, and Dionysus resuscitated (Rohde, p. 360, refers to Julian, *c. Chr.* p. 167, 7 ed. Neumann: Διονύσου μελῶν κολλήσεις). The myth was interpreted of rebirth: Plutarch, *Mor.* 389 A; 996 C; Proclus, *in Tim.* 313 C. Cf. also Plotinus, IV, 3, 12.

the door has been closed so that we may not give any consistent explanation which harmonizes and agrees in all respects with the scriptures
inspired by the divine Spirit dwelling in pure souls? Celsus does not understand the meaning of our scriptures at all. On this account his criticism
touches his own interpretation and not that of the Bible. If he had
understood what is appropriate for a soul which will have everlasting life,
and what is the right view of its essence and origin, he would not have
ridiculed in this way the idea of an immortal person entering a mortal
body; (our view here does not accept the Platonic doctrine of the transmigration of souls, but a different and more sublime view). He would
also have understood how because of His great love to man, God made
one special descent in order to convert those whom the divine scripture
mystically calls 'the lost sheep of the house of Israel',[1] which had strayed
down from the mountains; in certain parables[2] the shepherd is said to have
come down to them, leaving on the mountains those which had not gone
astray.

18. Although he has not understood these things, Celsus persists in
talking about them, and so is responsible for our repetitions, since we do
not want even to appear to have left any of his statements unexamined.
He next says: *Either God really does change, as they say, into a mortal body;
and it has already been said that this is an impossibility.*[3] *Or He does not
change, but makes those who see him think He does so, and leads them astray
and tells lies. Deceit and lying are in all other cases wrong except only when
one uses them as a medicine for friends who are sick and mad in order to heal
them, or with enemies when the intention is to escape danger.*[4] *But no sick or
mad man is God's friend, nor is God afraid of anyone so that he has to mislead
him to avoid danger.* My reply to this would argue partly from the nature
of the divine Word, who is God, and partly from the soul of Jesus.
Concerning the nature of the Word, just as the quality of food changes in
a mother into milk suitable for the nature of her infant, or is prepared by
a physician with the intention of restoring a sick man to health, while it is
prepared in a different way for a stronger man, who is more able to digest
it in this form; so also God changes for men the power of the Word,
whose nature it is to nourish the human soul, in accordance with the
merits of each individual. To one he becomes 'the rational milk which is
without guile',[5] as the Bible calls it; to another who is weaker he becomes
like a 'herb';[6] while to another who is perfect, 'solid food'[7] is given.

---

[1] Matt. xv. 24.   [2] Matt. xviii. 12–13; Luke xv. 4 ff.
[3] Read τὸ ἀδυνατεῖν with Herter and Bader.
[4] Celsus is quoting Plato, *Rep.* 382C; 389B; 459C, D.
[5] I Pet. ii. 2.   [6] Rom. xiv. 2.
[7] Heb. v, 12, 14.

Surely the Word is not false to his own nature when he becomes nourishment for each man according to his capacity to receive him; in so doing he does not mislead or tell lies.

Concerning Jesus' soul, if anyone supposes that there was a change when it entered a body, we will ask what he means by a 'change'. If he means a change of essence, we do not grant this, either of his soul, or of any other rational soul. But if he means that it undergoes something because it has been mixed with the body and because of the place into which it has come, then what difficulty is there if the Word out of great love to mankind brings down a Saviour to the human race? None of those who had previously claimed to cure men were able to do such a great work as this soul displayed by the miracles which he performed, even descending of his own free will to accept the limitations of humanity on behalf of our race. In reference to this the divine Word frequently speaks in several passages of the Bible. It is enough for the moment to quote one passage of Paul, which reads as follows: 'Have this mind in you which was also in Christ Jesus, who being in the form of God counted it not a prize to be on an equality with God, but emptied himself, taking the form of a servant; and being found in fashion as a man, he humbled himself, becoming obedient unto death, yea the death of the cross. Wherefore God also highly exalted him, and gave him a name which is above every name.'[1]

19. Others may agree with Celsus that He does not change, but makes those who see Him think that He has changed. But we, who are persuaded that the advent of Jesus to men was not a mere appearance, but a reality and an indisputable fact, are unaffected by Celsus' criticism. Nevertheless we will reply thus: Do you not say, Celsus, that sometimes it is allowable to use deceit and lying as a medicine? Why, then, is it unthinkable that something of this sort occurred with the purpose of bringing salvation? For some characters are reformed by certain doctrines which are more false than true, just as physicians sometimes use similar words to their patients. This, however, has been our defence on other points.[2] But further, there is nothing wrong if the person who *heals sick friends* healed the human race which was dear to him with such means as one would not use for choice, but to which he was confined by force of circumstances. Since the human race was mad, it had to be cured by methods which the Word saw to be beneficial to lunatics that they might recover their right mind. Celsus says that one also does this *with enemies when the intention is to escape danger.* But *God is not afraid of any so that He has to mislead* those who conspire against Him *in order to avoid danger.* It is entirely superfluous and unreasonable to reply to an assertion which is not made

---

[1] Phil. ii. 5–9.   [2] Cf. II, 24.

about our Saviour by anyone. In making our defence of other points we
have already dealt with the following remark: *But no sick or mad man is
God's friend.* We affirm in reply that providence has not done this for the
sake of sick men or lunatics who have already become friends, but for
those who, because their soul is diseased and their natural reasoning
powers distracted, are still enemies, so that they may become friends of
God. Moreover, Jesus is clearly said to have accepted everything for the
sake of sinners,[1] that he might deliver them from sin and make them
righteous.

20. He then represents the Jews, on the one hand, as finding reasons
for their belief that the advent of the Christ is still in the future, and the
Christians, on the other hand, as saying that the advent into human life
of the Son of God has already happened. Accordingly, let us give our
mind to this briefly, as far as possible: *The Jews say*, thinks Celsus, *that
as life is filled with all manner of evil it is necessary for God to send someone
down that the wicked may be punished and everything purified, as it was when
the first flood occurred.* Since he says that the Christians add other ideas to
these, he obviously thinks that these opinions are held by them as well.
Now why is it absurd to believe that the person who purifies the world
because of the flood of wickedness will come and deal with each man
according to his merits? It is not in accord with God's character not to
stop the spread of evil and bring moral renewal. The Greeks also have
a doctrine that the earth is periodically purified by a flood or by fire, as
Plato also says in one place as follows: 'And then the gods flood the earth,
purifying it with waters, some in the mountains...'[2] and so on. Should
it be said that if they say this the opinions put forward[3] are impressive and
significant, whereas if we also maintain doctrines similar to those approved
by the Greeks then they are good no longer? However, those who are
interested in the exactness and accuracy of everything in the Bible will try
to show not only the antiquity of the men who wrote these things, but also
the importance of what they say and the consistency of their teaching.

21. For some unknown reason he thinks that *the overthrow of the tower
had a similar purpose to that of the flood which*, according to the doctrine of
Jews and Christians, *purified the earth.* Supposing that *the story about the
tower* in Genesis[4] *contains no hidden truth but*, as Celsus thinks, *is obvious*,
even so its overthrow does not seem to have happened for the purification
of the earth—unless perhaps he imagines that the so-called confusion of
tongues was a purification of the earth. A competent student would explain

---

[1] Cf. Matt. ix. 13, etc.   [2] *Timaeus* 22D. Cf. I, 19; IV, 11, above.
[3] Read ἀπαγγελλόμενα with Bo., We., K. tr.
[4] Gen. xi. 1–9. For Origen's allegorical interpretation, cf. v, 29 ff.

this at a more opportune moment when it is his task to show both the literal sense of the passage and its mystical interpretation. He thinks, however, that *Moses who wrote about the tower* and the confusion of languages *corrupted the story about the sons of Aloeus when he composed the narrative about the tower.*[1] I reply that no one before Homer, I think, tells the story of the sons of Aloeus; whereas I am convinced that the story about the tower recorded by Moses is much earlier than Homer and even than the invention of the Greek alphabet.[2] Who, then, is more likely to have corrupted the stories of the other? Is it that those who tell the story of the sons of Aloeus are corrupting that of the tower, or that those who wrote of the tower and the confusion of languages are corrupting that of the Aloadae? Unprejudiced hearers, however, are of the opinion that Moses was more ancient than Homer.

Celsus also compares with *the story of Phaethon the narrative told* by Moses in Genesis *about Sodom and Gomorrah, that they were destroyed by fire on account of their sins.*[3] All that he has done is the consequence of one mistake: he failed to notice the evidence of Moses' antiquity. For those who relate the story of Phaethon seem to have been even more recent than Homer, who was far more recent than Moses. Accordingly, we do not deny the reality of the purifying fire and the destruction of the world to destroy evil and renew the universe, since we say that we have learnt these things from the prophets out of the sacred books. However, since, as we have said above,[4] the prophets who made many predictions of the future are proved to have spoken the truth concerning many events which have come to pass, and give proof that there was a divine Spirit in them, obviously we ought also to believe them, or rather the divine Spirit in them, concerning events which are still future.

22. According to Celsus: *Christians also add certain doctrines to those maintained by the Jews, and assert that the Son of God has already come on account of the sins of the Jews, and that because the Jews punished Jesus and gave him gall to drink they drew down upon themselves the bitter anger of God.*[5] I challenge anyone to prove my statement untrue if I say that the

---

[1] Homer, *Il.* v, 385–7; *Od.* XI, 305–20; Otus and Ephialtes, the tallest men on earth, tried to pile three mountains on top of one another, Ossa, Pelion, and Olympus, to make 'a pathway to the sky'; Apollo killed them. The similarity to the story of Babel is noted by Philo, *de Conf. Ling.* 4 (cf. *de Somn.* II, 284 f.), and Julian, *c. Chr.* pp. 181 ff. (ed. Neumann).

[2] The Priority of Moses is a favourite theme with both Jewish and Christian apologists. Cf. VI, 7; VII, 28, below; Tatian, 31.

[3] Gen. xix. 1–29. Helios allowed his son, Phaethon, to drive the chariot of the sun across the heavens one day; he was too weak to hold the horses and came too near the earth so that it was nearly burnt up; Zeus killed him. The story is first told by Euripides (*Hippol.* 735 ff.).

[4] Cf. I, 36–7; III, 2–4.

[5] Cf. Matt. xxvii. 34. Celsus plays on the words χολήν and χόλον.

entire Jewish nation was destroyed less than one whole generation later on
account of these sufferings which they inflicted upon Jesus. For it was,
I believe, forty-two years from the time when they crucified Jesus to the
destruction of Jerusalem.[1] Indeed, ever since the Jews existed, it has not
been recorded in history that they were ejected for so long a time from
their sacred ritual and worship, after they had been conquered by some
more powerful people. Even if sometimes they did seem to have been
deserted on account of their sins, nevertheless they were under God's care
and returned to resume their own property and to perform the customary
ritual without hindrance. Accordingly, one of the facts which show that
Jesus was some divine and sacred person is just that on his account such
great and fearful calamities have now for a long time befallen the Jews. We
will go so far as to say that they will not be restored again. For they
committed the most impious crime of all, when they conspired against the
Saviour of mankind, in the city where they performed to God the customary rites which were symbols of profound mysteries. Therefore that city
where Jesus suffered these indignities had to be utterly destroyed. The
Jewish nation had to be overthrown, and God's invitation to blessedness
transferred to others, I mean the Christians, to whom came the teaching
about the simple and pure worship of God. And they received new laws
which fit in with the order established everywhere. Those which had
previously been given were intended for a single nation ruled by men of
the same nationality and customs, so that it would be impossible for
everyone to keep them now.

23. After this he continues as usual by laughing at *the race of Jews and
Christians*, comparing them *all* to *a cluster of bats*[2] *or ants coming out of
a nest, or frogs holding council round a marsh,*[3] *or worms assembling in some
filthy corner, disagreeing with one another about which of them are the worse
sinners. They say: 'God shows and proclaims everything to us beforehand, and
He has even deserted the whole world and the motion of the heavens, and
disregarded the vast earth to give attention to us alone; and He sends messengers
to us alone and never stops sending them and seeking that we may be with Him
for ever.'* In the words which he invents he asserts that we are *like worms
who say: ' There is God first, and we are next after Him in rank since He has*

---

[1] Elsewhere Origen says that forty-two years were allowed for repentance (*Hom. in
Jerem.* XIV, 13). The same period is named by Clem. Al. *Strom.* I, 145, 5 (forty-two years,
three months). Possibly the source of this figure was Phlegon of Tralles (see note on
II, 14 above). In *Comm. ser. in Matt.* 40, Origen quotes him for the view that 'Jerusalem
was destroyed round about forty years after the fifteenth year of Tiberius Caesar'. (Here
Origen has reduced the period slightly in order to get a figure of thirty-five years between
the Passion and the destruction of the temple; he is led to this by his exegesis of Dan. ix. 27.)

[2] The phrase is from Homer, *Od.* XXIV, 6–8, quoted by Plato, *Rep.* 387A.

[3] The phrase 'ants or frogs round a marsh' is from Plato, *Phaedo,* 109B.

made us entirely like God, and all things have been put under us, earth, water, air, and stars; and all things exist for our benefit, and have been appointed to serve us.' Celsus' worms, that is we Christians, further[1] say: *'Since some among us are in error, God will come or will send His Son to consume the unrighteous, and that the rest of us may have eternal life with Him.'* And he adds to all this that *these assertions would be more tolerable coming from worms and frogs than from Jews and Christians disagreeing with one another.*

24. In reply we ask this question of those who approve of this attack upon us: Do you suppose that because God is superior to them all men are *a cluster of bats, or ants, or frogs, or worms?* Or do you hold that this comparison is not true of other men whom, on account of their rationality and established laws, you still regard as men, whereas Christians and Jews you disparage and compare to these animals merely because their opinions are not agreeable to you? In any event, whatever reply you give to our question, we will answer by attempting to show that it is not right to say this either of all men or of us. Let us suppose, in the first place, that you mean that in comparison with God all men are on a level with these mean animals, since they are small and in no way comparable with God's majesty. What do you mean by 'small'? Answer me, sirs. If you mean smallness of body, observe that by the true criterion superiority and inferiority are not to be judged by physical size. In that case griffins and elephants would be greater than we men; for they are larger and stronger, and live longer.[2] But no sensible person would say that these irrational animals are superior to rational beings on account of their bodies; for reason raises the rational being far above all irrational beings. Nor is this true of the good and blessed beings, whether, as you say, they are good daemons, or, as we usually call them, the angels of God,[3] nor of any other natures which are superior to men. For it is the rational element in them which has been perfected and endowed with every virtue.

25. If you disparage a man as of small stature not on account of his body but of his soul, thinking him inferior to other rational beings and especially to those who are good, and holding that the reason for his inferiority is the evil within him, why are the bad men among Christians and those Jews who live evil lives *a cluster of bats or ants or worms or frogs* any more than wicked men of other races? According to this view any man who is particularly far gone in the flood of sin is a bat, worm, frog, and ant in comparison with other men. Even if an orator was a Demosthenes and yet committed sin as he did and the actions which he

---

[1] Read δ' ἔτι with K. tr.   [2] Cf. Seneca, *de Benef.* 11, 29.
[3] Cf. v, 5 below. Philo, *de Gigant.* 6 'Those beings which other philosophers call daemons, Moses usually calls angels.'

did as a result of evil;[1] or even if another is thought to be an Antiphon who even denied providence in his work 'On Truth',[2] which has a title similar to that of Celsus' treatise; nevertheless they are worms wallowing in some filthy corner of uneducated ignorance. And yet, whatever is the nature of the rational being, it would not be reasonable to compare it to a worm, since it possesses tendencies towards virtue. These general inclinations towards virtue prohibit us from comparing with a worm those who potentially possess virtue, and who cannot entirely destroy its seeds.[3] It therefore appears that men, taken as a whole, cannot be mere worms in comparison with God. For the reason, which originates from the Logos of God, does not allow the rational being to be regarded as entirely alienated from God. Nor may those who are bad among Jews and Christians, who are not real Christians or Jews at all, be compared any more than other men to worms wallowing in some filthy corner. If the nature of the reason does not allow us to accept this, clearly we shall not insult human nature which has been made for virtue, even if it sins through ignorance, nor shall we liken it to animals such as these.

26. If, merely because the doctrines of Christians and Jews are not agreeable to Celsus, though he does not appear to know the first thing about them, they are worms and ants, while other people are not like that, let us examine the doctrines of Christians and Jews that are in themselves clearly intelligible to anyone. Let us set them beside[4] those of other people to see whether it will not seem clear, to those who for the moment accept that certain men may be worms and ants, that the people who really are worms and ants and frogs are those who have fallen from a sound notion of God, and with the semblance of piety worship either irrational animals, or images, or created things, when they ought to be moved by their beauty to admire their Maker and to worship Him. On the other hand, those people are human, and perhaps even more honourable than that, who following their reason have been able to rise up from stocks and stones, and also from silver and gold, the substances considered to be most valuable, and have also ascended from the beautiful things in the world to the Maker of the universe and have entrusted themselves to Him. For, since He alone is able to sustain everything that exists and to perceive the thoughts of all men and to hear the prayer of every man, they send up their prayers to Him. They do every action as in His sight; and, as if He

---

[1] Cf. [Plutarch], *Mor.* 847 E, F 'Some say that he (Demosthenes) lived licentiously, wearing women's clothes and revelling....' Aulus Gellius, I, 5, 1; I, 8, 3–6; Athenaeus, XIII, 592 E (cf. 588 c); Aeschines, III, 174; Macrobius, *Sat.* II, 2, 11.

[2] Origen here confuses Antiphon the sophist with the orator of the same name.

[3] For Origen's denial of total depravity, cf. II, 11 above.

[4] Read ⟨σὺν⟩ τοῖς.

were listening to what they say, they take care not to say anything that may not be reported to God without displeasing Him.

Perhaps such earnest devotion, which is subdued neither by pain nor by imminent death nor by plausible arguments, does not prevent those who have become so devoted from being compared to worms, even if this could fairly be said of them before they attained to this state. But[1] do we think that those people are the brothers of worms, the relatives of ants, and similar to frogs, who master the most violent desire for sexual pleasure, which has made the minds of many soft and pliable as wax,[2] and who master it for the reason that they have been persuaded that in no other way can they become intimate with God unless they ascend to Him by self-control? Is the radiance of righteousness, which observes the social rights of neighbours and relatives,[3] justice, love to humanity, and goodness, of no avail towards preventing such a person from being a bat? Are not the worms in the filth those who wander round licentious women (and most men are like that) and those who live with harlots as though it were a matter of indifference, even teaching that this is not at all contrary to any moral principle?[4] That they are worms is particularly clear when they are compared with those who have been taught not to take 'the limbs of Christ', and the body inhabited by the Word, and to make them 'the limbs of a harlot',[5] and who have already learnt also that the body of the rational being that is devoted[6] to the God of the universe is a temple[7] of the God whom they worship. It becomes this as a result of their pure conception of the Creator. They also take care not to corrupt the temple of God by unlawful sexual indulgence, and practise self-control as an act of piety towards God.

27. So far I have said nothing of the other sins of men from which not even those who seem to be philosophers easily keep themselves pure (for in philosophy there are many charlatans). Nor have I yet mentioned that such vices are frequent among people who are neither Jews nor Christians. But such things do not exist among Christians, if you examine strictly who is a true Christian; or if such sins were to be found, yet at least it would not be among those who *hold council* and come to the common prayers and are not excluded from them. I admit that perhaps someone of this sort might occasionally be found among the multitude. Accordingly, we are not *worms assembling together* when we oppose the Jews with arguments from the writings which they believe to be sacred, and show that

---

[1] Read ἄρά γε with We., K. tr.   [2] Verbal allusion to Plato, *Laws* 633 D.
[3] Read ὁμογενῆ with Hort, K. tr.
[4] Origen turns this Stoic doctrine to good account in IV, 45, below.
[5] I Cor. vi. 15.   [6] Read ἀνακειμένου with We., K. tr.
[7] I Cor. iii. 16; vi. 19; II Cor. vi. 16.

the person prophesied has come, that they have been deserted because of their dreadful sins, and that we who have accepted the gospel have the highest hopes with God on the ground both of our faith in Him and of our moral life which enables us to have communion with God, pure from all wickedness and evil. Therefore, if anyone calls himself a Jew or a Christian, he would not say without qualification that for us God made *the whole world and the motion of the heavens.* But anyone who is, as Jesus taught, pure in heart, meek, a peacemaker, and who gladly endures danger for the sake of his religion,[1] would with good reason be confident in God; and provided that he understood the doctrine found in the prophecies he could even say, '*God has shown and proclaimed all these things beforehand to us* who believe.'

28. He has made the Christians, whom he regards as worms, to say that '*God has deserted the motion of the heavens and disregarded the vast earth to give attention to us alone; and He sends messengers to us and never stops sending them and seeking that we may be with Him for ever*'. Our reply to this is that he attributes to us statements which we do not make. For we both read and know that God 'loves everything that exists and hates nothing that He has made; for He would never have made anything if He had hated it'.[2] And we have also read: 'But thou sparest all; for they are thine, O lover of souls. For thine incorruptible Spirit is in all things. Therefore thou convictest little by little those who fall from the right way, and, putting them in remembrance by the very things wherein they sin, thou dost admonish them.'[3] How can we say that *God has left the motion of the heavens and the whole world, and has disregarded the vast earth to give attention to us alone*, we who know that in our prayers we must say and believe that 'the earth is full of the Lord's mercy', and 'the Lord's mercy is upon all flesh', and that because God is good 'He makes His sun to rise upon the evil and the good and sends His rain upon the just and the unjust'?[4] Moreover, He exhorts us to do likewise that we may become His sons, and teaches us to extend our good works to all men as far as possible. He is also called 'Saviour of all men, especially of those who believe', and His Christ is 'a propitiation for our sins, but not for our sins only, but also for the whole world'.[5] Although they would not say what Celsus has written, perhaps there are some Jews who at any rate might make some other stupid statements. But they are certainly not the assertions of Christians who have been taught that 'God commends His love towards us in that while we were yet sinners, Christ died for us', although

---

[1] Matt. v. 8, 4, 9.
[2] Wisd. of Sol. xi. 25.
[3] Wisd. of Sol. xi. 27; xii. 1–2.
[4] Ps. xxxii. 5; Sirach xviii. 13; Matt. v. 45.
[5] I Tim. iv. 10; I John ii. 8.

'scarcely for a righteous man will one die; but for a good man someone would even dare to die'.[1] But now, according to our preaching, Jesus who is called the Christ of God by a certain traditional usage in the Bible has come on behalf of sinners in all places, that they may forsake their sin and entrust themselves to God.

29. Celsus probably misunderstood some of those whom he calls *worms* when he represents them as saying: *There is God first and we are next after Him in rank.* He behaves like those who attack a whole sect of philosophy because of certain assertions make by a rash youth who has studied with a philosopher for three days and exalts himself above other people as though they were beneath him and without any understanding of philosophy. For we know that there are many beings more honourable than man. We have read that 'God stood in the congregation of the gods', though these gods are not those worshipped by others (for 'all the gods of the heathen are daemons').[2] And we have read that when God 'stands in the congregation of the gods, He judges among the gods'.[3] We know also that 'though there may be some which are called gods, whether in heaven or on earth, as there are gods many and lords many; yet to us there is one God, the Father, of whom are all things and we unto him, and one Lord Jesus Christ, through whom are all things and we through him'.[4] We know too that angels are so far superior to men that when men are made perfect they become equal to angels. 'For in the resurrection of the dead they neither marry nor are given in marriage, but the righteous are as the angels of heaven', and they become 'equal to angels'.[5] We know that in the order of the universe there are some which are called thrones, others called principalities, and others authorities, and others powers.[6] We also see that, though we men fall far short of these beings, we have hopes that by living a good life and doing everything according to reason we may ascend to the likeness of all these. And finally, since 'it is not yet made manifest what we shall be, we know that when he shall appear we shall be like God, and shall see him as he is'.[7] But if anyone should maintain the assertion made by some, whether they are intelligent, or whether they are lacking in understanding and have misunderstood sound doctrine, that *There is God first, and we are next after Him in rank,* even this I would accept interpreting the word 'we' to refer to the rational beings, and in particular, the good rational beings. For in our opinion the virtue of all blessed beings is the same, just as the virtue of both man and God is the same.[8] That is why we are taught to become 'perfect as our heavenly

---

[1] Rom. v. 7–8.   [2] Ps. xcv. 5.   [3] Ps. lxxx. 1.
[4] I Cor. viii. 5–6.   [5] Luke xx. 36.   [6] Cf. Col. i. 16.
[7] I John iii. 2.   [8] Stoic doctrine. Cf. vi, 48; *S.V.F.* iii, 245–54.

Father is perfect'.[1] No noble or good man, then, is a worm wallowing in filth. No pious man is an ant. No righteous man is a frog. And no one who is illuminated in his soul by the radiant light of the truth can reasonably be said to be like a bat.

30. Celsus also seems to me to have misunderstood the words 'Let us make man in our image and likeness';[2] I think this is the reason why he has made the worms say *we have been made by God and are like Him in every way*. However, if he had realized the difference between man being made in God's image and being made in His likeness, and that though God is recorded to have said 'Let us make man in our image and likeness' God only made man in the image of God, but not as yet in His likeness,[3] then he would not have made us say that *we are like God in every way*. We do not assert that even *the stars have been put under us*. For what is called the resurrection of the righteous, as it is understood by the wise, is compared to sun, moon, and stars, by him who says: 'There is one glory of the sun, another glory of the moon, and another glory of the stars; for one star differs from another in glory. So also the resurrection of the dead.'[4] Daniel also prophesied about this long ago.[5] But Celsus says that we maintain that *all things have been appointed to serve us*, perhaps because he did not understand some similar remark made by those of us who are intelligent, and perhaps also because he did not know the meaning of the saying 'He that is greatest among us is servant of all.'[6] When the Greeks say

> The sun and moon serve mortals[7]

they approve the saying and also give an interpretation of it. But Celsus falsely criticizes us also in this matter because such a statement as that which he attributes to us is either not made by us at all, or is meant in a different sense.

According to Celsus we, who in his view are worms, say: *Since some among us are in error, God will come or will send His Son to consume the unrighteous, and that the rest of us frogs may have eternal life with Him.* See how like a vulgar fellow the noble philosopher heaps mockery, ridicule, and abuse upon the divine promise of judgment and punishment for the unrighteous and of reward for the righteous.

And he adds on top of all this that *these assertions would be more tolerable coming from worms and frogs than from Jews and Christians*

---

[1] Matt. v. 48.　　　　　　　　　　　[2] Gen. i. 26.

[3] This is a traditional exegesis; cf. Irenaeus, v, 6, 1 (Harvey, 11, 334); Clem. Al. *Strom.* 11, 131, 6; Origen, *de Princ.* 111, 6, 1; *Comm. in Rom.* IV, 5.

[4] I Cor. xv. 41–2.　　　　　　　　　[5] Cf. Dan. xii. 3.

[6] Cf. Matt. xx. 26–7; xxiii. 11.

[7] Euripides, *Phoenissae*, 546 (quoted by Celsus in IV, 77).

disagreeing with one another. But we will not imitate him and say similar things about the philosophers who profess to know the nature of the universe, and who dispute with one another about the way in which the universe came to be, and how heaven and earth and all that is in them came into existence, and whether souls are unbegotten and not created by God, although they are ordered by Him,[1] and if they change from one body to another, or whether they are made at the same time as their bodies, and whether or not they survive death. For one could mock at this also, instead of speaking of them as worthy men and believing in the sincerity of those who have devoted themselves to discovering the truth. One might speak evil of them by asserting that they are worms in a filthy corner of human life because they do not recognize their limitations, and for this reason make statements about immense subjects as though they had understood them, and because they seriously maintain that they have perceived the truth about problems when they cannot be understood without superior inspiration and divine power. 'For no man knows the things of a man except the spirit of a man which is within him; so also no man has known things of God, except the Spirit of God.'[2] Furthermore, as we are not mad, we do not compare with the wriggles of worms, or anything else of that sort, the profound intelligence of men (I use the word 'intelligence' in the ordinary sense) who are engaged not in the vulgar affairs of the common people, but with the search for the truth. We candidly admit that some Greek philosophers did know God, since 'God made it plain to them'. But they did not 'glorify Him as God or give thanks, but became vain in their reasonings, and professing themselves to be wise they became fools, and changed the glory of the incorruptible God for the likeness of an image of corruptible man, and of birds, and four-footed beasts, and creeping things'.[3]

31. After this, from a desire to argue that Jews and Christians are no better than the animals which he mentioned above, he says: *The Jews were runaway slaves who escaped from Egypt; they never did anything important,*

---

[1] The former view, that souls are pre-existent, is Platonic. The view that body and soul come into being together is Stoic. For a good discussion of ancient ideas on this subject, see J. H. Waszink's commentary on Tertullian, *de Anima*, 27 (Amsterdam, 1947), pp. 342 ff. For Origen's own opinion see *Comm. in Cant. Cantic.* 2 (VIII, pp. 146 f., ed. Baehrens); *in Ep. ad Tit.* (vol. v, p. 291 Lomm.); *de Princ.* I, Praef. 5; *ibid.* I, 3, 3. In the last passage he says: 'It is proved by many declarations throughout the whole of Scripture that the universe was created by God and that there is no substance which has not received its existence from him; which refutes and dismisses the doctrines falsely taught by some, that there is a matter which is co-eternal with God, or that there are unbegotten souls, in whom they would have it that God implanted not so much the principle of existence as the quality and rank of their life' (Butterworth's translation). See further F. J. Dölger, *Antike und Christentum*, IV (1933), pp. 28 ff.
[2] I Cor. ii. 11.   [3] Rom. i. 19, 21–3.

nor have they ever been of any significance or prominence whatever.[1] We have
said earlier that they were neither runaway slaves nor Egyptians, but that,
although they lived in Egypt, they were Hebrews.[2] If he thinks that he
can argue that they were never of any significance or prominence from the
fact that *nothing about their history is to be found among the Greeks*, we will
say that if anyone were to study carefully their society in their early days
when the law was given, he would find that they were men who manifested
a shadow of the heavenly life upon earth.[3] Among them none was regarded
as God other than the supreme God, and none of those who made images
possessed citizenship. There were no painters or image-makers in their
society, since the law banished from it any people of this sort,[4] in order
that there might be no occasion for the making of images which takes hold
of unintelligent men and drags the eyes of their soul down from God to
earth. There was a law among them as follows: 'Do not break the law and
make for yourselves a graven image, any figure that is a likeness of male or
female, a likeness of any beast of those that are in the earth, a likeness of
any winged bird which flies under heaven, a likeness of any creeping thing
which creeps upon the earth, a likeness of any fish that is in the waters
under the earth.'[5] The intention of the law was that in everything they
should have the reality, and should not make up things which are different
from reality, and misrepresent what is truly male, or what is really female,
or the nature of beasts, or the species of birds, or creeping things, or fishes.
Impressive and magnificent also is their law: 'Do not look up to heaven
and see the sun and moon and stars, all the world of heaven, lest being led
astray thou worship them and serve them.'[6]

Such was the way of life of the whole nation that among them it was not
even possible for any effeminate person to appear. It is also admirable
that the harlots, who inflame the lust of young men, were removed from
their society.[7] Moreover, the law courts consisted of the most righteous
men who had given proof of their good life over a long period.[8] These
men were entrusted with the responsibility of giving judgments, and
because of their purity of character, surpassing human nature, they were

[1] This was a standing anti-Semitic argument: Apion ap. Josephus, *c. Ap.* II, 12, 135;
Apollonius Molon, *ibid.* II, 14, 148. The phrase οὔτ' ἐν λόγῳ οὔτ' ἐν ἀριθμῷ alludes to the
story that the Megarians asked the oracle who were the most important people in Greece, and
were told they were not even in the reckoning at all. Cf. Theocritus, XIV, 48; Callimachus,
Epigr. 25; Philo, *de Praem. et Poen.* 111; Plutarch, *Mor.* 682F; Julian, 249D; Agathias in
Anth. Pal. V, 6; Suidas *s.v.* ὑμεῖς ὦ Μεγαρεῖς; Iamblichus, *V.P.* 259; Libanius, *Orat.* XXXI,
27. Clem. Al. *Strom*, VII, 110, wrongly ascribes the lines of the oracle to Theognis.
[2] Cf. III, 5–8.   [3] Cf. Heb. x. 1.
[4] Similarly Philo, *de Gigantibus* 59.   [5] Deut. iv. 16–18.
[6] Deut. xi. 19.   [7] Deut. xxiii. 1, 17.
[8] Exod. xviii. 21–2; Deut. i. 15.

called 'gods' by a traditional Jewish usage.[1] It was possible to see an entire nation studying philosophy; and in order that they might have leisure to hear the divine laws, the days called Sabbaths and their other feasts were instituted. And why need I mention the appointment of their priests and sacrifices, which contain countless symbols which are explained by those who are learned?

32. However, as nothing in human nature is permanent, even that society had to be gradually done away with and altered. Providence changed their noble doctrine in those respects in which it was in need of change[2] so that it would be suitable for people everywhere, and instead gave the noble religion of Jesus to those who believe in all places. He was endowed not only with intelligence but also with divine honour, and overthrew the teaching about the daemons on earth, who delight in frankincense and blood and the odours rising from burnt sacrifices,[3] and drag men down from the true conception of God, like the Titans or Giants of mythology. Without paying any attention to their conspiracy (for they plot particularly against good people) he gave laws, so that those who live in accordance with them will be blessed, without needing to pay any flattery at all to daemons by sacrifices. They utterly despise them, seeing that the Word of God helps those who look up even to God.[4] Because God wanted the word of Jesus to succeed among men, daemons have been powerless, even though they have exerted every effort, to put a stop to the further existence of Christians. For they have stirred up the emperors, and the Senate, and the local governors everywhere, and even the populace, who do not perceive the irrational and wicked activity of the daemons, to oppose the Gospel and those who believe in it. But the word of God is mightier than them all, and although it has been hindered it has taken the hindrance as nourishment by which it is increased, so that it has advanced and won over more souls.[5] For this was the will of God.

Even if this has been a digression on our part, yet I think it has been necessary. For we wanted to reply to Celsus' assertion about the Jews that they *were runaway slaves who escaped from Egypt*, and that the men beloved by God *never did anything of importance*. Furthermore, to his remark that *they were of no significance or prominence whatever*, we reply that, as they were 'a chosen race and a royal priesthood',[6] they withdrew themselves and avoided contact with the multitude lest their morals

---

[1] Cf. Ps. lxxxi. 1; Exod. xxii. 28.
[2] K. tr. proposes κατα⟨σκευάσασα καὶ⟩ τὰ δεόμενα.
[3] Cf. III, 28 above.   [4] Perhaps a reminiscence of Celsus' words in III, 62.
[5] Cf. Tertullian, *Apol.* 50 'semen est sanguis Christianorum'.
[6] I Pet. ii. 9.

should be corrupted, and that they were protected by divine power. They neither possessed the ambition, like most men, to annex other kingdoms, nor were they so forsaken that they became an easy prey to attack because of their insignificance, and were utterly destroyed as a result. This protection of God continued so long as they were still worthy of it. But whenever, because the whole nation were sinning, they needed to be converted to their God by suffering, they were forsaken sometimes for a long time, sometimes for a short time, until under the Romans, because they had committed their greatest sin in killing Jesus, they were entirely abandoned.

33. After this Celsus attacks the first book of Moses entitled Genesis, saying that *they shamelessly[1] undertook to trace their genealogy back to the first offspring of sorcerers and deceivers, invoking the witness of vague and ambiguous utterances concealed in some dark obscurity, which they misinterpreted to uneducated and stupid people, in spite of the fact that throughout the length of past history such an idea has never even been claimed.[2]* In these words he seems to me to have expressed his meaning very obscurely. But it is probable that obscurity on this subject suited his purpose since he saw the strength of the evidence which proves that the Jewish nation is descended from ancient ancestors. On the other hand, he did not want to appear ignorant of the facts about the Jews and their ancestry which may not be lightly passed over. In any event, it is clear that the Jews trace their genealogy back to the three fathers Abraham, Isaac, and Jacob. Their names are so powerful when linked with the name of God that the formula 'the God of Abraham, the God of Isaac, and the God of Jacob'[3] is used not only by members of the Jewish nation in their prayers to God and when they exorcise daemons, but also by almost all those who deal in magic and spells. For in magical treatises it is often to be found that God is invoked by this formula, and that in spells against daemons His name is used in close connexion with the names of these men. I think that these arguments, which are adduced by Jews and Christians to prove that Abraham, Isaac, and Jacob, the Fathers of the Jewish race, were holy men, were not entirely unknown to Celsus, but that he did not express himself clearly because he was unable to meet the argument.

34. We ask all those who use such invocations of God: Tell us, sirs, who Abraham was, and how great a man was Isaac, and what power was possessed by Jacob, that the name 'God' when attached to their names performs such miracles? And from whom did you or could you learn about these men? And who undertook to write the history about them, whether

---

[1] Read perhaps ⟨ἀναισχύντ⟩ως with K. tr. (cf. IV, 34-5).

[2] In the last phrase Origen is abbreviating Celsus' words, the meaning of which is clearer from the full quotation in IV, 35, below.

[3] See I, 22, 24; V, 45.

directly exalting the men because of their mysterious power, or giving veiled hints of certain great and wonderful truths to those who are able to perceive them? Then, whenever in answer to our question no one can show any history as the source of the stories about these men, either Greek or barbarian, or, if not history, at least some secret treatise, we produce the book called Genesis, which contains the acts of these men and the oracles of God uttered to them. And we say: Is not the divine character of these men shown by the fact that you use the names of these three progenitors of the nation who, as experience shows, compel the performance of considerable miracles when their names are invoked? We receive the traditions about them from no other source than from the sacred books of the Jews. Furthermore, 'the God of Israel', and 'the God of the Hebrews', and 'the God who drowned the king of Egypt and the Egyptians in the Red Sea',[1] are formulae which are often used to overcome daemons or certain evil powers. We learn from the Hebrews the history of the events mentioned in these formulae and the interpretation of the names, since in their traditional books and language they pride themselves on these things and explain them. How, then, was it *shameful* of the Jews to *try*[2] *to trace their genealogy back to the first offspring of* those whom Celsus supposes to have been *sorcerers and deceivers*, and to trace themselves and their origin to these men whose names, being Hebrew, bear witness that the Hebrews, whose sacred books are written in the Hebrew language and alphabet, are a nation related to them? Moreover, to this day Jewish names are in the language of the Hebrews, and are taken either from the scriptures themselves, or in general from words the meaning of which is made clear by the Hebrew language.

35. Let the reader of Celsus' book consider also whether he does not hint at this when he says: *They undertook to trace their genealogy back to the first offspring of sorcerers and deceivers, invoking the witness of vague and ambiguous utterances concealed in some dark obscurity.* These names may be obscure, and many have not the enlightenment and knowledge to understand them, but in our view they are not ambiguous, even if they are used in this way by people alien to our religion. Yet by Celsus for some unknown reason they have been cast aside, without him giving any example of the ambiguity of the words. But if he had wanted to give an honest refutation of the genealogy which he regarded as having been used most *shamefully* by the Jews when they have boasted of Abraham and his

---

[1] For an invocation of 'the Lord God of the Hebrews' in a pagan papyrus cf. Preisendanz, *Pap. Gr. Mag.* 22B 18. Jewish influence on magical literature was strong. See W. L. Knox, 'Jewish Liturgical Exorcism', in *Harv. Theol. Rev.* XXXI (1938), pp. 191–203; idem, *St Paul and the Church of the Gentiles* (1939), pp. 208 ff.

[2] Read with K. τr. ἅτε ἐπιχειρήσαντες.

descendants, he ought to have made a full statement of the matter, and
first advocated the view which he thinks convincing, and after this to
have given a respectable refutation of the relevant points on the ground
of the truth as he sees it and the arguments in its favour. But neither
Celsus, nor anyone else who discusses the problem of the nature of names
used for miracles, will be able to give a precise account of these matters
and to prove that no attention need be paid to men whose names alone
have such power, not only among people of their own nationality but
even among others.

He ought to have explained how we *misinterpret* these names to
uneducated and stupid people, and *deceive*, as he thinks, those who listen to
us, and how he, who boasts that he is neither uneducated nor stupid, gives
the true interpretation of them. And in what he says about these names
from which the Jews trace their descent, he asserts that although *throughout the length of past history no claim has ever been made about such names,
yet now the Jews make claims about them in answer to certain others* (who
they are he does not specify). I challenge anyone to point to any who
make a counter claim and put forward even any plausible argument against
the Jews which proves that what Jews and Christians maintain about the
names of the men in question is not true, but that others have given the
wisest and truest account of them. However, we are convinced that they
will not be able to do this, because it is beyond doubt that the names were
taken from the Hebrew language, which is to be found among the Jews
alone.

36. After this Celsus quotes from literature outside the divine Scripture
the stories about *the men who claimed antiquity, such as the Athenians,
Egyptians, Arcadians, and Phrygians, who hold that some among them were
born of earth, and each of whom produce evidence for these assertions.*[1] He
says that *the Jews, being bowed down in some corner of Palestine,*[2] *were totally
uneducated and had not heard of these things which were sung in poetry long
before by Hesiod and thousands of other inspired men. They composed a most
improbable and crude story that a man was formed by the hands of God and
given breath, that a woman was formed out of his side, that God gave commands, and that a serpent opposed them and even proved superior to the*

---

[1] For the notion that the first men were born of earth cf. the Stoic opinion quoted by
Origen in I, 37. Various races claimed to be the most ancient on earth. Cf. Cicero, *de Rep.*
III, 15, 25 (Arcadians and Athenians); Dio Chrys. LXIV, 12 (Athenians); Strabo, VIII, 1, 2,
p. 333 (Athenians); *idem*, VIII, 8, 1, p. 388 (Arcadians); Diodorus Sic. I, 9, 3 (Egyptians);
Pausanias, II, 14, 4 (Athenians); Clem. Al. *Protr.* VI, 4 (Phrygians, Arcadians, Egyptians);
similarly the Naassene in Hippolytus, *Ref.* v, 7, 3; Censorinus, *de Die Nat.* IV, 11; Aelius
Aristides, *Orat.* 23 (42), 26 (Keil, II, 38); Cosmas Hieros., *ad Carm. S. Greg. Theol.* LX, 131
(*P.G.* XXXVIII, 477); Lucian, *Philops.* 3.

[2] Cf. VI, 78.

ordinances of God[1]—*a legend which they expound to old women, most impiously making God into a weakling right from the beginning, and incapable of persuading even one man whom He had formed.* In these remarks the well-read and learned Celsus, who accuses both Jews and Christians of ignorance and want of education, clearly shows how accurate was his knowledge of the dates of each writer, Greek and barbarian. He really imagines that *Hesiod and thousands of others* whom he calls *inspired* were earlier than Moses and his writings, Moses, who is proved to have lived long before the Trojan war.[2] It was not, therefore, the Jews who *composed a most improbable and crude story* about the man born of earth, but the men who according to Celsus were *inspired, Hesiod* and his *thousands of others,* who had never learnt or heard of the far older and more sacred traditions to be found in Palestine, and wrote stories about the ancients, Eoiae and Theogonies,[3] attributing birth to gods by their statements, and thousands of other absurdities. [Plato quite rightly expelled from his Republic Homer and those who wrote poems of this kind because they harm the young.[4]] But Plato obviously did not think the men who left poems such as these to have been *inspired.* However, Celsus the Epicurean, if, at least, he is the one who also composed two other books against the Christians,[5] is a more competent judge than Plato, though it is probable that *he only called them inspired in order to attack us, and did not really think that they were inspired.*

37. He criticizes us for introducing the idea that *man was formed by the hands of God.* But the book of Genesis does not mention God's hands either at the making of man or at his forming. It is Job and David who say 'Thy hands have made me and fashioned me.'[6] We have much to say on this point to show the meaning of those who said this, not only concerning the distinction between making and fashioning, but also concerning God's hands. People who have not understood this and similar sayings in the divine scriptures imagine that we attribute to the supreme God a form like the human body. In their opinion we must think that God has a body with wings because, when interpreted literally, the scriptures also say this of Him.[7] But our present task does not require us to explain these things, for they have received primary consideration, to the best of our ability, in the commentary on Genesis.

---

[1] Gen. ii. 21 ff. [2] Cf. IV, 21.

[3] Read with Del., K. tr. Ὁοίας. These are titles of Hesiod's works. The phrase is perhaps a gloss which has come into the text.

[4] *Rep.* 379 C, D. Wifstrand (*Bull. Soc. Roy. Lund* (1939), p. 28) regards this sentence as a marginal gloss, breaking the connexion.

[5] See Introduction, p. xxvi. [6] Cf. Job x. 8; Ps. cxviii. 73.

[7] Cf. Exod. xix. 4, etc.

See, then, the wicked character of Celsus in what follows. For our scripture says of the forming of man: 'And he breathed into his face the breath of life and man became a living soul.'[1] But in his usual wicked way he wants to throw ridicule on the words 'he breathed into his face the breath of life', of which he has not even understood the meaning, and has written that *they composed the story that man was formed by the hands of God and given breath*, so that anyone would think that the words 'given breath' were meant in a similar sense to that of skins being inflated, and would laugh at this idea that 'he breathed into his face the breath of life'. But this is meant allegorically and needs an explanation which shows that God imparted a share of His incorruptible spirit to man, according to the saying: 'And thine incorruptible spirit is in all things.'[2]

38. Then, as it was his purpose to attack the Bible, he also ridicules the words 'God brought a trance upon Adam and he slept; and He took one of his ribs and closed up the flesh in its place; and He made the rib which He took from Adam into a woman',[3] and so on. But he does not quote the passage which one has only to hear to understand that it is to be interpreted allegorically. In fact, he wanted to pretend that such stories are not allegories, although in what follows he says that *the more reasonable Jews and Christians are ashamed of these things and try somehow to allegorize them*.[4] Are, then, the stories related by your *inspired* Hesiod in the form of a myth about the woman to be interpreted allegorically when they say that she was given to men by Zeus as an evil, as the price of the fire, whereas you think that there is no deeper and hidden meaning at all in the story that the woman was taken and made by God from the rib of the man who fell asleep after a trance?

But it is not treating the matter fairly to refuse to laugh at the former as being a legend, and to admire the philosophical truths contained in it, and yet to sneer at the biblical stories and think that they are worthless,[5] your judgment being based upon the literal meaning alone. If one may criticize simply on the ground of the literal sense what is expressed by veiled hints, consider whether it is not rather the stories of Hesiod which deserve to be laughed at, though he was, as you say, an inspired man. This is what he wrote:[6]

But Zeus who gathers the clouds said to him in anger, Son of Iapetus, surpassing all in cunning, you are glad that you have outwitted me and stolen fire, a great plague to you yourself and to men that shall be. But I will give men as

---

[1] Gen. ii. 7.   [2] Wisd. of Sol. xii. 1.
[3] Gen. ii. 21–2.   [4] Cf. IV, 89; I, 17; IV, 48–50.
[5] Read with K. tr. ἔχεσθαι.
[6] Hesiod, *Op.* 53–82. The translation above is that of Evelyn-White in the *Loeb Classical Library*, adapted to verbal differences.

the price of fire an evil thing in which they may all be glad of heart while they embrace their own destruction. So said he, and the father of men and gods ceased and ordered famous Hephaestus make haste and mix earth with water, and to put in it the voice and strength of human kind, and fashion a sweet lovely maiden-shape, like to the immortal gods in face; and Athene to teach her needlework and the weaving of the varied web; and golden Aphrodite to shed grace upon her head and cruel longing and cares that weary the limbs. And he charged Hermes, the guide, the slayer of Argus, to put in her a shameless mind and a deceitful nature. So he ordered. And they obeyed the Lord Zeus, the son of Kronos. Forthwith the famous lame god moulded clay in the like of a modest maid, as the son of Kronos purposed. And the goddess bright-eyed Athene girded and clothed her, and the divine Graces and queenly Persuasion put necklaces of gold upon her, and the rich-haired Hours crowned her head with spring flowers. And Pallas Athene bedecked her form with all manner of finery. Also the Guide, the slayer of Argus, contrived within her lies and crafty words and a deceitful nature at the will of the loud thundering Zeus, and the Herald of the gods put speech in her. And he called this woman Pandora, because all who dwelt on Olympus gave each a gift, a plague to men who eat bread.

The passage about the jar is also obviously ludicrous:[1]

For ere this the tribes of men lived on earth remote and free from ills and hard toil and heavy sicknesses which bring the Fates upon men; for in misery men grow old quickly. But the woman took off the great lid of the jar with her hands and scattered all these and her thought caused sorrow and mischief to men. Only Hope remained there in an unbreakable home within under the ruin of the great jar, and did not fly out of the door; for ere that the lid of the jar stopped her.

In reply to the man who gives a profound allegorical interpretation of these verses, whether his allegory is successful or not, we will say this: Are the Greeks alone allowed to find philosophical truths in a hidden form, and the Egyptians too, and all barbarians whose pride is in mysteries and in the truth which they contain? And do you think that the Jews alone, and their lawgiver, and the authors of their literature, are the most stupid of all men, and that this nation alone had no share at all of God's power, although it had been taught so magnificently to ascend to the uncreated nature of God, and to look upon Him alone, and to base its hopes only on Him?

39. Celsus also makes fun of the story of the serpent, saying that it opposed God's commands to the man, imagining that this is a legend like those told to old women. He intentionally says nothing either of the paradise of God, or of the way in which God is said to have planted it 'in *Eden eastward*', and after this made to arise '*out of the ground every tree*

[1] Hesiod, *Op.* 90–8.

214

that is pleasant to the sight and good for food, the tree of life also in the middle of the garden, and the tree of the knowledge of good and evil'.[1] He does not mention the account given of these things, which in itself is able to lead the kindly disposed reader to see that all these things have a significant allegorical meaning. Come, then, let us compare what is said by Socrates about Eros in Plato's *Symposium*. The passage is attributed to Socrates because he was more important than any of those who talk about Eros in the *Symposium*. The words of Plato read as follows:[2]

When Aphrodite was born, the gods gave a banquet, and besides the others Porus the son of Metis was there. When they had dined, Penia who was a beggar came near as there was a feast, and stood by the doors. Now Porus became drunk with the nectar (for wine did not yet exist) and entering into the garden of Zeus he became heavy and fell asleep. Penia then because of her distress thought out a plan to get a child by Porus; and she lay down beside him and conceived Eros. For this reason Eros became the attendant and servant of Aphrodite, because he was born on her birthday, and was also a lover by nature of beauty, since Aphrodite was beautiful. Now because Eros was son of Porus and Penia this became his lot; first, he is always poor, and far from being delicate and beautiful, as most people think; but he is hard, rough, barefoot, and homeless; he is always lying on the ground and has no covering, sleeping in doorways and roads in the open air, having his mother's nature in that he always lives in company with want. But, on the other hand, he takes after his father in plotting against the beautiful and good things, being brave, bold, and courageous, an expert hunter, always devising schemes, a lover of intelligence and resourceful, a philosopher throughout his whole life, an expert sorcerer, poisoner, and sophist. And his nature is neither immortal nor mortal, but on the same day at one time he flourishes and lives, when he is in good circumstances, while at another time he dies, though he comes to life again through his father's nature. His provisions are always flowing in and out, so that Eros is never either in adversity or in wealth. And again he is midway between wisdom and ignorance.

If readers of this were to imitate the malice of Celsus (which no Christian would do) they would ridicule the myth and would make a mock of so great a man as Plato. But if they could find Plato's meaning by examining philosophically what he expresses in the form of a myth, they would admire the way in which he was able to hide the great doctrines as he saw them in the form of a myth on account of the multitude, and yet to say what was necessary for those who know how to discover from myths the true significance intended by their author. I quoted this myth of Plato because he mentions 'the garden of Zeus', which seems to bear a certain resemblance to the paradise of God, and Penia, who is like the serpent of the Bible, and Porus who was conspired against by Penia, who is like the

---

[1] Gen. ii. 8–9.   [2] *Symp.* 203 B–E.

man against whom the serpent conspired. It is not quite clear whether Plato happened to hit on these matters by chance, or whether, as some think, on his visit to Egypt[1] he met even with those who interpret the Jews' traditions philosophically, and learnt some ideas from them, some of which he kept, and some of which he slightly altered, since he took care not to offend the Greeks by keeping the doctrines derived from the wisdom of the Jews without making any change. For they are popularly criticized for the strange character of their laws and their peculiar society. However, it is not now the right time to explain the myth of Plato, nor the story about the serpent and the paradise of God, and all the events which according to the Bible occurred in it. To the best of our ability we dealt with them as our primary concern in the commentary on Genesis.

40. When he asserts that the narrative of Moses represents God *most impiously, making Him into a weakling right from the beginning, and incapable of persuading even one man whom He had formed*, to this also we will reply that his remark is much the same as if one were to object to the existence of evil because God has been unable to prevent even one man from committing sin in order that just one individual might be found who has had no experience of evil from the beginning.[2] Just as in this matter those who are concerned to defend the doctrine of providence state their case at great length and with arguments of considerable cogency, so also the story of Adam and his sin will be interpreted philosophically by those who know that Adam means *anthropos* (man) in the Greek language, and that in what appears to be concerned with Adam Moses is speaking of the nature of man. For, as the Bible says, 'in Adam all die', and they were condemned in 'the likeness of Adam's transgression'.[3] Here the divine Word says this not so much about an individual as of the whole race. Moreover, in the sequence of sayings[4] which seem to refer to one individual, the curse of Adam is shared by all men. There is also no woman to whom the curses pronounced against Eve do not apply. And the statement that the man who was cast out of the garden with the woman was clothed with 'coats of skins',[5] which God made for those who had sinned on account of the transgression of mankind, has a certain secret and mysterious

---

[1] Cf. Cicero, *de Fin.* v, 29, 87; Plutarch, *Mor.* 354E; Diogenes Laert. III, 6; Clem. Al. *Strom.* I, 66, 3; Philostratus, *V.A.* I, 2.

[2] Cf. IV, 3.   [3] I Cor. xv. 22; Rom. v. 14.

[4] I.e. the curses enumerated in Gen. iii. 17–19.

[5] Gen. iii. 21. The Gnostics interpreted the coats of skins as bodies; cf. Cassianus ap. Clem. Al. *Strom.* III, 95, 2; Irenaeus, I, 5, 5 (Harvey, I, 50); Tertullian, *de Resurr. Carnis*, 7; Clem. Al. *Exc. Theod.* LV, 1. It is taken to be Origen's opinion by Methodius, *de Resurr.* I, 4, 2; I, 23, 3. But in *Sel. in Gen.* (vol. VIII, p. 58 Lomm.) Origen says this is possible but by no means certain. His disciple, Gregory of Nyssa, interprets it to mean a change for the worse in the physical state of man; cf. K. Holl, *Amphilochius von Ikonium* (1904), p. 202.

meaning, superior to the Platonic doctrine of the descent of the soul which loses its wings and is carried hither 'until it finds some firm resting-place'.[1]

41. He next speaks as follows: *Then they tell of a flood and a prodigious ark holding everything inside it, and that a dove and a crow were messengers. This is a debased and unscrupulous version of the story of Deucalion,[2] I suppose they did not expect that this would come to light, but simply recounted the myth to small children.* Here also see the unphilosophical hatred of the man towards the very ancient scripture of the Jews. For he had nothing to say against the story of the flood; and he did not even realize what he could have said against the ark and its measurements. For if we follow the opinion of the multitude and accept the statement that the ark was three hundred cubits long, fifty wide, and thirty high, it is impossible to maintain that it had room for all the animals on earth, fourteen of each clean and four of each unclean animal. He merely says it was *prodigious, holding everything inside it.* But what was *prodigious* about it? It is related to have taken a hundred years to build; at the bottom its length was three hundred cubits and its breadth fifty cubits, and it contracted in dimensions until at the top, which was thirty cubits high, it ended by being one cubit square. Should we not rather admire a construction which resembled a very large city? For when we square the measurements, the result is that it was ninety thousand cubits long at the bottom, and two thousand five hundred broad.[3] Should we not admire the planning which made it firmly built and able to endure a storm which brought such a flood? Moreover, it was not smeared with pitch or any such substance,

---

[1] Plato, *Phaedrus* 246B, C; Cf. VI, 43 below.
[2] For Noah as Deucalion cf. IV, 11; Philo, *de Praem. et Poen.* 23; Justin, *Apol.* II, 7, 2; Theophilus, *ad Autol.* III, 19.
[3] The difficulty of the inadequate size of the ark was raised by Apelles, Marcion's pupil (cf. V, 54). Origen quotes his views in *Hom. in Gen.* II, 2; the Greek text of this passage is preserved both in Catenae and in Procopius of Gaza (see Baehrens' edition in the Berlin Corpus, VI, pp. 23 ff.). There Origen answers that he has learnt from a learned Jew that the cubits are to be understood as geometrical cubits, so that the measurements should be squared, giving a floor area of 90,000 by 2500 and a height of 900 cubits. 'And it would be quite absurd if one who had been educated in all the wisdom of the Egyptians, who are particularly expert in geometry, and had been brought up in the king's house, had not perceived that if the 300 cubits of length, the 50 of breadth, and 30 of height, had been ordinary cubits, there would probably not have been room even for four elephants and their food for a year, whereas God commanded that two of all unclean animals should go into the ark.' The Latin text, however, has a sentence corresponding to nothing in the Greek fragment (Baehrens, p. 29): 'Apud geometras enim secundum eam rationem quae apud eos virtus (= δύναμις) vocatur, ex solido et quadrato vel in sex cubitos unus deputatur, si generaliter, vel in trecentos, si minutatim deducatur.' The statement that according to the geometricians one cubit equals either six or three hundred does not fit the interpretation in the Greek fragment. But it explains Augustine's comments (*Quaest. in Hept.* I, 4 (Migne, *P.L.* XXXIV, 549); *de Civ. Dei*, XV, 27) that according to Origen the measurements of the ark are reckoned in geometrical cubits one of which equals six ordinary cubits.

but was made watertight with asphalt. Is it not amazing that survivors
of every species were brought inside by the providence of God in order
that the earth might again possess the seeds of all animals, and that God
used a most righteous man to be the father of all born after the flood?

42. To give the appearance of having read the book of Genesis Celsus
alludes to the story of the dove, though he was unable to say anything to
prove that the account of the dove is fictitious. Then, as he habitually
changes the words of the Bible to something ridiculous, he has altered the
raven to a crow, and he thinks that when Moses wrote this story he *gave
a debased and unscrupulous version of the story of Deucalion* current among
the Greeks—unless perhaps he thinks that the book is not by Moses but by
several authors, for this appears to be implied by the words *they gave
a debased and unscrupulous version of the story of Deucalion,* and by the
words *I suppose they did not expect that this would come to light.* But how
could people who gave writings to a whole nation not expect that they
would come to light, when they even prophesied that this religion would be
preached to all nations? And when Jesus said to the Jews 'the kingdom of
God shall be taken from you and given to a nation bringing forth the
fruits thereof',[1] was not his purpose simply that by divine power he might
bring forth to light the whole Jewish scripture which contains the mysteries
of the kingdom of God? Accordingly, when people read the theogonies of
the Greeks and the stories about the twelve gods,[2] they make them sacred
by allegories. But if they want to ridicule our histories, they say that they
are *recounted simply to small children.*

43. *Utterly absurd also,* he says, *is the begetting of children when the
parents were too old,* and though he does not say so he obviously means the
case of Abraham and Sarah.[3] He rejects also *the conspiracies of the brothers,*
referring either to Cain's plot against Abel, or both this and that of Esau
against Jacob.[4] He mentions the *father's grief,* perhaps referring to that of
Isaac at the departure of Jacob, but perhaps also to that of Jacob when
Joseph was sold into Egypt.[5] When he writes of *the treacheries of mothers,*
I think he means Rebecca when she contrived that the blessings of Isaac
should not come to Esau but to Jacob.[6] If we say that *God entered into the
closest contact with* these men, why are we doing anything *absurd*? For we
are convinced that His divinity is never absent from those who are devoted
to Him and live a good and healthy life. He has ridiculed the property
which Jacob acquired when he was with Laban, because he did not under-

[1] Matt. xxi. 43.
[2] Cf. O. Weinreich in W. H. Roscher, *Lexikon der griechischen und römischen Mythologie,*
VI, 764–848; W. K. C. Guthrie, *The Greeks and their Gods* (1950), pp. 110–12.
[3] Gen. xxi. 1–7.   [4] Gen. iv. 8; xxv. 29–34; xxvii. 18–29.
[5] Gen. xxviii. 1–5; xxxvii. 33–5.   [6] Gen. xxvii. 5–17.

stand the reference in the words 'And the unbranded sheep were Laban's and the branded sheep were Jacob's.'¹ He says that *God made a present to the sons of asses, sheep, and camels.* He did not see that 'all these things happened to them for an example, and were written for our sake upon whom the ends of the ages have come'.² In our view the different nations³ become branded and are ruled by the Word of God, since they have been given as a possession to Him who is allegorically called Jacob. For the story in the Bible about Laban and Jacob refers to those Gentiles who believe in Him.

44. He has missed the meaning of the Bible when he says that *God also gave wells to the thirsty.*⁴ He did not notice that the righteous do not construct reservoirs; they dig *wells,*⁵ seeking to find the inner source and origin of good refreshment,⁶ because they have received the command, also to be interpreted allegorically, which says: 'Drink waters out of thine own vessels, and from thine own wells of water. Do not let thy waters overflow outside thy wall, but let thy waters pass through thy level places. Let them be for thee alone and let no stranger share them with thee.'⁷ In many passages the Word made use of stories about actual events and recorded them to exhibit deeper truths, which are indicated by means of hints. Of this sort are the stories about the *wells,* and *the marriages,* and *the intercourse of* righteous *men with* different *women.* Concerning these one would attempt to give an explanation at a more suitable time in commentaries upon these very points. That wells have been made by the righteous in the land of the Philistines, as recorded in Genesis, is clear from the wonderful wells which are shown at Ascalon, which are worth mentioning on account of their strange and extraordinary style of construction in comparison with other wells.⁸

¹ Gen. xxx. 42.   ² I Cor. x. 11.
³ Read ἔθνη with K. tr. The allusion is perhaps to Ps. ii. 8. Possibly Origen may have connected the story with the Good Shepherd who obtains other sheep, not of his own fold, i.e. Gentile believers.
⁴ Cf. Gen. xvi. 14; xxi. 19; xxvi. 22. E. Stein (in *Eos,* xxxiv (1933), p. 214 n. 25) proposed διψίοις for δικαίοις.
⁵ Origen follows Philo, *de Fuga et Inventione,* 200, who says that the impious do not dig wells (φρέατα) like the wise Abraham and Isaac, but reservoirs (λάκκοι) which need supplying from without.
⁶ Verbal allusion to Plato, *Phaedrus* 243D.   ⁷ Prov. v. 15–17.
⁸ Eustathius of Antioch (*de Engastrim.* 21, p. 48 Klostermann) complains of Origen's allegorizing of the wells dug by Abraham, 'when even to this day the wells in the land are still to be seen'. For wells at Ascalon cf. Eusebius, *Onomasticon* (p. 168, ed. Klostermann). In the account of a pilgrimage to the Holy Land about A.D. 570 known as the *itinerarium* of Antoninus Placentinus the author says of the Philistine country that 'in these places are the wells which Abraham and Jacob digged'. He goes on to say: 'We went on to Ascalon. There is the well of peace which is greater in width and is made like a theatre, in which one goes down to the water by steps' (text in P. Geyer, *Itinera Hierosolymitana* (C.S.E.L. 39), p. 180). Cf. William of Tyre (twelfth century) in Migne, *P.L.* cci, 697A.

It is not we who teach that *brides and maidservants* are to be interpreted allegorically, but we have received this from wise men before us. One of them, when urging the hearer to understand an allegorical meaning, said: 'Tell me, you who read the law, do you not hear the law? For it is written that Abraham had two sons, one by the handmaid and one by the free woman. But the child by the handmaid is born after the flesh; but the son by the free woman is born through the promise. These things contain an allegory. For these women are two covenants, one from Mount Sinai bearing children unto bondage, which is Hagar.' And a little later he says: 'The Jerusalem which is above is free, which is our mother.'[1] Anyone who likes to take up the Epistle to the Galatians will know how the stories about the marriages and the intercourse with the maidservants may be allegorized. For the Word does not want us to emulate those who did these things in respect of their physical acts, as they are commonly supposed, but to emulate their spiritual actions, as they are usually called by the apostles of Jesus.

45. Although Celsus ought to have approved of the honesty of the authors of the divine scriptures, who did not even conceal discreditable events, and ought to have been won over also to regard even the other more remarkable stories as being not fictitious, yet he did the opposite. Concerning the story of Lot and his *daughters*, where he neither examined its ordinary meaning, nor looked into its mystical interpretation, he says that the story is *more iniquitous than Thyestian sins*. However, it is not necessary to discuss now the allegorical meaning of the passage, and to explain what Sodom means, and what the saying of the angels meant when they said to him who was escaping from the place: 'Do not look behind you, nor stand in all the plain; escape to the mountain lest you should be consumed',[2] and to explain what is meant by Lot, and his wife who became a pillar of salt because she turned to look behind her, and who are his daughters, who made their father get drunk that they might become mothers by him. However, let us briefly endeavour to soften down the discreditable features of the story. The Greeks have examined the nature of actions, good, bad, and indifferent. Those who are successful in this hold that it is only the motive which determines whether actions are good or bad;[3] and they maintain that all actions proved to have been done without a motive are, strictly speaking, indifferent, and that the motive is laudable when the actions are rightly performed, but blameworthy when they are not. Concerning things indifferent they say, therefore, that

---

[1] Gal. iv. 21–4, 26.   [2] Gen. xix. 17.
[3] For this Stoic doctrine, cf. Epictetus, *Diss.* III, 10, 18; Clem. Al. *Strom.* IV, 113, 6; II, 66, 1.

strictly speaking it is a matter of moral indifference to have intercourse
with one's daughters, although one ought not to do such a thing in civilized
society. And for the sake of argument, to show that such action is morally
indifferent they suppose that the wise man has been left with his daughter
alone and that all the rest of mankind has been destroyed; and they ask if
it would be compatible with moral principle for the father to have sexual
intercourse with his daughter to avoid the whole human race coming to
an end, as would occur in the instance here assumed.

Are the Greeks right in this opinion which is advocated by the important sect of the Stoics? But when young girls, who had heard something
of the world-conflagration but had no clear idea about it, saw that a sole
surviving spark of the human race had been left in their father and themselves, and when, having accepted this assumption, they desired that the
world should continue to exist:[1] are they to be inferior to the wise man in
the instance taken by the Stoics who, when all men have been destroyed,
has sexual intercourse with his daughters without infringing moral
principle? I am aware that some people have been offended at the desire of
Lot's daughters, and have supposed that their action was impious and
said that accursed nations, the Moabites and Ammonites, originated from
unlawful intercourse.[2] And, it is true, the divine Scripture is not to be
found giving clear approval of this act and indicating that they did right;
nor does it criticize and find fault with it. Yet, however the event is to be
understood, it has an allegorical meaning, though in some degree it is
also capable of defence as it stands.

46. Celsus objects to the *hatred*, referring, I think, to that of Esau
towards Jacob.[3] Esau is a man admitted by the Bible to be bad. And
without clearly quoting the story, he attacks that of Simon and Levi who
went forth because of the insult to their sister after she had been forced by
the son of the king of Shechem.[4] He speaks of *brothers trading*, meaning
Jacob's sons, and of *a brother sold*, meaning Joseph, and *a father who was
deceived*, meaning Jacob who suspected nothing when his sons showed
Joseph's coat of many colours, but believed them and mourned Joseph as
dead although he was a slave in Egypt.[5] See the hostile and unphilosophical way in which Celsus collects points from the history. Where he
thinks the narrative contains an opening for criticism, he quotes it. But
where impressive self-control was displayed, as when Joseph did not yield

---

[1] Origen follows Philo, *Quaest. in Genes.* IV, 56; the presbyter of Irenaeus, IV, 31, 2
(Harvey, II, 252–3). Origen's allegorical interpretation in *Hom. in Gen.* V, 4–5 rejects that
of Irenaeus' presbyter in Iren. IV, 32, 1.
For the Stoic opinion quoted, cf. *S.V.F.* III, 743–56.
[2] Cf. Gen. xix. 37–8.　　　　　　[3] Gen. xxvii. 41–5.
[4] Gen. xxxiv. 2, 25–31.　　　　　[5] Gen. xxxvii. 26–36.

to the passion of his supposed mistress, both when she pleaded and when she threatened him, he has not even mentioned the story.[1] If he had done so, we should have seen that Joseph was far superior to the actions related of Bellerophon,[2] since he chose to be shut up in prison rather than lose his modesty.[3] In fact, although he could have defended himself and pleaded his cause against the woman who accused him, he nobly kept silence and committed his cause to God.

47. After this, for form's sake, Celsus makes exceedingly obscure references to the *dreams* of the chief butler and the chief baker of Pharaoh, and to *their explanation*, as a result of which Joseph was brought out from the prison to be entrusted by Pharaoh with authority of the second rank among the Egyptians.[4] What is *absurd* about the narrative, even when taken literally, that he should make it part of his accusation? (For although he entitled his book *The True Doctrine* it contains no positive doctrines, but just criticizes Jews and Christians.) And he says that *the one who was sold was kind to his brothers who sold him when they were hungry and had been sent with the asses to do some trading,*[5] though Celsus does not specify what he did for them. He also mentions *the time when* Joseph *made himself known*, though I have no idea what his intention is in so doing, and what absurdity he produces from the fact that he made himself known. Not even Momus himself,[6] as one might say, could reasonably criticize this story; for apart from its allegorical meaning it possesses several attractive features. And he says that Joseph, *the man who was sold to be a slave, was set free and with a solemn procession returned to his father's tomb.*[7] He thinks that the story contains a ground for an objection when he says: *By him* (clearly meaning Joseph) *the distinguished and marvellous race of the Jews, which in Egypt had increased to be a multitude, were commanded to live somewhere outside and to tend their flocks in land that was valueless.* It was his hostile purpose which led him to add that *they were commanded to tend their flocks in land that was valueless.* But he did not show in what respect Goshen,[8] the home of the Egyptians, is valueless. He has called the departure of the people from Egypt a *flight*, not even mentioning at all what is written in the Exodus about the Hebrews' departure from the land of Egypt. We have quoted these instances to show that Celsus has not said anything that seems worth calling a criticism even of

---

[1] Gen. xxxix. 7–12.

[2] Homer, *Il.* VI, 155–95. Bellerophon committed murder and fled to the king of Argos, whose wife fell in love with him. He rejected her advances and she then accused him to her husband of having approached her.

[3] Read ἀπολέσθαι τὸν σώφρονα with A, We. For the idiom Wendland compares Epict. I, 28, 23.   [4] Gen. xl–i.   [5] Gen. xlii–iv.

[6] Momus: the genius of criticism. Cf. Plato, *Rep.* 487A; Lucian, *Hist. Conscr.* 33.

[7] Gen. l. 4–14.   [8] Gen. xlvii. 1–5.

the literal interpretation in his accusations and mockery. For he has not shown by any argument what he thinks to be wrong with our scriptures.

48. Then, as though he had devoted himself only to hatred and hostility towards the doctrine of Jews and Christians, he says that *the more reasonable Jews and Christians allegorize these things.*[1] He asserts that *because they are ashamed of them, they take refuge in allegory.* One might say[2] to him that if any stories of myths and legends may be said to be shameful on the ground of their literal meaning, whether they were composed with a hidden interpretation or in any other way, what stories deserve to be so regarded more than those of the Greeks? In these divine sons castrate their divine fathers. Divine fathers swallow their divine sons. A divine mother gives a stone instead of a son to the father of men and gods. A father has sexual intercourse with his daughter. And a wife binds her husband, employing the brother of the person bound and his daughter to help her with the bonds.[3] Why need I enumerate the outrageous stories of the Greeks about the gods which are obviously shameful even if they are to be interpreted allegorically? At any rate, in one place Chrysippus of Soli, who is considered to have adorned the Stoic school of philosophers by his many intelligent treatises, expounds the meaning of a picture at Samos, in which Hera is portrayed as performing unmentionable obscenities with Zeus. This honourable philosopher says in his treatises that matter receives the generative principles of God, and contains them in itself for the ordering of the universe. For in the picture at Samos matter is Hera and God is Zeus.[4] It is because of these myths and thousands of others like them that we are unwilling to call the supreme God Zeus, or even to use the name, or to call the sun Apollo and the moon Artemis. But we practise a pure piety towards the Creator and praise the beautiful things which He has created, without defiling the things of God even by a name. We approve Plato's saying in the *Philebus*, when he refused to allow that pleasure was a god: 'For my reverence, Protarchus,' he says, 'for the names of the gods is profound.'[5]

---

[1] Cf. I, 17; IV, 38.   [2] Read εἴποι with K. tr.

[3] Cf. I, 25. Kronos castrated Ouranos (Hesiod, *Theogony*, 164–82) and swallowed Zeus (*ibid.* 453–67). Gaia gave Kronos a stone to swallow instead of a baby (*ibid.* 481–91). It was an Orphic legend that Zeus raped Persephone (see H. J. Rose, *Handbook of Greek Mythology* (1928), p. 51). Hera, Poseidon, and Athena plotted to bind Zeus (Homer, *Il.* I, 400). Cf. Lucian, *Philops.* 2.

[4] Criticism of Chrysippus' interpretation also appears in Diog. Laert. VII, 187–8; Theophilus, *ad Autol.* III, 8; *Clem. Hom.* V, 18. Cf. Dio Chrys. XXXVI, 55 (Celsus in VI, 42). For the sacred marriage of Zeus and Hera cf. A. B. Cook, *Zeus*, III, pp. 1027ff. In the confession of the magician, Cyprian of Antioch, the marriage of Zeus and Hera is interpreted as the union of aether and air. Cf. M. P. Nilsson, 'Greek Mysteries in the Confession of St Cyprian of Antioch', in *H.T.R.* XL (1947), pp. 167ff. Also Doxopater, *Hom. in Aphthon.* II, 151 Walz.   [5] *Philebus*, 12B, C, already quoted in I, 25.

Accordingly, we truly have reverence for the name of God and the names of the beautiful things which He has created, so that we do not accept any myth which might harm the young[1] even if it is to be understood allegorically.

49. If Celsus had read the Bible impartially, he would not have said that our writings *are incapable of being interpreted allegorically*. For from the prophecies, in which events of history are recorded, it is possible to be convinced in a way which would not come from the history alone that the histories also were written with an eye to an allegorical meaning, and were arranged very wisely to be exactly suited both to the multitude of simple-minded believers and to the few who have the desire or the capacity to examine the questions with intelligence. If those Jews and Christians who allegorize the Bible, who in Celsus' opinion are *reasonable*, are thought to be only those of our own time, perhaps Celsus might be supposed to have said something plausible. But since the very authors of the doctrines themselves and the writers interpreted these narratives allegorically, what else can we suppose except that they were written with the primary intention that they should be allegorized?

We will quote a few examples out of a great number in order to show that Celsus falsely accuses the Bible to no purpose when he says that it cannot be interpreted allegorically. Paul, the apostle of Jesus, says: 'It is written in the law, Thou shalt not muzzle the ox that treadeth out the corn. Does God care for oxen? Or does He say this altogether on our account? For on our account it was written, because he that ploughs ought to plough in hope, and he that threshes ought to thresh in hope of partaking.'[2] And in another place the same man says: 'For it is written that for this cause a man shall leave his father and his mother and shall cleave unto his wife, and the two shall become one flesh. This is a great mystery; but I speak concerning Christ and his church.'[3] And again in another passage: 'And we know that all our fathers were under the cloud, and all passed through the sea, and were all baptized unto Moses in the cloud and in the sea.'[4] Then he interprets the story of the manna and of the water which is recorded to have come miraculously out of the rock, saying as follows: 'And they all ate the same spiritual meat, and they all drank the same spiritual drink; for they drank of the spiritual rock which followed them; and the rock was Christ.'[5] Asaph showed that the stories in Exodus and Numbers are 'problems' and 'parables', as it is written in the book of Psalms. For when about to recount these narratives he prefaces *his*

---

[1] It is on the ground that they harm the young that Plato expels Homer and the poets from his Republic (377-8).

[2] I Cor. ix. 9-10.

[3] Eph. v. 31-2.

[4] I Cor. x. 1-2.

[5] I Cor. x. 3-4.

account in this way: 'Give ear, O my people, to my law, incline your ears
to the words of my mouth. I will open my mouth in parables, I will utter
problems of old, which we have heard and read, and our fathers have told
us.'¹

50. Furthermore, had the law of Moses contained within it nothing to
be interpreted as containing hidden meaning, the prophet would not have
said to God in his prayer 'Open thou mine eyes, that I may understand
thy wonders out of thy law.'² Here he knew that there is a veil of ignorance
lying upon the heart of those who read and do not understand the
allegorical meaning.³ This veil is taken away by God's gift, when He
perceives a man who has done everything in his own power,⁴ and by use
has exercised his senses to distinguish good and evil,⁵ and has unceasingly
said in his prayer 'Open thou mine eyes, that I may understand thy
wonders out of thy law.' And who that reads of a dragon living in the
river of Egypt and of the fishes lurking in its scales, or of the mountains of
the Egyptians being filled with Pharaoh's excrement, is not at once
persuaded to find out who it is who fills the mountains of the Egyptians
with so much of his foul excrement, and what is meant by the mountains
of the Egyptians, and the rivers in Egypt, of which the Pharaoh just
mentioned boasts, saying 'the rivers are mine and I made them',⁶ and
what meaning, corresponding to the interpretation given of the rivers, is
to be assigned to the dragon and to the fishes in its scales? But why do
I need to argue at length about matters which need no argument?
Concerning these things it is said: 'Who is wise, and will understand these
things? Or who is intelligent and will know them?'⁷

I have ventured upon an extended discussion from a desire to show that
Celsus is incorrect when he says that *the more reasonable Jews and Chris-
ians try somehow to allegorize them, but they are incapable of being explained in
this way, and are manifestly very stupid fables.* But the truth is much rather
that it is the legends of the Greeks which are not only *very stupid*, but also
very impious. For our scriptures have been written to suit exactly the
multitude of the simple-minded, a consideration to which no attention
was paid by those who made up the fictitious stories of the Greeks. For
this reason it was not mere ill will which led Plato to banish from his
Republic myths and poems of this character.⁸

¹ Ps. lxxvii. 1–3.   ² Ps. cxviii. 18.
³ Cf. II Cor. iii. 13–16.
⁴ There is no need to emend the MS. reading τῷ παρ' ἑαυτόν. Wifstrand proposes
τῷ ⟨τὰ⟩ παρ' ἑαυτοῦ (or ἑαυτῷ). Cf. VII, 42 (193, 19).
⁵ Cf. Heb. v. 14.   ⁶ Ezek. xxix. 3; xxxii. 6.
⁷ Hos. xiv. 9.
⁸ *Rep.* 379C, D. Plato is criticized for his arrogance in banishing Homer by Dionysius
of Halicarnassus, *Ep. ad Pomp.* 756 (ed. Roberts, p. 94).

51. He seems to me to have heard also that there are treatises containing allegories of the law. But if he had read them he would not have said: *At any rate, the allegories which seem to have been written about them are far more shameful and preposterous than the myths, since they connect with some amazing and utterly senseless folly ideas which cannot by any means be made to fit.* He appears by this to mean the works of Philo or even writers still earlier such as the writings of Aristobulus.[1] But I hazard the guess that Celsus has not read the books, for I think that in many places they are so successful that even Greek philosophers would have been won over by what they say. Not only have they an attractive style, but they also discuss ideas and doctrines, making use of the *myths* (as Celsus regards them) in the scriptures. I am also aware that Numenius the Pythagorean,[2] a man who expounded Plato with very great skill and maintained the Pythagorean doctrines, quotes Moses and the prophets in many passages in his writings, and gives them no improbable allegorical interpretation, as in the book entitled 'Hoopoe' (Epops) and in that 'Concerning Numbers' and in that 'Concerning Place'. In the third book 'Concerning the Good' he even quotes a story about Jesus, though without mentioning his name, and interprets it allegorically; whether his interpretation is successful or not we may discuss at another time. He also quotes the story about Moses and Jannes and Jambres.[3] It is not that this is a source of pride to us, but that we approve of him because he had a greater desire than Celsus and other Greeks to examine even our writings in a scholarly way, and was led to regard them as books which are to be interpreted allegorically and which are not foolish.

52. After this, out of all the writings which contain allegories and interpretations written with a literary style, he has chosen one that is worthless, which although it could be of some help to the simple-minded multitude in respect of their faith, certainly could not impress the more intelligent, saying: *I know a work of this sort, a Controversy between one*

---

[1] Writings ascribed to Aristobulus, teacher of Ptolemy Philometor (cf. II Macc. i. 10), are quoted by Clem. Al. (*Strom.* v, 97, 7) and Eusebius (*P.E.* VIII, 10; XIII, 12); their theme seems to have been the debt of Aristotle and the Peripatetics to the O.T., the anthropomorphisms of which are freely allegorized. His work does not survive. Whether it was an authentic work of Aristobulus himself is a disputed question; but there is reason to think that it was a Jewish pseudepigraphic production like the epistle of Aristeas, and is to be dated before Philo.   [2] *Frag.* XXIV Thedinga; *frag.* 19 Leemans. Cf. I, 15 above.
[3] Eusebius preserves this passage, *P.E.* IX, 8, 411 D: 'Next, Jannes and Jambres, Egyptian sacred scribes, men judged to be inferior to none in the art of magic, lived at the time when the Jews were being driven out of Egypt. In fact, these were the men elected by the multitude of the Egyptians to oppose Musaeus, the leader of the Jews, a man who was very powerful in prayer to God; and they were seen to be capable of stopping the most violent of the plagues which Musaeus brought upon Egypt.' For the story, known to Pliny (*N.H.* XXX, 11) and Apuleius (*Apol.* 90), see the commentaries on II Tim. iii. 8.

Papiscus and Jason,[1] *which does not deserve ridicule but rather pity and hatred. It is not, therefore, my duty to refute this nonsense; for it is obvious to everyone, I presume, and especially to anyone who has had the patience and endurance to give his attention to the actual writings. But I would prefer to teach about the order of nature and say that God made nothing mortal. Whatever beings are immortal are works of God, and mortal beings are made by them.*[2] *And the soul is God's work, but the nature of the body is different. In fact, in this respect there will be no difference between the body of a bat or a worm or a frog or a man. For they are made of the same matter, and are equally liable to corruption.* Nevertheless, I could wish that everyone who hears Celsus' clever rhetoric asserting that the book entitled 'A Controversy between Jason and Papiscus about Christ' deserves not laughter but hatred, were to take the little book into his hands and have *the patience and endurance to give his attention* to its contents. He would then at once condemn Celsus, for he would find nothing in the book deserving of hatred. If anyone reads it impartially he will find that the book does not even move him to laughter. In it a Christian is described as disputing with a Jew from the Jewish scriptures and as showing that the prophecies about the Messiah fit Jesus; and the reply with which the other man opposes the argument is at least neither vulgar nor unsuitable to the character of a Jew.

53. For some unknown reason he connects feelings which are incompatible and which cannot occur simultaneously in human experience when he says that the book *deserves pity and hatred.* For everyone will admit that anyone who is the object of pity is not felt to be the object of hatred at the time when he is being pitied; and anyone who is hated is not pitied at the time when he is being hated. For this reason, however, Celsus says that it is not his *duty to refute this,* because he thinks *it is obvious to everyone,* even before any reasoned refutation is produced, that it is bad and *deserves pity and hatred.* But we invite the reader of this defence we have written in reply to Celsus' criticism to have the patience and to give his attention to our books and to exert all his powers to find out from the writings the purpose of the authors, and their honesty and sincerity. For he will find men who contend ardently for what they have received, and that some of them show that they are writing about history of which they were

---

[1] The dialogue is not extant; Clement apparently ascribed it to Luke (cf. Stählin's edition, III, p. 199). It was known to Jerome. A Latin translation was made by one Celsus, an African, probably of the late third century (Harnack, *Chronologie,* II, 391); his covering letter is extant in the Appendix to Cyprian (ed. Hartel, III, pp. 119 ff.). According to Maximus Confessor (seventh century) the dialogue was written by Aristo of Pella (cf. Eus. *H.E.* IV, 6, 3). See Harnack, *Gesch. d. altchr. Litt.* I, i, 92–5; A. L. Williams, *Adversus Judaeos* (1935), pp. 28–30.

[2] Cf. Plato, *Timaeus,* 69 C, D.

eye-witnesses, and which they understood to be miraculous and worthy of being recorded for the benefit of future hearers. I challenge anyone to dare to assert that it is not the source and origin of every benefit to have believed in the God of the universe and to do every action with the object of pleasing Him, whatever it may be, and not even to desire anything displeasing to Him, since not only words and works but even thoughts will be open to His judgment. And what other teaching would be more effective in converting mankind to live a good life than the belief or the conviction that the supreme God sees everything that we say and do, and even what we think? I challenge anyone to produce any comparable method which both converts and improves not merely one or two but a very large number of people, so that by comparing both the methods one may understand exactly which doctrine disposes men towards goodness.

54. In the passage which I quoted from Celsus, which is a paraphrase of the Timaeus, he made certain remarks to the effect that God made nothing mortal, but only immortal beings, and mortal beings are the work of others. *And the soul is God's work, but the nature of the body is different. And a man's body will be no different from the body of a bat or a worm or a frog. For they are made of the same matter, and they are equally liable to corruption.* Let us briefly deal with this, and prove either that he is pretending not to hold his Epicurean opinion, or, as someone might say, that he has undergone a belated conversion for the better, or even, as might be said,[1] that he is only a namesake of the Epicurean. Seeing that he has put forward views which contradict not only us but also the not undistinguished sect who are disciples of Zeno of Citium,[2] he ought to have shown that the bodies of animals are not the works of God and that their intricate design did not originate from the supreme Mind. And concerning the great and varied number of plants which are nourished by an inherent nature, incapable of perception, and which were made to perform the important function in the universe of serving men and the animals which minister to men, or[3] whatever else they may do, he ought not merely to have asserted his own opinion, but also to have *taught* why it was not a perfect Mind which created the numerous qualities[4] in the matter constituting the plants.

Once he had made gods the creators of all bodies while the soul alone is the work of God, would it not have been logical for him who apportions the vast number of created things and assigns them to numerous gods, to have given some convincing argument to explain the difference

---

[1] Read ὡς ἂν λέγοιτο with Preuschen.
[3] Read ζῴων ⟨ἢ⟩ ὅπως with Wif.
[2] Cf. *S.V.F.* II, 1152–67.
[4] Cf. IV, 56–7.

between the various gods, and how some make human bodies while others, for example, make the bodies of domestic animals, and others those of wild animals? And if he regarded gods as the creators of dragons and asps and basilisks, and some of them as creators of each species of insect,[1] and others of the form of each creature and each plant, he ought to have given the reasons for this division of labour. For perhaps if he had devoted himself to an accurate study of the subject either he would have retained the belief that one God is the creator of all, and has made each thing for a certain purpose and for a certain reason; or if he did not retain this, he would have seen the reply which he ought to have made to the criticism that in its own nature destructibility is a matter of indifference,[2] and that there is no difficulty about holding that, although the world is composed of dissimilar elements, it originated from one Artificer, who constructed the various forms for the benefit of the whole. Or, finally, if he did not intend to argue in support of the views which he professed to *teach*, he ought not even to have made any assertion at all on such an intricate subject—unless perhaps he who criticizes people who profess a simple faith[3] himself wanted us to believe his assertions, even though he has claimed not to have asserted but to have *taught* them.

55. I have not yet mentioned the fact that if he had had *the patience and endurance to give his attention*, as he says, to the books of Moses and the prophets, he would have considered why the phrase 'God made' is applied to heaven and earth and to the so-called firmament, and also to the planets and stars, and after these to great fishes and 'every soul of the creeping animals which the waters brought forth after their kind', and to 'every winged bird after its kind', and following these to the beasts of the earth after their kind, and every creeping thing upon the earth after its kind, and finally to man; whereas the words 'He made' are not said of other things.[4] At the creation of light the Word is content to say 'Let there be light', and at the gathering together into one place of all the water beneath all the heaven to say 'And it was so.' Similarly also of the things that grew from the earth it merely says: 'The earth brought forth a herb of grass which sows seed after its kind and after its likeness, and a fruit-tree that produces fruit, whose seed is in itself after its kind upon the earth.' He would have raised the question also to what being or beings God's commands in the

---

[1] Read ἔντομον with K. tr.
[2] The Stoics held that the world was periodically destroyed by fire; therefore destructibility must be a matter of moral indifference.
[3] Cf. Celsus in I, 9 ff.
[4] Cf. Gen. i. 1 ff. Read comma for full stop before μή with We., K. tr. (also before ὁμοίως, 328, 16).

Bible about the making of each part of the world were addressed;[1] and he would not have rashly accused of being silly and of having no secret meaning the account written of these matters either by Moses, or, as we would say, by the divine Spirit in Moses, by whose inspiration he also prophesied. For

He knew the present and the future and the past[2]

better than those seers said by the poets to have known these things.

56. Moreover, Celsus says that *the soul is God's work, but the nature of the body is different. In fact, in this respect there will be no difference between the body of a bat, or a worm, or a frog, or a man. For they are made of the same matter, and they are equally liable to corruption.* To this argument of his I reply that if, because the same matter underlies the body of a bat, or a worm, or a frog, or a man, these bodies will not differ from one another, obviously the bodies of these will be no different from sun or moon or stars or heaven, or anything else which is called by the Greeks a visible god.[3] For the same matter which underlies all bodies is strictly speaking without qualities and shape,[4] though by what agency Celsus thinks it receives its qualities I do not know since he will not accept the view that anything corruptible is God's work. By Celsus' own argument the corruptible part of anything whatever which is composed of the same underlying matter must necessarily be similar. But perhaps in that case, because he is in difficulties, Celsus would turn away from Plato who makes the soul originate from a bowl,[5] and would take refuge with Aristotle and the Peripatetics, who think that the aether is immaterial and is composed of a fifth nature other than the four elements.[6] Against this doctrine both the Platonists and the Stoics have rightly stood firm.[7] And we who are despised by Celsus will also stand firm, since we are required to expound and defend the following saying of the prophet: 'The heavens shall perish, but thou remainest; they all shall wax old as a garment, and as a vesture shalt thou fold them up and they shall be changed. But thou art the same.'[8] However, this is a sufficient reply to Celsus' assertion that *the soul is God's*

---

[1] Omit εἰ with We. Cf. II, 9 where Origen says that these commands were addressed to the Logos; *Ep. Barn.* v, 5; Tatian in VI, 51 below. The argument was useful against the Rabbis, who had to reply that God was talking to Himself just as men do sometimes (Justin, *Dial.* 62). For Philo's view see W. L. Knox, *St Paul and the Church of the Gentiles*, p. 83.

[2] Homer, *Il.* I, 70.　　　　　　　　　　[3] See v, 10 below.

[4] Cf. III, 41 above.　　　　　　　　　　[5] *Timaeus*, 41 D, E.

[6] For this doctrine, see the references collected by W. Scott, *Hermetica*, III, pp. 39–41.

[7] For Platonic opposition, cf. Atticus ap. Eus. *P.E.* xv, 7; for Stoic opposition, cf. Zeno ap. Cicero, *Acad. Post.* I, 11, 39; *de Fin.* IV, 5, 12.

[8] Ps. ci. 26–8.

work, but the nature of the body is different. For it follows from his view that the body of a bat or a worm or a frog is no different from the matter of the aether.

57. Consider whether one ought to agree with a man who criticizes the Christians when he puts forward such doctrines, and if one should abandon a philosophy which accounts for the diversity of bodies by the hypothesis that different qualities are given to them. For we also know that there are 'both heavenly bodies and earthly bodies' and that there is one glory of heavenly bodies and another of earthly bodies, and that not even that of heavenly bodies is the same; for there is one glory of the sun and another glory of the stars, and even among themselves 'one star differs from another in glory'. Therefore also, as we believe in the resurrection of the dead, we affirm that changes occur in the qualities of bodies, since some of them which have been 'sown in corruption are raised in incorruption, and some sown in dishonour are raised in glory', and some sown in weakness are raised in power, and bodies sown natural are raised spiritual.[1] All of us who have accepted the existence of providence maintain that the underlying matter is capable of receiving the qualities which the Creator wills to give it. And by God's will a quality of one kind is imposed upon this particular matter, but afterwards it will have a quality of another kind, one, let us say, which is better and superior.

Moreover, as from the beginning to the end of the world changes in bodies occur according to ways that have been appointed, possibly a new and different way may succeed after the destruction of the world, which our writings call the consummation;[2] so it is not remarkable if at the present time, *as the popular opinion has it, a snake is formed out of a dead man, originating from the marrow of the spine,[3] and a bee from an ox,[4] and a wasp from a horse, and a beetle from an ass,[5] and in general worms from most animals.* But Celsus thinks that this supports his opinion that none of these are God's work, and that the qualities which by some unknown agency have been appointed to change from one character to another, are *not the work of any divine Logos who changes the qualities in matter.*

[1] Cf. I Cor. xv. 40–4. See III, 41 above.
[2] Cf. Matt. xiii. 39; Heb. ix. 26. συντέλεια is not used by pagan writers in this sense. Read with Bo., K. tr. διαδεξομένης in 330, 13, and omit the second καὶ with K. tr. in 330, 14.
[3] Ovid, *Metam.* xv. 389–90; Pliny, *N.H.* x, 188; Aelian, *N.A.* I, 51.
[4] The process of rotting the carcass to get bees is described by Vergil, *Georg.* IV, 281 ff., and Florentinus ap. Cassianus Bassus, *Geoponica* xv, 2, 22 ff. Cf. Aelian, *N.A.* II, 57; Porphyry, *de Antro Nymph.* 18; Varro, *de Re Rust.* II, 5, 5; Philo, *de Sp. Leg.* I, 291.
[5] Archelaus ap. Varro, *de Re Rust.* III, 16, 4; Aelian, *N.A.* I, 28. With the whole sentence, cf. Pliny, *N.H.* xI, 70; Plutarch, *Cleomenes,* 39; Philo, *Vita Mos.* II, 260; *de Prov.* II, 104; Clement. *Recog.* VIII, 25; Plotinus, III, 4, 6; Augustine, *de Civ. Dei* xIX, 12. Previous editors have not taken these words to be a quotation from Celsus.

58. We have a further point to make to Celsus' remark, *The soul is God's work, but the nature of the body is different,* that he has thrown out a large dogmatic statement not only without a shred of proof but even without defining his terms. For he has not made it clear whether every soul is God's work or only the rational soul. Accordingly we say to him: If every soul is God's work, obviously this includes the meanest irrational animals, so that every body has a nature which is different from that of the soul. Indeed, later where he says that *the irrational animals are dearer to God* than we are *and have a purer idea of the Deity,*[1] he seems to suggest not only that the soul of man is God's work, but that the soul of the irrational animals is far more so. This follows from his remark that they are dearer to God than we are. But if only the rational soul is God's work, my first objection is that he did not make this clear; and secondly, it follows from what he has said about the soul without defining his terms that, if it is not every soul but only the rational soul which is God's work, it is not true that every body has a nature which is different from that of the soul. And if every body has not a nature which is different, but the body of each animal corresponds to its soul, then obviously the body of a being whose soul is God's work would be superior to a body in which a soul dwells which is not God's work. Thus it will be wrong to say that the body of a bat, or a worm, or a frog, will in no respect differ from that of a man.

59. Moreover, it is absurd that some stones and buildings should be regarded as more pure or impure than other stones and buildings because they have been built for the honour of God or for the use of the most dishonourable and polluted bodies if there is no difference between one body and another, the difference depending upon whether they are inhabited by rational or irrational beings, and by the better kind of rational beings or by the worst men.[2] At any rate, the assumption that there is such a difference has made some go so far as to deify the bodies of outstanding people because they received a good soul, and to reject or dishonour the bodies of very bad men. I do not mean to say that this has been entirely right. But it originated from an idea which was right to a certain extent. After the death of Anytus and Socrates would a wise man pay similar attention to the tomb of Anytus' body as to that of Socrates, and would he build a similar tomb or sepulchre for both? I have made these remarks because he says that *none of these are God's work,* the word 'these' referring to the human body, or to that of snakes which come from the body, and to that of the ox or the bees which come from the body of the ox, and to that of a horse or an ass and to the wasps that come from a horse

---

[1] Cf. IV, 88 below.   [2] Cf. V, 24 below; Augustine, *de Cura pro Mortuis,* 5.

and the beetles from an ass. It was because of these instances that we were compelled to return to Celsus' assertion that *the soul is God's work, but the nature of the body is different.*

60. Then he next says: *All the bodies I have mentioned have a single common nature which passes through changes into many forms and returns again to what it was.* I reply to this that from what I have said earlier it is obvious that this nature is held in common not only by the bodies he has mentioned but also by the heavenly bodies. And if this is so, it is clear that in Celsus' opinion (whether this is his real opinion I do not know) *the single nature of all bodies passes through changes into many forms and returns again to what it was.* Clearly this is the case in the view of those who think that the world is destructible.[1] And those also who do not think it is destructible and do not admit a fifth substance[2] will try to show that in their opinion too *the single nature of all bodies passes through changes into many forms and returns again to what it was.* Thus even that which is perishable persists through the process of change; for matter, the substance which underlies the perishable quality, remains constant in the opinion of those who hold that it is uncreated. If, however, any argument could show that it is not uncreated but was brought into existence for a certain purpose, obviously it will not have the same constant nature as it would have on the assumption that it is uncreated. But it is not our task now to discuss the nature of the world when we are replying to the attacks of Celsus.

61. He says also that *No product of matter is immortal.* To this the reply will be made that if no product of matter is immortal, then either the whole world is immortal, and so not a product of matter, or, if it is a product of matter, then it is not an immortal thing at all. Now if the world is immortal, which is the opinion of those who say that only the soul is *God's work* and that it originated from a bowl,[3] let Celsus show that it did not originate from matter which has no qualities, remaining consistent with his opinion that *no product of matter is immortal.* But if, since the world is a product of matter, the world is not immortal, then is the world mortal and destined for destruction or not? For if it is destined for destruction, it will be destroyed although it is God's work. Then let Celsus tell us what the soul, which is God's work, will do at the destruction of the world. But if he will pervert the concept of immortality and affirm that it is immortal in that, although it is liable to destruction, it is not to be destroyed in fact, and on the ground that although it is capable of dying it does not actually die, obviously he will think it to be something which is at once mortal and immortal because it is capable of both mortality

---

[1] I.e. the Stoics.   [2] I.e. the Platonists.   [3] Plato, *Timaeus*, 41 D, E.

and immortality; it will be mortal although not dying, and that which is not by nature immortal by a peculiar usage may be called immortal because it does not in fact die.[1] What meaning, then, will he attach to his statement that *no product of matter is immortal?* You see that when the ideas in his book are subjected to precise definition and examination they are shown up as not containing doctrine which is unimpeachable and beyond contradiction.

He goes on to say this: *So much is sufficient on this subject. And if anyone is capable of understanding and inquiring further, he will acquire that knowledge.* Let us therefore, who in his opinion are *stupid,* see what has been the result of our ability for even a little *understanding and inquiry.*

62. After this he thinks he can enable us to learn in a few words the various problems about the nature of evils which have been the subject of many important discussions, and which have received different answers, saying: *In the existing world there is no decrease or increase of evils either in the past or in the present or in the future. For the nature of the universe is one and the same, and the origin of evils is always the same.*[2] This he seems to have paraphrased from the words of the Theaetetus, where according to Plato Socrates says: 'But neither is it possible for evils to be destroyed from men, nor for them to find a place among the gods'[3] and so on. I do not think that he has even understood Plato correctly, although he embraces all the truth in this one treatise and entitles his book against us *The True Doctrine.* For the passage in the Timaeus which says 'And when the gods purify the earth'[4] has shown that when the earth is cleansed by water it has fewer evils than it had during the time before it was purified. And in agreement with the opinion of Plato we maintain that at times evils are less, on account of the passage in the Theaetetus that says 'evils cannot be destroyed from men'.

63. I do not know how, although he accepts providence by implication in the words of this book, he says that evils are neither more nor less, but

---

[1] This passage is intelligible against the background of the debates in contemporary Platonism about the interpretation of the *Timaeus.* The orthodox Academy understood the *Timaeus* allegorically, not as describing the creation of the world, but as affirming that the world although eternal was dependent upon God. This view was held by the Middle Platonists of the second century, Albinus and Taurus. But another school, represented by Plutarch and Atticus, held that the *Timaeus* was to be understood literally, that the world was created, and was only eternal by the will of God; for this they appealed to *Tim.* 41 A ('the things which have been made by me are indestructible because I will it so'). For an account of the debate see K. Praechter in P.-W. VA, 63 ff. *s.v.* 'Tauros'; Hal Koch, *Pronoia und Paideusis,* p. 261. Origen alludes to it in *de Princ.* II, 3, 6. Cf. Celsus in IV, 79; VI, 52. The terminology is commonplace: Aetius, *Placita,* II, 3, 1–2 (*Dox. Gr.* 330–1); Galen, *Hist. Phil.* 17 (*ibid.* 609); Philo, *Q.R.D.H.* 246; *Decal.* 58; Irenaeus, II, 34, 2 (Harvey, I, 382); Arnobius, II, 56; Augustine, *de Civ. Dei,* XI, 4; Alex. Aphrod. *Quaest.* I, 18. See also Grant, *Miracle and Natural Law,* pp. 35 ff.
[2] Cf. Seneca, *de Benef.* I. 10; M. Aurelius VII. 1; Alexander Lycop. 12.
[3] *Theaetetus,* 176A. Cf. Celsus in VIII, 55.   [4] *Timaeus,* 22D.

as it were fixed, abolishing the excellent doctrine that evil and evils are not fixed and are, strictly speaking, indeterminate.[1] And from the view that evils have been, or are, or will be neither less nor more it seems to follow that, just as in the view of those who hold that the world is indestructible the equilibrium of the elements is maintained by providence which does not allow any one of them to predominate lest the world should be destroyed,[2] so some providence, as it were, has determined that however many evils there are, they become neither more nor less.

Celsus' statement about evils is refuted in another way by the philosophers who have examined the question of good and evil. They have shown from history that at first prostitutes hired themselves out to those who desired them outside the city and wore masks. Then later they disdainfully laid aside their masks, though as they were not allowed by the laws to enter the cities, they lived outside them. But as perversion increased every day they ventured even to enter the cities. This is said by Chrysippus in his 'Introduction to the subject of Good and Evil'. It is possible to argue that evils do increase and decrease from the fact that the so-called 'doubtful' men[3] were at one time prostitutes, being subject to and arranging for and serving the lusts of those who came to them; but later the public authorities expelled them. And concerning the countless vices which have entered human life from the flood of evil, we can say that earlier they did not exist. At any rate, the most ancient histories, even though they make innumerable criticisms of those who went astray, know nothing of people who committed unmentionable enormities.

64. In the light of these and similar facts does not Celsus appear ludicrous when he supposes that *evils could never either increase or decrease?* For even if *the nature of the universe is one and the same*, the origin of evils is not by any means always the same. Although the nature of some particular individual man is one and the same, things are not always the same where his mind, his reason, and actions are concerned. At one time he may not even have the capacity for reason, while at another time his reason is vitiated by evil, and this varies in its extent either more or less; and sometimes he may have been converted to live virtuously and is making more or less progress, and at times reaches perfection and comes to virtue itself by more or less contemplation. So also even more may this

---

[1] Cf. Plotinus, I, 8, 9; Gregory of Nyssa, *de Hom. Opif.* 21 (*P.G.* XLIV, 211 B, C).

[2] Critics of the Stoic theory of conflagrations (cf. VIII, 72) held that the four elements were continually being transformed into one another, earth into water, water into air, air into fire, and then back again by the reverse process, so that constant equilibrium was maintained. See Philo, *de Aetern. Mundi*, 107–12, 116; Seneca, *N.Q.* III, 10, 3; III, 29, 5; Cicero, *de Nat. Deor.* II, 84–5; Plotinus II, 1, 1; Greg. Nyss. *c. Eunom.* III, ii, 142 (ii. 93 Jaeger).

[3] I.e. eunuchs, so called because their sex is doubtful.

be said of the universe, that, even if it remains one and the same generically, yet the events which happen to the universe are not always the same nor of the same kind. For there are not periods of productivity or of famine all the time, nor always of heavy rain or drought. In this way neither are there determined periods of fertility or famine in the life of good souls; and the flood of bad souls increases or decreases. In fact, for those who want to have the most accurate knowledge of everything that they can, it is an unavoidable doctrine that evils do not always remain the same in number on account of the providence which either watches over earthly affairs or cleanses them by floods and conflagrations,[1] and probably not only earthly things but also those of the whole universe which is in need of purification whenever the evil in it becomes extensive.

65. After this Celsus says: *It is not easy for one who has not read philosophy to know what is the origin of evils; however, it is enough for the masses to be told that evils are not caused by God,[2] but inhere in matter and dwell among mortals;[3] and the period of mortal life is similar from beginning to end, and it is inevitable that according to the determined cycles the same things always have happened, are now happening, and will happen.*[4] Celsus maintains that *it is not easy for one who has not read philosophy to know the origin of evils*, as though anyone who is a philosopher is easily able to know their origin, while for anyone who is not a philosopher it is not easy to perceive the origin of evils although it is possible for him to know it, even if only after much hard work. We reply to this that it is not easy even for one who has read philosophy to know the origin of evils, and probably it is impossible even for these men to know it absolutely, unless by inspiration of God it is made clear what are evils, and shown how they came to exist, and understood how they will be removed. At any rate, since ignorance of God is also among the number of evils, while one of the greatest evils is not to know the way to worship God and of piety towards Him, even Celsus would have to admit that some of those who have read philosophy have been totally ignorant of this, as is clear from the different sects in philosophy. But in our view no one will be able to know the origin of evils if he has not realized that it is an evil to suppose that piety is preserved by keeping the established laws of states in the ordinary sense of the word. And no one will be able to know the origin of evils who has not grasped the truth about the so-called devil and his angels, and who he was before he became a devil, and how he became a devil, and what caused his so-called angels to rebel with him. Anyone

[1] H. von Arnim (*S.V.F.* II, 1174) thinks that in this chapter Origen is adapting and quoting Chrysippus' work, to which he has referred in 63.
[2] Cf. Plato, *Rep.* 379C.   [3] *Idem, Theaetetus,* 176A.
[4] *Idem, Politicus,* 269C–270A. Cf. IV, 11; VIII, 53.

who intends to know this must possess an accurate understanding of daemons, and be aware that they are not God's creation in so far as they are daemons, but only in so far as they are rational beings of some sort. And he must understand how they came to be such that their mind put them in the position of daemons. Accordingly if there is any subject among those that need[1] study among men which is baffling to our comprehension, the origin of evil may be reckoned as such.

66. Then, as if he had certain more secret things to say about the origin of evils but omits them because he is saying what is suitable for the multitude, he says *it is enough for the masses to be told* concerning the origin of evils *that they are not caused by God, but inhere in matter and dwell among mortals.*[2] It is true that evils are not caused by God. For according to our Jeremiah it is clear that 'out of the Lord's mouth evil and good do not proceed'.[3] But in our view it is not true that *the matter which dwells among mortals* is responsible for evils.[4] Each person's mind is responsible for the evil which exists in him, and this is what evil is. Evils are the actions which result from it. In our view *nothing else is strictly speaking evil.* However, I know that the problem requires an extended discussion and argument which, by the grace of God illuminating the mind, can be done by one who is judged by God to be worthy even of knowledge of this subject.

67. I do not know why Celsus in writing against us thought it profitable to throw out an opinion which needs much proof, or at least a plausible argument, to show as convincingly as possible that *the period of mortal life is similar from beginning to end, and it is inevitable that according to the determined cycles the same things always have happened, are now happening, and will happen.* If this is true, free will is destroyed. For if *it is inevitable that in the period of mortal life according to the determined cycles the same things always have happened, are now happening, and will happen,* it is obviously inevitable that Socrates will always be a philosopher and be accused of introducing new deities and of corrupting the youth; Anytus and Meletus will always be accusing him, and the council on the Areopagus will vote for his condemnation to death by hemlock.[5] Thus also it is inevitable that according to the predetermined cycles Phalaris will always be a tyrant, Alexander of Pherae will commit the same atrocities, and

---

[1] Read δεομένων with K. tr.

[2] For this popular dualism, taught but not really believed by some Platonists, cf. W. R. Inge, *The Philosophy of Plotinus,* I, pp. 148 f.

[3] Lam. iii. 37.   [4] Cf. III, 42, above.

[5] The instances in this argument are commonplace: cf. v, 20; Tatian, 3; Eusebius, *Theophan.* II, 21; Nemesius, *de Nat. Hom.* 38; Augustine, *de Civ. Dei,* XII, 13. Origen gives the argument with Biblical instances in *de Princ.* II, 3, 4.

those condemned to the bull of Phalaris will always groan inside it. If this is admitted, I do not see how free will can be preserved, and how any praise and blame can be reasonable. The reply to this assumption of Celsus will be that if *the period of mortal life is similar from beginning to end*, and if *it is inevitable that according to the determined cycles the same things always have happened, are now happening, and will happen*, then it is inevitable that according to the determined cycles Moses will always come out of Egypt with the people of the Jews; Jesus will again come to visit this life and will do the same things that he has done, not just once but an infinite number of times according to the cycles. Furthermore, the same people will be Christians in the determined cycles, and again Celsus will write his book, though he has written before an infinite number of times.

68. Celsus affirms that it is only *the period of mortal life* which *according to the determined cycles* has of necessity always been, and is now, and will be identical. But most of the Stoics say that this is true not only of the period of mortal life, but also of immortal life and of those whom they regard as gods.[1] For after the general conflagration of the universe, which has happened and will happen an infinite number of times, the same order of all things from beginning to end not only has happened but also will happen. In attempting to remedy the absurdities in some way the Stoics say that in every cycle all men will be in some unknown way indistinguishable from those of former cycles. To avoid supposing that Socrates will live again, they say that it will be some one indistinguishable from Socrates, who will marry some one indistinguishable from Xanthippe, and will be accused by men indistinguishable from Anytus and Meletus.[2] But I do not know how the world can always be the same, and one world not merely indistinguishable from another, while the things in it are not the same but are indistinguishable. However, the primary argument in reply to the words of Celsus and the Stoics will be discussed elsewhere at a more convenient time, since at the present moment it is not relevant to our immediate object to give a further discussion here.

69. After this he says that *neither has the visible world been given to men, but each particular thing both comes into existence and perishes for the sake of the whole according to the process of change from one thing to another*[3] *of which I spoke earlier*.[4] It is superfluous to spend further time in refuting this assertion, since that has already been done to the best of our ability. This too has been answered: *And neither good nor bad can increase among mortals*. We have also discussed this: *God has no need to have a new*

---

[1] The Stoic gods are not exempt from the process of *ekpyrosis* and *diakosmesis*. Cf. Philo, *de Aetern. Mundi*, 45–51.

[2] Cf. v, 20; *de Princ.* II, 3, 4; Nemesius, *de Nat. Hom.* 38.

[3] Celsus follows Plato, *Laws*, 903 B–E.   [4] Celsus in IV, 57, 60.

reformation. Moreover, *God does not inflict correction on the world like a man who has built something defectively and created it unskilfully, when he purifies it by a flood or a conflagration.* But He does this to prevent the flood of evil from spreading further; and I think that in an orderly way He is even making it disappear entirely for the advantage of the universe. But whether or not there is reason to suppose that after evil has disappeared it rises again, such a problem will be discussed in a book dealing primarily with this subject.[1] By a *new reformation,* then, God always wants to make good that which is wrong. Even though everything had been arranged by Him at the creation of the universe to be very beautiful and very steadfast, yet nevertheless He has had to apply some medical treatment to people sick with sin and to all the world as it were defiled by it. In fact, nothing has been or will be neglected by God, who at each season makes what He should be making in a world of alteration and change. And just as at different seasons of the year a farmer[2] does different agricultural jobs upon the earth and its crops, so God cares for whole ages as if they were years, so to speak. In each one of them He does what is in itself reasonable for the universe, which is most clearly understood and accomplished by God alone since the truth is known to Him.

70. Now Celsus has made the following remark about evils: *Even if something seems to you to be evil, it is not yet clear whether it really is evil; for you do not know what is expedient either for you or for someone else or for the universe.* This remark shows some discretion; but he suggests that the nature of evils is not entirely pernicious because something which is thought to be evil for a particular individual may possibly be of advantage to the universe.[3] However, lest anyone should misunderstand my opinion and find in it an excuse for crime on the ground that his sin is, or at any rate could be, beneficial to the world as a whole, I will say that while God preserves the free will of each man He makes use of the evil of bad men for the ordering of the whole, making them useful to the universe; yet such a man is none the less guilty, and as such he has been appointed to perform a function which is repulsive to the individual but beneficial to the whole.

---

[1] Cf. VIII, 72, and my remarks in *J.T.S.* XLVIII (1947), pp. 41 f.

[2] For the comparison of God with a farmer cf. *de Princ.* III, 1, 14; Numenius ap. Eus. *P.E.* XI, 18, 14, 538C; and Festugière's note on *Corp. Herm.* IX, 6.

[3] This argument is drawn from the Stoic theodicy; cf. Plutarch, *Mor.* 1050E, 1065B (see also the references given by P. Wendland, *Philos Schrift über die Vorsehung* (Berlin, 1892), p. 78 n. 2). For Origen's use of it, cf. *de Princ.* II, 9, 2; *Hom. in Jerem.* XII, 5 'So also God *does not care just for one man, but for the whole world; he administers things in heaven, and things on earth everywhere. Accordingly, he has an eye to what is expedient for the whole world and for everything that exists; so far as it is possible he also has an eye for what is expedient for the individual, but not so that what is expedient for the individual causes loss to the world.*'

It is, to take an illustration from cities, as though one said that a man, who
had committed certain crimes and on that account was sentenced to do
certain public services of benefit to the community, was doing something
of benefit to the whole city, although he himself was engaged in a repulsive
task and in a position in which no one even of slight intelligence would
want to be.[1]

Moreover, Paul the apostle of Jesus teaches us that even the very worst
men may contribute something to the advantage of the whole, though in
themselves they will be engaged in the most repulsive acts, while the very
good men will be of most benefit to the whole and on their own account
will be appointed to the best position. He says: 'And in a great house
there are not only vessels of gold and silver but also of wood and earthen-
ware, and the one are to honour and the other to dishonour; therefore if
any man cleanse himself, he will be a vessel unto honour, sanctified and
meet for the master's use, prepared unto every good work.'[2] I think it
was necessary to quote this in reply to his remark: *Even if something
seems to you to be evil, it is not yet clear whether it is evil; for you do not
know what is expedient either for you or for someone else.* For I wanted to
avoid giving anyone an excuse for sinning in what I have said on this
subject, on the ground that he would be benefiting the community by
his sin.

71. After this because Celsus failed to understand them, he ridicules
passages in the Bible which speak of God as though He were subject to
human passions, in which *angry utterances* are spoken against the impious
and *threats* against people who have sinned. I reply that, just as when we
are talking with little children we do not aim to speak in the finest
language possible to us, but say what is appropriate to the weakness of
those whom we are addressing, and, further, do what seems to us to be of
advantage for the conversion and correction of the children as such, so
also the Logos of God seems to have arranged the scriptures, using the
method of address which fitted the ability and benefit of the hearers. In
fact, in Deuteronomy it is quite generally stated concerning this type of
address which is attributed to God, in these words: 'The Lord thy God
bare with thy ways, as a man might bear with his son.'[3] The Logos speaks
like this because he assumes, as it were, human characteristics for the
advantage of men. There was no need for the multitude that the words
put into God's mouth, which were intended to be addressed to them,
should correspond to His real character. However, anyone interested in
the exposition of the divine scriptures, by comparing spiritual things with

[1] Origen uses the same illustration for the same point in *Hom. in Num.* XIV, 2.
[2] II Tim. ii. 20–1.   [3] Deut. i. 31.

spiritual,[1] as it is said, will discover from them the meaning of the sayings addressed to the weak and of those spoken to the intelligent, while often both meanings lie in the same text for him who knows how to understand it.

72. When we speak of God's wrath, we do not hold that it is an emotional reaction on His part, but something which He uses in order to correct by stern methods those who have committed many terrible sins. That the so-called wrath of God and what is called His anger has a corrective purpose, and that this is the doctrine of the Bible, is clear from the words of Psalm vi: 'Lord, do not rebuke me in thine anger, nor correct me in thy wrath',[2] and of Jeremiah: 'O Lord, correct us but with judgment; not in thine anger, lest thou bring us low.'[3] Anyone who has read in the second book of the Kingdoms how the wrath of God urged David to number the people, and that in the first book of Chronicles the devil is said to have done this,[4] and who compares the passages with one another, will see for what purpose the anger is determined. It is this wrath of which Paul says that all men were children, when he says 'We were by nature children of wrath even as the others.'[5]

That God's wrath is not an emotional reaction, but that each man brings this on himself by his sins, will be clear from Paul's words: 'Or do you despise the riches of his goodness and forbearance and long-suffering, not knowing that the goodness of God leads you to repentance? But by your hardness and impenitent heart you are treasuring up for yourself wrath in the day of wrath and revelation of the righteous judgment of God.'[6] How can each man 'treasure up for himself wrath in the day of wrath' if wrath is understood as an emotional reaction? And how could the emotion of wrath be corrective? Furthermore, the word teaches us not to be angry at all, and says in Psalm xxxvi: 'Cease from anger and forsake wrath',[7] and says also in Paul: 'You too must put aside these, wrath, anger, evil, blasphemy, shameful talk.'[8] The word would not, then, have attributed to God himself the emotion which he wants us to abandon altogether. It is obvious that the statements about God's wrath are to be interpreted allegorically from what is also recorded of His sleep. As though waking Him from sleep, the prophet says: 'Rise up Lord, why sleepest thou?'

---

[1] I Cor. i. 13. Omit the comma after πνευματικοῖς.

[2] Ps. vi. 2.   [3] Jer. x. 24.

[4] II Sam. (II Regn.) xxiv. 1; I Chron. xxi. 1.   [5] Eph. ii. 3.

[6] Rom. ii. 4–5. For Origen's view that wrath is what each man brings on himself, cf. *Hom. in Ezech.* III, 7 'deus non facit poenas, sed ea quae patimur ipsi nobis praeparamus'; *de Princ.* II, 10, 4 'unusquisque peccatorum flammam sibi ipse proprii ignis accendat....'. Iamblichus, *de Myst.* I, 13, explains that the wrath of the gods is not, as some think, an inveterate anger, but is due to the fact that we turn away from their beneficent care and bring darkness upon ourselves, as if we hid ourselves at midday and so deprived ourselves of the good gift of the gods.   [7] Ps. xxxvi. 8.   [8] Col. iii. 8.

And again he says: 'And the Lord arose as one out of sleep, and like a mighty man that shouted by reason of wine.'¹ Therefore if sleep means something else and not what is indicated by the superficial interpretation of the word, why should not wrath also be understood in a similar way?

Moreover, the *threats* are simply proclamations of what will happen to bad men. Similarly one might call the words of a physician threats when he says to patients 'I will cut you and apply cauterizing irons if you do not obey my orders and regulate and conduct yourself in this way and that.'² Therefore we do not attribute human passions to God, nor do we hold impious opinions about Him, nor are we in error when we produce explanations concerning Him from the scriptures themselves by comparing them with one another. The task of those of us who give an intelligent account of Christianity is simply to deliver our hearers from stupidity as well as we can and to make them sensible.

73. As a result of the fact that he has not understood what is written of God's wrath, he says: *Is it not ridiculous that when a man was angry with the Jews and destroyed them all from the youth upwards and burnt down their city, in this case they were annihilated; yet when the supreme God, as they say, was angry and wrathful and sent His Son with threats, he suffered such indignities?* If after treating Jesus in the way in which they dared to act against him, the Jews were destroyed from the youth upwards and their city burnt down with fire, the cause of their suffering these things was simply the wrath which they treasured up for themselves; there came to pass God's judgment against them which had been fixed by God's appointment, this judgment being called 'wrath' by a traditional Hebrew usage. And if the Son of the supreme God suffered, he did so willingly for the salvation of men, as we have said earlier to the best of our ability.³

After this he says: *However, that the discussion may not be confined to the Jews alone (for that is not my theme) but may concern the whole of nature, as I promised,*⁴ *I will show what has just been said with greater clarity.* What ordinary reader of these words, who realizes the weakness of humanity, would not wince at the offensive arrogance of a fellow who *promised* to give an account of *the whole of nature*, and who was so proud as to give his book a title such as that which he has ventured to give his? Let us see now what it is which he promises to say about the whole of nature, and what he will show clearly.

74. He next embarks on a lengthy discussion, criticizing us on the ground that we *assert that God made all things for man*. From the history

¹ Ps. xliii. 24; lxxvii. 65.
² Cf. II, xxiv. For the words put into the mouth of the physician, cf. *Hom. in Jerem.* xx, 3.
³ Cf. I, 54-5, 61; II, 16, 23.   ⁴ Cf. Celsus in IV, 52.

of animals and from the sagacity which they display he wants to show that *everything was made just as much for the irrational animals as for men.*[1] He seems to me to talk rather like the people who, because of their hostility to their enemies, accuse them of the things for which their best friends receive credit. For as in this example hostility blinds men from perceiving that they are accusing even their best friends by the attacks which they suppose they are making against their enemies, so also in the same way Celsus, being muddle-headed, did not see that he is also criticizing the Stoic school of philosophers. They quite rightly put man and the rational nature in general above all irrational beings, and say that providence has made everything primarily for the sake of the rational nature. Rational beings which are the primary things have the value of children who are born; whereas irrational and inanimate things have that of the afterbirth which is created with the child.[2] I think, moreover, that just as in cities those who are in charge of the stalls and the market-place are concerned only with men, though dogs and other irrational animals share the surplus food; so providence primarily cares for the rational beings, while the fact that the irrational animals also share in what is made for men has been a subsidiary result. And just as a man is wrong who says that the market authorities are no more concerned for men than for dogs since dogs also share the surplus food on the market stalls, so also Celsus and those who agree with him act far more impiously against the God who cares for the rational beings when they say: *Why were these things made for man's nourishment any more than for plants, trees, grass, and thorns?*

75. He thinks in the first place that *thunders and lightnings and rainstorms are not made by God,* at last displaying his Epicurean views more clearly. And in the second place he says that *even if one were to allow that these things are made by God, they are not created for the nourishment of us men any more than for plants, trees, grass, and thorns,* admitting that these things happen by chance and not by providence, like a true Epicurean. For if these things do not benefit us any more than plants, trees, grass, and thorns, it is obvious that these things do not come from providence, or at least from a providence which cares any more for us than for trees and grass and thorns. But either of these alternatives is obviously impious, and it would be silly to counter arguments such as these in opposing a man

---

[1] This subject is discussed from here to the end of the fourth book. For the background and sources of the material see the Introduction, p. x, and my remarks in *J.T.S.* XLVIII (1947), at pp. 36 f. Masterly discussion in M. Pohlenz, *Die Stoa* (1948), I, pp. 81 ff.

[2] Origen's summary of the Stoic view explains the sentence quoted from Chrysippus by Plutarch, *Mor.* 1000F (*S.V.F.* II, 1158): 'The man who provides the seed is not called father of the afterbirth although it is derived from the seed.' For the Stoic view generally, see *S.V.F.* II, 1152–67.

who accuses us of *impiety*. It is manifest to anyone from his remarks who is the one who is impious.

Then he says: *Even if you say that these things grow for men* (evidently meaning the plants, trees, grass, and thorns) *why do you say that they grow for men any more than for the wildest of irrational animals?* Let Celsus say clearly that the enormous variety of things that grow on earth is not made by providence, but that some chance meeting of atoms has made the vast number of qualities, and that it is by chance that so many species of plants and trees and grass resemble one another, and that no designing reason caused them to exist, and that they did not originate from a Mind surpassing all admiration. We Christians, however, who are devoted to the only God who created these things, acknowledge our gratitude for them to their Creator, because He has prepared such a home for us and, with a view to our benefit, for the animals which serve us. 'He causes the grass to grow for the cattle and herb for the service of man; that he may bring forth food out of the earth, and that wine may gladden man's heart and that his face may shine with oil, and that bread may strengthen man's heart.'[1] Even if He also made nourishment for the wildest of animals, there is nothing remarkable about that; for other philosophers have said that even these animals were made for the exercise of the rational being.[2] One of our wise men somewhere says: 'Do not say, What is this? What use is that? For he has made all things for their uses'; and 'Do not say, What is this? What use is that? For everything will be sought out in its time.'[3]

76. After this Celsus wants to make out that providence has not made the things that grow on earth any more for us than for the wildest animals, saying: *Though we struggle and persevere we sustain ourselves only with difficulty and toil, whereas for them 'everything grows without sowing and tillage'.*[4] He does not see that from a desire that human understanding should be exercised everywhere, in order that it might not remain idle and ignorant of the arts, God made man a needy being, so that by his very need he has been compelled to discover arts, some for food and others for protection.[5] Moreover, for those who would not seek for the things of God and study philosophy it was better that they should be in distress in order that they might use their intellect to discover arts than that by being in prosperity they should entirely neglect their intellect. Need of the necessities of life, in fact, was the origin of the art of agriculture and of the cultivation of vineyards, the arts of gardening, carpentry and of the blacksmith, which made tools for the arts which serve to feed mankind. Need

---

[1] Ps. ciii. 14–15.　　　　[2] Cf. IV, 78, below. This is the Stoic view.
[3] Sir. xxxix. 21, 17.　　　[4] Homer, *Od.* IX, 109; cf. Lucretius, V, 218 ff.
[5] For necessity as the mother of civilization cf. Vergil, *Georg.* I, 121 ff. (referred to by A. D. Nock, *Sallustius*, p. xliv n. 31); Diod. Sic. I, 8, 5–9.

of protection introduced the art of weaving after that of wool-carding and spinning, and that of building; and in this way the mind also advanced to architecture. Lack of the necessities of life has also made things, which originate in other places, to be transported to those men who do not possess them by the arts of sailing and navigation; so that for these reasons one might admire the providence which made the rational creature for his benefit more needy than the irrational animals. For the irrational animals have their food ready for them because they have nothing to urge them to practise arts; and they also have natural protection, for they are covered with hair or with wings or with scales or with a shell.[1] Let this, then, be our reply to Celsus' words: *Though we struggle and persevere we sustain ourselves only with difficulty; whereas for them 'everything grows without sowing or tillage'.*

77. After this, forgetting that his object is to accuse Jews and Christians, he replies to a supposed objection to his view in the iambic line of Euripides which contradicts his opinion. He attacks the verse and criticizes it as being wrong. Celsus' words are as follows: *But if you were to quote the verse of Euripides[2] that*

> *Sun and night serve mortals*

why do they exist for us any more than for ants and flies? For in their case too the night is for rest and the day for seeing and doing. Clearly then it is not just some Jews and Christians who have said that the sun and the other heavenly bodies serve us, but also the philosopher of the stage, as some call him,[3] who heard Anaxagoras' lectures on nature. He illustrates this by taking one example of a rational being, man, and says that the things in the universe are appointed to serve all rational creatures, the former being represented again by the sun and the moon which he takes as instances. Or perhaps also the tragedian called the day 'sun' because it makes the day, to teach that those beings in particular need of day and night are the beings below the moon, and that other beings are not in the same position in this respect as those upon earth. Therefore, if day and night serve mortals, they exist for the sake of the rational beings. If the benefits of day and night, which have been made for men, are shared by ants and flies which work during the one and rest during the other, we ought not to say that day and night exist for ants and flies, nor for anything else; but we ought to think that they were made by providence for the sake of mankind.

---

[1] Cf. Plato, *Protag.* 321 A, B; Cicero, *de Nat. Deor.* II, 47, 121; Plutarch, *Mor.* 98 D.

[2] *Phoenissae,* 546 (quoted by Origen in IV, 30).

[3] Clem. Al. *Strom.* V, 70, 2; Athenaeus, 158 E, 561 A; Sextus Emp. *adv. Math.* I, 288. That he was a pupil of Anaxagoras is mentioned by numerous writers (Diog. Laert. II, 10; Strabo, XIV, 1, 36 (p. 645); Cicero, *Tusc.* III, 14, 30; Gellius, *N.A.* XV, 20, 4).

78. After this he refers to the objections to his view which point to the superiority of men and hold that on their account the irrational animals have been created. He says that *if anyone were to call us rulers of the irrational animals*[1] *because we hunt them and feast on them, we will reply by asking why rather were we not made on their account since they hunt and eat us? Furthermore, we need nets and weapons and many men and dogs to help us against the hunted prey. Whereas to them nature has given weapons from the start in their natural powers, making it easy for them to subdue us.* But it is just here that you may see how great a help is given to us in our intelligence, superior to any weapon which wild beasts are thought to possess. Although indeed we are physically weaker than many[2] of the animals, and in comparison with some are extremely small, we overcome wild beasts by intelligence. We hunt enormous elephants. Those which can be domesticated we subject to our taming, while against those which are not capable of being tamed, or which we do not think would serve any useful purpose if they were domesticated, we protect ourselves in such a way that when we wish we have the largest wild beasts imprisoned, and when we need the food from their bodies we slaughter them just as we do with the animals which are not wild. The Creator, then, has made everything to serve the rational being and his natural intelligence. And for some purposes we need dogs, for example for guarding flocks or herds of cattle or goats, or as house-dogs; for others we need oxen as for agriculture, while for others we use beasts to carry burdens or baggage.[3] Similarly the species of lions and bears, leopards and boars, and animals of this sort, are said to have been given to us in order to exercise the seeds of courage in us.[4]

79. Then he addresses the kind of men who are aware of the fact that mankind is superior to the irrational animals, saying: *In reply to what you say, that God gave us the ability to catch the wild beasts and to make use of them, we will say that it is likely that before the existence of cities and arts and the formation of societies of this kind, and before there were weapons and nets, men were captured and eaten by wild beasts and that it was very rare for beasts to be caught by men.* Notice on this point that even if men catch beasts and beasts carry off men, there is a lot of difference between those who use intelligence to overcome animals which are superior in wildness and fierceness, and those that do not use intelligence to avoid suffering any

[1] Read τῶν ἀλόγων, ἐπεὶ ἡμεῖς τὰ ἄλογα ζῷα...with Φ.
[2] Read πολλῶν with Wif.
[3] Cf. the Stoic in Cicero, *de Nat. Deor.* II, 60, 150–2 'Efficimus etiam domitu nostro quadrupedum vectiones, quorum celeritas atque vis nobis ipsis adfert vim et celeritatem. nos onera quibusdam bestiis, nos iuga imponimus, nos elephantorum acutissimis sensibus, nos sagacitate canum ad utilitatem nostram abutimur...'; Maximus Tyr. XXXI, 4 (Hobein, p. 364). For dogs and oxen, cf. also Cicero, *loc. cit.* II, 63, 158–9.
[4] Cf. IV. 75, and for Stoic parallels, *J.T.S.* XLVIII (1947), p. 38 n. 2.

harm from wild beasts. However, in speaking of the time *before the exis-*
tence of cities and the formation of societies of this kind, I think he has
forgotten what he said earlier, that *the world is uncreated and indestructible,*
and only things on earth are subject to floods and conflagrations, and not all of
them meet with these catastrophes at the same time.[1] Just as those who
maintain that the world is uncreated cannot speak of its beginning, so also
they cannot speak of a time when there were not yet any cities or arts to be
found. However, suppose that we allow him this point since it is in
harmony with our doctrines though not with his as he stated them earlier.
What then has this got to do with the fact that at the beginning it was
always the case that men were carried off and eaten by wild beasts while
beasts were not caught by men? For if the world came into being through
providence, and if God gave existence to the universe, it was necessary
that the sparks[2] of the human race should from the beginning be under
some care from superior beings, so that at the beginning there was
intercourse between the divine nature and men. The Ascraean poet also
perceived this when he said:[3]

> For then there were common banquets and common councils
> Between immortal gods and mortal men.

80. Moreover, the divine Scripture written by Moses represented the
first men as hearing a divine voice and oracles, and sometimes having
visions of angels of God who came to visit them. And it is probable that
at the beginning of the world human nature received more help until men
had progressed in intelligence and the other virtues, and in the discovery
of the arts, and were able to live independently, not needing those beings
who minister to God's will always to be looking after them and caring for
them with some miraculous appearance. It follows from this that it is
untrue that at the beginning *men were carried off and eaten by wild beasts and*
that it was very rare for beasts to be caught by men.

From these considerations it is obvious that this statement of Celsus is
also wrong: *Therefore in this respect at least it is truer to say that God*
subjected men to the wild beasts. God did not make men subject to the wild

___

[1] Origen has not quoted these words before; they may come from Celsus' discussion of
the antiquity of traditions among the different races (I, 14, 16). For world-catastrophes,
cf. Celsus in I, 19; IV, 41. He does not give an opinion about the eternity of the world in
VI, 52. That not all parts of the world suffer at the same time is probably a deduction from
Plato, *Tim.* 22E, where the Egyptian priest tells Solon that the Nile saves Egypt from the
periodical floods. For Egypt's exemption, cf. Diod. Sic. I, 10, 4; Varro ap. Aug. *de Civ. Dei*
XVIII, 10. According to the Platonic tradition the catastrophes were partial, thus allowing
for the survival of a few men. Lucretius, V, 324 ff., forms a good commentary upon
Origen's argument. Cf. also Macrobius, *In Somn. Scip.* II, 10.

[2] Cf. Plato, *Laws* 677B (of the survivors of the deluge).

[3] Hesiod, *fr.* 82 (216), ed. Rzach.

beasts; but He made the wild beasts to be liable to capture through men's intelligence and through the devices for catching them devised by intelligence. For it was not without divine aid that men devised means of protecting themselves from the wild beasts and attained the mastery over them.

81. This distinguished fellow, not seeing how many philosophers there are who believe in providence and say that it makes all things on account of the rational beings, destroys as far as he can doctrines which are of value together with Christianity, which in these points agrees with philosophy. Nor does he perceive the extent of the harm done and the hindrance to piety which results from believing that in God's sight man is no better than ants and bees. He says that *if the reason why men appear to be better than the irrational animals is that they live[1] in cities and have a state and positions of authority and leadership, this proves nothing at all. For ants and bees do this too.[2] At any rate, the bees have a leader, they have attendants and servants,[3] wars and conquests, they slay[4] the vanquished, they have cities[5] and even suburbs,[6] they pass work on from one to another, they condemn the idle and wicked—at least they drive out and punish the drones.[7]* Here too he has not seen the difference between actions done as a result of reason and thought[8] and those which are the product of irrational nature and are merely natural characteristics. The cause of these actions cannot be any reason inherent in those who do them (for they do not possess it); but the supreme Son of God, king of all that exists, has made an unreasoning instinct which, as such, helps those beings not worthy of reason.

Cities with many arts and with legislation have come to exist only among men. States and positions of authority and leadership among men are either what are properly speaking called good dispositions and activities, or what are more loosely so called because of their very close resemblance to the former.[9] Successful lawgivers had them in view when they intro-

---

[1] Read ᾤκισαν with cod. C, K. tr.
[2] Ants and bees are stock examples, similarly associated in Philo, *de Prov.* I, 25.
[3] Cf. Pliny, *N.H.* XI, 53.   [4] Read ἀναιρέσεις with K.
[5] Cf. Dio Chrys. XLVIII, 16; *Geoponica*, XV, 3, 2.
[6] This is apparently a *hapax legomenon* of πρόπολις = suburb (προάστιον). It usually means 'bee-glue' or 'propolis', a resinous substance which the worker bees extract from tree buds and use as a cement in the hive (cf. Varro, *de Re Rustica*, III, 16, 23; Pliny, *N.H.* XI, 16). Celsus (or the author of his source) may not have understood the word. It is of interest that in Artemidorus (IV, 22) there is a story of a man suffering from gout, who dreams that he is walking in the suburbs (ἐν τοῖς προαστείοις); he is told to apply as a remedy bee-glue, *propolis*. (I owe the reference to C. Blum in *Eranos* XLI (1943), p. 29.)
[7] For punishment of drones, cf. Pliny, XI, 27–8; Varro, *op. cit.* III, 16, 8; *Geoponica* XV, 3, 19. For the wars of the bees, Vergil, *Georg.* IV, 67–87; Varro, III, 16, 9; Pliny, XI, 58; Aelian, *N.A.* V, 11; Philo, *Alexander*, 21.
[8] Read λογισμοῦ with Φ, We., K. tr.
[9] Origen is quoting a Stoic school definition.

duced the best states and positions of authority and leadership. None of
these are to be found among irrational animals, even though Celsus takes
the names applied to a rational society, city, states, positions of authority
and leadership, and applies them to ants and bees. We ought not to praise
ants and bees for these since they do not act from reason. But we ought to
admire the divine nature which has gone so far as to give irrational beings
the ability to copy, as it were, the rational beings, perhaps in order to put
the latter to shame, that by considering ants they may become more
industrious and thrifty with things which are useful to them, and that by
understanding the ways of bees they may obey their rulers and divide
among themselves the work beneficial to the state which will preserve
their cities.[1]

82. Probably also in the so-called wars of the bees there lies teaching
that among men wars, if they are ever necessary, are to be just and ordered.
There are no cities and suburbs among bees, but they have hives and
hexagonal cells, do work and pass it on from one to another, because men
need honey for many things, for healing sick bodies[2] and for a pure food.
But the attacks of the bees on the drones should not be compared with the
condemnations of idle and wicked men in cities and the punishment
inflicted on them. But, as I said before, we ought to admire nature in
these things, and believe that man who is able to think everything out and
to arrange everything in order, seeing that he is working together with
providence, does works which are the product not merely of the natural
instincts with which he is endowed by the providence of God but also of
his own independent thought.

83. After Celsus has spoken of the bees, so that by the force of his
argument he treats as of no account the cities, states, positions of authority
and leadership, and wars fought for one's country, not only of us Christians
but of all men, he then continues by delivering a eulogy of ants. His aim
in eulogizing them is to disparage men's care for food and[3] by his words
about the ants to throw aside human forethought for the winter as being
in no way superior to the unreasoning *forethought which* he thinks *ants
possess.* Might not Celsus discourage by his words a person of the simple
sort, who do not know how to look into the nature of all things, from
helping people weighed down with burdens and from sharing their
troubles, when he says of *ants* that *they undertake one another's burdens
when they see anyone in toil?* For someone lacking in education in argument

[1] For Origen's reply here, cf. Seneca, *Ep.* cxxi, 21–3; *de Clementia*, i, 19, 3–4; Philo,
Alexander, 78.
[2] Pliny, *N.H.* xxii, 108, says that honey is an excellent remedy for throat trouble and
tonsillitis. Cf. Dioscorides, *de Materia Medica*, ii, 82.
[3] Read καταβάλῃ ⟨καὶ⟩ τῷ with K. tr.

and knowing nothing about it might say: Since then we are no better than ants, even when we help people in trouble because they are carrying very heavy burdens, is anything gained if we do this? Although ants, in that they are irrational animals, would not be lifted up to think proudly because their actions are compared to those of men, yet men because of their reason can understand how their helpfulness to one another is disparaged, and might receive harm from the implication of Celsus' words. He has not seen that in his desire to turn readers of his book away from Christianity he is also turning away the sympathy of those who are not Christians towards people who carry very heavy burdens. If he had been a philosopher with any sense of obligation to his fellow-men, he ought to have avoided destroying with Christianity the helpful beliefs which are commonly held among men, and should have given his support, if he could, to the fine doctrines which Christianity has in common with the rest of mankind.

Even if *the ants do pick out the growths of the fruits which are produced so that they should not ripen, but remain for their sustenance through the year*,[1] we ought not to suppose that the reason for this is any rational process in ants. It is due to nature, the mother of all,[2] which also orders the irrational animals, not even forsaking the smallest which bears any trace of the law of nature. Perhaps, however, Celsus means to hint that every soul is of the same shape[3] (for in many points he likes to follow Plato), and that the soul of man is no different from that of ants and bees. This is the view of him who brings the soul down from the vaults of heaven not only to the human body but even to other bodies also.[4] Christians will not believe these doctrines, for they have already been told that the human soul was made in the image of God, and they perceive that it is impossible for the soul that has been made in the image of God entirely to abandon its characteristics and to assume others, I know not what, which are made after the image of some sort of irrational beings.

84. He also says that *for the ants which die the living set apart some particular place, and that is their ancestral graveyard.*[5] I reply that the more he eulogizes the irrational animals, the more he magnifies without meaning

---

[1] Cf. Pliny, *N.H.* xi, 109; Plutarch, *Mor.* 968 A; Aelian, *N.A.* ii, 25; Cassianus Bassus, *Geoponica* xv, 1, 26; Basil, *Hexaemeron* ix, 3 (*P.G.* xxix, 196 A). For ants' preparation for winter, cf. Philo, *Alexander*, 42; Greg. Naz. *Orat. Theol.* ii, 25 (Mason, p. 61).

[2] Cf. Clem. Al. *Paed.* ii, 85, 3, and the magical invocation in Preisendanz, *P.G.M.* iv, 2917.

[3] Cf. Celsus in iv, 52, paraphrasing *Timaeus*, 69 C, D; Plotinus, vi, 5, 9; Albinus, *Epit.* 25, says that while bodies have many forms, soul is μονοειδής.

[4] According to Plato, *Phaedrus*, 246 B–247 B, in the process of transmigration a fallen soul may enter an animal body.

[5] Pliny, *N.H.* xi, 110; Cleanthes ap. Plutarch, *Mor.* 967 E; Aelian, *N.A.* vi, 43, and 50 where he says he witnessed an ants' funeral procession.

to do so the work of the Logos that ordered all things, and shows the skill of men which is capable of ruling by reason the superior natural powers of the irrational animals. But why do I say 'the irrational animals' when those which are called irrational according to the universal notions of everyone do not seem irrational to Celsus? At least, he who professed to give an account of *the whole of nature*[1] and boasted of knowing the truth in the title of his book, does not even think that the ants are irrational. For he speaks of the ants as though they had discussions with one another, saying as follows: *And in fact when they meet together they have discussions with one another, and this is why they do not lose their way;*[2] *accordingly they also have a completely developed rational faculty, and universal notions of certain general matters, and a voice to make clear their experiences and meaning.* If a person is to have a discussion with another this must take place by means of a voice which makes clear some meaning, and which often may recount what he calls experiences. When this is said to be true of ants, is it not the very height of absurdity?

85. He is not even ashamed to continue after this, so that he may display to people who will live after him his disgraceful views: *Come then, if anyone were to look out from heaven at the earth, what difference would appear between what is done by us and by ants and bees?* To take his instance, when the one who looks from heaven at the earth sees what is done by men and by ants, does he consider just the bodies of men and ants and fail to comprehend that the rational mind is impelled by reasoning, while on the other hand the irrational mind is impelled by instinct and unreasoning suggestion and by a sort of basic natural constitution? Surely not. It is preposterous to suppose that the one who looks from heaven upon earthly things would want to consider the bodies of men and ants from such a distance, and not want much rather to see the natures of the minds and the source of the impulses, whether rational or irrational. Once he saw the source of all impulses, obviously he would also see the pre-eminence and superiority of men, not only above the ants, but also above the elephants. He who looks from heaven upon the irrational animals, even though their bodies may be large, will not see any origin for their impulses other than irrationality, so to speak. But when he looks at the rational beings, he will see reason which is common to men and to divine and heavenly beings, and probably also to the supreme God Himself. This explains why he is said to have been made in the image of God; for the image of the supreme God is His reason (Logos).[3]

---

[1] Celsus in IV, 73.
[2] Pliny, *N.H.* XI, 109–10, says that the ants collect food from various places and have fixed days when they come together to take stock and meet.   [3] Cf. Col. i. 15.

86. After this, as though striving still further to degrade the human race and liken it to the irrational animals, and wanting to avoid omitting any of the stories told of animals which point to their superiority, he even says that some animals possess powers of sorcery, so that not even in this may men take undue pride or wish to have the pre-eminence over the irrational animals. This is what he says: *And if men take any pride in sorcery, yet even in this matter snakes and eagles are wiser. At any rate, they know many antidotes and prophylactics, and furthermore, the powers of certain stones to keep their young from harm. If men fall in with these, they think they have some wonderful possession.* In the first place, I do not know why he gave the name of *sorcery* to the knowledge possessed by animals of natural antidotes, whether it is found by experience or due to some natural perception. The name 'sorcery' has regularly been applied in another sense. But perhaps he wants, as an Epicurean, to make a secret attack on the entire practice of this art by implying that it depends upon the claims of sorcerers. However, suppose he is right in thinking that men are proud of their knowledge of these matters, whether they are sorcerers or not. How are snakes wiser than men in this respect if they use fennel[1] to see clearly and to move quickly, when they receive their natural power not from reasoning but only from the way they are made? Men do not attain to such ability from mere nature like snakes, but partly from experience and partly from reason, and sometimes as a result of inference based on knowledge. Thus, even if to keep their young safe in the nest eagles bring to it the so-called eagle-stone,[2] why conclude that eagles are wise and wiser than men? For what is given to eagles as a natural aid men have discovered by experience on account of their reasoning and have made intelligent use of it.

87. Supposing also that other antidotes are known to animals, is this any evidence that it is not nature but reason in the animals which finds out these things? If the discovery were due to reason, one particular antidote would not be found exclusively among snakes, or even a second or a third supposing they existed, and another particular one among eagles, and so on with the other animals. But they would have as many as men have. However, from the fact that each animal has by nature inclined to use exclusively one particular aid, it is obvious that they do not possess wisdom or reason but a certain natural constitution made by the Logos, which inclines them to particular antidotes which cure them.

---

[1] Cf. Pliny, *N.H.* VIII, 99; Aelian, *N.A.* IX, 16; Plutarch, *Mor.* 974B; Basil, *Hexaemeron* IX, 3 (*P.G.* XXIX, 193A).

[2] For the legend that eagles bring this stone to the nest to help the female to lay eggs, cf. M. Wellmann, 'Der Physiologus', in *Philologus*, Suppl. Bd. XXII, 1 (1931), pp. 88 f. It is mentioned by Pliny, *N.H.* X, 12; XXXVI, 149–51; Aelian, *N.A.* I, 35; Philostratus, *V.A.* II, 14; Aetius Amidenus, II, 32 (*Corp. Medic. Gr.* VIII, 1 (1935), p. 166).

And yet, if I wanted to join issue with Celsus on this point, I would have discussed Solomon's words from Proverbs which read as follows: 'There are four things that are very little on the earth, but these are wiser than the wise: the ants who have no strength, who prepare their food in summer; the coneys, a people not strong, who make their houses in the rocks; the locust has no king, and it wages war in good order with one command; the lizard, though leaning on its hands and easy to catch, lives in king's strongholds.'[1] However, I am not concerned with the obvious sense of the words, but in accordance with the title (for the book is entitled Proverbs) I examine these words to find out their hidden meanings. For it is the habit of these men to distinguish between things that have an obvious meaning and those which have a hidden interpretation, and to divide them into many classes one of which is proverbs. That is why our Saviour is recorded in the gospels to have said: 'I have spoken these things to you in proverbs; but the time is coming when I will speak to you in proverbs no longer.'[2] It is not, then, the literal ants who are even wiser than the wise, but those alluded to under a proverbial form. This may be also said of the other animals. But Celsus thinks the books of Jews and Christians are utterly crude and illiterate, and supposes that those who allegorize them force the meaning of the authors in so doing.[3] Let this, then, be our proof that Celsus attacks us to no purpose, and let this be the refutation also of his argument about snakes and eagles, making out that they are wiser than men.

88. He further wants to argue at length that even the ideas of God among the human race are no more remarkable than those of all other mortal beings, but that some of the irrational animals have ideas of God, though there have been great disagreements about Him among the most intelligent men everywhere, Greeks and barbarians. He says: *If because man has laid hold of notions of God he is thought to be superior to the other animals, let those who maintain this realize that many of the other animals would lay claim to this. And quite reasonably. For what would anyone say to be more divine than to foreknow and declare the future?*[4] *Well then, men learn this from the other animals, and especially from birds; and those who understand the indications which they give are diviners. If then the birds and all other prophetic animals which are given foreknowledge by God teach us by means of signs, they seem to be naturally so much nearer in communion with God and to be wiser and dearer to God. Intelligent men say that the birds have associations, obviously more sacred than ours, and that somehow they know what the birds say and show in practice that they do know by the fact that,*

---

[1] Prov. xxiv. 59–63.   [2] John xvi. 25.
[3] Cf. Celsus in I, 17; IV, 38, 51.   [4] Cf. Origen in VI, 10.

after they have previously said that the birds declared they would go away to
some place and would do this or that, they show that they have gone and done
what in fact they foretold.[1] *No animal appears to keep oaths better than*
elephants, or to be more faithful to the Deity, no doubt because they have
knowledge of Him.[2] See here how he jumps to conclusions and puts
forward as recognized truths statements which are problems discussed by
the philosophers not only of the Greeks but also of the barbarians, who
either discovered, or learnt from certain daemons, about birds and the
other animals from which certain powers of divination are said to have
come to men. In the first place, it is an open question whether or not
an art of augury and that of divination by animals in general have any
real existence at all. And secondly, among those who do believe that
divination by birds is real, no agreement has been reached as to the
cause of the method of divination, since some say that the movements
of the animals are due to certain daemons or prophetic gods, impelling
birds to different flights and different utterances, and other animals to
this or that sort of movement, whereas others think that their souls are
divine to a greater degree and are adapted for this purpose, which is very
improbable.[3]

89. Therefore, if Celsus wanted by the words which we are considering
to prove that the irrational animals are more divine and wiser than men,
he ought to have given an extended argument to show that divination of
this kind genuinely exists, and after that to have shown his grounds of
defence more clearly, and to have provided some proof to overthrow the
arguments of those who deny the reality of this kind of divination, and to
have given a logical refutation of the arguments of those who say that
daemons or gods move the animals to give prophecies; and after that he
ought to have supported his view that the souls of irrational animals are
divine to a greater degree. Had he done this to the best of our ability we
would have opposed his plausible arguments, if he had displayed philosophical skill in handling such difficult questions. We would have refuted
the assertion that the irrational animals are wiser than men, and exposed
the falsity of the statement that they have notions of God more divine
than ours, and that they have certain sacred associations with one another.
In fact, he who criticizes us for believing in the supreme God asks us to

[1] Philostratus (*V.A.* IV, 3) tells such a story of Apollonius. Cf. Porphyry, *de Abstinentia*,
III, 5 'Birds understand the gods more quickly than men, and when they have understood
declare it as far as they are able and are heralds of the gods to men, one bird of one god,
another of another, the eagle of Zeus, the hawk and raven of Apollo, the stork of Hera, the
corn-crake and owl of Athena, as also the crane of Demeter, and so on with each god.'
[2] See note on IV, 98 below.
[3] The former view is Stoic, the latter Peripatetic. Cf. Cicero, *de Divin.* I, 38, 81, where
Aristotle is credited with the view that divination is real but not supernatural.

believe that the souls of birds have notions more divine and clear than those of men. If this is true, birds have far clearer ideas of God than Celsus —and that would not be remarkable in his case since he disparages man so much. It follows from Celsus' opinion that the birds have ideas which are superior and more divine, I do not say merely than those held by us Christians or by the Jews who use the same scriptures as we do, but also superior to those among the Greeks who taught about God; for they also were men. According to Celsus, therefore, the species of prophetic birds understood the nature of God better than Pherecydes, Pythagoras, Socrates, and Plato! And we ought to have resorted to the birds as our teachers so that, just as they teach us the future by divination according to Celsus' notion, so also they may set men free from doubt about God and pass on the clear conception of Him which they have received.

It would accordingly be logical of Celsus, since he thinks birds superior to men, to use birds as teachers and none of the Greek philosophers.

90. We, however, have a few things to say out of many arguments on the question before us to show that his false opinion is ungrateful to his Maker. For 'man' (that is Celsus) 'being in honour has not understood',[1] and for this reason 'is compared' not even to the birds and the other irrational animals which he regards as prophetic; but he has yielded them the first place even more than the Egyptians who worship the irrational animals as gods, and degraded himself and, by the implication of his words, even the entire human race as having a worse and inferior understanding of God than the irrational animals.

Let us now primarily consider the question whether divination by birds and by the other animals believed to be prophetic is genuine or not. The argument advanced on either side is not lightly to be discarded. On the one side the argument would dissuade us from accepting it so that the rational being may not abandon the miraculous oracles and turn from them to use birds. On the other side, the argument points to the indisputable facts to which many bear witness, that many have been delivered from very great dangers because they have believed in divination by birds. For the moment let us assume that augury is a reality, that on this hypothesis I may show to people who have been prejudiced that even if this is granted man has a great superiority over the irrational animals and even over those with powers of divination, and is in no way comparable with them. I should say, then, that if some divine instinct was in them which gave them foreknowledge of the future and was so rich in this respect that out of their abundance they could show the future to any man who so desired, obviously they would have known of their own future long

[1] Ps. xlviii. 13, 21.

before knowing that of others. And had they known their own future they would have taken care not to fly into a place where men had set traps and nets for them, or where archers would take aim and shoot arrows at them as they flew.[1] Surely also, if eagles had foreknown the designs against their young, whether those of snakes creeping up to them and destroying them or those of some men who capture them for amusement or for some other use and service, they would not have built their nest where they were liable to be exposed to attack. And in general, none of these animals would ever have been caught by men if they had been more divine and wiser than men.

91. Moreover, if birds fight with birds and, as Celsus says, prophetic birds and the other irrational animals have a divine nature, and notions of God and foreknowledge of the future, and if they had declared these things beforehand to others, the sparrow in Homer would not have built her nest where the serpent could consume her and her young, nor would the serpent in the same poet have failed to avoid being caught by the eagle. For Homer, the wonderful poet, speaks as follows of the former:

Then there was seen a great portent; a snake blood-red on the back, terrible, whom the god of Olympus himself had sent forth to the light of day, sprang from beneath the altar and darted to the plane-tree. Now there were there the brood of a sparrow, tender little ones, upon the topmost branch, nestling beneath the leaves; eight were they and the mother of the little ones was the ninth, and the snake swallowed these cheeping pitifully. And the mother fluttered around wailing for her little ones; but he coiled himself and caught her by the wing as she screamed about him. Now when he had swallowed the sparrow's little ones and the mother of them, the god who revealed him made of him a sign; for the son of crooked counselling Kronos turned him to stone, and we stood by and marvelled to see what was done. Thus then the dread portent brake in upon the hecatombs of the gods.[2]

And of the latter he says:

For as they were eager to pass over a bird had appeared to them, an eagle of lofty flight, skirting the host on the left hand. In its talons it bore a blood-red monstrous snake, alive and struggling still; yea, not yet had it forgotten the joy of battle, but writhed backward and smote the bird that held it on the breast, beside the neck, and the bird cast it from him down to the earth in sore pain,

[1] Origen is probably thinking of the story quoted by Josephus (c. *Ap.* 1, 22, 201–4) from Hecataeus: a competent archer named Mosollamus shot a bird which was being observed by a seer; when the seer protested he replied that if the bird had had any ability for knowing the future, it would not have come to the place where it would be killed by his arrow.

[2] Homer, *Il.* 11, 308–21 (the translation is that of Lang, Leaf, and Myers). The passage is also quoted for the same point by Cicero, *de Divin.* 11, 30, 63–4.

and dropped it in the midst of the throng; then with a cry sped away down the gust of the wind. And the Trojans shuddered when they saw the gleaming snake lying in the midst of them; an omen of aegis-bearing Zeus.[1]

Had the eagle, then, prophetic powers but not the serpent, though the augurs use this animal too? Since it is easy to prove that it is merely arbitrary to select one and not the other, is it not proved that neither of them has prophetic powers? If the serpent had possessed prophetic powers, would it not have avoided suffering these things from the eagle? One could also find thousands of other examples to show that animals do not in themselves have a prophetic soul. But according to the opinion of the poet and the majority of men it was

> Olympian Zeus himself who sent it forth to the light of day.

And with some symbolical meaning Apollo also uses as messenger a hawk. For it is said that 'the hawk of Apollo is a swift messenger'.[2]

92. We hold that there are certain evil daemons and, if I may so say, Titans or Giants who have become impious towards the true God and the angels in heaven, and have fallen from heaven to roam about the grosser bodies on earth which are unclean. They have some perception of the future, in that they are unclothed by earthly bodies; and they engage in this sort of activity because they want to lead the human race away from the true God. They creep into the most rapacious wild beasts and other very wicked animals and impel them to do what they want when they so desire, or turn the images in the minds of such animals towards flights and movements of a particular sort. Their desire is that men may be caught by the prophetic power in the irrational animals and not seek God who contains the whole world, or search out the pure way of worshipping Him, but may fall in their reasoning to the level of earth and the birds and serpents, and even to foxes[3] and wolves. For it has been noticed by experts in these matters that the future is known with greater clarity by means of such animals as these, because the daemons have not such power with the milder animals as they have with them. This is because animals of this sort have something about them resembling evil, and although it is not evil yet it is like it.[4]

[1] Homer, *Il.* XII, 200–9, also quoted by Plato, *Ion*, 539 B–D, and Cicero, *op. cit.* I, 47, 106. Evidently these two passages from Homer were stock instances in the debates about divination.

[2] Homer, *Od.* XV, 526. Cf. Porphyry, *de Abst.* III, 5 (quoted above on IV, 88).

[3] For the use of foxes in augury cf. Pliny, *N.H.* VIII, 103.

[4] This is Stoic; cf. Seneca, *de Ira*, I, 3, 8 (of wild animals): 'ex eo procursus illorum tumultusque vehementes sunt, metus autem sollicitudinesque et tristitia et ira non sunt, sed his quaedam similia.' Unlike Aristotle and Posidonius, the ancient Stoa denied that emotions, such as wrath, could be attributed to animals. Cf. J. H. Waszink on Tertullian, *de Anima*, XVI (pp. 233–4). Porphyry (*de Abst.* III, 22) disagreed.

93. On this account, whatever else about Moses I have admired, I would assert that the following fact is worthy of admiration, that he understood the different natures of animals, and, either because he had learnt from God about them and about the daemons related to each animal, or because he had discovered about them himself as he advanced in wisdom, in his legislation about animals he said that all the animals which are regarded as having prophetic powers by the Egyptians and the rest of mankind are unclean, and that broadly speaking those not so regarded are clean. Among those which Moses calls unclean are the wolf, fox, serpent, eagle, hawk, and those like them.[1] And broadly speaking you would find not only in the Law but also in the prophets that these animals are mentioned to illustrate the worst things,[2] and that a wolf or fox is never referred to with a good connotation. There seems, therefore, to be some sort of kinship between the form of each daemon and the form of each animal. And just as among men some are stronger than others, though this has nothing at all to do with their moral character, in the same way some daemons probably have more power than others in things morally neutral, and some use these animals to deceive men in accordance with the will of 'the prince of this world'[3] as he is called in our scriptures, while others use another form to show the future. See too how repulsive the daemons are, when some even use weasels to declare the future.[4] But judge for yourself which of the two views it is better to accept, that the supreme God and His Son influence the birds and the other animals to prophesy, or that the beings who influence animals of this kind (not men, though men are present) are evil and, as our holy scriptures call them, unclean daemons.[5]

94. If, however, the soul of birds is divine because the future is foretold by them, why should we not rather say that, since omens are received by men, the soul of those through whom we hear the omens is divine? According to this principle the female slave in Homer who ground the corn was some divinely inspired person when she said of the suitors:

May they dine here for the last and final time.[6]

[1] Lev. xi.

[2] Cf. Isa. xi. 6; lxv. 25; Jer. v. 6; Ezek. xii. 4; xxii. 27; Ps. lxii. 11; Cant. ii. 15.

[3] John xii. 31; xiv. 30; xvi. 11; II Cor. iv. 4.

[4] To meet a weasel in one's path was a bad ómen; cf. Aristophanes, *Eccles.* 792; Theophrastus, *Charact.* 16; Ammianus Marcellinus, xvi, 8, 2. Aelian, *N.A.* vii, 8, says that if weasels squeak it indicates a severe winter. Cf. also H. Bolkestein, *Theophrastos' Charakter der Deisidaimonia als religionsgeschichtliche Urkunde* (1929), p. 18, who quotes one of the 'symbola Pythagoreorum' (Mullach, *Frag. Philos. Gr.* i, 510) 'Mustela e transversa offensa redeundum, i.e. fugiendi delatores. nam mustelam ore parere affirmant.' For the assignment of animals to daemons, cf. Plato, *Politicus,* 271 D, E; the notion that evil daemons dwell in harmful animals appears in Iamblichus, *de Myst.* ii, 7.

[5] Cf. Matt. x. 1; xii. 43, etc.

[6] Homer, *Od.* iv, 685 (cf. xx, 105 ff.).

And though she was divinely inspired, yet the great Odysseus, the friend
of the Homeric Athene, was not so, but merely rejoiced when he understood
the words of omen uttered by the divinely inspired grinder, as the poet
says   And noble Odysseus rejoiced at the omen.[1]

Consider now. If birds really have a divine soul and a perception of God,
or as Celsus would say, of the gods, then obviously also when we men
sneeze we do so as a result of some divinity in us and some prophetic
power in our soul. For this too is testified by many. For this reason also
the poet says   And he sneezed as she prayed.

So too Penelope says

    Dost thou not see that my son has sneezed at thy words?[2]

95. For the knowledge of the future the true God uses neither irrational animals nor ordinary men, but the most sacred and holy human souls
whom He inspires and makes prophets. For this reason we should
reckon the following command to be among the most admirable sayings
in the Mosaic law: 'You shall not employ augury nor study the omens of
birds',[3] and in another place: 'For the nations, which the Lord thy God
shall utterly destroy before thy face, will listen to omens and divination;
but as for thee, the Lord thy God has not allowed this.' Then he next says
'The Lord thy God shall raise up a prophet for thee from thy brethren.'[4]
When God once wanted to turn them away from augury by means of an
augurer, He made a spirit in the augurer say: 'For there is no augury in
Jacob nor divination in Israel; in due time it shall be told to Jacob and
Israel what God will do.'[5] Since we know these injunctions and others
like them, we want to keep the commandment which says with mystical
meaning 'Keep thy heart with all diligence.'[6] We do not want any daemon
to get a place in our mind, or any hostile spirit to turn our imagination
where he wills. But we pray that there may shine in our hearts the light
of the knowledge of the glory of God,[7] by the Spirit of God dwelling in
our imagination and representing to us the things of God. 'For as many
as are led by the Spirit of God, they are the sons of God.'[8]

96. It is necessary to realize that foreknowledge of the future is not
necessarily divine;[9] for in itself it is morally neutral and happens to bad

---

[1] Homer, *Od.* xx, 120 (cf. xviii, 117).

[2] Homer, *Od.* xvii, 541, 545. For sneezing as an omen, cf. Cicero, *de Divin.* ii, 40, 8
(see A. S. Pease's commentary *ad loc.*).

[3] Lev. xix. 26.   [4] Deut. xviii. 14, 12, 15.   [5] Num. xxiii. 23 (Balaam).

[6] Prov. iv. 23.   [7] II Cor. iv. 6.   [8] Rom. viii. 14.

[9] Cf. iii, 25. But in vi, 10 'the proclamation of future events is the mark of divinity'.
Porphyry (*Ep. ad Aneb.* 46) says: 'Those who have the divine gift of divination foresee
the future, but are not blessed; for though they foresee the future, they do not know how
to use this rightly.'

and good. At any rate, physicians foreknow certain things as a result of their medical skill, though they may be morally bad men. So also pilots, though they may be wicked, foreknow changes in the weather and severe gales and alterations in atmospheric conditions as a result of some experience and observation.[1] I do not suppose that anyone would say they were divine on this account, if their moral character should happen to be wicked. Therefore, Celsus' statement is untrue—*What would anyone say to be more divine than to foreknow and declare the future?* And it is not true that *many of the animals would claim to have ideas of God;* for none of the irrational animals has any idea of Him. It is also a lie that *the irrational animals are nearer in communion with God.* In fact, even those men who advance to the summit of spiritual progress are still evil and far from close communion with God. Only those who are truly wise and genuinely pious are nearer to communion with God. Such is the character of our prophets and of Moses, of whom the scripture testified on account of his great purity that 'Moses alone shall draw near to God, while the others shall not draw near'.[2]

97. Is it not impious of this fellow who accuses us of impiety to say that *the irrational animals are* not only *wiser than* the nature of *men* but even that they are *dearer to God?* And who would not be repelled if he gave attention to a man who says that a serpent, fox, wolf, eagle, and hawk are dearer to God than the nature of men? It follows from his view that if these animals are dearer to God than man obviously they are dearer to God than Socrates, Plato, Pythagoras, Pherecydes, and the men who taught about God whose praises he was singing a short while ago.[3] Indeed, one might utter this wish for him and say: If these animals are dearer to God than men, may you be dear to God with them and become like those who in your opinion are dearer to God than men are. Let him not suppose that this is a curse; for who would not pray that he may become entirely like those whom he believes to be dearer to God in order that he too may become loved by God just as they are?

Since Celsus wants to make out that *the associations of animals are more sacred than ours,* he attributes this story not to ordinary people but to the *intelligent.* But it is good men who are in reality intelligent; for no bad man is intelligent. This, then, is the way he talks: *Intelligent men say that the birds have associations, obviously more sacred than ours, and that somehow they know what the birds say and show in practice that they do know by the fact*

---

[1] For parallels see *J.T.S.* xlviii (1947), p. 38 n. 1, and to the references there given add Plutarch, *Mor.* 581 f; Athanasius, *Vita Antonii,* 33; Augustine, *de Civ. Dei,* x, 32; *de Divinat.* v, 9 (*C.S.E.L.* xli, 607). Macrobius (*Sat.* 1, 20, 5) remarks that medicine and divination are related sciences, because the physician foresees the future.

[2] Exod. xxiv. 2.   [3] Cf. Celsus in 1, 16.

that, after they have previously said that the birds declared they would go away
to some place and would do this or that, they show that they have gone and
done what in fact they foretold. In truth, however, no intelligent man has
related anything of the kind, and no wise man says that the associations of
irrational animals are more sacred than those of men. If, for the sake of
examining the views of Celsus, we look at the conclusion which follows
from them, it is obvious that in his opinion the associations of irrational
animals are more sacred than the distinguished associations of Pherecydes,
Pythagoras, Socrates, Plato, and the philosophers. It is self-evident that
this is not only absurd but quite outrageous. But supposing we were to
believe that some have learnt from the unintelligible sound of the birds
that the birds will go away and do this or that, and that they predict this,
we would say that this too has been shown to men by daemons through
outward signs with the aim that man may be deceived by the daemons, and
that his mind may be dragged from heaven and from God down to earth
and lower still.

98. I do not know how Celsus heard also of an oath of elephants, and
that they are more faithful to God than we are and have knowledge of God.
For though I know many amazing things are told of the nature of the
animal and of its docility, yet I am certainly not aware that anyone has
spoken of the elephant's oaths.[1] Unless perhaps it is their docile nature
and the way in which they keep an agreement when once they have, as it
were, made one with men which he called fidelity to an oath.[2] But even
that is actually untrue. For though it happens rarely, yet at least it is on
record that after they have apparently become docile elephants have
savagely attacked men and killed them, and for this reason have been
condemned to death as no longer of any use.

After this to prove, as he thinks, that *storks are more pious than men,* he
uses the story about *the bird* that it *returns affection and brings food to its*

---

[1] Pliny (*N.H.* VIII, 2–3) and Dio Cassius (XXXIX, 38) tell the story that elephants worship
the moon, and will not go on board ship until they have received a solemn oath from their
drivers that they will return. That elephants worship sun and moon is alleged by Aelian,
N.A. VII, 44; IV, 10. Cf. F. J. Dölger, *Sol Salutis* (2nd ed. 1925), p. 31. F. Münzer,
Beiträge zur Quellenkritik der Naturgeschichte des Plinius (Berlin, 1897), pp. 411–22, argues
that Pliny's immediate source in *N.H.* VIII was the learned king Juba II of Mauretania
(c. 50 B.C.–c. A.D. 23), who also seems to have been a main source of Aelian (cf. M. Wellmann
in *Hermes*, XXVII (1892), pp. 389–406). Origen's statement is taken to show that Celsus is
dependent directly or indirectly upon Juba's work, and that Origen himself had not read it,
by M. Wellmann, 'Der Physiologus', in *Philologus*, Suppl. Bd. XXII, 1 (1931), pp. 7–9.
That this does not necessarily follow seems clear from Origen's next sentence. In Juba the
drivers do the swearing; in Celsus it is apparently the elephants themselves. It is the latter
idea of which Origen says he has never heard. In any event, it may be noted that F. Jacoby,
Die Fragmente der griechischen Historiker, IIIA (1943), p. 343, is doubtful how far Juba was
a chief source of Pliny and Aelian even in the story about elephants only.
[2] Read γενομένην. For the *clementia* of elephants, cf. Pliny, *N.H.* VIII, 23.

parents.[1] I may reply that here too the storks do not do this as a result of thinking out what is morally right, or by reasoning, but by instinct, because their natural constitution is intended to set an example among irrational animals that is able to put men to shame in the matter of paying their debt of gratitude to their parents. Had Celsus realized the extent of the difference between doing these things by reason and doing them without thinking and by instinct, he would not have said that storks are more pious than men.

Still striving to show the piety of irrational animals, Celsus uses *the Arabian bird, the phoenix, which after many years visits Egypt, and brings its dead father, buried in a ball of myrrh, and puts him in the shrine of the sun.*[2] This is the story. But even if it is true, it is possible that this also happens by instinct. For the providence of God created so many different varieties of animals in order to show to men the diversity which exists in the constitution of the things in the world, which extends also to the birds. And if He made a 'unique'[3] creature, it was in order that by this also He might make men to admire not the creature but Him who made it.

99. To all this Celsus adds the following remark: *Accordingly, all things have not been made for man any more than for the lion or the eagle or the dolphin, but so that this world, as God's work, may be made complete and perfect in all its parts. For this purpose all things have been proportioned, not for one another except incidentally, but for the universe as a whole.*[4] *And God takes care of the universe, and providence never abandons it, nor does it become more evil; nor does God turn it back to Himself after a time, nor is He angry because of men any more than He is because of monkeys or mice; nor does He threaten them. For each of them has received his destiny in his turn.* Let us answer this one just briefly. I think I have shown by what has already been said how all things have been made for man and every rational creature; for all things have been created primarily on account of the rational being. Celsus may say if he likes that creation is not for man any more than for the lion or those which he mentions; but we will say that the Creator has not made these things for the lion or eagle or dolphin,

[1] Aristotle, *Hist. Anim.* x, 13 (615 b 23), mentions this as a popular story. It is repeated by Philo, *Alexander*, 61; *de Decal.* 116; Plutarch, *Mor.* 962E; Aelian, *N.A.* III, 23; x, 16; Pliny, *N.H.* x, 63; Artemidorus, II, 20; Basil, *Hexaemeron*, VIII, 5; Horapollon, *Hierogl.* II, 58.

[2] The story appears in numerous writers from Herodotus (II, 73) onwards. For references see J. B. Lightfoot, *The Apostolic Fathers*, part I, ii, pp. 84 f. Aelian, *N.A.* VI, 58, argues like Celsus that the intelligence of the phoenix is superior to that of man. See also P.-W. *s.v.* 'Phoenix', and J. Hubaux and M. Leroy, *Le mythe du Phénix dans les littératures grecque et latine* (Liège, 1939).

[3] See Lightfoot, *op. cit.* p. 87 on I Clement xxv.

[4] Read with Wif. ἀλλήλων, ἀλλ' εἰ μὴ πάρεργον, ἀλλὰ τοῦ ὅλου.

but has created everything for the rational being, and *so that this world as God's work may be made complete and perfect in all its parts.* For we should agree that in this point he was right. But God does not take care, as Celsus imagines, only of *the universe as a whole,* but in addition to that He takes particular care of every rational being. And providence will never abandon the universe. For even if some part of it becomes very bad because the rational being sins, God arranges to purify it, and after a time to turn the whole world back to Himself. Furthermore, he is not angry because of monkeys and mice; but He inflicts judgment and punishment upon men, seeing that they have gone against the impulses of nature. And He threatens them through prophets and through the Saviour who came to visit the whole human race, in order that by means of the threat those who hear may be converted, while those who neglect the words aimed at their conversion pay penalties according to their deserts. It is right that God should impose these according to His will to the advantage of the whole world upon people who need healing and correction of this kind and of such severity.

However, the fourth book has also become long enough, and here we will end its argument. May God grant that through His Son who is divine Logos, Wisdom, Truth, Righteousness, and every other divine title which the holy scriptures give to him, we may also begin the fifth book to help those who will read it, and may successfully complete that one also with His Logos dwelling in our soul.

BOOK V

1. Holy Ambrose, we now begin a fifth book in reply to Celsus'
treatise, not with any desire to talk a great deal—which is forbidden since
by so doing we would not avoid sin[1]—but attempting as far as possible not
to leave any of his statements unexamined, and especially where he might
seem to some people to have brought clever charges against us or the
Jews. And if it were possible for us with our argument to penetrate the
consciousness of every single reader of his treatise and to extract each dart
which wounds anyone who has not been completely protected by the
whole armour of God,[2] and to apply a spiritual medicine which would
heal the wound made by Celsus which causes people who pay attention to
his arguments to be unhealthy in their faith,[3] then we would have done so.
But it is God's work to dwell invisibly by His Spirit and by the Spirit of
Christ in those in whom He judges it right to dwell. Whereas it is our task,
since we try to confirm men's faith by arguments and treatises, to do all in
our power that we may be called 'workmen who need not to be ashamed,
handling rightly the word of truth'.[4] One of all these tasks seems to us to
be that of demolishing Celsus' plausible arguments to the best of our
ability, and to perform faithfully the work which you have enjoined upon
us. Let us quote, then, the next points after the arguments of Celsus
which we have already tackled (the reader will decide whether we also
refuted them), and let us produce the reply to them. May God grant that
we may not come to the task with our mind and reason merely human and
without any divine inspiration, that the faith of those who, we pray, may
be helped may not be in the wisdom of men, but that we may receive the
mind of Christ[5] from His Father who alone gives it, and be helped to
share in the Logos of God, and may throw down 'every high thing that
exalts itself against the knowledge of God',[6] even the pride of Celsus who
exalts himself against us and against our Jesus, and furthermore against
Moses and the prophets. We desire that He who gives 'the word to those
who preach with great power'[7] may furnish this also to us, and grant this
great power so that by the word and power of God faith may spring up
in those who will read this reply.

2. It is our object now to refute his words which read as follows: *Jews
and Christians, no God or child of God either has come down or*[8] *would have
come down. And if it is certain angels of which you speak, whom do you mean*

---

[1] Prov. x. 19.   [2] Eph. vi. 11.   [3] Titus ii. 2.
[4] II Tim. ii. 15.   [5] I Cor. ii. 5, 16.   [6] II Cor. x. 5.
[7] Ps. lxvii. 12.   [8] K. tr. proposes οὔτ᾽ ⟨ἂν⟩ κατέλθοι.

by them, gods or some other kind of being? You presumably mean some other kind—the daemons. Celsus is repeating himself (for earlier he has frequently said this already),[1] and it is unnecessary to discuss it at length; what we have said on this point will be enough. But we will make a few remarks out of many which could be made, which we think to be in line with what has already been said, yet which have not entirely the same content. In these we will show that by asserting as a general principle that *no God or child of God has come down to men* he rules out the opinions held by most people about God's manifestation which he too has mentioned earlier.[2] For if Celsus is right in maintaining as a general principle that no God or child of God has or would have come down, obviously the idea is ruled out that there are gods upon earth who have come down from heaven either to give oracles to men or that they may heal them by means of oracular utterances. Neither the Pythian Apollo nor Asclepius nor any other one of those supposed to do these things could be a god who has come down from heaven; or if he were a god, it would be his lot always to inhabit the earth and to be, as it were, an exile from the abode of the gods, or he would be one of those who have no right to have fellowship with the gods there; or Apollo and Asclepius and all those who are believed to effect something on earth would not be gods, but certain daemons, far inferior to wise men who ascend on account of their virtue even to the vault of heaven.[3]

3. Notice that through his desire to demolish our doctrines he who throughout all his treatise has not admitted that he is an Epicurean is convicted of changing to Epicurus' opinions. It is now for you who read Celsus' arguments and agree to what has already been said either to reject the idea of God's advent and providential care for men individually, or to affirm belief in this and prove Celsus' doctrine to be wrong. If you entirely reject providence, in order to maintain that your opinion is true you will prove his arguments wrong where he affirms belief in gods and providence.[4] But if none the less you affirm belief in providence, so that you do not agree with Celsus when he says that no God or child of God has or will come down to men, why do you not look carefully into what we have said about Jesus and into the prophecies about him to find out who ought rather to be regarded as a God or child of God who has come down to men? Should we regard as divine Jesus who accomplished and performed such great miracles, or those who by means of oracles and divination fail to reform the morals of those who are healed and, what is more, depart from the pure and holy solemn worship of the Creator of the universe, and by means of a worship of several gods tear the souls of

---

[1] Cf. IV, 2–23.
[2] Celsus in III, 22–5.
[3] Cf. Plato, *Phaedrus*, 247 B.
[4] Cf. Celsus in I, 57; IV, 4, 99; VII, 68; VIII, 45.

people who pay attention to them away from the one and only manifest and genuine God?

4. After this, as though Jesus or Christians would have answered that those who come down to men are angels, he says: *And if it is certain angels of which you speak.* And he goes on to ask: *Whom do you mean by them, gods or some other kind of being?* Then again he supposes that the answer would *presumably* be that they are *some other kind, the daemons.* Let us now consider this point also. Admittedly we do speak of angels who are 'ministering spirits sent forth to do service for the sake of those who will inherit salvation'.[1] They ascend bringing the prayers of men into the purest heavenly region of the universe,[2] or even to places purer than these beyond the heavens.[3] And again they descend from there bringing to each individual according to his merits some benefit which God commands them to administer to those who are to receive His favours. Though we have learnt to call them angels from their activity, because they are divine we find that they are sometimes called 'gods'[4] in the sacred scriptures, but not in the sense that we are commanded to reverence and worship instead of God those who minister and bring to us His blessings. We have to send up every petition, prayer, intercession, and thanksgiving[5] to the supreme God through the high-priest of all angels, the living and divine Logos. We will even make our petitions to the very Logos himself and offer intercession to him and give thanks and also pray to him, if we are capable of a clear understanding of the absolute and the relative sense of prayer.[6]

5. It is unreasonable to invoke angels without having received superhuman knowledge about them. But even supposing for the purposes of argument some wonderful and secret knowledge about them had been grasped, since this knowledge would show their nature and the purposes for which each one has been appointed, it would forbid us from venturing to pray to any other than the supreme God, who is sufficient for all things, through our Saviour, the Son of God. He is Logos, Wisdom, Truth and every other title which the scriptures of the prophets of God and the

[1] Heb. i. 14.
[2] In *de Princ.* I, 8, 1 this is the particular function of the archangel Michael, as also in Jewish tradition (see W. Bousset and H. Gressmann, *Die Religion des Judenthums* (1926), p. 327).
[3] Allusion to Plato, *Phaedrus*, 247C.
[4] Cf. Ps. xlix. 1; lxxxi. 1; lxxxv. 8; xcv. 4; cxxxv. 2.   [5] Cf. I Tim. ii. 1.
[6] In *de Oratione*, 15-16 Origen argues that strictly speaking prayer ought to be offered only to the Father, 'not even to Christ himself' since he too prayed. But our prayers to the supreme God have to be made through the high-priest. Prayer to Christ is therefore justifiable, but the sense of it is relative not absolute. See Origen in VII, 26 and 36 below, and C. Bigg, *The Christian Platonists of Alexandria* (2nd ed. 1913), pp. 228-9, who quotes from the Latin homilies a number of 'ejaculatory and brief' prayers to the Son.

apostles of Jesus give to him. In order that the holy angels of God may be gracious to us and that they may do all they can on our behalf, it is enough that our attitude to God, as far as possible for human nature, should be one of imitating their devotion, since they imitate God, and that our idea of His Son, the Logos, so far as possible should not be in disaccord with the clearer idea which the holy angels have of him, but should be daily progressing towards theirs in clarity and distinctness.[1] Because he has not read our holy scriptures Celsus replies to his own question as though he were giving our view, as if we say that the angels who come down from God for the benefit of men are *some other kind of being*; and he says that *presumably* we would have meant *daemons*. Celsus fails to notice that the name of daemons is not morally neutral like that of men, among whom some are good and some bad; nor is it good like the name of gods, which is not to be applied to evil daemons[2] or to images or to animals, but by those who know the things of God to beings truly divine and blessed. The name of daemons is always applied to evil powers without the grosser body, and they lead men astray and distract them, and drag them down from God and the world beyond the heavens to earthly things.[3]

6. After this he writes the following statement about the Jews. *The first thing about the Jews which may well cause amazement is that although they worship the heaven and the angels in it,[4] yet they reject its most sacred and powerful parts, the sun, moon, and the other stars, both the fixed stars and the planets. They behave as though it were possible that the whole could be God but its parts not divine, or that one might quite rightly worship beings which are alleged to draw near to people blinded in darkness somewhere as a result of black magic, or who have dreams of obscure phantoms. But as for those beings who prophesy so clearly and distinctly to everyone, through whom showers and heat, clouds and thunders, which they worship, and lightnings and fruitfulness and all productivity are controlled,[5] by whom God is revealed to them, the clearest heralds of the powers above, the truly heavenly messengers (angels), these are thought to be of no account.* In these remarks Celsus seems to me to have been muddled, and to have based his statements on hearsay which he did not understand. For to those who examine the ideas of the Jews and associate with them those of the Christians, it is obvious that the Jews follow the law where God is represented as saying: 'Thou shalt have none

---

[1] Porphyry says that angels should be imitated rather than invoked: de Regressu Animae, frag. 6 Bidez (Aug. de Civ. Dei, x, 26).

[2] Read with K. tr. ἐπὶ φαύλων δαιμονίων.

[3] Origen is aware that in the Greek Bible the word δαίμων is never used in a good sense. Cf. Augustine, de Civ. Dei, IX, 19.   [4] See note on I, 26.

[5] For the heavenly bodies as controllers of the weather, cf. Varro ap. Tertullian, ad Nat. II, 5. Cf. also [Plato,] Epinomis, 984 E. For the value of prayer to the sun and stars, cf. Plotinus, IV, 4, 30.

other gods but me; thou shalt not make to thyself an idol nor any likeness
of anything in the heaven above and in the earth beneath and in the waters
under the earth; thou shalt not bow down to them nor worship them.'¹
And they worship none other than the supreme God who made heaven
and everything else. It is clear, then, that since those who live according
to the law reverence Him who made the heaven, they do not reverence
the heaven together with God. Furthermore, none of those who serve
the Mosaic law worship the angels in heaven; and in the same way that
they do not worship the sun, moon, and stars, 'the world of heaven', they
avoid worshipping heaven and the angels in it, obeying the law which
says: 'And thou shalt not look up to heaven and see the sun and moon and
stars, all the world of heaven, and be led astray to bow down to them and
worship them which the Lord thy God divided unto all the nations.'²

7. Moreover, after taking for granted that the Jews regard heaven as
God he continues by saying this is absurd, criticizing them for worshipping the heaven but not the sun, moon, and stars, in that the Jews do this
as though it were possible for the whole to be God but its parts not divine. By
the whole he seems to mean the heaven, and by its parts the sun, moon,
and stars. However, it is clear that neither Jews nor Christians say that
the heaven is God. But let us assume that he is right that the Jews affirm
that the heaven is God, and suppose also that the sun, moon, and stars are
parts of the heaven (which is not absolutely true any more than that the
animals and plants on earth are parts of the earth). Even following the
opinion of the Greeks how can it be true that if a particular whole is God
then its parts are also divine? Certainly they say that the whole world is
God. The Stoics say it is the first God,³ the Platonists the second,⁴ and
some of them call it the third.⁵ Is it the view of these men that since the
world as a whole is God, then also its parts are divine, so that not only men
but also all the irrational animals are divine, since they are parts of the
world, and ·in addition to these the plants as well? And if the mountains,
rivers, and seas are parts of the world, then since the world is God, are
the rivers and seas also gods?⁶ No. And no Greeks maintain this, though

¹ Exod. xx. 3–5.   ² Deut. iv. 19.
³ Cf. Cicero, *de Nat. Deor.* II, 17, 45; Seneca, *N.Q.* II, 45, 3; Diog. Laert. VII, 137–40;
Diels, *Dox. Gr.* 464.
⁴ Cf. Diels, *Dox. Gr.* 305.
⁵ Origen is probably thinking of Numenius of Apamea, who believed in three gods,
'calling the first Father, the second Maker, the third Product; for in his opinion the cosmos
is the third god...' (Proclus, *in Tim.* 93 A = Numenius, *frag.* 36 Thedinga, *frag.* 24
Leemans). Proclus alludes to this doctrine also in 268 A, B = *frag.* 39 Thedinga.
⁶ J. Geffcken, *Zwei griechische Apologeten*, p. 263, observes that Origen's remarks are
similar to those of Carneades, as quoted by Sextus Emp. *adv. Math.* IX, 182–90 'If Zeus is
a god, Poseidon also is a god....And if Poseidon is a god, Achelous too will be a god;
and if Achelous, Neilos; and if Neilos, every river as well; and if every river, the streams

perhaps they would say that the beings, whether they are daemons or gods as they call them, who have charge of rivers and seas are gods. Even in the opinion of the Greeks who believe in providence Celsus' sweeping statement would be untrue, that if some particular whole is God, the parts of this whole are necessarily divine. It follows from Celsus' remark that if the world is God, everything in it is divine as being parts of the world. According to this conception even animals will be divine, flies, fleas, worms, and every kind of snake, and furthermore birds and fishes. Not even those who maintain that the world is God hold that view. But even if those Jews who live according to the Mosaic law do not know how to interpret the hidden meaning of the words of the law which express some secret doctrine, they do not say that either the heaven or the angels are gods.

8. We said that he has been muddled as a result of misunderstanding what he learnt from hearsay. Let us, then, make this clear also to the best of our ability, and let us show that while Celsus thinks that it is Jewish practice to worship heaven and the angels in it, this is not Jewish at all, but it is a transgression of the law of Judaism, just as it is in the case of the worship of sun, moon, and stars, and of images too. At any rate, you will find particularly in Jeremiah that the word of God through the prophet finds fault with the people of the Jews because they worship these and sacrifice to the queen of heaven and to all the host of heaven.[1] And when the scriptures of the Christians accuse the Jews of their sins, they make it clear that when God forsook that people because of certain sins this sin was among those which they had committed. For in the Acts of the Apostles it is written of the Jews that 'God turned, and gave them up to serve the host of heaven; as it is written in the book of the prophets, Did you offer unto me slain beasts and sacrifices forty years in the wilderness, O house of Israel? And you took up the tabernacle of Moloch and the stars of the god Rompha, the figures which you made to worship them.'[2] Paul, who received a meticulous education in Jewish doctrines and later became a Christian as a result of a miraculous appearance of Jesus, says these words in the Epistle to the Colossians: 'Let no man rob you of your prize of his own mere will, by humility and worshipping of angels, taking his stand upon things which he has seen, vainly puffed up by his fleshly mind, and not holding fast the Head, from whom all the body, being supplied and knit together through the joints and bands, increases with

also will be gods; and if the streams the torrents; but the streams are not gods; neither then is Zeus a god. But if there had been gods, Zeus would have been a god. Therefore there are no gods...' (R.G. Bury's translation in *Loeb Class. Libr.*). Similarly Cicero, *de Nat. Deor.* III, 17, 44 ff.; Lactantius, *Div. Inst.* II, 5.

[1] Cf. Jer. li, 17; vii. 17–18; xix. 13.   [2] Acts vii. 42–3.

the increase of God.'[1] As Celsus had neither read nor heard of these things, for some unknown reason he has made out that the Jews do not transgress the law if they worship the heaven and the angels in it.

9. Because he was still muddled and did not carefully consider the subject, he supposed that the Jews were led on to worship the angels in heaven by the spells used in trickery and sorcery as a result of certain phantoms which the spells cause to appear to people who pronounce them. He did not realize that here also those who do these things break the law which says: 'You shall not follow ventriloquists, and you shall not cleave to wizards to be defiled by them; I am the Lord your God.'[2] Therefore, since he observed that the Jews keep the law,[3] and said that they are those who live according to the law, either he ought not to have attributed this to the Jews at all or, if he did so, ought to have shown that they are Jews who transgress the law if they do such things. Furthermore, just as they are transgressors of the law who *worship beings* because they are *blinded in darkness somewhere as a result of black magic* and *who have dreams of obscure phantoms*, and who reverence beings which are *alleged to draw near* to such people; so also those who sacrifice to sun, moon, and stars, are *quite rightly* regarded as law-breakers. It was not sensible for the same man to say that Jews avoid the worship of sun, moon, and stars, and yet to say that they do not avoid doing so to heaven and the angels.

10. If we, who equally do not worship the angels and the sun, moon, and stars, ought to defend our attitude in refusing to worship those visible and sensible gods as the Greeks call them,[4] we will say that the Mosaic law knows that these have been allotted by God 'to all the nations under the heaven', but not to those who have been chosen by God for a special 'portion'[5] above all the nations upon earth. At any rate, it is written in Deuteronomy: 'And thou shalt not lift up thine eyes unto heaven and see the sun, moon and stars, all the world of heaven, and be led astray to worship them and serve them, which the Lord thy God divided to all the nations under the whole heaven; but the Lord God took us and led us out of the iron furnace, from Egypt, to be a people for his inheritance as at this day.'[6] The people of the Hebrews, then, were called by God to be 'an elect race', 'a royal priesthood', 'a holy nation', and 'a people for His possession'.[7] Concerning them the prediction was given to Abraham by

---

[1] Col. ii. 18–19.   [2] Lev. xix. 31.   [3] Cf. Celsus in v, 25.

[4] Cf. iv, 56. Philo, *de Opif.* 27, says that heaven is the home of 'visible and sensible gods'. Also *de Sp. Leg.* I, 13–14; *de Aetern. Mundi*, 46.

[5] Cf. Deut. xxxii. 9.

[6] Deut. iv. 19–20. The Alexandrines interpret this to mean that God gave the heavenly bodies to the heathen to be worshipped so that they might not be entirely without belief in God and might rise to higher things; cf. Clem. Al. *Strom.* VI, 110, 3; Origen, *Comm. in Joann.* II, 3.   [7] I Pet. ii. 9.

the voice of the Lord to him: 'Look up to the heaven and number the
stars, if you can count them. And he said to him, So shall your seed be.'[1]
A nation which had the hope to become as the stars in heaven would not
have worshipped them; for they were to become like them as a result of
understanding and keeping the law of God. Moreover, it was said to
them: 'The Lord your God has multiplied you, and behold, you are this
day as the stars of heaven in number.'[2] In Daniel also there is this prophecy
about them at the resurrection: 'And in that day thy people shall be saved,
every one that has been written in the book; and many of those who sleep
in the dust of the earth shall rise up, some to eternal life, and some to
shame and eternal contempt; and the wise shall shine forth as the brightness of the firmament, and from the many righteous men radiance shall
shine as the stars for ever and ever.'[3] This is also the reason why when
Paul deals with the resurrection he says: 'And there are heavenly bodies
and earthly bodies; but the glory of the heavenly bodies is one, and that
of the earthly is another. There is one glory of the sun, and another glory
of the moon, and another glory of the stars; for one star differs from
another star in glory. So also is the resurrection of the dead.'[4]

For those, then, who have been taught to rise nobly above all created
things and to hope for the best blessings for themselves from God as
a result of living a very good life, and who have heard the sayings 'You
are the light of the world', and 'let your light so shine before men that
they may see your good works and glorify your Father who is in heaven';[5]
who train themselves to obtain the shining and undefiled wisdom, or even
have obtained that which is an effulgence of eternal light:[6] it is unreasonable
that they should have been amazed at the visible light of the sun, moon
and stars, to such an extent that because of their visible light they should
somehow regard themselves as beneath them and worship them. For
they possess a great intellectual light of knowledge and a 'true light', and
a 'light of the world', and a 'light of men'.[7] If they ought to worship
them, they ought not to do so because of the visible light which amazes the
masses, but because of the intellectual and true light, supposing that the
stars in heaven are also rational and good beings[8] and have been enlightened

---

[1] Gen. xv. 5.   [2] Deut. i. 10.   [3] Dan. xii. 1–3.
[4] I Cor. xv. 40–2.   [5] Matt. v. 14, 16.   [6] Cf. Wisd. of Sol. vi. 13; vii. 26.
[7] John i. 9; viii. 12; ix. 5; i. 4.
[8] That the stars are spiritual beings was held by Plato (*Tim.* 40 B) and the Stoics (*S.V.F.*
II, 686 ff.). Origen found it in Job xxv. 5 'The stars are not clean in his sight', since it
implies that they must be capable of sin (*Comm. in Joann.* I, 35). Cf. VIII, 67 below; *de Princ.*
I, 7, 2; *Comm. in Matt.* XIII, 20. He is not so positive in *de Princ.* II, 11, 7, where it is
a question to be answered when the saints reach heaven. For discussion, see Huet's
Origeniana II, 8 (Lommatzsch, XXIII, 115 ff.). It is of interest that Ambrose (*Ep.* XXXIV, 7)
takes Origen's view.

by the light of knowledge from the wisdom which is 'an effulgence of eternal light'.[1] Furthermore, their visible light is the work of the Creator of the universe, while it is probable that their intellectual light comes from the freedom of choice which they possess.

11. However, not even their intellectual light ought to be worshipped by anyone who sees and understands the true light, since even the stars have been given their light only[2] by participation in the true light, not by anyone who sees God, the Father of the true light; it is well said of Him that 'God is light, and in him is no darkness at all'.[3] Those who worship sun, moon and stars because their light is visible and heavenly would not worship a spark of fire or a lamp on earth, because they see that the lights which they consider worthy of worship possess an incomparable superiority over the light of sparks and lamps. Similarly those who have realized how 'God is light', and who have comprehended how the Son of God is 'the true light, which lightens every man coming into the world',[4] and have also understood what he meant when he said 'I am the light of the world',[5] would not reasonably worship the light in the sun, moon and stars which is like a dim spark compared with God who is light of the true light.

We do not say these things about the sun, moon and stars with the intention of disparaging the vast creations of God, nor because we say with Anaxagoras that they are 'masses of hot metal',[6] but because we perceive the superiority of the divinity of God which is beyond description and also that of His only-begotten Son who is far above all things. Because we are convinced that the sun itself and the moon and stars pray to the supreme God through His only-begotten Son, we consider that we ought not to pray to beings who pray themselves, since even they wish to refer us to the God to whom they pray rather than to bring us down to their level or to take the power of answering our prayers away from God and arrogate it to themselves.

I will also use this illustration of my point concerning them.[7] When our Saviour and Lord once heard the words 'Good master', he referred the man who said this on to his Father, saying 'Why do you call me good? There is none good but one, God the Father.'[8] If the Son of the Father's love[9] was right in saying this, he being the image of God's goodness, how much more would the sun say to its worshippers: 'Why do you worship

---

[1] Wisd. of Sol. vii. 26.   [2] Read καὶ ταῦτ' εἰ ἄρα with We., K. tr.
[3] I John i. 5.   [4] John i. 9.   [5] John viii. 12.
[6] Diog. Laert. 11, 8 'He maintained that the sun is a mass of hot metal and larger than the Peloponnese.' Cf. Diels, *Dox. Gr.* 348; Josephus, *c. Ap.* 11, 265, etc.
[7] Origen has the same point with the same illustration in *Exh. Mart.* 7.
[8] Mark x. 17–18; Luke xviii. 18–19.   [9] Col. i. 13.

me? For "thou shalt worship the Lord thy God and him only shalt thou
serve".¹ I and all my associates worship and serve Him.' And if someone is
less exalted than the sun, such a man should no less pray to the Logos of
God who is able to heal him, and far more to his Father who also to the
righteous men of earlier times 'sent forth his Word and healed them and
delivered them from their distresses'.²

12. God in His goodness comes down to men not spatially but in His
providence,³ and the Son of God was not only with his disciples at that
particular time, but is also with them always, in fulfilment of his promise
'Lo, I am with you all the days until the end of the world.'⁴ And if
'a branch cannot bear fruit if it does not abide in the vine',⁵ obviously the
disciples of the Logos, the spiritual branches of the true vine, the Logos,
are not able to bear the fruits of virtue unless they abide in the true vine,
the Christ of God, who is even with us who are down on earth in space.
He is with those everywhere who cling fast to him and furthermore is even
with those everywhere who do not know him. This is made clear by John
the author of the Gospel when he quotes the words of John the Baptist,
saying 'There stands one in your midst whom you do not know, coming
after me.'⁶ He has filled the heaven and the earth, and says 'Do not I fill
the heaven and the earth? saith the Lord';⁷ and he is with us and near us
(for I believe Him when he says 'I am a God at hand, and not a God far
off, saith the Lord').⁸ It is wrong, then, to attempt to pray to a being who
does not permeate the whole world such as the sun or moon or one of the
stars.

But, to quote Celsus' actual words, suppose that *the sun, moon, and
stars do prophesy showers and heat, clouds and thunders.* Ought we not
therefore, if they prophesy such important matters, to worship God whom
they serve by prophesying, and reverence Him rather than His prophets?
Suppose that they also prophesy *lightnings and fruitfulness and all productivity,* and that all things of this nature are under their control; yet we
would not on this account worship beings who themselves worship God,
just as we would not worship Moses and those after him who prophesied
by divine inspiration of matters more important than showers and heat,
clouds and thunder, lightnings, fruitfulness, and all productivity of the
physical world. Moreover, even if the sun, moon and stars were able to
prophesy about more important things than showers, not even so would
we worship them but the Author of the prophecies which are in them, and
the Logos of God who mediates them.

¹ Matt. iv. 10. ² Ps. cvi. 20.
³ Cf. IV, 5, 12, above; Philo, *de Conf. Ling.* 134 ff.
⁴ Matt. xxviii. 20. ⁵ John xv. 4–6. ⁶ John i. 26–7; see II, 9.
⁷ Jer. xxiii. 24. ⁸ Jer. xxiii. 23.

Furthermore, supposing that they are His *heralds* and *the truly heavenly messengers*, ought we not therefore to worship the God whom they proclaim and announce rather than His heralds and angels?

13. Celsus assumes that we think the sun, moon and stars are *of no account*. We believe about them that even they are waiting for the 'revelation of the sons of God', having been subjected to the futility of material bodies for the time being 'on account of him who subjected them in hope'.[1] If Celsus had read also countless other things which we say about the sun, moon and stars, such as 'Praise him all ye stars and light', and 'Praise him ye heavens of heavens',[2] he would not have attributed to us the assertion that the vast bodies which mightily praise God are of no account. Nor did Celsus know the saying: 'For the earnest expectation of the creation waits for the revelation of the sons of God; for the creation was subjected to futility, not of its own will, but by reason of him who subjected it, in hope that the creation itself also shall be delivered from the bondage of corruption into the liberty of the glory of the children of God.'[3]

With this we may come to an end of our defence in reply to the charge that we do not worship the sun, moon and stars. And let us quote the next passage, that after this by God's grace we may give the reply to it which shall be given to us from the light of the truth.

14. This is what he says! *It is foolish of them also to suppose that, when God applies the fire (like a cook!),*[4] *all the rest of mankind will be thoroughly roasted and that they alone will survive, not merely those who are alive at the time but those also long dead who will rise up from the earth possessing the same bodies as before.*[5] *This is simply the hope of worms. For what sort of human soul would have any further desire*[6] *for a body that has rotted? The fact that this doctrine is not shared by some of you [Jews] and by some Christians*[7] *shows its utter repulsiveness, and that it is both revolting and impossible. For what sort of body, after being entirely corrupted, could return to its original nature and that same condition which it had before it was dissolved? As they have nothing to say in reply, they escape to a most*

---

[1] Rom. viii. 19-20, similarly interpreted in *de Princ.* I, 7, 5; *Exh. Mart.* 7; *Comm. in Rom.* VII, 4.

[2] Ps. cxlviii. 3-4.   [3] Rom. viii. 19-21.

[4] For hell-fire, cf. Celsus in IV, 23; VII, 9.

[5] Cf. Celsus in VIII, 49. The usual Church view is represented by Tertullian, *Apol.* 48; *de Anima*, 56; *de Carnis Resurr.* etc.

[6] Read ποθήσειεν ⟨ἄν⟩ with Bader.

[7] Among the Jews the doctrine of resurrection was rejected by the Sadducees, among others (see Bousset and Gressmann, *Die Religion des Judenthums* (1926), pp. 273 f.); among Christians by the Gnostics. Cf. Irenaeus, v, 13, 2 (Harvey, II, 356); Tertullian, *de Carnis Resurr.* 48-9.

outrageous refuge by saying that 'anything is possible to God'.[1] *But, indeed, neither can God do what is shameful nor does He desire what is contrary to nature. If you were to desire something abominable in your wickedness, not even God would be able to do this, and you ought not to believe at all that your desire will be fulfilled. For God is not the author of sinful desire or of disorderly confusion, but of what is naturally just and right. For the soul He might be able to provide an everlasting life; but as Heraclitus says, 'corpses ought to be thrown away as worse than dung'.*[2] *As for the flesh, which is full of things which it is not even nice to mention, God would neither desire nor be able to make it everlasting contrary to reason. For He Himself is the reason of everything that exists; therefore He is not able to do anything contrary to reason or to His own character.*

15. See now, to start with, how he pours ridicule upon the idea of the conflagration of the world, which is a doctrine maintained also by some Greeks whose philosophy cannot be despised,[3] and wants to make out that when we teach the doctrine of the world-conflagration we are making God like a cook. He has not realized that according to the opinion of some Greeks (probably borrowing from the very ancient nation of the Hebrews)[4] the fire that is brought on the world is purifying, and it is probable that it is applied to each individual who needs judgment by fire together with healing. The fire burns but does not consume utterly those who have no matter which needs to be destroyed by it, while it burns and does utterly consume those who have built 'wood, hay, or stubble'[5] on the building (as it is allegorically called) by their actions, words, and thoughts. The divine scriptures say that the Lord 'like the fire of a smelting-furnace and like a cleaner's herb'[6] will visit each individual who is in need, because they have been adulterated by the evil flood of matter, as it were, which results from sin; and I say that they need fire which, so to speak, refines those adulterated by copper, tin, and lead. Anyone who is interested may learn these things from the prophet Ezekiel.[7]

That we do not say *God applies fire like a cook*, but that God is a benefactor of those who are in need of pain and fire, the prophet Isaiah will also bear witness, where he is recorded to have said to a sinful nation: 'Because thou hast a coal-fire sit on it; it shall be a help to thee.'[8] The Logos, accommodating himself to what is appropriate to the masses who will read the Bible, wisely utters threatening words with a hidden meaning to frighten people who cannot in any other way turn from the flood of iniquities. Even so, however, the observant person will find an indication

[1] For discussion of this, cf. my remarks in *Harv. Theol. Rev.* XLI (1948), pp. 83 ff., and R. Walzer, *Galen on Jews and Christians* (1949), pp. 28 ff.   [2] *Frag.* 96 Diels.
[3] The Stoics.   [4] Cf. IV, 21, above.   [5] I Cor. iii. 12.
[6] Mal. iii. 2.   [7] Cf. Ezek. xxii. 18.   [8] Isa. xlvii. 14–15.

of the end for which the threats and pains are inflicted on those who suffer. At the present moment it is enough to quote from Isaiah, 'For my name's sake will I show mine anger, and I will bring my honours upon thee, so that I will not destroy thee.'[1] But we have been compelled to hint at truths which are not suitable for the simple-minded believers who need elementary words which come down to their own level, in order that we may not seem to allow Celsus' attack to pass without refutation when he says *When God applies the fire like a cook.*

16. From what has been said it will be clear to those who have some intelligence how we should meet this objection also: *All the rest of mankind will be thoroughly roasted and they alone will survive.* It is not remarkable if this sort of opinion has been held by those among us called by the word 'the foolish things of this world, and the base things, and the things that are despised, and that are not', whom 'through the foolishness of the preaching God was pleased to save,[2] since in the wisdom of God the world by wisdom knew not God', because they are not capable of a clear perception of the question nor willing to spend time searching the scriptures, though Jesus says 'search the scriptures'.[3] Nor is it amazing if they hold such ideas about the fire that is applied by God and about the things that will happen to sinners. Probably, just as some words are suitable for use with children and are appropriate for their tender age, in order to exhort them to be better, because they are still very young, so also with those whom the word calls 'the foolish things of this world and the base things and the things that are despised'[4] the ordinary interpretation of punishments is suitable because they have not the capacity for any other means of conversion and of repentance from many evils, except that of fear and the suggestion of punishment. The Bible accordingly says that only those who have been utterly pure in doctrine, morals, and mind will remain untouched by fire and punishments; whereas it says that people not of this character, who need the ministry of punishment by fire according to their merits, will suffer these punishments for an appointed end such as may be fittingly applied by God to those who, although made in His image, have lived contrary to the intention of the nature that is in His image. This is our reply to his remark that *all the rest of mankind will be thoroughly roasted and they alone will survive.*

---

[1] Isa. xlviii. 9.
[2] The MS. text here is very difficult, as Wendland saw (*G.G.A.* (1899), pp. 290, 621). There is, however, no need to follow him in assuming a lacuna. The problematic ἅτινα must be object to σῶσαι, and I would bracket τοὺς πιστεύοντας αὐτῷ as a scribal interpolation from I Cor. i. 21; alternatively it is possible to read πιστεύοντα αὐτῷ. In any event, the difficulty arises from the scribe's memory of the N.T. text.
[3] John v. 39.   [4] I Cor. i. 27–8.

17. Then after this, because he has misunderstood either the holy scriptures or people who have not understood them themselves, he asserts that we say that we Christians alone will survive at the time when judgment will be brought on the world by purifying fire, and *not only those of us who are living at the time, but also those long dead.* He did not understand what was said with a certain secret wisdom by the apostle of Jesus: 'We shall not all sleep, but we shall be changed in a moment, in the twinkling of an eye, at the last trumpet; for the trumpet shall sound, and the dead shall rise incorruptible and we shall be changed.'[1] And he ought to have attended to what the author of these words meant when, as being by no means dead himself, he distinguished between them and himself and people in the same state as himself. After saying 'and the dead shall rise incorruptible', he goes on 'and we shall be changed'. To confirm that this was the apostle's meaning when he wrote what I have quoted from the First Epistle to the Corinthians, I will also quote the passage from the First Epistle to the Thessalonians where, as a man who is alive and awake and different from those who are asleep, Paul speaks as follows: 'For I tell you this by the word of the Lord, that we who are alive who are left until the coming of the Lord shall not precede those who are asleep, because the Lord Himself shall descend from heaven with a shout, with the voice of an archangel and with the trump of God.' Then after this, as he knows that the dead in Christ are different from himself and people in the same state as himself, he goes on to say: 'The dead in Christ shall rise first, then we who are alive that are left shall together with them be caught up in the clouds to meet the Lord in the air.'[2]

18. He has further made fun of the resurrection of the flesh which, while preached in the churches, is understood more clearly by the intelligent. But it is not necessary to quote again his words which have been mentioned once already. Let us, then, state to the best of our ability and give a brief account of this problem in a form exactly suited to our readers, since this is a defence addressed to one foreign to the faith, and is written because of those who are still babes and who are tossed to and fro and carried about 'by every wind of doctrine, by the sleight of men, in craftiness after the wiles of error'.[3] Neither we nor the divine scriptures maintain that those long dead will rise up from the earth and live in the same bodies without undergoing any change for the better; and in saying this Celsus falsely accuses us. For we also hear many scriptures that speak of the resurrection in a way worthy of God. But for the moment it is enough to quote the words of Paul from the First Epistle to the Corinthians, where he says: 'But some one will say, How are the dead raised?

---

[1] 1 Cor. xv. 51–2.   [2] I Thess. iv. 15–17. Cf. II, 65 above.   [3] Eph. iv. 14.

And with what kind of body do they come? You foolish man, that which you yourself sow is not brought to life unless it dies, and what you sow is not the body that shall be, but a mere grain, it may be of wheat or of some other kind; but God gives it a body even as it pleased him, and to each seed a body of its own.'[1] Notice how he here says that 'the body that shall be' is not sown, but he says that as it were a resurrection takes place from that mere grain sown and cast in the earth, since God gives to each seed a body of its own. For from the seed that has been thrown down there is raised in some cases an ear of corn, and in others a tree[2] such as the mustard, or a still larger tree in the case of an olive-stone or one of the other fruits.

19. Accordingly 'God gives to each a body as he pleased', as with seeds that are sown so also with those who are sown, so to speak, in death, and who at the appropriate time out of the bodies that are sown take up the body which is appointed by God for each man in accordance with his merits. We also hear the Bible teaching by many passages that there is a difference between the body that is, as it were, sown, and that which is, as it were, raised from it. It says: 'It is sown in corruption, it is raised in incorruption; it is sown in dishonour, it is raised in honour; it is sown in weakness, it is raised in power; it is sown a natural body, it is raised a spiritual body.' Anyone who is able may further understand what is meant when it says: 'As is the earthy, such are they also who are earthy; and as is the heavenly, such are they also that are heavenly. And as we have borne the image of the earthy, so let us also bear the image of the heavenly.' Though the apostle wants to hide the secret truths on this point which are not appropriate for the simple-minded and for the ears of the common crowd who are led on to live better lives by their belief, nevertheless to prevent misunderstanding of his words he was later forced after the words 'let us bear the image of the heavenly' to say as follows: 'Now this I say, brethren, that flesh and blood cannot inherit the kingdom of God; neither does corruption inherit incorruption.' Then because he is aware that there is something secret and mysterious about this doctrine, and as it was fitting for one who left behind in writing for posterity the ideas which he had thought out, he goes on to say 'Behold, I tell you a mystery.'[3] This word is usually applied to the deeper and more mystical doctrines which are rightly concealed from the multitude. Thus it is also written in Tobit, 'it is good to hide a king's mystery'; but with reference to that which is glorious and suitable for the multitude it goes on 'it is

---

[1] I Cor. xv. 35–8.

[2] Read with Wif. στάχυος ἐν τοῖς τοιοῖσδε, ⟨δένδρου δὲ ἐν τοῖς τοιοῖσδε⟩ οἱονεὶ ἐν νάπῦι ἢ ἔτι μείζονος. . . . .

[3] I Cor. xv. 42–4, 48–9, 50–1.

good to reveal the works of God gloriously',[1] the truth being expressed by terms which are on their level.

Therefore, our hope is not one of *worms*, nor does our soul *desire a body that has rotted*. But though it may need a body in order to pass from one place to another, the soul that has studied wisdom, according to the saying 'the mouth of the righteous man will study wisdom',[2] understands the difference between the earthly house which is destroyed in which is the tabernacle, and the tabernacle itself in which those who are righteous groan being burdened, not because they desire to put off the tabernacle, but because they want to be clothed upon, in order that as a result of this 'mortality may be swallowed up by life'.[3] For since the nature of the body is to be entirely corruptible, this mortal tabernacle must put on incorruptibility, and its other part, which is mortal and capable of death which is the consequence of sin, must put on immortality; so that when corruptibility shall put on incorruptibility and mortality immortality, then shall come to pass that which was foretold long ago by the prophets, the destruction of death's victory,[4] in that it had conquered and subjected us to itself, and of the sting by which it stings the soul that has not been entirely protected and inflicts upon it the wounds resulting from sin.

20. Our doctrine of the resurrection, however, has been set forth in part so far as possible at the present time (for elsewhere we have written a treatise on the doctrine, in which we discussed the subject at length).[5] But now, as is reasonable, we have to tackle Celsus' assertions. He neither understood the teaching of our Bible, nor was able to judge that it is not right to think that the meaning of those wise men is represented by people who do not profess to have any more than mere faith in regard to Christian doctrine. Let us show, then, that utterly absurd ideas are believed by men, who on grounds of their rational insight and dialectical speculations may not be lightly regarded. And if one may jeer at anyone for believing in paltry stories fit for old women, it is more appropriate in their case than in ours.

The Stoics maintain that the universe periodically undergoes a conflagration and after that a restoration of order in which everything is indistinguishable from what happened in the previous restoration of the world. All those who have felt embarrassed by the doctrine[6] have said that

---

[1] Tobit xii. 7.   [2] Ps. xxxvi. 30.   [3] Cf. II Cor. v. 1–4.   [4] Cf. I Cor. xv. 53.

[5] This was an early work, mentioned in *de Princ.* II, 10, 1. Origen wrote two books and two dialogues on the resurrection, which together were reckoned as four books. Only fragments survive; they are printed in Lommatzsch, XVII, 53–64.

[6] For the doctrine, see IV, 67–8. Some later Stoics rejected it, notably Panaetius (Diog. Laert. VII, 142; Cicero, *de Nat. Deor.* II, 46, 118; Diels, *Dox. Gr.* 469) and Boethus (Philo, *de Aetern. Mundi*, 78 ff.). Clement suggests the correspondence with the Christian idea of resurrection (*Strom.* v, 9, 4).

there is a slight and very minute difference between one period and the events in the period before it. Now these men say that in the succeeding period it will be the same[1] again: Socrates will again be son of Sophroniscus and be an Athenian, and Phaenarete will again marry Sophroniscus and give birth to him. Therefore, although they do not use the word 'resurrection' at least they have the idea when they say that Socrates will rise again after originating from the seed of Sophroniscus and will be formed in the womb of Phaenarete, and after being educated at Athens will become a philosopher; and something like his previous philosophy will rise again and will similarly be indistinguishable from the one before. Moreover, Anytus and Meletus will again rise up as Socrates' accusers, and the council of the Areopagus will condemn him. And, what is more ludicrous than this, Socrates will put on clothes which will be indistinguishable from those of the previous period, and will be in poverty and in a city called Athens which will be indistinguishabie from that before. Phalaris will again be a tyrant, with a cruelty indistinguishable from that of the previous period, and will condemn men also indistinguishable from those before. But why need I enumerate the doctrine about these matters held by the Stoic philosophers, even though Celsus does not laugh at it but probably even respects it, since he thinks that *Zeno was wiser than Jesus*.

21. Furthermore, though the Pythagoreans and Platonists maintain that the whole is indestructible, yet they fall into similar absurdities. For when in certain fixed cycles the stars adopt the same configurations and relationships to each other, they say that everything on earth is in the same position as it was at the last time when the relationship of the stars in the universe to one another was the same.[2] According, then, to this doctrine it is inevitable that when after a long period the stars come into the same relationship to one another which they had in the time of Socrates, Socrates will again be born of the same parents and suffer the same attacks, and will be accused by Anytus and Meletus, and be condemned by the council of the Areopagus. Moreover, are the learned men among the Egyptians who have similar traditions respected and not laughed at by Celsus and his like? While as for us who say that the universe is cared for by God in accordance with the conditions of the free will of each man, and that as far as possible it is always being led on to be better, and who know that the nature of our free will is to admit various possibilities (for it cannot achieve the entirely unchangeable nature of God), do we appear to say nothing worthy of trial and study?

[1] Read οὗτοι δὴ with Wif. and ταὐτὰ ἔσεσθαι with K. tr.
[2] Cf. Plato, *Timaeus* 39 D. For the Great Year see the discussion in W. L. Knox, *St Paul and the Church of the Gentiles* (1939), pp. 2 ff.; W. Gundel, art. 'Planeten', in P.-W. xx, 2 (1950), 2095 f.

22. However, let no one suppose that because we say this we are among those who, although they are called Christians, deny the scriptural doctrine of resurrection. For the consequence of their opinion is that they are quite unable to show that, so to speak, the ear or tree rises up from a grain of corn or from one of the other seeds. But we are convinced that that which is sown is not brought to life unless it dies, and that it is not the body that shall be which is sown. For 'God gives it a body, as it pleased him'. After it was sown in corruption, He raises it in incorruption; and after it was sown in dishonour, He raises it in glory; and after it was sown in weakness, He raises it in power; and after it was sown a natural body, He raises it a spiritual body.[1] We preserve both the doctrine of the Church of Christ and the greatness of God's promise, establishing that it is a possibility not by mere assertion but by argument. For we know that even if heaven and earth and the things in them pass away, yet the words about each doctrine, being like parts in a whole or forms in a species, which were uttered by the Logos who was the divine Logos with God in the beginning,[2] will in no wise pass away. For we would pay heed to him who says: 'Heaven and earth shall pass away, but my words shall not pass away.'[3]

23. Therefore, we do not say that after the body has been corrupted it will *return to its original nature*, just as the grain of corn that has been corrupted will not return to be a grain of corn. For we hold that, as from the grain of corn an ear rises up, so in the body there lies a certain principle[4] which is not corrupted from which the body is raised in incorruption. But it is the Stoics who say that *after the body has been entirely corrupted it will return to its original nature*, because they believe in the doctrine that each world-period is indistinguishable; and it is they who say that it will again be composed in *that same first condition which it had before it was dissolved*, proving this, as they imagine, on the ground of logical necessities. And we do not *escape to a most outrageous refuge by saying that anything is possible to God*. We know that we may not understand the word 'anything' of things which do not exist or which are inconceivable.[5] But we do say that *God cannot do what is shameful*, since then God could not possibly be God. For if God does anything shameful He is not God.[6]

But when he affirms that God also *does not desire that which is contrary*

---

[1] Cf. I Cor. xv. 36–44.   [2] John i. 1.   [3] Matt. xxiv. 35.

[4] Cf. vii, 32, and further references in *Harv. Theol. Rev.* xli (1948), p. 101.

[5] For limits to divine omnipotence, cf. iii, 70; *de Princ.* ii, 9, 1; iv, 4, 8; *Comm. ser. in Matt.* 95 'quantum ad potentiam quidem dei omnia possibilia sunt sive iusta sive iniusta, quantum autem ad iustitiam eius...non sunt.'

[6] Euripides, *frag.* 292 (Nauck) εἰ θεοί τι δρῶσιν αἰσχρόν, οὐκ εἰσὶν θεοί. The quotation was hackneyed; cf. (Ps.-)Justin, *de Monarchia* 5; Plutarch, *Mor.* 21 A, 1049 F.

to nature, we have to make a distinction in his remark. If anyone says evil
is what is contrary to nature, we also hold that God does not desire
what is contrary to nature, neither what is the result of sin, nor what is
done irrationally. But if he means what is done according to the Word of
God and to His will, obviously that must not be contrary to nature; for
God's actions are not contrary to nature, even though they may be
miraculous or may seem to some people to be so. If we are forced to use
this terminology, we will say that compared with what is commonly[1]
regarded as nature some things which sometimes God might do transcend
nature, such as lifting man up beyond human nature and making him
change to a superior and more divine nature, and keeping him in this
position for so long as the man who is kept shows by his actions that he
desires Him to do this.

24. Having said once that God desires nothing that He cannot rightly
do, which would mean that he ceased to be God, we will say that if man in
his wickedness desires anything *abominable*, God would not be able to
grant this. But here we are not concerned to disagree with Celsus' statements; we give them an honest examination and would agree that *God is
not the author of sinful desire or of disorderly confusion, but of what is naturally
just and right*, seeing that He is author of everything good. What is more,
we admit that He *can provide an everlasting life for the soul*, and say not
only that He can but that He actually does so. His last remarks cause us
not the least difficulty. Nor does the verse of Heraclitus which Celsus
quoted, that '*corpses ought to be thrown away as worse than dung*'. Yet
someone might say even of this that while dung should be thrown away,
yet human corpses should not be thrown away out of respect for the soul
that has dwelt within, and especially if it is a soul of a good character. For
according to good customs they are thought worthy of burial with all the
honour possible appropriate to their character so that, as far as possible,
we may not insult the soul that has dwelt within by casting out the body
when the soul has gone out of it, as we do with the bodies of beasts.[2] Let
us not, therefore, suppose that contrary to reason God wishes to make
everlasting either the grain of corn, rather than if at all[3] the ear which it
produces, or the body sown in corruption, rather than the body which
rises from it in incorruption. Further, in Celsus' view *the reason of
everything is God Himself.* But we believe it is His Son. In our philosophy
about him we say: 'In the beginning was the Logos, and the Logos was
with God, and the Logos was God.'[4] And we would also hold that *God
is not able to do anything contrary to reason or to His own character.*

---

[1] K. tr. proposes κοινότερον.   [2] Cf. IV, 59.
[3] Read with We. ἀλλ' εἰ ἄρα τὸν ἐξ αὐτοῦ στάχυν, μήτε....   [4] John i. 1.

25. Let us also look at Celsus' next passage which reads as follows: *Now the Jews became an individual nation, and made laws according to the custom of their country; and they maintain these laws among themselves at the present day, and observe a worship which may be very peculiar but is at least traditional. In this respect they behave like the rest of mankind, because each nation follows its traditional customs, whatever kind may happen to be established. This situation seems to have come to pass not only because it came into the head of different people to think differently and because it is necessary to preserve the established social conventions, but also because it is probable that from the beginning the different parts of the earth were allotted to different overseers, and are governed in this way by having been divided between certain authorities.[1] In fact, the practices done by each nation are right when they are done in the way that pleases the overseers; and it is impious to abandon the customs which have existed in each locality from the beginning.* Here Celsus affirms that the Jews, who were Egyptians in early times,[2] later became an individual nation and made laws which they still maintain. And, not to repeat the words of Celsus which we have quoted, he also says that it has come to pass that they observe their traditional rites just like the other nations who follow their own customs. And he states a more profound reason why it has come about that the Jews follow their traditional customs, giving a veiled hint that the laws of each people were made in collaboration with the lawgivers by those beings which obtained the lot of being overseers of the earth. He seems, therefore, to indicate that some being or beings watch over the land of the Jews and the nation inhabiting it, and that the laws of the Jews were appointed by him or them in collaboration with Moses.

26. One ought, he says, to keep the laws *not only because it came into the head of different people to think differently and because it is necessary to preserve the established social conventions, but also because it is probable that from the beginning the different parts of the earth were allotted to different overseers, and are governed by having been divided in this way.* Then as though he had forgotten what he said against the Jews, Celsus now includes them too in a general approval of all those who keep their traditional customs, saying: *In fact, the practices done by each nation are right when they are done in the way that pleases the overseers.* Consider whether it is not obvious from his statement that he wants the Jew who lives by his own laws not to abandon them because he would act impiously if he did so. For he says: *It is impious to abandon the customs which have existed in each locality from the beginning.*

---

[1] Cf. VIII, 35, 53, 67. See Introduction, p. xx.
[2] Cf. III, 5 ff.

In reply to this I would like to ask him or those who agree with him who then it might be who distributed the different parts of the earth to different overseers from the beginning, and in particular allotted the land of the Jews and the Jewish people to the being or beings who obtained it. Was it Zeus, as Celsus would call him, who assigned the Jewish nation and their land to some power or powers, and who wanted the one who obtained Judaea to make such laws for the Jews? Or did this occur contrary to His will? However he replies you perceive that the argument will be put into difficulties. And if the parts of the earth were not assigned to their overseers by someone, then each one took possession of his own division of the earth according to chance, at random, and without the commission of any superintendent.[1] But this is monstrous and to a large extent[2] does away with the providence of the supreme God.

27. Let anyone who likes explain how the parts of the earth have been divided between certain authorities and are governed by those who have oversight of them. And let him also inform us how the practices that are done by each nation are right when they are done in the way that pleases the overseers, and whether for example the Scythians' laws are right which allow parricide, or the Persians' laws which do not prohibit mothers from being married to their own sons or fathers to their own daughters. Why should I make a selection from the instances collected by those who have concerned themselves with the laws of the different nations to raise the objection as to how it can be right for each nation to keep the laws on the ground that they please the overseers? Let Celsus inform us how it is impious to break ancestral laws which allow men to marry their wives and daughters, or which say that it is blessed to depart this life by being strangled, or assert that complete purification is attained by those who surrender themselves to the flames and depart from life by means of fire. And how is it impious to break laws such as those for example among the Taurians, where strangers are offered as victims to Artemis, or among some Libyans, where they sacrifice children to Kronos?[3] Yet this is the logical consequence of Celsus' opinion that it is impious for the Jews to break the traditional laws which lay down that they ought not to worship any other God than the Creator of the universe. According to

---

[1] Cf. Origen's similar remarks about the angels in *Hom. in Iesu Nave*, XXIII, 3.

[2] Read ⟨οὐ⟩ μετρίως with We.

[3] Origen's four instances are stock examples in the traditional arguments about the relativity of moral codes and religious practices; cf. my remarks in *J.T.S.* XLVIII (1947), p. 35, and for the theme, e.g. Lucian, *Jupp. Trag.* 42. For the religious significance of death by hanging, cf. J. G. Frazer, *The Golden Bough* (3rd ed.), *Adonis, Attis, Osiris* (1914), I, pp. 288–97; for cremation as facilitating the soul's ascent at death cf. Cumont, *Lux perpetua*, p. 390, but this view was not universal; cf. A. D. Nock, 'Cremation and Burial in the Roman Empire', in *H.T.R.* xxv (1932), pp. 321–59.

his view piety will not be divine by nature, but a matter of arbitrary arrangement and opinion; for among some people it is pious to worship the crocodile and to eat some animal worshipped by others, and among others it is pious to worship the calf, and among others to regard the goat as a god. Thus the same person will be making things to be pious by the standard of one set of laws and impious by another, which is the most monstrous thing of all.

28. Probably, however, the reply would be made to this that the man who observes the traditional customs is pious and not at all impious provided that[1] he does not keep those of other people as well; and again, that the man thought to be impious among some people is not impious when he worships his own deities in accordance with the traditional customs and makes war against and consumes the deities of those who have laws of the opposite kind. Consider whether he does not show considerable confusion in his conception of what is righteous and holy and pious, in that it is not distinctly conceived and has not any unique nature, and does not mark as pious those who act in accordance with it. If piety and holiness and righteousness are reckoned to be relative, so that one and the same thing is pious and impious under differing conditions and laws, consider whether we should not logically reckon self-control also as relative, and courage, intelligence, knowledge, and the other virtues.[2] Nothing could be more absurd than this.

What has been said is enough as a simple and ordinary argument against the remarks of Celsus which we have quoted. But as we think that some of those who are more capable of examining these problems may read this book, let us take the risk and give an account of a few of the more profound truths which have a mystical and secret conception of the way in which different regions of the earth were divided from the beginning among different overseers. And to the best of our ability let us show that the doctrine is free from the absurdities which we have mentioned.

29. Celsus seems to me to have misunderstood certain very mysterious truths about the division of the regions of the earth. Even Greek history touches on them in some way when it introduces the idea that some of the supposed gods contended with one another over Attica,[3] and makes some of the supposed gods confess in the poets that some places are closely

---

[1] Read ἐπειδὴ τὰ with We.

[2] The Stoics denied that virtues and vices were relative; cf. Chrysippus ap. Galen, *de Hippocr. et Plat. decr.* 7, p. 583, ed. Müller (*S.V.F.* III, 259). See further *S.V.F.* II, 399–404.

[3] For the contest between Athena and Poseidon for Attica, see J. G. Frazer on Apollodorus, *Bibl.* III, 14, 1 (177–9); A. B. Cook, *Zeus* III, pp. 750 ff.

related to them. Barbarian history also, and especially that of the Egyptians, shows something of the kind in the matter of the division of the so-called nomes of Egypt, when it says that the same Athena who obtained Sais also possesses Attica.[1] Egyptian scholars may say countless things of this sort, though I do not know whether they include the Jews and their land in the division and assign them to the control of some power. But that is enough for the present about what is said outside the divine word.

We say that Moses, the prophet of God as we believe and His true servant, gives an account of the division of the peoples of the earth in the song in Deuteronomy where he speaks as follows: 'When the Most High divided the nations, as he scattered the sons of Adam, he set the boundaries of the nations according to the number of the angels of God; and the Lord's portion was Jacob his people, Israel the lot of his inheritance.'[2] In the book entitled Genesis the same Moses speaks about the division of the nations under the form of a story, as follows: 'And the whole earth was of one language and all had one speech. And it came to pass that as they moved from the east they found a plain in the land of Shinar; and they dwelt there.' And a little later 'the Lord', he says, 'came down to see the city and the tower which the sons of men had built. And the Lord said, Behold they are one race and have all one language; and this is what they have begun to do, and now nothing will escape from them which they may attempt to do. Come and let us go down and there confound their language, that each man may not understand his neighbour's speech. And the Lord scattered them from thence upon the face of all the earth, and they left off building the city and the tower. Therefore was its name called Confusion, because there the Lord God confused the languages of all the earth; and the Lord God scattered them from thence upon the face of all the earth.'[3] And in the book entitled the Wisdom of Solomon, speaking of wisdom and the people who lived at the time of the confusion of languages, when the division of the nations on earth took place, the following is said of wisdom: 'Moreover, when nations consenting together in wickedness had been confounded, she knew the righteous man and preserved him blameless unto God, and kept him strong when his heart yearned toward his child.'[4]

We have much of a mysterious nature to say about this, to which the quotation is appropriate that 'it is good to hide the mystery of a king'.[5] For we do not want the truth about the way in which souls became bound

[1] Cf. Celsus in v, 34. Neith, the goddess of Sais, was identified with Athena by Herodotus, II, 62; Plato, *Timaeus*, 21 E; Plutarch, *Mor.* 354C; Diod. Sic. v, 57; Pausanias, II, 36, 8; IX, 12, 2. See further O. Hoefer in Roscher's *Lexikon d. Mythologie*, IV, 275–6.
[2] Deut. xxxii. 8–9.   [3] Gen. xi. 1–2, 5–9.
[4] Wisd. of Sol. x. 5.   [5] Tobit xii. 7.

to a body (though not by reincarnation) to be cast before an uneducated audience, nor that holy things should be given to the dogs, nor that pearls be cast before swine.[1] For that would be impious, as it implies a betrayal of the secret oracles of the wisdom of God, of which it is finely written: 'Wisdom will not enter into a soul that devises evil, nor dwell in a body that is held in pledge by sin.'[2] It is enough to give an account of the doctrines which are obscurely set forth under the guise of a story by following the course of it, in order that those who have the ability may work out the meaning of the passage for themselves.

30. Let us conceive, then, that all the nations on earth are using one particular language, and as long as they agree with one another they continue using the divine language. And they remain without moving from the east as long as they pay attention to the things of light and of the effulgence of the everlasting light.[3] And when these people move themselves from the east and pay attention to things foreign to the east, they find 'a plain in the land of Shinar' which means 'a shaking of teeth',[4] as a symbol of the fact that they have lost that by which they are nourished, and they dwell there. Then they desire to collect material things and to join what cannot naturally be joined to heaven, in order that by means of material things they may conspire against immaterial things, saying: 'Come, let us make bricks and burn them with fire.' Therefore, they strengthen and harden material clay, and desire to make the brick into stone and the clay into asphalt, and by these methods to build a city and a tower, 'the top of which', as they suppose, 'will reach to heaven', like the high things that exalt themselves against the knowledge of God.[5] And each one is handed over to angels who are more or less stern and whose character varies in proportion to the distance that they moved from the east, whether they had travelled far or a little way, and in proportion to the amount of bricks made into stones and of clay into asphalt and to the size of the building made out of them. Under them they remain until they have paid the penalty for their boldness. And each one is led by angels, who put in them their native language, to the parts of the earth which they deserve. Some are led to parched land, for example; others to country which afflicts the inhabitants by being cold; and some to land that is difficult to cultivate; others to land that is less hard; and some to country full of wild beasts, and others to country that has them to a lesser degree.

[1] Matt. vii. 6.   [2] Wisd. of Sol. i. 4.
[3] Wisd. of Sol. vii. 26.
[4] It is so interpreted by Philo, de Conf. Ling. 68; the derivation is based on the Hebrew shēn = tooth, na'ar = shake.
[5] Cf. II Cor. x. 5.

31. Then if anyone has the ability to understand what is expressed in the form of a story which has both something true in its literal meaning and also indicates some secret truth, let him also consider those who have preserved the language from the beginning, who, because they have not moved from the east, continue in the east and with the eastern language. And let him understand that only those have become the Lord's portion and His people, who are called Jacob; and Israel has become the lot of His inheritance.[1] They alone are under the charge of a ruler who has not received his subjects for the purpose of punishment like the others. Let him see, so far as it is possible for human understanding, that in the society of these people who are assigned to the Lord as the superior portion sins were committed which at first were tolerable and of such a character that they did not deserve to be utterly forsaken, and that even though later their sins increased in number they were still tolerable. And let him realize that this happened for a long time, and that a remedy was always applied, and at intervals they turned back. Let him perceive that in proportion to their sins they were abandoned to those beings who had obtained other countries. At first, after they were punished and had paid the penalty to a small extent, and having been as it were chastised, they returned to their native land. And let him see how later they were handed over to sterner rulers, the Assyrians and then the Babylonians, as the scriptures would call them. Then let him notice that although remedies were applied nevertheless they sinned still more, and on this account were scattered in the other parts by the rulers of the other nations who carried them off. Their ruler purposely takes no notice of them when they are carried off by the rulers of the other nations, so that, as if avenging himself, he might with good reason exercise the power which he possessed of detaching those whom he could from the other nations, and might appoint laws for them and show them a life which they should follow, his purpose being to lead them on to the end to which he led those of the earlier nation who did not sin.

32. And by this let those who have the ability learn to see the great truth that the one who obtained as a possession those who did not sin among the earlier nation is far more powerful than the others, since he has been able to take chosen men from the portions of all the others, and to deliver them from the beings who had received them for the purpose of punishment, and to bring them to laws and to a life which helps them to forget the sins that they have previously committed. However, as we have already declared, we have made these remarks obscurely, to establish the truths misunderstood by those who say that *the different parts of the earth*

[1] Deut. xxxii. 9.

were allotted to different overseers, and are governed in this way by having been divided between certain authorities. Celsus borrowed from these ideas when he made the remarks which we have quoted.

Since those who moved from the east on account of their sins were given over 'to a reprobate mind' and 'to passions of dishonour' and 'to impurity in the lusts of their hearts',[1] in order that by being sated with sin they might hate it,[2] we would not agree with Celsus' opinion when he maintains that because of the overseers that have been allotted to the parts of the earth *the practices done by each nation are right.* Moreover, we do not want to do their practices *in the way that pleases them.* For we see that it is pious to break *customs which have existed in each locality from the beginning* and to adopt better and more divine laws given us by Jesus, as the most powerful being, 'delivering us from this present evil world', and from 'the rulers of this world who are coming to nought'.[3] On the other hand, it is impious not to cast oneself upon him who appeared and proved himself to be purer and more powerful than all rulers. To him, as the prophets foretold many generations before, God said: 'Ask of me, and I will give thee nations for thine inheritance and the uttermost parts of the earth for thy possession.'[4] And he became the hope[5] of us Gentiles who have believed in him and in the supreme God, his Father.

33. This is not only our reply to the words quoted about the overseers, but to some extent it anticipates what Celsus says to us in these remarks:[6] *Now let us take the second chorus. I will ask them where they have come from, or who is the author of their traditional laws. Nobody, they will say. In fact, they themselves originated from Judaism, and they cannot name any other source for their teacher and chorus-leader. Nevertheless they rebelled against the Jews.*[7] Each one of us *has come* 'in the last days',[8] when our Jesus came, 'to the visible mountain of the Lord', to the Word far above every word, and to the house of God which is 'the church of the living God, a pillar and ground of the truth'.[9] And we see how he built on 'the tops of the mountains' which are all the sayings of the prophets who are his foundation. This house is exalted 'above the hills' which are those men who seem to profess some exceptional ability in wisdom and truth. And 'all nations' are coming to it,[10] and 'many nations' go, and we exhort one another to the worship of God through Jesus Christ which has shone out in the last days,

---

[1] Rom. i. 28, 26, 24.

[2] Similarly *de Orat.* XXIX, 13, and of the Fall of the rational beings in VI, 44 and *de Princ.* II, 8, 3.

[3] Gal. i. 4; I Cor. ii. 6.　　　　[4] Ps. ii. 8.　　　　[5] Cf. Gen. xlix. 10.

[6] This fragment of Celsus is taken out of order; see V, 51. Originally it followed that in V, 41. Cf. Bader, p. 31.　　　　[7] Cf. III, 5.

[8] Isa. ii. 2–4, on which text the next section is a small homily.

[9] I Tim. iii. 15.　　　　[10] Read ἐπ' αὐτόν with K. tr.

saying: 'Come, and let us go up to the mountain of the Lord and to the house of the God of Jacob, and he will proclaim to us his way and we will walk in it.' For from those in Sion a spiritual law has come forth and changed from them to us. Moreover, 'the word of the Lord' came forth from that Jerusalem that He might hold sway and judge 'between the nations' everywhere, choosing out those whom he sees to be obedient, and that He may reprove 'many people' who are disobedient.

To those who would ask us where we have come from or who is our author we reply that we came in accordance with the commands of Jesus to beat the spiritual swords that fight and insult us into ploughshares, and to transform[1] the spears that formerly fought against us into pruning-hooks. No longer do we take the sword against any nation, nor do we learn war any more, since we have become sons of peace[2] through Jesus who is our *author*[3] instead of following the traditional customs, by which we were 'strangers to the covenants'.[4] We receive a law for which we give thanks to him who delivered us from error and say: 'Because our fathers have inherited lying idols, and there is none among them that sends rain.'[5] Our *chorus-leader and teacher* came forth from the Jews to control the whole world by the word of his teaching. We have taken this remark of Celsus out of its proper sequence, though it is added after many others, and refuted it to the best of our ability taken together with his words which we quoted.

34. That we may not pass by the remarks which Celsus has made in between these last two, let us also quote these: *One might also call Herodotus as witness for this, when he speaks as follows:* 'Now the people of the cities Marea and Apis who live in the part of Egypt bordering on Libya, thinking that they were Libyans and not Egyptians, objected to the worship of the temples, not wanting to abstain from eating cows; so they sent to Ammon, saying that they had nothing in common with the Egyptians, for they lived outside the Delta and did not agree with them; and they wanted Ammon to allow them to taste all meats. But the god did not allow them to do this, saying that land which the Nile passed over and watered was Egypt, and that those who lived below the city of Elephantine and drank from this river were Egyptians.'[6] *This is the story of Herodotus. Ammon is not any less competent to give an account of the things of God than the angels of the Jews. Thus there is nothing wrong if each nation observes its own laws of worship. Actually we will find that the difference between each nation is very considerable, and nevertheless each one of them appears to think its own by far the best.*

---

[1] Read μετασκευάζειν with K. tr.   [2] Cf. Luke x. 6.
[3] Cf. Acts iii. 15; v. 31; Heb. ii. 10; xii. 2.
[4] Eph. ii. 12.   [5] Jer. xvi. 19; xiv. 22.
[6] Herodotus, II, 18.

The Ethiopians who live at Meroe worship only Zeus and Dionysus.[1] *The Arabians worship only Ourania and Dionysus.*[2] *The Egyptians all worship Osiris and Isis;*[3] *the people of Sais Athena;*[4] *the Naucratites, though they did not begin long ago, invoke Sarapis;*[5] *and the rest act in each case according to their respective laws. Some abstain from sheep,*[6] *reverencing them as sacred, others from goats, others from crocodiles,*[7] *others from cows;*[8] *and they abstain from pigs because they loathe them.*[9] *Indeed, among the Scythians cannibalism is a good thing;*[10] *and there are some Indians who think they are acting piously when they eat even their fathers. And the same Herodotus says this somewhere (and I will again quote his actual words to guarantee its genuineness). He tells the following story: 'For if anyone were to propose to call men and to tell them to choose which of all laws were the best, on consideration each would choose his own. Therefore, it is not likely that anyone but a lunatic would make a mock of these things. But that all men have believed this of their laws can be concluded by this proof among many others. While he was ruler Darius called the Greeks who were with him, and asked for how much money they would be willing to feed on their dead fathers. They said that they would not do this at any price. After this Darius called those Indians called Calatians who feed on their parents, and in the presence of the Greeks, and learning their reply through an interpreter, he asked for what money they would be ready to burn their dead fathers with fire. But they uttered a loud cry and told him to keep silence. These customs have in fact existed, and Pindar seems to me to have been right when he said that custom is king of all.'*[11]

35. From these facts the argument seems to Celsus to lead to the conclusion that all men ought to live according to their traditional customs and should not be criticized for this; but that since the Christians have forsaken their traditional laws and are not one individual nation like the Jews they are to be criticized for agreeing to the teaching of Jesus. Let him tell us, then, whether philosophers who teach men not to be super-stitious would be right in abandoning the traditional customs, so that they even eat of things forbidden in their own countries, or would they act contrary to moral principle in so doing? For reason persuades them not to busy themselves about images and statues or even about the created things of God, but to ascend above them and to present the soul to the

---

[1] *Idem*, II, 29.   [2] *Idem*, III, 8; I, 131.   [3] *Idem*, II, 42.

[4] *Idem*, II, 28, 59, 169–70, 175. Cf. v, 29 above.

[5] For the worship of Sarapis there, cf. Strabo, XVII, 1, 23, p. 803. According to Tacitus (*Hist.* IV, 81) and Plutarch (*Mor.* 361–2) the cult was introduced by Ptolemy I (*c.* 367–283 B.C.).

[6] Herodotus II, 42.

[7] *Idem*, II, 69; Strabo, XVII, 1, 39 (p. 812), 44 (p. 814).

[8] Herodotus, II, 41.   [9] *Idem*, II, 47.

[10] *Idem*, I, 216; IV, 26. See on v, 27 above.

[11] *Idem*, III, 38 (cf. 99); Pindar, *frag.* 152 Bowra.

Creator. If Celsus or those who approve of his views were to try to defend
the view which he has set forth by saying that one who has read philosophy
would also observe the traditional customs, that implies that philosophers,
for example, among the Egyptians would become quite ridiculous if they
took care not to eat onion in order to observe the traditional customs or
abstained from certain parts of the body such as the head and shoulders in
order not to break the traditions handed down to them by their fathers.
And I have not yet said anything of those Egyptians who shiver with fear
at the trivial physical experience of flatulence.[1] If one of their sort became
a philosopher and were to keep the traditional customs, he would be
a ridiculous philosopher because he would be acting unphilosophically.
So then, he who is brought by the Logos to worship the God of the universe,
and for the sake of the traditional customs remains at some inferior level
among images and human statues, not wanting to advance in devotion to
the Creator, would become like those who have learnt philosophy, but
still fear things which are not alarming and think that to eat particular
foods is impiety.

36. What sort of a being is Herodotus' Ammon anyway, whose words
Celsus has quoted to prove that each nation ought to keep its traditional
customs? For their Ammon does not allow the people of the cities Marea
and Apis who live in the land bordering on Libya to be indifferent towards
the use of cows, although this is a matter which is not only in its nature
morally neutral, but which also does not hinder anyone from being noble
and good. And if their Ammon prohibited the use of cows because the
animal is useful for farming, and besides this because their species is
propagated particularly through the females, perhaps the doctrine might
be plausible. But in fact he simply wants to say that people who drink of
the Nile ought to keep the Egyptian laws about cows. With this in mind
Celsus mocked at the angels of the Jews, who give an account of the things
of God, and said that *Ammon is not any less competent to give an account of
the things of God than the angels of the Jews.* He did not examine their
utterances and appearances to see what they mean. For he would have
seen that 'God is not concerned about oxen'[2] even where He seems to be
laying down laws about oxen or other irrational animals. But laws which

---

[1] Cf. Minucius Felix, xxviii, 9 'Idem Aegyptii cum plerisque vobis non magis Isidem
quam ceparum acrimonias metuunt, nec Serapidem magis quam strepitus per pudenda
corporis expressos contremescunt.' Jerome, *Comm. in Isai.* xiii, 46 (Migne, *P.L.* xxiv,
467 A): '...ut taceam de formidoloso et horribili cepe et crepitu ventris inflati, quae
Pelusiaca religio est.' *Clem. Hom.* x, 16; *Clem. Recog.* v, 20; Theophilus, *ad Autol.* i, 10.
For the onion cf. Pliny, *N.H.* xix, 101; Plutarch ap. Gellius, *N.A.* xx, 8, 7; *Mor.* 353F;
Cyril of Jerusalem, *Catech.* vi, 10. Discussion in T. Hopfner, *Plutarch über Isis und Osiris*
(Monographien des Archiv Orientální ix, Prague, 1940), i, pp. 71–2; A. B. Cook, *Zeus* ii
(1925), pp. 986–7.   [2] I Cor. ix. 9.

in outward appearance are concerned with irrational animals were written
for the sake of men and contain certain teaching about nature.

Celsus says that *each nation does no wrong* when it desires *to observe its
own laws of worship.* It follows from his view that the Scythians do no
wrong when they indulge in cannibalism according to the traditional
customs. And those Indians also who eat their fathers and think that they
act piously are right in Celsus' opinion, or at least they do no wrong. At
any rate, he quotes a passage from Herodotus which agrees that each nation
is morally right in following the traditional customs, and he seems to give
his approval to the Indians called Calatians in the time of Darius who fed
on their parents, who, in reply to Darius' question for how much money
they would be willing to abandon this custom, uttered a loud cry and told
him to keep silence.

37. Now there are two kinds of law for our consideration. The one is
the ultimate law of nature, which is probably derived from God, and the
other the written code of cities.[1] Where the written law does not contradict the law of God it is good that the citizens should not be troubled by
the introduction of strange laws. But where the law of nature, that is of
God, enjoins precepts contradictory to the written laws, consider whether
reason does not compel a man to dismiss the written code and the intention
of the lawgivers far from his mind, and to devote himself to the divine
Lawgiver and to choose to live according to His word, even if in doing
this he must endure dangers and countless troubles and deaths and shame.
Moreover, if the actions which please God are different from those
demanded by some of the laws in cities, and if it is impossible to please
both God and those who enforce laws of this kind, it is unreasonable to
despise actions by means of which one may find favour with the Creator
of the universe, and to choose those as a result of which one would be
displeasing to God, though one may find favour with the laws that are not
laws, and with those who like them.

If in other instances it is reasonable to prefer the law of nature, as being
God's law, before the written law which has been laid down by men in
contradiction to the law of God, should we not do this even more in the
case of the laws which concern the worship of God? We will not follow
the *Ethiopians who live round Meroe, in worshipping only Zeus and
Dionysus* as they like to do, nor will we honour at all Ethiopian gods as
the Ethiopians do. Nor will we follow the Arabians in thinking that only
Ourania and Dionysus are gods. We think that they are not even gods at

[1] For the antithesis, which is a Stoic commonplace, see VIII, 26 and *S.V.F.* III, 314–26;
Maximus Tyr. VI, 5 (Hobein, p. 72); Porphyry, *de Abst.* I, 28; Dio Chrys. LXXX, 5–6;
Cicero, *de Leg.* I, 15, 42–3. Cf. Plato, *Laws,* 793 A.

293

all; for in them the male and female sexes are glorified (the Arabians worship Ourania as female and Dionysus as male).[1] Nor will we follow all the Egyptians in regarding Osiris and Isis as gods, nor will we reckon Athena with them in accordance with the opinion of the people at Sais. Even if the earlier Naucratites thought fit to worship other gods, while those of recent times have begun to worship Sarapis who never used to be a god, this is no reason why we should say that a new god, that was not formerly a god and was not even known to men, really exists. However, even if the Son of God, 'the firstborn of all creation',[2] seems to have become man recently, yet he is not in fact new on that account. For the divine scriptures know that he is oldest of all created beings, and that it was to him that God said of the creation of man: 'Let us make man in our image and likeness.'[3]

38. I want to show how unreasonable it is of Celsus to say that each nation worships its native and traditional deities. For he says that the Ethiopians who live at Meroe recognize only two gods, Zeus and Dionysus, and worship only them, and that the Arabians also have only two, Dionysus (like the Ethiopians) and Ourania who is peculiar to them. By his account neither do the Ethiopians worship Ourania nor the Arabians Zeus. Accordingly, if an Ethiopian had come to live among the Arabians by some circumstances and was thought to be impious because he did not worship Ourania, and on this account was in danger of his life, would it be right for the Ethiopian to die rather than to break his traditional customs and to worship Ourania? If it would be right for him to break his traditional customs, he would not be doing what is pious according to the arguments of Celsus. But if he were carried away to be put to death, let Celsus show that it would be reasonable to choose death; I do not know whether the Ethiopians have a doctrine which teaches them to think philosophically about the immortality of the soul and the reward for piety, if they reverence the alleged gods according to the traditional laws. We could say the same thing of the Arabians too, if by some circumstance they came to live among the Ethiopians round Meroe. For since they too have been taught only to worship Ourania and Dionysus, they will not worship Zeus with the Ethiopians. Let Celsus inform us what would be their reasonable course of action if they were thought to be impious and were carried away to be put to death.

It is superfluous for us to recount now the myths about Osiris and Isis, and it is not the right time. But even if the myths are interpreted allegorically, they will teach us to worship inanimate water and earth which is the element underlying men and all animals. For in this way, I believe, they

---

[1] Herodotus, III, 8.   [2] Col. i. 15   [3] Gen. i. 26; cf. II, 9 above.

interpret Osiris as water and Isis as earth.[1] Concerning Sarapis the story is lengthy and discrepant.[2] It was only recently that he appeared through some trickery of Ptolemy who wanted to show to the Alexandrians as it were a visible god. We have read in Numenius the Pythagorean about the formation of Sarapis, where he says that he partakes of the being of all the animals and plants cared for by nature, so that he appears to be set up as a god with the aid of impious rites and with the magic spells that invoke daemons, not merely by image-makers but also by magicians and sorcerers and the daemons who are bound by their spells.[3]

39. We must try to find what may appropriately be eaten and not eaten by a rational and civilized person who does all things after deliberation; and we should not at random worship sheep or goats or cows. To abstain from these animals is not a bad thing, for men derive great benefit from them. But to have respect for crocodiles and to think they are sacred to some unknown god of mythology—is not this utterly silly? For it is quite mad to have respect for animals who have no respect for us, and to treat with honour animals that feast on men. But Celsus approves of folk who worship and honour crocodiles according to certain traditional customs and writes not a word against them. Yet in his eyes Christians are at fault

---

[1] Cf. Plutarch, *Mor.* 366A; 376F; Hippolytus, *Ref.* V, 7, 23; Porphyry ap. Eus. *P.E.* III, 11, 51, 116A; *Clem. Recog.* X, 27; Heliodorus, *Aethiopica*, IX, 9.

[2] Clem. Al. *Protr.* 48 gives three differing accounts of Sarapis' origin. For the introduction by Ptolemy, cf. note on V, 34; for modern views about the origin of the cult, see the summary in A. B. Cook, *Zeus*, I (1914), p. 188, and discussion by U. Wilcken, *Urkunden der Ptolemäerzeit*, I (1927), pp. 82 ff.; A. D. Nock, *Conversion* (1933), pp. 35 ff.; now also P. Jouguet, 'Les premiers Ptolémées et l'Hellénisation de Sarapis', in *Hommages à J. Bidez et à F. Cumont* (Brussels, n.d.), pp. 159–66.

[3] Numenius (*frag.* 33 Leemans) is referring to the setting-up of Sarapis' image. For Sarapis' relation to animals and plants, cf. Aelius Aristides, *Orat.* XLV (8), 32 (Keil, 361.23), who says of him προέστηκε δὲ καὶ πάντων ζῴων γενέσεως καὶ τροφῆς....

If any image was to be set up more than craftsmen were necessary; it had to be made of the right materials, such as stones with magical properties, and spells were needed to compel the god to inhabit the image. Knowledge of these matters was the most secret lore of the priests. For these ideas cf. the fragment 'On setting-up of gods' by the astrologer Julian of Laodicea (c. A.D. 500) in *Cat. Codd. Astr.* VIII, 4, pp. 252f.; the Neoplatonist Proclus 'On the priestly art' (ed. Bidez in *Catalogue des Manuscrits Alchimiques Grecs*, VI, pp. 150 f.) who writes: καὶ ἀγάλματα πολλάκις κατασκευάζουσι σύμμικτα καὶ θυμιάματα, φυράσαντες εἰς ἓν τὰ μερισθέντα συνθήματα καὶ ποιήσαντες τέχνῃ ὁποῖον κατ' οὐσίαν τὸ περιληπτικὸν καθ' ἕνωσιν τῶν πλειόνων δυνάμεων. Similarly Psellus' treatise *de Op. Daem.* (ed. Bidez, *ibid.* pp. 128 f.). Porphyry, *de Abst.* II, 49, says that 'the priest of any of the gods is skilled in the technique of setting up images'. Iamblichus, *de Myst.* V, 23 'It is not that we must abhor all matter, but only that which is alien to the gods; that which has affinities with them we should choose out, because it is suitable to be used for buildings of the gods and for setting up images and also for the performance of the sacrifices.' See also Origen in III, 36; VIII, 61; and the remarks of E. R. Bevan, *Holy Images* (1940), pp. 31 ff.; Festugière's commentary on *Corp. Herm.*, *Asclepius*, 37–8 (Nock-Festugière, II, pp. 347 ff.); Cumont, *Lux perpetua*, pp. 436–43; for Plotinus, M. P. Nilsson, *Greek Piety* (1948), p. 169.

in that they are taught to regard evil as abominable and to avoid the
actions caused by sin, and to reverence and honour virtue as having been
made by God and as God's Son. For we ought not to imagine that
because of the feminine name wisdom and righteousness are feminine in
their being.[1] In our view the Son of God is these things, as his genuine
disciple showed when he said of him: 'Who was made unto us wisdom
from God, and righteousness, and sanctification, and redemption.'[2] Therefore, though we may call him a second God, it should be understood by
this that we do not mean anything except the virtue which includes all
virtues, and the Logos which includes every logos whatsoever of the
beings which have been made according to nature, both those which are
primary and those that exist for the benefit of the whole.[3] We say that this
Logos dwelt in the soul of Jesus and was united with it in a closer union
than that of any other soul, because he alone has been able perfectly to
receive the highest participation in him who is the very Logos and the
very Wisdom, and the very Righteousness himself.

40. Celsus then goes on to say this of the different laws: *Pindar seems
to me to have been right when he said that law (custom) is king of all.* Let us
discuss this too. What law, sir, do you say is king of all? If you mean the
laws of each city, that is a lie; for all men are not ruled by the same law,
and if you meant that you should have said: 'Laws are kings of all.' For
each individual nation has a law which is king of all its citizens. But if you
understand law in the proper sense, this is by nature king of all, even if
some are like robbers who revolt from the law and deny this, living the
life of a robber and a criminal. We Christians, then, recognize that law is
by nature king of all when it is the same as the law of God; and we try to
live in accordance with it, having declared our renunciation of the laws
which are no laws.

41. Let us see what Celsus has to say next, where there is very little
about the Christians but a great deal about the Jews. He says: *If indeed
in accordance with these principles the Jews maintained their own law, we
should not find fault with them but rather with those who have abandoned their
own traditions and professed those of the Jews.*[4] *If, as though they had some
deeper wisdom, they are proud and turn away from the society of others on the
ground that they are not on the same level of piety,*[5] *they have already heard*

---

[1] Similarly Philo, *de Fuga* 51.

[2] I Cor. i. 30. For the Logos as second God, cf. vi, 61; vii, 57.

[3] Cf. iv, 74 ff.; *de Princ.* I, 2, 2 '...ea quae principaliter exsistunt vel ea quae accidunt
consequenter....'

[4] For pagan hatred of Gentile proselytes, cf. Tacitus, *Hist.* v, 5; Juvenal, *Sat.* xiv, 100 ff.

[5] For Jewish ἀπανθρωπία, cf. Hecataeus ap. Diod. Sic. xL, 3 (= Photius, *Bibl.* 244);
Posidonius, *frag.* 109 Jacoby = Diod. Sic. xxxiv, 1 (Photius, *loc. cit.*); Dio Cassius, xxxvii,
17, 2; Apollonius Molon, ap. Jos. *c. Ap.* ii, 148; Philostratus, *V.A.* v, 33.

*that not even their doctrine of heaven is their own but, to omit all other
instances, was also held long ago by the Persians, as Herodotus shows in one
place. 'For their custom', he says, 'is to go up to the highest peaks of the
mountains to offer sacrifice to Zeus, and to call the whole circle of heaven
Zeus.'*[1] *I think, therefore, that it makes no difference whether we call Zeus
the Most High, or Zen, or Adonai, or Sabaoth,*[2] *or Amoun like the Egyptians,
or Papaeus like the Scythians.*[3] *Moreover, they would certainly not be holier
than other people because they are circumcised; for the Egyptians and Colchians
did this before they did.*[4] *Nor because they abstain from pigs; for the Egyptians
also do this, and in addition abstain also from goats, sheep, oxen, and fish.*[5]
*And Pythagoras and his disciples abstain from beans and from all living
things.*[6] *Nor is it at all likely that they are in favour with God and are loved
any more than other folk, and that angels are sent to them alone, as though
indeed they had been assigned some land of the blessed. For we see both the
sort of people they are and what sort of a land it was of which they were
thought worthy.*[7]

*Let this chorus depart, then, after suffering the penalty of their arrogance.
For they do not know the great God, but have been led on and deceived by
Moses' sorcery and have learnt about that for no good purpose.*[8]

42. It is obvious that here he accuses the Jews of falsely supposing
themselves to be an elect portion[9] of the supreme God preferred before
any other nation. At any rate, he charges them with arrogance for
boasting of the great God, while they do not know Him, but have been
led on by Moses' sorcery and deceived by him, and have learnt from him
to no good purpose. In what we have previously said[10] we gave a partial
account of the holy and peculiar society of the Jews at the time when it
exhibited to them the symbol of the city of God, and of His temple, and
the sacerdotal worship in it at the altar. If anyone were to apply his mind
to an examination of the lawgiver's intention and the society which he
founded, and were to compare them with the present conduct of other
nations, he would admire none more, since as far as it is humanly possible
they removed everything not of advantage to mankind, and accepted only
what is good. For this reason there were no gymnastic contests or
theatrical shows or horse-racing among them; nor were there women who
sold their beauty[11] to anyone who desired sexual relations without having

[1] Herodotus, I, 131.
[2] Cf. Celsus in I, 24. For Hypsistos as title of Zeus, cf. A. B. Cook, *Zeus* II, pp. 876–90;
III, pp. 1162–4.
[3] Cf. Herodotus, II, 18, 42; IV, 59; Plutarch, *Mor.* 354C.
[4] Celsus in I, 22.   [5] See V, 34 above.
[6] Cf. Diels, *Dox. Gr.* 557, 20 ff.; 590, 10; Diog. Laert. VIII, 34, etc.; Celsus in VIII, 28.
[7] Cf. Celsus in VIII, 69.   [8] Cf. Celsus in I, 23.   [9] Deut. xxxii. 9.
[10] Cf. IV, 31.   [11] Cf. Lev. xix. 29; Deut. xxiii. 17–18.

children and wished to outrage the natural purpose of human sexual powers.

What an admirable thing it was for them that they were taught even from childhood to ascend above all sensible nature and not to think that God is established in any part of it, but even to seek for Him beyond material things! And what a splendid thing that almost as soon as they were born, when they were fully capable of understanding, they were taught about the immortality of the soul and the courts of judgment under the earth[1] and the rewards for people who live good lives! These truths were proclaimed still under the form of a story because they were children and only had the understanding of children; but now to those who seek for the meaning and wish to advance in it, what hitherto were myths, if I may use the word, have been transformed into the inner truth which had been hidden from them. I think that they deserved to be called God's portion because they despised all divination on the grounds that it kept men spellbound in vain, and that it proceeded from wicked daemons rather than from some superior nature, and because they sought to know the future from souls who received inspiration from the supreme God on account of their high purity.

43. Why do I need to point out how reasonable is the law which prohibits any Jew from being the slave of a fellow-believer for more than six years,[2] and how this harms neither master nor slave? Accordingly, if the Jews observe their own law it is not because they follow the same principles as the other nations. For they would be at fault and guilty of failure to understand the superiority of their laws if they imagined that they had been written like the laws of all other nations. Though Celsus will not agree, the Jews do possess *some deeper wisdom*, not only more than the multitude, but also than those who seem to be philosophers, because the philosophers in spite of their impressive philosophical teachings fall down to idols and daemons, while even the lowest Jew looks only to the supreme God. In this respect at least they are right to be proud and to avoid the society of others as polluted and impious. Would that they had not sinned and broken the law, both earlier when they killed the prophets and also later when they conspired against Jesus![3] Otherwise we might have an example of a heavenly city such as even Plato attempted to describe,[4] although I doubt whether he was as successful as Moses and his successors when they trained an 'elect nation' and a 'holy people',[5] devoted to God, by means of doctrines which were free from all superstition.

---

[1] Plato, *Phaedrus*, 249 A.   [2] Exod. xxi. 2; Deut. xv. 12; Jer. xli. 14.
[3] Cf. Matt. xxiii. 37.
[4] Plato, *Rep.* 369–72, 427–34. Cf. Clem. Al. *Strom.* iv, 172, 3.   [5] I Pet. ii. 9.

44. As Celsus wants to put the sacred laws of the Jews on a level with the laws of certain races, let us consider this also. He thinks that the doctrine of heaven is no different from that of God, and says that the Persians offer sacrifices to Zeus like the Jews, going up to the highest peaks of the mountains. He does not see that just as the Jews recognized only one God, so also they had only one holy house of prayer, and one altar for whole burnt-offerings, and one censer for incense, and one high-priest of God.[1] The Jews, then, had nothing in common with the Persians who go up and offer sacrifices on the highest peaks of the mountains, of which there are many, and have nothing resembling the sacrifices of the Mosaic law. According to this the priests of the Jews served 'a pattern and shadow of the heavenly things',[2] discussing in secret the meaning of the law about sacrifices and the truths of which they were symbols. Suppose, then, that the Persians do call the whole circle of heaven Zeus; we say that the heaven is neither Zeus nor God. For we know that even some of the lesser creatures of God have ascended above the heavens and all sensible nature. This is how we understand the words: 'Praise God ye heavens of heavens, and the water that is above the heavens; let them praise the name of the Lord.'[3]

45. However, since Celsus imagines that *it makes no difference whether we call Zeus the Most High, or Zen, or Adonai, or Sabaoth, or Amoun like the Egyptians, or Papaeus like the Scythians*,[4] let us briefly discuss this too, at the same time reminding the reader of what was said earlier on this question when Celsus' remarks led us to deal with these matters.[5] Accordingly, now we say also with regard to the nature of names that they are not arbitrary conventions of those who give them, as Aristotle thinks. For the languages in use among men have not a human origin, which is clear to those able to give careful attention to the nature of spells which were adapted by the authors of the languages in accordance with each different language and different pronunciation. We briefly discussed this question above when we said that if names whose nature it is to be powerful in some particular language are translated into another tongue they no longer have any effect such as they did with their proper sounds. This phenomenon is also to be found with men's names. For if we translated the name of some man or other who from birth has had a name in the Greek language into

---

[1] For this theme as conventional in Hellenistic-Jewish literature see W. L. Knox, *St Paul and the Church of the Gentiles*, p. 194.

[2] Heb. viii. 5.

[3] Ps. cxlviii. 4–5. Cf. VI, 19 below.

[4] With Celsus' opinion, cf. Seneca, *de Benef.* IV, 7, 1–2; Ps.-Aristotle, *de Mundo* 7; Augustine, *de Civ. Dei* IV, 11, and E. Peterson, Εἷς θεός (Göttingen, 1926), p. 254. Introduction, p. xvii.   [5] See I, 24–5.

the language of the Egyptians or Romans or some other nation, we would not bring about the experience or action which would happen if he were called by the name first given to him. Nor, if we translated into the Greek language the name of a man called in the first instance by a Roman name, would we effect what the spell is professed to do if the first name by which he was called is preserved.

If this is true of human names, what ought we to think in the case of names that are applied for whatever reason to God? For example, something of the word Abraham may be translated into Greek, and something is signified by the name Isaac, and there is a meaning in the sound Jacob. If anyone who utters an invocation or oath names 'the God of Abraham, and the God of Isaac, and the God of Jacob',[1] he would effect something, either because of the nature of these names, or even because of their power; for daemons are overcome and made subject to him who says these things. But if he were to say: the God of the chosen father of the echo,[2] and the God of laughter,[3] and the God of the man who strikes with the heel,[4] in this case the recitation would have no effect as it would be no different from the names which have no power at all. Thus if we were to translate the name Israel into Greek or another language, we would effect nothing. But if we keep it as it is, linking it on to those words with which experts in these matters have thought fit to connect it, then something would happen in accordance with the power which such invocations are said to possess when a formula of this kind is pronounced. We would say the same also of the word Sabaoth, which is frequently used in spells,[5] because if we translate the name into 'Lord of the powers' or 'Lord of hosts' or 'Almighty' (for its interpreters explain it differently)[6] we would effect nothing; whereas if we keep it with its own sounds, we will cause something to happen, according to the opinion of experts in these matters. We may say the same too of Adonai. If, then, neither Sabaoth nor Adonai have any effect when translated into what they seem to mean in Greek, so much the more would they have no effect and be powerless with people who think that *it makes no difference whether we call Zeus the Most High, or Zen, or Adonai, or Sabaoth.*

[1] See IV, 33-4. For Abraham, Isaac, and Jacob in magical spells, cf. K. Preisendanz, *Pap. Gr. Mag.* IV, 1230 ff., XIII, 815 f., 975-6; XII, 287 f.; Justin, *Dial.* 85; a gnostic amulet published by Villefosse in *Florilegium Melchior de Vogüé* (1909), pp. 289-90.

[2] Cf. Philo, *de Gig.* 64; *de Abrah.* 82; *de Mut. Nom.* 66, 71, etc.

[3] Philo, *Leg. Alleg.* I, 82; *de Mut. Nom.* 137, 157, etc.

[4] Philo, *Leg. Alleg.* I, 61; III, 15; *de Mut. Nom.* 81; Clem. Al. *Strom.* VI, 60, 3.

[5] Cf. Preisendanz, *op. cit.* II, 15, 116; III, 55, 76 f., 446 f., and *passim.*

[6] 'Lord of the powers' is the translation common in the Septuagint and Theodotion; 'Lord of hosts' is that of Aquila; 'Almighty' is common in the Septuagint. Cf. Origen, *Hom. in Isa.* IV, 1.

46. Because Moses and the prophets understood these things and similar secret doctrines, they prohibit the people from naming 'the name of other gods'[1] with a mouth that has studied to pray to the only supreme God, and from remembering them with a heart that is taught to be free from all vanity of thought and speech. For this sort of reason we choose to endure any outrage rather than to admit that Zeus is a god. For we do not suppose that Zeus and Sabaoth are identical. On the contrary, we hold that there is nothing divine about Zeus at all, but that a certain daemon delights in being so called, who is no friend to men or to the true God. Even if the Egyptians offer us Amoun with threats of punishment, we will die rather than call Amoun God; for the name is probably used in certain Egyptian spells which invoke this daemon. Suppose too that the Scythians say Papaeus is the supreme God; yet we will not believe it. We affirm belief in the supreme God, but we do not call God Papaeus as if it were His correct name, for we regard it as a name loved by the daemon who has obtained control of the Scythian desert and of their nation and language. However, if any individual calls God by the title by which He is known in Scythian, or in Egyptian, or in any language in which he may have been brought up, he will not be doing wrong.

47. The reason for the Jews' circumcision is not the same as the reason for that of the Egyptians and Colchians, and on this ground the circumcision could not be regarded as identical. Just as a man who sacrifices does not sacrifice to the same God even though he seems to sacrifice in a similar way, and just as a man who prays does not pray to the same God even if he makes the same petitions in his prayers, so anyone who is circumcised is entirely different from one who is circumcised for another purpose. For the purpose and law and intention of the man who performs the circumcision put the thing into a different category.[2] To make this point still more clearly understood, we might say that the word 'justice' is the same among all the Greeks. But justice as Epicurus conceived it is manifestly one thing, and another thing as conceived by the Stoics, who deny that the soul is tripartite,[3] and another in the opinion of the Platonists who hold that justice is an individual act of the parts of the soul.[4] So also the courage of Epicurus, who endures troubles to avoid more of them, is one thing, and that of the Stoic, who chooses all virtue for its own sake, another; and that of the Platonist[5] is another, for he holds that it is a virtue of the spirited part of the soul and appoints a place for it round about

---

[1] Exod. xxiii. 13; Ps. xv. 4.   [2] Similarly *Hom. in Jerem.* v, 14.

[3] The Stoic soul had eight parts: Diog. Laert. VII, 110.

[4] For this definition, cf. Clem. Al. *Strom.* VI, 125, 6; Porphyry, *Sent.* XL, 6; Iamblichus, *de Myst.* IV, 5; Greg. Thaum. *Paneg.* XI, 139; Athenag. *Res.* 22. It summarizes Plato, *Rep.* 441–3.   [5] Read ἡ ⟨τοῦ⟩ ἀπὸ Πλάτωνος with K. tr.

the abdomen.¹ Thus circumcision is different according to the different
doctrines of the people who practise the rite. But in a book of this character
it is not necessary to discuss this now. If anyone wants to consider further
our opinions on this point, he may read about it in our commentary on
Paul's Epistle to the Romans.²

48. Although the Jews may be *proud* of circumcision they would
distinguish it not only from that of the Colchians and Egyptians, but also
from that of the Ishmaelite Arabs, even though Ishmael was born of their
forefather Abraham and was circumcised with him. The Jews maintain
that the circumcision which was performed on the eighth day was correct,
while that which was not performed at that age occurred merely through
chance circumstances.³ Perhaps the command was given because of some
angel hostile to the Jewish nation who had power to injure those of them
who were not circumcised, but who was powerless against those circumcised. One might say that this is indicated by what is written in Exodus,
where the angel had power to act against Moses before the circumcision
of Eliazar, but after he was circumcised he could effect nothing. It was
because she had learnt this that 'Zipporah took a pebble and circumcised'
her child, and according to the usual manuscripts she is recorded to have
said 'the blood of my child's circumcision is checked'; but according to
the Hebrew text: 'A bridegroom of bloodshed art thou to me.'⁴ For she
knew the truth about this angel who had power before the blood was shed
and was checked by the blood of the circumcision. That is why she said
to him: 'A bridegroom of bloodshed art thou to me.'

However, although what I have said so boldly seems somehow to be
rather curious and unsuited to the ear of the common crowd, I will add
this one further point as more distinctively Christian, and then change to the
next subject. This angel, I believe, had power against those of the people
who were not circumcised, and in general against all who worship only
the Creator; and he had this power so long as Jesus had not assumed
a body. But when he did that, and his body was circumcised, all his
power against those who are uncircumcised⁵ and who follow this religion
was taken away. For Jesus destroyed him by an indescribable divine
power. This is why his disciples are forbidden to be circumcised, and why
they are told: 'If you are circumcised, Christ shall profit you nothing.'⁶

¹ Plato, *Rep.* 442 C; *Timaeus* 69 E–70 A.
² *Comm. in ep. ad Rom.* II, 12–13 (Lommatzsch, VI. 116–43). The commentary on Romans,
also mentioned in VIII, 65, was probably written three or four years before the *contra Celsum*.
³ Josephus, *Antiq.* I, 12, 2, 214, contrasts the Jewish rite on the eighth day with the Arab
practice of postponing it till the thirteenth year, Ishmael having been circumcised at that age.
⁴ Exod. iv. 24–6. The first translation is that of the Septuagint. Cf. F. Field, *Origenis
Hexaplorum quae supersunt* (1875), I, p. 87.
⁵ Read ταύτῃ ⟨μὴ⟩ with Bo., K. tr.   ⁶ Gal. v. 2.

49. Furthermore, the Jews are not proud of their abstinence from pigs as though the pig were some great thing, but because they have learnt[1] the nature of clean and unclean animals and know the reason for this distinction, and that the pig is reckoned among the unclean animals. These were symbols of certain truths before the advent of Jesus. But after his time, to his disciple who did not yet understand the truth about these things and said 'Nothing common or unclean has entered my mouth', it was said 'What God has cleansed, do not make common.'[2] Therefore, it is nothing to do with either the Jews or us that the Egyptian priests abstain not only from pigs but *in addition from goats, sheep, oxen, and fish.* But since 'it is not that which goes into the mouth that defiles a man',[3] and since 'meat does not commend us to God',[4] we are not proud because we do not eat; nor do we come to meals with gluttonous motives. So then, for all we care, let the Pythagoreans continue as they like in abstaining from living things. But notice also the difference in the reason for the abstention from living things between the Pythagoreans and the ascetics among us.[5] For they abstain from living things on account of the myth about the soul's reincarnation. And who would

> Lift up his own son
> And slay him with an imprecation, the great fool?[6]

But if we are abstemious, we do this because we bruise the body and bring it into subjection and want to 'mortify our members that are on earth, fornication, impurity, licentiousness, passion, evil desire'; and we do everything in our power to mortify the deeds of the body.[7]

50. Celsus makes this further remark about the Jews: *Nor is it likely that they are in favour with God and are loved any more than other folk, and that angels are sent to them alone, as though indeed they had been assigned some land of the blessed. For we see both the sort of people they are and what sort of a land it was of which they were thought worthy.*[8] We will refute this also by saying that this race is shown to have been in favour with God from the fact that the supreme God is called the God of the Hebrews even by people alien to our faith.[9] And because they were in favour with God so long as they were not forsaken, though they were few in number, they continued to be protected by divine power, so that not even in the time of Alexander of Macedon did they suffer anything at his hands, in spite of the fact that because of certain agreements and oaths they would not take

---

[1] K. tr. proposes μεμαθηκέναι (after Guiet), and two lines later reads μεθ' ἥν.

[2] Acts x. 14–15.   [3] Matt. xv. 11, 17.   [4] I Cor. viii. 8.   [5] Cf. VII, 48.

[6] Empedocles, *frag.* 137 Diels. Belief in metempsychosis into animals (so Pythagoras and Empedocles) meant that if a man killed an animal for food he might be killing a relative.

[7] Cf. I Cor. ix. 17; Col. iii. 5; Rom. viii. 13.

[8] Cf. Celsus in VIII, 69.   [9] Magicians; cf. IV, 34.

up arms against Darius. They say also that at that time the high-priest put
on his sacerdotal vestment and that Alexander bowed before him, saying
that he had had a vision of a man in this very dress[1] who proclaimed to him
that he would bring the whole of Asia under his rule. Accordingly we
Christians say that while they surely experienced favour with God and
were loved more than any others, yet this care and grace changed to us
when Jesus transferred the power at work among the Jews to those Gentiles who believed in him. That is why, although the Romans have wanted
to do much against the Christians to prevent their further existence, they
have not been able to achieve this. For the hand of God was fighting for
them and wanted to scatter the word of God from one *corner*[2] in the land
of Judaea to the whole of mankind.

51. However, as we have given the best reply that we can to Celsus when
he brings the charges we have quoted against the Jews and their doctrines,
let us now quote the next passage, and show that neither are we *arrogant*
when we profess to *know the great God*, nor as Celsus supposes are we *led
on by the sorcery of Moses* or even by that of our Saviour Jesus himself.
Moreover, it is for a *good purpose* that we both listen to God in Moses'
writings and accept Jesus as Son of God, who is testified by the former to
be God; and we hope for the best rewards when we live according to his
word.

We will intentionally omit any reply to the words that we quoted
earlier when we taught *where we have come from*, and *whom we have as our
author*, and what is *the law* that he gave.[3] And, if Celsus wants to make out
that there is no difference between us and the Egyptians who worship the
goat, or the ram, or the crocodile, or the ox, or the hippopotamus, or the
dog-faced baboon, or the cat,[4] that is the concern of him and anyone who
is in agreement with him on this point. But to the best of our ability we
have made our defence concerning the worship of our Jesus by several
arguments before now, and have shown that we have found something
better. And when we alone affirm that the truth which is pure and uncontaminated by error consists in the teaching of Jesus Christ, we do not
recommend ourselves but the teacher to whom testimony is borne by the
supreme God in many ways, both by the prophecies in the Jewish scriptures and by the self-evident nature of the facts themselves. For a man who
has been able to do works of such magnitude is obviously not unaided by
God.

[1] For the corrupt ἑωρακέναι K. tr. proposes περιβεβλημένον. The (legendary) story is
from Josephus, *Antiq.* XI, 8, 3–5, 317–39.
[2] Cf. Celsus in VII, 68; IV, 36.   [3] See V, 33.
[4] Bader (p. 134) is right, as against Koetschau, in holding that this is not a new fragment
of Celsus; Origen is referring back to V, 34.

52. The passage of Celsus which we now want to examine reads as follows: *We leave on one side the many arguments which refute what they say about their teacher; and let us assume that he really was some angel. Was he the first and only one to have come? Or were there also others before him? If they were to say that he is the only one, they would be convicted of telling lies and contradicting themselves. For they say that others also have often come, and, in fact, sixty or seventy at once, who became evil and were punished by being cast under the earth in chains. And they say that their tears are the cause of hot springs.*[1] *Furthermore, they say that an angel came to the tomb of this very man (some say one angel, some two),*[2] *who replied to the women that he was risen. The Son of God, it seems, was not able to open the tomb, but needed someone else to move the stone. What is more, an angel came to the carpenter to defend Mary when she was pregnant, and another angel that they might rescue the infant and escape.*[3] *And why should I give a careful list of them all and enumerate those alleged to have been sent to Moses and to others of them? If therefore others also were sent, obviously Jesus too came from the same God. Apparently he had a mission of greater significance because, for example, the Jews were doing something wrong, or were debasing their religion, or were behaving impiously;*[4] *for these things are hinted at.*

53. What we have already said when we examined particular points concerning our Saviour Jesus Christ is an adequate reply to Celsus' words. But lest we should seem to leave out intentionally some passage of his book as though we were incapable of refuting him, even if we will be repeating ourselves, as Celsus provokes us to do this, let us give an abbreviated discussion as well as we can. Perhaps by going over the same ground again we may put the matter in a clearer light or look at it from a new angle. Now he says that he *leaves on one side the many arguments which refute what* Christians *say about their teacher.* But he does not leave out anything which he was able to say. This is clear from what he said earlier; and elsewhere he does this after the manner of a rhetorical trick.[5] Furthermore, that we are not refuted in what we say about our mighty Saviour, although our accuser may seem to refute us, will be clear to those who read all the prophecies and records about him honestly and carefully.

Next, as he supposes that he can say of the Saviour by way of a concession *Let us assume that he really was some angel*, we say that we do not

---

[1] As Origen points out, Celsus' source (whether direct or indirect) is Enoch vi–x, and lxvii–ix. For springs cf. lxvii. 11. The number seventy derives from Enoch lxxxix. 59 ff.; for later rabbinic traditions cf. Strack-Billerbeck, *Kommentar zum Neuen Testament aus Talmud und Midrasch*, III, pp. 48 f.

[2] Matthew (xxviii. 2) and Mark (xvi. 5) say one, Luke (xxiv. 4) and John (xx. 12) two.

[3] Matt. i. 20; ii. 13. Cf. Celsus in I, 66.

[4] Cf. Celsus in IV, 22.   [5] Cf. II, 13; III, 78.

accept this from Celsus as a concession. But we consider the work of him
who visited the whole human race by his word and teaching, according as
each one of those who believe him was able to receive him. This was not
the work merely of an angel but, as the prophecy about him says, of 'the
angel of the great counsel'.[1] For he proclaimed to men the great counsel
of the God and Father of the universe concerning them, that those who
yield to a life of pure religion ascend to God by their great actions, and
that those who do not believe alienate themselves from God and are on
the road to destruction[2] through unbelief about God.

Then next he says: If he was an angel who came to men, *was he the first
and only one* to have come? *Or were there also others before him?* He thinks
he can meet either alternative with several arguments, although no real
Christian says that Christ is the only one who has visited mankind; and
if we were to say that he is the only one, Celsus replies that others have
appeared to men.

54. Then he meets his own objection as he would have it: *So far is he
from being the only one related to have visited mankind, that those who
because of the teaching of the name of Jesus have departed from the Creator as
an inferior being, and have gone to a God whom they regard as superior, who
is Father of him who came, say that even before him some have visited mankind
from the Creator.*[3] As we are studying the subject honestly we will observe
that Apelles, Marcion's disciple, who became the author of a heresy and
thought that the writings of the Jews were legendary, says that Jesus alone
has visited mankind.[4] As, therefore, he says that Jesus alone has come from
God to visit men, it would not be reasonable for Celsus to reply to him
that *others too have come*. For Apelles, as we have already said, does not
believe the books of the Jews which relate miracles. He will much less
admit what Celsus seems to have affirmed because he misunderstood what
is written in the book of Enoch. Nobody, then, convicts us of telling lies
and of contradicting ourselves as if we said both that only our Saviour has
come and that none the less many others have often come. However,
because he was hopelessly muddled in his discussion about the angels who
have come to men, he uses the instances, which he failed to understand,
that were suggested to him by what is written in the book of Enoch. He
seems neither to have read them nor to have been aware that the books
entitled Enoch are not generally held to be divine by the churches,[5]

---

[1] Isa. ix. 6.   [2] Cf. Matt. vii. 13.
[3] Celsus has in mind the Marcionites (cf. Harnack, *Marcion*, 2nd ed. p. 275 *); cf. v, 62;
VI, 74; VII, 18.
[4] The fragments of Apelles are collected by Harnack, *op. cit.* pp. 404*-20*. Cf. IV, 41.
[5] For patristic views of Enoch, see R. H. Charles, *Apocrypha and Pseudepigrapha of the
O.T.* II, pp. 181-4.

although perhaps he took from this source his statement that sixty or seventy angels came down at once and became evil.

55. However, let us be open-minded and grant him that according to the words of Genesis which he did not notice 'the sons of God saw that the daughters of men were fair, and took to themselves wives of all whom they chose'; nevertheless even here we shall convince those who are able to understand the meaning of the prophet that one of our predecessors referred these words to the doctrine about souls who were afflicted with a desire for life in a human body, which, he said, is figuratively called 'daughters of men'.[1] Yet whatever the truth may be concerning the sons of God who desired daughters of men, the idea does not help him at all towards showing that Jesus, if an angel, is not the only one who has visited men. Indeed, he has manifestly become Saviour and benefactor of all who change their lives from the flood of iniquity.

Then he muddles and confuses what he has somehow heard, and what is written in some book or other, whether believed by Christians to be divine or not, saying that *sixty or seventy angels came down at once, and were punished by being cast down under the earth in chains.* And he quotes as from Enoch, though he does not name it, *their tears are the cause of hot springs*, a notion neither mentioned nor heard of in the churches of God. For no one has been so stupid as to imagine that the tears of the angels that came down from heaven were physical tears like those of men. If we may be frivolous about objections which Celsus seriously brings against us, we would remark that nobody would say that warm springs, most of which are fresh water, are angels' tears since tears are naturally salt— unless perhaps Celsus' angels weep tears of fresh water![2]

56. Then he next combines statements which are incompatible, and compares to one another things that are incomparable. For after his words about the sixty or seventy angels who, as he says, came down, and whose tears in his opinion are hot springs, he goes on to say that according to some two angels are related to have come to the tomb of Jesus himself, while others say only one. I do not think he noticed that Matthew and Mark have one, while Luke and John have two angels. But these statements are not contradictory. The writers that have one angel say that this one was he who rolled back the stone from the sepulchre,[3] whereas those

---

[1] Gen. vi. 2; see Philo, *de Gig.* 6–18. Cf. Origen, *Comm. in Joann.* VI, 42 (25).

[2] The Valentinians held that all wetness was derived from the tears of Achamoth; Irenaeus (*adv. Haer.* I, 4, 2–4, Harvey, I, 35 f.) replies with the same jest made here by Origen about fresh water. It appears also in Tertullian, *adv. Val.* 15. With more plausibility the Pythagoreans held that the sea was caused by the tears of Kronos: Clem. Al. *Strom.* V, 50, 1.

[3] Matt. xxviii. 2; cf. Mark xvi. 4.

that have two say they stood in shining raiment before the women
who came to the tomb, or that they were seen 'sitting in white robes'
within it.[1] However, while it would be possible to substantiate now each
of these statements, both as historical events and as manifesting some
allegorical meaning which concerns the truths which are made clear to
people who have been prepared to see the resurrection of the Logos, it is
not relevant to the present undertaking but rather to commentaries on
the gospel.

57. Some Greeks have also related that miraculous events have been seen
by men; and these tales are told not only by those who might be suspected
of inventing legends, but even by those who have shown in many ways[2]
that they are genuine philosophers, and who give an honest account of
the stories which have come to their ears. We have read such stories in the
books of Chrysippus of Soli and some in those of Pythagoras, and also of
some more recent writers who were born in modern times, such as in the
book of Plutarch of Chaeronea on the soul,[3] and in the second book on
the indestructibility of the soul by Numenius the Pythagorean.[4] If Greeks
discuss such stories, and especially the philosophers among them, are
their accounts not to be thought absurd and ridiculous, nor to be *fictitious
and mythical*,[5] while as for those who are devoted to the God of the
universe and accept any outrage to the point of death rather than tell a lie
with their voice about God, if they profess to have seen appearances of
angels, are they judged unworthy of credit, and are their words not to be
reckoned among those which are true?

But it is not reasonable to decide in this arbitrary way whether people
are telling the truth or falsehood. For those who practise avoiding all
mistakes take great pains to search and examine the statements on each
subject and give their opinion rather slowly and carefully when they are
deciding that one group of people is telling the truth and another telling
falsehood in their narratives about miraculous happenings. For not all
men give clear evidence of their credibility, nor do all men make it manifest
that they have told men *fictitious stories and myths*. This may further be
said of the resurrection of Jesus from the dead, that it is not remarkable if
one or two angels appeared at the time to announce that he had risen and
was caring by his providence for those who to their own benefit believe
in this miracle. It does not seem to me unreasonable that at all times those
who believe in the resurrection of Jesus, and who show considerable fruit

---

[1] Luke xxiv. 4; John xx. 12.   [2] Read οἱ ἀνὰ πολὺ with Wif.
[3] Only fragments survive. Eusebius preserves such a story from this work in *P.E.* xi,
36, 1, 563-4. See Bernardakis' edition of Plutarch, vii, 18 ff.
[4] *Frag.* 31 Leemans; 45 Thedinga.   [5] Cf. Celsus in iii, 27.

from their faith in that their moral life is healthy and that they have been
converted from the flood of iniquity, should be accompanied by angels
who help to bring about their conversion to God.

58. Celsus also objects to the words which say that an angel rolled away
the stone from the tomb where the body of Jesus was, like a young fellow
at school who has been given the task of pulling some argument to pieces.
And, as if he had found some clever criticism to make against the gospel,
he says: *The Son of God, it seems, was not able to open the tomb, but needed
someone else to move the stone.* Lest I should say anything irrelevant on
this matter and seem to choose the wrong moment for explaining these
things philosophically by giving an allegorical interpretation here, I will
say of the story as it stands that it appears in itself more dignified for the
inferior servant to have rolled away the stone than for him who was rising
again for the benefit of men to have done this. I say nothing of the fact
that those who conspired against the Logos and wanted to kill him and
show to all men that he was dead and of no importance, did not at all
desire his tomb to be opened lest anyone should see the Logos alive after
their plot. But the *angel* of God[1] who comes for the salvation of men
co-operated with the other angel and, being stronger than those who
conspired against him, rolled away the heavy stone; in order that those
who had been under the impression that the Logos had died might be
convinced that he is not with the dead but is alive, and that he goes before
those who are willing to follow him, that he may show the truths of the
next stage of progress, which follow those that he has showed before, to
those who had not yet the capacity for deeper truths at the time when they
were first converted.

Then after this for some unknown reason he comes out with the words
that an angel came to Joseph about Mary's pregnancy, and again in order
that they might rescue the infant which had been born because there was
a conspiracy against it, and might escape to Egypt, though I do not know
how this seems useful for his purpose. This also is a subject which we have
discussed earlier in reply to his remarks.[2] What is Celsus' object in saying
that according to the Bible angels are related to have been sent to Moses and
others? It seems to me not to help him at all towards his aim, and particularly since none of them strove with all his power to turn the human race
from their sins. Therefore, let us grant that *others have been sent from God*,
and that Jesus *had a mission of greater significance* and that, *because the Jews
were doing something wrong* and *were debasing their religion* and *behaving
impiously* he transferred the kingdom of God to 'other husbandmen',[3]
those everywhere who are in charge of the churches and do all in their

---

[1] Jesus (Celsus in v, 52).   [2] Cf. 1, 34–8.   [3] Matt. xxi. 41, 43.

power to bring others[1] to follow the leading of Jesus' teaching by living a pure life and by speech consistent with the life which is directed towards the God of the universe.

59. Then Celsus next says: *Therefore both the Jews and these people have the same God,* clearly by the latter meaning the Christians. And as if he were drawing a conclusion which would not be accepted, he says this: *Obviously the members of the great Church confess this, and believe that the story of the making of the world current among the Jews is true even in respect of the six days and the seventh in which,* according to the Bible, God ceased from His work[2] and retired into the contemplation of Himself,[3] though Celsus, because he did not read the scriptures carefully and did not understand them, says that *God rested,* which is not the word used. However, we could say much that is mysterious, profound, and hard to explain,[4] about the making of the world and the sabbath rest for the people of God which remains after it.[5]

Then he seems to me to want to fill up his book and to make it look big. For he irrelevantly adds some words such as these about the first man, to the effect that we *say he was the same man as the Jews do, and* we *trace the genealogical descent from him like them.* But we know nothing about *a plot of brothers against one another,*[6] although we do know that Cain plotted against Abel and Esau against Jacob. For Abel did not plot against Cain, nor Jacob against Esau. Had this been the case, Celsus would have been right in saying that we *tell of the same plots of brothers against one another as the Jews do.* Suppose also that we do talk of *the same departure to Egypt as they do, and the same* return *from there* (it was not a *flight* as Celsus thinks). Why does this help to criticize us or the Jews? And where he thinks he can mock us by the story about the Hebrews he uses the word *flight;* but where it was his task to examine the story about the plagues which, according to the Bible, came upon Egypt from God, he was intentionally silent.

60. If we may give an exact answer to Celsus' words when he thinks that we hold the same opinions as the Jews about the stories he quotes, we will say that we both confess that the books were written by divine inspiration, but concerning the interpretation of the contents of the books we no longer speak alike. In fact, the reason why we do not live like the Jews is that we think the literal interpretation of the laws does not contain the meaning of the legislation. We maintain that 'when Moses is read, a veil lies upon their heart' because the meaning of the Mosaic law has been

---

[1] Read with K. τr. τοῦ ⟨καὶ ἄλλους κατὰ⟩ τάς.   [2] Gen. ii. 2–3. Cf. VI, 61.
[3] Origen quotes Plato, *Politicus,* 272 E. Bader is right as against Koetschau in thinking that these words are not from Celsus (I withdraw my note in *J.T.S.* XLVIII (1947), p. 48 n. 2).
[4] Heb. v. 11.   [5] Heb. iv. 9.   [6] Cf. Celsus in IV, 43 above.

hidden from those who have not eagerly followed the way through Jesus Christ. We know that 'if anyone shall turn to the Lord (now the Lord is the Spirit), the veil is taken away' and 'with unveiled face he reflects' as it were 'the glory of the Lord' which is in the thoughts hidden in the text, and transmutes the so-called divine glory into his own glory.[1] The word 'face' is used figuratively, and more simply, as one might say, means the mind; in this is the face 'according to the inner man'[2] which is filled with light and glory when the true meaning of the law is understood.

61. After this he says: *Let no one imagine I do not know that some of them will agree that they have the same God as the Jews, while some think there is another God to whom the former is opposed, and that the Son came from the latter.*[3] If he thinks it is a charge against Christianity that there are several sects among Christians, on this analogy would it not be considered a charge against philosophy that among the sects of philosophers there is disagreement not just about small and trivial matters but about the most important subjects? We could also criticize medicine because of the sects within it.[4] But let us grant that there are some among us who do not say that God is the same God as that of the Jews. Yet that is no reason why they are to be criticized who prove from the same scriptures that there is one and the same God for Jews and Gentiles. So also Paul, who came to Christianity from the Jews, says clearly: 'I thank my God whom I serve from my forefathers in a pure conscience.'[5]

We may admit also that *a third kind exists, and they call some natural and others spiritual*—I think he means the Valentinians.[6] What has this to do with us who belong to the Church, who find fault with those who maintain that natures are saved or lost in consequence of the way they are made? Let us admit that *there are some too who profess to be Gnostics,*[7] like the Epicureans who call themselves philosophers. But neither can those who abolish providence really be philosophers, nor can those be Christians who introduce strange new ideas which do not harmonize with the traditional doctrines received from Jesus. Let us admit that *some also accept Jesus* and on that account boast that they are Christians *although they still want to live according to the law of the Jews like the multitude of the Jews.* These are the two sects of Ebionites, the one confessing as we do that Jesus was born of a virgin, the other holding that he was not born in

---

[1] See II Cor. iii. 15–18.   [2] Rom. vii. 22.   [3] Cf. v, 54.
[4] See III, 12.   [5] II Tim. i. 3.
[6] Cf. Irenaeus, I, 7, 5 (Harvey, I, 64–6); Clement, *Exc. Theod.* 54; Tertullian, *adv. Val.* 29.
[7] The term seems to have been applied first to the Ophites who 'called themselves Gnostics, claiming to be the only ones to know the depths' (Hippolytus, *Ref.* v, 6, 4). See R. P. Casey in *J.T.S.* xxxvi (1935), pp. 45 ff.

this way but like other men.[1] What criticism is there in this against those
who belong to the Church, whom Celsus calls *those of the multitude?*[2] He
says that *some are also Sibyllists*, perhaps because he misunderstood some
who were criticizing people who think the Sibyl a prophetess, and called
the latter Sibyllists.[3]

62. Then he pours on us a heap of names, saying that he *knows of some
also who are Simonians, who reverence as teacher Helena or Helenus and are
called Helenians.*[4] But Celsus fails to notice that Simonians do not admit
that Jesus is God's Son at all, but maintain that Simon is a power of God,[5]
and relate some incredible tales about him. For he thought that if he
pretended to do miracles like those which he thought Jesus pretended to
do, he too would have as much power among men as Jesus had with the
multitudes. However, neither Celsus nor Simon was able to understand
how Jesus as a 'good husbandman'[6] of the Word of God has been able to
spread his teaching through most of Greece and barbarians' lands, and to
fill them with doctrines which change the soul from all evil and lead on to
the Creator of the universe. Celsus *knows also of Marcellians who follow
Marcellina,*[7] *and Harpocratians who follow Salome,*[8] *and others who follow
Mariamme,*[9] *and others who follow Martha.* But although by giving all
our strength to study we have examined not only the doctrines in Christianity and the different views held within it, but also to the best of our
ability have honestly looked well into the teachings of the philosophers,
yet we have never met with these. Celsus also mentioned *Marcionites who
take Marcion as their leader.*

---

[1] Cf. II, 1; v, 65.   [2] Cf. 'the great Church' in v, 59.
[3] The Jewish Sibylline Oracles were much quoted by some Christian apologists such as
Clement. Cf. Celsus in VII, 53. Nothing is known of a specific sect of 'Sibyllists'. Origen
himself evidently did not regard the Sibylline Oracles with respect; he never quotes from
them in his works.
[4] Cf. Justin, *Apol.* I, 26; Irenaeus, I, 23, 2 (Harvey, I, 191); Tertullian, *de Anima*, 34;
Hippolytus, *Ref.* VI, 19; Epiphanius, *Panar.* 21-2. For Simon, see Lietzmann in P.-W.
III A, 180-4, and for Helen, Bousset, *Haupt probleme der Gnosis*, pp. 78 ff.; G. Quispel,
Gnosis als Weltreligion (1951), pp. 45-70.
[5] Acts viii. 10.
[6] James v. 7.
[7] Marcellina was a follower of Carpocrates, the Egyptian Gnostic; she came to Rome in
the time of Pope Anicetus and led many astray (Irenaeus, I, 25, 6, Harvey, I, 210). Cf.
Epiphanius, *Panar.* XXVII, 6, 1; Augustine, *de Haeresibus* 7.
[8] Celsus may have confused the Egyptian god Harpocrates (- Horus) with Carpocrates.
In a text of the third century A.D. the god Harpocrates is named Carpocrates; cf. A. D. Nock
in *Class. Philol.* XLV (1950), p. 50. Salome figured in the Gospel according to the Egyptians
(Clement Al. *Strom.* III, 45, 63, 66, 92); both Salome and Martha appear in *Pistis Sophia*.
[9] The Ophites held that their doctrines were taught to Mariamme by James the Lord's
brother (Hippolytus, *Ref.* v, 7, 1; x, 9, 3). Her connexion with them appears in the Acts of
Philip (M. R. James, *Apocryphal N.T.* p. 446) where Philip and Mariamme go to the land
of the Ophites.

63. Then in order that he may give the appearance of knowing others beside those whom he mentions by name, he says in accordance with his usual habit that *some have found as their leader[1] one teacher and daemon, and others another, for they go astray in evil ways and wander about in great darkness more iniquitous and impure than that of the revellers of Antinous in Egypt.*[2] In touching on these matters he seems to me to have said something true in his remark that *some have found as their leader one daemon, and others another, for they go astray in evil ways and wander about in the great darkness* of ignorance. But we have previously spoken of the worshippers of Antinous when he compared him with our Jesus, and we will not repeat ourselves.

And these, he says, *slander one another with dreadful and unspeakable words of abuse. And they would not make even the least concession to reach agreement; for they utterly detest each other.* We have replied to this objection that bitter strife between sects is to be found both in philosophy and in medicine. However, we who follow the word of Jesus and have practised his teaching in thought, word, and deed, 'being reviled we bless, being persecuted we endure, being defamed we entreat'.[3] We would not utter *unspeakable words of abuse* about those who hold opinions other than those that we have accepted. But if we can we do everything possible to convert them to a better life so that they rely on the Creator alone and do every action as men who will be judged. If the heretics are not won over, we observe the word which directed that they should be treated as follows: 'A man that is heretical after a first and second admonition refuse, knowing that such a one is perverted and sins being self-condemned.'[4] Furthermore, those who have understood the sayings 'Blessed are the peacemakers', and 'Blessed are the meek',[5] would not *detest* those who *debase* Christian doctrines, nor would *they call* people who are in error *Circes and wily agitators.*[6]

64. He seems to me to have misunderstood the words of the apostle which say: 'In later times some shall fall away from the faith, giving heed to seducing spirits and doctrines of daemons, through the hypocrisy of men that speak lies, branded in their own consciences as with a hot iron, forbidding to marry, and commanding to abstain from meats which God created to be received with thanksgiving by believers.'[7] He also appears to have misunderstood those who have used these words of the apostle

---

[1] Read with K. tr. ⟨εὑραντο προστάτην⟩ κατά.

[2] For Antinous cf. III, 36–8; for the immorality of the Carpocratians see Clem. Al. *Strom.* III, 10: after their feasts the light was overturned and enormities followed.

[3] I Cor. iv. 12–13.   [4] Titus iii. 10–11.   [5] Matt. v. 9, 4.

[6] Clem. Al. *Strom.* VII, 95, 1, compares heretics to those drugged by Circe in Homer.

[7] I Tim. iv. 1–3.

against men who have debased Christian doctrines. This explains why Celsus says that among Christians *some are called 'branding-irons of hearing'.*[1] And he says that *some are called 'enigmas'*, a thing of which we know nothing. Certainly the word 'stumbling-block' is common in these writings; for it is a word we normally use of those who pervert the simple folk who are easily led astray from sound teaching. But we do not know of *some called Sirens who are cheats of disgraceful conduct, who seal up the ears of those whom they win over, and make their heads like those of pigs.*[2] Nor, I imagine, does anyone else know of them, whether he is a member of the Church or of the sects.

However, he who professes to know everything also says this: *And you will hear all those*, he says, *who disagree so violently and by their strife refute themselves to their utter disgrace, saying 'The world is crucified unto me and I to the world.'*[3] This is the only phrase of Paul that Celsus seems to have remembered.[4] But is there any reason why we should not quote countless other passages such as this: 'For though we walk in the flesh, we do not fight according to the flesh; for the weapons of our warfare are not carnal but mighty before God to the casting down of strongholds, casting down imaginations and every high thing that is exalted against the knowledge of God'[5]?

65. As he says *you will hear all those who disagree so violently saying 'The world is crucified unto me and I unto the world'*, we will prove that even this is untrue. For there are some sects who do not accept the epistles of the apostle Paul, such as the two kinds of Ebionites and those who are called Encratites.[6] Those, then, who do not use the apostle and do not regard him as a blessed and wise man would not say *'the world is crucified unto me and I unto the world'*. Here too, therefore, Celsus lies. And he dwells on his criticism of the difference between the sects; but he does not seem to me to have any clear idea at all of what he means, nor to have looked into them carefully, nor to have understood how *Christians who have made some progress in education say that they know more than the Jews,*

[1] According to Heracleon (ap. Clement, *Ecl. Proph.* xxv, 1 = *frag.* 49 Brooke), 'some brand with fire the ears of those whom they seal'. Irenaeus, I, 25, 6 (Harvey, I, 210), says that some of the Carpocratians 'brand their disciples in the back parts of the lobe of the right ear'. Cf. Hippolytus, *Ref.* vii, 32, 8; Epiphanius, *Panar.* xxvii, 5, 9. Discussion by F. J. Dölger, 'Die Sphragis als religiöse Brandmarkung im Einweihungsakt der gnostischen Karpokratianer', in *Antike und Christentum*, I (1929), pp. 73–8. For tattooing in religious initiations cf. A. B. Cook, *Zeus*, II (1925), p. 123.
[2] Cf. Homer, *Od.* x, 239, where Circe turns Odysseus' men into swine.
[3] Gal. vi. 14, quoted by the Valentinians according to Irenaeus, I, 3, 5 (Harvey, I, 30).
[4] But cf. Celsus in I, 9.   [5] II Cor. x. 3–5.
[6] For Ebionites cf. II, 1; v, 61. For the Encratites as followers of Tatian cf. Irenaeus, I, 28, 1 (Harvey, I, 220); Eusebius, *H.E.* IV, 29. They rejected Paul (Hippolytus, *Ref.* VIII, 20, 1) and the Acts (Eusebius, *H.E.* IV, 29, 5).

for he does not specify whether they accept the scriptures but explain
the meaning differently, or if they do not even accept the books of the
Jews. For we would find both these views held among the sects.

After this he says: *However, even if they have no authority for their
doctrine,*[1] *let us examine the actual teaching. Now first we must speak of all
the misunderstandings and corruptions of the truth which they have made
through ignorance.*[2] *For they vulgarly discuss fundamental principles and
make arrogant pronouncements about matters of which they know nothing. The
following are examples.* And he immediately contrasts certain phrases which
are continually being used by believers in Christian doctrine with quotations from the philosophers, wanting to make out that the opinions which
Celsus thinks to be right in the doctrines held by the Christians have been
expressed both better and more clearly by the philosophers, so that he may
draw away to philosophy those who are impressed by doctrines that in
themselves are manifestly good and religious. And as here we have come
to the end of the fifth book, let us begin the sixth with this next passage.

[1] Cf. Celsus in III, 14; V, 33.   [2] Cf. Celsus in III, 16.

BOOK VI

1. In this sixth book which we are beginning in reply to Celsus' attack on Christianity it is not our intention, pious Ambrose, to wrestle in it against the opinions he expresses which are derived from philosophy, as some one might perhaps suppose. For Celsus has quoted several passages especially from Plato, comparing them with extracts from the holy scriptures such as could impress an intelligent person, saying that *these ideas have been better expressed among the Greeks, who refrained from making exalted claims and from asserting that they had been announced by a god or the son of a god.* We say that it is the task of those who teach the true doctrines to help as many people as they can, and as far as it is in their power to win everyone over to the truth by their love to mankind—not only the intelligent, but also the stupid, and again not just the Greeks without including the barbarians as well. It is a very excellent thing[1] if someone is able to convert even *the most stupid and uneducated yokels.* Obviously, therefore, when such teachers speak they have to take pains to use a type of vocabulary that will help everybody and can command a hearing with anyone. On the other hand, all those who have abandoned the uneducated as being low-class and incapable of appreciating the smoothness of a literary style and an orderly description, and who pay attention only to people educated in learning and scholarship, confine what should be of benefit to the community to a very narrow and limited circle.

2. I have said this in reply to the criticism of Celsus and others that the scriptures have a mean style, which appears to be put in the shade by the brilliance of a literary composition.[2] For our prophets, and Jesus and his apostles, were careful to use a method of teaching which not only contains the truth but is also able to win over the multitude. After conversion and entrance into the Church each individual according to his capacity can ascend to the hidden truths in the words which seem to have a mean style. If I may venture to say so, the beautiful and refined style of Plato and those who write similarly benefits but a few, if indeed it benefits anybody; whereas that of teachers and writers with a meaner style which was practical and exactly suited to the multitude has benefited many. At any

---

[1] Read πολὺ δὲ τὸ εὐήμερον with Wif. No satisfactory sense is given either by the reading of A (ἥμερον), kept by Koetschau in his text (1899), or by that of the *Philocalia* (ἡμέτερον), preferred by Wendland, Winter, and Koetschau in his translation (1926).
[2] For pagan criticism of the vulgar style of the scriptures, cf., for example, Lactantius, *Div. Inst.* v, 1, 15–16; Jerome, *Ep.* xxii, 30; Aug. *Conf.* iii, 5, 9.

rate, Plato can only be seen in the hands of men who seem to be learned,[1] while Epictetus is admired even by common folk, who have an inclination to receive benefit because they perceive the improvement which his words effect in their lives.

We do not say this in criticism of Plato (for the great world of mankind has derived help from him also), but to elucidate the meaning of those who say: 'And my word and my preaching were not in persuasive words of wisdom, but in demonstration of the spirit and of power, that our faith may not be in the wisdom of men but in the power of God.'[2] The divine scripture says that the spoken word, even if it is true in itself and very persuasive, is not sufficient to affect a human soul unless some power is also given by God to the speaker and grace is added to what is said; and it is only by God's gift that this power is possessed by those whose preaching is successful. So in the sixty-seventh psalm the prophet says that 'the Lord will give a word to those who preach with great power'.[3]

Supposing that it is granted that in some respects the Greeks and those who believe our doctrines hold the same views, yet they have not the same power to win over souls and to confirm them in these teachings. For this reason the disciples of Jesus, who were uneducated so far as Greek philosophy is concerned, travelled through many nations of the world, influencing each of their hearers according to his merits as the Logos willed; and their converts became far better men in proportion to the inclination of their free will to accept a good life.

3. Let us allow, then, that *ancient and wise men reveal*[4] *their meaning to those able to understand it,* and also that *Plato the son of Ariston points out the truth about the highest good in one of his epistles when he says that the highest good cannot at all be expressed in words, but comes to us by long familiarity and suddenly like a light in the soul kindled by a leaping spark.*[5] When we hear this, we also agree that this is well said; for God revealed to them these things and all other truths which they stated rightly. That is why we say that those who have grasped the truth about God, but have not in practice worshipped God in a way worthy of the truth about Him, are subject to the punishments inflicted on sinners. Paul speaks of such people in these very words: 'The wrath of God is revealed from heaven against all ungodliness and unrighteousness of men, who hold down the truth in unrighteousness, because that which may be known of God is manifest among them; for God revealed it to them. For the invisible

[1] Plutarch remarks (*Mor.* 328 E): 'Few of us read Plato's *Laws.*' (Contrast 711 C, on children learning by heart simple Platonic dialogues.) Gellius, XIX, 1 (pocket Epictetus).
[2] I Cor. ii. 4–5.   [3] Ps. lxvii. 12.
[4] Read with *Philocalia* (We., Wif.) δηλούτωσαν.
[5] Celsus quotes Plato, *Ep.* VII, 341 C.

things of him since the creation of the world are clearly seen, being
perceived through the things that are made, even his everlasting power
and divinity, that they may be without excuse; because that knowing God
they glorified him not as God, neither gave thanks; but became vain in
their reasonings, and their senseless heart was darkened. Professing
themselves to be wise, they became fools, and changed the glory of the
incorruptible God for the likeness of an image of corruptible man, and of
birds, and fourfooted beasts, and creeping things.'[1] It is 'holding down
the truth', as our scripture testifies, when they think that *the highest good
cannot at all be expressed in words*, and say that 'it comes suddenly by
long familiarity with the subject itself and by living with it, like a light in
the soul kindled by a leaping spark, which after it has come into being
feeds itself'.[2]

4. However, those who wrote such passages as this about the highest
good go down to Piraeus to pray to Artemis as a goddess, and to see the
festival celebrated by uneducated people.[3] And those who taught such
profound philosophy about the soul and the future course of the soul that
has lived a good life, abandon the great truths that God revealed to them
to attend to mean and trivial things, and give a cock to Asclepius.[4]
Although they had been shown the invisible things of God and the ideas
from the creation of the world and the sensible universe, from which they
ascend to the intelligible world, and though they finely perceived His
eternal power and divinity, nevertheless they became vain in their
reasonings; and their senseless heart wallows in darkness and ignorance
where the worship of God is concerned. It is even possible to see those
who pride themselves on their wisdom and idea of God bowing down to
a 'likeness of an image of corruptible man' and saying that it honours
God,[5] and sometimes even descending with the Egyptians to birds, or
fourfooted animals, or creeping things. Even if some seem to have risen
above these things, yet they will be found to have changed the truth of God
into a lie and to worship and serve the creation rather than the Creator.[6]
Therefore, because the wise men and scholars among the Greeks were in
error about God in their religious practices, 'God chose the foolish things
of the world' to put the wise to shame, and the base things, and the weak
things, and the things that are despised, and the things that are not, that

[1] Rom. i. 18–23.
[2] Origen quotes the full text of the Platonic passage, no doubt (as Bader rightly observes)
in order to show that he knows Celsus' source at first hand himself.
[3] See Plato, *Rep.* 327 A. Max. Tyr. v, 8 a, defends Socrates' prayer as philosophic.
[4] See Plato, *Phaedo*, 118 A. Similarly Tert. *Apol.* XLVI, 5; *de An.* I, 6; Prudentius, *Apoth.*
203 ff.
[5] For φησιν K. tr. reads φασιν. For the idea, cf. Celsus in VII, 62.
[6] Cf. Rom. i. 20–5.

He may bring to nought the things that are, and indeed that no flesh may boast before God.[1]

Our wise men, Moses who was the most ancient and the prophets who succeeded him, were the first to understand that '*the highest good cannot at all be expressed in words*', when, seeing that God manifests Himself to those who are worthy and ready to receive Him, they wrote that God appeared to Abraham, for instance, or to Isaac, or to Jacob.[2] But who it was that appeared, and what sort of a person, and in what way, and to which[3] of those among us, are questions which they have left for the examination of people who can show themselves to be like the men to whom He appeared. For they saw Him not with the eyes of the body, but with a pure heart. In the words of our Jesus, 'blessed are the pure in heart; for they shall see God'.[4]

5. The idea that '*a light suddenly arrived in the soul as though kindled by a leaping spark*' was known before Plato by the Word, saying in the prophets: 'Light for yourselves a light of knowledge.'[5] And John who lived after Jesus says: 'That which has come into being in the Logos was life, and the life was the light of men', which is 'the true light that lightens every man' coming into the true and intelligible world, and that makes him a 'light of the world'.[6] This light has 'shone in our hearts to give the light of the gospel of the glory of God in the face of Jesus Christ'.[7] So a very ancient prophet, who prophesied many generations before the reign of Cyrus (he was more than fourteen generations earlier than he),[8] says: 'The Lord is my light and my salvation, whom shall I fear?' And 'thy law is a lamp to my feet and a light to my path'. And 'the light of thy face has been shown upon us, O Lord'. And 'in thy light shall we see light'.[9] The Word in Isaiah exhorts us to this light, saying 'Be enlightened, be enlightened, O Jerusalem; for thy light is come, and the glory of the Lord has risen upon thee.'[10] This same man, in the place where he prophesies about the coming of Jesus, who makes us abandon the worship of idols and images and daemons, says that 'to those who sit in the land and shadow of death a light has arisen'; and again, 'a people that sat in darkness saw a great light'.[11]

See then the difference between Plato's fine utterance about the highest good and what the prophets said about the light of the blessed. And notice that, though what Plato said was true, it did not help his readers towards a pure religion at all, nor even Plato himself, in spite of the fact

[1] Cf. I Cor. i. 27–9.   [2] Cf. Gen. xii. 7; xxvi. 2; xxxv. 9.
[3] K. tr. proposes ἐν ἡμῖν ⟨ὅμοιος⟩, 'like to which of those...'.
[4] Matt. v. 8.   [5] Hos. x. 12.   [6] John i. 3–4, 9; Matt. v. 14.
[7] II Cor. iv. 6.   [8] Deduction from Matt. i. 17.
[9] Ps. xxvi. 1; cxviii. 1–5; iv. 7; xxxv. 10.   [10] Isa. lx. 1.   [11] Isa. ix. 2.

that he taught such profound philosophy about the highest good. But
the mean style of the divine scriptures has made honest readers inspired
by it. And this light is sustained in them by the oil mentioned in a certain
parable as keeping alight the torches of the five wise virgins.[1]

6. Celsus also quotes another passage from the epistle of Plato which
reads as follows: '*And if it seemed to me that these matters ought to be
described in writing or orally at some length for the masses, what finer thing
in life could we do than to describe what is of great benefit to mankind and to
bring out its nature to the light for all men?*'[2] Let us briefly discuss this. The
question whether or not Plato had something more sacred than the
doctrines which he wrote down and more divine than those which he left
behind, we will leave for each man to study to the best of his ability. We
will show, on the other hand, that our prophets also had certain truths in
their minds that were too exalted to be written down and which they did not
record. For Ezekiel receives a roll of a book with writing within and
without, in which there was mourning, lamentation, and woe;[3] and when
the Word commanded him he ate the book lest he should write it down
and betray its contents to people who were unworthy. John also is
recorded to have seen and done a similar thing.[4] Moreover, Paul heard
unspeakable words which it is not lawful for man to utter.[5] Jesus, who
was superior to all these men, is said to have spoken the Word of God to
his disciples privately,[6] and especially in places of retreat. But what he
said has not been recorded. For it did not seem to them that '*these matters
ought to be described at some length or orally for the masses*'. And, if it is not
an impertinence to speak the truth about such great men, I affirm that,
because they received their thoughts by the grace of God, these men saw
better than Plato what truths should be committed to writing, and how
they should be written, and what ought under no circumstances to be
written for the multitude, and what may be spoken, and what is not of
this nature. And again, John teaches us the difference between matters
that may and that may not be written down when he says that he heard
seven thunders teaching him about certain subjects, and forbidding him to
commit their words to writing.[7]

7. Much is to be found in Moses and the prophets, who are not only
earlier than Plato but also than Homer and the discovery of writing among
the Greeks,[8] which is worthy of the grace of God given to them and is
filled with profound meaning. They did not say these things, as Celsus
thinks, *because they misunderstood Plato*. How could they have heard

[1] Matt. xxv. 1 ff.   [2] Plato, *Ep.* VII, 341 D.   [3] Ezek. ii. 9–10; iii. 1–2.
[4] Rev. x. 9–10.   [5] II Cor. xii. 4.   [6] Mark iv. 34.
[7] Rev. x. 4.   [8] Cf. IV, 21.

a man who had not yet been born? But supposing that anyone were to apply Celsus' argument to the apostles of Jesus, who were more recent than Plato, consider whether it is not manifestly unconvincing to say that Paul the tentmaker and Peter the fisherman and John who left his father's nets taught such doctrines about God because they misunderstood what was said by Plato in his epistles. And, although Celsus has often babbled about Christians *requiring immediate belief*,[1] he says it again as if it were something new in addition to what he has already said. However, the reply we have made to this is sufficient.

He also quotes another phrase of Plato where he says that through '*the use of questions and answers*'[2] *understanding illuminates those who follow his philosophy*. Let us show, then, from the holy scriptures that the divine Word also exhorts us to study dialectics. Solomon says in one place 'Education that is unchallenged goes wrong.'[3] In another place Jesus the son of Sirach, who left us the book of Wisdom, says 'The knowledge of an unwise man is unexamined words.'[4] Accordingly '*proofs are friendly*'[5] even more among us who have learnt that a leader of the gospel must be 'able to refute the adversaries'.[6] If, however, some are idle, and do not take the trouble to give heed to Bible-reading, and to search the scriptures,[7] and do not obey Jesus' command to seek[8] for the meaning of the scriptures and to ask God about them and to knock for the truths locked up inside them, that is no reason for supposing that there is no wisdom in scripture.

8. After other words of Plato to the effect that *the Good is known* '*to a few*' *since, when the multitude are filled with* '*a wrong contempt and a high and conceited ambition because they have learnt some sacred truths*',[9] *they say that certain things are true*, he then says: *After Plato has said this, nevertheless he does not relate some incredible tale, nor does he check the tongue of the man who wants to inquire*[10] *what in fact it is which he professes, nor does he at once order people to* '*start by believing that God is like this and He has a Son like that, and that the latter came down and talked with me*'.[11] I reply to this that Aristander, I believe, wrote of Plato that he was not the son of Ariston, but of a visionary figure who came to Amphictione in the form of Apollo.[12]

---

[1] Cf. I. 9; VI, 10–11.   [2] Plato, *Ep.* VII, 344B.   [3] Prov. x. 17.
[4] Sir. xxi. 18.   [5] Plato, *Ep.* VII, 344B.   [6] Titus i. 9.
[7] John v. 39.   [8] Matt. vii. 7; Luke xi. 9.   [9] Plato, *Ep.* VII, 341E.
[10] Read προσερέσθαι with Bo. (K. tr. proposes πρόσθεν ἐρέσθαι.)
[11] Cf. Hermas, *Mand.* I, 1 'First of all believe that God is one....'
[12] Aristander is probably the soothsayer of Alexander the Great (Clem. Al. *Strom.* I, 134, 4; Lucian, *Philopatris* 21–2) who wrote a book full of incredible miracles (Pliny, *N.H.* XVII, 243). For his story of Plato cf. Plutarch, *Mor.* 717E–718B; Diog. Laert. III, 2; Apuleius, *de Plat.* I, 1; Olympiodorus, *Vita Plat.* I (in Hermann's *Plato*, VI, 191, 2); Suidas, *s.v.* 'Plato'; Jerome, *adv. Jovin.* I, 42.

Many other Platonists also have told this story in narrating Plato's life.
What should we say too of Pythagoras, who told a vast number of
fantastic tales, and to a whole crowd of Greeks showed his thigh to be
made of ivory, and said that he recognized the shield which he used when
he was Euphorbus, and who is alleged to have appeared in two cities on
one day?[1] Anyone who wants to criticize a story of Plato and Socrates as
an incredible tale would quote the story of the swan which associated with
Socrates in a dream and of the master saying, when the young man was
introduced to him, 'This then was the swan.'[2] Furthermore, the third eye
which Plato saw himself to possess may be regarded as an incredible tale.[3]
Malicious folk, who want to find fault with the visionary experiences of
men whose character surpasses that of the majority, would find plenty of
points to attack and to criticize. They might also mock at the daemon of
Socrates as being a fiction.[4]

We, therefore, tell no incredible tales when we explain the doctrines
about Jesus, nor did his genuine disciples record stories of this kind about
him. But Celsus, who professes to know everything and quotes much from
Plato, says nothing (intentionally, I think) of the saying about the Son of
God, uttered by Plato in the epistle to Hermeias and Coriscus. The words
of Plato read as follows: 'And swear by the God of all things, who is
ruler of all that is and that shall be, and by the Father and Lord of the mind
and cause, whom if we really are philosophers we shall all know clearly as
well as possible for blessed men.'[5]

9. Celsus also quotes another passage from Plato which reads like
this: '*It has come into my mind to speak at still greater length about this
subject; for probably the things of which I speak would be clearer if I did so.
For there is a true doctrine,*[6] *which meets anyone who ventures to write
anything at all about such matters, of which I have often spoken before, but*

---

[1] Origen is slightly confused here; the usual story was that the shield was ivory, the
thigh golden (Diog. Laert. VIII, 5, 11). Cf. Amm. Marc. XXII, 16, 21. For the Euphorbus
story cf. E. Rohde, *Psyche* (E.T.) pp. 598 f. with his numerous references; for the golden
thigh, A. B. Cook, *Zeus*, II (1925), p. 223 n. 6. (Origen makes it ivory, perhaps through
confusion with the ivory shoulder of Pelops: cf. *ibid.* p. 224.) For Pythagoras' achievement of bilocation cf. Porphyry, *Vita Pythag.* 27 (copied by Iamblichus, *Vita Pythag.*
XXVIII, 134), who says that Pythagoras appeared on one and the same day at Metapontum
in Italy and at Tauromenium in Sicily.

[2] Cf. Pausanias, I, 30, 3; Diog. Laert. III, 5; Apuleius, *de Plat.* I, 1; Tert. *de Anima*,
XLVI, 9; Suidas, *s.v.* 'Plato'; Olympiodorus, *Vita Plat.* 4.

[3] Cf. the late Anon. *Vita Platonis* in the Didot *Diogenes Laertius*, app. 9, 13.

[4] Meletus ridiculed it in his indictment (Plato, *Apol.* 31 D).

[5] Plato, *Ep.* VI, 323 D, quoted as referring to the Father and the Son by Clem. Al. *Strom.*
V, 102. For the Neoplatonic exegesis, cf. A. E. Taylor, *The Parmenides of Plato* (1934),
pp. 145 ff.

[6] Cf. Introduction, p. xxi.

which seems to need stating now also. Each thing that exists has three factors by which knowledge of it must necessarily come; and the knowledge itself is a fourth, and we must define the fifth as that which is knowable and true. Of these the first is the name, the second the word, the third the image, and the fourth is the knowledge.[1] We might follow this definition and say that it corresponds to the 'name' of which Plato speaks that John was introduced before Jesus as 'a voice crying in the wilderness';[2] and that it corresponds to the 'word' of Plato that 'the second' after John was Jesus, to whom John drew attention and to whom are applied the words 'The Word became flesh.'[3] Plato says that '*the third is the image*'. We apply the word 'image' with greater precision to something else;[4] but we might say that after the Word there is marked upon the soul the impress of the wounds, and that this is the Christ in each individual, derived from Christ the Word.[5] And a person with ability might carefully consider also whether Christ, whom we believe to be the wisdom 'in those who are perfect',[6] corresponds to the fourth which is 'knowledge'.

10. Then he says: *You see how Plato, though he strongly affirms that it cannot be 'described in words',*[7] *nevertheless gives a reason for this difficulty lest he should appear to retreat by putting the matter beyond discussion; for perhaps even the nature of Nothing could be defined in words.* As Celsus mentions this to substantiate his view that it is needful not merely to believe but also to give a reason for one's belief, we also will quote a phrase of Paul where he criticizes the man who believes by giving a random assent saying 'except you have believed at random'.[8]

By his repetitions Celsus forces us to repeat ourselves when, like a boaster, after the arrogant words he has just uttered he says: *Plato is not arrogant, nor does he tell lies, asserting that he has found something new, or that he has come from heaven to proclaim it; but he confesses the source from which these doctrines come.* Anyone seeking a reply to Celsus would say to this that even Plato is arrogant when in the Timaeus he puts these words into the mouth of Zeus: 'Gods of gods, whose Creator and Father I am...'[9] and so on. If, however, someone were to defend this on the

---

[1] Plato, *Ep.* VII, 342 A, B.   [2] Matt. iii. 3.
[3] John i. 14. Origen is using the recognized distinction between λόγος (a rational utterance) and φωνή (a cry), familiar since Plato, *Theaet.* 203 B. He writes similarly in *Comm-in Joann.* II, 32 (26), though he will not accept Heracleon's use of the distinction (*ibid.* VI, 20 (12)). For the history of the distinction and its use in Christian theological writing see Lightfoot on Ignatius, *Rom.* ii. 1; F. J. Dölger, *Antike u. Christentum*, V (1936), pp. 218–23.
[4] In Jewish-Christian usage εἴδωλον is applied to pagan deities.
[5] Origen is probably being deliberately obscure. For Christ in each individual Christian, cf. VI, 79, below; *Comm. in Joann.* VI, 6 (3). In *Comm. in Cant. Cantic.* III, 76 (VIII, 194) he has an elaborate mystical interpretation of the text 'I am wounded with love', which may help to explain the reference to 'the wounds'. Possibly the allusion is to Gal. vi. 17.
[6] I Cor. ii. 6.   [7] Plato, *Ep.* VII, 341 C.   [8] I Cor. xv. 2.   [9] *Tim.* 41 A.

ground that it is the thought of Zeus which Plato represents him as declaring, why should not he who studies the meaning of the words of the Son of God, or of the Creator in the prophets, have something more significant to say than Zeus' speech in the Timaeus? The proclamation of future events is the mark of divinity, since they are not foretold by a natural human faculty;[1] and from the consequent events we draw the conclusion that it was a divine Spirit which proclaimed these things.

We do not *say to every one who comes to us, 'First believe that the person of whom I am telling you is God's Son.'* But we put the gospel before each man in a form suited to his character and condition; for we have learnt to 'know how we ought to answer each individual'.[2] There are some people to whom we preach only an exhortation to believe, since they are incapable of anything more; but with others we do all we can to approach them with rational arguments 'by questions and answers'.[3] We certainly do not say what Celsus mockingly attributes to us, '*Believe that the person of whom I am telling you is God's Son, although he was most dishonourably arrested and punished to his utter disgrace, and though quite recently he wandered about most shamefully in the sight of all men.*'[4] Nor do we say: '*This is all the more reason for believing.*'[5] For we try to give each individual even more extensive arguments than those which we have set forth earlier.

II. After this Celsus says: *If these people* (meaning the Christians) *proclaim Jesus, and others proclaim someone else, and if they all have the common and glib slogan 'Believe if you want to be saved, or else away with you', what will those do who really want to be saved? Are they to throw dice in order to divine where they may turn, and whom they are to follow?* To this we hasten to reply on the ground of the self-evident nature of the facts. If there had been many like Jesus related to have visited human life as sons of God, and if each of them had attracted some to follow him; so that, because of the similarity of their claims, it became a moot point which of the persons to whom testimony was borne by the people who believed in them actually was Son of God: then he would have been justified in saying *If these people proclaim Jesus, and others proclaim someone else, and if they all have the common and glib slogan 'Believe if you want to be saved, or else away with you'*, and so on. But, in fact, Jesus has been preached in all the world because he is the only Son of God who has visited the human race. Those who like Celsus supposed that Jesus performed incredible frauds, and on this account wanted to do the same as he, as if they too might have

---

[1] Cf. III, 25; IV, 96; Celsus in IV, 88.   [2] Col. iv. 6.
[3] Cf. Plato, *Ep.* VII, 344B.   [4] Cf. Celsus in I, 62; II, 9.
[5] For the view that the shame of the Incarnation is a reason for believing in it the *locus classicus* is Tertullian, *de Carne Christi*, 5.

similar powers over men, were proved to be of no significance. They were
Simon the Samaritan magician, and Dositheus who came from the same
country as the former; the one said that he was the so-called Great
Power of God,[1] while the other said that he himself was son of God.
There are no Simonians anywhere in the world, although to gain more
adherents Simon relieved his disciples of any risk of death, which Christians have been taught to prefer, by teaching them to regard idolatry as
a matter of indifference. Moreover, the Simonians have not been subject
to any organized opposition at all; for the evil daemon who plots against
the teaching of Jesus knew that none of his particular intentions would be
frustrated by Simon's teaching. The Dositheans also did not flourish even
in their early days; at the present time their numbers have become
exceedingly few, so that their whole number is said not to amount to
thirty.[2] Judas the Galilean also, as Luke wrote in the Acts of the Apostles,
wanted to make out that he was some great person, and before him there
was Theudas. But as their teaching was not of God they were killed and
all who believed them were suddenly scattered.[3] We do not, therefore,
throw dice in order to divine where we may turn and whom we are to follow, as
if there were several men who could lead us off with the claim that they
had come from God to visit the human race. That, however, is enough on
this topic.

12. So we pass on to another objection of Celsus who, because he does
not know the actual text of our scriptures but misunderstands them, says
we *say that the wisdom possessed by men is foolishness with God*. Paul's
words are 'the wisdom of the world is foolishness with God'.[4] And
Celsus asserts that *the reason for this has been mentioned long ago. The reason*,
he thinks, why we use this phrase is that we *aim to convert only the uneducated
and stupid*. But, as he himself has indicated, he has *made the same point
earlier*,[5] and we met the argument as well as we could. Nevertheless, he

---

[1] Acts viii. 10. Cf. I, 57; *Comm. in Joann.* XIII, 27 'From the Samaritans one Dositheus
arose and asserted that he was the prophesied Christ; there are Dositheans to this day who
originate from him; they read books by Dositheus and interpret certain myths about him
to the effect that he did not taste death, but is still alive somewhere.' Origen has other
allusions to him in *Comm. ser. in Matt.* XXXIII; *Hom. in Luc.* XXV; *de Princ.* IV, 3, 2.

[2] In I, 57 the Simonians are said to number 30. The confusion may be explained from
Clement. Recog. II, 8–11, where after the death of the Baptist Dositheus advanced his
heresy with a fixed circle of thirty disciples; Simon Magus applied for entry and was admitted
when a vacancy occurred by death; he ultimately ousted Dositheus and became head of the
sect. (The account in *Clement. Hom.* II, 23–4 is closely parallel; but here John the Baptist is
said to have had thirty disciples.) In this connexion it is important to note that Origen
seems to have known the second-century document lying behind the Clementine writings,
which in their present form date from the fourth century.

[3] Cf. Acts v. 36–7.   [4] I Cor. iii. 19. Cf. Celsus in I, 9.

[5] Cf. Celsus in I, 27; III, 44, 50, 55, 59, 74, 75; VI, 13–14.

wanted here to show both that *this notion was invented by us*, and that *it was taken over from the Greek wise men who said that human wisdom is one thing and divine wisdom another*. So he quotes verses of *Heraclitus*—one where he says '*The character of man has no common sense, but that of God has*', and another where he says '*A man has the reputation of being a fool before a god just as a child before a man.*'[1] He also quotes this from the Apology of Socrates which Plato wrote: '*For I, men of Athens, have come to have this name for no other reason than that of wisdom. But what sort of wisdom is this? It is a wisdom that is perhaps attainable by man; for in truth I venture to affirm that I am wise in that respect.*'[2] These are the quotations that Celsus gives. For my part I will add these words from Plato's epistle to Hermeias, Erastus, and Coriscus: 'Now although I am an old man, I say that for this beautiful wisdom of the Forms Erastus and Coriscus need wisdom which will protect them from wicked and unrighteous men, and a certain power of self-defence. For because they have spent much of their life with us who are moderate men and not evil, they are inexperienced. That is why I said that they need these powers so that they are not forced to neglect the true wisdom, and to attend more than they ought to human and necessary wisdom.'[3]

13. These words, then, distinguish between a wisdom that is divine and one that is human. Human wisdom is what we call 'the wisdom of the world', which is 'foolishness with God'.[4] But the divine wisdom, which is different from the human if it really is divine, comes by the grace of God who gives it to those who prove themselves to be suitable persons to receive it,[5] and especially to those who, because they have realized the difference between the two kinds of wisdom, say in their prayers to God: 'For even if a man be perfect among the sons of men, yet if the wisdom that comes from above is not with him, he shall be held in no account.'[6] We maintain that human wisdom is a means of education for the soul, divine wisdom being the ultimate end. So the latter is said to be 'solid food' for the soul by the writer who says: 'But solid food is for fullgrown men, who by reason of use have their senses exercised to discern between good and evil.'[7]

It is true that this opinion is ancient; but it is not true, as Celsus thinks, that *the antiquity of this distinction goes back to Heraclitus and Plato*. Before their time the prophets had distinguished between the two kinds of wisdom. At this moment it is enough to quote from the words of David

---

[1] Heraclitus, *fragg.* 78–9 Diels.   [2] Plato, *Apol.* 20 D.
[3] Plato, *Ep.* VI, 322 D, E.   [4] I Cor. iii. 19.
[5] For the knowledge of God as only attainable by grace, cf. VII, 44.
[6] Wisd. of Sol. ix. 6.   [7] Heb. v. 14.

the saying about the man who is wise in the divine wisdom, who, he says,
'will not see corruption when he sees wise men die'.[1] Divine wisdom,
which is not the same thing as faith, is first of what are called the spiritual
gifts of God; the second place after it, for those who have accurate understanding of these matters, is held by what is called knowledge; and faith
stands in the third place, since salvation must be available also for the
simple folk who advance in religion as far as they can comprehend. So
Paul has it: 'For to one is given through the Spirit the word of wisdom;
and to another the word of knowledge according to the same Spirit; and
to another faith, in the same Spirit.'[2] For this reason you would not find
ordinary people partaking of divine wisdom, but those whose ability is
superior and stands out among all those who are adherents of Christianity.
And no one would *expound the truths of divine wisdom to those who are very
uneducated or slaves or quite ignorant.*

14. Celsus describes as *very uneducated* and as *slaves* and as *quite ignorant*
those who do not understand what he has to say[3] and have not been
educated in the learning of the Greeks. But the people whom we call very
uneducated are those who are not ashamed to address lifeless objects,[4] who
invoke what is diseased that it may grant them good health, who ask what
is dead to give life, and who beseech what is quite helpless for succour.
Even if some maintain that these objects are not gods but imitations of the
true gods and symbols of them,[5] none the less they too are *uneducated and
slaves and ignorant* because they imagine that the hands of artisans can
make imitations of the divinity.[6] So we say that the most insignificant of
us Christians has been delivered from this lack of education and ignorance,
whereas the most intelligent understand and comprehend the divine hope.
But we also maintain that it is not possible for a man who has not been
trained in human wisdom to receive the more divine, and hold that all
human wisdom is foolishness in comparison with divine wisdom.

Instead of arguing, as he ought, in support of his assertion, he calls us
sorcerers, and says that we *flee headlong from cultured people because they are
not prepared to be deceived; but we trap illiterate folk.*[7] He did not see that
right from the beginning our wise men were educated in the learning of
foreign peoples—Moses in all the wisdom of the Egyptians,[8] and Daniel,
Ananias, Azarias, and Misael, in all the writings of the Assyrians,[9] so that
they were found to know ten times as much as all the wise men there. And,
though they are few in proportion to the multitudes, there are even at the

---

[1] Ps. xlviii. 10–11.   [2] I Cor. xii. 8–9.
[3] Read πράγματα with A. For the argument, cf. Celsus in III, 44 ff.
[4] Cf. Wisd. of Sol. xiii. 17–18.   [5] Cf. III, 40; Celsus in VII, 62.
[6] Cf. I, 5.   [7] Cf. I, 27.
[8] Acts vii. 22.   [9] Dan. i. 17 ff.

present time wise men in the churches who have been converted after having been educated in what we call carnal wisdom; and there are also men who have passed on from that to the divine wisdom.

15. Then after this, because Celsus knows only by hearsay of our teaching about humility, and has not taken the trouble to understand it, he tries to malign our doctrine. He imagines that it is *a misunderstanding of the words of Plato who says somewhere in the Laws:* '*God, as the ancient saying goes, having the beginning, end, and middle of all that exists, advances on a straight course and goes about according to nature. And with him justice always follows as avenger of transgressions of the divine law, and he who will be happy follows her closely, humble and orderly.*'[1] He does not see that men far earlier than Plato prayed: 'Lord, my heart would not have been uplifted, nor mine eyes lofty; neither would I have gone into great matters nor into things too wonderful for me, if I had not been humble.'[2] This passage also clearly proves the falsity of his remark that *the humble man humiliates himself in a disgraceful and undignified manner, throwing himself headlong to the ground upon his knees, clothing himself in a beggar's rags, and heaping dust upon himself.*[3] For according to the prophet the humble man walks in great and wonderful things that are beyond him, which are the truly great doctrines and wonderful insights, because he humbles himself 'under the mighty hand of God'.[4]

If, however, because of their lack of education some have not a clear idea of the doctrine of humility and behave in the way he describes, it is not the gospel that is at fault. But we ought to make allowances for the lack of education of those who, though they mean well, fail because of this defect. More humble and orderly than the man whom Plato regards as humble and orderly is the man who is orderly because he 'walks in great matters which are too wonderful for him', and who is humble because even when his mind is uplifted by these insights he voluntarily humbles himself, not under any ordinary man but 'under the mighty hand of God', through Jesus who teaches him these doctrines. 'He counted it not a prize to be on an equality with God, but emptied himself, taking the form of a servant, and being found in fashion as a man he humbled himself,

---

[1] Plato, *Laws*, 715 E.   [2] Ps. cxxx. 1–2.
[3] Celsus describes the Christian penitential system. Sackcloth and ashes and the self-abasement before the presbyters of the church are a necessary part of this process as described by Tertullian, *de Paenitentia*, 9. It is evident from what Tertullian goes on to say (*ibid.* 11) that many Christians recoiled from the practice as shameful and disgusting.
The Greeks regarded prostration as a mark of barbarous superstition. It is characteristic of the Superstitious Man, says Theophrastus (*Char.* 16), 'to fall on his knees'. Similarly Plutarch, *Mor.* 166A. Evidence on the Greek dislike of *proskynesis* is collected by A. Alföldi in *Mitteil. d. Deutschen Archäol. Inst., röm. Abt.* XLIX (1934), pp. 11 ff., 46 ff.
[4] I Pet. v. 6.

becoming obedient unto death, yea, the death of the cross.'[1] So great is the doctrine of humility that we have no common teacher to instruct us in it, but it is our great Saviour himself who says: 'Learn of me; for I am meek and humble of heart; and you shall find rest for your souls.'[2]

16. After this he says that *Jesus' judgment against the rich, when he said 'It is easier for a camel to go through the eye of a needle than for a rich man to enter the kingdom of God'*,[3] *was manifestly borrowed from Plato*, and that *Jesus corrupts the Platonic saying where Plato says that 'It is impossible for an outstandingly good man to be exceptionally rich.'*[4] What person, even if he were only able to give slight attention to the facts, would not laugh at Celsus, not only if he were a believer in Jesus but even if he were one of the rest of mankind, when he hears that Jesus (who was born and bred among the Jews, and was thought to be the son of Joseph the carpenter, and had not even learnt the writings either of the Greeks or of the Hebrews, as the scriptures written by his followers frankly testify[5]) had read Plato, and approved of the remark which Plato made about the rich, that 'It is impossible to be exceptionally rich and good', and that he corrupted it to make the saying: 'It is easier for a camel to go through the eye of a needle than for a rich man to enter the kingdom of God'?

If Celsus were honest and had read the Gospels without hatred and hostility, he would carefully have considered why it is a camel, the animal which is crooked by its natural constitution, which he compared to a rich man, and what he who said that the way leading to life is narrow and strait[6] meant by the narrow eye of the needle. He would have observed that this animal was reckoned by the law to be unclean, because it has a certain tendency to chew the cud, and is also objectionable because it does not divide the hoof.[7] He would also have examined how often a camel is mentioned in the divine scriptures, and in what contexts, that he might perceive the meaning of the saying about the rich men. Also he would not have left unexamined Jesus' pronouncements about the blessedness of the poor[8] and the miserable lot of the rich,[9] to see whether these sayings were spoken of those who are poor and rich in respect of sensible things, or

---

[1] Phil. ii. 6–8.   [2] Matt. xi. 29.
[3] Matt. xix. 24; Mark x. 25; Luke xviii. 25.   [4] Plato, *Laws* 743 A.
[5] Matt. xiii. 54; Mark vi. 2; John vii. 15.   [6] Matt. vii. 14.
[7] Lev. xi. 4. Cf. Origen, *Hom. in Lev.* VII. 6, and especially *Comm. in Matt.* XV, 20 where the discussion is very similar. Philo, *de Agric.* 131 f., remarks that the Levitical law marking the camel as unclean because it chews the cud and does not divide the hoof is quite irrational if interpreted literally; he proceeds to give an elaborate allegorical exegesis.
[8] Matt. v. 3; Luke vi. 20.
[9] Luke vi. 24; xvi. 19–31. Cf. Clem. Al. *Strom.* IV, 25, 4 'It is not the poor without qualification whom he pronounces blessed, but those who have desired to become poor for righteousness' sake.' Similarly *Quis Dives*, XVII, 4.

whether the Word has in mind a poverty which is blessed without qualification and a wealth which is without qualification blameworthy. For not
even a stupid person would praise the poor indiscriminately; the majority
of them have very bad characters. But that is enough on this point.

17. Next, because he wants to disparage what our scriptures say about
the kingdom of God,[1] he quotes none of these sayings, as though they were
not even worth recording in his book, though perhaps it was because he
did not even know them. And he quotes passages of Plato *from the
Epistles and the Phaedrus* as if these were *inspired utterances*, and our
scriptures nothing of the sort. Let us, then, compare a few instances and
contrast them with the words of Plato which, though they are not unconvincing, certainly did not dispose the philosopher towards a behaviour
worthy even of himself in the matter of piety towards the Maker of the
universe. For he ought not to have polluted and adulterated his religion
by what we call idolatry, or, to use the word employed in popular usage,
by superstition.

It is said of God in the seventeenth Psalm that 'God made darkness his
hiding-place'.[2] This is a Hebrew way of showing that the ideas of God
which men understand in accordance with their merits are obscure and
unknowable, since God hides Himself as if in darkness from those who
cannot bear the radiance[3] of the knowledge of Him and who cannot see
Him, partly because of the defilement of the mind that is bound to a human
'body of humiliation',[4] partly because of its restricted capacity to comprehend God. To make it clear that the experience of the knowledge of God
comes to men on rare occasions, and is to be found by very few people,
Moses is said in scripture to have entered into 'the darkness where God
was'.[5] And again of Moses: 'Moses alone shall draw near to God; but the
others shall not draw near.'[6] And again, that the prophet may show the
depth of the doctrines about God, which is unfathomable to people who
do not possess the Spirit that searches all things, and searches even the
deep things of God,[7] he says: 'The great deep like a garment is his
covering.'[8]

Moreover, our Saviour and Lord, the Logos of God, shows the depth
of the knowledge of the Father, and that, although a derived knowledge
is possessed by those whose minds are illuminated by the divine Logos
himself, absolute understanding and knowledge of the Father is possessed
by himself alone in accordance with his merits, when he says: 'No man

---

[1] Cf. Celsus in I, 39; III, 59; VIII, 11.   [2] Ps. xvii. 12.
[3] Verbal allusion to Plato, *Rep.* 518A; cf. IV, 15 above.   [4] Phil. iii. 21.
[5] Exod. xx. 21, understood of God's transcendence by Philo, *de Post. Caini* 14; *de Mut.
Nom.* 7; Clem. Al. *Strom.* II, 6, 1.   [6] Exod. xxiv. 2.
[7] I Cor. ii. 10.   [8] Ps. ciii. 6.

has known the Son save the Father, and no man has known the Father save the Son, and him to whom the Son will reveal him.'[1] Neither can anyone worthily know the uncreated and firstborn of all created nature[2] in the way that the Father who begat him knows him; nor can anyone know the Father in the same way as the living Logos who is God's wisdom and truth. By participation in him who took away from the Father what is called darkness, which he made 'his hiding-place', and what is called his covering, 'the great deep', thus revealing the Father, anyone whatever who has the capacity to know Him may do so.

18. I have thought fit to adduce these few examples from the vast number of sayings about God which holy men have thought out, to show that, for those who have eyes that are able to perceive the profound truths of the Bible, the sacred writings of the prophets have something more profound about them than the words of Plato admired by Celsus. The passage from Plato which Celsus quoted reads as follows: '*All things centre in the King of all, and are for his sake, and he is the cause of all that is good. The second things centre in the Second, and the third things centre in the Third. The human soul, then, yearns to learn about these things to find what is their nature, by looking at the things that are related to itself, none of which are perfect. Now where the king and the principles which I mentioned are concerned, there is nothing of this sort.*'[3] I could quote the statements about the seraphim, as they are called by the Hebrews, described by Isaiah as hiding the face and the feet of God, and about what are called cherubim, which Ezekiel portrayed, and of their shapes, as it were, and of the way in which God is said to be carried upon the cherubim.[4] But, as these things are expressed in a very obscure form because of the unworthy and irreligious who are not able to understand the deep meaning and sacredness of the doctrine of God, I have not thought it right to discuss these matters in this book.

19. After this Celsus says: *It is because certain Christians have misunderstood sayings of Plato that they boast of a God who is above the heavens and place Him higher than the heaven in which the Jews believe.*[5] Here he does

---

[1] Matt. xi. 27; Luke x. 22.   [2] Cf. Col. i. 15.

[3] Plato, *Ep.* II, 312E, interpreted of the Trinity by Justin, *Apol.* I, 60, 7; Clem. Al. *Strom.* v, 103, 1. Cf. Athenagoras, *Leg.* 23. According to Hippolytus (*Ref.* VI, 37, 5) Valentinus got his idea of the Pleroma from this passage. For Neoplatonist exegesis, cf. A. E. Taylor, *The Parmenides of Plato*, pp. 145 ff., and Numenius of Apamea (ap. Eus. *P.E.* XI, 18).

[4] Isa. vi. 2; Ezek. i. 5–27; x. 1–21.

[5] Jewish preference for the number seven led to the location of their God in the seventh sphere; the Christians, working on a system of eight, could identify God's dwelling with the eighth region, the sphere of the fixed stars above the seven planets. See W. L. Knox, *St Paul and the Church of the Gentiles*, pp. 6 ff.; F. Dölger, 'Die Achtzahl in der altchristlichen Symbolik', in *Antike u. Christentum* IV (1934), pp. 153–87.

not make it quite clear whether they place Him higher than the God of the Jews, or only higher than the heaven by which they swear.[1] It is not, however, our task to speak now of those who proclaim a God other than that worshipped by the Jews, but to defend ourselves and to show that the Jewish prophets, in whom we believe, could not have taken anything from Plato. For they were earlier than he. Therefore we did not borrow from Plato the saying that 'All things centre round the King of all and are for his sake.' On the contrary, we have learnt from the prophets doctrines that are better expressed than this, since Jesus and his disciples explained the meaning of the Spirit that spoke in the prophets (which was none other than the Spirit of Christ). Nor was the philosopher the first to state the truth of a region above the heavens. Long ago David showed the profundity and the magnitude of the visions of God possessed by those who rise beyond sensible things when he said in the book of Psalms: 'Praise God, ye heavens of heavens, and the water that is above the heavens; let them praise the name of the Lord.'[2]

I do not doubt that Plato learnt the words of the *Phaedrus* from some Hebrews and that, as some writers have said,[3] it was after studying the sayings of the prophets that he wrote the passage where he says '*No earthly poet either has sung or will sing of the region above the heavens as it deserves*', and the following passage in which this also occurs: '*Ultimate being, colourless, formless, and impalpable, visible only to the mind that is guide of the soul, round which is the species of true knowledge, lives in this place.*'[4] At any rate, our Paul, who was educated in those prophetic writings and desired the things of the other world and the region beyond the heavens, and did every action in the light of those things that he might attain to them, says in the Second Epistle to the Corinthians: 'For our light affliction which is but for a moment works for us more and more exceedingly an eternal weight of glory; while we look not at the things that are seen, but at the things which are not seen; for the things that are seen are temporal; but the things which are not seen are eternal.'[5]

20. To those who can understand he obviously means the sensible world, though he calls it 'the things that are seen', and the intelligible world which is comprehensible by the mind alone,[6] though he calls it 'the things

---

[1] Cf. Matt. v. 34.   [2] Ps. cxlviii. 4–5.

[3] That Plato and the Greek philosophers plagiarized the Hebrew prophets and Moses was a commonplace of Jewish apologetic, taken over by Christian writers. Cf. Josephus, *c. Ap.* II, 36, 256–7; Justin, *Apol.* I, 59–60. The theme is especially common in Clement; cf. W. Bousset, *Jüdisch-christlicher Schulbetrieb in Alexandria und Rom* (1915), pp. 205 ff., who thinks Clement used a connected source dealing with this subject.

[4] Plato, *Phaedrus* 247 C.   [5] II Cor. iv. 17–18.

[6] Allusion to *Phaedrus*, 247 A.

that are not seen'. He also knows that sensible things are temporal and
visible, while intelligible things are eternal and invisible. Desiring to
continue in the contemplation of these things and being helped by his
longing for them, he regarded all affliction as nothing and as something
light. Even at the very time of affliction and troubles he was in no way
weighed down by them, but made light of every difficulty because he was
contemplating these things. For we have a great high priest who by the
greatness of his power and of his mind 'has passed through the heavens,
Jesus the Son of God',[1] who told those that had genuinely learnt the things
of God and who lived lives worthy of them that he would lead them on to
the things beyond this world. So he says: 'That where I go, you may be
also.'[2] On this account we hope that *after the 'troubles and strivings'*[3] *here
we shall come to the topmost heavens*, and according to the teaching of Jesus
will receive 'springs of water springing up to everlasting life',[4] and will
have the capacity for rivers of visions, and will be with the waters that are
said to be 'above the heavens' which 'praise the name of the Lord'.[5] As
long as we praise Him,[6] we shall not be *carried about away from 'the
circumference of the heaven'*,[7] but we shall always be engaged in the *contemplation* of the invisible things of God, which will no longer be
understood by us 'from the creation of the world by the things that are
made'[8] but, as the genuine disciple of Jesus expressed it, when he said 'But
then face to face'; and 'When that which is perfect is come, that which is
in part shall be done away.'[9]

   21. The scriptures accepted in the churches of God do not declare that
there are *seven heavens*,[10] or indeed any definite number of them at all,
though the Bible does seem to teach that there are heavens, perhaps
meaning the spheres of the planets of which the Greeks speak or perhaps
something else more mysterious. Celsus also follows Plato in saying that
the way for the souls to and from the earth passes through the planets.[11] But
Moses, our most ancient prophet, says that in a divine dream our forefather[12] Jacob had a vision in which he saw a ladder reaching to heaven and
angels of God ascending and descending upon it, and the Lord standing
still at its top;[13] perhaps in this story of the ladder Moses was hinting at these

---

[1] Heb. iv. 14.   [2] John xiv. 3.   [3] *Phaedrus*, 247B.
[4] John iv. 14.   [5] John vii. 38; Ps. cxlviii. 4–5.
[6] Cf. my remarks in *J.T.S.* XLVIII (1947), pp. 41 f.
[7] Plato, *Phaedrus*, 247C.   [8] Rom. i. 20.   [9] I Cor. xiii. 12, 10.
[10] Clem. Al. (*Strom.* IV, 159, 2) speaks of 'the seven heavens which some reckon as being
one on top of another'. Cf. Porphyry ap. Eus. *P.E.* IX, 10, 5, 413C. For the Rabbis,
Strack-Billerbeck, *Kommentar z. N.T.* III, p. 532. Origen (*de Princ.* II, 3, 6) knows of some
who 'appeal to the Book of Baruch in support of this doctrine'.
[11] *Phaedrus* 248C-E; *Timaeus* 41D-42E. Cf. Origen, *de Princ.* II, 11, 6.
[12] Read προπάτορος with Wendland.   [13] Gen. xxviii. 12–13.

333

truths or at yet more profound doctrines. Philo also composed a book about this ladder, which is worthy of intelligent and wise study by those who wish to find the truth.[1]

22. After this from a desire to parade his erudition in his attack on us Celsus also describes some Persian mysteries, where he says: *These truths are obscurely represented by the teaching of the Persians and by the mystery of Mithras which is of Persian origin. For in the latter there is a symbol of the two orbits in heaven, the one being that of the fixed stars and the other that assigned to the planets, and of the soul's passage through these. The symbol is this. There is a ladder with seven gates and at its top an eighth gate. The first of the gates is of lead, the second of tin, the third of bronze, the fourth of iron, the fifth of an alloy, the sixth of silver, and the seventh of gold. They associate the first with Kronos (Saturn), taking lead to refer to the slowness of the star; the second with Aphrodite (Venus), comparing her with the brightness and softness of tin; the third with Zeus (Jupiter), as the gate that has a bronze base and which is firm; the fourth with Hermes (Mercury), for both iron and Hermes are reliable for all works and make money and are hard-working; the fifth with Ares (Mars), the gate which as a result of the mixture is uneven and varied in quality; the sixth with the Moon as the silver gate; and the seventh with the Sun as the golden gate, these metals resembling their colours.*[2]

[1] Philo, *de Somniis*.
[2] For the Mithraic conception of the soul's ascent through the planets, cf. F. Cumont, *The Mysteries of Mithra* (1903), pp. 144 f. Of the considerable literature on this passage the most important discussions are these: W. Bousset, 'Die Himmelreise der Seele' in *Archiv für Religionswissenschaft* IV (1901), pp. 136–69 and 229–73, who discusses the theme of the soul's ascent from the point of view of comparative religion; A. B. Cook, *Zeus*, II (1925), pp. 114–40; P. Wendland, *Die hellenistisch-römische Kultur* (3rd ed. 1912), pp. 170–5; Cumont, *Textes et Monuments figurés relatifs aux Mystères de Mithra*, I (1899), pp. 117 f.; *Lux perpetua*, pp. 282 ff., and in *Rev. d'hist. des Rel.* CIII (1931), pp. 46 ff. The system described by Celsus is similar to that of the Mithraeum discovered at Ostia in 1885 (described in Cumont, *Textes et Mon.* II, pp. 243–5), where there is a succession of seven doors with planetary figures painted by each; there was probably a prayer to be recited before each door. Porphyry (*de Antro Nympharum*, 6) speaks of Mithraic worshippers in the cave (the cult-chamber) 'bearing symbols of the planets and of ladders'. Cf. *ibid.* 29 where 'the theologians say that the sun and moon are gates for the souls, which ascend through the sun and descend through the moon' (cf. Macrobius, *in Somn. Scip.* I, 12, 1–3). In the *Logia Chaldaica* (on which cf. Bidez in *Camb. Anc. Hist.* XII, p. 637) there is mention of a 'staircase with seven gates' (text quoted by Bousset, p. 265). Amulets in the shape of small bronze ladders have been found in tombs (Cook, p. 125). The theme is traced by Cook in Orphism, the second-century orator and hypochondriac Aelius Aristides, Babylonian religion, in the *Passio S. Perpetuae* and many later saints, and in Dante's ascent with Beatrice. Cf. G. G. Coulton in Cook, II, p. 1215 for the theme in Franciscan sources. In the Moslem 'liber Scalae Machometi' (early thirteenth century), which inspired Dante's *Divina Commedia*, Mahomet is conducted by Gabriel up through eight heavens with opening doors. The heavens are of metals and precious stones: (1) iron; (2) bronze; (3) silver; (4) gold; (5) pearl; (6) emerald; (7) ruby; (8) topaz. For the text see E. Cerulli, *Il Libro della Scala e la questione delle Fonti arabo-spagnole della Divina Commedia* (Studi e Testi 150, Vatican City, 1949). Professor H. W. Bailey draws my attention to the important discussion

He next examines the reason for this particular *arrangement of the stars which is indicated by means of symbols in the names of the various kinds*[1] *of matter.* And he connects *musical theories* with *the theology of the Persians* which he describes. He waxes enthusiastic about these and gives a *second explanation* which again contains *musical ideas*.[2] It seemed to me that to quote Celsus' words here would be absurd, for it would be to do what he himself has done when, for the purpose of criticizing Christians and Jews, he inappropriately compared their teaching not merely with the remarks of Plato, with which he might have rested content, but also, as he says, with *the mysteries of the Persian Mithras and their interpretation of them.* Leaving on one side the question whether this is a false or true account of what the Persians say who maintain the doctrines of Mithras, why did he describe these rather than one of the other mysteries with its interpretation? The Greeks do not think the mysteries of Mithras have anything exceptional about them compared with those of Eleusis or with those of Hecate which are revealed to people who are initiated in Aegina.[3] If he wanted to describe barbarian mysteries with their interpretation, why did

of this work by G. Levi della Vida, 'Nuova Luce sulle Fonti islamiche della Divina Commedia', in *Al-Andalus*, XIV, 2 (1949), pp. 377–407.

The obvious modern example of the association of planets with certain metals is mercury. Parallels to Celsus' text are adduced from the Byzantine world by Cook, *op. cit.* I (1914), pp. 625 f. Lists varied, and no other list corresponds exactly to that of Celsus: (i) a scholiast on Homer in Cramer, *Anecd. Paris.* III, 113, 4 ff. gives Kronos—bronze, Zeus—gold, Ares—iron, Helios—*elektron* (alloy of gold and silver), Aphrodite—tin, Hermes—lead, Selene—silver. A list more commonly found is (ii) Helios—gold, Selene—silver, Ares—iron, Kronos—lead, Zeus—*elektron*, Hermes—tin, Aphrodite—bronze. So Proclus, *in Tim.* I, 43, 5 ff. Diehl, and the scholiast *ad loc.* in *ibid.* I, 460, 22 ff.; Olympiodorus, *in Arist. meteor.* III, 6 on 377a 29 (Stuve, pp. 266 f.); Schol. Pindar, *Isthm.* V, 2 (Drachmann, III, p. 242); and the list printed by C. O. Zuretti, *Catalogue des manuscrits alchimiques grecs,* VIII (1932), p. 1. (iii) E. Piccolomini in *Rivista di Filologia*, II (1874), published a collection of excerpts from profane and ecclesiastical writers made by the thirteenth-century Byzantine monk, Maximus Planudes (cf. Wendel in P.-W. XX, 2 (1950), 2202–53). *Fr.* 57, p. 158, has a list with interlinear comments by a corrector assigning animals also to each planet: Kronos—lead—ass, Zeus—silver—eagle, Ares—iron—wolf, Helios—gold—lion, Aphrodite—tin—dove, Hermes—bronze—snake, Selene—crystal—bull (cf. Celsus in VI, 30 below). For planetary characteristics cf. Servius *ad Aen.* VI, 714 'torporem Saturni, Martis iracundiam, libidinem Veneris, Mercurii lucri cupiditatem, Iovis regni desiderium...'. For Saturn's slowness, [Plato], *Epinomis* 987C; Albinus, *Epit.* 14; Vettius Valens, VI, 2, etc.

[1] Read ποικίλης with K. tr.

[2] The order of the planets in this Mithraic list is not the usual order based on the ancient view of their distance from the earth (Saturn, Jupiter, Mars, Sun, Venus, Mercury, Moon), but that of the days of the week. Evidently Celsus mentioned explanations of this order derived from Pythagorean musical theory. Dio Cassius (XXXVII, 18–19) also gives two explanations of the planetary week. The second is now regarded as correct. The first is based on the principle of the tetrachord, and is no doubt one of the two mentioned by Celsus. See F. H. Colson, *The Week* (1926), pp. 43 ff., 75 ff.; A. D. Nock in *Amer. Journ. Arch.* L (1946), pp. 153, 164. See also Introduction, p. xxix.

[3] For the cult of Hecate at Aegina cf. Pausanias, II, 30, 2, and P.-W. VII, 2781.

he not prefer those of the Egyptians on which many pride themselves, or those of the Cappadocians who worship Artemis at Comana,[1] or those of the Thracians,[2] or even those of the Romans themselves who initiate the noblest members of the Senate?[3] But if he thought it inappropriate to bring forward one of these, since they are of no value for the purpose of criticizing Jews or Christians, why did it not also seem inappropriate to him to describe the Mithraic mysteries?

23. If anyone should want to have suggestions of the deeper truths about the way in which the soul enters into the divine realm, derived not from the most insignificant sect which he has mentioned,[4] but from the books, some of which are Jewish and are read in their synagogues, and in which Christians also believe, and some of which are only Christian, let him read the visions seen by the prophet Ezekiel at the end of his prophecy where different gates are depicted, conveying in veiled form certain doctrines about the various ways in which the more divine souls enter into the higher life.[5] Let him also read from the Apocalypse of John about the city of God, the heavenly Jerusalem, and about its foundations and gates.[6] And if he is also able to learn by means of symbols the way indicated for those who will journey to the divine realm, let him read the book of Moses entitled Numbers; and let him ask anyone competent to initiate him into the statements about the encampments of the children of Israel, of what nature were those fixed on the eastern side which are mentioned first, and of what sort were those on the south-west or south, and what were those which faced the sea, and what were those on the north side which are mentioned last.[7] For he will perceive truths of considerable profundity in the passages and not, as Celsus thinks, *matters only fit for fools and slaves to listen to*. He will comprehend who are the people referred to here, and

---

[1] The Cappadocian goddess Ma was identified with Artemis; cf. G. Wissowa, *Religion und Kultus der Römer* (2nd ed. 1912), pp. 348–50. For the mysteries at Comana, cf. Strabo, XII, 2, 3 (p. 535). Procopius, *Hist. Bell.* I, 17, 13, gives an aetiological account of the founding of Artemis' temple, and remarks that the two temples at Comana were turned into Christian churches without any change.

[2] For the Thracian mysteries of Sabazios cf. Wissowa, *op. cit.* pp. 375 f., and P.-W. *s.v.*

[3] The cult of the Great Mother had a strong traditional following among the Roman aristocracy, as has been shown by S. Aurigemma, 'La protezione speciale della Gran Madre Idea per la nobiltà Romana', in *Bullettino della Commissione Archeologica comunale di Roma*, XXXVII (1909), pp. 31–65 (I owe the reference to Cumont, *Religions Orientales* (1929), p. 221). Cf. also H. Graillot, *Le Culte de Cybèle* (1912), pp. 108 ff.

[4] The Ophites; cf. below.   [5] Ezek. xlviii. 31–5.

[6] Rev. xxi.

[7] Num. ii. In *Hom. in Num.* I, 3 Origen interprets the position of the tribes at the four points of the compass as referring to the resurrection of the dead; cf. *ibid.* III, 3 where it means the four ranks in heaven mentioned in Heb. xii. 18–23 (some reach Mount Sion, some the heavenly Jerusalem, some the multitude of angels, while the best reach the church of the first-born).

what is the true nature of the numbers enumerated in these places as belonging to each tribe. But I have not thought it appropriate to explain these matters now.

However, let Celsus and the readers of his book realize that *seven heavens* are nowhere mentioned in the scriptures which we believe to be genuine and divine. Nor is it *because they borrowed from the Persians or the Cabeiri*[1] that our prophets, or the apostles of Jesus, or the Son of God himself, say certain things.

24. Following the section which he borrowed from the Mithraic mysteries Celsus claims that *if one cares to study a mystery of the Christians side by side with that of the Persians which has been mentioned, contrasting them with one another and laying bare also the teaching of the Christians, one may then see*[2] *the difference between them.* Where he knew that he could give the names of sects, he did not hesitate to mention those which he seemed to know. But where it was his bounden duty to have done this if he knew the name, and where he ought to have informed us what sect it is which uses *the diagram* drawn by them, he has failed to do so.

It seems to me from what follows that his account of the diagram which he describes in part is based upon misunderstandings of the Ophites, a most undistinguished sect in my opinion. After industrious researches we managed to obtain this,[3] and we found in it what Paul calls the inventions of men 'who creep into houses and lead captive silly women laden with sins, led away by various lusts, ever learning and never able to come to the knowledge of the truth'.[4] The diagram has been so completely unconvincing that it has not even persuaded the women who are so easily deceived, nor the most stupid yokels, who are liable to be convinced by anything with the least plausibility. At any rate, although I have travelled through many places in the world and have inquired in all

---

[1] For the mysteries of the Cabeiri at Samothrace, cf. L. R. Farnell in Hastings' *Enc. Rel. Eth.* VII (1914), col. 628 ff.; O. Kern in P.-W. x (1919), cols. 1399 ff.; B. Hemberg, *Die Kabiren* (Uppsala, 1950).

[2] Read θεάσεσθαι with We.

[3] There are differences in the accounts given of the diagram by Celsus and Origen (cf. VI, 30), and it is not certain that the identical document lay before them. E. de Faye (*Gnostiques et Gnosticisme* (2nd ed. 1925), p. 359) remarks that if the names of the 'archontes' in VI, 30 had been before Celsus, it is strange that he did not mention them. W. Bousset (*Hauptprobleme der Gnosis* (1907), p. 10) thinks Origen nearer the original than Celsus. I reproduce a reconstruction of the Ophite diagram by T. Hopfner in *Charisteria Alois Rzach dargebracht* (1930), pp. 86–98. The place of magical diagrams in such Gnostic systems is shown by the Books of Jeu in the Bruce papyrus (C. Schmidt, *Koptisch-gnostische Schriften*, I, 1905, pp. 257–334). For a useful summary on the Ophites, see Salmon in *Dict. Chr. Biogr. s.v.*, and F. Legge, *Forerunners and Rivals of Christianity*, II, pp. 25–82. Also H. Leisegang, *Die Gnosis* (3rd ed. 1941), pp. 111–85.

[4] II Tim. iii. 6–7.

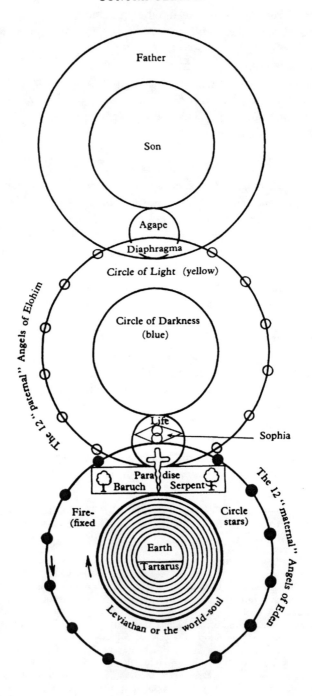

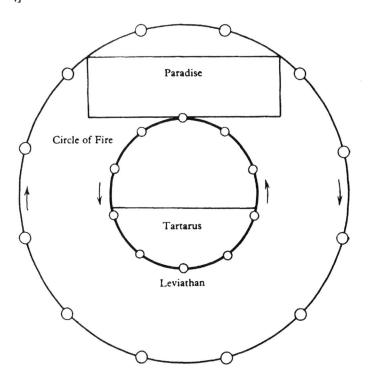

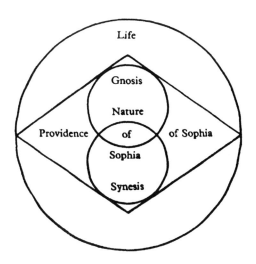

places of those who professed to be learned, I have not met with anyone
who believed in the teachings of the diagram.

25. *It contained a drawing of ten[1] circles, which were separated from one
another and held together by a single circle, which was said to be the soul of
the universe and was called Leviathan.*[2] The Jewish scriptures, with
a hidden meaning in mind, said that this Leviathan was formed by God as
a plaything. For in the Psalms we find: 'Thou hast made all things in
wisdom; the earth is filled with thy creation. This is the sea great and wide;
there go the ships, small animals and great, this serpent which thou didst
form to play with him.'[3] Instead of the word 'serpent' the Hebrew text
read 'Leviathan'. The impious diagram said that the Leviathan, which
was clearly so objectionable to the prophet, is the soul that has permeated
the universe. We also found that Behemoth[4] is mentioned in it as if it were
some being fixed below the lowest circle. The inventor of this horrible
diagram depicted Leviathan upon the circumference of the circle and at
its centre, putting in the name twice.

Celsus further says that *the diagram was divided by a thick black line,*

[1] R. A. Lipsius (in *Zeitschr. f. wiss. Theol.* VII (1864), p. 38 n. 1) and Hopfner (*loc. cit.*
p. 87) read ἑπτά to make this statement agree with VI, 35.
[2] Leviathan is an *ophis* in Isa. xxvii. 1 (cf. Job iii. 8; xli. 1; Ezek. xxxii. 2). For the
Gnostic idea that the world is surrounded by a great serpent cf. *Pistis Sophia*, 126 (Schmidt,
op. cit. p. 207; Horner's Eng. trans. p. 160): 'The outer darkness is a great dragon with his
tail in his mouth, being outside the whole world and going round all the world.' In the
Acts of Thomas 32 (James, *Apocr. N.T.* p. 379; cf. G. Bornkamm, *Mythos und Legende in
den Thomasakten* (1933), pp. 28 f.) the serpent that meets the apostle says 'I am son to him
that girdeth about the sphere; and I am kin to him that is outside the ocean, whose tail is
set in his own mouth.' A. B. Cook, *Zeus*, I (1914), pp. 191–2, figures a bronze disk, first
published by Cumont, showing Zeus surrounded by a snake coiled in a circle with its tail
in its mouth. Cook also quotes Horapollon, *Hierogl.* I, 2 'Wishing to describe the world
they depict a snake eating its own tail'; Macrobius, *Sat.* I, 9, 12 'When the Phoenicians in
their sacred art expressed the world pictorially, they depicted a snake drawn in a circle and
eating its own tail, symbolizing the fact that the world is nourished of itself and returns
upon its course'; Lydus, *de Mensibus* III, 4 'The Egyptians following sacred tradition
engrave on the pyramids a serpent eating his tail' (symbolizing the cycle of the year);
Mythogr. Vatic. III, 1, 1 (Mai, *Class. auct. e vatic. codicibus tom.* III, p. 162), where Saturn is
symbolized by a fire-breathing dragon eating its tail. For the magical papyri, cf. K. Preisendanz, *P.G.M.* I, 145; VII, 586 (with plate i. 4). Cook also figures a 'Gnostic' gem with the
same type of device. (For the frequency of the type cf. Campbell Bonner, *Studies in Magical
Amulets*, p. 250.) A gem of similar type is discussed by J. H. Iliffe in *Amer. Journ. Arch.*
XXXV (1931), pp. 304–9 (I owe the reference to Cook, III, p. 1137). The initiate of *Corp.
Herm.* I, 4 (according to A. D. Nock's probable restoration of the text) has a vision of
darkness like to a snake. For the soul, or *pneuma*, pervading the world as a snake cf.
Horapollon, *Hierogl.* I, 64. For the world-soul as a circle cf. Plotinus IV, 4, 16. I have not
seen K. Preisendanz, 'Aus der Geschichte des Uroboros', *Festschr. f. E. Fehrle* (1940),
pp. 194–209.
[3] Ps. ciii. 24–6.
[4] In I Enoch lx. 7 f. Leviathan is a female monster dwelling in the ocean, Behemoth
a male dwelling in a desert east of paradise; cf. IV Ezra vi. 49–52; II Baruch xxix. 4.

and asserts that they informed him that *this was Gehenna, also called Tartarus*. Finding Gehenna described in the gospel as a place of punishment,[1] we searched to find out if it was mentioned anywhere in the ancient books, especially in view of the Jews' use of the word. We found that in one passage the scripture mentions a Chasm of the son of Ennom; but we are informed that instead of the word 'Chasm', though with the same meaning, the Hebrew text reads 'the Chasm of Ennom and Gehenna'.[2] By careful study of the texts we also find that Gehenna or the Chasm of Ennom is included in the property assigned to the tribe of Benjamin,[3] of which Jerusalem was also a part. And by considering the inference from the fact that there is a heavenly Jerusalem with[4] the chasm of Ennom belonging to the property assigned to Benjamin, we find an allusion to the doctrine of punishments which are transformed into the means by which certain souls are purified through torment. So scripture says: 'Behold the Lord cometh like the fire of a smelting-furnace and as a fuller's herb; and he shall come down to refine and purify as it were gold and silver.'[5]

26. And the punishments that occur round Jerusalem are for those who are being refined; for they have taken into the very essence of their soul the works caused by evil, which somewhere is allegorically called lead. So in Zechariah iniquity was seated upon a 'talent of lead'.[6]

It is not right to explain to everybody all that might be said on this subject. Nor is this an appropriate moment. It is risky to commit to writing the explanation of these matters, because the multitude do not require any more instruction than that punishment is to be inflicted upon sinners. It is not of advantage to go on to the truths which lie behind it because there are people who are scarcely restrained by fear of everlasting punishment from the vast flood of evil and the sins that are committed in consequence of it.

The doctrine of Gehenna, therefore, was understood neither by the diagram nor by Celsus. For, had they known it, neither would the Ophites have solemnly made pictures and diagrams as though they displayed the truth by this means, nor would Celsus in his book against the Christians have included among his criticisms of them opinions which are not held by Christians at all, but merely by some who probably do not exist any longer and have entirely disappeared, or who, if they do survive,[7]

---

[1] Matt. v. 22, etc.
[2] The Masoretic Hebrew text has nothing of the kind. Cf. Jer. vii. 31 f.; xxxix (xxxii). 35.
[3] Joshua xviii. 16. Similar exegesis in *Comm. ser. in Matt.* 16.
[4] Read μετά with K. tr.　　　　[5] Mal. iii. 2–3.
[6] Zech. v. 7.
[7] With Wif. omit comma after τινων and read ⟨ἢ⟩ καὶ εἰς πάνυ.

consist of a very few people of no significance. Just as it is not proper for
Platonic philosophers to defend Epicurus and his impious doctrines, so
we are under no obligation to defend the diagram and to reply to Celsus'
objections to it. Consequently we leave on one side what Celsus has said
on this subject as superfluous and irrelevant. For if we met those who
have been overcome by such doctrines, we should find fault with them
more than Celsus has done.

27. What he has to say following the discussion of the diagram is not
derived even from misunderstandings of the teaching about *the Seal*, as it
is called by church people.[1] He is inventing out of his own head when he
mentions strange doctrines and *a dialogue in which the one who administers
the seal is called Father and the one who is sealed is called young man and
Son; and he answers 'I have been anointed with white ointment from the tree
of life.'*[2] Not even among the heretics have we heard that this takes place.
Then, giving the precise number, he says that *those who impart the seal say
that there are seven angels standing on either side of the soul when the body is
dying, the one group being angels of light and the other of what are called
archontic angels.*[3] And he says that *the chief of those called archontic angels
is said to be an accursed God.*

[1] The term 'seal' is applied by early Christian writers to baptism or to that part of the
initiation ceremony commonly called confirmation, which included anointing or chrism.
Cf. G. W. H. Lampe, *The Seal of the Spirit* (1951).
[2] Celsus may be drawing on the same 'heavenly dialogue' as that mentioned in VIII, 15.
That the reference is to a Gnostic version of Jesus' baptism is suggested by *Clement. Recog.*
I, 45 where the reason why the Son of God is called Christ is that 'him first the Father
anointed with oil which was taken from the tree of life'. The notion that oil is derived from
the tree of life appears in unorthodox Judaism; cf. *Vita Adae et Evae*, 36 where Adam sends
Eve and Seth to approach paradise as penitents: 'Perchance God will have pity and send his
angel across to the tree of his mercy whence floweth the oil of life, and will give you a drop
of it to anoint me with it that I may have rest from these pains...'; *Acta Pilati* 3 (19)
(James, *Apocr. N.T.* p. 127) where Seth is sent by Adam 'to make supplication unto God
hard by the gate of paradise, that he would lead me by his angel unto the tree of mercy, and
I should take the oil and anoint my father, and he should arise from his sickness...', etc.
In II Enoch viii. 3–5 oil is a fruit of the tree of life. Cf. *Apoc. Mos.* IX, 3 (in R. H. Charles,
Apocr. and Pseudepigr. II, p. 143); *Acta Thomae* 157. For the view that this notion is
implied in Ignatius, *Ephes.* XVII, 1 cf. W. L. Knox, *St Paul and the Church of the Gentiles*,
p. 157 n. 2. For sacraments of anointing, common among the Gnostic sects, cf. Irenaeus, I,
21, 4; Clem. Al., *Exc. Theod.* 82; Hippolytus, *Ref.* v, 9, 22. Discussion in Bousset, *Hauptprobleme der Gnosis*, pp. 297ff.
[3] The sentence is obscure; it may be taken to mean that it is the angels who give the seal.
Origen has so abbreviated Celsus' text here that the precise meaning cannot be determined.
With the statement that there are two groups of angels on either side, we may compare the
Valentinian doctrine of good angels of the Right and bad angels of the Left: Clement,
Exc. Theod. XXIII, 3, XXVIII, XXXIV, XXXVII, XLVII, 2; Irenaeus, I, 30, 2–3. The notion appears
in the Peratic Gnostics of Hippolytus, *Ref.* v, 14, 7–8 (where Raphael and Suriel are among
the powers of the Left), the Nicolaitans (Filastrius, 33), and *Pistis Sophia*, cc. 139–40. Also
Bardesanes, *de Fato*, 21 (ed. Nau in *Patr. Syr.* II (1907), at p. 577). The role of the archontic

He then objects to this expression and with good reason criticizes those who venture to say this. On this ground we too share the annoyance of those who find fault with such people, if any there are, who *maintain that the God of the Jews is accursed, being the God who sends rain and thunder, and who is the Creator of this world and the God of Moses, described in his account of the creation of the world.* In these words, however, Celsus seems not to have been quite fair in his intentions, but indeed to have been deeply prejudiced as a result of his hatred of us, so unbecoming to a philosopher. He wanted the readers of his book who have no knowledge of our teaching to attack us as if we hold that the good Creator of this world is an accursed God. He seems to have behaved in much the same way as the Jews who, when the teaching of Christianity began to be proclaimed, spread abroad a malicious rumour about the gospel, to the effect that Christians sacrifice a child and partake of its flesh, and again that when the followers of the gospel want to do the works of darkness they turn out the light and each man has sexual intercourse with the first woman he meets.[1] This malicious rumour some time ago unreasonably influenced a very large number and persuaded people knowing nothing of the gospel that this was really the character of Christians. And even now it still deceives some who by such stories are repelled from approaching Christians even if only for a simple conversation.

28. Celsus appears to me to have done something of this sort when he asserted that *Christians say the Creator is an accursed God,* his intention being that the man who believes him when he says these things against us may, if possible, immediately convict Christians of being the most impious of all men. That he is confusing the issue is shown when he gives the reason why the God of the Mosaic cosmogony is said to be accursed. For he says that *such a God even deserves to be cursed in the opinion of those who*

---

angels is much developed in the fourth-century sect, the Archontici, 'evidently a branch of the old Ophites' (Hort in *Dict. Chr. Biogr. s.v.*), for whom cf. Epiphanius, *Panarion* XL; summary in Theodoret, *Haer. Fab. Comp.* I, 11. They held that Sabaoth, the God of the Jews, was lord of the seventh heaven, and that the devil was his son. (On these see now H.-C. Puech in *Reallexikon für Antike und Christentum* I, *s.v.* 'Archontiker'.)

[1] Cf. VI, 40 below (and Celsus in V, 63 of Gnostics). For the charges cf. Aristides, 17 (Syriac); Justin, *Apol.* I, 26, 7; II, 12; *Dial.* 10; Tatian, 25; Athenagoras, *Leg.* III, 31; Theophilus, *ad Autol.* III, 4; Minucius Felix IX, 28; Eus. *H.E.* V, I, 14, 52; Tertullian, *Apol.* IV, 11; Salvian, *de Gub. Dei* IV, 17. Discussion in J.-P. Waltzing, 'Le crime rituel reproché aux chrétiens du IIe siècle', in *Académie Royale de Belgique: Bulletins de la Classe des Lettres* (1925), pp. 205–39, and especially F. J. Dölger in *Antike und Christentum*, IV (1934), pp. 188–228.

It is worth noting that Celsus is well informed and never makes the charges against 'the great church'. There is, however, a probable reference in the astrologer Vettius Valens (IV, 15) who says that at certain times 'some deny the deities and follow another worship or even eat things that are not meet' (ἀρνοῦνται τὰ θεῖα καὶ ἑτεροσεβοῦσι ἢ ἀθεμιτοφαγοῦσιν). Cf. A. D. Nock, in *Journ. Bibl. Lit.* LXVII (1948), p. 153.

*hold this view of him, because he cursed the serpent which imparted to the first
men knowledge of good and evil.*[1]

He ought to have known that those who have taken the story of the
serpent to mean that he did right in conspiring with the first men, and who
go beyond the Titans and Giants of mythology and on this account are
called Ophites, are so far from being Christians that they object to Jesus
no less than Celsus; and they do not admit anyone into their meeting unless
he has first pronounced curses against Jesus.[2] You see, then, how quite
unreasonably Celsus has behaved in making his criticisms of Christians,
since he takes as Christians those who do not want even to hear the name
of Jesus, if only to admit that he was a wise person or a man with a character
marked by moderation.[3] What, therefore, could be *sillier or crazier* not
only than those who have chosen to take their name from the serpent,
believing him to be the originator of good gifts, but also than Celsus when
he thought that charges against the Ophites were charges against Christians? Some time ago the Greek philosopher who loved poverty and set
an example of a happy life to show that he was not prevented from being
happy by being entirely without possessions, called himself a Cynic.[4]
But these impious men pride themselves on being called Ophites, taking
their name from the snake, which is a reptile very hostile to men and very
dreadful, as though they were not men, to whom the serpent is an enemy,
but snakes. And they boast that a certain Euphrates was the man who
taught them their impious doctrines.[5]

29. Then next, as though it were the Christians upon whom he is
pouring scorn when he criticizes those who say that the God of Moses and
his law is accursed, and imagining that those who hold these views are
Christians, he says: *What could be sillier or crazier than this blockheaded
wisdom? For why did the Jews' lawgiver make a mistake?*[6] *And if he did, why
do you accept his cosmogony or the law of the Jews interpreting it as an*

[1] Cf. Ps.-Tertullian, *adv. Omn. Haer.* 2 'Besides these there are those heretics who are
called Ophites. For they exalt the serpent to such a degree that they even prefer him to
Christ himself. For it was he, they say, who originally gave us the knowledge of good and
evil. ...'; Epiphanius, *Panar.* xxxvii, 3, 1 'And these so-called Ophites attribute to this
serpent all knowledge, saying that he was the first to impart knowledge to men. ...'
[2] Cf. Origen, *Catena fragm.* 47 *in I Cor.* xii. 3 (ed. Jenkins, *J.T.S.* x (1909), p. 30):
'There is a certain sect which does not admit a convert unless he pronounces anathemas on
Jesus; and that sect is worthy of the name which it has chosen; for it is the sect of the so-
called Ophites, who utter blasphemous words in praise of the serpent.'
[3] Omit ἤ before ἄνθρωπος with Bo., K. tr.
[4] I.e. Dog-man. Origen is thinking of Crates (cf. II, 41), mentioned in very similar words
in *Comm. in Matt.* xv, 15.
[5] Hippolytus (*Ref.* IV, 2, 1; V, 13, 9; X, 10, 1) mentions Euphrates as one of the two chief
sources of the Peratic system. The Peratics also took a marked interest in the serpent
(*Ref.* V, 16, 6 ff.). No doubt both the Ophites and the Peratics derived much of their
doctrine from a book by Euphrates.   [6] Read ἐσφάλη with Bader.

allegory, as you say, while you only grudgingly praise the Creator of the world, you most impious fellow, though he promised the Jews everything, declaring that he would increase their race to the ends of the earth[1] and would raise them up from the dead with the same flesh and blood,[2] and inspired the prophets; and yet you pour abuse on him? But when you are put in difficulties by the Jews, you confess that you worship the same God. Yet when your master Jesus and Moses, in whom the Jews believe, lay down contradictory laws,[3] you try to find another God instead of this one who is the Father.

Here too that most noble philosopher Celsus obviously accuses Christians falsely when he says that the same people, whenever the Jews put them in difficulties, confess that they have the same God, but when Jesus lays down contradictory laws to Moses, try to find another in his place. Whether we are disputing with Jews or are amongst ourselves, we acknowledge one and the same God, whom the Jews both used to worship long ago and profess to worship now, and in no way do we act impiously towards Him. Nor do we say that God will raise up people from the dead with the same flesh and blood, as we have said above.[4] For we do not maintain that the natural body, which is sown in corruption and in dishonour and in weakness, is raised up in the same form in which it was sown.[5] However, we spoke at moderate length about these matters earlier.

30. Then he next returns to *the seven archontic daemons* which are not *mentioned by Christians* but which are, I believe, spoken of by the Ophites. In the diagram which we too obtained on their account we found the arrangement set out in a similar way to that which Celsus describes. Celsus said that *the first is formed in the shape of a lion;*[6] but he does not inform us what these people, who are really *the most impious* ones, call it.

---

[1] Cf. Gen. viii. 17; ix. 1, 7; xii. 2–3; xv. 5, etc.
[2] Cf. Celsus in v, 14.   [3] Cf. Celsus in vii, 18.
[4] iv, 57; v, 18–19, 23.   [5] I Cor. xv. 42–4.
[6] It is remarkable that in this passage Celsus does not mention the angelic names, except in the case of the seventh, and perhaps in the version before him the names were not present. On the other hand in vii, 40 he mentions 'those who have wretchedly learnt by heart the names of the doorkeepers', which suggests that he may have known the names given by Origen. Possibly his version had a system such as that of vi, 31 with the names of vi, 30.
For archons with animal heads and shapes cf. R. Wünsch, *Sethianische Verfluchungstafeln aus Rom* (1898), pp. 86 f. (Typhon-Seth with an ass's head); C. Schmidt, *Kopt.-gnost. Schr.* 334. In *Pistis Sophia* 126 (Schmidt, p. 207) we have a system of twelve archons with animal forms. Theodore bar Kuni (late eighth century) describes the Ophite system with ten heavens controlled by angelic powers in animal shapes; the lowest heaven is under Samiel, in the form of a pig; the second under Pharon, like a lion, etc. (H. Pognon, *Inscriptions Mandaïtes des Coupes de Khouabir* (1898), pp. 212–14.) Cf. Epiphanius, *Panar.* xxvi, 10, 6 'Some say that Sabaoth has the shape of an ass, others of a pig.'

However, we found that the angel of the Creator, who in the holy scriptures is spoken of with honour, was affirmed by that foul diagram to be Michael the lion-like. Again, Celsus said that *the next, the second, is a bull.* The diagram in our possession said that Suriel[1] is the bull-like. Then Celsus said that *the third was a sort of double being and hissed dreadfully,* while the diagram said that the third is Raphael, the serpent-like. Again, Celsus said that *the fourth has the form of an eagle,* while the diagram says that Gabriel is the eagle-like. Celsus then said that *the fifth has the face of a bear;* the diagram says that Thauthabaoth is the bear-like. Celsus then said that *the sixth is asserted by them to have the face of a dog;* the diagram said that he is Erathaoth. Then Celsus said that *the seventh has the face of an ass,* and that *he is called Thaphabaoth or Onoel;*[2] but in the diagram we found that this one is called Onoel or Thartharaoth, and has the shape of an ass. We thought it right for us also to set out these things accurately, that we may not appear ignorant of what Celsus professed to know, and also that we may show that we Christians know them more accurately than he does, and that they are not the teachings of Christians, but of people entirely alien to salvation who do not recognize Jesus as Saviour or God or Master or Son of God at all.

31. If anyone wishes to learn even the inventions of those sorcerers, which they use with the aim of leading men astray by their teaching, pretending to the possession of certain secret truths, though they have met with little success, let him hear what they are taught to say at the eternally chained gates of the Archons after passing through what they call 'the Barrier of Evil'.[3]

---

[1] Suriel (or Uriel) is said to be 'lord of the second heaven' in the Gnostic amulet from Beirut published by A. H. de Villefosse, in *Florilegium Melchior de Vogüé* (Paris, 1909), pp. 287–95. But he is lord of the third heaven in Preisendanz, *Pap. Gr. Mag.* XXXV, 4. Cf. E. Peterson in *Rhein. Mus.* LXXV (1926), p. 418.

[2] Peterson (*loc. cit.* p. 409) compares the mention of 'Ornoel' in *Cat. Cod. Astr.* X, 81, 30.

[3] It is a common Gnostic notion that the lower regions of the cosmos, the kingdom of darkness, are divided from the upper, the kingdom of light, by a barrier (*phragmos*); thus the firmament in the system of Basilides, Horus in that of Valentinus, etc. Discussion in H. Schlier, *Christus und die Kirche im Epheserbrief* (1930), pp. 22 f. who gives Mandean parallels, and finds the idea in St Paul (Eph. ii. 14). Also *Acta Thomae*, 32 (cf. Bornkamm, *Mythos und Legende*, p. 29) where the serpent tells the apostle, 'I am he that entered through the *phragmos* into paradise and spake with Eve the things which my father bade me speak unto her.'

It appears that Origen's list of passwords starts at the top with the eighth and supreme sphere, not at the bottom, so that he has the Ophite liturgy in the reverse order. The first power to be met by the Ophite soul on its ascent would be Horaeus. For the general theme of the soul's ascent cf. note on VI, 22; Plotinus, I, 6, 7 'To those that approach the Holy Celebrations of the Mysteries, there are appointed purifications and the laying aside of the garments worn before, and the entry in nakedness—until, passing, on the upward way, all that is other than God, each in the solitude of himself shall behold that solitary-dwelling Existence, the Apart, the Unmingled, the Pure, that from Which all things depend, for

Solitary King, bond of blindness, unconscious oblivion, I hail thee, the supreme Power, preserved by the spirit of providence and wisdom; from thee I am sent in purity, being already part of the light of Son and Father. May grace be with me; yea, father, let it be with me.

And they say that the Powers of the Ogdoad come from him. Then as they pass through the one they call Ialdabaoth they are taught to say next:

And thou, Ialdabaoth, first and seventh, born to have power with boldness, being ruling Word of a pure mind, a perfect work for Son and Father, I bear a symbol marked with a picture of life,[1] and, having opened to the world the gate which thou didst close for thine eternity, I pass by thy power free again. May grace be with me, father let it be with me.

And they say that the star Saturn is in sympathy with the lion-like Archon.[2] Then they think that the person who has passed through Ialdabaoth and reached Iao must say:

And thou, Archon of the hidden mysteries of Son and Father, who shinest by night, thou Iao,[3] second and first, lord of death, portion of the guiltless, I bear already thine own...[4] as a symbol, and am ready to pass by thy power; for by a living word I have prevailed over him that was born of thee. May grace be with me, father, let it be with me.

Then next comes Sabaoth, to whom they think one should say:

Archon of fifth authority, mighty Sabaoth, defender of the law of thy creation which grace is destroying, by a more potent pentad,[5] look upon a blameless

Which all look and live and act and know, the Source of Life and of Intellection and of Being' (Mackenna's trans.). Cf. Cumont, *Religions orientales* (1929), p. 292 n. 69, and Festugière's note on *Corp. Herm.* I, 25.

For the idea of the ascending soul passing through doors, cf. Odes of Solomon XVII, 8.

[1] An amulet is necessary as well as the right formula if the soul is to pass the Archon. Even Clem. Al. (*Strom.* IV, 116, 2) says that the good man shows to the angels in charge of the upward ascent 'a holy symbol' which is the shining mark of righteousness. For the necessity of passwords cf. Irenaeus, I, 21, 5; Plotinus, II, 9, 14.

[2] Ialdabaoth also has the form of a lion in *Pistis Sophia*, 31 (Schmidt, p. 28; Horner, p. 24). In Mithraic art Saturn is commonly represented with the head of a lion; cf. Cumont, *Textes et Monuments*, I, p. 78. For the identification Ialdabaoth–Saturn–Kronos cf. Bousset, *Hauptprobleme der Gnosis*, pp. 351–5.

[3] Cf. E. Peterson, Εἷς θεός (1926), p. 307, for evidence that Iao was identified with the Sun and with Light (cf. Macrobius, *Sat.* I, 18, 19 f.; A. B. Cook, *Zeus*, I, pp. 233 ff.). Peterson interprets the phrase 'first and second' to refer to the notion that the sun not only gives light in heaven during the day but also illumines Hades at night (cf. Vergil, *Aen.* VI, 641 and for Pindar, Rohde, *Psyche* (E.T.), p. 444 n. 38. Also Macrobius, *Sat.* I, 21, 22). For νυκτοφάνεια as epithet of Hecate–Selene–Artemis cf. Preisendanz, *Pap. Gr. Mag.* IV, 2523, 2819 f., with the remarks of T. Hopfner in *Pisciculi f. F. J. Dölger* (1939) at p. 129.

[4] The Vatican MS. has φέρων ἤδη τὸν ἴδιον ὑπήνουν σύμβολον. K. tr. proposes ὑπή-⟨κοον⟩ νοῦν (and would read παροδεύειν in next phrase).

[5] The five books of the Mosaic Law suggest the association of pentad and Sabaoth; for pentadic mysticism, cf. the references collected by W. L. Knox, *St Paul and the Church of the Gentiles*, p. 155 n. 1; add Irenaeus, II, 24, 4, and the Coptic Gnostic fragment published by W. E. Crum in *J.T.S.* XLIV (1943), pp. 176–9.

symbol of thine art, and let me pass by, preserved by the image of a picture, a body set free by the pentad. May grace be with me, father, let it be with me.

* * * * * * *[1]

And after him comes Astaphaeus, to whom they believe one should say the following formula:

Archon of the third gate, Astaphaeus, overseer of the original source of water, look on one initiate, and let me pass who have been cleansed by a virgin's spirit, and see the world's essence. May grace be with me, father, let it be with me.

And after him comes Ailoaeus, to whom they think it right to speak as follows:

Archon of the second gate, Ailoaeus, let me pass as I bring to thee a symbol of thy mother,[2] a grace hidden by the powers of the principalities. May grace be with me, father, let it be with me.

Finally they mention Horaeus, and think fit to say to him:

Thou who hast fearlessly passed beyond the wall of fire,[3] who hast been assigned the power over the first gate, Horaeus, look upon a symbol of thy power vanquished by a picture of the tree of life, taken[4] by an image made in the likeness of a guiltless man, and let me pass by. May grace be with me, father, let it be with me.

32. It is Celsus' so-called learning, which is rather futile nonsense, which has led us to discuss these matters, since we wanted to show to the reader of his book and of the reply we have written to it that no difficulty to us is caused by Celsus' learning which he uses to make a false attack upon the Christians, who neither believe in these things nor know of them, even if in our case we have taken the trouble to get to know them and to quote them. But we have done so in order that the sorcerers may not, by claiming to know something more than we do, succeed in deceiving those who are swept off their feet by the parading of names. By quoting several other examples we could also show that, while we do know what the deceivers teach, yet we deny it as alien to us and blasphemous and not in agreement with the doctrines of genuine Christians which we confess to the point of death.

[1] The password for Adonai has fallen out of the text (cf. VI, 32).
[2] For the figure of the Mother in the Gnostic systems cf. Bousset, *Hauptprobleme*, pp. 58–83.
[3] The wall of fire (the *phragmos*) separates the kingdom of light from the kingdom of darkness. Cf. Bornkamm, *Mythos und Legende in den apokryphen Thomas-Akten*, p. 78, who compares *Acta Thomae*, 124 where the heavenly marriage is said to be 'founded on the bridge of fire upon which is sprinkled grace'.
[4] K. tr. proposes ληφθέντι. But a participle in the accusative masculine singular is more probable.

It is necessary, however, to realize that those who composed these formulas muddled everything without any understanding of the art of magic or any clear idea of the divine scriptures. From magic they took Ialdabaoth, Astaphaeus, and Horaeus. From the Hebrew scriptures they took Iao,[1] the name used by the Hebrews, Sabaoth, Adonai, and Eloaeus.[2] But the names taken from the Bible are titles of one and the same God.[3] God's enemies did not understand this, as even they admit, and thought that Iao was one God, Sabaoth another, and Adonaeus a third besides (the scriptures call him Adonai), and Eloaeus, whom the prophets call in Hebrew Eloai, yet another.

33. Then Celsus describes other fables to the effect that *some return into the archontic forms so that some become lions, some bulls, and others serpents or eagles or bears or dogs.*[4] In the diagram which we had we also found what Celsus called *a rectangular figure,* and what those wretches say about *the gates of paradise.* The flaming sword, as guarding the trees of knowledge and of life, was drawn as the diameter of a circle of fire. Celsus, however, was unwilling or unable to quote the passwords which, according to the fables of these impious people, are to be recited at each gate by those who pass through them. But we have done this, that we may show to Celsus and the readers of his book that the purpose of the impious mystery is alien to the Christians' pious worship of God.

[1] K. tr. reads 'Ιαώ for the MS. 'Ιαωία. Cf. K. Preisendanz, *Pap. Gr. Mag.* IV, 3257 where the papyrus has ια..ιφ. Wessely, Eitrem, and Deissmann (*Bible Studies* (1903), p. 325) read here ιαωια, Preisendanz ιαωιω.

[2] For these names, cf. Irenaeus, I, 30, 11 (Harvey, I, 237), and 30, 5 where he says that the Gnostics (here Ophites or Sethites) say: 'Him who is first derived from the Mother is called Ialdabaoth; the one who is derived from him, Iao; the one from him, Sabaoth; the fourth Adoneus, and the fifth Eloeus, and the sixth Oreus; while the seventh and last of all is Astaphaeus.' According to the Coptic Gnostic treatise, *Apocryphon Johannis* (still unpublished), which was Irenaeus' source in *adv. Haer.* I, 29 (C. Schmidt, in *Philotesia P. Kleinert dargebracht* (1907), pp. 317–36), the lords of the seven heavens are Iaoth, with the shape of a lion; Eloaeus with the shape of an ass; Astaphaeus with the shape of·a hyena; Iao with the shape of a seven-headed serpent; Adonaeus with the shape of a dragon; Adoni with the shape of . . . (lost); Sabbataeus with a shape of flaming fire. But almost immediately afterwards the text goes on to give the seven names as Iaoth, Eloaeus, Astaphaeus, Iao, Sabaoth, Adonaeus, Sabbataeus (Schmidt, pp. 332–3). Cf. also the Ophite amulet discussed by Campbell Bonner, *Studies in Magical Amulets* (1950), pp. 135–8, with plate IX, no. 188. On the obverse there is a lion-headed god with Ialdabaoth inscribed to the right, Aariel to the left (probably Ariel is interpreted to mean Lion of God); on the reverse are the names Ia, Iao, Sabaoth, Adonai, Eloai, Horeos, Astapheos.

[3] Irenaeus, II, 35, 3 (Harvey, I, 384–6) makes the same point.

[4] This is probably to be explained by supposing that the Ophite initiates wore masks shaped according to the animal forms of the Archons. It appears from Porphyry, *de Abstinentia*, IV, 16 (Nauck 254, 4 ff.) that the Mithraic initiates wore such masks (the text is corrupt), and some grades of initiate in the Mithraic mysteries bore animal names. (Jerome, *Ep.* CVII, 2, says that Mithraic worshippers were initiated by the names of raven, bridegroom, soldier, lion, Persian, courier of the Sun, and father.) Cf. Cumont, *Textes et Monuments*, I, p. 315; Wendland, *op. cit.* p. 173.

34. After he has set out the words we have quoted, and matters like them which we have added, Celsus says this: *They have further added one on top of another sayings of prophets, and circles upon circles, and emanations of an earthly Church, and of Circumcision, and a power flowing from a certain virgin Prunicus,*[1] *and a living soul, and heaven slain that it may have life, and earth slain with a sword and many men slain that they may have life, and death in the world being stopped when the sin of the world dies, and a narrow descent again, and gates that open of their own accord.*[2] *And everywhere they speak in their writings of the tree of life*[3] *and of resurrection of the flesh by the tree—I imagine because their master was nailed to a cross and was a carpenter by trade.*[4] *So that if he had happened to be thrown off a cliff, or pushed into a pit, or suffocated by strangling, or if he had been a cobbler or stonemason or blacksmith, there would have been a cliff of life above the heavens, or a pit of resurrection, or a rope of immortality, or a blessed stone, or an iron of love, or a holy hide of leather. Would not an old woman who sings a story to lull a little child to sleep have been ashamed to whisper tales such as these?*[5] Here Celsus seems to me to confuse ideas that he has misunderstood. It seems that he may have heard some catch-phrase of some sect or other, and did not clearly see what it really meant, but heaped up the phrases, in order to show to people who know nothing either of our doctrines or of those of

[1] Prunicus, as Origen remarks (VI, 35), is the name given to Sophia by the Valentinians who saw an allegory of her in the woman with the issue of blood healed by Jesus. For Prunicus as a name of Sophia cf. Irenaeus, *adv. Haer.* I, 29, 4; 30, 3–9. Irenaeus gives no explanation of the name. The word is used in ordinary Greek usage to mean a 'bearer', or, as an adjective, to mean 'lewd', 'lustful'. Epiphanius, *Panar.* I, 25, 3–4, interprets Prunicus in the latter sense as obscene. M. P. Nilsson, 'Sophia-Prunikos' in *Eranos*, XLV (1947), pp. 169–72, observes that the Church Fathers were anxious to give the word an obscene meaning to discredit the Gnostics, but that in Gnostic thought the word was used in the sense of 'bearer', because Sophia brought something from the divine realm into the material world. It is, however, probable that the Gnostics used the word because of its double meaning. The lustfulness of Sophia is an important feature in Valentinian doctrine. And Nilsson's suggestion that the reference of the word to sexual lust was made by the Church Fathers and not by the Gnostics is rendered improbable by the *Apocryphon Johannis* (Schmidt, *op. cit.* p. 329) where we hear of τὸ προύνικον in Sophia.
[2] Automatically opening gates are common in magic; cf. II, 34, and J. Kroll, *Gott und Hölle* (1932), pp. 482–5. The notion is also common in Gnostic treatises, e.g. *Pistis Sophia* 11 (Schmidt, p. 12; Horner, p. 10).
[3] For mystical exegesis of the tree of life in Gnostic circles, cf. Celsus in VI, 27, with the note; Justin the Gnostic in Hippolytus, *Ref.* V, 26, 6; *Pistis Sophia*, 99, 134 (Schmidt, pp. 158, 229). For the Cross of Christ as the tree of life cf. Ignatius, *Trall.* XI, 2; *Smyrn.* 1; Justin, *Dial.* 86; Clem. Al. *Paed.* III, 25, 3; *Strom.* V, 72, 3; Tertullian, *adv. Jud.* 13.
[4] Justin, *Dial.* 88, remarks that as a carpenter Jesus made ploughs and yokes—symbols of righteousness and an active life. Cf. *Gospel of Philip*, 91.
[5] For a *garrula nutrix* as a source of unreliable religious instruction, cf. Prudentius, *Apotheosis*, 297. Eustathius of Antioch (*de Engastrim.* 29, p. 61 Klostermann) comments on the tendency of such nurses to be inebriated, as Celsus does (VI, 37).

the sects that he knew all the doctrines of the Christians.[1] This is made clear by the passage before us.

35. It is true that we make use of *the sayings of the prophets* to prove that Jesus is the Christ proclaimed by them beforehand, and to show from the prophecies that the events recorded of Jesus in the gospels fulfilled them. But the phrase *circles upon circles* perhaps belongs to the sect mentioned earlier which included within one circle, which, they say, is the soul of the universe and Leviathan, the seven circles of the archontic powers.[2] Perhaps also it is a misunderstanding of the saying in Ecclesiastes: 'The wind goes in circles of circles, and the wind returns upon its circles.'[3]

The phrase about *emanations of an earthly Church and of Circumcision* was perhaps taken from some who speak of a certain heavenly Church, and say that the church on earth is an emanation from a higher world,[4] and that the circumcision described in the Law is a symbol of a circumcision which has taken place in some heavenly rite of purification. *Prunicus* is the name given to Wisdom by the Valentinians, according to their own deceived wisdom; and they want to make out that the woman who had an issue of blood for twelve years is a symbol of Wisdom.[5] It was because this fellow, who muddles together everything from Greeks, barbarians, and heretics, misunderstood this that he spoke of *a power flowing from a certain virgin Prunicus*.

A living soul is perhaps the term used in secret by some of the Valentinians to apply to the 'psychic Creator' as they call him.[6] Perhaps also there are some who, in antithesis to a dead soul, speak of the soul of the man who is being saved as a living soul; this is not objectionable. But I do not know that any one has mentioned *a heaven slain*, or *earth slain with a sword and many men slain that they may have life*. It is not unlikely that Celsus produced these ideas out of his own head.

36. Perhaps we could say that *death in the world is stopped when the sin of the world dies* in explaining the mysterious words of the apostle that read as follows: 'And when he has put all his enemies under his feet, then death, the last enemy, shall be destroyed.'[7] It is also said: 'When this corruptible body puts on incorruption, then the word that is written shall come to pass, Death is swallowed up in victory.'[8] But it is perhaps those who hold the doctrine of reincarnation who would speak of *a narrow*

---

[1] Cf. Celsus in I, 12.　　　[2] Cf. VI, 25, where there are ten circles.
[3] Eccles. i. 6.
[4] Ecclesia (Church) was the eighth member of the Valentinian Ogdoad: Irenaeus I, 1, 1; I, 2, 2; I, 5, 6; Tertullian, *adv. Val.* 25, etc.
[5] Cf. Irenaeus, I, 3, 5; II, 20, 1; II, 23, 1–2; Epiphanius, *Panar.* I, 31, 14, 10.
[6] Gen. ii. 7 is a more likely source. Cf. Celsus in VIII, 49.
[7] I Cor. xv. 25–6.　　　　　　　　[8] I Cor. xv. 54.

descent again. And it is not improbable that *gates which open of their own accord* have been mentioned by some who were using obscure phrases when explaining the text 'Open to me the gates of righteousness that I may go into them and give thanks unto the Lord; this is the gate of the Lord; the righteous shall enter into it.'[1] Again it is said in the ninth Psalm 'Thou exaltest me from the gates of death, that I may proclaim all thy praises in the gates of the daughter of Zion.'[2] The Word says that the sins that carry men to destruction are gates of death, even as, on the contrary, good actions are gates of Zion.[3] So also there are gates of righteousness, which are equivalent to the gates of virtue. For these are readily opened to the man who eagerly tries to do virtuous actions.

It would be a more suitable time to explain *the tree of life* if we were interpreting the story recorded in Genesis about the paradise of God which He planted. However, Celsus has frequently mocked at the *resurrection* which he did not understand; yet not satisfied with what has been said, he now says that we speak of a *resurrection of the flesh from the tree*, I imagine because he has misunderstood the symbolical saying that through a tree came death and through a tree came life, death in Adam and life in Christ.[4] He then mocks the phrase about the tree, and pours ridicule on it on two grounds, suggesting that the actual reason why we speak of the tree is either that our *master was nailed to a cross*, or that he *was a carpenter by trade.* But he failed to see that the tree of life is described in the writings of Moses. Furthermore, he did not observe that Jesus himself is not described as a carpenter anywhere in the gospels accepted in the churches.[5]

37. He also imagines that we have invented the tree of life in order to allegorize the story of the cross; and in consequence of his mistake on this point he says that *if he had happened to be thrown off a cliff, or pushed into a pit, or suffocated by strangling*, we should have invented *a cliff of life above the heavens, or a pit of resurrection, or a rope of immortality.* And again, he says that if the tree of life had been invented because he was a carpenter, it would have followed that, had he been a cobbler, the story would have been about *a holy hide*; or, if a stonemason, about *a blessed stone*; or, if a blacksmith, about *an iron of love.* Who does not at once see how worthless his criticism is? He merely pours abuse upon the men whom he professed himself to be *trying to convert as being misguided.*

[1] Ps. cxvii. 19–20.   [2] Ps. ix. 14–15.
[3] Similarly *Comm. in Matt.* XII, 12.
[4] Cf. Rom. v. 12 ff.; I Cor. xv. 21–2.
[5] At Mark vi. 3 ('Is not this the carpenter?') Origen's text agrees with many authorities, such as the Old Latin, in assimilating the text to Matt. xiii. 55 ('Is not this the carpenter's son?').

His next remark after this would be appropriate to those who invented the lion-like, ass-headed, and serpent-shaped Archons and to anyone who has concocted similar nonsense, but certainly not to Church people. It is true, *even a drunken old woman would have been ashamed to sing such a tale to lull a little child to sleep*, and *to whisper* to a child nonsense such as that made up by the men who invented the ass-headed powers and the passwords, so to speak, to be pronounced at each gate. But the doctrines held by members of the Church were unknown to Celsus. Only very few have taken the trouble to understand them. They are those who have devoted their entire life, as Jesus commanded,[1] to searching the scriptures, and have laboured to study the meaning of the sacred scriptures more than Greek philosophers have done to acquire some supposed knowledge.

38. The worthy fellow, not content with the account of the diagram, in order to swell his charges against us, who have nothing in common in that diagram, wanted to bring some other objections by way of parenthesis, and then returned to the doctrines of the heretics as if they were ours. He says: *That is not the least remarkable thing about them. For they interpret certain words inscribed between the upper circles above the heavens, and in particular two among others, a larger and a smaller circle, which they interpret of Son and Father.* In this diagram we found the larger and the smaller circles, on the diameter of which was inscribed 'Father' and 'Son'. And between the larger circle, within which was the smaller one, and another which was compounded of two circles, the outer circle being yellow and the inner blue, we found inscribed a barrier shaped like a double axe.[2] Above it there was a small circle touching the greater of the first two circles, which had been inscribed with the word 'Love'; and below it next to the circle there was written the word 'Life'. In the second circle, within which were intertwined and enclosed two other circles and another figure in the shape of a rhombus, there was inscribed 'Providence of Wisdom'. And inside the sector common to them there was written 'Nature of Wisdom'. Above the sector common to them there was a circle in which was inscribed the word 'Knowledge' (*Gnosis*), and

---

[1] John v. 39.

[2] For the axe as a cult-symbol, see A. B. Cook, *Zeus*, II (1925), pp. 513–704, especially at 610–11 where this passage is discussed. He suggests that 'the colouration of the concentric circles, yellow and blue, may have been suggested by the zones of *aither*, the "burning sky", and *aer*, the "moist sky"'. Cook also quotes an invocation of the Vine from the Kyranides (a magico-medical compilation prior to A.D. 408): '...Thou bringest to light all that is in the souls of mortal men, and of them that have mystic thoughts in secret thou, O Vine, having knowledge unutterable wilt reveal all that is wrought by writings unique or sovereign remedies, yea all the hidden meaning of knife or double axe.' (On the Hermetic character of the Kyranides, cf. A. J. Festugière, *La Révélation d'Hermès Trismégiste*, I (2nd ed. 1950), pp. 201 ff.)

below it another in which was inscribed the word 'Understanding' (*Synesis*).

We have included these remarks in our refutation of Celsus that we may show our readers that we know better than he does, and not from hearsay, about the doctrines which are also subject to criticism from our side. But whether those who pride themselves on such doctrines *profess also some magical sorcery, and this is the summit of wisdom to them*, we do not know for certain, for we have not found any such statement. Celsus, who has often already been found guilty of false witness and of unreasonable accusations, would know whether he is also lying here, or[1] if he had learnt anything of this sort from certain people who are alien and foreign to the faith, who were his source for the statements in his treatise.

39. Then as for those who, as he says, *use some sort of magic and sorcery and invoke certain daemons with barbarous names*,[2] he says that *these men do much the same as those who, while invoking the same daemons in various languages, bamboozle people who do not know that their names have one form among the Greeks and another form among the Scythians*. He then takes from Herodotus his affirmation that *the Scythians call Apollo Gongosyrus, Poseidon Thagimasada, Aphrodite Argimpasa, and Hestia Tabiti*.[3] Anyone who has the ability will examine this to see whether even in this matter both Celsus and Herodotus are not partly wrong, seeing that the Scythians do not have the same conceptions as the Greeks concerning the supposed gods. What convincing argument is there to show that Apollo is called Gongosyrus among the Scythians? I do not think that when translated into Greek Gongosyrus indicates the etymology of Apollo, or that Apollo means Gongosyrus in the language of the Scythians. So also of the other names one[4] could not say that they have the same meaning. For the Greeks began from one set of ideas and etymologies, and so gave names to the beings supposed by them to be gods; but the Scythians began from another, and so also the Persians from another, and the Indians, or Ethiopians, or Libyans from others, each nation giving names in its own individual way. This was a consequence of the fact that they had given up holding to the pure idea of the Creator of the universe which they had possessed at first. However, we said enough on this subject earlier when we endeavoured to show that Sabaoth and Zeus are not the same, when also we quoted from the divine scriptures passages bearing on

---

[1] Read ἤ for εἰ with Bo., and πάρα for περί with K. tr.

[2] Irenaeus, I, 21, 3 (Harvey, I, 183–5), preserves such formulas in Hebrew used by the Gnostics, and remarks that their purpose is to impress their initiates. Cf. Jerome, *Ep.* LXXV, 3.

[3] Herodotus, IV, 59. Cf. E. H. Minns, *Scythians and Greeks* (1913), p. 85.

[4] Read τις with K. tr.

the question of languages. Therefore we intentionally pass over these things where Celsus would tempt us to repeat ourselves.

Then again, he makes some muddled remarks about magical sorcery. Probably there is no one to whom his objection applies, since there are no magicians who practise their art under pretence of a religion which is of this moral character, though perhaps he was thinking of some who use such methods to deceive the gullible so that they may give the impression of doing some miracle by divine power. He says: *Why need I enumerate all those who have taught rites of purification, or spells which bring deliverance, or formulas that avert evil, who produce noisy crashes,*[1] *or pretended miracles, or all the various prophylactics of clothes, or numbers, or stones, or plants, or roots, and other objects of every sort?*[2] Seeing that we are not suspected of such practices even to any slight extent, reason does not demand that we should make our defence in these matters.

40. After this he seems to me to do something like those who, because of their hostility to Christians, assert before those who know nothing whatever of the practices of Christians that they have found *by experience* that Christians eat the flesh of little children and indulge in unrestrained sexual intercourse with the women among them.[3] These allegations are now condemned even by the multitude and by people entirely alien to our religion as being a false slander against the Christians. Similarly it would be found that Celsus' assertions are also lies when he affirmed that he *has seen among certain elders who were of our opinion books containing barbarian names of daemons and magical formulas.*[4] And he asserted that *these men* (the alleged elders of our opinion) *profess nothing good, but everything that is harmful to men.* I wish that all Celsus' objections to the Christians were like this. For they would be refuted by the masses who have found *by experience* that such charges are false, since, although they have lived with very many Christians, yet they have not even heard anything of the kind about them.

41. After this, as if he had forgotten that it is his object to write against the Christians, he remarks that *a certain Dionysius, an Egyptian musician, who had some conversation with him, told him that magical arts were effective*

---

[1] Herter (ap. Bader, p. 160 n.) suggests that these were intended to have an apotropaic effect. Bader himself follows the unnecessary emendation of K. tr. and reads κ(αινοὺς) τύπους.

For the use of clashing metals to scare away evil spirits, cf. J. G. Frazer, *Folk-lore in the Old Testament*, III (1918), pp. 446 ff.; A. B. Cook, 'The Gong at Dodona', in *Journ. Hell. Stud.* XXII (1902), pp. 5–28.

[2] For magical use of plants and stones, cf. VIII, 61.

[3] See VI, 27 and note.

[4] This is probably to be explained by Celsus' acquaintance with Gnosticism, where magic is an important element. In the text no comma should be read after βάρβαρα.

with uneducated people and with men of depraved moral character, but that with people who had studied philosophy they were not able to have any effect, because they were careful to lead a healthy way of life.[1] If it were now our task to discuss magic, we might have added a few remarks on this subject besides what we said about it earlier.[2] But we have to keep to what is relevant to our reply to Celsus' book. So on the subject of magic we say that anyone interested in examining whether or not even philosophers have sometimes been taken in by it may read what has been written by Moiragenes of the memoirs of Apollonius of Tyana, the magician and philosopher.[3] In them the author, who is not a Christian but a philosopher, observed that some not undistinguished philosophers were convinced by the magic of Apollonius, although when they went to him they regarded him merely as a charlatan. Among such, so far as I remember, he included even the well-known Euphrates[4] and a certain Epicurean. However, we affirm that we know *by experience* that those who worship the supreme God through Jesus according to the way of Christianity, and live according to his gospel, and who use the appointed prayers continually and in the proper way day and night, are not caught either by magic or by daemons.

[1] Cf. Plotinus, IV, 4, 43 'In the soul he [the wise man] is immune from magic; his reasoning part cannot be touched by it, he cannot be perverted. But there is in him the unreasoning element, which comes from the (material) All, and in this he can be affected, or rather this can be affected in him.' *Idem* IV, 4, 44 'Alone in immunity from magic is he who, though drawn by the alien parts of his total being, withholds his assent to their standards of worth, recognizing the good only where his authentic self sees and knows it, neither drawn nor pursuing, but tranquilly possessing and so never charmed away' (Mackenna's trans.). Philostratus, *Vit. Sophist.* p. 590 Boissonade 'An educated man would not be led astray into the practices of magicians.' Cf. the story of Plotinus and Olympius told by Porphyry, *V. Plot.* 10.

[2] Cf. II, 51; IV, 33; VI, 32.

[3] Moiragenes (2nd cent. A.D.) wrote a life of Apollonius in four books, in which he evidently represented him as a sorcerer. Philostratus, who wrote his *Life of Apollonius* with the express purpose of showing his hero to have been a philosopher, not a sorcerer, strongly criticized Moiragenes' work (*V.A.* I, 3; III, 41). He may be the same Moiragenes as the Athenian of Plutarch, *Mor.* 671 c ff., who tries to show that the God of the Jews is Dionysus (cf. E. Meyer, *Kleine Schriften*, II, p. 150 n. 1). Moiragenes' work is also mentioned by Tzetzes, *Chiliades*, II, 60. For the controversy concerning Apollonius cf. Jerome, *Ep.* LIII, 1 'Apollonius—sive ille magus, ut vulgus loquitur, sive philosophus, ut Pythagorici tradunt....' The popular view that he was a magician is shown by the spell to which his name is attached in Preisendanz, *Pap. Gr. Mag.* XIa; cf. Lucian, *Alexander*, 5; Dio Cassius, LXVII, 8; LXXVII, 18; Augustine, *Ep.* CII, 32; Isid. Pelus. *Ep.* I, 398 (*P.G.* LXXVIII, 405 B). For a good summary see K. Gross in *Reallexikon für Antike und Christentum, s.v.* 'Apollonius v. Tyana' (1942), and the remarks of Wilamowitz, *Der Glaube der Hellenen*, II, p. 487.

[4] Euphrates of Tyre, a preacher of popular Stoic philosophy who died in A.D. 118 (Dio Cass. LXIX, 8), held in high regard by the younger Pliny (*Ep.* I, 10) and Epictetus (III, 15, 8; IV, 8, 17 ff.), is alleged by Philostratus to have carried on an intrigue against Apollonius and to have accused him of being a sorcerer (*V.A.* I, 13; V, 33, 37 etc.). Little confidence is placed in Philostratus' story by von Arnim, in P.-W. *s.v.* 'Euphrates' (4). Pohlenz (*Die Stoa*, II, p. 146) thinks the conflict between Euphrates and Apollonius 'certainly historical', but that it was worked up with legends by Philostratus.

For in truth 'the angel of the Lord will encamp round about those who fear him and will deliver them'[1] from all evil. And the angels of the little ones in the church, who are also appointed to be their guardians, are said to behold continually the face of the Father in heaven[2]—whatever may be meant by 'face', and whatever it may mean to 'behold'.

42. After these remarks Celsus brings the following objections against us from another angle: *That they make some quite blasphemous errors is also shown by this example of their utter ignorance, which has similarly led them to depart from the true meaning of the divine enigmas, when they make a being opposed to God; devil, and in the Hebrew tongue, Satanas are the names which they give to this same being. At all events these notions are entirely of mortal origin, and it is blasphemy to say that when the greatest God indeed wishes to confer some benefit upon men, He has a power which is opposed to Him, and so is unable to do it.*[3] *The Son of God, then, is worsted by the devil, and is punished by him so that he may teach us also to despise the punishments which he inflicts on us.*[4] *He declares that even Satan himself will appear in a similar way to that in which he has done and will manifest great and amazing works, usurping the glory of God. We must not be deceived by these,*[5] *nor desire to turn away to Satan, but must believe in him alone. This is blatantly the utterance of a man who is a sorcerer, who is out for profit and is taking precautions against possible rivals to his opinions and to his begging.*

Then after this he wants to give an account of the *enigmas* which he thinks we have *misunderstood* when we teach the doctrine about Satan, saying that *the ancients hint at a sort of divine war. For Heraclitus speaks as follows: 'But one must know that war is a mutual thing, and justice is strife, and that everything comes into being through strife and necessity.'*[6] *And Pherecydes, who was far earlier than Heraclitus, relates a myth of an army drawn up in battle against another army, and says that Kronos was leader of the one and Ophioneus of the other; he tells of their challenges and their contests, and that they made agreements that whichever of them fell into Ogenus should be the vanquished party, while the party which drove the other*

---

[1] Ps. xxxiii. 8.   [2] Matt. xviii. 10.

[3] For Celsus' objection to dualism (after Plato, *Politicus*, 270A), cf. VIII, 11. For the devil as a figure causing some embarrassment to Christian apologists cf. Athenagoras, *Leg.* 24.

[4] Cf. Celsus in II, 38, 45, 47, 73. For begging, cf. I, 9; II, 55.

[5] Read οἷς οὐ χρῆναι βουκοληθέντας with Wifstrand.

[6] Heraclitus, *frag.* 80 Diels, reading χρεών with Diels, an emendation confirmed by the quotation of this fragment in Philodemus, *de Pietate*, discovered at Herculaneum; cf. Philippson in *Hermes* LV (1920), p. 254, a reference I owe to the kindness of Mr G. S. Kirk. For other references to Heraclitus' opinion cf. Aristotle, *Eth. Nicom.* VIII, 2 (1155 b 6); Plutarch, *Mor.* 370D; Diog. Laert. IX, 8.

out and conquered should possess the heaven.[1] Celsus says that *this is also the meaning contained in the mysteries which affirm that the Titans and Giants fought with the gods, and in the mysteries of the Egyptians which tell of Typhon and Horus and Osiris.*[2]

After he has made these remarks, although he does not explain how these myths contain a profound meaning, nor yet how our doctrines are misunderstandings of them, he pours abuse on us saying that *these myths are not like the tales which tell of a devil who is a daemon, or (and here they are nearer the truth) which speak of a man who is a sorcerer and proclaims opposing opinions.*[3] He also understands *Homer* in this sense, saying that he *hints at the same truths as Heraclitus and Pherecydes and as those who teach the mysteries of the Titans and Giants, in these words which Hephaestus addresses to Hera:*

> *For once already, when I intended to defend you, he took me by the foot and hurled me from the·divine threshold.*[4]

And similarly in the words of Zeus to Hera:

> *Dost thou not remember when thou wert hanging from on high, and I let two anvils hang from his two legs and threw golden and unbroken chains around thine arms? And thou wast hanging in the aether and the clouds. And the gods struck from far Olympus, but they could not set him free though standing by; but I took him and seizing him threw him from the threshold until he came powerless to earth.*[5]

[1] Pherecydes of Syros, *frag.* 4 Diels (whose delimitation of the words deriving from Pherecydes is corrected by H. O. Schröder in *Hermes*, LXXIV (1939), pp. 108–10). For the myth of Kronos' victory over the world-ruler, Ophioneus (cf. Tert. *de Cor.* 7), see the discussion by E. Wüst in P.-W. XVIII, 1 (1939), 643–6. Philo of Byblus (= Sanchuniathon) ap. Eus. *P.E.* I, 10, 50, 41 D, remarks that 'Pherecydes took his ideas from the Phoenicians in his theology concerning the god called by him Ophion and the Ophionidae'. A confused reference also in Maximus Tyrius, IV, 4 (p. 45 Hobein). For Ogenus (= Oceanus), cf. Pherecydes ap. Clem. Al. *Strom.* VI, 9, 4.

[2] For the Titans cf. Celsus' remarks on the *peplos* of Athena, below. The Isis-Osiris myth is similarly interpreted by Plutarch, *Mor.* 371 A, B: 'The fact is that the creation and constitution of this world is complex, resulting, as it does, from opposing influences, which, however, are not of equal strength, but the predominance rests with the better. Yet it is impossible for the bad to be completely eradicated, since it is innate, in large amount, in the body and likewise in the soul of the universe, and is always fighting a hard fight against the better. So in the soul Intelligence and Reason, the Ruler and Lord of all that is good, is Osiris, and in earth and wind and water and the heavens and stars that which is ordered, established, and healthy, as evidenced by the seasons, temperatures, and cycles of revolution, is the efflux of Osiris and his reflected image. But Typhon is that part of the soul which is impressionable, impulsive, irrational, and truculent, and of the bodily part the destructible, diseased, and disorderly as evidenced by abnormal seasons and temperatures, and by observations of the sun and disappearances of the moon, outbursts, as it were, and unruly actions on the part of Typhon' (F. C. Babbitt's trans.). Also Proclus, *in Tim.* 20D (I, 77, 15 Diehl).

[3] I.e. the Antichrist.   [4] *Il.* I, 590–1.

[5] *Il.* xv, 18–24.

Commenting on the words of Homer he says that *the words of Zeus to Hera are the words of God to matter,*[1] and that *the words to matter vaguely hint that at the beginning it was in chaos and God divided it in certain proportions, bound it together, and ordered it,*[2] *and that he cast out all the daemons round it which were arrogant, inflicting on them the punishment of being sent down here to the earth.* He maintains that *Pherecydes understood*[3] *these words of Homer in this way, when he said: 'Beneath that land is the land of Tartarus, and it is guarded by the daughters of Boreas, the Harpies and Thyella; there Zeus casts out any of the gods if ever one becomes arrogant.'*[4] And he says that *such ideas are expressed by the robe of Athena which is seen by every spectator at the procession of the Panathenaea.*[5] *For,* he says, *it indicates that a goddess, who has no mother and is undefiled,*[6] *overcomes those born of earth who are overbold.*

Accepting the legends invented by the Greeks he goes on to attack our doctrines as follows: *The punishment of the Son of God by the devil*[7] *is to teach us that when we are punished by the same being we should endure it patiently. All this also is ludicrous. In my opinion he ought to have punished the devil; certainly he ought not to have pronounced threats against the men who had been attacked by him.*

43. Consider whether he who accuses us of making *quite blasphemous errors,* and of having been *led to depart from the true meaning of the divine enigmas,* does not obviously make a mistake himself, since he has failed to comprehend the fact that it is the writings of Moses, which are not only

---

[1] For Zeus as God, Hera as matter, cf. Chrysippus in IV, 48, above.

[2] A reminiscence of Plato, *Timaeus* 37A ἀνὰ λόγον μερισθεῖσα καὶ ξυνδεθεῖσα (of the world-soul).

[3] Read νοήσαντα with Guiet, and Stählin, *Philol. Wochenschr.* (1942), 6.

[4] Pherecydes, *frag.* 5 Diels. For Hephaestus cast down by Zeus to Tartarus, cf. Hesiod, *Theogony*, 868; for the wind-spirits, the Harpies and Aello or Thyella, *ibid.* 267. This appears to be the only place where the Harpies appear as Boreas' daughters; the usual story is that they were daughters of Thaumas and Electra, and sisters of Iris. Cf. H. J. Rose, *A Handbook of Greek Mythology* (1928), pp. 27–8; O. Gruppe, *Griechische Mythologie*, p. 846 n. 5. S. Eitrem, 'Sonnenkäfer und Falke in der synkretistischen Magie', in *Pisciculi f. F. J. Dölger* (1939), pp. 94–101 with Plate VIII. 1, publishes a magic crystal stone with the figure of a beetle, above which is inscribed ΦΛΟΞ, below ΘΥΕΛΛΑ. The script is datable to the late hellenistic or early Roman periods.

[5] At the Panathenaea, an annual festival held at Athens on the birth-day of Athena, there was a procession in which an embroidered robe was brought to the goddess in a ship on wheels. The robe (*peplos*) was decorated with scenes from the battle with the Giants. Cf. L. R. Farnell, *The Cults of the Greek States*, I (1896), pp. 294 ff., and the article 'Panathenaia' in P.-W. XVIII, 3 (1949), 459 f. (L. Ziehen); for ancient representations of Athena fighting the Giants cf. Waser in P.-W., Suppl. Bd. III (1918), 678 ff.

[6] For Athena as παρθένος ἀμήτωρ, cf. Julian 352B. On the birth of Athena from Zeus, cf. A. B. Cook, *Zeus*, III (1940), pp. 662 ff. For her perpetual virginity, *ibid.* p. 224.

[7] Read ⟨τὸ⟩ θεοῦ with Wc., K. tr. and (113. 9) πάντα with Schmidt (*Gnomon* 3 (1927), p. 121). For the idea, cf. Celsus in II, 38, 45, 73.

far older than Heraclitus and Pherecydes, but even earlier than Homer,[1] which taught the existence of this wicked power who fell from the heavens. Some such doctrine is hinted at in the story that the serpent, which was the origin of Pherecydes' Ophioneus, was the cause of man's expulsion from the divine paradise, and deceived the female race with a promise of divine power and of attaining to greater things; and we are told that the man followed her also. And who else could be the destroyer in Exodus,[2] which Moses wrote, except the one who is the cause of destruction to those who obey him and who do not resist and struggle against his wickedness? Further, the averter in Leviticus, which the Hebrew text called Azazel,[3] is none other than he. The goat upon whom the lot fell had to be sent forth in the desert so that it should avert evil. For all who, on account of their sin, belong to the portion of the evil power and who are opposed to the people of God's inheritance,[4] are deserted by God. Moreover, take the sons of Belial in Judges.[5] Who other than he can be the one whose sons they are said to be because of their wickedness? A clearer instance than any of these is that in the book of Job, who was even earlier than Moses himself. It is there written that the devil stands near God, and asks for power against Job that he may encompass him with very severe calamities, first by the destruction of all his possessions and his children, and secondly by afflicting Job's whole body with a violent attack of the disease called elephantiasis.[6] I omit the passages from the gospels about the devil tempting the Saviour, that I may not appear to reply to Celsus with arguments on the question which are drawn from more recent scriptures.[7] Moreover, in the last chapters of Job, where the Lord spoke to Job through a whirlwind and clouds the sayings recorded in the book bearing his name, several passages could be taken which deal with the serpent.[8] I have not yet mentioned also the examples from Ezekiel[9] where he speaks, as it were, of Pharaoh, or of Nebuchadnezzar, or of the prince of Tyre, or the passage from Isaiah where the dirge is sung for the king of Babylon.[10] From these scriptures one would learn not a little about evil, of the character of its origin and beginning, and how that evil came to exist because of some who lost their wings and followed the example of the first being who lost his wings.[11]

---

[1] Cf. IV, 21.   [2] Exod. xii. 23; cf. Origen, de Princ. III, 2, 1.
[3] Lev. xvi. 8, 10.
[4] Deut. xxxii. 9. For the interpretation of Lev. xvi, cf. Hom. in Lev. IX, 4–5.
[5] Jud. xix. 22; xx. 13.
[6] Job i. 6–ii. 7.   [7] Matt. iv. 1–11; Mark i. 12–13; Luke iv. 1–13.
[8] Job xl. 1, 20.   [9] Ezek. xxvi–xxxii.
[10] Isa. xiv. 4 ff.
[11] Allusion to Plato, Phaedrus, 246B, C; cf. IV, 40, above.

44. It is not possible for that which is good accidentally and conse-
quentially to be good in the same sense as that which is good in its own
nature;[1] goodness in the former sense will never be absent from the man
who, so to speak, receives the living bread for his preservation. If it is
absent, the reason for this is that the man neglected to partake of the living
bread and the true drink.[2] When the wing is given these for food and drink
it is restored, even as the most wise Solomon teaches when he says of the
man who is rich with the true wealth: 'For he made for himself wings as
an eagle and returns to the house of his leader.'[3] It was necessary for God,
who knows how to use for a needful end even the consequences of evil, to
put those who became evil in this way in a particular part of the universe,
and to make a school of virtue to be set up for those who wished to strive
lawfully[4] in order to obtain it. His purpose was that when, like gold in the
fire, they had been tried by the evil on earth, and done everything possible
that they might let nothing impure enter their rational nature, they might
appear worthy of progressing to the divine realm and be drawn up by the
Logos to the supreme blessedness of all and, if I may so express it, to the
mountain-summit of goodness.

The word Satan in Hebrew, which some spell in a more Hellenic fashion
as *Satanas*, means adversary when translated into Greek.[5] Every man who
has chosen evil and to live an evil life so that he does everything contrary
to virtue is a Satan, that is, an adversary to the Son of God who is
righteousness, truth, and wisdom.[6] But speaking more strictly, the Adversary is the first of all beings that were in peace and lived in blessedness who
lost his wings and fell from the blessed state. According to Ezekiel he
walked blameless in all his ways until iniquity was found in him, and being
'a seal of likeness and a crown of beauty'[7] in the paradise of God he
became, as it were, sated with good things[8] and came to destruction, as the

---

[1] For the distinction, cf. *de Princ.* II, 9, 2 (of the rational beings at their creation)
'Whatever may have been the goodness that existed in their being, it existed in them not by
nature, but as a result of their Creator's beneficence. What they are, therefore, is something
neither their own nor eternal, but given by God.' *Ibid.* I, 2, 4 'Some of those who were
created would prove unable, in consequence of the good being within them as an accident
and not by nature, that is, not essentially (οὐσιωδῶς, *substantialiter*), to remain firm and
stedfast and to abide for ever in the just and temperate use of their original blessings...'
(Butterworth's trans.); *Comm. in Matt.* xv, 10.

[2] John vi. 51.

[3] Prov. xxiii. 5. Read αὐτῷ with Del., K. tr.

[4] II Tim. ii. 5.   [5] Luke x. 18; II Thess. ii. 4.

[6] The three nouns should be in the dative (so Wifstrand).

[7] Ezek. xxviii. 15, 12–13.

[8] Similarly *de Princ.* II, 8, 3, in the text reconstructed by Koetschau from the anathemas
of the Council of Constantinople (553): the rational creatures 'were seized with weariness
of the divine love and contemplation, and changed for the worse, each in proportion to his
inclination in this direction' (Butterworth's trans. p. 125). Contrast v, 32 above.

Word tells us which mysteriously says to him: 'Thou didst become destruction and shalt not exist for ever.'[1]

However, although we have boldly and rashly committed these few remarks to writing in this book, perhaps we have said nothing significant. But if anyone with the time to examine the holy scriptures were to collect texts from all sources and were to give a coherent account of evil, both how it first came to exist and how it is being destroyed, he would see that the meaning of Moses and the prophets with regard to Satan has not even been dreamt of by Celsus or by any of the people who are dragged down by this wicked daemon and are drawn away in their soul from God and the right conception of Him and from His Word.

45. As Celsus also objects to the doctrine about the figure called Antichrist, though he has read neither the passages about him in Daniel, nor those in Paul, nor the Saviour's prophecies in the gospels concerning his coming,[2] we have to say a little about this also. 'Just as faces are unlike other faces, so also the hearts of men are unlike one another.'[3] Obviously differences exist in the hearts of men, both among those who have inclined to goodness, since they have not all been moulded and shaped equally and like each other in their propensity towards it, and among those who because of their neglect of what is good rapidly pass to the opposite extreme;[4] for among the latter also there are some who have been overwhelmed by the flood of evil, while others have sunk less far. Why, then, is it absurd that among men there should be two extremities, if I may so say, the one of goodness, the other of the opposite, so that the extremity of goodness exists in the human nature of Jesus,[5] since from him the mighty work of conversion, healing and improvement flowed to the human race, whereas the opposite extremity exists in him who is called Antichrist? God comprehended all this by His foreknowledge, and, seeing that there were these two extremes, willed to tell men about these things through the prophets, in order that those who understood their words might be made lovers of what is better, and be on their guard against the opposite. It was right, also, that one of the extremes, the best, should be called Son of God because of his superiority, and that the one diametrically opposed to him should be called son of the evil daemon, who is Satan and the devil. Then, since the time when the wickedness of the flood of evil is at its height is marked by the fact that it feigns what is good, on this account, through the co-operation of his father the devil, the wicked one

---

[1] Ezek. xxviii. 19.
[2] Dan. viii. 23 ff.; xi. 36; II Thess. ii. 3–4; Matt. xxiv. 27; Luke xvii. 24.
[3] Prov. xxvii. 19.
[4] For neglect as the origin of sin, cf. *de Princ.* II, 9, 6.
[5] For the Greek phrase, cf. II, 25 above.

is accompanied by signs and wonders and false miracles.[1] For the aid given by daemons to sorcerers who deceive men for the most iniquitous purposes is surpassed by the assistance which the devil himself gives in order to deceive the human race.

Paul speaks of this person called Antichrist in his teaching when he shows, in rather guarded language, how he will come to the human race and when and why. Consider also whether Paul does not give a very impressive account of these truths which does not merit even the slightest ridicule.

46. This is what he says:

Now we beseech you, brethren, touching the coming of our Lord Jesus Christ, and our gathering together unto him, to the end that you may not be quickly shaken from your mind, nor yet be troubled, either by spirit, or by word, or by letter as from us, as that the day of the Lord is now present. Let no man beguile you in any way; for it will not be unless the falling away comes first, and the man of sin is revealed, the son of perdition, he that opposes and exalts himself against all that is called God or that is worshipped, so that he sits in the temple of God, setting himself forth as God. Do you not remember that when I was with you, I told you these things? And now you know that which restrains, to the end that he may be revealed in his own time. For the mystery of lawlessness is already at work, only until he that now restrains is taken out of the way. And then shall be revealed the lawless one, whom the Lord Jesus shall slay with the breath of his mouth, and bring to nought by the manifestation of his coming; even he, whose coming is according to the working of Satan with all power and signs and lying wonders, and with all deceit of unrighteousness for them that are perishing; because they did not receive the love of the truth that they might be saved. And for this cause God sends them a working of error, that they should believe a lie, that they all might be judged who believed not the truth, but had pleasure in unrighteousness.[2]

To explain each point in this passage is not relevant to our present concern. There is also the prophecy about him in Daniel, which is able to persuade an intelligent and honest reader to admire the words as truly *inspired*[3] and prophetic, in the passage where he prophesies about the future kingdoms, beginning from the times of Daniel down to the destruction of the world.[4] Although anyone interested can read it, nevertheless I quote the passage about the Antichrist which is as follows: 'And at the end of their reign, when the number of their sins is fulfilled, a king of shameless face shall arise who understands problems; and his power shall be mighty, and he shall destroy wonderful things and shall prosper and succeed and destroy mighty men and a holy people. And the

---

[1] Cf. II Thess. ii. 9.   [2] II Thess. ii. 1–12 (R.V. with minor changes).
[3] Cf. Celsus in IV, 36; VI, 80; VII, 41; VIII, 45.   [4] Dan. vii.

yoke of his collar shall prosper; craft shall be in his hand and he shall
magnify himself in his heart and destroy many by craft; and he shall stand
for the destruction of many, and shall crush them as eggs in his hand.'[1]
And the event mentioned by Paul in his words which I have quoted,
where he says 'so that he sits in the temple of God, setting himself forth
as God', is also mentioned by Daniel in these words: 'And at the temple
an abomination of desolations, and at the end of time an end shall be given
to the desolation.'[2]

I have thought it reasonable to quote these out of several passages in
order that the hearer may understand a little, at least, of the meaning of
the divine words which teach about the devil and the Antichrist. Content
with these passages which bear on this matter let us consider also another
sentence from Celsus and refute it to the best of our ability.

47. After the words that I quoted he makes the following remark: *But
I can tell you how even this idea that they should call him Son of God occurred
to them. Men of olden times used to call this world God's child and a demigod*[3]
*on the ground that it originated from Him. Jesus and that child of God are,
indeed, very alike.* He imagines that we call him Son of God in imitation of
what is said of the world on the ground that it originated from God and is
His son and is God. He was incapable of studying the dates of Moses and
the prophets to see that in general the prophets of the Jews prophesied
the existence of a Son of God before the Greeks and those whom Celsus
calls *men of olden times*. Nor did he want to quote the saying of Plato in
the Epistles which we have quoted above,[4] to the effect that the one who
ordered this universe was son of God, so that he might not be compelled
by Plato, whom he often mentions with respect, to admit himself that the
Creator of this universe is God's Son and that the first and supreme God
is his Father.

There is nothing amazing about it if, when we affirm that the soul of
Jesus was united by a supreme participation with the majesty of the Son of
God, we do not make any further distinction between them. For the
sacred words of the divine scriptures also mention other things which in
their own nature are two, but which are reckoned to become, and really
are, one with each other. For instance, of man and woman it is said that
'they are no longer two, but one flesh'.[5] And of the perfect man who is
joined to the true Lord, the Logos and wisdom and truth, it is said that
'he who is joined to the Lord is one spirit'.[6] If then 'he who is joined to

---

[1] Dan. viii. 23–5.   [2] Dan. ix. 27.
[3] Read ἡμίθεον (so K. tr., Schmidt, Bader). For the divinity of the cosmos, cf. v, 7.
[4] vi, 8.   [5] Gen. ii. 24; Matt. xix. 6.
[6] I Cor. vi. 17; similarly in II, 9, above. Also *Dial. c. Heracl.* 3, pp. 124 f. Scherer
(*Publ. Soc. Fouad I de Papyrologie, Textes et Doc.* IX, Cairo, 1949).

the Lord is one spirit', who has been joined more closely than the soul of Jesus, or even to any comparable extent, to the Lord who is the very Logos, wisdom, truth, and righteousness? If this is the case, the relation of the soul of Jesus to the firstborn of all creation,[1] the divine Logos, is not that of two separate beings.

48. If the philosophers of the Stoa say that man and God have the same virtue, and that the supreme God is not happier than their wise man but that the happiness of both is equal,[2] Celsus does not pour mockery or ridicule on the doctrine. But if the divine scripture affirms that the perfect man cleaves to the Logos himself by his virtue and is united with him, so that by this principle we go on to conclude that no separation is to be made between the soul of Jesus and the firstborn of all creation, he laughs at the affirmation that Jesus is Son of God, because he does not see that there is a secret and profound meaning in the words used about him in the divine scriptures.

To persuade a man who wishes to pursue doctrines to their conclusions and to derive benefit from them that this doctrine is acceptable, we say that according to the teaching of the divine scriptures the body of Christ, the soul of which is the Son of God, is the whole Church of God,[3] and that the limbs of this body, which is to be regarded as a whole, are those who believe, whoever they may be. For a soul gives life to a body and moves it, since it has not the power of self-movement like a living being; so also the Logos, which moves and acts upon the whole body for needful purposes, moves the Church and each limb of the members of the Church who do[4] nothing apart from the Logos. If, then, this illustration which in my opinion is worthy of consideration, is a good analogy, what difficulty is there in supposing that the soul of Jesus, indeed Jesus without qualification, by virtue of his supreme and unsurpassed communion with the very Logos himself, was not separated from the only-begotten and the firstborn of all creation, and was not distinct from him?[5] So much, however, for this problem.

49. Let us also consider the next remarks where he objects to the Mosaic story of the creation of the world with a single bare assertion without even saying anything plausible. *Besides, the cosmogony too is very silly.* If he had brought forward some reason why it seemed to him that it was silly, and had produced some plausible arguments, we would have

---

[1] Col. i. 15.

[2] Cf. IV, 29; Seneca, *Ep.* LXXIII, 15 'Iuppiter quo antecedit virum bonum? Diutius bonus est; sapiens nihilo se minoris existimat, quod virtutes eius spatio breviore cluduntur...sic deus non vincit sapientem felicitate, etiam si vincit aetate.'

[3] Col. i. 24.   [4] Read πραττόντων with We.

[5] Read ἕτερόν τι with We.

argued against them. But I do not think it reasonable to argue in reply to his assertion to explain why it is not silly.

If anyone wants to see the reasons that persuade us to believe the Mosaic story of the creation of the world, which are supported by the arguments that seemed right to us, let him take our studies in Genesis from the beginning of the book down to the words 'This is the book of the generation of men.'[1] In them we have tried to argue from the divine scriptures themselves what was the heaven that was made 'in the beginning', and the earth, and the invisible and unformed part of the earth, and what was the great deep, and the darkness upon it, and what was the water, and the Spirit of God that was borne upon it, and what was the light which was created, and what was the firmament as distinct from the heaven made in the beginning, and so on.

He asserted that *the record of the origin of man is also very silly*, without either quoting the texts[2] or combating with them. For I imagine he had no arguments able to refute the saying that man was made in God's image.[3] Furthermore, he does not understand *the paradise planted by God, and the life which the man lived in it in the first place, and that which came to pass through force of circumstances when the man was banished on account of his sin and made to live opposite the paradise of luxury.* Let the fellow who says that *these statements are very silly* first pay attention to each point, in particular to this: 'He placed the cherubim and the flaming sword that turned itself to guard the way of the tree of life.'[4] But perhaps *Moses wrote these stories because he understood nothing, but did much the same as the poets of the Old Comedy who mockingly wrote 'Proetus married Bellerophon, and Pegasus came from Arcadia.'*[5] Yet they composed this from a desire to raise a laugh. But it is not plausible that the man who left writings for a whole nation, and who wanted the people for whom he made laws to believe that they derived from God, should have written pointless stories, and that he should have had no conviction when he said: 'He placed the cherubim and the flaming sword that turned itself to guard the way of the tree of life', or any of the other statements about the origin of mankind which are understood philosophically by the wise men among the Hebrews.

---

[1] Gen. v. 1. Origen's commentary on Genesis expounded only the first four chapters; cf. Jerome, *Ep.* xxxvi, 9, where we learn that Origen commented on Gen. iv. 15 in the twelfth and thirteenth books of the Commentary. The Commentary contained thirteen books according to Jerome ap. Rufin. *Apol. adv. Hier.* II, 20, twelve books according to Eus. *H.E.* vi, 24, 2. For the surviving fragments cf. Preuschen in Harnack, *Geschichte der altchristlichen Litteratur,* I, pp. 343 f.   [2] Read λέξεις with We., K. tr.
[3] Gen. i. 27.   [4] Gen. iii. 24. Read τῷ δέ with K. tr.
[5] T. Kock, *Comicorum Atticorum Fragmenta,* III, p. 406, *frag.* 42. For the story of Bellerophon and his horse Pegasus, see H. J. Rose, *Handbook of Greek Mythology,* pp. 270 f.

50. After this he piles up mere assertions about *the different views concerning the origin of the world and of mankind held by some of the ancients whom* he has *mentioned*,[1] and says that *Moses and the prophets who left our books had no idea what the nature of the world and of mankind really is, and put together utter trash.* If he had stated the reason why he thought the divine scriptures were *utter trash*, we should have tried to demolish the arguments which seemed to him to be plausible which led him to believe that they were *utter trash*. But now we shall do as he does; we also will mockingly assert that Celsus had no idea of the nature of the meaning and doctrine of the prophets, and put together utter trash, boastfully entitling it *The True Doctrine*.

He then produces an objection about *the days of the creation of the world,* as if he had understood their meaning clearly and accurately; some of these passed before the existence of the light and of the heaven and before the sun, moon, and stars, while some passed after these had been made.[2] We will reply to him with this single observation. Did Moses forget that he had just said that the created world was completed in six days, and was it because he had forgotten this that he went on to say: 'This is the generation of men, in the day in which God made heaven and earth'?[3] It is not in the least plausible that it was because Moses understood nothing that after speaking of six days he should have said 'In the day in which God made heaven and earth.' If anyone thinks that the latter saying can be referred to the words 'In the beginning God made the heaven and the earth',[4] let him realize that the words 'In the beginning God made the heaven and the earth' occur before the words 'Let there be light and there was light' and before 'God called the light day.'[5]

51. It is not our present task to explain the doctrine about intelligible and sensible things, and the way in which the natures of the days have been divided between both forms, or to study the text of the passage. We would need whole treatises to explain the Mosaic account of the creation of the world. We did this as well as we could a long time before writing the present treatise against Celsus, using such ability as we possessed many years ago to discuss the Mosaic account of creation.[6] However, it must be realized that the Word proclaims to the righteous through Isaiah that there will be a restoration with days in which not the sun but the Lord himself shall be to them an everlasting light and God shall be their glory.[7]

---

[1] Origen omits Celsus' remarks here. Read εἰρημένων with We. and Stählin, *Philol. Wochenschr.* (1942), 6.

[2] Cf. Celsus in VI, 60, below.   [3] Gen. v. 1; ii. 4.

[4] Gen. i. 1.   [5] Gen. i. 3, 5.

[6] Origen's Commentary on Genesis (cf. IV, 37; VI, 49) was written about eighteen years before the *contra Celsum*.   [7] Isa. lx. 19.

But I think he has misunderstood some wicked heresy that wrongly interpreted the words 'Let there be light' as if they were uttered by the Creator as a prayer,[1] when he says: *Moreover, the Creator did not use light from above, like people who borrow lamps from their neighbours.* And it was because he misunderstood some other impious heresy that he said: *If it was an accursed God[2] opposed to the great God who made these things contrary to his will, why did he lend him the light?* So far are we from defending this that we would make more thoroughgoing criticisms of their erroneous opinion and would attack not what we do not know about them like Celsus, but that of which we have accurate knowledge, partly from what we have heard[3] from the heretics themselves, and partly from careful reading of their books.

52. After this Celsus says: *But I say nothing now about the beginning and the destruction of the world, whether it is uncreated and indestructible, or created and indestructible, or vice versa.[4]* For this reason neither do we speak now about these questions, for the treatise that we have in hand does not require this. However, we do not say that *the Spirit of the supreme God came among men on earth as to strangers[5]* when we say that 'the Spirit of God was borne above the water'. Nor do we say that *some things were devised by another Creator, different from the great God, against his Spirit while the higher God restrained himself, and that they needed to be destroyed.* Accordingly, we may dismiss those who hold these opinions and Celsus who fails to make any competent criticisms of them. For Celsus either ought not to have mentioned these notions, or he should have given a careful account of them in the way which he thought to be of benefit to men, and have combated their assertions. Nor have we ever heard that *after the great God has given the Spirit to the Creator, He asks for it to be returned.*

Then against such[6] impious words he next brings a foolish criticism: *What God gives anything which he will ask to be returned to him? For to ask*

---

[1] This was the opinion of Tatian, *frag.* 7–8 Schwartz = Clement, *Ecl. Proph.* XXXVIII, 1 'Against Tatian who says that the words "Let there be light" are a prayer: if then he who uttered the prayer was aware of a God higher than himself, why does he say "I am God and there is none other but I"?'; and Origen, *de Orat.* XXIV, 5 'Because Tatian failed to perceive that the imperative "Let there be" does not always signify a request but is sometimes a command, he held a most blasphemous opinion about the God who said "Let there be light", believing that he was praying rather than commanding that light be made, "for the reason", as he puts it with his atheistic mind, "that the God was in darkness".'
[2] Cf. Celsus in VI, 27.   [3] Read ἀκούσαντες with Bo., Guiet.
[4] Cf. IV, 61 and 79. 'Uncreated and destructible' would be Stoic doctrine.
[5] The good God of Marcion was called by him 'the Stranger', and those whom he redeemed 'the strangers' (cf. VI, 53). I cannot agree with Bader (and Keim) that the quotation from Gen. i. 2 is also taken from Celsus.
[6] Read ἑξῆς ⟨τοιούτοις⟩ with K. tr.

for something is the action of one who is in need, while God is in need of nothing.[1] And as though he were saying something clever against certain folk he adds to this: *Why, when he lent his Spirit, was he ignorant that he was lending to an evil being?* He also remarks: *Why does he put up with an evil Creator opposing him?*

53. He then, I think, muddles some sects with others, and does not notice that some are the doctrines of one sect and some of another. For he brings forward our objections to Marcion, though probably even of these he has got a distorted version from some who criticize the doctrine with shoddy and vulgar arguments, and certainly not with any intelligence. He sets forth the objections that are brought against Marcion without observing that it is Marcion whom he is addressing,[2] saying: *Why does he secretly send to destroy the creations of this God? Why does he force his way in by stealth and beguile and lead astray? Why does he lead off those whom, as you say, the Creator has condemned and cursed,*[3] *and carry them away like a slave-dealer? Why does he teach them to escape from their master? Why should they flee from their father? Why does he adopt them as his children without the consent of their father? Why does he lay claim to be the father of the strangers?*[4] And he adds to these questions, as if it were some wonderful saying: *An impressive God, indeed, who desires to be the father of sinners condemned by another and of poor wretches who, as they say themselves, are but dung,*[5] *and who is incapable of taking vengeance upon the Creator when he has caught the one whom he had sent out to bring them to himself.*[6]

After this, as if he were addressing us who believe that this world is not the creation of some *alien and strange God,* he speaks as follows: *But if*

---

[1] A commonplace. Cf. Celsus in VIII, 21.

[2] For Celsus' knowledge of Marcion, cf. v, 54, 62. Discussion in Harnack, *Marcion: Das Evangelium vom fremden Gott* (2nd ed. 1924), pp. 325* ff., who thinks it not improbable that Celsus had read anti-Marcionite polemic.

[3] Marcion said that the Lord descended to Hades to save Cain, Korah, Dathan, Abiram, Esau, and all the nations who had not obeyed the God of the Jews, such as the Sodomites and the Egyptians. Cf. Irenaeus, I, 27, 3; Epiphanius, *Panar.* XLII, 4.

[4] Cf. VI, 52 and note; for 'the Stranger' as the name of the good God in Marcion's doctrine, cf. Harnack, *op. cit.* p. 265*. Irenaeus, *adv. Haer.* IV, 33, 2 (Harvey, II, 257), has a similar series of questions addressed to Marcion: 'How can he be good who draws the strangers (*alienos homines*) away from him who made them, and calls them to his kingdom? And why is his goodness defective in that he does not save all men? And why is he good so far as men are concerned, but most unfair to him who made men, since he deprives him of that which is his?...' etc. For the idea, cf. H. C. Puech, *Le Manichéisme* (1949), pp.152–3 n. 273.

[5] According to Harnack (*op. cit.* pp. 126*, 312*) Marcion understood Paul to be referring to himself in Phil. iii. 8 (ἡγοῦμαι σκύβαλα εἶναι), for which view Harnack appeals to this passage from Celsus. This is a dubious conclusion. Celsus may only have in mind the tendency to self-depreciation seen, for example, in Ignatius' description of himself as an 'offscouring' (Ign. *Ephes.* 18; similarly *Ep. Barn.* IV, 9; VI, 5). He may not have only the Marcionites in mind. [6] Read αὐτοὺς ὑπεξάξοντα and omit commas with K. tr.

these are the Creator's works, how can it be that God should make what is evil? And how can he be incapable of persuading and admonishing men? How can he repent when they become ungrateful and wicked,[1] and find fault with his own handiwork, and hate and threaten and destroy his own offspring? Or where is he to banish them out of the world which he himself made? Here too, I think, because he has failed to make clear what are evil things, although even among the Greeks there are many differences of opinion about good and evil, he jumps to the conclusion[2] that from our affirmation that even this world is the work of the supreme God it follows that we believe God to be the maker of what is evil.

Whatever the truth may be about evil, whether God made it, or whether, if He did not, it has come into being as a by-product of the primary creations,[3] we are not concerned with that now. But I wonder whether the conclusion that God has made evil which, he thinks, follows from our affirmation that even this world is the work of the supreme God, does not by implication follow from what he even says himself. For one might say to Celsus—If these are the Creator's works, how can it be that God should make what is evil? And how can he be incapable of persuading and admonishing men? It is the greatest fault in argument when a man criticizes those who differ from him as being unsound in certain doctrines that they hold, while he himself in his own doctrines is far more open to the same criticisms.

54. In the light of the divine scriptures let us briefly consider the question of good and evil, and see what reply we should make to his remark: *How can it be that God should make what is evil? And how can he be incapable of persuading and admonishing men?* According to the divine scriptures it is the virtues and virtuous actions that are good in the strict sense, just as their opposites are bad in the strict sense.[4] For the present we may be content with words from the thirty-third Psalm which shows this as follows: 'They that seek out the Lord shall not be deprived of any good thing. Come, children, listen to me, I will teach you the fear of the Lord. What man is there who desires life and loves to see good days? Keep thy tongue from evil and thy lips from speaking guile. Depart from

---

[1] Cf. Gen. vi. 6–7. (Cf. the criticisms of this passage answered by Philo, *Quod Deus sit imm.* 21.)

[2] Read συναρπάζειν with We., K. tr.

[3] Cf. VI, 55 (with note); VII, 68; VIII, 68. The distinction is Stoic. Chrysippus (ap. Aulus Gellius, *N.A.* VII, 1, 7 ff. = *S.V.F.* II, 1170) held that diseases did not exist by nature, but only as a consequential effect of nature. For further references and discussion cf. my remarks in *J.T.S.* XLVIII (1947), pp. 38 f.

[4] Origen means that strictly speaking it is only moral, not physical evil which is bad, and that goodness and badness are moral not physical terms. For parallels, cf. *J.T.S. loc. cit.* p. 45.

evil and do good.'[1] The words 'Depart from evil and do good' refer
neither to physical good or evil things as they are called by some, nor to
external things, but to the good and evil of the soul.[2] He who has departed
from what is evil in this sense and who has done good actions of this kind,
as desiring to see the true life, will come to possess it. And he[3] who 'loves
to see good days', of which the Logos is the sun of righteousness,[4] will
attain unto them, since God delivers him out of this present evil world[5]
and from the evil days which Paul mentioned when he said: 'Redeeming
the time because the days are evil.'[6]

55. In a looser sense it would be found that in respect of both physical
and external things those which contribute to the life according to nature
are considered good, and those contrary to this bad. In this sense Job
says to his wife: 'For if we have received good from the Lord's hand, shall
we not submit to evil?'[7] Accordingly, it is to be found in the divine scriptures that in one place God is represented as saying, 'I am he that makes
peace and creates evil', while again in another place it is said of Him, 'Evil
came down from the Lord to the gates of Jerusalem, a noise of chariots and
horsemen.'[8] These texts have disturbed many readers of the Bible because
they are unable to see what is meant when the Bible speaks of good and
evil. It is probably because of this that Celsus raised the difficulty when
he said *How can it be that God should make what is evil?* or it may be that
he wrote the words I have quoted because he heard someone who
expounded these matters in a very unenlightened way.

We affirm that God did not make evils, metaphysical evil and the
actions which result from it. If God had made what is really evil, how
could the message of His judgment be preached with boldness, seeing
that it teaches that bad men are punished for their evil deeds in proportion
to the sins that they have committed, and that those who have lived
virtuous lives or who have done virtuous actions are blessed and will
attain to the rewards bestowed by God? I am well aware that people who
are willing to venture the assertion that even evil originated from God will
quote certain texts from the Bible, though they cannot display a coherent
series of scriptural texts.[9] For while the Bible blames sinners and approves
those who do right, nevertheless it also makes those statements which,

---

[1] Ps. xxxiii. 11–15.
[2] According to the Aristotelian school there were three kinds of good, moral, physical,
and external. Cf. Diog. Laert. v, 30; Hippol. *Ref.* 1, 20, 5 (Diels, *Dox. Gr.* 570, 25 ff.). The
Platonists held that physical and external good was not strictly speaking good, but only
loosely so described (*Dox. Gr.* 568, 29 f.).
[3] Read ⟨καὶ ὁ⟩ ἀγαπῶν and omit the inserted καὶ with K. tr.
[4] Mal. iv. 2.   [5] Gal. i. 4.   [6] Eph. v. 16.
[7] Job ii. 10.   [8] Isa. xlv. 7; Micah i. 12–13.
[9] Similarly Clem. Al. *Strom.* VII, 96, 2.

since they are not few in number, seem to distract unlearned readers of the divine scriptures. However, I have not thought it relevant to the treatise which we have in hand to give an account now of the distracting passages, as they are numerous and to explain them would require a lengthy discussion.

God, then, has not made evils if one understands the word to be used here in a strict sense. But evils which are few in comparison with the orderly arrangement of the universe have been the consequence of the works which were His primary intention, just as spiral shavings and sawdust are a consequence of the primary works of a carpenter, and as builders may seem to cause the mess that lies beside buildings such as the dirt that falls off the stones and the plaster.[1]

56. If anyone mentions those things which are loosely described as evils, namely physical and external evils, we may grant that sometimes God has made some of these in order that by this means he may convert certain men. What can be amiss with this doctrine? Just as when, to speak loosely, we understand as evils the pains inflicted on those who are being educated by fathers and teachers and schoolmasters, or by doctors on those who undergo operations or cauterizations in order to cure them, we say that the father does evil to his sons or that the schoolmasters or teachers or doctors do so, and yet do not regard those who inflict the beating or perform the operation as doing anything reprehensible; so also if scripture says that God inflicts pains of this nature in order to convert and heal those who are in need of such punishment, there can be no ground for objection to what the Bible says, even if we read that 'evil came down from the Lord to the gates of Jerusalem'.[2] The evil has concrete form in the distress caused by the enemies, but the distress itself is inflicted for remedial purposes. Similarly when we read that He visits with a rod the iniquities of those who forsake the law of God, and their sins with stripes,[3] or that He says 'Thou hast a coal fire; sit upon it, it shall be a help to thee.'[4] In this way also we explain the words 'I am he that makes peace and creates evil.'[5] For He creates physical or external evils to purify and educate those who are unwilling to be educated by reason and sound teaching. So much for our reply to his question, *How can it be that God should make what is evil?*

57. In reply to the question, *How can he be incapable of persuading and admonishing men?* we have already remarked that, if this is an objection at

---

[1] The same point with the same illustrations in Maximus Tyrius, XLI, 4; Marcus Aurelius, VIII, 50. Cf. *J.T.S. loc. cit.* pp. 38 f., and add Sextus Emp. *P.H.* I, 129; Plotinus, IV, 4, 41.
[2] Micah i. 12.   [3] Ps. lxxxviii. 33, 31.
[4] Isa. xlvii. 14-15.   [5] Isa. xlv. 7.

all, Celsus' words are applicable to all who believe in providence.[1] One might reply, however, that God is not incapable of admonishing men. For He warns those who hear Him throughout all scripture and through those who teach by the grace of God. But perhaps some particular meaning is attached to the word 'admonish' to the effect that it also means that the word of the teacher is successful in the person who is admonished,[2] though this is contrary to the idea of the meaning established by common usage.

In reply to the question, *How can he be incapable of persuading?*, an objection which would also be applicable to all who believe in providence, this is what we have to say. The persuasion of a man is similar to the relationships which are called 'reciprocal', like a man who has his hair cut who is active in that he offers himself to the barber.[3] Because of this there is need not only for the action of the one who persuades but also for submission, so to speak, to the one who persuades or for acceptance of what he says. That is why we may not say that people who are unconvinced fail to be persuaded because God is incapable of convincing them. The reason is rather that they do not accept God's persuasive words.

If anyone applies this also to men, who are called 'creators of persuasion',[4] he would not be wrong. For it is possible even for a man who has grasped in the highest degree the principles of rhetoric, and who uses them in the right way, to do all in his power to persuade men, and yet, because he fails to gain the will of the man who ought to be persuaded, he seems to be unconvincing. And that, even if the persuasive words are given by God, yet the act of assent to them is not caused by God, is clearly taught by Paul when he says: 'The persuasion is not from him who calls you.'[5] This is also the sense of the words: 'If you are willing and listen to me, you shall eat the good things of the earth; but if you are unwilling and will not listen to me, a sword shall devour you.'[6] For in order that a man may will what the person who admonishes him tells him, so that by listening to him he may become worthy of the promises of God, it is necessary to have the will of the hearer and his assent to what is said. This, I think, is the reason why it is emphatically stated in Deuteronomy: 'And now Israel, what does the Lord thy God require of thee but to fear the Lord thy God and to walk in all his ways and to love him and to keep his commandments?'[7]

---

[1] Cf. IV, 3, 40; VI, 53.   [2] Read ἀκούεσθαι with K. tr.
[3] A grammatical commonplace to illustrate the use of the Middle Voice: Philo, *Leg. Alleg.* III, 201; *de Cherub.* 79; Diog. Laert. VII, 64–5 (where R. G. Hicks' translation misses the point). Cf. Zeller, *Philos. d. Gr.* III, i (4th ed.), p. 91 n. 1.
[4] Plato, *Gorgias*, 453Aff.; cf. Plutarch, *Mor.* 801C.
[5] Gal. v. 8.   [6] Isa. i. 19–20.   [7] Deut. x. 12–13.

58. Then we have next to reply to the question: *How can he repent when they become ungrateful and wicked, and find fault with his own handiwork, and hate and threaten and destroy his own offspring?* Here he misrepresents the words written in Genesis which read like this: 'And the Lord God saw that the evils of the people upon the earth were multiplied, and every single person thought carefully in his heart about evil continually. And God was angry that he had made man upon the earth; and God considered in his heart and said, I will destroy the man whom I made from the face of the earth, from man to beast and from creeping things to the fowls of the heaven. For I was angry that I made them.'[1] Celsus asserts something which is not written in the Bible as if it were indicated by the scriptures. For a repentance on God's part is not mentioned in these words; nor that *he finds fault with and hates his own handiwork.*

If God appears to threaten the flood, and to destroy His own offspring in it, we would say that, since the soul of men is immortal, the words taken to be a threat are intended to convert the hearers, while the destruction of men by the flood is a purification of the earth, as also some distinguished Greek philosophers have said in the words 'When the gods purify the earth.'[2] In regard to the words which are applied to God as if He had human feelings we have also spoken earlier at some length.[3]

59. Next, because Celsus suspects or perhaps even himself understands the answer that could be made by those who reply to the question about the people destroyed by the flood, he says: If he does not destroy his own offspring, *where is he to banish them out of the world which he himself made?* We reply to this that He does not take those who suffered in the flood out of the world which consists of heaven and earth. He delivers them rather from the life in the flesh and, at the same time as He sets them free from their bodies, He also delivers them from existence on earth, which in many places in the Bible is usually called the world. And especially in the gospel according to John it is possible to find the earthly region frequently called the world, as in the saying 'He was the true light that lights every man coming into the world', and 'In the world you shall have tribulation; but be of good cheer, I have overcome the world.'[4] If, then, one understands the phrase *he banishes them out of the world* to refer to the earthly region, there is no great difficulty about the remark. But if one calls the frame of heaven and earth the world, those who suffered in the flood are certainly not taken out of the world in this sense. And yet, if a man has understood the saying that 'we look not on the things that are seen but on the things that are not seen', and that 'the invisible things are clearly seen from the

---

[1] Gen. vi. 5-7.   [2] Plato, *Timaeus* 22D. Cf. IV, 11-12, 20-1, 62, 64, 69.
[3] Cf. I, 71; IV, 71-2.   [4] John i. 9; xvi. 33.

creation of the world, being perceived through the things that are made',[1]
he might say that if he is among the things that are invisible and, in general,
those called unseen, he has gone out of the world, since the Logos takes
him out from this earthly existence and transfers him to the region beyond
the heavens for the contemplation of the realm of beauty.[2]

60. After the passage we have examined, as though it were his object
to fill his book somehow with lengthy verbosity, he makes a remark
which, though in different words, is to the same effect as that which we
examined a little above,[3] where he said: *But far more silly is to have
allotted certain days to the making of the world before days existed. For
when the heaven had not yet been made, or the earth yet fixed, or the sun
borne round it, how could days exist?*[4] What difference is there between
these words and this remark: *Moreover, taking the question from the
beginning, let us consider this. Would it not be absurd for the first and
greatest God to command, Let this come into existence, or something else, or
that, so that He made so much on one day and again so much more on the
second, and so on with the third, fourth, fifth, and sixth?*[5]

We gave the best reply we could also to the words *to command, Let this
come into existence, or something else, or that,* when we quoted the text 'He
spake and they were made, he commanded and they were created',[6] and
when we explained that the immediate Creator and, as it were, direct
Maker of the world was the Son of God, the Logos, but that the Father
of the Logos was the primary Creator because He commanded His Son,
the Logos, to make the world.

Concerning the statements that the light came into existence on one
day; the firmament on the second; the waters below the heaven that were
gathered together into their meeting-places on the third, so that the earth
produced the plants which are controlled by nature alone; on the fourth
day the luminaries and stars; on the fifth the creatures that swim; on the
sixth the animals that live on earth and man; these we discussed to the
best of our ability in our studies on Genesis. In what we said earlier we
criticized those who follow the superficial interpretation and say that the
creation of the world happened during a period of time six days long,
when we quoted the text 'This is the book of the generation of heaven and

---

[1] II Cor. iv. 18; Rom. i. 20.   [2] Cf. Plato, *Phaedrus* 247C.
[3] VI, 50-1.
[4] For this difficulty, cf. Philo, *Leg. Alleg.* I, 2-3; Augustine, *de Civ. Dei* XI, 5-7; XII, 15.
In the *Timaeus* (39B, 47A) Plato says that days were made first as a unit of measurement:
'Days and nights and months and years did not exist before the heaven was made' (37E).
[5] Cf. Galen's criticisms of the doctrine of divine omnipotence implied in the Genesis
creation-story, *de Usu Partium*, XI, 14 (Helmreich, pp. 158-9). Discussion in R. Walzer,
Galen on Jews and Christians, pp. 23-37; Grant, *Miracle and Natural Law*, p. 130.
[6] Ps. xxxii. 9; cxlviii. 5; cf. II, 9 above.

earth when it came into being, in the day in which God made the heaven and the earth.'¹

61. Then again, he fails to understand this saying: 'And on the sixth day God completed his works which he made; and he ceased on the seventh day from all his works which he made. And God blessed the seventh day, and hallowed it, because in it he ceased from all his works which God began to make.'² He thought that to say 'He ceased on the seventh day' was the same as 'He rested on the seventh day',³ saying: *After this, indeed, God, exactly like a bad workman, was worn out and needed a holiday to have a rest.* He does not even know the meaning of the day after the making of the world which is the object of His activity so long as the world exists, the day⁴ of the sabbath and the cessation of God, in which those who have done all their works in the six days will feast together with God; and because they have not neglected any of the responsibilities they will ascend to the contemplation of God and the assembly of the righteous and the blessed who are engaged in this.

Then, as if it were either what the scriptures say or what we ourselves expound them to say about God, that He rested because He was tired, he says: *It is not right for the first God to be tired or to work with his hands or to give orders.*⁵ Now Celsus affirms that it is not right for the first God to be tired. But we would say that neither is the divine Logos tired, nor any of those who belong to the rank that is already superior and spiritual. For

¹ Gen. ii. 4; cf. VI, 50. So *de Princ.* IV, 3, 1 'What person of any intelligence would think that there existed a first, second, and third day, and evening and morning, without sun, moon, and stars?'; *Comm. in Matt.* XIV, 9, where Origen argues against those who think the Last Judgment takes place in time: 'If anyone disbelieves in the speed of God's power in this respect, he has not yet understood that the God who made the whole world did not need time to make the mighty creation of heaven and earth and of all that is in them. For even if these things seem to have been made in six days, intelligence is required to understand in what sense the words "in six days" are meant because of this saying...' (Gen. ii. 4); *Sel. in Genes.* VIII, p. 54 Lomm.

² Gen. ii. 2–3.

³ Cf. V, 59 above. The distinction goes back to Aristobulus ap. Eus. *P.E.* XIII, 12, 11, 667B, C, followed by Philo, *Leg. Alleg.* I, 5–6; Clem. Al. *Strom.* VI, 141, 7; Augustine, *de Civ. Dei* XI, 8.

⁴ With Wif. omit comma and ἥ.

⁵ For the view that it is inappropriate for God to be too intimately involved in the making and administration of the world cf. Ps.-Aristotle, *de Mundo* 6 (398b 1 ff.) 'If it was beneath the dignity of Xerxes to appear himself to administer all things and carry out his own wishes and superintend the government of his kingdom, such functions would be still less becoming for a god. Nay, it is more worthy of his dignity and more befitting that he should be enthroned in the highest region, and that his power, extending through the whole universe, should move the sun and moon and make the whole heaven revolve and be the cause of permanence to all that is on this earth....It is most characteristic of the divine to be able to accomplish diverse kinds of work with ease and by simple movement...' etc. (trans. E. S. Forster). 'Le roi règne, mais il ne gouverne pas.' Discussion in Peterson, *Monotheismus*, pp. 16ff. Cf. Introduction, p. xviii.

tiredness is an attribute of those living in the body.[1] However, you might inquire whether this is the case with people in whatever sort of body they are, or only with those in the earthly body and in one a little better than this. Further, it is not right also for the first God to work with his hands. And if you understand the words 'to work with one's hands' in the strict sense, neither does this apply to the second God,[2] nor to any other of the divine powers. But let us suppose that the words 'to work with one's hands' are used loosely or figuratively, for so we would explain the text 'The firmament proclaims the work of his hands', and 'His hands established the heaven',[3] and any other similar saying. For we interpret God's hands and limbs allegorically. Why, then, is it absurd that God should work with His hands in this sense? Just as it is not absurd for God to work with His hands in this sense, so also it is not absurd for Him to give orders, that the works performed by the one who receives the orders may be beautiful and praiseworthy because it is God who has directed their making.

62. Again, perhaps because Celsus misunderstood the words 'For the mouth of the Lord has spoken these things',[4] and perhaps also because some of the uneducated have been hasty in interpreting sayings like this, and because he did not understand with what object the Bible uses the names of physical limbs in reference to the powers of God, he says *He has neither mouth nor voice*. It is true that God will have no voice if the voice is vibrated air, or a percussion of air, or a kind of air, or any other definition which experts in these matters may give to the voice.[5] But what is called the voice of God is said to be seen as such by the people in the text: 'All the people saw the voice of God.'[6] The word 'saw' is taken spiritually, if I may use the normal terminology of the Bible. Moreover, he says *Nor does God have any other of the characteristics of which we know*. But he does not make clear what he means by *the characteristics of which we know*. If he means limbs we agree with him, assuming that the characteristics of which we know are only physical and those known by ordinary sense-perception. But if we understand the words *of which we know* as applying to everything, we know of many characteristics which may be predicated of God.[7] For

---

[1] Cf. the Stoic in Cicero, *de Nat. Deor.* II, 23, 59, who remarks (after Plato, *Timaeus*, 33 A, B) that the universe and the stars do not grow weary because they have no veins, nerves, bones, and digestive organs; because Epicurus' gods had human form, he had to make them do nothing.   [2] For the Logos as a second God, cf. v, 39; VII, 57.

[3] Ps. xviii. 2; ci. 26.   [4] Isa. i. 20.   [5] See II, 72 and note.

[6] Exod. xx. 18, so interpreted by Philo, *de Decal.* 47; *de Migr. Abr.* 47; Clem. Al. *Strom.* VI, 34. Cf. Origen, *Hom. in Lucam*, 1; Basil, *Hexaem.* II, 7; III, 2.

[7] The text is corrupt, and the lacuna is taken to be beyond repair by Wifstrand (*Bull. Soc. Roy. Lund* (1941–2), p. 36). The translation gives what must be the general sense. Perhaps we might read πολλῶν ⟨ὧν⟩ ἡμεῖς ἴσμεν ἐξακούομεν ⟨περὶ τοῦ θε⟩οῦ, or πολλῶν ἡμεῖς ἴσμεν ⟨ὧν⟩ ἐξακούομεν ⟨περὶ τοῦ θε⟩οῦ.

He possesses virtue and blessedness and divinity. But if anyone were to understand in a more transcendent sense the words *of which we know*, since all that we know is inferior to God as He really is, it is not wrong that we also should accept the view that God has no characteristics of which we know. The attributes of God are superior to any which are known not only by human nature, but even by the nature of beings who have risen beyond it. If he had read the words of the prophets, where David says, 'But thou art the same' and where Malachi, if I remember rightly, says, 'And I change not',[1] he would have seen that none of us say that change takes place in God either in action or in thought. Remaining the same He controls the things that are subject to change, as that is their nature; and reason itself compels us to hold that they are under His control.

63. Then Celsus failed to see the difference between what is 'in the image of God'[2] and His image.[3] He did not realize that the image of God is the firstborn of all creation, the very Logos and truth, and, further, the very wisdom Himself, being 'the image of his goodness',[4] whereas man was made 'in the image of God', and, furthermore, every man of whom Christ is head is God's image and glory.[5] Moreover, he failed to understand to what characteristic of man the words 'in the image of God' apply, and that this exists in the soul which either has not possessed or possesses no longer 'the old man with his deeds', and which, as a result of not possessing this, is said to be in the image of the Creator.[6] He says: *Nor did he make man his image; for God is not like that, nor does he resemble any other form at all.* Is it possible to suppose that the part in the image of God is located in the inferior part of the composite man, I mean the body, and that, as Celsus interpreted it, the body should be that which is in His image?[7] If the nature that is in the image of God is in the body alone, the superior part, the soul, is deprived of being in the image, and this exists in the corruptible body. Not one of us holds this view. But if the words 'in the image of God' apply to both together, God must be composite[8] and, as it were, must consist of soul and body Himself, so that the superior part has its image in the soul, and the inferior and corporeal part in the body. And none of us says that. The remaining possibility is that that which is made in the image of God is to be understood of the inward man, as we call it, which is renewed and has the power to be formed in the image of the

---

[1] Ps. ci. 28; Mal. iii. 6.   [2] Gen. i. 27.   [3] Col. i. 15.
[4] Wisd. of Sol. vii. 26.   [5] I Cor. xi. 3, 7.   [6] Col. iii. 9.
[7] Cf. Philo, *Opif.* 69; *Leg. Alleg.* i, 31-2.
[8] Cf. Origen, *de Princ.* i, 1, 6 'God, who is the beginning of all things, must not be regarded as a composite being.' For Christians who believed God to be corporeal, cf. *Clement. Hom.* xvii, 8; Clem. Al. *Exc. Theod.* 10-17.

Creator,[1] when a man becomes perfect as his heavenly Father is perfect,[2] and when he hears 'Be holy because I the Lord your God am holy', and when he learns the saying 'Become imitators of God'[3] and assumes into his own virtuous soul the characteristics of God. Then also the body of the man who has assumed the characteristics of God, in that part which is made in the image of God, is a temple,[4] since he possesses a soul of this character and has God in his soul because of that which is in His image.

64. Again, he continues by making further remarks as if they were what we should agree to, although none of those Christians who have any intelligence would agree to them. Not one of us says that *God participates in shape or colour*.[5] Nor does He *partake of movement*; because it is His nature to be established and firm, He calls the righteous man to imitate Him in this respect when He says: 'But as for thee, stand with me.'[6] If, however, some texts suggest that there is movement of some sort on His part, as for example that which says 'They heard the Lord God walking in the garden in the evening',[7] we should understand such sayings in the sense that God is regarded as being moved by those who have sinned; or we should interpret such texts in the same way as we do when there is a figurative reference to God's sleep or His anger or anything of this sort.[8]

Moreover, *God does not even participate in being.*[9] For He is participated in, rather than participates; and He is participated in by those who possess the Spirit of God. Our Saviour also does not participate in righteousness; but being righteous, he is participated in by the righteous. However, there is much to say which is hard to perceive about being, and especially if we take 'being' in the strict sense to be unmoved and incorporeal. We would have to discover whether God 'transcends being in rank and power',[10] and grants a share in being to those whose participation is according to His Logos, and to the Logos himself, or whether He is

---

[1] Eph. iii. 16; Col. iii. 10.   [2] Matt. v. 48.
[3] Lev. xi. 45; Eph. v. 1.   [4] I Cor. vi. 19; iii. 16.
[5] Cf. Plato, *Phaedrus*, 247C 'the colourless and shapeless and intangible essence'; Origen, *de Princ.* I, 1, 6 'Mind does not need physical space in which to move and operate, nor does it need a magnitude discernible by the senses, nor bodily shape or colour' (trans. Butterworth). Justin, *Dial.* 4 'the originator of all intelligible things, having no colour, no shape, no magnitude, nor any other attribute that the eye can see; it is something which is beyond all being...'; Max. Tyr. XI, 11.
[6] Deut. v. 31, so interpreted by Philo, *Post. Ca.* 27; *Gigant.* 48; *Quod Deus sit imm.* 23; *Conf. Ling.* 30; *Somn.* II, 227; Clem. Al. *Strom.* II, 51, 6; Origen, *Catena frag. in Joann.* 125.
[7] Gen. iii. 8.   [8] Cf. IV, 72.
[9] The Good is beyond Being: Plato, *Rep.* 509B.
[10] Plato, *Rep.* 509B; cf. VII, 38 below; *Comm. in Joann.* XIX, 6 'No one understands God or sees Him, and comprehends the truth afterwards; he first knows the truth and in this way comes to perceive the being or the power and nature of God which are beyond being.'

Himself being, in spite of the fact that He is said to be invisible by nature in the words that say of the Saviour: 'Who is the image of the invisible God.'[1] That He is incorporeal is indicated by the word 'invisible'. We would also inquire whether we ought to say that the only-begotten and firstborn of all creation is being of beings, and idea of ideas, and beginning, and that his Father and God transcends all these.

65. Celsus affirms of God that *all things are derived from him*, although for some unknown reason he had separated all things from him.[2] But our Paul says that 'from him and through him and unto him are all things',[3] referring to the beginning of the existence of all things in the words 'from him', to their maintenance in 'through him', and to their end in 'unto him'. It is true that *God is derived from nothing*. But when he says *Neither is he attainable by reason*, I draw a distinction in the meaning and say: If you mean the reason that is in us, whether conceived or expressed,[4] we too would say that God is not attainable by reason. But if, because we have understood that 'in the beginning was the Logos, and the Logos was with God, and the Logos was God',[5] we affirm that God is attainable by this Logos, and is comprehended not by him alone, but also by any man to whom he reveals the Father,[6] we would prove that Celsus' words were untrue when he says *Neither is God attainable by reason*.

The assertion that *he cannot be named*[7] also needs precise definition. If he means that none of the descriptions by words or expressions can show the attributes of God, the affirmation is true. There are, however, many qualities which cannot be named. For who can express in words the difference between the quality of the sweetness of a date and that of a dried fig? Who can find a name to distinguish their tastes and to show the peculiar quality of each? It is therefore in no way remarkable if God cannot be named in this sense. But if you take the word to mean that it is possible by names to show something about His attributes in order to guide the hearer and to make him understand God's character in so far as some of His attributes are attainable by human nature, then it is not wrong at all to say that He can be named.

---

[1] Col. i. 15.   [2] Cf. Celsus in IV, 52 'God made nothing mortal.'   [3] Rom. xi. 36.
[4] The distinction between the *logos endiathetos* and the *logos prophorikos*, implied in Plato, *Theaet.* 189E, *Soph.* 263E, and Aristotle, *Post.* 76b 25, became common coin through the debates between the Stoics and the Academy. Cf. Zeller, *Philos. d. Gr.* III, i (4th ed.), p. 68 n. 4; M. Pohlenz in *Nachr. d. Gött. Ges. d. Wiss.*, phil. hist. Kl., Fachgruppe I (N.F.), III, 6 (1939), pp. 191–8; and my remarks in *J.T.S.* XLVIII (1947), pp. 36 f.
[5] John i. 1.   [6] Matt. xi. 27.
[7] Cf. Celsus in VII, 42; Justin, *Apol.* II, 6; Clem. Al., *Strom.* v, 82, 1; Cicero, *de Nat. Deor.* I, 12, 30 (Diels, *Dox. Gr.* 537); Dio Chrys. XII, 78; Max. Tyr. VIII, 10; *Corp. Herm.* v, 1 'He who is too great to be called God' (cf. *ibid.* 10). For Philo, cf. H. A. Wolfson, *Philo* (Cambridge, Mass. 1947), II, pp. 110–26, and my remarks in *The Classical Review*, LXIII, 1 (May 1949), p. 24.

In this way also we would make a distinction in the words *For he has no experience which can be comprehended by a name.* And it is also true that *God is outside any emotional experience.*[1] So much, then, for that.

66. Let us also consider his next remarks in which, as it were, he puts words into someone's mouth, who after hearing what he has said speaks as follows: *How then can I know God? And how can I learn the way to him? And how can you show him to me? For now you are throwing darkness before my eyes, and I see nothing distinctly.* Then he as it were answers the person who is in this difficulty, and supposes that he gives the reason why darkness has been poured down upon the eyes of the person who utters the previous words when he says: *If anyone leads people out of darkness into a bright light, they cannot endure the radiancy and think that their sight is injured and damaged and incapacitated.*[2] We would say to this that all those who look at the evil productions of painters and sculptors and image-makers sit in darkness and are settled in it, since they do not wish to look up and ascend in their mind from all visible and sensible things to the Creator of all who is Light; and that everyone who has followed the rays of the Logos is in light, for the Logos has shown him how great was the ignorance and impiety and lack of knowledge about God which caused these objects to be worshipped instead of God, and has led the mind of the man who wants to be saved to the uncreated and supreme God. 'For the people that sat in darkness', the people of the Gentiles, 'have seen a great light, and to those that sat in the region and shadow of death a light has arisen',[3] that is the God Jesus.

Therefore, no Christian would reply to Celsus or to any other critic of the divine Word, by saying *How can I know God?* Each of them, in accordance with his capacity, has known God. And no one says: *How can I learn the way to him?* For he has heard the one who says, 'I am the way, the truth, and the life',[4] and by travelling along the way has experienced the benefit that the journey brings. And no Christian would say to Celsus: *How can you show me God?*

67. In Celsus' remarks before us this at any rate is true, that anyone who heard his words and saw that his words are words of darkness would answer 'You are throwing darkness before my eyes.' Celsus and those like him wish to throw darkness before our eyes; but with the light of the Word we make the darkness of impious doctrines to disappear. Celsus says nothing distinct or impressive, and a Christian might say to

---

[1] Cf. Origen in IV, 72.

[2] Cf. the myth of the cave in Plato, *Rep.* 518 A, where just as anyone passing from darkness to light cannot see, so the soul that passes from ignorance to knowledge, or vice versa, is blinded and stupefied by the radiance. For the Christian difficulty, cf. Celsus in VII, 33.

[3] Matt. iv. 16; Isa. ix. 2.   [4] John xiv. 6.

him 'I see nothing distinct in your words.' Celsus is not leading us from darkness to a bright light; he wants to transfer us from light to darkness, 'making the darkness light and the light darkness', and becoming subject to the excellent saying of Isaiah, to this effect: 'Woe unto them that put darkness for light and light for darkness.'[1] But since the Logos has opened the eyes of our soul, we see the difference between light and darkness and in every way prefer to stand in the light, and do not want to enter the darkness at all. The true Light,[2] because he is living, knows to whom it will be right to show the radiance, and to whom only light, not showing his brilliance because of the weakness still inherent in the man's eyes.[3]

If we may say of anyone that his sight is injured and damaged, whose eyes should we describe as suffering in this respect but of the man who is afflicted by ignorance of God, and who is hindered by his passions from seeing the truth? Now Christians certainly do not think that they are blinded by Celsus' words or by those of anyone alien to the true worship of God. But let those who perceive that they are blinded by following the crowds of deluded people and the nations of those who celebrate festivals in honour of daemons approach the Logos who gives sight, that they may be shown mercy like the poor and blind men who threw themselves down by the roadside and were healed by Jesus because they said to him 'Son of David, have mercy upon me',[4] and may receive the new and good eyes created by the Logos of God.

68. Accordingly, if Celsus asks us *how we think we can come to know God, and how we imagine we shall be saved by him,* we reply that the Logos of God is sufficient; for he comes to those who seek him or accept him when he appears to make known and reveal the Father, who before his coming was not visible. And who but the divine Logos can save and lead the soul of man to the supreme God? He 'was in the beginning with God';[5] but because of those who had cleaved to the flesh and become as flesh, he became flesh,[6] that he might be received by those incapable of seeing him in his nature as the one who was the Logos, who was with God, who was God. And being spoken of under physical forms,[7] and being proclaimed to be flesh, he calls to himself those who are flesh that he may make them first to be formed like the Logos who became flesh, and after that lead them up to see him as he was before he became flesh; so that they may be

---

[1] Isa. v. 20.   [2] I John ii. 8.
[3] Cf. II, 64 f.; *de Princ.* I, 2, 7 'This brightness (of the Logos) falls softly and gently on the tender and weak eyes of mortal man and little by little trains and accustoms them, as it were, to bear the light in its clearness...', etc. (trans. Butterworth).
[4] Matt. xx. 31; cf. *Comm. in Matt.* XVI, 11.
[5] John i. 1.   [6] John i. 14.   [7] Cf. IV, 15.

helped and may advance from the first stage which is that of the flesh and
say: 'Even if we have known Christ after the flesh, yet now we know him
so no more.'[1] Accordingly he became flesh, and having become flesh he
tabernacled among us and was not apart from us. But even while he
tabernacled and lived among us he did not remain with his primary form.
After leading us up to the spiritual 'high mountain', he showed us his
glorious form and the radiance of his clothing, and not that of himself only,
but also that of the spiritual law, which is Moses who appeared in glory
with Jesus. He also showed us all prophecy, which did not even die after
his incarnation, but was received up into heaven, of which Elijah was
a symbol.[2] He, then, who has seen these things may say: 'We beheld his
glory, a glory as of the only-begotten of the Father, full of grace and truth.'[3]
Celsus, however, ignorantly invented the reply which he imagined we
would make to his question *How do we think we can come to know God, and
how do we imagine we shall be saved by him?* But we would give the answer
we have set forth.

69. Nevertheless, Celsus says that we reply as follows, and affirms that
he *makes a probable conjecture at our answer*[4] in these words: *Since God is
great and hard to perceive, he thrust his own Spirit into a body like ours, and
sent him down here, that we might be able to hear and learn from him.* But in
our opinion the God and Father of the universe is not the only being who
is great; for He gave a share of Himself and His greatness to the only-
begotten and firstborn of all creation,[5] that being himself an image of the
invisible God he might preserve the image of the Father also in respect of
His greatness. For it was impossible that, so to speak, a rightly proportioned and beautiful image of the invisible God should not also show the
image of His greatness.

Furthermore, in our view because God is not corporeal He is invisible.
But He may be perceived by those who can perceive with the heart, that
is the mind, though not with an ordinary heart, but with a pure heart.[6] It
is not right for a heart that has been defiled to look upon God; that which
can deservedly perceive Him who is pure must be pure also. Let us grant
that *God is hard to perceive.* Yet He is not the only being hard for a person
to perceive. For the divine Logos is hard to perceive; and the same is true
of the wisdom in which God has made all things.[7] For who can perceive

---

[1] II Cor. v. 16.   [2] Matt. xvii. 1–3.
[3] John i. 14.
[4] The correct interpretation of this sentence was first seen by Wifstrand, *Bull. Soc. Roy.
Lund* (1941–2), p. 416.
[5] Col. i. 15.   [6] Matt. v. 8.
[7] Ps. ciii. 24. With Wif. omit καθ' ἕκαστον τῶν πάντων (139, 17–18) as a dittography
of the next line.

the wisdom in which God has made each individual thing? Therefore, it was not because God is hard to perceive that He sent a Son who was easy to perceive. It was because Celsus failed to understand this that he remarked, as though it were our answer: *Because he is hard to perceive he thrust his own Spirit into a body like ours, and sent him down here, that we might be able to hear and learn from him.* But, as we have observed, the Son also is hard to perceive, seeing that he is the divine Logos through whom all things were made, who tabernacled among us.

70. If Celsus had understood what we say about God's Spirit, and that 'as many as are led by the Spirit of God, they are the sons of God',[1] he would not have invented a reply for us that *God thrust his own Spirit into a body and sent him down here.* God is always giving a share of His own Spirit to those who are able to partake of Him, though he dwells in those who are worthy not by being cut into sections and divided up.[2] For the Spirit in our opinion is not corporeal, just as the fire is not corporeal which God is said to be in the text 'Our God is a consuming fire.'[3] All these expressions are allegorical, and are meant to show the nature of the intelligible world by the terms usually applied to corporeal things.

Just as if sins are said to be wood, hay, and stubble, we would not say that sins are material, and if upright conduct is said to be gold, silver and precious stone,[4] we would not say that upright conduct is material: so, even though God is said to be a fire consuming the wood, hay, stubble, and every sinful substance, we would not think Him corporeal. Just as when He is called fire we do not think Him corporeal, so also if God is called Spirit, we do not hold that He is material.[5] By way of antithesis to sensible things, the scripture usually calls intelligible things spirit and spiritual. For example, Paul says 'But our sufficiency is of God, who also made us sufficient as ministers of a new covenant, not of the letter but of the spirit, for the letter kills, but the spirit gives life.'[6] He calls the sensible interpretation of the divine scriptures 'the letter' and the intelligible interpretation 'the spirit'.

It is the same with the text 'God is Spirit'. Because both Samaritans and Jews were fulfilling the commands of the law literally and outwardly,

---

[1] Rom. viii. 14.

[2] Cf. *de Princ.* I, 1, 3 'Although many saints partake of the Holy Spirit, he is not on that account to be regarded as a kind of body, which is divided into material parts and distributed to each of the saints, but rather as a sanctifying power, a share of which is said to be possessed by all who have shown themselves worthy of being sanctified through his grace' (trans. Butterworth); *ibid.* I, 2, 6; *Hom. in Num.* VI, 2. For the idea, Philo, *Gigant.* 25; Justin, *Dial.* 61, 128; Athenag. *Leg.* 10; Tert. *Apol.* 21; Clem. Al. *Strom.* VII, 5, 5.

[3] Deut. iv. 24; ix. 3; Heb. xii. 29.   [4] I Cor. iii. 12.

[5] Cf. *Comm. in Joann.* XIII, 21 (expounding John iv. 24 'God is a Spirit').
II Cor. iii. 5-6.

the Saviour said to the Samaritan woman: 'The hour is coming when
neither in Jerusalem nor in this mountain shall you worship the Father;
God is Spirit, and they that worship him must worship him in spirit and
in truth.'[1] By these words he taught that God must not be worshipped in
the flesh and carnal sacrifices, but in spirit. Moreover, Jesus himself would
be understood to be spirit in proportion to the degree in which a man
worships him in spirit and with the mind. Furthermore, the Father must
not be worshipped by external signs but in truth, the truth which came by
Jesus Christ[2] after the law given by Moses. 'For whenever we turn to the
Lord (and the Lord is the Spirit) the veil lying upon the heart whenever
Moses is read is taken away.'[3]

71. Because Celsus has not comprehended the doctrine about the Spirit
of God ('for a natural man does not receive the things of the Spirit of God,
for they are foolishness to him, and he cannot know them because they
are spiritually discerned')[4] he takes into his head the notion that when we
say *God is spirit, there is in this respect no difference between us and the Stoics
among the Greeks who affirm that God is spirit that has permeated all things
and contains all things within itself.*[5] The oversight and providence of God
does permeate all things, but not like the spirit of the Stoics. Providence
does contain all things subject to providential care and comprehends them;
but it does not contain them as a containing substance, since it is corporeal
matter which is contained, but as a divine power which has comprehended
the things which are contained.[6]

According to the opinion of the Stoics, who maintain that the first
principles are corporeal, and who on this account hold that everything is
destructible and venture even to make the supreme God Himself destructible[7] (unless this seemed to them to be utterly outrageous), even the
Logos of God that comes down to men and to the most insignificant
things is nothing other than a material spirit. But in the view of us
Christians, who try to show that the rational soul is superior to any
material nature and is an invisible and incorporeal being, the divine Logos
is not material. Through him all things were made, and in order that all
things may be made by the Logos, he extends not to men only but even to
the things supposed to be insignificant which are controlled by nature.
The Stoics may destroy everything in a conflagration if they like. But

---

[1] John iv. 21, 24.	[2] John i. 17.
[3] II Cor. iii. 15–17.	[4] I Cor. ii. 14.
[5] Cf. Cleanthes ap. Tert. *Apol.* XXI, 10; Galen, *Introd. medic.* 9 (XIV, 698 Kühn = *S.V.F.*
II, 416); Alexander Aphrod. *de Mixtione*, p. 216 Bruns = *S.V.F.* II, 473, etc.
[6] Philo (*Quod det. pot. insid.* 83) remarks that the Stoics conceive the soul to be mobile
air (ἀέρα κινούμενον) whereas its real nature is a sort of impress of divine power (τύπον
τινὰ καὶ χαρακτῆρα θείας δυνάμεως).
[7] Cf. *S.V.F.* II, 1049–56. Cf. IV, 68, note.

we do not recognize that an incorporeal being is subject to a conflagration, or that the soul of man is dissolved into fire,[1] or that this happens to the being of angels, or thrones, or dominions, or principalities, or powers.

72. Because Celsus does not know the doctrine of the Spirit of God, he makes the pointless remark that *since the Son is a spirit derived from God who was born in a human body, even the Son of God himself would not be immortal.* Again, in his confusion he invents the notion that *some of us would not admit that God is spirit, but assert that the Son is.* And he thinks he can meet this by observing that *the nature of spirit is certainly not such that it survives for ever.* In the same way, if we were to say that 'God is a consuming fire',[2] he would say that 'the nature of fire is certainly not such that it survives for ever'.[3] For he does not see what we mean by saying that our God is a fire, and that the things which He consumes are sins and evil. For it is right that a good God,[4] after each individual has made clear by his efforts what sort of a struggle he can make, should destroy evil by the fire of punishments.

Then again he attributes to us out of his own head a view which is not held by us, that *it was necessary for God to regain[5] his spirit. And it follows from this that Jesus could not have risen with his body; for God would not have received back the spirit which he gave after it had been defiled by the nature of the body.* It is silly for us to reply to statements put into our mouths which we should never say.

73. He next repeats himself, though he made many remarks earlier when he mocked the birth of God from a virgin to which we replied as well as we could,[6] saying: *And if he did wish to send down a spirit from himself, why did he have to breathe it into the womb of a woman? He already knew how to make men. He could have formed a body for this one also without having to thrust his own spirit into such foul pollution.[7] In that case*

[1] According to Zeno, the soul of man consisted of fire which was absorbed into the divine fire at the world-conflagration: cf. Cicero, *de Fin.* IV, 5, 12; *Tusc. Disp.* I, 9, 19.

[2] Heb. xii. 29.

[3] For the background of this argument in the Academic-Stoic debate, cf. my remarks in *J.T.S.* XLVIII (1947), p. 36.

[4] For Origen's view that all punishment is ultimately a sign of God's grace and goodness, see the excellent discussion of Hal Koch, *Pronoia und Paideusis* (1932), pp. 112–45.

[5] Misled by Koetschau's mistranslation of this sentence, Bader wishes to emend to ἐκπεπνευκέναι. The reference is not to God breathing out His spirit, but to receiving it back again at the Resurrection.

[6] Cf. I, 32–7.

[7] Compare Origen's criticisms of the inspiration of the Pythian priestess, III, 25; VII, 3. Celsus' difficulty was felt by Marcion (Tert. *adv. Marc.* III, 10 f.). For the Hellenistic feeling that the body was unclean, cf. Celsus in V, 14; Porphyry, *Vita Plotini*, 1 'Plotinus... seemed ashamed of being in the body.'

he would not have been disbelieved, had he been begotten directly from above.
He said this because he did not realize that the body which was to minister
to the salvation of men had a pure birth from a virgin and was not the
result of any immorality. Though he quotes Stoic doctrine and indeed[1]
claims to have learnt about things indifferent, he supposes that the divine
nature was thrust into defilement and polluted, either if it existed in
a woman's body until the body was formed for it, or if it assumed a body.
He does much the same as those who think that the rays of the sun are
defiled by dung-heaps and by stinking bodies, and that even there they do
not remain pure.[2]

Even if we follow Celsus' hypothesis and suppose that the body had
been formed[3] for Jesus without birth, those who saw the body would not
have believed at once that it was not produced by birth. For that which
is seen does not also proclaim the nature of its origin. For example,
supposing that there was some honey which was not produced by bees,
nobody could tell from taste or sight that bees had not produced it. So
not even honey produced by bees indicates its origin to the senses; but it
is experience which shows that they produce this. So also it is experience
which teaches us that wine comes from the vine; for taste does not show
that it is derived from the vine. In the same way, then, the sensible body
does not tell us the way in which it came to exist. You will be persuaded to
accept this view if you consider the heavenly bodies. When we look at
them, we perceive their existence and radiance. But our senses do not
suggest to us whether they are created or uncreated. In fact this is
a question which has given rise to different schools of thought; furthermore, those who say they are created do not agree about the way in which
they are created. For our perception of them does not suggest how
they came to be made, even if reason compels us to find that they are
created.

74. He next returns to the opinion of Marcion of which he has frequently
spoken already, and in part he gives a correct account of Marcion's

---

[1] Read καὶ μὴν with K. tr. The Stoics regarded marriage and sex as indifferent for the
wise man: Clem. Al. *Strom.* II, 138, 5. The passage in Celsus discussing this notion is not
quoted by Origen (cf. Introduction, p. xxiii).

[2] Cf. Diog. Laert. VI, 63 of Diogenes the Cynic: 'Some one having reproached him for
going into dirty places, his reply was that the sun too visits cesspools without being defiled'
(trans. R. G. Hicks); Julian, 140D (in praise of King Helios) 'Not even the light which
comes down nearest to the earth from the sun is mixed with anything, nor does it admit
dirt and defilement, but remains wholly pure and without stain...' (trans. W. C. Wright).
The illustration is frequent in later writers: Eus. *D.E.* IV, 1, 3, 170A; *Theophaneia*, III, 39;
Laus Constant. 14; Macarius Magnes IV, 28; Synesius, *Ep.* 57 (*P.G.* LXVI, 1396c); Cyril
Alex. *in Ev. Jo.* 12 (*P.G.* LXXIV, 643B); Prudentius, *c. Symm.* II, 831; Augustine, *de Civ. Dei*
IX, 16; Nemesius, *de Nat. Hom.* 44 (*P.G.* XL, 805A); etc.

[3] Read περιεπλάσσετο (περιεπλάσσατο A, περιεπλάσατο Kö., περιέπλασε We.).

teaching, but in part he misunderstands it. This it is not necessary for us to answer or even to prove wrong. Then again he goes on to give the arguments for and against Marcion, saying *they evade some of the criticisms, but fall at others.* And when he wants to agree with the opinion which affirms that Jesus was spoken of by the prophets,[1] so that he may attack Marcion and his followers, he says: *By what argument can a man who was punished as he was be proved to be the Son of God, unless it was foretold that this would happen to him?*

Then again he mocks and, in his usual manner, ridicules, introducing *two divine sons,* one of the Creator and another of Marcion's God; he describes *their single combats,* saying that *these and the battles between the divine fathers are like those of the quails.*[2] And he says that *since on account of their old age the fathers themselves are useless and in their dotage, they do nothing to one another, but allow their sons to fight.* We will say to him what he said earlier:[3] What old woman lulling a child to sleep would not be ashamed to say such things as he has done in his book entitled *The True Doctrine?* He ought to have made a competent attack upon the doctrines. But he leaves the facts and pours out mockery and low abuse, and thinks fit to write caricatures or jests of a sort. He did not see that such a method of argument conflicts with his purpose, since it was his aim to make us abandon Christianity and adopt his doctrines. If he had been serious about them, perhaps they might have been more convincing. But as he pours out ridicule and mockery and low abuse, we will say that it was through lack of serious arguments (for he did not have any, or even know of any) that he lapsed into such foolish drivel.

75. Following this he says that *if a divine spirit was in a body, it must certainly have differed from other bodies in size or beauty or strength or voice or striking appearance or powers of persuasion. For it is impossible that a body which had something more divine than the rest should be no different from any other.*[4] *Yet Jesus' body was no different from any other, but, as they say, was*

---

[1] Marcion believed that the Christ foretold by the O.T. prophets was not Jesus, who was the Christ of the Strange God and appeared without previous notice or warning in the fifteenth year of Tiberius Caesar. Cf. Harnack, *Marcion* (2nd ed. 1924), p. 283*. Accordingly, both the good and the just God had sons called Christ.

[2] For the ancient practice of quail-fighting, cf. D'Arcy Thompson, *A Glossary of Greek Birds* (2nd ed. 1936), p. 217; Epictetus, III, 25, 5; Plutarch, *Mor.* 207B; 487E; Lucian, *Anacharsis,* 37; etc.
Three coins from Tarsus in the British Museum bear the inscription ὀρτυγοθήρα (G. F. Hill, *Catalogue of the Greek Coins of Lycaonia, Isauria, and Cilicia* (1900), pp. 182–3, nos. 123–5). According to Hill (introd. p. lxxvii) this 'awaits elucidation'; he takes it as a proper name. Dr A. B. Cook suggested to me that it means quail-trap; possibly Tarsus had some close connexion with the sport.

[3] VI, 34.

[4] Contrast Origen's remarks in I, 32; Celsus in I, 69–70.

little and ugly and undistinguished.[1] Here too it seems that if he wants to criticize Jesus he quotes the scriptures that seem to him to provide opportunities for criticism, as though he believed them. But where by the same scriptures someone might think that statements were made which contradicted those used for the purposes of criticism, he would pretend not even to know them.

Admittedly it is written that the body of Jesus was ugly, but not, as he asserted, that it was also undistinguished; nor is there any clear indication that he was little. The passage written in Isaiah, when he was prophesying that Jesus would come to the multitude not with a beautiful form, or with any surpassing beauty, reads as follows: 'Lord, who has believed our report? And to whom was the arm of the Lord revealed? We proclaimed before him as a child, as a root in a thirsty land; there is no form nor glory in him. And we saw him, and he had not form or beauty; but his form was dishonourable and deserted more than the sons of men.'[2] Celsus paid heed to these words, since he thought they would be useful to him with a view to attacking Jesus; but he did not pay any attention to the words of the forty-fourth Psalm where it is said: 'Gird thy sword upon thy thigh, mighty one, with thy beauty and fairness; and exert thyself and ride on and rule.'[3]

76. Let us assume that he had not read the prophecy or, if he had done so, that he was led astray by those who misinterpret it as though it were not a prophecy about Jesus Christ.[4] What would he say about the gospel in which after ascending a high mountain he was transfigured before his disciples and appeared in glory, when also Moses and Elijah appeared in glory and spoke of his death which he would fulfil at Jerusalem?[5] If a prophet says 'We saw him and he had not form or beauty' and so on, Celsus accepts this prophecy as referring to Jesus, although he is blind in spite of his approval of the saying and does not see that the belief in Jesus as Son of God, even if he seemed to be without form, finds considerable support in the fact that many years before his birth even his form was a subject of prophecy. But if another prophet says that there is 'beauty and fairness' about him, is he no longer willing to believe that the prophecy refers to Jesus Christ? And if it were possible to find clear evidence in the gospels that 'he had not form or beauty, but his form was dishonourable,

---

[1] Cf. Clem. Al. *Paed.* III, 3, 2 'That the Lord himself had a dishonourable face is testified by the Spirit through Isaiah...' (Isa. lii. 14; liii. 2–3).

For Celsus' view that Jesus' voice ought to have been different, cf. the remarks of F. J. Dölger, *Antike und Christentum* V (1936), pp. 218–23; for God's voice as very loud he compares Ignatius, *Philad.* VII, 1; Lucian, *Icaromenippus*, 23; *Acta Philippi*, 22.

[2] Isa. liii. 1–3.   [3] Ps. xliv. 4–5.
[4] Cf. I, 55, above.   [5] Matt. xvii. 1–3.

deserted more than the sons of men', someone might say that Celsus did
not base his statements on the prophecy but on the words of the gospels.
In fact, however, neither the gospels nor even the apostles give any
evidence that he had no form or beauty. Obviously, then, he must
necessarily accept the words of the prophecy as being true of Christ. And
this puts his criticisms of Jesus out of court.

77. Again when he said, *If a divine spirit was in a body, it must certainly
have differed from other bodies in size or voice or strength or striking appearance
or powers of persuasion,* how did he fail to notice that his body differed in
accordance with the capacity of those who saw it, and on this account
appeared in such form as was beneficial for the needs of each individual's
vision?[1] It is not remarkable that matter, which is by nature subject to
change, alteration, and transformation[2] into anything which the Creator
desires, and is capable of possessing any quality which the Artificer wishes,
at one time possesses a quality of which it is said 'He had not form or
beauty', and at another time a quality so glorious and striking and
wonderful that the three apostles who went up with Jesus and saw the
exquisite beauty fell on their faces.

But he will say that these stories are fictitious and no better than legends,
just like the other stories of Jesus' miracles.[3] To this charge, however, we
replied at length in the previous pages. The doctrine has an even more
mysterious meaning since it proclaims that the different forms of Jesus
are to be applied to the nature of the divine Logos. For he did not appear
in the same way both to the multitude and to those able to follow him up
the high mountain which we have mentioned. To those who are still down
below and are not yet prepared to ascend, the Logos 'has not form nor
beauty'. His form to such people is dishonourable and deserted more than
the teaching which has originated from men, which this passage allegorically describes as 'the sons of men'. We would say that the teachings of
philosophers, which are 'sons of men', appear far more beautiful than the
Logos of God as he is preached to the multitude. What he shows to them
is the foolishness of preaching;[4] and because of the apparent foolishness

[1] For this notion, see II, 64 f.; IV, 16; VI, 68. Cf. *Comm. ser. in Matt.* 100 'A tradition
about Jesus has come down to us to the effect that there were not only two forms in him,
one according to which everybody saw him, and another according to which he was transfigured before his disciples on the mount when also his face shone like the sun; but that he
even appeared to each individual in the form of which he was worthy...'. That this
'tradition' had Gnostic origins is suggested by the Acts of John 93 where St John says,
'Sometimes when I would lay hold on him, I met with a material and solid body, and at
other times, again, when I felt him, the substance was immaterial and as if it existed not
at all' (James, *Apocr. N.T.* p. 252). Cf. E. von Dobschütz, *Christusbilder* (1899), p. 105*,
comparing Augustine, *de Trin.* VIII, 4, 7; *Enarr. in Ps.* CXXVII, 8.
[2] A dictionary definition: cf. III, 41; *Dox. Gr.* 307a. 23.
[3] Cf. Celsus in III, 27; V, 57.   [4] I Cor. i. 21.

of preaching those who see only this say 'we saw him and he had not form or beauty'. However, to those who by following him have received power to go after him even as he is ascending the high mountain, he has a more divine form. Anyone who is a Peter sees this; for Peter was capable of having the Church built upon him by the Logos and attained such ability that no gate of hell could prevail against him;[1] the Logos lifted him up from the gates of death that he might proclaim all the praises of God in the gates of the daughter of Zion.[2] And if there are some whose birth is from loud-sounding words, they will not lack anything in spiritual thunder.[3]

But how can Celsus and those hostile to the divine Word, who do not examine the teachings of Christianity with a desire to find the truth, realize the meaning of the different forms of Jesus? And I would include also the different stages of his life, and any of the actions which he did before he suffered and after he rose again from the dead.

78. Celsus next says something to this effect: *Furthermore, if God, like Zeus in the comic poet, woke up out of his long slumber and wanted to deliver the human race from evils, why on earth did he send this spirit that you mention into one corner?*[4] *He ought to have breathed into many bodies in the same way and sent them all over the world. The comic poet wrote that Zeus woke up and sent Hermes to the Athenians and Spartans*[5] *because he wanted to raise a laugh in the theatre. Yet do you not think it is more ludicrous to make the Son of God to be sent to the Jews?* Here also you notice the irreverence of Celsus. In a manner unbecoming to a philosopher he quotes a poet of the Comedy who wanted to raise a laugh, and compares our God, the Creator of the universe, with Zeus in the play who was woken up and sent Hermes. We observed earlier that it was not as if God had risen up from long slumber when He sent Jesus to the human race; although now, for good reasons, he has accomplished[6] the work of his incarnation, he has

---

[1] Matt. xvi. 18. The same argument with the same examples in *Comm. in Matt.* XII, 32.

[2] Ps. ix. 14–15.

[3] Cf. Mark iii. 17, and *Comm. in Matt.* XII, 32, where Origen says that 'the sons of thunder are begotten of the loud voice of God who thunders and shouts great things from heaven to those who have ears to hear and are wise'.

At this point in his text Koetschau inserts a long passage from the *Philocalia* (XV, 19), assuming it to have fallen out of the Vatican MS. But the style and content are rather those of a homily (cf. Wendland in *G.G.A.* (1899), pp. 283 f.), and in his translation Koetschau omits it.

[4] For the comparison with Comedy, cf. Celsus in VI, 49; for 'one corner', IV, 36; for the inactivity of God, IV, 7. Geffcken (*Zwei griechische Apologeten*, p. 256) points out that Celsus is adapting the Epicurean argument against the Stoic notion of the making of the world; the Epicurean in Cicero, *de Nat. Deor.* I, 9, 21, asks 'cur mundi aedificatores repente extiterint, innumerabilia saecula dormierint'.

[5] T. Kock, *Comicorum Atticorum Fragmenta*, III, p. 406, *frag.* 43.

[6] Read ἐπιπληρώσαντα with Bo., We.

always been doing good to mankind. For nothing good has happened among men without the divine Logos who has visited the souls of those who are able, even if but for a short time, to receive these operations of the divine Logos.[1]

Moreover, though the advent of Jesus was apparently in one corner, it was quite reasonable; since it was necessary that the one prophesied should visit those who had learnt that there was one God, and who were reading His prophets and learning of the Christ they preached, and that he should come at a time when the doctrine would be poured forth from one corner all over the world.

79. For this reason also there was no need for many bodies to be in several places and to have many spirits like Jesus, so that the whole world of men might be enlightened by the Word of God. For the one Word was enough, who rose up as a 'sun of righteousness'[2] to send forth from Judaea his rays which reach the souls of those who are willing to accept him. If anyone should want to see many bodies filled with a divine spirit, ministering to the salvation of men everywhere after the pattern of the one Christ, let him realize that those who in many places teach the doctrine of Jesus rightly and live an upright life are themselves also called Christs by the divine scriptures in the words: 'Touch not my Christs and do my prophets no harm.'[3]

Moreover, just as we have heard that 'antichrist is coming', and have learnt no less that there are 'many antichrists' in the world,[4] in the same way knowing that Christ has come we see that because of him there have been many Christs in the world, who like him have 'loved righteousness and hated iniquity'; and on this account God, the God of Christ, has even anointed them with the oil of gladness.[5] But he loved righteousness and hated iniquity more than his fellows and took the first-fruits of the anointing, even, so to speak, the whole anointing of the oil of gladness; whereas his fellows, each one as he had the capacity, shared in his anointing. That is why, since Christ is the head of the Church,[6] so that Christ and the Church are one body, the oil on the head descended upon the beard of Aaron, the signs of a full-grown man, and why this oil descended till it reached the skirts of his garment.[7]

This is my reply to the irreverent saying of Celsus that *he ought to have breathed into many bodies in the same way and sent them all over the world.* The comic poet, then, made Zeus sleep and wake up and send Hermes to

---

[1] Cf. Justin, *Apol.* I, 46. [2] Mal. iv. 2.
[3] Ps. civ. 15; similarly *Comm. in Joann.* VI, 6 (3); Methodius, *Symp.* VIII, 8, 191.
[4] I John ii. 18. [5] Ps. xliv. 8; Heb. i. 9.
[6] Col. i. 18. [7] Ps. cxxxii. 2.

the Greeks wanting to raise a laugh. But let the Word that understands the sleepless nature of God teach us that all the time God is caring for the affairs of the world, as reason demands. It is not, however, remarkable if, because the judgments of God are great and hard to explain, uneducated souls go astray[1] and Celsus with them. Accordingly there is nothing ludicrous in the fact that the Son of God has been sent among the Jews with whom the prophets lived, so that beginning from there in bodily form he might rise with power and spirit upon the world of souls which no longer wanted to be deserted of God.

80. After this Celsus thought fit to say that *the Chaldeans have been a race endowed with the highest inspiration from the beginning*, though it was from them that the deceitful art of astrology spread among men. Celsus also reckons *the Magi* among the most inspired races, though from them magic, which takes its name from their race, has come to other nations as well, to the destruction and ruin of those who use it. *The Egyptians*, whom Celsus also mentioned earlier,[2] went astray in having impressive precincts about their supposed temples, but inside nothing but cats or crocodiles or goats or snakes or some other animals. Yet now Celsus thought fit to remark that *the nation of the Egyptians* is also endowed with the highest inspiration,[3] and that from the beginning, probably because from the beginning they fought against the Jews. *The Persians*, who marry their mothers and have sexual intercourse with their daughters, appear to Celsus to be an inspired race;[4] and *the Indians* also of whom in the previous pages he said that some had tasted human flesh.[5] But although the Jews, especially those of early times, did none of these things, not only does he not call them *endowed with the highest inspiration* but even says that *they will presently perish*.[6] He makes this assertion about them as if he were a prophet. He does not see all the care of God for the Jews and for their ancient and sacred society, and that because of their fall salvation has come to the Gentiles, and that 'their fall is the riches of the world and their loss the riches of the Gentiles, until the fulness of the Gentiles comes in', that after this 'all Israel', of the meaning of which Celsus has no comprehension, 'may be saved'.[7]

81. For some unknown reason he says of God that *He who knows all did not realize that he was sending his son to evil men who would sin and punish him.* But here he seems to have intentionally ignored the saying which says that by a divine Spirit the prophets of God foresaw everything

---

[1] Wisd. of Sol. xvii. 1.
[2] Cf. Celsus in I, 14, 20.
[5] Celsus in V, 34.
[7] Rom. xi. 11–12, 25–6.

[3] Celsus in III, 17.
[4] Cf. V, 27 and note.
[6] Cf. Celsus in VIII, 69.

that Jesus would suffer and prophesied them.[1] It is inconsistent with this
to say that God did not know that he was sending His Son to evil men who
would sin and punish him. Yet he immediately says that we defend this by
asserting that *these events were foretold long ago.*[2]

However, our sixth volume has become long enough, and we will here
end its argument and, God willing, begin the seventh. There he thinks he
can meet our affirmation that the prophets foretold everything about
Jesus. As this is an extensive subject and needs a lengthy reply to deal
with it, we do not wish either to be compelled to cut it short by the size of
this book, or by avoiding abbreviation of the argument to make the sixth
volume too large and beyond appropriate dimensions.

[1] Cf. Luke xxiv. 26–7.   [2] Celsus in VII, 2.

BOOK VII

1. In the six previous books, holy brother Ambrose, we have wrestled to the best of our ability against Celsus' criticisms of the Christians, and have done all in our power to avoid allowing anything to pass by untested and unexamined, and have left nothing to which we have not[1] replied as well as we could. After calling on God through that same Jesus Christ who is accused by Celsus, asking that, as he is the truth, he may cause to shine in our hearts[2] the arguments which can successfully refute the falsehood, we begin a seventh book also, quoting that saying of the prophet in prayer to God 'Destroy them by thy truth',[3] obviously meaning by 'them' the doctrines opposed to the truth. For these are destroyed by God's truth, that after they have been destroyed those who have been set free from all[4] distraction may say the words that follow—'I will gladly sacrifice to thee'—and may offer a rational and smokeless sacrifice to the God of the universe.

2. It is Celsus' object to criticize the assertion that the history of Christ Jesus was prophesied by the prophets among the Jews. As a start we first examine his idea that those who teach the existence of another God beside the God of the Jews can make no reply at all to his difficulties, and that we, who have kept the same God, take refuge for our defence in the prophecies about Christ. To this he says: *Let us see how they will find an excuse. Those who teach the existence of another God have none to give, while those who keep the same God will again say the same thing—that intelligent reply that 'it was inevitable for events to happen in this way', and the proof is that 'these things were foretold long ago'.*[5] We would reply to this that the remarks he made about Jesus and the Christians a little while before this[6] are so weak that even those who teach the existence of another God, and on this account are blasphemers, could easily answer Celsus' words. And if it were not wrong to give the weaker folk openings for accepting bad doctrines, we also would have made such an answer so that we might prove it a lie that those who teach the existence of another God have no defence at all before the criticisms of Celsus. But let us now make a reply to his point about the prophets and add to what we said earlier on this subject.[7]

3. He says: *The predictions of the Pythian priestess or of the priestesses of Dodona or of the Clarian Apollo or at Branchidae or at the shrine of Zeus*

---

[1] Read πρὸς ὃ ⟨οὐχ⟩ ὡς with We. (293).   [2] Cf. John xiv. 6; II Cor. iv. 6.
[3] Ps. liii. 7–8.   [4] Read παντός with K. tr.
[5] Cf. vi, 81.   [6] Cf. vi, 72–5, 78.
[7] Cf. i, 35–7, 48; ii, 28–9, 37; iii, 2–4; vi, 19–21.

Ammon,[1] *and of countless other prophets, are reckoned of no account, although it is probable that by them the whole earth became inhabited.*[2] *But the predictions, whether they were actually spoken or not, made by the people in Judaea after their usual manner, as even now is customary with those who live round about Phoenicia and Palestine,*[3] *are thought to be wonderful and unalterable.* We may observe with regard to the oracles enumerated that it would be possible to collect from Aristotle and the Peripatetic philosophers[4] much which we might say in order to overthrow the claim that is made for the Pythian and the other oracles. We could also quote the statements of Epicurus and those who welcome his doctrine[5] on the same matters to show that some Greeks also reject the supposed prophetic oracles which have been admired throughout Greece.

However, let us suppose that the prophecies of the Pythian priestess and the other oracles are not inventions of men who pretend to possess divine inspiration. Let us consider whether it cannot be proved by those who honestly examine the matter that even for the man who accepts the view that these oracles are genuine there is no necessity to admit that they are caused by certain gods. On the contrary, it is more likely that they are caused by certain evil daemons and spirits hostile to the human race, who hinder the soul's ascent and journey by means of virtue, and a restoration of true piety towards God. Indeed, of the Pythian priestess—the oracle that seems to be more distinguished than the others—it is related that while the prophetess of Apollo is sitting at the mouth of the Castalian cave she receives a spirit through her womb;[6] after being filled with this she

---

[1] The oracle of the Pythian priestess was at Delphi; Dodona, the oldest oracle of Zeus, in Epirus; Branchidae, the oracle of Apollo, in Ionia; Ammon is the Libyan Zeus. For remarks on these oracles, cf. Strabo, XVII, 1, 43 (p. 814), where he says that in his time oracles were much neglected; Lucian, *Alex.* 8.

[2] For the importance of consulting oracles before undertaking the serious hazards of sending out a colony, cf. H. W. Parke, *A History of the Delphic Oracle* (1939), pp. 47–87 (esp. p. 49 n. 1); also Celsus in VIII, 45.

[3] Cf. Celsus in VII, 9.

[4] Divination depended upon divine providence, the activity of which Aristotle denied in the sublunary sphere; he accordingly denied divination. Cf. Eus. *P.E.* IV, 2, 13, 136A; IV, 3, 14, 139B. For a naturalistic explanation of oracles cf. Ps.-Arist. *de Mundo* 4, 395 b 26 ff. Cf. also VIII, 45 below.

[5] H. Usener, *Epicurea, frag.* 395, p. 261. Cf. Origen's remarks (I, 24) on the Peripatetic and Epicurean view of magic, and Oenomaus ap. Eus. *P.E.* V, 19.

[6] Cf. III, 25; Chrysostom, *Hom. in I Cor.* XXIX, 1; perhaps also Strabo, IX, 3, 5 (p. 419) 'They say that the place where the oracles are given is a cave, hollow and deep but not very wide, and that from it there arises a spirit which brings on frenzy; over its mouth is set a high tripod upon which the Pythian priestess ascends to receive the spirit....' For the Pythia as the bride of Apollo see the discussion in A. B. Cook, *Zeus*, II, pp. 207–9 (and *ibid.* p. 1216 for a reference to Plutarch, *Mor.* 566 D, where Themis on the Delphic tripod is impregnated by the central pillar of light = Apollo). Cf. also Preisendanz, *Pap. Gr. Mag.* VIII, 2 'Come to me, Lord Hermes, as babes come into their mother's wombs', with the

utters oracular sayings, supposed to be sacred and divine. Consider, then, whether this does not indicate the impure and foul nature of that spirit in that it enters the soul of the prophetess, not by open and invisible pores which are far purer than the womb, but through the latter part which it would be wrong for a self-controlled and sensible man to look upon or, I might add, even to touch.[1] And this happens not just once or twice (for perhaps this might have seemed to be more tolerable), but every time she is believed to have prophesied under the inspiration of Apollo.

Furthermore, it is not the work of a divine spirit to lead the alleged prophetess into a state of ecstasy and frenzy so that she loses possession of her consciousness. The person inspired by the divine spirit ought to have derived from it far more benefit than anyone who may be instructed by the oracles to do that which helps towards living a life which is moderate and according to nature, or towards that which is of advantage or which is expedient. And for that reason he ought to possess the clearest vision at the very time when the deity is in communion with him.[2]

4. From this ground, by collecting evidence from the sacred scriptures, we prove that the prophets among the Jews, being illuminated by the divine Spirit in so far as it was beneficial to them as they prophesied, were the first to enjoy the visitation of the superior Spirit to them. Because of the touch, so to speak, of what is called the Holy Spirit upon their soul they possessed clear mental vision and became more radiant in their soul, and even in body, which no longer offered any opposition to the life lived according to virtue, in that it was mortified according to 'the mind of the flesh' as we call it. For we are convinced that 'the deeds of the body' and the enmities which originate from 'the mind of the flesh' which is opposed to God are put to death by a divine Spirit.[3]

If the Pythian priestess is out of her senses and has not control of her faculties when she prophesies, what sort of spirit must we think it which poured darkness upon her mind and rational thinking? Its character must be like that of the race of daemons which many Christians drive out of

---

remarks of Rohde, *Psyche* (E.T.), pp. 312 f. P. Amandry, *La Mantique Apollinienne à Delphes* (1950), pp. 21–3 dismisses Origen's story as tendentious. It is, however, more than improbable that Origen himself invented it.

[1] Read with Wifstrand οὔπω λέγω ὅτι [ἢ] καὶ ἅπτεσθαι.

[2] According to the Platonic view divine inspiration clarifies rather than confuses the mind. Cf. Plato, *Timaeus*, 71, *Phaedrus*, 244, and Apuleius' comments on the priests of Dea Syria (*Met.* VIII, 27) 'There was one more mad than the rest, that fetched many deep sighs from the bottom of his heart, as though he had been ravished in spirit, or replenished with divine power, and he feigned a swoon and frenzy, as if (forsooth) the presence of the gods were not wont to make men better than before, but weak and sickly' (trans. Adlington-Gaselee).

[3] Rom. viii. 6–7, 10, 13.

people who suffer from them, without any curious magical art or sorcerer's device, but with prayer alone and very simple adjurations and formulas such as the simplest person could use.[1] For generally speaking it is uneducated people who do this kind of work. The power in the word of Christ shows the worthlessness and weakness of the daemons; for it is not necessary to have a wise man who is competent in the rational proofs of the faith in order that they should be defeated and yield to expulsion from the soul and body of a man.

5. Moreover, not only Christians and Jews, but also many other Greeks and barbarians have believed that the human soul lives and exists after separation from the body, and show this by the doctrine that the pure soul, which is not weighed down by the leaden weights of evil,[2] is carried on high to the regions of the purer and ethereal bodies, forsaking the gross bodies on earth and the pollutions attaching to them;[3] whereas the bad soul, that is dragged down to earth by its sins and has not even the power to make a recovery, is carried here and roams about, in some cases at tombs where also apparitions of shadowy souls have been seen,[4] in other cases simply round about the earth. What sort of spirits must we think them to be which for whole ages, so to speak, are bound to buildings and places, whether by some magical incantations[5] or even because of their own wickedness? Reason demands that we should think such spirits to be wicked, for they use their power to know the future, which is morally neither good nor bad,[6] to deceive men and to distract them from God and pure piety towards Him. That this is the character[7] of the daemons is also made clear by the fact that their bodies, nourished by the smoke from sacrifices and by the portions taken from the blood and burnt-offerings in which they delight,[8] find in this, as it were, their heart's desire, like vicious men who do not welcome the prospect of living a pure life without their bodies, but only enjoy life in the earthly body because of its physical pleasures.

If the Delphic Apollo were a god, as the Greeks imagine, ought he not rather to have chosen as his prophet some wise man or, if such a man could not be found, at least one who had made progress in that direction? And why did he not prefer to prophesy through a man rather than a woman? If, however, he even preferred the female, perhaps because he was unable

---

[1] Cf. I, 6, above.   [2] Cf. II Cor. v. 4; Plato, *Phaedrus*, 246–7; *Rep.* 519B.
[3] Cf. Celsus in VI, 73.
[4] Plato, *Phaedo* 81 C, D; cf. II, 60 above; Cumont, *Lux perpetua* (1949), pp. 81 f.
[5] For magic as a means of forcing a daemon to inhabit a particular shrine, cf. III, 34; V, 38; VII, 64.
[6] Similarly III, 25; IV, 96.   [7] Read δηλοῖ δὲ τὸ τοιούτους αὐτοὺς with We., K. tr.
[8] Cf. III, 28.

to prophesy through a man[1] or because his sole source of delight was in
the private parts of women, ought he not to have chosen a virgin rather
than a married woman to prophesy his will?

6. In fact the Pythian Apollo admired by the Greeks did not adjudge
any wise man, or indeed any man at all, to be worthy of what the Greeks
take to be divine inspiration. And from the female sex he did not choose
a virgin or a wise person who had been helped by philosophy, but some
vulgar woman.[2] Probably people of the better type were too good to
receive his inspiration. Moreover, if he was a god, he ought to have used
his foreknowledge as an incentive, so to speak, for the conversion and
healing and moral reformation of men. In fact, however, history says
nothing of the kind about him. Even though he said that Socrates was
wisest of all men,[3] the force of his praise was destroyed by the words he
uttered about Euripides and Sophocles in the line

Sophocles is wise, but Euripides is wiser.[4]

Thus, although Socrates is thought to be superior to tragic poets who
were called wise by the oracle, since the former strive for the vulgar prize
on the stage and the orchestra,[5] and sometimes make the spectators sad
and unhappy and at other times cause irreverent laughter (for such is the
object of satirical plays), this judgment on Socrates does not in any way
base its estimate of his worth and its praise of him upon the ground
of his philosophy and the truth of his opinions. Probably he said that
he was wisest of all men not so much for his philosophy as for the sacrifices and the burnt-offerings which he brought to him and to the other
daemons.[6]

The daemons seem to perform the petitions of those who bring requests
to them more because of the sacrifices they offer than because of their
virtuous actions. That is why when Homer, the best of poets, was
describing what takes place and was teaching what things especially
persuade the daemons to perform the desires of people who offer them
sacrifice, he introduced Chryses as obtaining by means of a few garlands
and thigh-bones of bulls and goats that which he asked for his daughter's
sake, that the Greeks might be plagued by a pestilence and give Chryseis

[1] Something has fallen out of the MS. text; I follow K. tr. and read δυνάμενος ⟨τῷ ἄρρενι
χρῆσθαι⟩ ἢ . . . .
[2] At first the Pythian priestess was a young woman; but after the outrage of Echecrates
of Thessaly she was a woman over fifty years old dressed as a virgin; cf. A. B. Cook,
Zeus, II, p. 209 n. 3; Parke, History of the Delphic Oracle, p. 257.
[3] Plato, Apol. 21 A.
[4] Suidas, s.v. σοφός, quotes: 'Sophocles is wise; Euripides is wiser; but Socrates is wiser
than all men.' Discussion and further references in Parke, op. cit. pp. 412 ff.
[5] I.e. the place where the chorus danced.   [6] Cf. VI, 4.

up to him.¹ I remember having read in a certain Pythagorean² who wrote a book about the doctrines expressed in veiled form by the poet, that the words of Chryses to Apollo and the pestilence which Apollo sent upon the Greeks teach that Homer knew how certain evil daemons, that delight in burnt-offerings and sacrifices, grant to those who offer them sacrifices the destruction of other people as their reward, if this is requested by their worshippers.

And he also 'who rules from stormy Dodona',³ whose prophets 'have unwashed feet and sleep on the ground', has rejected the male sex for the purposes of prophecy and uses *the priestesses of Dodona*, as Celsus himself has pointed out. But even if we grant that there is an oracle at Claros similar to these, and another at Branchidae, and another at the shrine of Zeus Ammon, or at any other place on earth where there are oracles, how can it be shown that they are gods and not certain daemons?

7. Of the Jewish prophets some were wise before they received the gift of prophecy and divine inspiration, while others became wise after they had been illuminated in mind by the actual gift of prophecy itself. They were chosen by providence to be entrusted with the divine Spirit and with the utterances that He inspired on account of the quality of their lives, which was of unexampled courage and freedom;⁴ for in face of death they were entirely without terror. And reason demands that the prophets of the supreme God should be such people. They make the courage of Antisthenes, Crates, and Diogenes appear as child's play.⁵ Indeed, because they spoke the truth and freely rebuked sinners, 'they were stoned, sawn asunder, tempted, were killed by the sword; they went about in sheepskins, in goatskins, being destitute, evil entreated, wandering in deserts and mountains and caves and the holes of the earth; of whom earthly honour was not worthy.'⁶ They always looked upon God and the invisible things which are not seen with the eyes of the senses, and on that account are eternal.⁷

¹ Homer, *Il.* 1, 34-53.
² This is attributed to Numenius of Apamea (cf. I, 15; IV, 51; V, 38, 57) by Thedinga (*frag.* 64) and K. S. Guthrie, *Numenius of Apamea* (Grantwood, New Jersey, 1917), p. 50. Numenius certainly interpreted Homer allegorically; cf. Porphyry, *de Antro Nympharum*, 34. But if Origen were quoting Numenius, he would be more likely to give his name as he does elsewhere; this is not included among the fragments of Numenius by Leemans.
³ That is, Zeus: Homer, *Il.* XVI, 234-5. For priestesses at Dodona cf. K. Buresch, *Klaros* (1889), p. 36 n. 5. Origen, however, seems to be mistaken in supposing that there were no priests there also. Cf. Cosmas Hieros. *ad Carm. S. Greg.* LXIV, 257 (Migne, *P.G.* XXXVIII, 500).
⁴ Similarly *Hom. in Jerem.* XV, 1 'From many passages we might gather the exceptional qualities of the prophets—their freedom, their courage, their watchfulness...', etc.
⁵ Antisthenes founded the Cynic school; for Crates and Diogenes cf. II, 41.
⁶ Heb. xi. 37-8.   ⁷ II Cor. iv. 18.

The life of each prophet is to be found in the Bible. But at the present moment it is enough to mention the life of Moses (for there are also prophecies by him which are to be found written in the law), and that of Jeremiah, described in the prophecy bearing his name, and that of Isaiah, who surpassed every ascetic practice when he went naked and barefoot for three years.[1] Notice also the strong life of the youths, Daniel and his companions, and read of the way in which they drank water and how that their sustenance was pulse since they abstained from animal food.[2] If you are able, observe also what happened before their time, how Noah prophesied and Isaac prophetically blessed his son, and Jacob said to each of the twelve 'Come that I may tell you what shall come to pass at the last days.'[3] These and countless others prophesied unto God and foretold the story of Jesus Christ. That is the reason why we reckon of no account the predictions uttered by the Pythian priestess, or by the priestesses of Dodona, or by the oracle of Apollo at Claros, or at Branchidae, or at the shrine of Zeus Ammon, or by countless other alleged prophets; whereas we admire those of the prophets in Judaea, seeing that their strong, courageous, and holy life was worthy of God's Spirit, whose prophecy was imparted in a new way which had nothing in common with the divination inspired by daemons.

8. I do not know why, to the words *the utterances made by the people in Judaea after their usual manner*, Celsus added *whether they were actually spoken or not*, as if he did not believe it, and was asserting that possibly they were not even spoken at all and that perhaps the Bible includes utterances which were never said. He did not notice the dates, or that they uttered countless predictions many years beforehand, and spoke also about Christ's advent. Again, as he wants to misrepresent the ancient prophets, he says that they prophesied in this manner *such as is customary even now with those who live round about Phoenicia and Palestine*. But he did not make it clear whether he is referring to certain people alien to the doctrine of Jews and Christians, or to people within Judaism who prophesy according to the pattern of the prophets. Whatever he may mean, it can be proved that he is wrong. Neither have any of those alien to the faith done anything like the prophets, nor are there any of modern times, who have lived since the advent of Jesus, who are related to have prophesied among the Jews. For the Holy Spirit, as people are well aware, has forsaken them because they acted impiously against God and against the one prophesied by the prophets among them. But signs of the Holy Spirit were manifested at the beginning when[4] Jesus was teaching, and after his

---

[1] Isa. xx. 2–3.
[2] Dan. i. 11–16.
[3] Gen. ix. 25–7; xxvii. 27–9; xlix. 1.
[4] Read μὲν ⟨ἐπὶ⟩ τῆς with Wif.

ascension there were many more, though later they became less numerous. Nevertheless, even to this day there are traces[1] of him in a few people whose souls have been purified by the Logos and by the actions which follow his teaching. 'For a Holy Spirit of discipline will flee from deceit, and will start away from thoughts that are without understanding.'[2]

9. As Celsus professes to describe the style of prophecy in Phoenicia and Palestine as though he had *heard it and had a thorough first-hand knowledge of it*, let us also consider this. He first says that *there are several kinds of prophecies*, but he does not give any instances; for he did not possess any, but merely *brandished* this phrase as a piece of bluff. Let us see what he asserts to be *the most perfect type among the men in that region. There are many*, he says, *who are nameless, who prophesy at the slightest excuse for some trivial cause both inside and outside temples;*[3] *and there are some who wander about begging*[4] *and roaming around cities and military camps; and they pretend to be moved as if giving some oracular utterance. It is an ordinary and common custom for each one to say: 'I am God (or a son of God, or a divine Spirit). And I have come.*[5] *Already the world is being destroyed. And you, O men, are to perish because of your iniquities. But I wish to save you. And you shall see me returning again with heavenly power. Blessed is he who has worshipped me now! But I will cast everlasting fire upon all the rest, both on cities and on country places. And men who fail to realize the penalties in store for them will in vain repent and groan. But I will preserve for ever those who have been convinced by me.'*[6] Then after that he says: *Having brandished*

---

[1] Cf. I, 2; II, 8, 33, for the occasional survival of miracles in the Church in Origen's time. For the development of Christian thought here, cf. K. Holl, *Gesammelte Aufsätze* II, p. 89 n. 2: Irenaeus (*adv. Haer.* II, 31, 2, Harvey, I, 370) treats miracles as a matter still of some frequency in the Church, and says that very often (*saepissime*) at the prayer of the brotherhood the spirit of a dead man has returned. 'What the real state of things was at that time one may conclude from the fact that the Montanist prophets never made any attempt to prove the truth of their proclamation by means of miracles' (Holl). Origen (*Hom. in Jerem.* IV, 3) treats miracles as a thing of the past. Eusebius (*H.E.* V, 7) only quotes Irenaeus as evidence for miracles after the N.T. period. For the *Vita Antonii* cf. Augustine, *Conf.* VIII, 6, 14. Chrysostom, *Hom. in Matt.* XXXII, 7 (*P.G.* LVII, 386–7) is significant.

[2] Wisd. of Sol. i. 5.   [3] Cf. Maximus Tyrius, XIII, 3 c, quoted above on I, 68.

[4] Cf. Celsus in I, 9; II, 55 *ad fin.*

[5] For the solemn formula ἥκω Reitzenstein (*Poimandres* (1904), pp. 222 f.) compares John viii. 42 ff. 'I came forth from God and have come (καὶ ἥκω)... Why do you not understand my speech? It is because you cannot hear my word. You are of your father the devil and desire to do the lusts of your father...', etc. Cf. also E. Norden, *Agnostos Theos* (1913), pp. 188 ff., and especially O. Weinreich in *Archiv für Religions-wissenschaft* XVIII (1915), pp. 34 ff. for numerous parallels where such types of utterance are attributed to saviour-gods, e.g. the epigram of Artemidorus beginning ἥκω Πρίαπος...(p. 43), on which cf. H. Herter, *de Priapo* (Giessen, 1932), pp. 233 ff. (It is perhaps worth noting that by a slip Weinreich (p. 42) quotes the words from Celsus and attributes them to the Hermetic tractate *Poimandres*.)

[6] The literature on this famous passage is immense. That such wandering prophets were common in Syria is likely enough (cf. the evidence of the *Didache*; and for such characters

these threats they then go on to add incomprehensible, incoherent, and utterly
obscure utterances, the meaning of which no intelligent person could discover;
for they are meaningless and nonsensical, and give a chance for any fool or
sorcerer to take the words in whatever sense he likes.

10. If he were sincere in his criticism, he ought to have quoted the
prophecies word for word, whether the passages where the speaker
claimed to be God Almighty, or where the person speaking believed
himself to be a son of God or the Holy Spirit. By this method he might[1]
have attempted to demolish the utterances and shown that the words were
not inspired which turn men from their sins and rebuke them for their
present state and foretell the future. It was because of this that the prophets'
contemporaries wrote down their prophecies and saw to it that when
posterity read them they should admire them as the words of God, and be
benefited not only by the words of rebuke and exhortation but also by the
predictions, being convinced by the resulting events that it was a divine
Spirit that foretold them, and might continue in the practice of religion
according to the teaching of the Word, being persuaded by the law and
the prophets.

The prophets, according to the will of God, said without any obscurity
whatever could be at once understood as beneficial to their hearers and
helpful towards attaining moral reformation. But all the more mysterious
and esoteric truths, which contained ideas beyond the understanding of
everyone, they expressed by riddles and allegories and what are called
dark sayings, and by what are called parables or proverbs.[2] Their purpose
was that those who are not afraid of hard work but will accept any toil to
attain to virtue and truth might find out their meaning by study, and after
finding it might use it as reason demands. But the worthy Celsus, as if in
a rage because he did not comprehend these sayings of the prophets,
poured abuse on them saying that *having brandished these threats they then*
go on to add incomprehensible, incoherent, and utterly obscure utterances, the
meaning of which no intelligent person could discover; for they are meaningless
and nonsensical, and give a chance for any fool or sorcerer to take the words in
whatever sense he likes. I think he said this out of deliberate wickedness
because he wanted to do all in his power to prevent readers of the prophecies from examining and studying their meaning. His behaviour

as Alexander of Abonuteichos and Peregrinus Proteus, cf. E. Fascher, Προφήτης (Giessen,
1927), pp. 190 ff.). But the content of their proclamation is 'Celsus' parody of perfectly
good ante-Nicene Christian preaching of a rather enthusiastic type' (W. L. Knox, *Hellenistic
Elements in Primitive Christianity* (1944), p. 83 n. 2). Cf. G. P. Wetter, *Der Sohn Gottes*
(1916); Reitzenstein, *Die hellenistischen Mysterienreligionen* (1927), p. 316 (Celsus' prophets
not Montanist); A. E. J. Rawlinson, *The N.T. Doctrine of the Christ*, pp. 69 f.
  [1] Read perhaps with K. tr. οὕτω γὰρ κἂν . . .and (line 26) τότε with Guiet and K. tr.
  [2] Cf. Num. xii. 8; I Cor. xiii. 12; Prov. i. 6; III, 45 above.

resembles that of those who said of a certain prophet when he came in to
a person and foretold the future to him 'Why came this mad fellow to
you?'¹

11. Probably there are arguments far beyond the skill of my brains
which could prove that in these words Celsus was lying and that the
prophecies are inspired. Nevertheless we have done the best we could
when verse by verse we explained *the incoherent and utterly obscure
utterances*, as Celsus calls them, in our studies on Isaiah and Ezekiel and
some of the twelve prophets.² And if God grants us further understanding
of his Word, at the time that He chooses, we shall add to those already
composed on these books commentaries either on those that remain or on
those at least for which we shall have time.³ And there are others also who
desire to study the Bible and possess intelligence; they would be able to
find out its meaning. For though it is true that in many places it is obscure,
yet it is certainly not *meaningless*, as Celsus asserts. Neither could *any fool
or sorcerer* smooth away the difficulties or *take the words in whatever sense
he likes*. It is only a person who is wise and truly in Christ who could give
as a connected whole the interpretation of the obscure passages in the
prophets by 'comparing spiritual things with spiritual'⁴ and by explaining
each phrase he found in the text from the common usage of that phrase
elsewhere in scripture.

Celsus is not to be believed when he says that he has heard such men
with his own ears. For in Celsus' time there were no prophets like the
ancients, since if there had been their prophecies would have been
written down afterwards by those who believed and admired them, just
as the ancient scriptures were. To me it seems quite obvious that Celsus is
lying when he says that *the alleged prophets whom he has heard with his own
ears were cross-examined* by Celsus, and *admitted* to him *that they were
a fraud, and that their words, meaning now one thing and now another, were
their own invention*. He ought also to have given the names of the people
whom, he asserts, he *heard with his own ears*, so that from the names, if he
were able to give them, it might be clear, to those competent to judge,
whether he was speaking the truth or lying.

12. He also thinks that *those who base their defence of the doctrine of
Christ upon the prophets have not a word to say if one points out some utterance
about God which is wicked, or disgraceful, or impure, or abominable*. Accord-
dingly, as if there was no reply, he goes on to give countless conclusions

¹ II Kings (IV Regn.) ix. 11.
² These commentaries were written during Origen's Caesarean period (Eus. *H.E.* VI, 32),
probably A.D. 238-44 (Harnack, *Chronologie*, II, p. 34). They are not extant.
³ The *contra Celsum* was Origen's last major work.
⁴ I Cor. ii. 13.

based on premisses which are not granted. He ought to realize that those
who desire to live in accordance with the divine scriptures, and who know
that 'the knowledge of the fool is as unexamined words',[1] and have read
the saying 'Being always ready to give an answer to everyone that asks us
for a reason of the hope that is in us',[2] do not merely take refuge in
affirming that these matters were predicted. They also attempt to solve
the apparent absurdities, and to show that in the words there is nothing
wicked, or disgraceful, or impure, or abominable, but that they only
appear so to people who do not know the right way to understand the
divine scripture.[3] He ought to have quoted from the prophets what
appeared to him to be wicked in them, or what seemed to him disgraceful,
or what he supposed to be impure, or what he assumed to be abominable,
if he had noticed such sayings in the prophets. His argument would have
been more impressive and effective towards attaining his object. In fact,
however, he gave no instances, but merely *brandished* his threatening
assertion that such sayings occur in the Bible, bringing an accusation
against it which is false. There is, therefore, no rational consideration
which demands that we reply to mere empty words in order to show that
there is in the words of the prophets nothing wicked or disgraceful or
impure or abominable.

13. Moreover, *God* does not *do or suffer the most shameful things*, nor
does He *minister to evil.* Nothing of this sort was *predicted.* If he says that *it
was predicted that God should minister to evil, or should do and suffer the most
shameful things,* he should have quoted the passages from the prophets to
this effect, and not try to defile the minds of his hearers without reason.
What Christ was to suffer the prophets did foretell; and they gave the
reason why he was to suffer; and God knew what His Christ was to suffer.
But why should this be *most abominable and impure,* as Celsus says?
However, he thinks he will teach us how the sufferings that he endured
were *most abominable and impure* when he says *For when God eats the flesh
of sheep*[4] *or drinks vinegar or gall,*[5] *what else is he doing but eating filth?* But
in our opinion it is not God that eats the flesh of sheep. Even supposing
that it appears that Jesus ate, he only ate because he had assumed a body.
Furthermore, with regard to the vinegar and the gall, which were
prophesied in the words 'They gave vinegar for my meat, and gave me
gall to drink for my thirst',[6] we spoke about them earlier; and it is Celsus
who forces us to repeat ourselves. It is always true that those who take

[1] Sirach xxi. 18.   [2] I Pet. iii. 15.
[3] Read with Wifstrand τοιοῦτον φαίνεσθαι τοῖς ὡς χρὴ ἐκδέχεσθαι μὴ συνιεῖσι . . .
[4] Celsus refers to the Passover; cf. I, 70.   [5] Cf. Celsus in II, 37.
[6] Ps. lxviii. 22.

405

counsel against the word of truth bring to the Christ of God the vinegar
of their own evil and the gall of their own turning aside to evil ways; and
when he has tasted it, he does not wish to drink.[1]

14. Then after this, with the aim of overthrowing the faith of those
who believe the story of Jesus because it has been prophesied, he says: *If
the prophets foretold that the great God (to mention nothing else more
offensive) would serve as a slave and be sick and die, would it necessarily
follow from the fact that it was predicted, that God must die and serve as
a slave and be sick, in order that by his death it might be believed that he
was God? But the prophets could not have foretold this. For it is wicked and
impious. So we should not consider either whether they did or whether they did
not foretell it, but whether the act is worthy of God and is good. And we should
disbelieve what is disgraceful and evil, even if all men should seem to predict it
in a state of frenzy. How, then, is it anything but blasphemy to assert that
the things done to Jesus were done to God?*

He appears from these words to have imagined that the argument that
Jesus was prophesied is influential in persuading the hearers; and he tries
to overthrow it with another plausible phrase when he says *So we should
not consider either whether they did or whether they did not foretell it.* But if
he wanted to oppose the assertion without any fallacious reasoning but by
proving his case, he ought to have said: 'So we must prove that they did
not foretell it, or that what they said about Christ was not fulfilled in
Jesus in the way that they predicted.' And he ought then to have added
the proof that seemed right to him. In that case it would have been made
clear both what it is which the prophecies say, which we refer to Jesus,
and how he misrepresents our interpretation. And it would have been
discovered whether he is acting from noble motives in overthrowing
words from the prophets which we apply to the doctrine about Jesus, or
if he is caught in a shameless desire to deny by violent language the truth
of that which is obviously true.

15. He assumes that certain things are impossible and improper for
God to do, saying: *If these things were prophesied about the supreme God,
ought we then to believe such things about God because they are predicted?*
And he thinks he can argue that *even if it is really true that the prophets
foretold such things about God's son, it would be impossible to believe in the
predictions that he should suffer and do these things.* We may reply that his
assumption is mistaken and would make hypothetical premises result in
contradictory conclusions. This is shown as follows: (i) If the prophets of
the supreme God were to say that God will serve as a slave or will be sick
or even[2] that He will die, these things will happen to God, since the

---

[1] Matt. xxvii. 34.   [2] Read (for ἀεὶ ἤ) ἤ καί.

prophets of the great God must necessarily speak the truth. (ii) On the
other hand, if the true prophets of the supreme God say these same things,
since things that are intrinsically impossible are not true, what the
prophets say of God would not happen. But when two hypothetical
premisses result in contradictory conclusions by the syllogism known as
the syllogism of two propositions,[1] the antecedent of the two premisses is
denied, which in this instance is that 'the prophets foretell that the great
God will serve as a slave or will be sick or will die'. The conclusion is
therefore that the prophets did not foretell that the great God will be
a slave or will be sick or will die. The argument runs like this: If *A* is true,
B is true also; if *A* is true, *B* is not true; then *A* is not true.

The Stoics give the following concrete illustration of this when they
say: If you know that you are dead, you are dead; if you know that you
are dead you are not dead; it follows that you do not know that you are
dead. This is the way in which they make up the premisses. If you know
that you are dead, what you know is true; then it is true that you are dead.
And on the other hand, if you know that you are dead, then it is also true
that you know that you are dead.[2] But since a dead man knows nothing,
obviously if you know that you are dead, you are not dead. And as I said
before, it follows from both premisses that you do not know that you are
dead. The same sort of argument is implicit in Celsus' assumption when he
makes the remark we have quoted.

16. However, what we have used for the purposes of argument bears
no resemblance to the prophecies about Jesus. The prophecies did not
foretell that God would be crucified when they say of him who accepted
death: 'And we saw him, and he had not form or beauty; but his form
was dishonourable, deserted more than the sons of men; being a man in
affliction and trouble and knowing how to bear sickness.'[3] Notice how
they clearly say that he who suffered human sorrows was a man. And
Jesus himself, who knew precisely that it was a man who was to die, said
to the men who conspired against him: 'And now you seek to kill me,
a man who told you the truth, which I heard from God.'[4] If there was
something divine in his human nature, it was the only-begotten Son of
God and the firstborn of all creation, who says 'I am the truth', and 'I am
the life', and 'I am the door', and 'I am the way', and 'I am the living
bread that came down from heaven'.[5] Indeed, the person and essence of
the divine being in Jesus is quite a different matter from that of his human
aspect.

---

[1] Cf. Sextus Emp. *P.H.* II, 3; Galen, *de Hippocr. et Plat. placit.* II, 3 (p. 182, ed. Müller, =
S.V.F. II, 248).

[2] Read with K. τr. εἰ ἐπίστασαι ὅτι τέθνηκας, καὶ ἔστιν τὸ ἐπίστασαι ὅτι τέθνηκας.

[3] Isa. liii. 2–3.   [4] John viii. 40.   [5] John xiv. 6; x. 9; xiv. 6; vi. 51.

Consequently not even Christians who are very simple, who have not been educated in dialectical subtleties, would say that it was the truth, or the life, or the way, or the living bread that came down from heaven, or the resurrection, that died. It was he who dwelt in the apparently human Jesus who said that he was the resurrection when he taught 'I am the resurrection.'[1] Furthermore, none of us is so idiotic as to say that the life died, or that the resurrection died. But Celsus' argument would have had some justification if we maintained that the prophets had foretold that the divine Logos, or the truth, or the life, or the resurrection, would die, or if they had said this of any of the other titles by which the Son of God calls himself.

17. It is, therefore, only in one point that Celsus is right on this subject, when he says *But the prophets would not have predicted this; for it is wicked and impious.* What does he mean by *this* except that *the great God will serve as a slave or will die?* But what the prophets predicted is *worthy of God*; for they prophesied that a certain 'effulgence and image'[2] of the divine nature would come to human life together with the holy incarnate soul of Jesus, so that a doctrine might be spread abroad which would make a friend of the God of the universe anyone who received it into his own soul and cultivated it, and which would lead him on to the ultimate goodness, if he possessed in himself the power of the divine Logos who was to come to dwell in a human body. But this would happen in such a way that it was not true that his rays were enclosed in that man alone, or that it could be supposed[3] that the light, which is the divine Logos, which causes these rays, existed nowhere else.

So then, the things that were done to Jesus, in so far as they are understood to apply to the divine element[4] in him, are pious, and not in conflict with the accepted notion of God. But in so far as he was a man, who more than anyone else was adorned by sublime participation in the very Logos and wisdom himself, he endured as a wise and perfect man what must needs be endured by a man who does all in his power on behalf of the entire race of men and of rational beings as well. There is nothing objectionable in the fact that a man died, and in that his death should not only be given as an example of the way to die for the sake of religion, but also should effect a beginning and an advance in the overthrow of the evil one, the devil, who dominated the whole earth.[5] And signs of his over-

---

[1] John xi. 25. For Origen's expressions here to describe the humanity of Christ, cf. my remarks in *H.T.R.* XLI (1948), p. 100 n. 30.
[2] Wisd. of Sol. vii. 26 (Heb. i. 3).
[3] Read μηδὲ νομίζεσθαι with Hoeschel, K. tr. For the idea, cf. II, 9.
[4] Read θεότητι ⟨τῇ⟩ ἐν αὐτῷ with Wif.
[5] Cf. Heb. ii. 14-15; I John v. 19; Rev. xii. 9.

throw are the people in many places who on account of the advent of
Jesus have escaped the daemons who held them fast and who, because
they have been liberated from bondage to them, devote themselves to God
and to a piety towards Him which, so far as it is in their power, advances
in purity every day.

18. After this Celsus continues as follows: *Will they not ponder that
again? If the prophets of the God of the Jews foretold that Jesus would be his
son, why did he give them laws by Moses that they were to become rich and
powerful[1] and to fill the earth[2] and to massacre their enemies, children and all,
and slaughter their entire race,[3] which he himself did, so Moses says,[4] before
the eyes of the Jews? And besides this, if they were not obedient, why does he
expressly threaten to do to them what he did to their enemies?[5] Yet his son, the
man of Nazareth, gives contradictory laws, saying that a man cannot come
forward to the Father if he is rich or loves power or lays claim to any intelligence or reputation,[6] and that he must not pay attention to food or to his store-
house any more than the ravens, or to clothing any more than the lilies, and that
to a man who has struck him once he should offer himself to be struck once
again.[7] Who is wrong? Moses or Jesus? Or when the Father sent Jesus had
he forgotten what commands he gave to Moses? Or did he condemn his own
laws and change his mind, and send his messenger for quite the opposite
purpose?*

Here Celsus, who professes to know everything,[8] has fallen into a very
vulgar error concerning the meaning of the Bible. He thinks that in the
law and the prophets there is no deeper doctrine beyond that of the literal
meaning of the words. He fails to notice that the Word would not have
promised material wealth to those who live upright lives, since that would
be obviously unconvincing; very righteous people have manifestly lived
in extreme poverty. In fact, the prophets, who received the divine Spirit
because of their purity of life, 'went about in sheepskins, in goatskins,
being destitute, afflicted, evil entreated, wandering in deserts and mountains and caves and the holes of the earth'.[9] As the Psalmist says, 'many
are the afflictions of the righteous'.[10]

If Celsus had read the Mosaic law he would probably have thought that
the words 'Thou shalt lend to many nations, but thou shalt not borrow',[11]

---

[1] Deut. xv. 6; xxviii. 11–12.   [2] Gen. viii. 17; ix. 1, 7, etc. Cf. VI, 29 above.
[3] Exod. xvii. 13–16; Num. xxi. 34–5; Deut. xxv. 19.
[4] Exod. xxxiv. 11; Deut. xxix. 2–3.   [5] Deut. i. 26–45; vii. 4; ix. 14; xxviii. 15–68.
[6] Matt. xix. 24; xx. 25–7. (Cf. Celsus in VI, 16 above.) Matt. xi. 25.
[7] Matt. vi. 26–9; v. 39. It seems that Celsus is drawing upon Marcionite sources (cf.
Origen's remarks in VII, 25).
[8] Cf. Celsus in I, 12.   [9] Heb. xi. 37–8.
[10] Ps. xxxiii. 20.   [11] Deut. xv. 6; xxviii. 12.

which are addressed to the man who keeps the law, are to be understood
as a promise made to the righteous man that he would amass so much
blind wealth[1] that, on account of the quantity of his possessions, he would
lend not only to Jews, nor even to any other single nation, nor to two or
three only, but to many nations. If, then, the righteous man received
possessions as a reward for righteousness in accordance with the law, how
much wealth would he have had to acquire in order that he might lend to
many nations? From such an interpretation it follows that we should also
suppose that the righteous man never borrows, since it is written 'But
thou shalt not borrow.' Accordingly, would the nation have remained
faithful to the Mosaic religion for so long a time when they would clearly
see that the lawgiver, if Celsus is right, was not speaking the truth? No one
is related to have amassed so much wealth that he lent to many nations.
But it is not likely that after being taught to understand the law in this
sense, as Celsus imagined, and after clearly seeing that the promises in the
law were untrue, they would have fought for the law.

However, if anyone should take the sins of the people, described in
scripture, as proof that they despised the law, perhaps because they
rejected it as untrue, we should say to him that he ought to read of the
occasions when the whole people, after they had done evil in the sight of
the Lord, are recorded to have been converted to living a better life and
to worshipping God according to the law.

19. Moreover, if the law promised that they would be powerful, when
it says 'Thou shalt rule many nations, but they shall not rule thee',[2] and
if nothing more profound is indicated by these words, obviously the
people would have had an even stronger reason for rejecting the promises
of the law. Celsus gives a paraphrase of certain words which indicate
that the whole earth will be filled by the Hebrew stock. This happened as
a historical event after the advent of Jesus because God was angry, so to
speak, rather than because He was granting blessings. Furthermore,
concerning the promise to the Jews to the effect that they would massacre
their enemies we would say that, if one reads and studies the words
carefully, one finds that the literal interpretation is impossible. It is enough
at present to quote from the Psalms where the righteous man is introduced
as saying this, among other things: 'Every morning I killed all the sinners
on earth, to destroy from the city of the Lord all the workers of iniquity.'[3]
Notice the words and the intention of the speaker, and consider whether
it is possible that, after having previously related great deeds in a passage
which can be read by anyone interested, he should continue by saying
what the text could be taken to mean—that at no other time of day but

[1] Cf. Plato, *Laws,* 631 c, and 1, 24 above.   [2] Deut. xv. 6; xxviii. 12.   [3] Ps. c. 8.

the morning he destroyed all the sinners on earth so that he left none of them alive. And consider whether he destroyed out of Jerusalem every man whatsoever who was working iniquity. You would also find many sayings of this sort in the law, such as this: 'We did not leave any of them to be taken alive.'[1]

20. Celsus also states that *it was foretold to them that if they disobeyed the law, they would suffer the same fate as that which they inflicted upon their enemies.* Before Celsus produces any argument on this point and quotes sayings from the teaching of Christ which, as he supposes, contradict the law, we must speak of his earlier remarks. We maintain that the law has a twofold interpretation, one literal and the other spiritual, as was also taught by some of our predecessors.[2] And it is not so much we as God, speaking in one of the prophets, who described the law literally understood as 'judgments that are not good' and 'statutes that are not good'; and in the same prophet God is represented as saying that the law spiritually understood is 'judgments that are good' and 'statutes that are good'.[3] The prophet is obviously not making contradictory statements in the same passage. It is consistent with this when Paul also says that 'the letter kills', which is equivalent to the literal interpretation; whereas 'the spirit gives life',[4] which means the same as the spiritual interpretation. In fact, one can find in Paul something analogous to the statements in the prophet which Celsus would suppose to be contradictions. In one sentence Ezekiel says: 'I gave them judgments that were not good and statutes that were not good, in which they will not live in them'; but in another 'I gave them judgments that were good and statutes that were good, in which they will live in them', or at least words to the same effect as these. So also Paul, in one place where he wants to attack the literal interpretation of the law, says: 'If the ministration of death written and engraven upon stones came with glory, so that the children of Israel could not look stedfastly on the face of Moses for the glory of his face, which glory was to pass away, how shall not the ministration of the Spirit be even more glorious?'[5] But in another place he admires and approves of the law and calls it spiritual, saying 'And we know that the law is spiritual', and he speaks of it in terms of approval in the words 'So the law is holy, and the commandment holy and righteous and good.'[6]

21. If, then, the letter of the law promises[7] wealth to the righteous, Celsus may follow the letter that kills and think that the promise is speaking

<hr/>

[1] Deut. ii. 34; Num. xxi. 35.   [2] E.g. Philo, *de Spec. Leg.* 1, 287, and passim.
[3] Ezek. xx. 25.   [4] II Cor. iii. 6.   [5] II Cor. iii. 7–8.   [6] Rom. vii. 14, 12.
[7] Wendland (*G.G.A.* (1899), p. 291) emends the MS. reading ἐπαγγέλλεται (indicative after ἐάν) to ἐπαγγέλληται. For the vulgar use of the indicative, however, cf. Blass-Debrunner, *Grammatik des neutest. Griechisch* (7th ed. 1943), Anhang p. 61, §372, 1 a.

of blind wealth. But we regard it as the riches that have keen sight,[1] according as a person is rich 'in all utterance and all knowledge', and as we 'exhort those who are rich in this present world, that they be not high-minded, nor have their hope set on the uncertainty of riches, but on God who gives us all things richly to enjoy, that they do good, that they be rich in good works, that they be ready to distribute, willing to communicate'.[2] Moreover, according to Solomon the man that is rich in things which are genuinely good is 'a ransom of a man's soul', while the poverty which is the opposite of this is ruinous—the poverty on account of which 'the poor man will not submit to a threat'.[3]

We should give a similar interpretation to that which we gave of the saying about wealth for that concerning the power by which one righteous man is said to pursue thousands, and two to remove tens of thousands.[4] If this is the interpretation of the sayings about riches, would it not be consistent to interpret the promise of God to mean that the man who is rich 'in all utterance and all knowledge'[5] and in all wisdom and every good work, lends out of his wealth of utterance and wisdom and knowledge to many nations, just as Paul lent to all the nations that he visited when from Jerusalem round about to Illyricum he fully preached the gospel of Christ?[6] And since the divine truths were made known to him by revelation and he was illuminated in his soul by the divinity of the Logos, for this reason he did not borrow, nor did he need anyone to minister the word to him. And in this sense also we take the scripture, 'Thou shalt rule many nations, but they shall not rule thee.' By the power conferred by the Logos he subjected the Gentiles to the teaching of Christ Jesus and ruled them, and was never made subject even for an hour[7] to any men as his superiors. And it was in this sense that he 'filled the earth'.

22. If we may explain the massacre of enemies at the same time as we interpret the righteous man's power over all things, we would say that in the words 'Every morning I killed all the sinners on earth, to destroy from the city of the Lord all the workers of iniquity', he allegorically calls the flesh 'earth', the mind of which is enmity towards God;[8] and by 'the city of the Lord' he means his own soul in which was a temple of God,[9] because it possessed a right opinion and conception of God so as to become an object of admiration to all who see it. Accordingly, at the same time as the rays of 'the sun of righteousness'[10] were illuminating his soul, he was, as it were, being empowered and strengthened by them; and so he

---

[1] Plato, *Laws*, 631 c.   [2] I Cor. i. 5; I Tim. vi. 17–18.   [3] Prov. xiii. 8.
[4] Deut. xxxii. 30.   [5] I Cor. i. 5.   [6] Rom. xv. 19.
[7] Read with Bo. οὐδὲ πρὸς ὥραν (from Gal. ii. 5). That the emendation is correct is shown by the allusions to Galatians here (i. 11–12).
[8] Rom. viii. 7.   [9] I Cor. iii. 16–17; II Cor. vi. 16.   [10] Mal. iv. 2.

destroyed every 'carnal mind',[1] here called 'the sinners upon earth', and destroyed from the city of the Lord in his soul all the thoughts that are 'workers of iniquity' and the desires hostile to the truth.

It is in this sense also that the righteous destroy everything remaining alive of the enemies which originate from evil, so that there is left not even an infant sin which has only just become implanted. Thus also we understand the saying in the 136th Psalm which reads as follows: 'O daughter of Babylon, thou wretched one, blessed is he who shall repay thee thy reward which thou didst repay to us; blessed is he who shall take hold of thy infants and dash them against the rock.'[2] The infants of Babylon, which means confusion,[3] are the confused thoughts caused by evil which have just been implanted and are growing up in the soul. The man who takes hold of them, so that he breaks their heads by the firmness and solidity of the Word, is dashing the infants of Babylon against the rock; and on this account he becomes blessed. Supposing, then, that God does command men to kill the works of iniquity, *children and all*, and *to slaughter their entire race*, His teaching in no way contradicts the proclamation of Jesus. And we may also grant that *before the eyes of* those who are *Jews* in secret[4] God brings about the destruction of their enemies and of all the works caused by evil. And we may take it that this is the meaning when those who are disobedient to God's law and word are compared to *enemies*; for their characters are moulded by evil so that they suffer the penalties which are deserved by people who forsake God's words.

23. It is obvious from this that Jesus, *the man of Nazareth*, does not lay down laws in contradiction to those we have quoted concerning wealth and the people who give it up, when he says that it is hard for a rich man to enter the kingdom of God,[5] where one may take 'a rich man' either in the simple sense to mean the man who is distracted by wealth and hindered, as if by its thorn, from bearing the fruits of the word,[6] or as meaning the man who is rich in false opinions, of whom it is written in Proverbs: 'A poor man who is righteous is better than a rich man who is a liar.'[7]

It is probably from the words 'He who wishes to be first among you, let him be servant of all', and 'The rulers of the Gentiles lord it over them', and 'Those who have authority among them are called benefactors',[8] that Celsus has taken the notion that Jesus forbade any love of power. But this is not to be regarded as contradicting the words 'Thou shalt rule many

[1] Rom. viii. 7.   [2] Ps. cxxxvi. 8–9.
[3] Cf. F. Wutz, *Onomastica Sacra* (*T.U.* 41, 1914), p. 153.
[4] Rom. ii. 29.   [5] Matt. xix. 23.   [6] Cf. Matt. xiii. 22.
[7] Prov. xxviii. 6.   [8] Matt. xx. 25–7; Luke xxii. 25.

nations, but they shall not rule thee', chiefly for the reasons which we have given in explaining this text.

After this Celsus produces an objection about wisdom. He thinks that Jesus teaches that a wise man cannot *come to the Father*. We may say to him: What sort of wise man? If you mean the man who is moulded in accordance with what is called the wisdom of this world which is foolishness with God,[1] we also would affirm that a man wise in this sense cannot come to the Father. But if by wisdom one understands Christ, since Christ is the power of God and the wisdom of God,[2] we say not only that a man wise in this sense can come to the Father, but also that the man adorned with the spiritual gift called 'the word of wisdom',[3] which is conferred by the Spirit, is far superior to people who are not so adorned.

24. Again, we say that the claim to fame among men is forbidden not only by the teaching of Jesus but also by the Old Testament. At any rate, when one of the prophets is invoking curses on himself if he has been guilty of sins, he says that worldly glory is the greatest evil that could happen to him. His words are as follows: 'O Lord my God, if I have done this, if there is unrighteousness in my hands, if I have repayed evil to those who repayed me, may I fall away empty from my enemies; let the enemy persecute and capture my soul, and let him trample my life down to the earth, and make my glory rest on dust.'[4]

Furthermore, the sayings, 'Take no thought what you shall eat or drink; consider the birds of the heaven, or consider the ravens, that they sow not nor reap, and your heavenly Father sustains them; how much more are you better than the birds?' and 'Why be anxious about raiment? Consider the lilies of the field',[5] and the sayings that follow this, are not in contradiction to the blessings of the law, which teach the righteous man to eat to repletion,[6] and to the saying of Solomon which reads as follows: 'A righteous man eats and fills his soul, but the souls of the impious are in need.'[7] We ought to notice that it is food of the soul which is indicated in the blessing in the law. It is not the composite man (body and soul) who is filled by it, but the soul alone. From the gospel we should take perhaps two interpretations, the one profound, the other simple, the latter being that one must not be worried in the soul by anxieties about food and clothing, but must practise a simple life and believe that one is under God's providential care, being concerned only for what is necessary.

25. Celsus does not quote any passages from the law which are apparently in contradiction to what stands in the gospel, so that we might

[1] I Cor. iii. 19. [2] I Cor. i. 24. [3] I Cor. xii. 8.
[4] Ps. vii. 4–6. [5] Matt. vi. 25–8.
[6] Cf. Lev. xxvi. 5 'Ye shall eat your bread to the full.' [7] Prov. xiii. 25.

compare them. He says: *And to a man who has struck one once one should offer oneself to be struck again.* But we will say that we are aware that 'it was said to them of old time, An eye for an eye and a tooth for a tooth', and that we have read also the words 'But I say unto you, to him that strikes you on one cheek offer the other one also.'[1] However, as I imagine that Celsus derived some vague notions from those who say that the God of the gospel is different from the God of the law, and so made remarks like this, I would reply to his objection that the Old Testament also knows the doctrine that to him that strikes you on the right cheek you should offer[2] the other one also. At any rate, it is written in the Lamentations of Jeremiah: 'It is good for a man when he bears a yoke in his youth, he will sit alone and in silence when he has taken it on himself. He will give a cheek to the man who smites him and shall be filled with reproaches.'[3] The gospel, then,[4] does not lay down laws in contradiction to the God of the law, not even if we interpret literally the saying about a blow on the jaw. And neither Moses nor Jesus *is wrong.* Nor did the Father *forget when he sent Jesus the commands which he had given to Moses.* Nor did He *condemn His own laws, and change His mind, and send His messenger for the opposite purpose.*

26. If we may say a little about the manner of life which the Jews formerly used to follow according to the prescriptions of the law of Moses, and which Christians now wish to correct to conform to the teaching of Jesus, we will observe that it did not fit in with the calling of the Gentiles that they should conduct their society according to the literal interpretation of the law of Moses, since they were subject to the Romans. Nor was it possible for the structure of life of the ancient Jews to remain without any modification if, for instance, they were to obey the form of life enjoined by the gospel. It was impossible for Christians to follow the Mosaic law in killing their enemies or those who acted illegally and were judged to be deserving of death by fire or by stoning, although, in fact, even the Jews were not able to inflict these punishments on them,[5] as the law commanded, even if they wanted to do so. Again, if you took away from the Jews of that time, who had their own political life and country, the power to go out against their enemies and to fight for their traditional customs, and to take life, or at any time to punish adulterers or murderers or people who had committed any such crime, the inevitable consequence would have been their complete and utter destruction when their enemies attacked the nation, because by their own law they would have been

---

[1] Matt. v. 38–9.   [2] Read παρέχειν with A (K. tr.).
[3] Lam. iii. 27–9.   [4] Read οὖν for θεοῦ with K. tr.
[5] Read κατ' ἐκείνων with Bo., K. tr.

deprived of strength and prevented from resisting their enemies. But the providence which long ago gave the law, but now has given the gospel of Jesus Christ, did not wish that the practices of the Jews should continue, and so destroyed their city and temple and the service of God in the temple offered by means of sacrifices and the prescribed worship. Just as providence did not want them to be performed, and destroyed them, in the same way it increased the success of the Christians and added daily[1] to the multitude, and also granted boldness in spite of the fact that there were countless hindrances to the spread of the teaching of Jesus in the world. But because it was God who wanted the Gentiles also to be helped by the teaching of Jesus Christ, every human design against the Christians has been frustrated; and the more emperors and rulers of nations and peoples in many places have humiliated them, the more they have increased in number so that 'they have become exceedingly strong'.[2]

27. After this Celsus quotes at length statements about God which we do not make, as though they were a fair representation of our views, to the effect that *He is corporeal by nature and has a body like the human form.*[3] As he endeavours to overthrow notions which we do not maintain, it is superfluous to quote these remarks or to give them any refutation. If we said what he maintains we affirm about God, and if this had been the object of his attack, it would have been necessary for us to quote his words and to argue in support of our doctrines and to demolish his. But if he invents out of his own head ideas which he heard from nobody, or, to grant that he heard them from somebody, notions which he derived from some simple and naïve folk who do not know the meaning of the Bible, there is no need for us to concern ourselves with unnecessary argument. The Bible clearly says that God is incorporeal. That is why 'No man has seen God at any time', and 'the firstborn of all creation' is said to be an 'image of the invisible God'[4]—using 'invisible' in the sense of 'incorporeal'. However, in what has gone before we have spoken at moderate length about God, when we examined the sense in which we take the words 'God is spirit, and they that worship him must worship him in spirit and in truth.'[5]

[1] Acts ii. 47.   [2] Exod. i. 7.
[3] Cf. VI. 62–4 above; and for Origen's polemic against church members who conceived of God anthropomorphically, *Comm. in Rom.* I, 19 (VI, 66 Lommatzsch): '...those members of the church who say that the corporeal form of man is the image of God'. Tertullian often insists that nothing is real which is not corporeal (a Stoic point): *adv. Prax.* 7; *de Carne Christi* 11. Cf. *Clement. Hom.*, XVII, 7 ff. where Peter refutes the view of Simon Magus that God has no shape; Clement, *Exc. Theod.* 10–16, discussed by Collomp in *Revue de Philologie et Litt. et d'Hist. anc.* XXXVII (1913), pp. 19 ff., and Bousset, *Jüdisch-christlicher Schulbetrieb in Alexandria und Rom* (1915), pp. 155 ff.
[4] John i. 18; Col. i. 15.   [5] John iv. 24; cf. VI, 70 above.

28. After the remarks about God in which he misrepresents us, he asks us: *Where will we go to? And what hope have we?* And as if it were our reply, he alleges that we say words like this: *To another earth, better than this one.* To this he says: *Divinely inspired men of ancient times related that there is a happy life for fortunate souls. Some called it the Islands of the Blessed;*[1] *others the Elysian Fields because they were there set free from the evils of the world. Thus Homer says*

> *But immortals will send thee to the Elysian Fields*
> *And the ends of the earth where life is very easy.*[2]

And Plato, who thinks the soul immortal, quite openly calls that region where the soul is sent a land, when he says: ' *The world is quite enormous, and we inhabit the part from the Phasis to the pillars of Hercules which is but a small fraction, like ants or frogs round a marsh, living round the sea; and many other people live elsewhere in many similar places. For in many places round the earth there are several hollows of various shapes and sizes, into which the water and the mist and the air have poured together. But the land itself is pure and lies in the pure heaven.*'[3]

Celsus, then, supposes that we have taken the doctrine about the other earth, which is better and far superior to this one, from certain men of ancient times whom he regards as divinely inspired, and in particular from Plato, who in the Phaedo spoke philosophically about a pure earth lying in a pure heaven. He fails to see that Moses, who is far earlier even than the Greek alphabet,[4] taught that God promised a pure earth, which was 'good and large, flowing with milk and honey',[5] to those who lived in accordance with His law. And the good land was not, as some think, the earthly land of Judaea, which indeed lies in the earth which was cursed from the beginning by the works of Adam's transgression. For the saying, 'Cursed is the earth by thy works; in grief shalt thou eat of it all the days of thy life',[6] refers to the entire earth, of which every man who has died in Adam eats in grief, that is in troubles; and it is so that he eats all the days of his life. And because it is cursed, all the earth will bring forth thorns and thistles all the days of the life of the man who, in Adam, was cast out of paradise; and every man eats his bread by the sweat of his brow until he returns to the earth from which he was taken. However, there is much to be said about this whole subject which could be adduced in order to explain these texts. But at present we are content with a brief discussion;

---

[1] Cf. Hesiod, *Op.* 171.
[2] Homer, *Od.* IV, 563–5. For ancient derivations of Elysium (here from *lysis* = 'setting free'), cf. the remarks of Rohde, *Psyche* (E.T.), p. 82 n. 15.
[3] Plato, *Phaedo*, 109 A, B.   [4] Cf. IV, 21; VI, 7.
[5] Exod. iii. 8.   [6] Gen. iii. 17; I Cor. xv. 22.

we only wish to dispel any mistaken notion which supposes that the sayings about a good land which God promises to the righteous were spoken about the land of Judaea.

29. If, therefore, the whole earth itself was cursed by the works of Adam and those who died in him, obviously all its parts also share in the curse, among which is also the land of Judaea. Consequently, the words 'to a land good and large, flowing with milk and honey' cannot be made to refer to it, even if Judaea and Jerusalem are shown to be a symbolical shadow of the pure land which is good and large and lies in a pure heaven, in which is the heavenly Jerusalem. The apostle discusses this land, as one who is risen with Christ who seeks the things that are above[1] and has found a meaning not contained by any Jewish mythological interpretation,[2] when he says 'But you have come to mount Sion and to the heavenly Jerusalem, the city of the living God, and to an innumerable company of angels.'[3]

If anyone wants to be convinced that we are not speaking in contradiction to the meaning of the divine Spirit concerning the Mosaic land which is good and large, let him pay attention to all the prophets who teach that there will be a return to Jerusalem for those who have gone astray and fallen from it,[4] and, in general, that they will be restored to what is called the place and city of God by the one who says 'His place is in holy peace', and who affirms that 'Great is the Lord, and much to be praised in the city of our God, in his holy mountain, a well-rooted joy of all the earth.'[5]

It is enough at present to quote the words from the thirty-sixth Psalm about the land of the righteous which read as follows: 'But they who wait on the Lord shall inherit the earth.' And a little later 'The meek shall inherit the earth and delight in much peace.' And a little further on 'Those who bless him shall inherit the earth.' And again 'The righteous shall inherit the earth and shall dwell for ever therein.' And is not the existence of the pure earth in the pure heaven indicated to those able to understand by the following words in the same Psalm: 'Wait upon the Lord and keep his way, and he shall exalt thee to inherit the earth'?[6]

30. I think that Plato took the idea of the stones which on earth are regarded as precious, which, he says, are an emanation from the stones in the better land,[7] from the words written in Isaiah about the city of God, of which it is written: 'I will set thy battlements of jasper and thy stones of crystal and thy border of choice stones.' And again, 'I will lay thy

---

[1] Col. iii. 1.   [2] Cf. Tit. i. 14.   [3] Heb. xii. 22.
[4] For Origen's teaching about the final restoration, cf. VIII, 72.
[5] Ps. lxxv. 3; xlvii. 2–3.   [6] Ps. xxxvi. 9, 11, 22, 29, 34.
[7] Plato, *Phaedo*, 110 D, E.

foundations with sapphire.'¹ Those who understand in an exalted sense
the teachings of the philosopher explain Plato's myth as an allegory. But
those who have lived a life akin to that of the prophets and under divine
inspiration, and who have devoted all their time to studying the sacred
scriptures, will explain the prophecies, from which we conjecture Plato
also borrowed, to people who are suitable because their life is pure and
because they desire to learn about the things of God.

It has been our object to show that we did not take the idea of the holy
land from the Greeks or from Plato. But since the Greeks were more
recent, not only than Moses who was of the greatest antiquity, but also
than most of the prophets, they made certain statements about the better
land either because they misunderstood² some sayings which hint obscurely
at these truths, or because they read the sacred scriptures and modified
them. Now Haggai clearly shows that the dry land is one thing and the
earth another, when he calls this world in which we are dry land. He speaks
as follows: 'Yet once, and I will shake the heaven and the earth and the dry
land and the sea.'³

31. He draws back from explaining Plato's myth, found in the Phaedo,
by saying this: *It is not easy for anyone to know what he means by these
words, unless he is able to understand what he refers to when he says that 'by
weakness and slowness we cannot pass through to the topmost air, and if
nature were able to bear the vision we would realize that that is the true heaven
and the true light'*.⁴ Following his example, as we do not think it consistent
with the plan of the present work to explain the holy and good earth and
the city of God in it, we leave that for the commentaries on the prophets,
having in part discussed the city of God as well as we could in our studies
on the forty-fifth and forty-seventh Psalms.⁵ The very ancient doctrine of
Moses and the prophets is aware that the true things all have the same name
as the earthly things which are more generally given these names. For
example, there is a 'true light', and a 'heaven' which is different from the
firmament, and 'the sun of righteousness'⁶ is different from the sun
perceived by the senses. In general, in contrast to the sensible things, none
of which are real, the scripture says, 'God, his works are true'⁷—
assigning the works of God to the category of true things,⁸ while those
called 'the works of his hands'⁹ belong to an inferior category. At any
rate, when He is finding fault with certain people, He says by Isaiah: 'They

---

¹ Isa. liv. 12, 11.   ² Cf. Celsus in v, 65; vi, 22. For the priority of Moses, cf. iv, 21.
³ Hag. ii. 6.   ⁴ Plato, *Phaedo*, 109, D, E.
⁵ The surviving fragments of these studies (xii, 329 ff. Lommatzsch) do not include any
discussion of the city of God.
⁶ I John ii. 8; Gen. i. 6–8 (cf. vi, 49 above); Mal. iv. 2.
⁷ Dan. iv. 34.   ⁸ Read ἐπ' ἀληθινῶν with K. tr.   ⁹ Ps. ci. 26.

do not see the works of the Lord, and do not understand the works of his hands.'¹ So much, then, for this matter.

32. Celsus did not understand the doctrine of the resurrection, which is deep and hard to explain,² and needs a wise man of advanced skill more than any other doctrine in order to show that it is worthy of God and that the doctrine is a noble conception. It teaches that the tabernacle³ of the soul, as it is called in the Bible, possesses a seminal principle.⁴ And in this tabernacle those who are righteous groan, being weighed down, and desiring not to put it off but to be clothed on top of it.⁵ Celsus' failure to understand this is caused by the fact that he has heard about it from uneducated people who are incapable of supporting it by any argument at all, and so he mocks at the affirmation. It is worth adding to our previous remarks on this subject⁶ this one observation about the doctrine. We do not talk about the resurrection, as Celsus imagines, because we have *misunderstood the doctrine of reincarnation*, but because we know that when the soul, which in its own nature is incorporeal and invisible, is in any material place, it requires a body suited to the nature of that environment.⁷ In the first place, it bears this body after it has put off the former body which was necessary at first but which is now superfluous in its second state. In the second place, it puts a body on top of that which it possessed formerly, because it needs a better garment for the purer, ethereal, and heavenly regions. When it came to be born into this world, it put off the afterbirth, which was useful for its formation⁸ in the womb of the mother so long as it was within it; and underneath that it put on what was necessary for one that was about to live on earth.

Then again, since there is⁹ an earthly house of the tabernacle, which is somehow necessary to the tabernacle, the Bible says that the earthly house

¹ Isa. v. 12.   ² Cf. Heb. v. 11.   ³ II Cor. v. 4.
⁴ Origen's phrase (λόγον σπέρματος) is reminiscent of the Stoic *logos spermatikos*. Cf. my remarks in *H.T.R.* XLI (1948), at p. 101. I cannot agree with Bader that the phrase was used by Celsus.
⁵ II Cor. v. 4.   ⁶ Cf. II, 55–67; v, 18–20; 57–8.
⁷ Cf. Origen, ap. Method. *de Resurrectione* I, 22, 4–5 'For it is necessary for the soul that is existing in corporeal places to use bodies appropriate to those places. Just as if we became aquatic beings, and had to live in the sea, it would no doubt be necessary for us to adopt a different state similar to that of the fish, so if we are to inherit the kingdom of heaven and to exist in superior places, it is essential for us to use spiritual bodies. This does not mean that the form of the earlier body disappears, though it may change to a more glorious condition' (cf. on this *H.T.R. loc. cit.* p. 99).
⁸ Read κυούσης ⟨διάπλασιν⟩, with K. tr. For the idea, cf. Strabo, xv, 1, 59 (p. 713): 'The Brahmans have much conversation about death. They think that this life is like the period of the embryo in the womb, and that for students of philosophy death is a birth unto the true and happy life.' Similarly Seneca, *Ep.* CII, 23; M. Aurelius, IX, 3, 4; Porphyry, *ad Marcellam*, 32; Eusebius, *Theophaneia*, I, 72.
⁹ For the language here, cf. II Cor. v. 1 ff.

of the tabernacle is being dissolved, and that the tabernacle puts on 'a house not made with hands, eternal in the heavens'. The men of God say that 'that which is corruptible shall put on incorruptibility', which is different from that which is incorruptible, and that 'that which is mortal shall put on immortality',[1] which is not the same as that which is immortal. The relation of wisdom to that which is wise, of righteousness to that which is righteous, and of peace to that which is peaceable, is the same as that of incorruptibility to that which is incorruptible, and of immortality to that which is immortal. Notice, then, the character of the life set before us by the Bible, when it says that we shall put on incorruptibility and immortality which, like garments on the man who puts them on and is surrounded by these clothes, do not allow the person who wears them to suffer corruption or death. We have ventured to say this because he did not understand what we mean by resurrection, and for this reason ridiculed and laughed at a doctrine which he does not comprehend.

33. Thinking that we maintain the doctrine of the resurrection because we shall *know and see God*, he continues by inventing notions out of his own head; this is what he says: *When indeed they are shut in on all sides and their position has been refuted, as though they had not understood anything they return again to the same question:* '*How then are we to know and see God? And how shall we go to him?*'[2] Anyone interested should realize that we need a body for various purposes because we are in a material place, and so it needs to be of the same character as that of the nature of the material place, whatever that may be; and as we require a body, we put the qualities previously mentioned on top of the tabernacle. But in order to know God we need no body at all. The knowledge of God is not derived from the eye of the body, but from the mind which sees that which is in the image of the Creator and by divine providence has received the power to know God. And that which sees God is a pure heart, from which evil thoughts no longer proceed, nor murders, nor adulteries, nor fornications, nor thefts, nor false witnessings, nor blasphemies, nor an evil eye, nor any other evil deed.[3] That is why it is said: 'Blessed are the pure in heart, for they shall see God.'[4] However, since our will is not sufficiently strong for us to be entirely pure in heart, and because we need God to create it entirely pure, the man who prays with understanding says 'Create in me a clean heart, O God.'[5]

34. Moreover, we would not address a question to anyone as if God were in a place, saying *How shall we go to God?* God is superior to all place, and comprehends everything whatsoever; and there is nothing that

---

[1] I Cor. xv. 53.   [2] Cf. Celsus in VI, 66.   [3] Matt. xv. 9; Mark vii. 21-2.
[4] Matt. v. 8.   [5] Ps. l. 12.

contains God.[1] The command to go to God is not enjoined upon us in any corporeal sense in the words 'Walk after the Lord thy God.'[2] Nor does the prophet mean that he cleaved to God physically when he says in his prayer 'My soul cleaved after thee.'[3] Accordingly, Celsus is criticizing us on false grounds when he says that we *believe we shall see God with the eyes of the body and hear his voice with our ears and touch him with our sensible hands.*[4] We are aware that the divine scriptures speak of eyes which bear the same name as the eyes of the body, and similarly also of ears and hands; and, what is more remarkable than these, they speak of a divine sense which is different from that commonly so called by popular usage. When the prophet says 'Open thou mine eyes that I may comprehend thy wonders out of thy law', or 'The commandment of the Lord is luminous, enlightening the eyes', or 'Enlighten my eyes, lest I sleep the sleep of death',[5] no one is so idiotic as to suppose that the wonders of the divine law are comprehended with the eyes of the body, or that the commandment of the Lord enlightens the bodily eyes, or that a sleep which produces death comes upon the physical eyes.

Furthermore, when our Saviour says 'He that hath ears to hear let him hear',[6] even the unintelligent man understands that this refers to spiritual ears. If scripture says the word of the Lord was in the hand of Jeremiah the prophet, or of anyone else, or the law in the hand of Moses,[7] or that 'I sought the Lord with my hands and was not deceived',[8] no one is such a blockhead as to fail to grasp that there are some hands which are given that name with an allegorical meaning. Of these John also says: 'Our hands have handled the Word of life.'[9] And if you wish to learn from the sacred Scriptures about the superior and incorporeal sense, listen to Solomon's words in Proverbs, 'Thou shalt find a divine sense.'[10]

35. We have no need, then, as if we sought God in this way, to *go off* where Celsus would send us—*to Trophonius, Amphiaraus, and Mopsus, where* he says *gods are to be seen in human form and,* so Celsus informs us, *are not deceitful impostors, but true manifestations.*[11] For we possess the

---

[1] Cf. Philo, *de Somniis* 1, 62 'God is called place because he contains all things, but is contained by nothing whatever.' Similarly *Leg. Alleg.* 1, 44; *Sobr.* 63; *Migr. Abr.* 182; *Somn.* 1, 185; *Conf. Ling.* 136.

[2] Deut. xiv. 4.   [3] Ps. lxii. 9.

[4] Cf. Celsus in VI, 64; VII, 27. Read ἀκούσεσθαι with P[2], Bo., Wi., K. tr., Bader.

[5] Ps. cxviii. 18; xviii. 9; xii. 4.   [6] Matt. xi. 15; xiii. 9, etc.

[7] Jer. i. 4, 9; Num. xvi. 40.   [8] Ps. lxxvi. 3.

[9] I John i. 1.   [10] Prov. ii. 5; cf. I, 48 above.

[11] For the shrines of these heroes cf. Celsus in III, 34. For the reality of the appearances, Celsus in III, 24, VIII, 45. For such cultus at this date cf. Rohde, *Psyche* (E.T.), p. 567 n. 104 citing a third-century inscription from Lebadeia (*I.G.* VII, 3426). Also Rohde, *op. cit.* p. 104 n. 5, and especially p. 106 n. 13 where he remarks, 'When inquiries are made of a god by

knowledge that these are daemons who feed on burnt-offerings and blood and the odours of the sacrifices,[1] and who are held down in the prisons made by their lust. The Greeks have supposed these to be temples of the gods; but we know that places such as these are habitations of deceitful daemons.

After this Celsus in his wicked way says of the gods he has mentioned as possessing, in his opinion, *human form*, that *one may see them, not merely making a single appearance in a stealthy and secretive manner like the fellow who deceived the Christians, but continually having communion with any who so desire.* It seems from these words that he supposed Jesus to have been a phantom[2] when he appeared to his disciples after his resurrection from the dead, as though he had merely made an appearance to them in a stealthy and secretive manner; whereas he thinks that the gods whom he describes as possessing *human form* are *continually having communion with any who so desire.* But how could a phantom which, as he says, appeared stealthily and secretively to deceive those who saw it, have such a great effect even after the actual moment of the vision had passed, and convert the souls of so many men[3] and implant in them a conviction that they ought to do every action in a way pleasing to God because they will be judged by Him? And how could a so-called phantom expel daemons and bring about other effects of considerable significance? For he has not been assigned to any particular place like Celsus' gods who possess human form, but goes throughout all the world and collects and draws by his divinity any whom he finds to be inclined towards living the good life.

36. After these remarks, to which we have made the best reply we can, Celsus again speaks as follows: *Again, too, they will say: 'How are they to know God unless they lay hold of him by sense-perception? How is it possible to have any knowledge except by sense-perception?'*[4] He then gives an answer to this question, saying: *This utterance is not that of a man or of the soul, but of the flesh. Nevertheless let them listen to me, if so cowardly and carnal a race are able to understand anything. If you shut your eyes to the world of sense and look up with the mind, if you turn away from the flesh and raise the eyes of the soul, only so will you see God. And if you look for some one to lead you along this path, you must flee from the deceivers and sorcerers who court*

Incubation the god must always appear in person; if he is absent no oracle can be given....
In the records of miracles of healing found in Epidauros the god himself regularly comes to the sleeper in the *adyton*....' Discussion by K. Latte, in P.-W. *s.v.* 'Orakel', xviii, 1 (1939), 833–5.   [1] Cf. iii, 38.
[2] Cf. Celsus in ii, 70; iii, 22.   [3] Read τῶν τοσούτων with K. tr.
[4] Cf. Celsus in vi, 66; vii, 33. For his objection to the Christian estimate of the body and of matter, cf. v, 14; vii, 42, 45; viii, 49.

phantoms. For you make yourselves a laughing-stock in the eyes of everybody when you blasphemously assert that the other gods who are made manifest are phantoms,[1] while you worship a man who is more wretched than even what really are phantoms, and who is not even any longer a phantom, but is in fact dead;[2] and when you look for a father like him.

The first point I have to make in reply to the words which he puts into our mouth, attributing to us statements purporting to be what we say in defence of the resurrection of the flesh, is that it is a virtue in a writer who puts words into the mouth of someone else to preserve consistency in the meaning and character of the person to whom the words are attributed; and it is a fault when anyone attributes to the mouth of the speaker words which are inappropriate. Equally blameworthy are those who, in putting words into the mouth of a person, attribute philosophy which the author has learnt to barbarians and illiterate people or slaves, who have never heard philosophical arguments and have never given a proper account of them. It is unlikely that the person to whom the ideas are attributed would have known them. And, on the other hand, those people are also blameworthy who attribute to persons assumed to be wise, and who have had knowledge of the things of God, statements such as are made by illiterate folk moved by vulgar passions, and assertions resulting from ignorance. This is the reason why Homer is admired by many. He keeps the characters of the heroes the same as they were when he started, such as that of Nestor, or Odysseus, or Diomedes, or Agamemnon, or Telemachus, or Penelope, or one of the others.[3] But Euripides is made a fool of by Aristophanes for writing inappropriate verses, because he often attributed to barbarian women or slave-girls words containing ideas which he had learnt from Anaxagoras or some other wise man.[4]

37. If this is a correct account of what is right and what is wrong in the art of attributing words to a person, would not one have good reason to laugh at Celsus when he attributes to Christians statements which they do not make? If he was inventing ideas supposed to be held by the common people, how can such folk distinguish sense-perception from the mind and sensible things from intelligible? Are we to suppose that they formulate their doctrines like the Stoics who deny the existence of intelligible realities, and say that the things of which we have comprehension are

[1] *Eidōlon* is commonly used in ordinary Greek usage to mean 'phantom', but it is used in the Septuagint and the New Testament to mean 'idol'. Cf. Büchsel in Kittel, *Theol. Wörterbuch z. N.T. s.v.*   [2] Cf. Celsus in VII, 68.
[3] Cf. Theon, *Progymn.* 1 (Walz, *Rh. Gr.* i, 148–9): 'We praise Homer for putting appropriate words into the mouth of each of his characters, but we find fault with Euripides because he unsuitably makes Hecuba discuss philosophy.'
[4] Aristophanes, *Acharnians*, 393 ff. For Anaxagoras, cf. IV, 77 above.

comprehended by the senses and that all comprehension is based on sense-perception?[1] If, on the other hand, he was inventing statements supposed to be made by those who interpret the doctrines of Christ philosophically and do all in their power to study them carefully, he has not made the words appropriate to them either. No one who has learnt that God is invisible and that there are certain invisible, that is, intelligible creations, would say in order to defend the resurrection, *How are they to know God unless they lay hold of him by sense-perception? Or How is it possible to have any knowledge except by sense-perception?* It is written, not in recondite writings which are read only by a few scholars, but in popular literature that 'the invisible things of God are clearly seen from the creation of the world, being understood by the things that are made'.[2] By this we may know that even though men in this life have to begin from the senses and from sensible things when they intend to ascend to the nature of intelligible things, yet they must on no account remain content with sensible things. Nor would they say that it is impossible to have any knowledge of intelligible things except by sense-perception. And if they were to ask the question 'Who is able to have knowledge without sense-perception?' yet they would prove that there is no good reason for Celsus' further addition: *This utterance is not that of a man or of the soul, but of the flesh.*

38. Since we affirm that the God of the universe is mind, or that He transcends mind and being,[3] and is simple and invisible and incorporeal, we would maintain that God is not comprehended by any being other than him made in the image of that mind. To quote the words of Paul, we comprehend Him 'through a glass and in a riddle, but then face to face'.[4] And if I say 'face', let no one base upon the word a false charge against the meaning indicated by this word. Let him learn from the words 'with unveiled face reflecting as in a glass the glory of the Lord and being transformed into the same image from glory to glory',[5] that it is not a sensible face to which these words refer, but one which is understood by allegorical interpretation, just as eyes, and ears, and all the other things which, as we have shown above, bear the same name as parts of the body.[6]

A *man*, that is a soul using a body,[7] the soul being called 'the inner man',[8] and a *soul* also, would never make the reply which Celsus has written, but that which the man of God himself teaches. And no Christian would

---

[1] Cf. *S.V.F.* II, 105–21. Against the Sceptics who denied the possibility of certain knowledge, the Stoics affirmed that reality was material, that sense-perception was the source of all knowledge, and that the criterion of knowledge was the καταληπτικὴ φαντασία, an impression on the mind the validity of which was not open to doubt. Cf. I, 42.

[2] Rom. i. 20. [3] Plato, *Rep.* 509 B; cf. VI, 64 above.

[4] I Cor. xiii. 12. [5] II Cor. iii. 18. [6] Cf. VI, 61–2; VII, 34.

[7] A standard definition—e.g. Origen, *de Princ.* IV, 2, 7 (14); Julian, *Or.* VI, 183 B.

[8] Rom. vii. 22; II Cor. iv. 16; Eph. iii. 16.

speak an *utterance of the flesh,* since he has learnt to mortify by the Spirit the deeds of the body and to bear about always the dying of Jesus,[1] and has the command: 'Mortify your members that are upon earth.'[2] He knows what is meant by the saying: 'My Spirit shall not abide among these men for ever because they are flesh.'[3] He is aware also that 'those who are in the flesh cannot please God',[4] and on this account does all in his power in order that he may be in the flesh no longer, but in the spirit alone.

39. Let us also see what it is to which he invites us that we may hear from him how we are to know God. He thinks here that no Christian could understand his words; for he says: *Nevertheless let them listen to me, if they are able to understand anything.* We must understand then what words of his he, the philosopher, wants us to listen to. He ought to be teaching us; but he pours abuse on us. He ought to have shown his good-will towards his hearers at the beginning of his arguments; but he says that those who would go to death rather than renounce Christianity even by a word, and who are prepared for any outrage and any kind of death, are *a cowardly race.* He asserts that we are also *a carnal race,* though we affirm that 'even if we have known Christ after the flesh, now we know him so no longer'.[5] We put the body aside so lightly for the sake of religion that a philosopher would not more easily take off his garment.

Accordingly, he says to us: *If you shut your eyes to the world of sense and look up with the mind, if you turn away from the flesh and raise the eye of the soul, only so will you see God.* He imagines that the idea (that of the two eyes, I mean) which he took from the Greeks[6] had not previously been thought of by us. We may point out that in Moses' description of the making of the world he introduces man sometimes as seeing before his transgression and sometimes as not seeing. He is described as seeing in the words about the woman: 'The woman saw that the tree was good for food, and that it was pleasing for the eyes to look upon and beautiful to lay hold of.'[7] But the man is represented as not seeing, not only in the words of the serpent to the woman which imply that their eyes were blind —'For God knew that in the day that you ate of it, your eyes would be opened'—but also in the words: 'They ate, and the eyes of both of them were opened.'[8] Their eyes which were opened were those of the

---

[1] Rom. viii. 13; II Cor. iv. 10.   [2] Col. iii. 5.   [3] Gen. vi. 3.
[4] Rom. viii. 8.   [5] II Cor. v. 16.
[6] Cf. Plato, *Symp.* 219A; *Soph.* 254A; *Rep.* 519B, 533D; *Phaedo,* 99E.
[7] Gen. iii. 6.
[8] Gen. iii. 6–7. For the idea cf. Philo, *Quaest. in Genes.* I, 39 'That they [Adam and Eve] were not created blind is manifest from this fact, that as all other things, both animals and plants, were created in perfection, so also man must have been adorned with the things which are his most excellent parts, namely, eyes. And we may especially prove this, because a little

426

senses, which they rightly shut that they might not be distracted or
hindered from seeing with the eye of the soul. But it was the eyes of
the soul, with which for a time they saw while they rejoiced in God and
His paradise, which they closed, I think, because of their sin.

That is also the reason why our Saviour, knowing that these two kinds
of eyes belong to us, says, 'For judgment came I into this world, that
those who do not see may see and that those who see may become blind.'[1]
By those who do not see he is obscurely referring to the eyes of the soul,
to which the Logos gives the power of sight, and by those who see he
means the eyes of the senses. For the Logos blinds the latter, that the soul
may see without any distraction that which it ought to see. Therefore, the
eye of the soul of any genuine Christian is awake and that of the senses is
closed. And in proportion to the degree in which the superior eye is
awake and the sight of the senses is closed, the supreme God and His Son,
who is the Logos and Wisdom and the other titles, are comprehended and
seen by each man.

40. After the passage we have examined, Celsus, as though addressing
all Christians, puts forward an argument which, if used at all, might be
appropriately addressed only to those who confess that they are entirely
alien to the teaching of Jesus. For those who *court phantoms, deceivers,
and sorcerers,* are the Ophites who, as we remarked earlier,[2] deny Jesus
altogether, or any others who hold opinions similar to theirs. And it is
they who have *wretchedly learnt by heart the names of the doorkeepers.* It is
therefore futile for him to say to Christians: *And if you look for some one to
lead you along this path, you must flee from deceivers and sorcerers, who
court phantoms.* Not realizing that, because they are sorcerers, such
people agree with him and malign Jesus and all his religion no less than
he does, he confuses us with them in his argument, saying: *You make
yourselves a laughing-stock in the eyes of everybody when you blasphemously
assert that the other gods who are made manifest are phantoms, while you
worship a man who is more wretched even than what really are phantoms, and
who is not even any longer a phantom, but is in fact dead; and when you look
for a father like him.*

That Celsus does not know what is said by the Christians and what by
the inventors of such fables, but believes that the objections which he
brings against them apply to us, and that he says things to us which have

while before the earth-born Adam was giving names to all the animals on the earth. Therefore it is perfectly plain that he saw them before doing so. Unless, indeed, Moses used the
expression "eyes" in a figurative sense for the vision of the soul, by which alone the
perception of good and evil, of what is elegant or unsightly, and, in fact, of all contrary
natures, arises' (trans. Yonge). *Clem. Hom.* III, 39.

[1] John ix. 39.   [2] VI, 28.

nothing to do with us, is clear from the following remarks: *It is because of* [1] *such gross deceit and those wonderful counsellors and the miraculous words addressed to the lion and the animal with double form and the one shaped like an ass and the other superhuman doorkeepers, whose names you poor unfortunates have wretchedly learnt by heart so that terrible madness has taken hold of you,. . .* [2] *that you are crucified.* He did not see that none of those who think that the lion-like and the ass-like and the double-formed archons are doorkeepers on the path upwards, stand firm to the point of death even for the truth as they regard it. But what we do to excess, if I may so say, for religion, in giving ourselves up to any kind of death and the suffering of crucifixion, he applies to those who suffer none of these things. And he reproaches us, who are crucified for religion, with their fables about the lion-like archon and the one with the double form and the rest. However, it is not on account of Celsus' criticisms that we avoid the doctrine about the lion-like archon and the rest. For we have never even held anything of the sort. We follow the teaching of Jesus and say the opposite to them, and do not agree that Michael has a face of one sort, and some other of those previously mentioned a face of a different sort.

41. We have also to consider who it is whom Celsus would have us *follow* so that we may not be at a loss to find ancient leaders and holy men. He refers us to *inspired poets*, as he calls them, *and wise men and philosophers* [3] without giving their names; and although he promises to show us the *guides*, he points to the inspired poets and wise men and philosophers without stating precisely whom he means. If he had given the names of each one of them, it might have seemed reasonable for us to contend that he is giving us as guides men who are blinded about the truth, with the consequence that we shall fall into error, or who, if they are not entirely blind, yet at any rate are wrong about many doctrines of the truth. Whoever he means by an *inspired poet*, whether Orpheus, or Parmenides, or Empedocles, or even Homer himself, or Hesiod, let anyone who likes show how those who use such guides travel a better road, and receive more help for the problems of life than people who, through the teaching of Jesus Christ, have abandoned all images and statues and, what is more, all Jewish superstition, and through the Logos of God look up to God alone, the Father of the Logos. And who also are the *wise men and*

---

[1] Reading ⟨διὰ⟩ τὴν μὲν with Sp., K. tr., Bader. The emendation is far from certain; but it seems the simplest solution of a difficult problem. Also with We. bracket καὶ τοὺς (191, 7). For the doorkeepers, cf. VI, 30–1.

[2] K. tr. is probably right in marking a lacuna here; he proposes δαιμονᾶτε, ⟨ἀπάγεσθε⟩ καὶ ἀνασκολοπίζεσθε, comparing Celsus in VIII, 39. The lacuna, however, is probably greater than this.

[3] For Celsus' appeal to the authority of ancient poets and philosophers, cf. Introduction, p. xvi.

philosophers from whom Celsus would have us *hear many divine truths?* For
he would have us leave Moses, God's servant, and the prophets of the
Creator of the universe, though they uttered countless prophecies by
genuine inspiration, and him who enlightened mankind and proclaimed
a way to worship God, and, as far as he was able, left no one without some
experience of his mysteries. On the contrary, because of his exceeding
love towards man he was able to give the educated a conception of God
which could raise their soul from earthly things, and nevertheless came
down to the level even of the more defective capacities of ordinary men
and simple women and slaves, and, in general, of people who have been
helped by none but by Jesus alone to live a better life, so far as they can,
and to accept doctrines about God such as they had the capacity to receive.

42. Then after this he refers us to *Plato* as *a more effective teacher
of the problems of theology,* quoting his words from the Timaeus as follows:
'*Now to find the Maker and Father of this universe is difficult, and after
finding him it is impossible to declare him to all men.*'[1] Then he adds to
this: *You see how the way of truth is sought by seers and philosophers,*[2] *and
how Plato knew that it is impossible for all men to travel it. Since this is
the reason why wise men have discovered it, that we might get some conception of the nameless*[3] *First Being which manifests him either by synthesis
with other things, or by analytical distinction from them, or by analogy,*[4]

---

[1] Plato, *Timaeus,* 28C; perhaps the most hackneyed quotation from Plato in Hellenistic
writers. A formidable (though not complete) list of references is given by Geffcken,
Zwei griech. Apologeten, pp. 174 f.
[2] Read with K. tr. καὶ ⟨φιλοσόφοις⟩ ἀληθείας.
[3] For the namelessness of God, cf. Celsus in VI, 65.
[4] For Celsus' view that God is knowable by synthesis, analysis, and analogy, compare
the Middle Platonist Albinus, *Epit.* x, 5–6 'We shall achieve the first idea of God by making
successive abstractions, just as we get the conception of a point by abstraction from what
is sensible, removing first the idea of surface, then that of line, till finally we have a point.
A second way of obtaining an idea of God is that of analogy, as follows: the relation which
the sun has to sight and to visible things is that, while not itself sight, it makes it possible
for the sight to see and for visible things to be seen. The same relation exists between the
first mind and the mind of the soul and the intelligible objects. It is not identical with the
mind of the soul but makes it possible for that mind to conceive and for the intelligible
things to be conceived, throwing light upon the truth concerning them. (Cf. Plato, *Rep.*
508B.) The third way of achieving an idea of God is this. One contemplates the beauty
of physical objects; after this one passes on to the beauty of the soul, from there to the
beauty of customs and laws, and so on to the vast ocean of the beautiful. After this one
conceives the good and the lovable and the desirable like a shining light which, as it were,
illumines the soul which is thus ascending. And God is comprehended together with the
good because of its superior excellence.' (Cf. *Symp.* 208E; *Ep.* VII, 341C–D.) See on this
R. E. Witt, *Albinus and the history of Middle Platonism* (1937), pp. 132 f.
For the method of analysis cf. Clem. Al. *Strom.* v, 11, 71 'We shall understand the method
of purification by confession, and the visionary method by analysis, attaining to the primary
intelligence by analysis, beginning at its basic principles. We take away from the body its
natural qualities, removing the dimension of height, and then that of breadth and then that

I would like[1] to teach about that which is otherwise indescribable. But I would be amazed if you were able to follow, as you are completely bound to the flesh and see nothing pure.[2]

I admit that Plato's statement which he quotes is noble and impressive. But consider whether there is not more regard for the needs of mankind when the divine word introduces the divine Logos, who was in the beginning with God, as becoming flesh,[3] that the Logos, of whom Plato says that after finding him it is impossible to declare him to all men, might be able to reach anybody. Plato may say that it is difficult to find the maker and father of this universe, indicating that it is not[4] impossible for human nature to find God in a degree worthy of Him, or, if not worthy of Him, yet at least in a degree higher than that of the multitude. If this were true, and God really had been found by Plato or one of the Greeks, they would not have reverenced anything else and called it God and worshipped it, either abandoning the true God or combining with the majesty of God things which ought not to be associated with Him. But we affirm that human nature is not sufficient in any way to seek for God and to find Him in His pure nature, unless it is helped by the God who is object of the search. And He is found by those who, after doing what they can,[5] admit that they need Him, and shows Himself to those to whom He

of length. The point that remains is a unit, as it were, having position; if we take away position, we have the concept of Monad. If then we take away everything concerned with bodies and the things called incorporeal, and cast ourselves into the greatness of Christ, and so advance into the immeasurable by holiness, we might perhaps attain to the conception of the Almighty, since we know not what he is but what he is not. For form and movement, standing, a throne, right hand or left hand, are certainly not to be predicated of the Father of the universe, even if it is written in the Bible.'

The emotional and mystical colouring, absent in Celsus and Albinus, is felt in Plotinus, VI, 7, 36 'Knowledge of The Good or contact with it, is the all-important: this—we read—is the grand learning, the learning we are to understand, not of looking towards it but attaining, first, some knowledge of it. We come to this learning by analogies, by abstractions, by our understanding of its subsequents, of all that is derived from The Good, by the upward steps towards it. Purification has The Good for goal; so the virtues, all right ordering, ascent within the Intellectual, settlement therein, banqueting upon the divine— by these methods one becomes, to self and to all else, at once seen and seer; identical with Being and Intellectual-Principle and the entire living all, we no longer see the Supreme as an external; we are near now, the next is That and it is close at hand, radiant above the Intellectual. Here, we put aside all the learning; disciplined to this pitch, established in beauty, the quester holds knowledge still of the ground he rests on but, suddenly, swept beyond it all by the very crest of the wave of Intellect surging beneath, he is lifted and sees, never knowing how . . . .' (trans. Mackenna-Page.) Cf. also Maximus Tyrius, XI, 8 (Hobein, pp. 138 f.); Sextus Emp. *adv. Math.* IX, 394–5.

[1] Read with K. tr. θέλω ⟨μέ⟩ν.   [2] Cf. Celsus in VII, 36.
[3] John i. 1–2, 14.
[4] Read ⟨οὐκ⟩ ἀδύνατον with Bo., K. tr.
[5] For the phrase, cf. IV, 50 (323, 9). Here Wendland proposes μετὰ τὸ ⟨πάντα⟩ παρ' αὐτοὺς ποιεῖν, Wifstrand μετὰ τὸ ⟨πᾶν τὸ⟩ κτλ.

judges it right to appear, so far as it is possible for God to be known to man and for the human soul which is still in the body to know God.

43. Moreover, when Plato says that it is impossible for the man who has found the maker and father of the universe to declare him to all, he does not say that he is *indescribable* and *nameless*, but that although he can be described it is only possible to declare him to a few. It is as though Celsus had forgotten the words of Plato which he quoted when he says that God is nameless, as follows: *Since this is the reason why wise men have discovered it, that we might get some conception of the nameless First Being.* But we affirm that it is not only God who is nameless, but that there are also others among the beings inferior to Him. Paul is striving to indicate this when he says that he 'heard unspeakable words which it is not lawful for man to utter',[1] where he is using the word 'heard' in the sense of 'understood' as in the phrase 'He that hath ears to hear let him hear.'[2]

We certainly maintain that it is difficult to see the Maker and Father of the universe. But He is seen, not only in the way implied in the words, 'Blessed are the pure in heart, for they shall see God',[3] but also in the way implied in the saying of the Image of the invisible God that 'He who has seen me has seen the Father who sent me'.[4] In these words no one of any intelligence would say that Jesus was here referring to his sensible body which was visible to men, when he said, 'He who has seen me has seen the Father who sent me.' For in that event God the Father would have been seen even by all those who said, 'Crucify him, crucify him', and by Pilate who received power[5] over his human nature, which is absurd. That the words, 'He who has seen me has seen the Father who sent me', refer not to the ordinary meaning is obvious from the words he said to Philip: 'Have I been such a long time with you without your having known me, Philip?' He said this to him when he asked: 'Show us the Father, and it is enough for us.'[6] Anyone, therefore, who has understood how we must think of the only begotten God, the Son of God, the firstborn of all creation, and how that the Logos became flesh,[7] will see that anyone will come to know the Father and Maker of this universe by looking at the image of the invisible God.

44. Celsus thinks that God is known *either by synthesis with other things*, similar to the method called synthesis by geometricians, *or by analytical distinction* from other things, *or also by analogy*, like the method of analogy used by the same students, as if one were able to come in this

---

[1] II Cor. xii. 4.
[2] Matt. xi. 15; xiii. 9.
[3] Matt. v. 8.
[4] John xiv. 9; cf. Col. i. 15.
[5] Luke xxiii. 21; John xix. 10.
[6] John xiv. 8–9.
[7] Col. i. 15; John i. 14.

way, if at all, 'to the threshold of the Good'.[1] But when the Logos of God
says that 'No man has known the Father except the Son, and the man to
whom the Son may reveal him',[2] he indicates that God is known by a certain
divine grace, which does not come about in the soul without God's action,
but with a sort of inspiration. Moreover, it is probable that the knowledge
of God is beyond the capacity of human nature (that is why there are such
great errors about God among men), but that by God's kindness and love
to man and by a miraculous divine grace the knowledge of God extends
to those who by God's foreknowledge have been previously determined,
because they would live lives worthy of Him after He was made known
to them. Such people in no way *debase their religious piety*[3] towards Him,
neither if they are led away to death by people who have no notion what
piety is, and make out that piety is anything other than that which it
really is, nor if they are thought to be *a laughing-stock*.[4]

I believe that because God saw the arrogance or the disdainful attitude
towards others of people who pride themselves on having known God
and learnt the divine truths from philosophy, and yet like the most vulgar
keep on with the images and their temples and the mysteries which are
a matter of common gossip, He chose the foolish things of the world, the
simplest of the Christians, who live lives more moderate and pure than
many philosophers, that He might put to shame the wise,[5] who are not
ashamed to talk to lifeless things as if they were gods or images of gods.

What intelligent person would not laugh at a man who, after studying
in philosophy the profoundest doctrines about God or gods, turns his
eyes to images and either prays to them or, by means of the sight of these
images, offers his prayer, indeed, to the God who is known spiritually,
imagining that he must ascend to Him from that which is visible and
external? Even an uneducated Christian is convinced that every place in
the world is a part of the whole, since the whole world is a temple of God;
and he prays in any place,[6] and by shutting the eyes of sense and raising
those of the soul[7] he ascends beyond the entire world. He does not stop
even at the vault of heaven, but comes in mind to the super-celestial
region,[8] being guided by the Divine Spirit, and being as it were outside
the world he sends up his prayer to God. His prayer is not concerned with
any everyday matters; for he has learnt from Jesus to seek for nothing

---

[1] Quoted from Plato, *Philebus*, 64C; similarly Clem. Al. *Strom.* VII, 45, 3.
[2] Matt. xi. 27; Luke x. 22.   [3] Celsus in v, 52.
[4] Celsus in VII, 36.   [5] I Cor. i. 27.
[6] I Tim. ii. 8. For the commonplace that prayer may be offered anywhere and not only
in temples, cf. Origen, *de Orat.* XXXI, 4; Clem. Al. *Strom.* VII, 43, 1; Lucian, *Demonax*, 27;
Alexander of Aphrodisias, *de Fato*, 1.
[7] Celsus in VII, 36.   [8] Allusion to Plato, *Phaedrus*, 247A–C.

small,[1] that is, sensible, but only for things that are great and truly divine which, as God's gifts, help in the journey to the blessedness with Him attained through the mediation of His Son who is the Logos of God.

45. Let us also see what he says he *will teach* us if we are *able to understand* it, where he says that we are *completely bound to the flesh*—we who, if we live aright and in accordance with Jesus' teaching, hear the saying 'You are not in the flesh but in the spirit if the Spirit of God dwells in you.'[2] He also says that we *see nothing pure*, though we try to avoid being defiled by the lusts of evil even in our thoughts, and say in our prayer 'Create in me a clean heart, O God, and renew a right spirit within my being',[3] in order that we may see God with a pure heart which alone has the power to see Him.[4]

This is what he says: *Being and becoming are, respectively, intelligible and visible. Truth is associated with being, error with becoming. Knowledge concerns truth, opinion the other. Thought is concerned with what is intelligible, and sight with what is visible.*[5] *For Mind knows that which is intelligible, the eye that which is visible. Accordingly, what the sun is to visible things, being neither the eye nor sight, but the cause of the eye's vision and of the existence of sight and of the possibility of seeing visible things, which is the cause of all sensible things becoming, and is in fact itself the thing which enables itself to be seen, this is what God is to intelligible things.*[6] *He is neither mind nor intelligence nor knowledge, but enables the mind to think and is the cause of the existence of intelligence and of the possibility of knowledge, and causes the existence of all intelligible things and of truth itself and of being itself, since he transcends all things and is intelligible by a certain indescribable power.*

These doctrines I have set forth for men of intelligence. If you understand any of them, you are doing well. And if you think that some spirit came down from God to foretell the divine truths, this may be the spirit which declares these doctrines. Indeed, it was because men of ancient times were touched by this spirit that they proclaimed many excellent doctrines. If you are unable to understand them, keep quiet and conceal your own lack of education, and do not say that those who see are blind and those who run are lame, when you yourselves are entirely lamed and mutilated in your souls and live for the body which is a dead thing.

---

[1] Origen is quoting a saying not found in the N.T. Cf. also *de Orat.* II, 2; XIV, 1; Clem. Al. *Strom.* I, 158, 3; IV, 34, 6. Allusions are collected by A. Resch, *Agrapha* (*T.U.* V, 4, 1889), p. 114. Discussion of authenticity in J. H. Ropes, *Die Sprüche Jesu* (*T.U.* XIV, 2, 1896), p. 140.

[2] Rom. viii. 9.   [3] Ps. l. 12.   [4] Matt. v. 8.

[5] Plato, *Rep.* 534 A; *Timaeus*, 29 C.

[6] Plato, *Rep.* 508 B; cf. Albinus, *Epit.* 10, quoted above on VII, 42; Philo, *de Praem. et Poen.* 45; Plotinus, V, 3, 17; Sallustius, *de Diis* 8 (Nock, p. 14, 21).

46. We are careful not to raise objections to any good teachings, even if their authors are outside the faith, nor to seek an occasion for a dispute with them, nor to find a way of overthrowing statements which are sound. This, then, is our reply. People who pour abuse on those who wish to do all in their power to live a life of piety towards the God of the universe, who approves the faith of common folk in Him and the rational piety towards Him of more intelligent people who send up their prayers to the Creator of the universe with thanksgiving, an offering of prayer which they make as by the mediation of a high priest[1] who has shown to men the pure way to worship God; and people who call them *lamed and mutilated in their souls*, and assert that they *live for the body which is a dead thing*, in spite of the fact that they say with conviction 'For though we live in the flesh, we do not fight according to the flesh, for the weapons of our warfare are not carnal but mighty through God':[2] such people should see to it that, when they speak evil in this very way of men who pray that they may belong to God, they do not make their own souls lame and mutilate their own inner man. By their malignant words against others who wish to live good lives, they mutilate the reasonableness and tranquillity of spirit which has been naturally implanted in the rational nature by the Creator. It is those who among other things have learnt from the divine scriptures (a command which they also put into practice) that they should bless when they are reviled and endure when persecuted and entreat when defamed,[3] who have ordered correctly the steps of their lives and who purify and restore their soul entirely. It is not merely a matter of theory when they distinguish between being and becoming and between what is intelligible and what is visible, and when they associate truth with being and by all possible means avoid the error that is bound up with becoming. They look, as they have learnt, not at the things which are becoming, which are seen and on that account temporal, but at the higher things, whether one wishes to call them 'being', or things 'invisible' because they are intelligible, or 'things which are not seen'[4] because their nature lies outside the realm of sense-perception.

It is in this way also that the disciples of Jesus look at the things that are becoming, so that they use them as steps to the contemplation of the nature of intelligible things. 'For the invisible things of God', that is, the intelligible things, 'are understood by the things that are made' and 'from the creation of the world are clearly seen' by the process of thought. And when they have ascended from the created things of the world to the invisible things of God they do not stop there. But after exercising their

[1] Cf. Heb. ii. 17, etc.   [2] II Cor. x. 3-4.
[3] I Cor. iv. 12-13.   [4] II Cor. iv. 18.

minds sufficiently among them and understanding them, they ascend to
the eternal power of God, and, in a word, to His Divinity. They know
that out of love to man God manifested the truth and that which may be
known of Himself, not only to those who are devoted to Him, but also
to some ignorant of pure worship and piety towards Him. But some of
those who by God's providence have ascended to the knowledge of such
profound truths do not behave worthily of the knowledge, and are impious,
and hold down the truth in unrighteousness. And because of their knowledge of these profound truths, they are not able to have any further
opportunity for an excuse before God.[1]

47. At any rate, the divine scripture testifies of those who have
comprehended the ideas of which Celsus gives an account, and who
profess to think philosophically in accordance with these doctrines,
saying that 'although they knew God, they did not glorify him as God,
neither were they thankful, but they became vain in their reasonings', and
after the great light of the knowledge of the ideas which God manifested
to them their heart quickly became foolish and was darkened.[2]

And it is possible to see how those who assert that they are wise exhibit
examples of crass stupidity. For after learning in the philosophical schools
the great doctrines about God and the intelligible things 'they changed
the glory of the incorruptible God for the likeness of an image of corruptible man, and of birds, and fourfooted beasts, and creeping things'. This
is the reason why they were forsaken by providence. They have not lived
worthily of the truths manifested to them by God, and wallow in the lusts
of their hearts to impurity, and their bodies are dishonoured by disgraceful
and licentious behaviour, because 'they changed the truth of God into
a lie and worshipped and served the creature rather than the Creator'.[3]

48. Those who are held of no account by them for their lack of education and are said to be fools and slaves, even if they entrust themselves only
to God and accept the teaching of Jesus, are so far from licentiousness and
any disgraceful sexual immorality that, just like perfect priests who have
turned away from all sexual experience, many of them remain entirely
pure, not merely in respect of sexual intercourse.[4] There is one hierophant,
I believe, among the Athenians, who not trusting his ability to be master
of his male desires and to overcome them by force of will, drugs his male
parts with hemlock and is thought to be pure for the ritual customary

---

[1] Rom. i. 18–20.   [2] Rom. i. 21.   [3] Rom. i. 22–5.
[4] Cf. the well-known testimony of Galen (I quote the translation of R. Walzer, *Galen on
Jews and Christians* (1949), p. 15): The Christians 'include not only men but also women
who refrain from cohabiting all through their lives; and they also number individuals who,
in self-discipline and self-control in matters of food and drink, and in their keen pursuit of
justice, have attained a pitch not inferior to that of genuine philosophers'.

among the Athenians.¹ But among Christians it is possible to see men who
do not need hemlock to worship God in purity; for them not hemlock but
a word is sufficient to drive out all lust from their mind as they worship
God with prayers. In the case of other supposed gods there are a very
small number of virgins (whether they are put under restraint by men or
not it is not my object to discuss now) who seem to continue in chastity
for the worship offered to the deity.² But among Christians they practise
complete virginity, not for honours among men, nor for reward or money
or for the slightest reputation. And as 'they have thought fit to retain God
in their knowledge' they are preserved by God with an approved mind,
even because they do that which is right, being filled with all righteousness
and goodness.³

49. I have not said this in a spirit of captious criticism of the fine ideas
of the Greeks, nor in order to object to sound doctrines, but from a desire
to show that these things, and others yet more profound and divine than
these, have been said by the *divinely inspired men,*⁴ God's prophets and
Jesus' apostles, and that they are studied by those who desire to be more
perfect Christians, who know that 'the mouth of a righteous man will take
care for wisdom, and his tongue will speak judgment; the law of God is in
his heart'.⁵ But even in the case of those to whom these things are not
clear whether on account of their serious lack of education, or because of

¹ For this use of hemlock, cf. Dioscorides, *de Materia medica*, IV, 78 (Wellmann, II, 240);
Pliny, *N.H.* xxv, 154. Origen has in mind the ritual of the Eleusinian mysteries, for his
knowledge of which he may have been directly indebted to Hippolytus, *Ref.* v, 8, 40
'...the hierophant himself is not castrated like Attis, but is rendered a eunuch by means
of hemlock and is separated from all carnal generation'. That castration was forbidden at
Athens appears from the *Etymologicum Magnum s.v.* ἀφελής: 'Among the Athenians none
was to be deprived of any part of his body, but was to be whole.' Servius (*ad Aen.* vi, 661)
remarks that priests 'used to be emasculated with certain herbs with the result that they
were no longer able to have sexual intercourse'. Also Julian, *Or.* v, 173C-D 'As in the
festival of the Mother the instrument of generation is severed, so too with the Athenians
those who take part in the secret rites are wholly chaste and their leader the hierophant
forswears generation' (trans. W. C. Wright); Jerome, *Ep.* cxxiii, 7 'hierophanta apud
Athenas eiurat virum et aeterna debilitate fit castus'. In *adv. Jovin.* I, 49 Jerome tells us that
the practice was still current in his own time: 'hierophantas quoque Atheniensium usque
hodie cicutae forbitione castrari, et postquam in pontificatum fuerint allecti, viros esse
desinere.' For a modern medical opinion concerning the effectiveness of hemlock in this
connexion see J. G. Frazer, *The Golden Bough* (3rd ed.), *The Magic Art*, II, p. 139 n. 1.
² Cf. Philo, *de Vita Contemplativa* 68 (of a feast of the Therapeutae): 'The feast is shared
by women also, most of them aged virgins, who have kept their chastity not under compulsion, like some of the Greek priestesses, but of their own free will in their ardent yearning
for wisdom' (trans. F. H. Colson). Prudentius comments similarly on the virtue of the
Vestal virgins (*c. Symm.* II, 1064 ff.); Ambrose (*Ep.* xviii, 11 f.) says they only preserve
their virginity for monetary reward. For the comparison of Christian and pagan virginity
cf. Tertullian, *Exh. Cast.* 13; *Monog.* 17. For Christian virgins cf. I, 26 above; Justin,
Apol. I, 15; Athenagoras, *Leg.* 33; Tertullian, *Apol.* IX, 19.
³ Rom. i. 28-9.   ⁴ Celsus in vii, 28, 58.   ⁵ Ps. xxxvi. 30-1.

their simplicity, or even by reason of the fact that they have had no one to encourage them towards a rational piety, because they believe the supreme God and His only-begotten Son who is Logos and God, you would find among them a reverence[1] and purity and unsophisticated habits and a simplicity which is often excellent, and which has not been attained by those who assert that they are wise and wallow in immorality with boys, 'men performing obscenities with men'.[2]

50. He did not make clear how *error is associated with becoming*, nor did he show what he meant that we might understand and compare his ideas with ours. But the prophets, giving obscure expression to some wise doctrine on the subject of becoming, say that a sacrifice for sin is to be offered even for new-born babes because they are not pure from sin.[3] They also say 'I was conceived in iniquity and in sins my mother bore me.' Moreover, they declare that 'sinners have been estranged from the womb', and utter the startling saying 'They were in error from the womb, they spoke lies.'[4]

In this sense our wise men speak disparagingly of all sensible nature, so that in one place our bodies are said to be 'futility' in the words: 'For the creation was made subject to futility, not of its own choice, but because of him who subjected it in hope.'[5] And in another place they are said to be 'vanity of vanities', of which the writer of Ecclesiastes said 'Vanity of vanities, all is vanity.'[6] Who has made so strong an indictment of the life of the human soul upon earth as he who said 'Yet all is vanity, every living man'?[7] He was in no doubt about the difference between the soul's life on this earth and that lived beyond earthly things, nor did he say

> Who knows if to live is to die
> And to die to live?[8]

But he is bold enough to tell the truth in the saying 'Our soul is humbled to dust', and 'Thou hast brought me down to the dust of death.'[9] Just as it is said, 'Who shall deliver me from this body of death?', so also, 'Who shall change the body of our humiliation'.[10] And it is a prophet who said, 'Thou didst humble us in a place of affliction',[11] meaning by a place

---

[1] Read ἂν ⟨τι⟩ σεμνότητος with K. tr.   [2] Rom. i. 22.

[3] Celsus has used *genesis* to mean 'becoming' in the philosophical sense; Origen takes it in its meaning 'birth', that being the Biblical usage. Cf. Lev. xii. 6, and for the appeal to this text as part of the justification of infant baptism, *Comm. in Rom.* v, 9 (VI, 397 Lomm.); *Hom. in Lev.* VIII, 3; *Hom. in Lucam*, 14. Discussion in Bigg, *The Christian Platonists of Alexandria* (1913), pp. 246 ff.

[4] Ps. l. 7; lvii. 4.   [5] Rom. viii. 20.

[6] Eccles. i. 2.   [7] Ps. xxxviii. 6.

[8] Euripides, *frag.* 638 Nauck; cf. Rohde, *Psyche* (E.T.), p. 435.

[9] Ps. xliii. 26; xxi. 16.   [10] Rom. vii. 24; Phil. iii. 21.

[11] Ps. xliii. 20 (Origen gives his standing exegesis of this text).

of affliction the earthly region into which Adam, which means man, came after being cast out of paradise for his sin. Consider also what profound insight about the different spheres in which the soul lives was possessed by the man who said 'Now we see through a mirror and in a riddle, but then face to face', and also 'while we are at home in the body we are absent from the Lord', so that 'we prefer to be absent from the body and to be at home with the Lord'.[1]

51. But why should I continue to quote more texts against Celsus' words to show that among us these doctrines were set forth long before, when we have made our point clear from what we have already said? However, here he lays it down as if it were a matter of principle saying that if a divine *spirit came down from God to foretell the divine truths, this may be the spirit which declares these doctrines; indeed, it was because men of ancient times were touched by this spirit that they proclaimed many excellent doctrines.* He did not see the difference between them and the truths which have been rightly set forth among us. For we say that 'Thy incorruptible spirit is in all things, wherefore God convicts little by little those who fall from the right way.'[2] And among other things we also affirm that the words 'Receive the Holy Spirit' point to a gift which is different in quantity from that indicated by the saying, 'You will be baptized by the Holy Spirit not many days hence.'[3]

What is difficult is to give careful consideration to these matters and to see the difference between those who only at long intervals have received comprehension of the truth and a limited conception of God and those who have been inspired to a greater degree and have always remained with God and are continually being led by the divine Spirit.[4] If Celsus had examined and understood this, he would not have accused us of a *lack of education*, nor commanded us not to say that those who think piety is manifested in the material works of human artists, in image-making, *are blind*. For no one who sees with the eyes of his soul worships God in any other way than that which teaches him to be always looking to the Creator of the universe, to offer every prayer to Him and to do everything as in the sight of God, before a spectator who sees even into our thoughts.

Therefore we pray even that we may see and be guides of the blind, until they come to the Logos of God and recover the sight of their soul which has been blinded by ignorance. And if our behaviour is worthy of him who said to his disciples 'You are the light of the world',[5] and of his saying which taught us that 'the light shines in the darkness',[6] we shall be

---

[1] I Cor. xiii. 12; II Cor. v. 6, 8.
[3] John xx. 22; Acts i. 5.
[5] Matt. v. 14.
[2] Wisd. of Sol. xii. 1–2.
[4] Cf. Rom. viii. 14; Gal. v. 18.
[6] John i. 5.

even a light to those in darkness, and we shall educate the stupid and instruct babes.

52. Celsus should not be annoyed when we say that people who hasten to the supposed holy places as if they were in truth holy, and who do not see that nothing made by artisans can be holy,[1] are lame and defective in the steps of their soul. But those who act piously according to the teaching of Jesus run until, on reaching the end of the course, they say with firm and genuine sincerity, 'I have fought a good fight, I have finished my course, I have kept the faith; henceforth there is laid up for me a crown of righteousness.'[2] Each one of us, in fact, runs in this way not in any uncertain manner, and in this way boxes against evil not like one beating the air,[3] but fighting against those who are under 'the prince of the power of the air, the spirit now active in the children of disobedience'.[4] Celsus may say too that we *live for the body which is a dead thing.* But we hear the saying, 'If you live according to the flesh, you shall die; but if by the spirit you mortify the deeds of the body, you shall live.' And we learn that 'if we live in the spirit, let us also walk in the spirit'.[5] And it would be possible for us to show by our works that he is lying when he says of us that *we live for the body which is a dead thing.*

53. Then after these remarks to which we have replied to the best of our ability, he says to us: *How much better it would have been for you, since you conceived a desire to introduce some new doctrine, to have addressed your attentions to some other man among those who have died noble deaths and are sufficiently distinguished to have a myth about them like the gods. For example, if Heracles and Asclepius and those who since early times have been held in honour[6] failed to please you, you had Orpheus, a man who, as all agree, possessed a pious spirit and also died a violent death. But perhaps he had been chosen by others before you.[7] At any rate you had Anaxarchus who, when cast into a mortar and while he was being beaten with great violence, nobly showed contempt for the punishment, saying 'Beat on, beat the pouch of Anaxarchus, for you are not beating him.'[8] The utterance is surely one of*

---

[1] Cf. Zeno in I, 5, above.   [2] II Tim. iv. 7–8.   [3] I Cor. ix. 26.

[4] Eph. ii. 2.   [5] Rom. viii. 13; Gal. v. 25.   [6] Cf. Celsus in III, 22, 42.

[7] Orpheus was torn in pieces by the Thracian women (Plato, *Rep.* 620 A, etc.) according to the usual story. Cf. K. Ziegler in P.-W. XVIII, 1 (1939), 1281–93; W. K. C. Guthrie, *Orpheus and Greek Religion* (1935), p. 32.

[8] Anaxarchus of Abdera, of the school of Democritus, taught the Sceptic Pyrrho, and was regarded as the father of Scepticism. See Zeller, *Philos. d. Gr.* I (6th ed. 1920), pp. 1188 ff. For the story of his heroic death at the hands of Nicocreon of Cyprus cf. Cicero, *Tusc.* II, 52; *de Nat. Deor.* III, 33, 82; Valerius Maximus, III, 3, ext. 4; Plutarch, *Mor.* 449 E; Diog. Laert. IX, 59; Philo, *Quod omnis probus,* 109; *de Provid.* II, 11 (Avkher 51); Pliny, *N.H.* VII, 87; Dio Chrys. XXXVII, 45; Clem. Al. *Strom.* IV, 56, 4; Tertullian, *Apol.* L, 6; Eusebius, *Theophan.* I, 64; Nemesius, *de Nat. Hom.* 30 (Migne, *P.G.* XL, 721 A); Greg. Naz. *Epist.* 32; *Carm.* I, 9, 688–91; *Epigr.* 4 (*P.G.* XXXVII, 72 A, 730 A; XXXVIII, 84 A).

some divine spirit. But some natural philosophers have preceded you in taking him for their master. What about Epictetus then? When his master was twisting his leg he smiled gently and calmly said ' You are breaking it.' And when he had broken it he said ' Did I not tell you that you were breaking it?' [1] *What comparable saying did your God utter while he was being punished? If you had put forward the Sibyl, whom some of you use, as a child of God you would have had more to be said in your favour. However, you have had the presumption to interpolate many blasphemous things in her verses,* [2] *and assert that a man who lived a most infamous life and died a most miserable death was a god. A far more suitable person for you than Jesus would have been Jonah with his gourd, or Daniel who escaped from wild beasts,* [3] *or those of whom stories yet more incredible than these are told.*

54. Since he refers us to Heracles, let him show us records of his teaching, and give an explanation of his undignified slavery with Omphale. Let him show whether a man was worthy of divine honour who took the ox of a farmer by force like a thief, and feasted on it, delighting in the curses which the farmer swore at him while he was eating, so that even to this day the daemon of Heracles is said to receive the sacrifice with certain curses.[4] In mentioning Asclepius he leads us to repeat ourselves; but since

[1] Epictetus refers to his lameness in *Diss.* I, 8, 14; I, 16, 20; cf. I, 12, 24. But Suidas (*s.v.* Epictetus) gives as the reason for it 'a flux', and Schenkl, in his introduction to his edition of Epictetus (q.v.), thinks that Suidas is more likely to give the true cause than Celsus 'whose story seems to me to have the colour of an apophthegm'. For other references see Schenkl's *testimonia* (pp. xix f.).

[2] For Christian appeals to the Sibyl, cf. Celsus in v, 61. The oracles are commonly quoted by some Christian apologists: Theophilus of Antioch, Clement of Alexandria, and especially Lactantius. She was a favourite for Constantine the Great. Celsus' criticisms here are more than justified. Jewish apologists had freely forged Sibylline oracles, and the Christians followed their example. For pagan complaints cf. Lactantius, *Div. Inst.* IV, 15, 26 'Certain persons, when overcome by these testimonies, are accustomed to take refuge in saying that they are not verses of the Sibyl but have been forged and composed by us'; Constantine, *Oratio ad Sanctos*, XIX, 1 (p. 181 Heikel, in the Berlin *Eusebius Werke*, I, 1902): 'But the majority of men disbelieve, and, though they admit that the Erythraean Sibyl was a prophetess, they suspect that these verses were written by someone of our religious persuasion possessing skill in writing poetry...'.

[3] Jonah iv. 6; Dan. vi. 16–23.

[4] Read with K. tr. μετά τινων άρῶν. The usual story is that Heracles came to Lindus in Rhodes with his son, and asked a farmer for food. When he refused, Heracles killed one of the oxen with which the man was ploughing, and ate it while the farmer cursed him from a safe distance. This aetiological legend was associated with the cult of Heracles at Rhodes. G. Knaack (*Hermes* XXIII (1888), pp. 139–41) thinks it goes back to Apollonius Rhodius' lost work on Rhodes. Cf. Conon, *frag.* I, 11 (Photius, *cod.* 186) = F. Jacoby, *Die Fragmente der griechischen Historiker*, I, p. 194; Philostratus, *Imagines*, II, 24; Lactantius, *Div. Inst.* I, 21, 31–7; Diogenes Cyn. *Ep.* 36 (R. Hercher, *Epistolographi Graeci*, p. 250); Amm. Marc. XXII, 12, 4; Tzetzes, *Chil.* II, 385–8; Cosmas Hieros. *ad Carm. S. Greg.* LXIV, 278 (*P.G.* XXXVIII, 511; cf. 550), esp. III, 486 (*ibid.* 400). For the proverb Λίνδιοι τήν θυσίαν cf. Leutsch-Schneidewin, *Paroemiogr. Gr.* I, pp. 113, 272, 303, 372; II, p. 506. On curses to promote fertility see my *Priscillian of Avila* (1976), p. 52.

we have already spoken about him we are content with that.[1] But what
did he admire in Orpheus when he says that, *as all agree, he possessed
a pious spirit* and lived a good life? I wonder whether Celsus does not sing
Orpheus' praises now because he wants to pick a quarrel with us, and
wishes to disparage Jesus, and whether, when he read his impious myths
about the gods, he did not turn away from the poems on the grounds that
they deserve to be banished from a good state even more than those of
Homer.[2] For Orpheus said much worse things about the supposed gods
than Homer.

I do not deny that it was heroic of Anaxarchus to say to Aristocreon[3]
the tyrant of Cyprus, '*Beat on, beat the pouch of Anaxarchus.*' But this is
the only admirable story which the Greeks know about Anaxarchus. And
even if, as Celsus thinks,[4] it might be right for certain people to reverence
a man for his virtue, it would not be reasonable to call Anaxarchus a god.
He also refers us to Epictetus, and admires his noble utterance. But it is
certainly not true that what he said while his leg was being broken is
comparable to Jesus' miraculous words and works which Celsus does not
believe. For when spoken with divine power to this day they convert[5]
not only some of the simple people but also many of the more intelligent.

55. After the list of distinguished men he says: *What comparable saying
did your God utter while he was being punished?* We would reply to him that
by his silence[6] under the scourge and many other outrages he manifested
a courage and patience superior to that of any of the Greeks who spoke
while enduring torture—if, at least, Celsus is willing to believe even this,
which has been honestly recorded by truthful men; for they related the
wonderful events without falsehood, and among such they reckoned his
silence under the scourge. Moreover, when he was being mocked and was
clothed in a purple robe, and the crown of thorns was put on his head, and
when he took the reed in his hand for a sceptre,[7] he showed the highest
meekness. For he said nothing either ignoble or angry to those who
ventured to do such terrible things to him.

Accordingly, it was not consistent with the character of him who by
his courage was silent under the scourge and who by his meekness endured
all the outrages inflicted by those who mocked him, that he should have
been led by any mean cowardice, as some think, to say: 'Father, if it be
possible, let this cup pass from me; nevertheless not as I will, but as thou

---

[1] Cf. III, 22–5.   [2] Cf. IV, 36; for Orpheus' myths, I, 16.
[3] He is called Nicocreon in other sources.
[4] Read with We., K. tr. εἰ καί, ὡς Κέλσος ἀξιοῖ, ἐχρῆν.
[5] Read with K. tr. ἐπιστρέφουσιν.
[6] Read with Wif. ὅτι ⟨τῇ⟩ παρά. For Origen's admiration of the silence of Jesus (Matt.
xxvi. 63), cf. Praef. 1, above.   [7] Matt. xxvii. 14, 28–9, 39.

wilt.'[1] What appears to be an attempt to excuse himself from what he calls the 'cup' contains a meaning which elsewhere we have investigated and interpreted at length.[2] But to give a simple interpretation of the saying, consider whether there was not a true religious feeling towards God in the prayer. Everyone thinks that trouble is to be avoided for preference, though he endures calamity which he would prefer to avoid, whenever the occasion demands. But the utterance was not that of a man who had given in. The words 'Nevertheless not what I will, but what thou wilt' are the utterance of one who was content with his circumstances and preferred the difficult situation caused by providence.

56. Then for some unknown reason he wanted us to call the Sibyl *a child of God* rather than Jesus, asserting that we have *interpolated many blasphemous things in her verses*, though he does not give any instance of our interpolations. He would have proved this point had he showed that the older copies were purer and had not the verses which he supposes to have been interpolated. Without having proved also that these are blasphemous, once again, not merely for the second or third time, but as he has done many times, he says that Jesus' life was *most infamous*.[3] He did not dwell on each action in his life which he supposes to be most infamous. When he says this, he seems not only to be making unsupported assertions, but also to be pouring abuse on someone he knows nothing about. If he had quoted those actions which seemed to him to be instances of his most infamous life, we would have dealt with each one of those which he thought to be such.

The charge that Jesus *died a most miserable death* could be applied both to Socrates and to Anaxarchus, whom he mentioned a little earlier, and to thousands of others. Or was the death of Jesus most miserable, but not theirs also? Or was their death not most miserable, while that of Jesus was such? Here also, you see, it was Celsus' object to pour abuse on Jesus, being impelled, I suppose, by some spirit which was overthrown and conquered by Jesus, that it may no longer have burnt-offerings and blood.[4] For nourished by these it used to deceive people who seek for God in earthly images and do not look up to the real and supreme God.

57. Then next, as if it were his object to fill up his book with padding, he wanted us to regard Jonah as a god rather than Jesus; he prefers Jonah who preached repentance to the single city of Nineveh before Jesus who preached repentance to the whole world and had more success than Jonah. He wanted us to regard as a god the man who performed the portentous and incredible feat of spending three days and three nights in the belly of

---

[1] Matt. xxvi. 39.   [2] *Exh. Mart.* 29; *Comm. ser. in Matt.* 92.
[3] Celsus in I, 62; III, 50.   [4] Cf. III, 28.

the whale.¹ But him who accepted death for mankind, to whom God bore
witness by the prophets, Celsus would not regard as worthy of the second
place of honour after the God of the universe,² the position given to him
on account of the great deeds which he did in heaven and on earth. And
it was because he fled to avoid preaching the message that God had
commanded him that Jonah was swallowed up by the whale. But it was
because Jesus taught what God wished that he suffered death for mankind.

He next says that Daniel, who went free from the lions, ought to be
worshipped by us rather than Jesus, who trampled down the fierceness of
every opposing power and gave us 'power to walk upon serpents and
scorpions and all the might of the enemy'.³ Then although he has no
other examples to mention, he says *Or men of whom stories yet more
incredible than these are told*, so that he pours abuse at the same time on
Jonah and Daniel. The spirit in Celsus did not know how to speak well
of righteous men.

58. After this let us also see his next remarks which read as follows:
*They have also a precept to this effect—that you must not resist a man who
insults you. Even, he says, if someone strikes you on one cheek, yet you should
offer the other one as well.⁴ This too is old stuff, and was better said before
them. But they expressed it in more vulgar terms. For Plato makes Socrates
speak the following conversation in the* Crito:⁵

Then we ought never to do wrong.
No, indeed.
*Not even ought we to repay when wronged ourselves, as most people think, since
we ought not to do wrong under any circumstances.*
It appears not.
What then? Ought we to do harm, Crito, or not?
We ought not, I suppose, Socrates.
*What now? Is it just to repay harm when we suffer evil, as most people say, or
unjust?*
That is not just at all.
For, I suppose, to do harm to men is no different from doing wrong.
You are right.
*Then we ought neither to take revenge nor to do harm to any man, not even if we
suffer anything from him.*
So says Plato. And again he continues as follows:

*Therefore you too, look well to see if you agree with me and it is acceptable to you,
and let us begin from there to think together, assuming that it is never right either
to do wrong or to take revenge, or for one who has suffered harm to resist and to
requite evil. Or will you refuse to assent and not agree with the premiss? For to me
this has seemed to be the truth for a long time. And it seems so still.*

¹ Jonah ii. 1.   ² Cf. v, 39; vi, 61.   ³ Luke x. 19.
⁴ Luke vi. 29; Matt. v. 39.   ⁵ Plato, *Crito*, 49 B–E.

This was the opinion of Plato. But these views were set forth still earlier by divinely inspired men. But what I have said on this point may be a sufficient example for all the other doctrines which they corrupt.[1] *And anyone who wishes to find further instances of this will recognize them.*[2]

59. To this, and to all the parallels which Celsus has quoted and which, because he is unable to disregard their truth, he maintains were also said by the Greeks, we would make the following reply. If the doctrine is beneficial and its intention sound, and if it has been stated among the Greeks by Plato or one of the Greek wise men, and among the Jews by Moses or one of the prophets, and among the Christians in the recorded words of Jesus or utterances of one of his apostles, we are not to suppose that any objection to the saying uttered by Jews or by Christians can be based on the fact that the doctrines were also set forth by the Greeks, and particularly if the writings of the Jews are proved to be earlier than those of the Greeks. Nor again are we to think that the same doctrine expressed in the beauty of Greek style is in any way superior to its expression in the poorer style and simpler language used by Jews and Christians. In any event, the original words of the Jews, which the prophets used in the books which they have left to us, were written in the Hebrew language; and they made an artistic use of the literary style of their language.

If we may show that the same doctrines, even if the statement seems incredible, have been better expressed by the prophets of the Jews and the teaching of the Christians, we would base our argument for this view on a certain illustration concerning food and the way it is prepared. Suppose that there is a wholesome food which implants strength in those who eat it, and that after being prepared in a certain way and seasoned with certain spices it is received, not by peasants who have not learnt[3] how to eat such things because they have been brought up in farm-houses and in poverty, but by rich and luxurious people only. And suppose that there are innumerable people who eat the same food prepared not in that way which is how the supposed better classes like it, but in the way that the poor and the simple folk and the majority of men have learnt to eat it. Let us also assume that it is only the supposed better classes who are strengthened by cooking of the former kind since none of the multitude have any inclination for such food, whereas cooking of the other kind brings better health to the majority of men. Which cooks shall we approve more in the matter of the benefit they confer upon their fellow-men in preparing wholesome food? Will we prefer those who prepare food for the benefit of the learned, or those who cook for the multitude? Although

[1] Celsus in VI, 15 ff.   [2] For the phrase, cf. Celsus in IV, 61.
[3] Read μαθόντες with Φ, We., Wi., K. tr.

the health and physical well-being which the food brings may be the same
whether the food is cooked in this way or in that (such being our assumption), yet it is obvious that humanity itself and the interest of mankind as
a whole suggest that the physician who has cared for the health of the
majority helps his fellow-men more than the physician who has cared for
the health of only a few.

60. If the illustration has been well taken, we must apply it to the
quality of the rational food of rational beings. Consider whether Plato
and the wise men of the Greeks do not resemble in their fine utterances
the physicians who have cared only for those supposed to be the better
classes, while they have despised the multitude of men. But the prophets
among the Jews and the disciples of Jesus, who renounced stylistic composition of words and, as the Bible puts it, the wisdom of men and the
wisdom according to the flesh,[1] obscurely referring to the language,
would be comparable to those who have taken pains to cook and to
prepare the same very wholesome quality of food by means of a literary
style which gets across to the multitude of men, and which is not strange
to their language, and does not by its strangeness turn them away from
listening to discourses of this kind because they are in an unfamiliar idiom.
Moreover, if the object is to make the man who eats the rational food, if
I may so say, long-suffering and meek, would not that doctrine be better
prepared which makes multitudes of people long-suffering and meek or,
at least, helps them to make some progress towards these virtues, rather
than that which makes a very few people long-suffering and meek,
supposing that it be granted that it does this at all?[2]

For example, if Plato had wished to help by sound doctrines people who
spoke Egyptian or Syriac, he, being a Greek, would have taken pains to
learn the language of those who were to be his hearers and, as the Greeks
say, to speak like a barbarian for the sake of improving the Egyptians and
Syrians rather than, by remaining a Greek, have no power to say anything
helpful to either of them. Similarly, the divine nature, which cares not
only for those supposed to have been educated in Greek learning but also
for the rest of mankind,[3] came down to the level of the ignorant multitude
of hearers, that by using the style familiar to them it might encourage the
mass of the common people to listen. After they have once been introduced to Christianity they are easily able to aspire to grasp even deeper[4]
truths which are concealed in the Bible. For it is obvious even to an
ungifted person who reads them that many passages can possess a meaning

---

[1] I Cor. ii. 5; i. 26; II Cor. i. 12.   [2] Cf. vi, 2 above.
[3] Bracket the second Ἑλλήνων (after λοιπῶν) with Bo., Del., K. tr.
[4] Read with We., Wif. πρὸς τὸ καὶ ⟨τὰ⟩ βαθύτερα.

deeper than that which appears at first sight, which becomes clear to those
who devote themselves to Bible study, and which is clear in proportion to
the time they spend on the Bible and to their zeal in putting its teaching
into practice.

61. It is, therefore, not an unfounded statement that when Jesus says,
as Celsus puts it, *in vulgar terms*, 'To him that strikes you on one cheek,
turn to him the other one also, and to him that would go to law with you
and take away your coat, let him have your cloak also', he expressed the
doctrine and illustrated it by these words in a way more beneficial to
mankind than the form in which Plato said it in the *Crito*. Uneducated
people are not even able to understand Plato; and it is only with difficulty
that he is understood by those who have had a general education before
being instructed in the profound philosophy of the Greeks. We ought
also to notice that the idea about being long-suffering is not *corrupted* by
the poor literary style. Here also Celsus is bringing a false charge against
the gospel when he says: *But what I have said on this point may be
a sufficient example for all the other doctrines which they corrupt. And
anyone who wishes to find further instances of this will recognize them.*

62. But let us look at the next passage also where he says this: *However,
let us leave this point. They cannot bear to see temples and altars and images.*[1]
The Scythians also do not tolerate this,[2] *nor do the Nomads of Libya,*[3] *nor the
Seres who believe in no gods,*[4] *nor other nations that are most impious and
have no regard for law. And that this view is taken by the Persians also is
related by Herodotus in these words:* 'Now I know that the Persians follow
these laws, and do not hold it legal for images and altars and temples to be
established, but even attribute stupidity to people who do so. The reason for
this, as it seems to me, is that they did not regard the gods as possessing
a nature like that of men as the Greeks did.'[5] *Moreover, Heraclitus somewhere affirms:* 'And they pray to these images just as if one were to have
conversation with houses, having no idea of the nature of gods and heroes.'[6]
*What indeed do they teach us which is wiser than Heraclitus? At all events he
hints in very obscure language that it is silly for anyone to pray to images if
he does not know the nature of gods and heroes.*

*Such is Heraclitus' meaning. But they openly dishonour the images. If
what they mean is that an image of stone or wood or bronze or gold which some
man or other has wrought cannot be a god, their wisdom is ludicrous. Who but
an utter infant imagines that these things are gods and not votive offerings*

---

[1] This is one of the complaints of the pagan Caecilius in the *Octavius* of Minucius Felix
(VIII, 4).

[2] Herodotus, IV, 59.   [3] Cf. perhaps Herodotus, IV, 188.

[4] According to Bardesanes, *de Fato* 26, the Seres forbid idol-worship.

[5] Herodotus, II, 131.   [6] Heraclitus, *frag.* 5 Diels; cf. I, 5 above.

and images of gods?[1] *But if they mean that we ought not to suppose that images are divine because God has a different shape, as the Persians also maintain, they have unwittingly refuted themselves. For they say that 'God made man his own image' and made man's form like his own.*[2] *But, although they will agree that these things are intended for the honour of certain beings, whether they resemble their shape or not, yet they think that those to whom they are dedicated are not gods but daemons, and that no one who worships God ought to serve daemons.*

63. To this my reply is that if *the Scythians* and *the Nomads of Libya* and *the Seres who*, Celsus affirms, *believe in no gods*, and *other nations that are most impious and have no regard for law*, and if *the Persians also cannot bear to see temples and altars and images*, this is no reason why their intolerance of these things should be based on the same grounds as ours. We have to examine the doctrines which led those who do not tolerate temples and images to take that view. Then the person who does not tolerate them may be praised if his intolerance is based upon sound doctrines, and censured if on mistaken doctrines.

It is possible for the same conclusion to be based on different doctrines. For instance, the philosophers who follow Zeno of Citium avoid adultery; but so do the Epicureans and also some who are quite uneducated. But consider what a difference there is between the reasons which lead such various people to avoid adultery. The Stoics, basing their view on the good of society, hold that it is contrary to nature[3] for a rational being to corrupt a woman already bound by the laws to another, and to ruin the home of another man. The Epicureans, however, do not avoid adultery—when they do abstain from it—on this ground, but because in their view pleasure is the highest good, and because there are many hindrances to pleasure which confront the man who has given himself up to enjoying the one pleasure of adultery; and sometimes he has to face prison or banishment or death, and often dangers also before these while watching for the departure from the house of the husband and those who look after his affairs.[4] So if we suppose that it were possible for an adulterer to escape

---

[1] The best discussion of the point at issue here is that of E. R. Bevan, *Holy Images* (1940).
[2] Gen. i. 26–7; cf. Celsus in VI, 63.
[3] Read καὶ ⟨τὸ⟩ παρὰ φύσιν with K. tr. (But perhaps with H. von Arnim, *S.V.F.* III, 729 διὰ τὸ ⟨μὴ⟩ κοινωνικὸν καὶ παρὰ φύσιν εἶναι.)
[4] Epicurus, *frag.* 535 (p. 322) Usener. Cf. the fragment from the Vatican Gnomologium (Wotke, *Wiener Studien* X (1888), p. 195, *frag.* 51 = C. Bailey, *Epicurus* (1926), p. 114) 'You tell me that the stimulus of the flesh makes you too prone to the pleasures of love. Provided that you do not break the laws or good customs and do not distress any of your neighbours or do harm to your body or squander your pittance, you may indulge your inclination as you please. Yet it is impossible not to come up against one or other of these barriers: for the pleasures of love never profited a man and he is lucky if they do him no harm' (trans. Bailey). Also Seneca, *de Otio*, VII, 3.

the notice of both the woman's husband and all his servants, and those among whom he would lose his reputation by committing adultery, then an Epicurean would commit adultery for the sake of the pleasure. If an uneducated person abstains from committing adultery when he has the opportunity, it would sometimes be found that the reason why he so abstains is the fear put into him by the law and the penalties involved; a man like this would not abstain from adultery because he sought for further pleasures. You see, then, that the action which is supposed to be the same, abstinence from adultery, becomes quite a different matter by reason of the intentions of those who abstain from it. For it depends whether they do so on the basis of sound doctrines, or from the very wicked and impious reasons which motivate an Epicurean or a vulgar person such as we took in our example.

64. Just as this one thing, abstinence from adultery, although it seems to be but one, is found to be many things by reason of the different doctrines and intentions, so also the same is true of those who cannot bear to worship God with altars and temples and images. The Scythians or the Nomads of Libya or the Seres who believe in no gods or the Persians are led to do this by different doctrines from those which lead Christians and Jews to be intolerant of such worship supposed to be offered to the deity. For none of the former are intolerant of altars and images because they want to avoid degrading or debasing the worship of God to matter such as this, which has been modelled in some particular way. Nor is it because they have held the belief that daemons have occupied these images and places, either because they have been invoked[1] by certain magical spells, or even because in some other way they have been able to get possession of places for themselves, where they greedily partake of the portions of the sacrifices[2] and seek for illicit pleasure and for lawless men. But Christians and Jews are led to avoid temples and altars and images by the command 'Thou shalt fear the Lord thy God and him only shalt thou serve', and by the words 'Thou shalt have none other gods but me', and 'Thou shalt not make to thyself any idol or likeness of anything that is in heaven above and in the earth beneath and in the water under the earth, thou shalt not bow down to them nor worship them', and by the command 'Thou shalt worship the Lord thy God and him only shalt thou serve',[3] and many more to the same effect as these. And not only do they avoid them, but when necessary they readily come to the point of death to avoid defiling their conception of the God of the universe by any act of this kind contrary to His law.

[1] Read κατακληθέντες with We. Cf. Numenius in v, 38.
[2] Cf. III, 38 above.　　　　　[3] Deut. vi. 13; Exod. xx. 3–5.

65. Concerning the Persians it was said earlier that they set up no temples but that they do worship the sun and the creations of God.[1] This is forbidden to us. We are taught not to 'serve the creation rather than the Creator', but to know that 'the creation will be set free from the bondage of corruption into the liberty of the glory of the children of God', and that 'the earnest expectation of the creation is waiting for the revelation of the sons of God', and that 'the creation was made subject to futility, not willingly but by reason of him who subjected it in hope'.[2] And we are taught that we certainly must not honour in place of God who needs nothing,[3] or of His Son who is the firstborn of all creation,[4] things which have been subjected to the bondage of corruption and futility, a state which they have with a view to a better hope. This, however, is enough about the race of the Persians as an addition to our earlier remarks, that while they avoid altars and images they worship the creation rather than the Creator.

Then he quotes the saying of Heraclitus which he interpreted as meaning that it is silly for anyone to pray to images if he does not know the nature of gods and heroes. My reply is that it is possible to know God and His only-begotten Son and those beings who have been honoured by God with the title of God and who partake of His divinity,[5] who are different from all the gods of the heathen who are daemons;[6] but it is quite impossible both to know God and to pray to images.

66. It is silly not only to pray to images, but also to pretend to pray to them in order to accommodate oneself to the multitude as is done by the Peripatetic philosophers and those who embrace the doctrines of Epicurus or Democritus.[7] Nothing insincere ought to have any place in the soul of the man who is genuinely pious towards God. We do not honour the images precisely because, as far as possible, we wish to avoid falling into the notion that the images are other gods. That is why we object to Celsus and all who admit that they are not gods, because, while they seem to be wise men, they also offer a semblance of worship to the images. And the multitudes who follow their example are in error because they do not

---

[1] Cf. v, 41, 44; VI, 22.   [2] Rom. i. 25; viii. 19–21.
[3] For this commonplace, cf. Celsus in VI, 52; VIII, 21; Wetstein on Acts xvii. 25.
[4] Col. i. 15.   [5] That is, the angels; cf. III, 37 above.   [6] Ps. xcv. 5.
[7] Origen, *Exh. Mart.* 6, compares the sincerity of the Christian who refuses to worship images with the insincerity of the person who does not believe in them but nevertheless worships them 'on account of cowardice, which he calls "accommodating himself", pretending to worship them for the sake of appearing to be pious like the multitude'. For this attitude cf. Sextus Empiricus, *adv. Math.* IX, 49 'Perhaps it would be safer for the Sceptic if he followed the traditional habits and customs in affirming the existence of gods and in performing all that pertains to their worship and to piety, while making no hasty affirmations so far as a philosophical enquiry is concerned.'

think that they are merely worshipping them on the principle of accommodating themselves, but fall down in their soul to the level of thinking that they are gods, and cannot even bear to hear that these images which they worship are not gods.

Celsus maintains that they are not thought to be gods, but only votive offerings of the gods, without proving that they are not offerings of men but, as he puts it, of the gods themselves. It is obvious that they are offerings of men who hold wrong views about God. Furthermore, we do not suppose that the images are divine likenesses because we do not depict in any shape a God who is invisible and incorporeal. But Celsus supposes that we fall into contradicting ourselves when we say that God does not possess human form and when we believe that God .made man His own image and made him in the image of God. My reply to this, as I also said earlier,[1] is that the part which is 'in the image of God' is to be found preserved in the rational soul which has the capacity for virtue. And yet Celsus, failing to see the difference between God's image and that which is made after the image of God, says that we affirm '*God made man his own image and made man's form like his own.*' To this we replied earlier.

67. Then he next says of Christians that *although they will agree that these things are intended for the honour of certain beings, whether they resemble their shape or not, yet they think that those to whom they are dedicated are not gods but daemons, and that no one who worships God ought to serve daemons.* If he had known the doctrine about daemons and the activity of each of them, whether each one is invoked by the experts in these matters, or if it is of its own choice that it devotes itself to the activity which it desires and can perform, and if he had thought out the truth about daemons which is profound and hard for human nature to understand, he would not have made it a charge against us that we say that no one who worships the supreme God ought to serve daemons. So far, indeed, are we from serving daemons that by prayers and formulas from the holy scriptures[2] we even drive them out of human souls and from places where they have established themselves, and sometimes even from animals. For frequently the daemons effect some device for the injury of these as well.

68. As we spoke at length about Jesus earlier[3] there is no need to repeat it now in reply to the objection: *However, they themselves are clearly refuted for the reason that they worship not a god, nor even a daemon, but a corpse.*[4] On this account we may at once leave this, and pass on to consider Celsus' next remarks where he says: *Firs: I would ask, Why should*

[1] Cf. vi, 63.
[2] For the superior potency of scriptural names, cf. Origen, *Hom. in Iesu Nave*, xx.
[3] Cf. i, 69–70; ii, 63–6; iii, 41–3; vi, 75–7; vii, 16–17, 35–6, 40, 45–6, 52.
[4] Cf. Celsus in vii, 36.

we not worship daemons? Are not all things indeed administered according to
God's will, and is not all providence¹ derived from him? And whatever there
may be in the universe, whether the work of God, or of angels,² or of other
daemons, or heroes, do not all these things keep a law given by the greatest
God? And has there not been appointed over each particular thing a being who
has been thought worthy to be allotted power? Would not a man, therefore,
who worships God rightly worship the being who has obtained authority from
*him? But it is impossible, he says, for the same man to serve several masters.*³

Notice here also how he jumps to conclusions on problems which need
considerable study and also knowledge of very profound and mysterious
doctrines about the administration of the universe. For with regard to the
assertion that all things are administered according to God's will, we have
to examine what is meant, and whether the administration extends even
to the sins which are committed or not. If the administration extends even
to the sins which are committed not only among men but also among
daemons and any other being without a body which is capable of sinning,
let the person who says this notice the difficulty in holding that all things
are administered according to God's will. For it follows from his statement that even the sins which are committed and all the consequences of
evil are administered according to God's will; and that is not the same as
saying that they happen⁴ because God does not prevent them. But if one
were to take the words 'are administered' in their strict sense, one would
say that even the consequences of evil are subject to the control of God's
administration (it being obvious that all things are administered according
to God's will); and thus anyone who sins does not commit an outrage
against the administration of God.

We also have to make a similar distinction concerning providence, and
say that there is an element of truth in the statement that *all providence is*
derived from him when providence is the cause of what is good. But if we
are saying without qualification that everything which takes place is
according to the will of providence, even if anything evil occurs, then it
will be untrue to say that all providence is derived from him—unless
perhaps one were to say that even the accidental results of the works of
God's providence were caused by the providence of God.⁵

---

¹ Cf. Celsus in I, 57; IV, 99; for Celsus' theology here, see Introduction, pp. xvi ff.
² It is of interest that Celsus uses the Jewish-Christian word 'angel'. Evidence collected
by Bousset in *Archiv für Religionswissenschaft*, XVIII (1915), pp. 168–72, suggests that the
term could be used by pagan writers without any Jewish or Christian influence. For the
importance of angels in the Neo-platonists, Porphyry and Proclus, cf. Andres in P.-W.,
Suppl. III (1918), 111 f. *s.v.* 'Angelos'.
³ For the MS. οὔτε, read with K. tr. and Bader οὗτοι. Cf. Matt. vi. 24; Luke xvi. 13.
⁴ Read γίνεσθαι with K. tr.   ⁵ Cf. VI, 53, 55.

He also affirms that *whatever there may be in the universe, whether the work of God, or of angels, or of other daemons, or heroes, all these things keep a law given by the greatest God.* But what he asserts is not a '*true doctrine*'. For when they transgress these beings are not keeping a law given by the greatest God. And the Bible shows that transgressors include not only evil men, but also evil daemons and evil angels.

69. It is not only we who say that there are evil daemons, but almost all people who hold that daemons exist. Therefore, it is not true that *all things keep a law given by the greatest God.* All beings who through their own neglect, evil, or wickedness, or ignorance of the good, fell from the divine law, do not keep the law of God, but (to coin a phrase, which is also scriptural) keep 'the law of sin'.[1] However, in the view of the majority of people who hold that daemons exist, it is only the evil daemons who do not keep the law of God but transgress it. But in our opinion all daemons have fallen from the way to goodness, and previously they were not daemons; for the category of daemons is one of those classes of beings which have fallen away from God. That is why no one who worships God ought to worship daemons.

The truth about daemons is also made clear by those who invoke daemons for what are called love-philtres and spells for producing hatred, or for the prevention of actions, or for countless other such causes. This is done by people who have learnt to invoke daemons by charms and incantations and to induce them to do what they wish. On this account the worship of daemons is foreign to us who worship the supreme God. The worship of the supposed gods is also a worship of daemons. For 'all the gods of the heathen are daemons'.[2] This is also clear from the fact that, for those supposed holy places which seem to be more powerful, curious spells[3] were used at the time when such statues and temples were first set up; and these were performed by those who devote their time to worshipping daemons by means of incantations. That is the reason why we have decided to avoid the worship of daemons like a plague. And we maintain that all the supposed worship of gods among the Greeks with altars and images and temples is a worship offered to daemons.

70. With respect to his remark, *Has there not been appointed over each particular thing a being who has obtained power from the greatest God, and who has been held worthy to perform* some particular task, very profound knowledge is required if we are to be able to show whether, like public executioners in cities and officers appointed for unpleasant but necessary

---

[1] Rom. viii. 2.   [2] Ps. xcv. 5.

[3] Read with We., K. tr. κατακλήσεις (here and 218, 32). For the idea, cf. VII, 64 above, and Numenius in v, 38.

work in states, wicked daemons are appointed for certain tasks by the divine Logos who administers the whole world;[1] or if, just as robbers in deserted places advance one individual to be their chief, so the daemons have formed, as it were, confederacies in various parts of the earth and have made one individual their chief, to lead them in doing the deeds which they have chosen to do in order to steal and rob the souls of men.

A man who is going to give a good answer on this point, in order to defend the Christians who avoid worshipping anything other than the supreme God and His Logos, the firstborn of all creation,[2] needs to explain the sayings, 'All who came before me were thieves and robbers, and the sheep did not hear them', and 'The thief does not come except to steal and to kill and to destroy',[3] and any other similar sayings in the holy scriptures, such as 'Behold, I have given you power to walk upon serpents and scorpions, and upon all the might of the enemy, and nothing at all shall harm you', and 'Thou shalt walk upon an adder and basilisk and thou shalt trample on a lion and serpent.'[4]

But Celsus knew nothing at all of these sayings. For if he had known, he would not have said: *And whatever there may be in the universe, whether the work of God, or of angels, or of other daemons or heroes, do not all these things keep a law given by the greatest God? And has there not been appointed over each particular thing a being who has been thought worthy to be allotted power? Would not a man, therefore, who worships God rightly worship the being who has obtained authority from him?* And to this he adds *But it is impossible for the same man to serve several masters.* We shall deal with this in the next book, seeing that the seventh volume which we have written in reply to Celsus' treatise has reached sufficient dimensions.

---

[1] Cf. v, 30–1; viii, 31.   [2] Col. i. 15.
John x. 8, 10.   [4] Luke x. 19; Ps. xc. 13.

BOOK VIII

1. I have already succeeded in completing seven books. But I now intend to begin an eighth. May God and His only-begotten Son the Logos be with us that Celsus' lies, which are wrongly entitled *The True Doctrine*, may receive a proper refutation and that the doctrines of Christianity may be mightily proved to be true by the effect of the defence. We pray that we may say with Paul's sincerity the words 'We are ambassadors for Christ, as though God did beseech you by us',[1] and may be ambassadors for Christ to men, as the Logos of God beseeches them to enter into friendship with himself, desiring to make at home with righteousness, truth, and the other virtues, those who before accepting the doctrines of Jesus Christ spent their life in darkness about God and ignorance about the Creator. And again, I would ask that God may give us the noble and true Word, the Lord powerful and mighty in battle[2] against evil. However, we now have to go on to the next passage of Celsus and give our reply to it.

2. Earlier he put the question to us, *Why do we not worship daemons?* And to his remarks about daemons we replied[3] in accordance with the meaning of the divine word as it appears to us. Then, because he wants us to worship daemons, he next introduces us as replying to his question '*It is impossible for the same man to serve several masters.*' This, he thinks, *is a rebellious utterance[4] of people who*, as he puts it, *wall themselves off and break away from the rest of mankind.[5]* He supposes that *people who say this are in effect attributing their own feeling to God.* For this reason he thinks that *in the sphere of human affairs, a man who is serving one master could not reasonably serve another man as well, as the other would be harmed by the service rendered to a different person; nor could someone who had already pledged himself to one man do the same to another as well, because he would do the one harm. And it is reasonable not to serve different heroes and daemons at the same time. But where God is concerned, whom neither harm nor grief can affect*, he thinks that *it is irrational to avoid worshipping several gods on principles similar to those which apply in the case of men and heroes and daemons of this sort.* He also says: *The man who worships several gods, because he worships some one of those which belong to the great God, even by this very action does that which is loved by him.* And he goes on to say that *it*

---

[1] II Cor. v. 20.   [2] Ps. xxiii. 8.   [3] VII, 68–70.
[4] Cf. Celsus in III, 5; VIII, 49.
[5] For this charge, commonly levelled against the Jews (cf. Celsus in V, 41 and note), cf. Tacitus, *Ann.* XV, 44 'odium humani generis'.

is not lawful to give honour to any to whom this right has not been granted by him. Therefore, he says, *anyone who honours and worships all those who belong to God does not hurt him, since they are all his.*

3. Before the next question let us consider whether we have not good reason for approving of the saying 'No man can serve two masters', which continues 'for either he will hate the one and love the other, or he will cleave to the one and despise the other', and after that 'You cannot serve God and mammon.'[1] The defence leads us to a profound and mysterious doctrine about gods and lords. The divine scripture knows that there is a great Lord above all the gods.[2] In this phrase we do not understand the word 'gods' to refer to those worshipped by the heathen, seeing that we have learnt that 'all the gods of the heathen are daemons'.[3] But we understand it of gods who have some sort of assembly known to the prophetic word. The supreme God judges these and appoints to each one the work for which he is fitted. For 'God stood in the assembly of the gods, and in the midst he judges gods'.[4] Moreover, the Lord is 'the God of gods', who by His Son 'called the earth from the rising of the sun to its setting'.[5] And we are commanded to 'give thanks to the God of gods', and have also learnt that 'God is not the God of the dead but of the living'.[6] The idea here is set forth not merely in the texts which I have quoted but also in innumerable others.

4. Such are the ideas which the divine scriptures teach us to study and think about the Lord and lords. In one place they say 'Give thanks to the God of gods, for his mercy endureth for ever; give thanks unto the Lord of lords, for his mercy endureth for ever'; and in another place that God is 'King of kings and Lord of lords'.[7] And the Bible knows some so-called gods, and some who actually are gods, whether so called or not. Paul teaches the same doctrine about those that really are lords, and those which are not, when he says, 'For though there may be some that are called gods in heaven or on earth, as there are gods many and lords many'.[8] Then, because through Jesus the God of gods 'calls from the east and west'[9] those whom He wishes to call to His own portion,[10] and because the Christ of God who is Lord shows that he is superior to every other lord by the fact that he has gone into the territory of every lord and calls to himself people from every territory, and because Paul understood this, he continues after the words which I have quoted: 'Yet to us there is one God, the Father, of whom are all things, and one Lord Jesus Christ, through

---

[1] Matt. vi. 24; Luke xvi. 13. [2] Ps. xcvi. 9. [3] Ps. xcv. 5.
[4] Ps. lxxxi. 1. [5] Ps. xlix. 1. [6] Ps. cxxxv. 2; Matt. xxii. 32.
[7] Ps. cxxxv. 2–3; I Tim. vi. 15. [8] I Cor. viii. 5.
[9] Ps. xlix. 1. [10] Deut. xxxii. 9.

whom are all things and we through him.' And perceiving that the
doctrine in this matter is a wonderful and mysterious one he adds: 'But
this knowledge is not in all men.'[1] Now when he says, 'Yet to us there is
one God, the Father of whom are all things, and one Lord Jesus Christ,
through whom are all things', by the words 'to us' he refers to himself
and to all who have ascended to the supreme God of gods and to the
supreme Lord of lords. The man who has ascended to the supreme God
is he who, without any divided loyalty whatever, worships Him through
His Son, the divine Logos and Wisdom seen in Jesus, who alone leads
to Him those who by all means try to draw near to God, the Creator of
all things, by exceptionally good words and deeds and thoughts. I think
it is for this and for similar reasons that the prince of this world, who is
transformed into an angel of light,[2] caused the words to be written—
'A host of gods and daemons follows him, arranged in eleven divisions',
where he says of himself and the philosophers, 'We are with Zeus, but
others are with the other daemons, some with one, some with another.'[3]

5. Well then, since there are many so called or actual gods, and
similarly also lords, we do all we can to ascend not only above those
worshipped as gods by the nations on earth, but also even above those
whom the scriptures hold to be gods. Nothing is known of the latter by
strangers to the covenants[4] of God given through Moses and Jesus our
Saviour, and by those alien to His promises made plain by them. He who
does no action loved by daemons rises above bondage to all daemons and
ascends above the portion of those said to be gods by Paul if he looks,
whether in the way that they do or in some other way, not at the things
which are seen but at the things which are not seen.[5] If anyone sees how
'the earnest expectation of the creation waits for the manifestation of the
sons of God, for the creation was made subject to futility, not willingly
but by reason of him who subjected it in hope',[6] and if he speaks well of
the creation because he perceives how it will all 'be delivered from the
bondage of corruption' and come to 'the liberty of the glory of the
children of God', he is not dragged away to serving God in conjunction
with some other deity beside Him, nor to serving two masters.

Accordingly there is no question of a *rebellious utterance* in the case of
those who in the light of these considerations do not wish to serve several
masters. That is why they are content with the Lord Jesus Christ, who
educates under his instruction those who serve him in order that, after
they have been trained and have become a kingdom[7] worthy of God, he

[1] I Cor. viii. 6–7.   [2] II Cor. xi. 14.   [3] Plato, *Phaedrus*, 246E–247A, 250B.
[4] Eph. ii. 12.   [5] II Cor. iv. 18.   [6] Rom. viii. 19–21.
[7] Rev. i. 6; v. 10.

may present them to his God and Father. But they do separate and break
themselves away from people alien to the commonwealth of God and from
strangers to His covenants with a view to exercising their citizenship in
heaven,[1] coming to the living God and 'to the city of God, the heavenly
Jerusalem, and to an innumerable company of angels and to the church of
the firstborn who are written in heaven'.[2]

6. Moreover we avoid serving any other deity than God, whom we
worship through the mediation of His Logos and His truth, not because
God would be harmed, just as a man is harmed by one who serves another
man beside him. Our intention is that we may not harm ourselves by
separating ourselves from the portion of the supreme God, since we live
as people akin to His blessed nature by an exceptional spirit of adoption.
This spirit is in sons of the heavenly Father, who utter not mere words
but facts when with exalted voice they secretly say, 'Abba, Father'.[3]
Admittedly, the Spartan ambassadors did not worship the emperor of the
Persians in spite of considerable pressure from the bodyguard because
they feared their one lord, the law of Lycurgus.[4] But those who are
ambassadors for the far greater and more divine embassy of Christ would
not worship the ruler of the Persians or of the Greeks or of the Egyptians
or of any race whatever, even though the bodyguard of the rulers, the
daemons and the devil's angels, wish to put pressure upon them to do this,
and to persuade them to renounce Him who is superior to any law on
earth. For Christ is lord of those who are ambassadors for Christ,[5] whom
they represent, and he is the Logos who was in the beginning, and is with
God and is God.[6]

7. Of those opinions which he held to be true Celsus then thought fit
to mention a very profound doctrine concerning heroes and certain
daemons. After the remarks about the service of men, saying that if a man
wishes to serve one master he does him harm if he chooses to serve
a second also, he observes that the same might be said[7] also of *heroes and
daemons of this sort.* We must ask him what he understands by *heroes* and
what sort of beings he holds *daemons of this sort* to be, so that a man who
serves a particular hero ought not to serve another as well, and so that one
who serves a particular daemon ought not to serve any other also. He
thinks that the daemon whom the man honoured at first is harmed in the
same way as men are harmed when a man who has been their servant
leaves them for other masters. Let him show, however, what harm in his
opinion is received by *heroes* or *daemons of this sort.* For he will be forced

[1] Phil. iii. 20.   [2] Heb. xii. 22–3.   [3] Rom. viii. 15; Matt. vi. 6 ff.
[4] The story is told by Herodotus, VII, 136.
[5] II Cor. v. 20.   [6] John i. 1.   [7] Read with We. ⟨λεχθ⟩είη.

either to fall into a sea of nonsense and to amend his statement and withdraw what he has said or, if he wants to avoid talking nonsense, to admit
that he does not know the nature either of heroes or of daemons. And to
his remark about men, that the previous masters receive harm if a slave
gives service to someone else, we should say—What sort of harm does
he affirm to be received by the former man if his servant wishes to serve
another as well?

8. If, like a vulgar and unphilosophical[1] person, he means that kind of
harm which affects his possessions, which we call external things, he
would be proved to have failed to pay attention to the fine saying of
Socrates, 'Anytus and Meletus can kill me, but not harm me; for it is not
allowable for that which is better to be harmed by that which is worse.'[2]
But if he were to say that by 'harm' he means a motion or state which is
according to evil,[3] it is obvious that, because wise men cannot be harmed
in this sense, a man may serve two such masters who live in different places.
If not even this is reasonable, it was futile for him to use the example he
does to condemn the saying, 'No man can serve two masters', and the
greater will be the force of the saying when applied to the service of the
God of the universe rendered only through the mediation of His Son who
leads men to God. Furthermore, we will not worship God as though He
needed it, or as if He will be grieved if we do not worship Him, but
because we ourselves receive benefit from worshipping God, and become
men who have no feelings of grief or emotion[4] as a result of serving the
supreme God through His only-begotten Logos and Wisdom.

9. See how ill-considered is his remark, *For if you would worship any other
being in the universe*, where he indicates that we may worship God without
any harm to ourselves simply by worshipping any of those beings subordinate to God. But as if he perceived that his view was not sound when
he said, *For if you would worship any other being in the universe*, he then goes
back and corrects what he has said in this: *It is not lawful to give honour to
any to whom this right has not been granted by him.* Now let us ask Celsus
about those who receive honour as gods or daemons or heroes. By what
argument, my good fellow, are you able to prove that the right to receive
honour has been granted to these beings from God, and that it is not the
result of ignorance and lack of knowledge on the part of men[5] who are in

---

[1] Read ἀφιλόσοφος with Bo., We., K. tr.   [2] Plato, *Apol.* 30 C–D.
[3] Read λέγοι ⟨τὴν⟩ κατὰ κακίαν with K. tr. (after We.). This is a Stoic definition (*S.V.F.*
III, 78) of the type discussed by Klostermann in *Z.N.W.* xxxvii (1938), pp. 54–61. Klostermann is surely mistaken in thinking that Origen quotes this from Celsus (p. 56).
[4] The phrase is remarkable as one of the few passages where Origen speaks of *apatheia*
as implied in the mystical ideal.
[5] Read perhaps with We. (and Bo.) ἀνθρώπων. But Wifstrand, *Eikota*, iv, p. 21, makes
a case for the MS. reading.

error and fallen away from Him who is the proper object of their worship? At all events, Hadrian's favourite is honoured as you, Celsus, remarked a short while ago.[1] And you would not, I presume, say that the right to receive honour as a god has been granted to Antinous by the God of the universe? We could say the same of the rest also, demanding proof of the assertion that the right to receive honour has been granted to them by the supreme God.

If a similar rejoinder is made to us in the case of Jesus, we would prove that the right to receive honour has been granted to him by God 'that all men may honour the Son as he honours the Father'.[2] For the prophecies before his birth were a confirmation of his right to receive honour. Furthermore, the miracles which he did, not by sorcery as Celsus thinks,[3] but by a divine power foretold by the prophets, had their testimony from God, in order that he who honours the Son, who is Reason (Logos), may do nothing irrational, and by giving him honour may derive benefit therefrom, and that he who honours him who is the Truth may become a better person as a result of honouring Truth, and similarly also by honouring Wisdom and Righteousness, and all the characteristics which the divine scriptures ascribe to the Son of God.

10. Do we not learn that honour is offered to the Son of God by a life of good conduct, and similarly also to God the Father, both from the saying, 'You who boast of the law, by your transgression of the law you dishonour God', and by the words 'Of how much more severe punishment, do you think, shall he be thought worthy who has trampled under foot the Son of God and counted the blood of the covenant by which he was sanctified an unholy thing, and has insulted the spirit of grace?'?[4] For if the man who transgresses the law dishonours God by his action, and if the man who does not accept the gospel tramples under foot the Son of God, it is obvious that he who keeps the law honours God, and that he worships God who is adorned with the word of God and with His works. If Celsus had known who belong to God, and that they alone are wise, and who are those alien to Him, and that all men are bad who do not in any way incline towards the acquisition of virtue, he would have seen in what sense he might say: *Therefore anyone who honours and worships all those who belong to him does not hurt God at all, since they are all his.*

11. After this he says: *What is more, he who affirms that only one being has been called Lord, speaking of God, impiously divides the kingdom of God and makes two opposing forces, as if there was one party on one side and*

---

[1] Celsus in III, 36, v, 63.   [2] John v. 23.
[3] Celsus in I, 6, 68; II, 49.   [4] Rom. ii. 23; Heb. x. 29.

another one at variance with it.[1] He might have made out a case for this had
he shown by logical proofs that those worshipped by the nations really
are gods, and that the beings thought to dwell around the images and
temples and altars are not in truth certain evil daemons. Moreover, with
regard to the kingdom of God, which we continually speak of in our speech
and our writings, we pray that we may understand it, and may come to be
such people that we are ruled by God alone, and that the kingdom of God
may become ours. But Celsus who teaches us to worship many gods
ought to speak of a kingdom of gods rather than of God if it were his aim[2]
to be consistent. There are, then, no parties with God. Nor is there any
god at variance with him, even if some, like Giants or Titans,[3] because of
their own wickedness wish to join Celsus and those who are accursed in
waging war on the God who in countless ways showed the truth about
Jesus, and on him who for the salvation of our race has given himself up,
as the Logos, to all the world as a whole, in accordance with the capacity
of each individual.

12. Some one might think that there is some plausibility in his next
criticism of us: *If these men worshipped no other God but one, perhaps they
would have had a valid argument against the others. But in fact they worship
to an extravagant degree this man who appeared recently,*[4] *and yet think it is
not inconsistent with monotheism if they also worship His servant.* I should say
to this that if Celsus had considered the saying, 'I and my Father are one',
and the prayer uttered by the Son of God in the words, 'As I and thou are
one', he would not have imagined that we worship another besides the
supreme God. 'For the Father', he says, 'is in me and I in the Father.'[5]

If, however, anyone is perturbed by these words lest we should be
going over to the view of those who deny that there are two existences
(*hypostases*), Father and Son, let him pay attention to the text 'And all
those who believed were of one heart and soul',[6] that he may see the
meaning of 'I and my Father are one'. Accordingly we worship but *one
God*, the Father and the Son, and we still *have a valid argument against the
others*. And we do not *worship to an extravagant degree a man who appeared
recently* as though he did not exist previously. For we believe him who
says, 'Before Abraham was I am', and who affirms, 'I am the truth.'[7]
None of us is so stupid as to suppose that before the date of Christ's
manifestation the truth did not exist. Therefore we worship the Father of
the truth and the Son who is the truth; they are two distinct existences,

[1] Celsus' objection to dualism: VI, 42. For 'the kingdom of God', cf. I, 39; III, 59; VI, 17.
[2] Read ἐσκόπει with K. tr.   [3] Cf. Origen in IV, 32; Celsus in VI, 42.
[4] Cf. Celsus in I, 26.   [5] John x. 30; xvii. 21–2; xiv. 10–11; xvii. 21.
[6] Acts iv. 32.   [7] John viii. 58; xiv. 6.

but one in mental unity, in agreement, and in identity of will.[1] Thus he who has seen the Son, who is an effulgence of the glory and express image of the Person of God, has seen God in him who is God's image.[2]

13. Then he thinks that because together with God we worship his Son it follows that in our opinion not only God but also his servants are to be worshipped. If he had in mind the true servants of God who rank after the only-begotten Son of God, Gabriel, Michael, and the other angels, and meant that they ought to be worshipped, perhaps we might have dealt with what he meant by worship and with the actions of the person who offers such worship, and, while being aware that we were discussing a very difficult question, we might have said what we were able to understand of the matter. But when in fact he thinks that the daemons worshipped by the heathen are God's servants, there is nothing in his argument which would lead us to worship these. For the Bible shows that they are servants of the evil one, the prince of this world,[3] who tries to persuade any whom he can win over to forsake God. Because we think that those whom other men worship are not God's servants, we avoid paying reverence and honour to any of them; for since we have been taught that they are not servants of the supreme God, we would say that they are daemons. That is why we worship the one God and His one Son, His Logos and image, with the best supplications and petitions that we can offer, bringing our prayers to the God of the universe through the mediation of His only-begotten Son. We bring them to him first, asking him who is a propitiation for our sins to act as a high-priest and to bear our prayers and sacrifices and intercessions to the supreme God.[4] Accordingly, our faith about God is through His Son, who confirms this faith in us. And Celsus cannot show that there is any *discord* in our belief about the Son of God. Indeed, we worship the Father by admiring His Son who is Logos, Wisdom, Truth, Righteousness, and all that we have learnt the Son of God to be—him, in fact, who was born of a Father of this nature. So much, then, for that.

14. Then again Celsus says: *If you taught them that Jesus is not his Son, but that God is father of all, and that we really ought to worship him alone, they would no longer be willing to listen to you unless you included Jesus as well, who is the author of their sedition. Indeed, when they call him Son of God, it is not because they are paying very great reverence to God, but because they*

---

[1] ὄντα δύο τῇ ὑποστάσει πράγματα, ἐν δὲ τῇ ὁμονοίᾳ καὶ τῇ συμφωνίᾳ καὶ τῇ ταυτότητι τοῦ βουλήματος. For the language cf. Origen, *Comm. in Matt.* XVII, 14; *Comm. in Joann.* x, 37 (21); II, 10; *de Orat.* xv, 1. The phrase here is echoed in the Second Creed of Antioch (A.D. 341).

[2] John xiv. 9; Heb. i. 3; Col. i. 15; II Cor. iv. 4.

[3] I Cor. ii. 6, 8; John xii. 31; xiv. 30; xvi. 11.

[4] Cf. I John iv. 10; ii. 2; Heb. ii. 17, etc.

are exalting Jesus greatly. We have learnt who the Son of God is, even that he is 'an effulgence of his glory and the express image of his person' and 'a breath of God's power and a clear emanation of the glory of the Almighty', and further 'an effulgence from everlasting light and an unspotted mirror of the working of God and an image of his goodness';[1] and we know that Jesus is the Son come from God and that God is his Father. There is nothing in the doctrine which is not fitting or appropriate to God, that He should cause the existence of an only-begotten Son of this nature. No one would persuade[2] us to think that such a person as Jesus is not the Son of the unbegotten God and Father.

If Celsus misunderstood certain people who do not confess that the Son of God is Son of Him who created this universe, that is a matter between him and those who agree with this doctrine. Jesus, then, is not an author of sedition but of all peace. For he says to his disciples: 'Peace I leave with you, my peace I give unto you.' Then as he knew that the men who are of the world and not of God would make war on us, he went on to say, 'Not as the world gives peace do I give peace to you.'[3] And although we may be troubled in the world, we take courage because of him who said: 'In the world you shall have tribulation, but be of good cheer, I have overcome the world.'[4] We affirm that this person is Son of God—yes, of God to whom, if we may follow Celsus' words, we *pay very great reverence*; and we know His Son who has been *greatly exalted* by the Father.

But we may grant that some of those among the multitude of believers take a divergent view, and because of their rashness suppose that the Saviour is the greatest and supreme God. But we at least do not take that view, since we believe him who said: 'The Father who sent me is greater than I.'[5] Consequently we would not make Him whom we now call Father subject to the Son of God, as Celsus falsely accuses us of doing.

15. After this Celsus says: *To show that I am not wide of the mark in forming this opinion, I will quote their own words. For in one place in the heavenly dialogue*[6] *they speak there in these words: 'If the Son of God is mightier, and the Son of man is his Lord (and who else will overcome the God who is mighty?), how is it that many are round the well and no one goes into it? Why, when you have come to the end of such a hard journey, are you lacking in daring?'—'You are wrong, for I have courage and a sword.' Thus it is not their object to worship the super-celestial God,*[7] *but him whom they suppose to be the Father of Jesus who is the central object of their society. They want to*

---

[1] Heb. i. 3; Wisd. of Sol. vii. 25–6.   [2] Read with K. tr. μετοαπείσειέ τις.
[3] John xiv. 27.   [4] John xvi. 33.   [5] John xiv. 28.
[6] Cf. VI, 27 and note. Is this a Gnostic version of Jesus' agony in Gethsemane? Cf. Luke xxii. 38. See *Gospel of Thomas*, 74.   [7] Cf. Celsus in VI, 19.

CONTRA CELSUM

worship only this Son of man, whom they put forward as leader under the
pretence that he is a great God. And they say that he is mightier than and
lord of the God who is mighty. It was from this that they took their precept
against serving two masters, in order that the interests of the party following
this one person might be preserved unharmed.

Here again he takes these notions from some unknown and very
undistinguished sect, and bases on them an objection to all Christians.
I say 'very undistinguished' since it is not clear even to us who have often
taken part in controversy with heretics which is the opinion from which
Celsus has taken these ideas—if, at least, he did take them from some
source, and did not invent them or add anything as an inference of his own.
It is obvious that we, who maintain that even the sensible world is made
by the Creator of all things, hold that the Son is not mightier than the
Father, but subordinate. And we say this because we believe him who said,
'The Father who sent me is greater than I.'[1]

None of us is so idiotic as to say, '*The Son of man is lord of God.*' We
affirm that the Saviour, especially when we think of him as divine Logos,
Wisdom, Righteousness, and Truth, is Lord of all that has been subjected
to him, in so far as he is these things, but not that he is also lord of the God
and Father who is mightier than he. And since the Logos is not master of
those who are unwilling, and as there are still some bad beings, not only
men but also angels and all daemons, we maintain that he is not yet made
master of these, since they do not yield to him of their own free will.
However, if we take 'master' in another sense, he is master even of them—
just as we say that man is master of the irrational animals without making
their mind subject to him because he tames and masters certain lions and
beasts which have been broken in. Yet he does all in his power to persuade
even those who do not now obey, that he may be master of them also.
Therefore in our opinion Celsus' words are false when he attributes to us
the saying *Who else will overcome that God who is mighty?*

16. Then I think he muddles things again by bringing from another
sect the following: *How is it that many are round the well and no one goes
into it?* And *Why, when you have come to the end of such a hard journey, are
you lacking in daring? You are wrong.* And *For I have courage and a sword.*
We who belong to the church named after Christ alone say that none of
these things is true. He seems to be attributing to us sayings which are
nothing to do with us in order to be consistent with what he said earlier.
It is our purpose not to worship any merely assumed God, but to worship
the Creator of this universe and of all else which is not sensible or visible.
But this is a matter for those who tread 'another road' and 'other paths',[2]

[1] John xiv. 28.   [2] Homer, *Od.* IX, 261.

463

who deny Jesus and have given themselves up to a new-fangled fiction and to a merely nominal God whom they suppose to be greater than the Creator, and for anyone else who says that *the Son is mightier than and lord of the mighty God.*

Concerning the question whether it is right to serve two masters, we gave an account of the answer which occurred to us, when we showed that no sedition could be proved in the case of the honour offered to Jesus as Lord against those who confess that they have ascended above every lord and serve only the Son of God, and Logos of God, as Lord.[1]

17. After this Celsus says that we *avoid setting up altars and images and temples,* since, he thinks, it is *a sure token of an obscure and secret society.* He does not notice that our altars are the mind of each righteous man, from which true and intelligible incense with a sweet savour is sent up, prayers from a pure conscience. That is why it is said by John in the Apocalypse 'And the incense is the prayers of the saints', and by the Psalmist 'Let my prayers be as incense before thee.'[2]

Images and votive offerings appropriate for God, which have not been made by vulgar workmen, but which are made clear and formed in us by the divine Logos, are the virtues which are copies of the firstborn of all creation. For in him there are patterns of righteousness, prudence, courage, wisdom, piety, and the other virtues. Accordingly, there are images in all who, according to the divine word, have made for themselves prudence, righteousness, courage, wisdom, piety, and the products of the other virtues. We are persuaded that it is fitting for them to give honour to the prototype of all images, 'the image of the invisible God', the only-begotten God.[3] Moreover, those who 'have put off the old man with its deeds and put on the new man, which is renewed in knowledge after the image of him who created it',[4] restore what is in the image of the Creator and make images of him in themselves of such a nature as the supreme God wishes.

Just as some image-makers do their work with wonderful success, as, for example,[5] Pheidias or Polycleitus or the painters Zeuxis and Apelles, while others make them less skilfully than these men, and other men even less skilfully than the second class, so that in general there is much variation in the construction of images and pictures: in the same way, there are some who make images of the supreme God in a superior way and according to perfect knowledge, so that there is no comparison between the Olympian Zeus wrought by Pheidias and him who is made in the image of God who created him. But of all the images in the whole

---

[1] VIII, 3–5. [2] Rev. v. 8; Ps. cxl. 2. [3] Col. i. 15; John i. 18.
[4] Col. iii. 9–10. [5] Read with We., K. tr. ὡς φέρ' εἰπεῖν.

creation by far the most superior and pre-eminent is that in our Saviour who said, 'My Father is in me.'[1]

18. In each of those who do all in their power to imitate him in this respect there is an image 'after the image of the Creator',[2] which they make by looking to God with a pure heart, having become imitators of God.[3] And speaking generally, all Christians try to set up such altars as we have mentioned, and images such as we have described. They do not set up images which are lacking in life and feeling, nor which receive daemons greedy for lifeless things, but images which receive the Spirit of God, who dwells in the images of virtue which we have mentioned, and in that which is in the image of the Creator because they are related to Him. So also the Spirit of Christ sits[4] upon those, so to speak, who are formed like him. Because the Word of God wished to show this, God is described as promising to the righteous: 'I will dwell among them and will walk among them, and I will be their God and they shall be my people.'[5] And the Saviour says: 'If any man hears my words and does them, I and my Father will come to him and will make our habitation with him.'[6]

Anyone interested may compare the altars which I have described with those of which Celsus speaks, and the images in the soul of those who are pious towards the God of the universe with those made by Pheidias and Polycleitus and similar artists. He will clearly recognize that the latter are lifeless and in time become corrupted, while the former abide in the immortal soul so long as the rational soul is willing for them to remain in it.

19. If we may also compare temples with temples, to show to those who accept Celsus' criticisms that we do not *avoid setting up temples* of the same sort as the images and altars of which we have spoken, but that we turn away from building lifeless and dead temples to the author of all life, let anyone interested hear how we are taught that our bodies are a temple of God;[7] and if anyone by licentiousness or sin corrupts the temple of God, that man will be destroyed because he is the one who is truly impious in his attitude to the true temple. But the sacred and pure body of our Saviour Jesus was a temple better than and superior to all the so-called temples. For because he knew that impious men were able to form designs against the temple of God within him, though it was certainly not the case that the purpose of the men who had such designs was stronger than the divine power which built the temple, he said to them 'Destroy this temple and in three days I will raise it up.' But 'this he said of the temple of his body'.[8]

Moreover, elsewhere the divine scriptures teach the doctrine of the

---

[1] John xiv. 10.   [2] Col. iii. 10.   [3] Matt. v. 8; Eph. v. 1.
[4] Cf. Acts ii. 3.   [5] II Cor. vi. 16.   [6] Matt. vii. 24; John xiv. 23.
[7] I Cor. iii. 16–17; vi. 19.   [8] John ii. 19, 21.

resurrection under a mysterious form to those who are capable of hearing
God's words with a divine power of hearing; and they say that the temple
will be rebuilt with living and precious stones. This obscurely refers to the
doctrine that each of those who are united through the same Logos, for
the piety which is in accord with his teaching, is a precious stone of the
entire temple of God. So Peter says: 'But you are built up, as living
stones and a spiritual house, into a holy temple to offer up spiritual
sacrifices acceptable to God through Jesus Christ.'[1] And Paul says 'Being
built upon the foundation of the apostles and prophets, Christ Jesus our
Lord being himself the corner-stone'.[2] Some such mysterious meaning is
contained in the passage in Isaiah addressed to Jerusalem, which reads as
follows: 'Behold I prepare for thee a carbuncle as thy stone and sapphire
as thy foundations, and I will make thy battlements of jasper and thy
gates stones of crystal and thy wall of chosen stones. And all thy sons
shall be taught by God, and thy children shall dwell in much peace, and
shall be built in righteousness.'[3]

20. Some of the righteous are a carbuncle stone, and others sapphire,
others jasper, and others crystal. And in this way every sort of chosen
and precious stone are the righteous. It is not at present the moment to
explain the meaning of the stones and the doctrine concerning their nature,
and what sort of soul is referred to by the name of each[4] precious stone.
But we had to mention briefly just the meaning of the temples as we understand them, and of the one temple of God made out of precious stones.
For just as if in every city each people was proud of its supposed temples
in contrast to others, those who were proud of their temples because of
their great value would mention the pre-eminent qualities of their own
to show up the defects of their inferiors; so in reply to those who criticize
us because we do not think that we ought to worship God with temples
which cannot feel, we contrast with them the temples as we conceive
them and show, at least to people who are not incapable of perception nor
like their senseless gods, that there is no comparison between our images
and those of the heathen, or between our altars and the incense ascending
from them, so to speak, and the heathen altars and the burnt offerings and
blood offered at them, nor, what is more, between our temples which we
have described and those of the senseless gods which are admired by
senseless men who have not even any idea of the divine perception by
which one may perceive God and the images of Him and temples and
altars which are fitting for Him.

Therefore it is not true that we avoid setting up altars and images
because this is *a sure token of an obscure and secret society*. We do so because

[1] I Pet. ii. 5.   [2] Eph. ii. 20.   [3] Isa. liv. 11–14.   [4] Read ἐκ⟨άσ⟩του with K. tr.

through the teaching of Jesus we have found the way to worship God. And so we avoid things which, though they have an appearance of piety, make impious those who have been led astray from the piety which is mediated through Jesus Christ. He alone is the way of piety and truly said 'I am the way, the truth, and the life.'[1]

21. Let us also look at Celsus' next remarks about God, and the way in which he encourages us to eat what are really sacrifices offered to idols or, so to speak, sacrifices offered to daemons, although, because he does not know what is truly sacred and what is the nature of true sacrifices, he himself would call them 'sacred offerings'. This is what he says: *God is surely common to all men. He is both good and in need of nothing,*[2] *and without envy.*[3] *What, then, prevents people particularly devoted to them from partaking of the public feasts?* I do not know why he should have taken it into his head to suppose that it follows from the fact that God is good and in need of nothing and without envy that people devoted to Him may partake of the public feasts. I say that it would follow from the fact that God is good and in need of nothing and without envy that they may partake of the public feasts only if it were proved that the public feasts contained nothing wrong, but were customs founded on perception of God's nature so as to be consistent with worship and devotion to Him.

If, however, the so-called public feasts have no rational interpretation to show that they are consistent with worship offered to God, and if they were proved to be inventions of people who somehow were led to make these customs by certain human stories, or even imagine that they include philosophical doctrines concerning water or earth or the fruits produced by it, then obviously those who wish to be careful about the way they worship God would be acting with good reason if they did not partake of the public feasts. For, as one of the Greek wise men rightly said, 'a feast is nothing but doing one's duty'.[4] In fact, he who is doing his duty is in reality keeping a feast; for he is always praying, continually offering bloodless sacrifices in his prayers to God.[5] For this reason also Paul seems to me to have said very finely: 'Do you observe days and

---

[1] John xiv. 6.   [2] Cf. Celsus in vi, 52; Origen in vii, 65.
[3] From Plato, *Phaedrus*, 247 A; *Timaeus* 29 E. Cf. Aristotle, *Met.* I, 2 (983 a 2). With Celsus' view that although God needs no sacrifices it is a good thing to offer them, cf. Dio Chrys. xxxi, 15 'Probably God needs none of these things like images and sacrifices; but these things are not futile, because they manifest our zeal and attitude towards the gods.'
[4] Thucydides, 1, 70, *ad fin.*
[5] Philo, *de Sp. Leg.* II, 46 'Rejoicing in the virtues they make their entire life the celebration of a feast'; imitated by Clem. Al. *Strom.* vii, 35 'It is neither in a definite place or special shrine, nor yet on certain feasts and days set apart, that the gnostic honours God, returning thanks to Him for knowledge bestowed and the gift of the heavenly citizenship; but he will do this all his life in every place, whether he be alone by himself or have with him some who share his belief....Accordingly all our life is a festival' (trans. Hort-Mayor).

months and times and years? I am afraid for you lest by any means I have bestowed labour on you in vain.'[1]

22. If anyone makes a rejoinder to this by talking of our observances on certain days, the Lord's Day which we keep, or the Preparation, or the Passover, or Pentecost,[2] we would reply to this that the perfect man, who is always engaged in the words, works, and thoughts of the divine Logos who is by nature his Lord, is always living in His days and is continually observing the Lord's Day. Moreover, since he is always making himself ready for the true life and abstaining from the pleasures of this life which deceive the multitude, and since he does not nourish 'the mind of the flesh', but buffets his body and makes it his slave,[3] he is always observing the Preparation. Furthermore, if a man has understood that 'Christ our passover was sacrificed', and that he ought to 'keep the feast'[4] by eating the flesh of the Logos, there is not a moment when he is not keeping the Passover, which means offerings before making a crossing.[5] For he is always passing over in thought and in every word and every deed from the affairs of this life to God and hastening towards His city. In addition to this, if a man is able to say truthfully 'we are risen with Christ', and also that 'he raised us up and made us sit with him in the heavenly places in Christ',[6] he is always living in the days of Pentecost, and particularly when, like the apostles of Jesus, he goes up to the upper room and gives time to supplication and prayer, so that he becomes worthy of the mighty rushing wind from heaven which compels the evil in men and its conse-quences to disappear, and so that he becomes worthy also of some share in the fiery tongue given by God.[7]

23. The multitude of those who seem to believe have not made such progress. And because they lack the desire or the ability to live in this way every day, they need sensible examples by way of a reminder to prevent them from neglecting the matter entirely. I think that this is what Paul had in mind when he called the feast that is held on days set apart from the others 'part of a feast';[8] he hinted by this phrase that the life which is continually being lived according to the divine word is not in 'part of a feast' but in an entire and continual feast. Accordingly consider from what we have said about our feasts, by comparing them with the public feasts of Celsus and the heathen, whether these are not far more sacred than the public feasts. For in the latter 'the mind of the flesh'[9]

---

[1] Gal. iv. 10-11.
[2] For these observances, cf. H. Lietzmann, *The Founding of the Church Universal* (2nd ed. 1950), pp. 133 ff.
[3] Rom. viii. 6-7; I Cor. ix. 27.
[4] I Cor. v. 7; cf. John vi. 52-6.
[5] Similarly Philo, *Vita Mos.* II, 224.
[6] Col. ii. 12; iii. 1; Eph. ii. 6.
[7] Acts i. 13-14; ii. 2-3.
[8] Col. ii. 16.
[9] Rom. viii. 6-7.

celebrates the feasts in a wanton manner, turning to drunkenness and licentiousness.

It would be possible here to say much about the question why the feasts prescribed by the law of God teach that men must 'eat the bread of affliction' or 'unleavened bread with bitter herbs', or why they say 'humble your souls'[1] or some similar command. For it is not even possible for the whole human personality to celebrate the feasts in his entirety so long as the flesh still 'lusts against the spirit, and the spirit against the flesh'.[2] Anyone who keeps a feast in the spirit afflicts the body which, on account of the 'mind of the flesh', is incapable of keeping the feast with the spirit. And anyone who keeps a feast according to the flesh is not able to keep the feast according to the spirit as well. However, for the present that is enough on the subject of feasts.

24. Let us look at the words which Celsus uses to encourage us to eat meats offered to idols and to take part in the public sacrifices at the public feasts. This is what he says: *If these idols are nothing, why is it terrible to take part in the high festival? And if they are daemons of some sort, obviously these too belong to God, and we ought to believe them and sacrifice to them according to the laws, and pray to them that they may be kindly disposed.* For an answer to this it would be helpful to take into our hands the First Epistle to the Corinthians and to explain the entire discussion of meats offered to idols which Paul there gives. In that passage he was replying to the view that 'an idol is nothing in the world' and established that harm comes from eating meats offered to idols, proving to those able to understand his words there that without doubt the man who partakes of meats offered to idols is doing something no less serious than murder. For he destroys his brethren for whom Christ died.[3] And after this when he affirms that the offerings are sacrificed to daemons, he shows that those who partake of the table of daemons become partakers of the daemons; and he shows that it is impossible for the same person to 'partake of the table of the Lord and the table of daemons'.[4]

However, since the commentary on these points in the Epistle to the Corinthians requires a whole treatise with an extended discussion, we will be content with these brief remarks. From them it will be clear to the man who studies them that, even if idols are nothing, it is none the less terrible to take part in the high festival of the idols. We have also spoken at moderate length about the point that, even if they are daemons of some sort to whom the offerings are sacrificed, we ought not to partake of them since we know the difference between the table of the Lord and the table

---

[1] Deut. xvi. 3; Exod. xii. 8; Lev. xvi. 29, 31.   [2] Gal. v. 17.
[3] I Cor. viii. 4, 11.   [4] I Cor. x. 20–1.

of daemons, and on account of our knowledge do all we can to partake always of the table of the Lord, while in every way we take care lest at any time we become partakers of the table of the daemons.

25. Celsus here says that the daemons *belong to God*, and that for this reason *we ought to believe them and sacrifice to them according to the laws and pray to them that they may be kindly disposed*. We must therefore inform those who are interested in this matter that the word of God is unwilling to call any evil being the possession of God, since it judges them unworthy of so great a Lord. That is why not all men are called men of God,, but only those who are worthy of God. Such were Moses and Elijah,[1] and anyone else who is·described as a man of God or who resembles those so described. Similarly not all angels are said to be angels of God,[2] but only the blessed angels, while those who have turned aside to evil are named the devil's angels,[3] just as bad men are called men of sin, or pestilent sons, or sons of iniquity.[4] Since then there are both good and bad men, for this reason some are said to be men of God and some of the devil; so also there are some angels of God and some of the devil. But the twofold division no longer holds good in the case of daemons; for they are all proved to be bad. On this account we would say that Celsus' words are false when he says: *And if they are daemons of some sort, obviously these too belong to God*. Let anyone who likes show either that the distinction in the case of men and angels is not a sound one,[5] or that a similar distinction could be proved to hold good of daemons also.

26. If, however, this is impossible, it is obvious that the daemons do not belong to God; for their ruler is not God but, as the divine scriptures say, Beelzebul.[6] [26] Nor ought we to believe daemons, even though Celsus exhorts us to do so, but we ought to die before believing daemons and, moreover, endure anything whatever in obedience to God. Similarly we ought not to sacrifice to daemons; for it is impossible to do this to evil beings hurtful to men. Further, what sort of laws does Celsus want us to follow in sacrificing to daemons? If he means those in force in the cities, let him prove that they are in harmony with the divine laws. But if he cannot do this (for the laws of most cities do not agree even with one another),[7] obviously we must say that they[8] are not strictly speaking laws at all or are laws made by evil men. And such we must not believe. For 'we ought to obey God rather than men'.[9]

---

[1] Deut. xxxiii. 1; II Kings (IV Regn.) i. 10.
[2] Matt. xxii. 30; Luke xii. 8.   [3] Matt. xxv. 41.
[4] I Sam. (I Regn.) ii. 12; x. 27; xxv. 17; Ezek. xviii. 10; II Sam. (II Regn.) iii. 34; vii. 10.
[5] Read with Wif. μὴ [λόγον] ὑγιῆ εἶναι, and in the next line λόγον ἔχουσαν.
[6] Matt. xii. 24.   [7] Cf. v, 37 above.
[8] Read with Wif. οὐδὲ κυρίως νόμους (λεκτέον αὐτούς) ἢ φαύλων.   [9] Acts v. 29.

Away with Celsus' advice when he says that *we ought to pray to daemons.*
We ought not to pay the slightest attention to it. We ought to pray to the
supreme God alone, and to pray besides to the only-begotten Logos of
God, the firstborn of all creation;[1] and we ought to beseech him, as a high-
priest, to bear our prayer, when it has reached him, up to his God and our
God and to his Father and the Father[2] of people who live according to the
word of God. We would not wish that men who want us to live lives as
wicked as theirs should be kindly disposed, if they happen to be kindly
disposed to no one who chooses the opposite to them. The reason for this
is that their goodwill makes us enemies of God, who probably does not
become kindly disposed towards those who want to have the goodwill of
men of that sort. In the same way those who have considered the nature
of daemons and their purpose and wickedness would never desire to have
their goodwill.

27. For even if the daemons were not kindly disposed towards them
they could not suffer any harm at their hands. Because of their piety they
are guarded by the supreme God who is kindly disposed towards them
and makes His divine angels stand over those worthy to be guarded so
that they suffer no harm at the hands of the daemons.[3] But the man who
has the goodwill of the supreme God because of his piety towards Him
and because he has accepted the Lord Jesus, the 'angel of the great counsel'[4]
of God, is content with the goodwill of God through Christ Jesus, and
because he will suffer no harm from all the army of daemons he may
boldly say: 'The Lord is my light and my saviour; whom shall I fear?
The Lord is the protector of my life; of whom shall I be afraid?' And he
would also say: 'If a host should be lined up against me, my heart will not
be afraid.'[5] So much, then, for our reply to his words that *if they are
daemons of some sort, obviously these too belong to God, and we ought to
believe them and sacrifice to them according to the laws, and pray to them
that they may be kindly disposed.*

28. Let us also quote his next remarks and again to the best of our
ability examine them. They read as follows: *If they follow a custom of their
fathers[6] when they abstain from particular sacrificial victims, surely they
ought also to abstain from the food of all animals—such is the view taken by
Pythagoras with the intention of honouring thereby the soul and its organs.[7]
But if, as they say, they abstain to avoid feasting with daemons,[8] I congratu-
late them on their wisdom, because they are slowly coming to understand that
they are always associating with daemons. They take pains to avoid this only*

---

[1] Col. i. 15.   [2] Cf. John xx. 17.   [3] Cf. i, 61, above.
[4] Isa. ix. 6.   [5] Ps. xxvi. 1, 3.   [6] Cf. Celsus in v, 25, 41.
[7] v, 41.   [8] I Cor. x. 20 ff. (cf. Lietzmann *ad loc.*).

at the time when they see a victim being sacrificed. But whenever they eat food, and drink wine, and taste fruits, and drink[1] even water itself, and breathe even the very air, are they not receiving each of these from certain daemons, among whom the administration of each[2] of these has been divided? I do not know why here he thought it logical for those whom he describes as *following a custom of their fathers* when they abstain from particular sacrificial victims, that they should abstain from the food of all animals. We do not take this view, because the divine scripture does not even suggest anything of the kind, although for the sake of a safer and purer life it says, 'It is good neither to eat flesh nor to drink wine nor to do anything whereby your brother stumbles', and again, 'Do not destroy with your meat the man for whom Christ died', and again, 'If meat makes my brother to stumble, I will eat no flesh for evermore to avoid making my brother to stumble.'[3]

29. However, we must realize that the Jews, who think they understand the law of Moses, take care to partake only of those meats regarded by them as clean and to abstain from unclean food, and also not to use for food the blood of an animal, nor those animals caught by wild beasts and others. There is much to be said about these matters, and for this reason it is not now a suitable time for the examination of the question. The teaching of Jesus, on the other hand, wanted all men to be called to the pure worship of God and to avoid hindering, by reason of the tiresome legislation about meats, many who could be helped by Christianity in their moral life; and so he declared that 'it is not that which goes into the mouth that defiles a man, but that which comes out of the mouth'. 'For', he says, 'the things which go into the mouth pass into the belly and are cast out into the draught', but the things which come out of the mouth are 'evil thoughts' which are spoken aloud, 'murders, adulteries, fornications, thefts, false witnesses, and blasphemies'.[4] Paul also says that 'meat will not commend us to God; for neither, if we eat, are we the better; nor, if we do not eat, are we the worse'.[5] Then since unless these matters are[6] defined precisely they are somewhat obscure, it seemed good to the apostles of Jesus and the elders assembled together in Antioch, and, as they put it, 'to the Holy Spirit', to write a letter to the Gentile believers, demanding that they should abstain only from what they called 'the essentials'. These are things sacrificed to idols, or things strangled, or blood.[7]

[1] The word 'drink' has fallen out here in the text. K. tr. proposes ⟨ὕδωρ πίνωσι⟩, Bader prefers ὕδωρ ⟨ῥοφῶσι⟩. For the idea cf. Celsus in VIII, 55; Clem. Al. *Strom.* III, 12, 3 (of the Marcionites).
[2] Read with K. tr. ἑκάστων. For the idea cf. Celsus, in V, 25; VII, 68.
[3] Rom. xiv. 21, 15; I Cor. viii. 13.   [4] Matt. xv. 11, 17, 19.   [5] I Cor. viii. 8.
[6] Read τύχοι with We., K. tr.; and in line 32, μόνα τά, ὡς... with Wif.
[7] Acts xv. 22, 28–9. (Origen perhaps puts the council at Antioch by a slip.)

30. That which is offered to idols is sacrificed to daemons, and a man of God ought not to become a partaker of the table of daemons. The Bible forbids things strangled because the blood has not been removed, which, they say, is the food of daemons who are nourished by the vapours rising from it, in order that we may not be fed on daemons' food, perhaps because if we were to partake of things strangled some spirits of this nature might be fed together with us.[1] From what has been said about things strangled the explanation for abstinence from blood can be clearly seen. It is not irrelevant for me to mention in this connexion a very graceful maxim written in the Maxims of Sextus which even the multitude of Christians read. It is as follows: 'It is a matter of moral indifference to eat living things, but abstinence is more rational.'[2] Therefore, it is not simply because we follow a custom of our fathers that we abstain from what are supposed to be victims sacrificed to the so-called gods, or heroes, or daemons, but for several reasons some of which I have set forth in part. Moreover, we ought not to abstain from the food of all animals in the way that we do from all evil and its results. But we ought to abstain not only from the food of animals, but also from everything whatever if it implies eating the food associated with evil and its consequences. For we ought to abstain from eating with gluttonous motives or merely because of a desire[3] for pleasure without having in view the health of the body and its restoration.

However, even if we do sometimes abstain from animals, it is certainly not for any reason similar to that of Pythagoras that we do not eat their flesh. For we do not hold the doctrine of the transmigration of the soul

[1] Cf. III, 28, above.
[2] Origen is the earliest witness to the existence of the collection of Sextus' Maxims, from which he quotes also in *Comm. in Matt.* XV, 3, where he speaks of the collection as 'a book accepted by many as sound'. At the end of the fourth century Rufinus produced a Latin translation, alleging in his preface that the Maxims were by Xystus II, bishop of Rome and martyr (A.D. 256–8). Jerome could quote from the collection with approval (*adv. Jovin.* I, 49, Vallarsi, II, 318); but in controversy with his former friend Rufinus he attacked the attribution to Xystus, insisting that it is a pagan collection of Maxims by Sextus a Pythagorean (*in Ierem.* IV, 22; *Ep.* CXXXIII, 3; *Comm. in Ezech.* VI on Ezek. xviii. 5; Vallarsi, IV, 993, I, 1030, V, 206). He may have had in mind Sextius, a Stoic contemporary of Julius Caesar, who had Pythagorean leanings (Seneca, *Ep.* LIX, 7; LXIV, 2, 5; LXXIII). Augustine (*de Nat. et Gr.* LXIV, 67) quotes the Maxims as the work of Xystus, but withdrew in his *Retractations* (II, 42). Nevertheless, the work continued to circulate in the Middle Ages in Rufinus' version, and was quoted as the work of the Christian bishop.
The Maxims are extant not only in Rufinus' version and a Syriac translation published by Lagarde (*Analecta Syriaca*, 1858), but also in Greek, first published by A. Elter (*Index Scholar. Bonn.* 1891/2). The origin of the Maxims is obscure. Wendland (*Theol.-Lit. Zeit.* (1893), col. 292 ff.) thought the collection a Christian revision of a pagan original. W. Kroll, in P.-W. *s.v.* 'Sextus' (5), dates the collection in the second century A.D.
The Maxim which Origen quotes here is no. 109 in Elter's edition.
[3] Read κατὰ τὸ ἄγεσθαι with We. (K. tr. proposes καθὸ ἄγεταί τις).

and its fall even to irrational animals.¹ We acknowledge honour to the
rational soul only, and commit its organs to the grave with honour
according to the customary ceremonies. For the dwelling of the rational
soul does not deserve to be cast aside without honour and in a casual
manner like that of the irrational animals.² Christians particularly hold
this view because they are convinced that the honour paid to the body
where a rational soul has dwelt is to be applied to the person who received
a soul which fought a good fight with this organ.³ However, concerning
the question 'How are the dead raised and with what body do they come?'⁴
we have briefly spoken earlier as the purpose of this book required.

31. After this Celsus quotes what, admittedly, Christians and Jews
say when they defend their abstinence from things sacrificed to idols and
affirm that people who are devoted to the supreme God ought not to
feast with daemons. In reply to this he said the words which we have
quoted. Now concerning food and drink, we think that a man cannot
feast with daemons except by eating what are popularly called sacred
offerings,⁵ and by drinking the wine of the libations made to the daemons.
But Celsus thinks that a man is feasting with daemons even when he
partakes of food and drinks some wine, and when he tastes fruits, and,
moreover, if he only drinks some water; even here, he says, the man who
drinks is associating with daemons. He adds to this that even the man who
breathes in the common air gets this from certain daemons, since the
daemons who have been given charge of the air grant it to living beings
for breathing.

I challenge anyone to defend Celsus' doctrine. Let him show how
those appointed to administer all the things just mentioned are not
certain divine angels of God, but are daemons, the entire race of whom is
evil. For we say that the earth bears the things which are said to be under
the control of nature because of the appointment of invisible husbandmen,⁶
so to speak, and other governors who control not only the produce of the
earth but also all flowing water and air. For this reason also the water in
the wells and in the natural springs becomes rain and circulates, and the
air is kept free from pollution, and becomes capable of giving life to those
who breathe it. We certainly do not maintain that these invisible beings
are daemons. But, if we may go so far as to say what, if not these,⁷ are the

¹ For Origen's view of transmigration, cf. Bigg, *The Christian Platonists* (1913), p. 241.
² Cf. IV, 59; V, 24; VIII, 50.
³ Read with Wif. ⟨τὸν⟩ δεξάμενον. Origen perhaps has in mind the ceremonies at the
tombs of martyrs, for which cf. E. Lucius, *Die Anfänge des Heiligenkults* (1904), pp. 71 f.,
282 ff.　　　　⁴ I Cor. xv. 35; cf. v, 18 above.　　　　⁵ Cf. VIII, 21, above.
⁶ Cf. Origen, *de Princ.* III, 3, 3; *Hom. in Iesu Nave*, XXIII, 3.
⁷ Read τίνα, εἰ μὴ ταῦτα, δαιμόνων.

works of daemons, we would say that they are responsible for famines, barren vines and fruit-trees, and droughts, and also for the pollution of the air, causing damage to the fruits, and sometimes even the death of animals and plague among men. Of all these things daemons are the direct creators; like public executioners,[1] they have received power by a divine appointment to bring about these catastrophes at certain times, either for the conversion of men when they drift towards the flood of evil, or with the object of training the race of rational beings. The purpose is that those who remain religious even in such great disasters and do not become worse may reveal their true character to the onlookers, visible and invisible, who hitherto have not seen this; whereas those who are inclined in the opposite way, but conceal the manifestation of their wickedness, are shown up by the catastrophes, and their character is displayed to those who, so to speak, look on.

32. That grim disasters are, by a divine appointment, directly caused by certain wicked angels is testified by the psalmist in the words: 'He sent forth the wrath of his anger against them, anger and wrath and trouble sent by means of wicked angels.'[2] Anyone who has the ability may examine the question whether the daemons are sometimes[3] allowed to cause other disasters beside these. For they are always wanting to do these things, but are not always able because they are prevented. And, so far as it is possible for human nature, he may obtain some idea of the divine judgment which allows the sudden separation of many souls from the body when they are following paths such as lead to death—a matter of moral indifference.[4] Moreover 'the judgments of God are great', and on account of this greatness it is not possible for a mind still bound to a mortal body to grasp them; and they are 'hard to explain', while 'uneducated souls' have not the least perception of them.[5] That is why hasty people, ignorant of these matters and because of their rashness opposed to God, multiply impious doctrines against providence.

Accordingly it is not from daemons that we receive each of the necessities of life, especially if we have learnt how to use them aright; nor do those who partake of food, wine, fruits, water, and air feast with daemons. The truth is rather that they are associating with the divine angels appointed in charge of these things, who are, so to speak, invited to the home of the religious man who has understood the saying which teaches as follows: 'Whether you eat or drink, do all to the glory of God.'[6]

---

[1] Read ⟨ὡς⟩ δήμιοι with K. tr. Cf. I, 31; VII, 70; VIII, 73; Porphyry, *de Abst.* II, 38 ff.
[2] Ps. lxxvii. 49.   [3] Read γίνεται ὅθ' οἱ with Wif.
[4] Stoic teaching: cf. Zeno, *S.V.F.* I, 190; III, 117; Origen, *Comm. in Joann.* XX, 39 (31); *Dial. c. Heracl.* p. 168 Scherer.
[5] Wisd. of Sol. xvii. 1.   [6] I Cor. x. 31.

And in another place we find the words 'Whether you eat or drink, do all in God's name.'[1] Therefore when we eat, drink, and breathe to the glory of God, and do every action in accordance with Christian principles, we are feasting not with any of the daemons, but with divine angels. Moreover, 'every creature of God is good and nothing is to be rejected, if it is received with thanksgiving; for it is sanctified by the word of God and prayer'.[2] But it would not have been good nor could it be sanctified if, as Celsus thinks, these things had been put under the charge of daemons.

33. From these remarks it is obvious that we have also replied to his next sentence which reads as follows: *Either we ought not to live at all anywhere on earth and not to enter this life, or, if we do enter this life under these conditions, we ought to give thanks to the daemons who have been allotted control over earthly things, and render to them firstfruits and prayers as long as we live that we may obtain their goodwill towards us.* Live we must; and we are to do so in accordance with the word of God, so far as it is possible and as it is granted to us to live in accordance with it; but this is granted when, 'whether we eat or drink, we do all to the glory of God'.[3] We must not refuse to eat with thanksgiving to the Creator the things He has created for us. And it is on these conditions that we were brought into this life by God rather than on those which Celsus supposes. And we are not subject to daemons, but to the supreme God through Jesus Christ who brought us to Him.

According to God's laws no daemon has been allotted control of earthly things. But through their own wickedness, perhaps, they divided[4] among themselves those regions where there is not to be found any knowledge of God or the life lived after His will, or where there are many alien to God. Perhaps, on the other hand, as worthy to govern and to punish the wicked, they were appointed by the Logos who administers the universe to rule those who have subjected themselves to evil and not to God. For reasons of this kind Celsus, as one who is ignorant of God, may render the offerings of thanksgiving to daemons. But we give thanks to the Creator of the universe and eat the loaves that are presented with thanksgiving and prayer over the gifts, so that by the prayer they become a certain holy body which sanctifies those who partake of it with a pure intention.[5]

34. Celsus wants us to dedicate firstfruits to daemons. But we do this to Him who said: 'Let the earth bring forth a plant of grass, a seed that

---

[1] Col. iii. 17.   [2] I Tim. iv. 4–5.
[3] I Cor. x. 31.   [4] Read διείλοντο with Bo., K. tr.
[5] For Origen's eucharistic theology see Bigg, *The Christian Platonists* (1913), pp. 264 f.; H. de Lubac, *Histoire et Esprit: L'Intelligence de l'Écriture d'après Origène* (1950), pp. 355 ff.

sows after its kind and likeness, and a fruitful tree that produces fruit, of
which its seed is in it after its kind upon the earth.'[1] He to whom we
render the firstfruits is also the one to whom we send up our prayers,
since we 'have a great high priest who has passed into the heavens, Jesus
the Son of God',[2] and we hold fast the confession *as long as we live*, as we
obtain the goodwill of God and of His only-begotten Son who is manifested to us in Jesus.

If we also want to have a multitude of beings whose goodwill we desire
to obtain, we learn that 'thousand thousands stood beside him, and ten
thousand times ten thousand ministered to him'.[3] These beings regard as
kinsmen and friends those who imitate their piety towards God, and assist
those who call upon God, and who truly pray, in obtaining their salvation.
They appear to them and think it their duty to hear their prayers, and as
it were by one consent to visit with blessing and salvation those who pray
to God, to whom they themselves also pray. For 'they are all ministering
spirits, sent forth to do service for the sake of them that shall inherit
salvation'.[4] *The wise men of the Greeks* may *say that the human soul is
allotted to daemons from birth;*[5] but when Jesus taught us not to despise
even the little ones in the church he said that 'their angels continually
behold the face of my Father who is in heaven'.[6] And the prophet says
'The angel of the Lord will encamp round about those who fear him and
deliver them.'[7]

Therefore, even we do not deny that there are many daemons on earth;
but we maintain that they exist and have power among bad men on account
of the wickedness of the latter, and that they have no power against those
who have put on the whole armour of God and have received strength to
withstand the wiles of the devil, and who are always being exercised in
struggles with them because they know that 'our wrestling is not with
flesh and blood but against principalities, against powers, against the
rulers of this darkness, against spiritual wickedness in heavenly places'.[8]

35. Let us consider also another passage of Celsus which runs as
follows: *The satrap and subordinate governor or officer or procurator of the
Persian or Roman emperor, and, furthermore, even those who hold lesser
positions or responsibilities or offices, could do much harm if they were slighted.
Would the satraps and ministers both in the air and on earth do but little
harm if they were insulted?*[9] Notice how he introduces anthropomorphic
satraps of the supreme God and subordinate governors, and officers, and

---

[1] Gen. i. 11.   [2] Heb. iv. 14.   [3] Dan. vii. 10.
[4] Heb. i. 14; for angelic help, cf. Origen, *de Orat.* xi, 3.
[5] For this belief, cf. Rohde, *Psyche* (E.T.), pp. 514 f.
[6] Matt. xviii. 10.   [7] Ps. xxxiii. 8.
[8] Eph. vi. 10–12.   [9] See Introduction, p. xix.

procurators, and those who hold lesser positions and responsibilities and offices, as if they did much harm to people who insult them. He does not notice that no wise man would want to harm anyone, but would do all in his power to convert and improve even people who insulted him. But perhaps in Celsus' view the satraps, subordinate governors, and officers of the supreme God are worse than Lycurgus, the lawgiver of the Spartans, and than Zeno of Citium. For when Lycurgus obtained power over a man who had struck out his eye, not only did he not take revenge, but he did not cease trying to win him over until he had persuaded him to study philosophy.[1] And to the man who said, 'I'll be damned if I will not take vengeance on you', Zeno replied, 'And I, if I do not make you my friend.'[2]

I have not yet mentioned those whose characters conform to the teaching of Jesus, who have heard the saying: 'Love your enemies and pray for those who despitefully use you, that you may become sons of your Father who is in heaven, who makes his sun to rise upon the evil and the good, and sends rain upon the just and on the unjust.'[3] And in the words of the prophets a righteous man speaks as follows: 'O Lord my God, if I have done this thing, if there is iniquity in my hands, if I have repaid evil to those who repaid it to me, then may I fall back empty from my enemies; let the enemy persecute my soul and catch it and trample my life to the earth.'[4]

36. The angels, the true satraps, subordinate governors, officers, and procurators of God, do no harm to those who slight them, as Celsus thinks. But if certain daemons inflict harm, of whom even Celsus had some notion, they do so because they are evil, and have not been entrusted by God with any position as satrap or officer or procurator. And they harm those who are under their power and have submitted themselves to them as masters. Perhaps it is also for this reason that people in each place are harmed when they break the law concerning foods which by custom may not be eaten, if they belong to those who are in the power of those daemons. But if they are not among those who are in their power, and have not submitted themselves to the daemon of the locality, they are free from suffering at their hands, and entirely renounce daemons of this sort; although if, because of their ignorance on other matters, they put themselves in the power of other daemons, they could suffer at their hands. But the Christian, the real Christian who has submitted himself to God alone and His Logos, would not suffer anything at the hands of daemons, since he is superior to them. And the reason why he would not suffer is that 'the

[1] The story is told by Plutarch in his life of Lycurgus (11); also Musonius, *frag.* 39 Hense (= Epictetus, *frag.* 5, p. 406 Schenkl).

[2] Plutarch, *Mor.* 462c (from which the true text here is restored). Plutarch tells the story also of Eucleides (489 D), saying that the story is 'hackneyed in the schools'.

[3] Matt. v. 44–5. [4] Ps. vii. 4–6.

angel of the Lord will encamp round about those who fear him and deliver
them', and his angel 'continually beholds the face of the Father in heaven'[1]
and is always bearing up his prayers to the God of the universe through
the mediation of the only High Priest. And the angel himself prays
together with the man who is under his charge.[2] Let not Celsus scare us,
then, by threatening that we shall be hurt by daemons if we slight them.
For even if daemons are slighted, they are able to do nothing to us who
are devoted to the Person that is alone able to help all those who deserve
it. He does no less than set His own angels over those whose lives are
devoted to him, that the opposing angels and the so-called ruler of this
world[3] who governs them may be unable to do anything against those who
are dedicated to God.

37. Then he forgets that he is talking to Christians who alone pray to
God through Jesus, and muddles together the notions of others which for
no reason whatever he connects with the Christians, saying: *If one
pronounces their name in a barbarian tongue, they will have power; but if in
Greek or Latin, they are no longer effective.*[4] I challenge anyone to show
what being we name in a barbarian tongue in order to call him to our aid.
He may be convinced that it was futile for Celsus to have said these things
against us when he observes that most[5] Christians do not even use in their
prayers the names applied to God which are found in the divine scriptures.
But the Greeks speak in Greek, and the Romans in Latin; and so each one
according to his language prays to God and sings his praises as he is able.
And the Lord of every language hears those who pray in every language
as though He were hearing one utterance, so to speak, the same meaning
being expressed by the various languages. For the supreme God is not
one of those that have been allotted a particular language, barbarian or
Greek, who no longer understand the rest or are no longer willing to pay
heed to those who speak in other languages.

38. Then after this, either because he has not heard any Christian or
has heard some lawless and uneducated fellow from the multitude, he says
that *Christians say, Look, I stand by the image of Zeus or Apollo or any god
indeed, and I blaspheme it and strike it; but it takes no vengeance on me.*[6] He
does not notice that in the divine legislation there is the command, 'Thou
shalt not speak evil of gods',[7] that our mouth may not get accustomed to

[1] Ps. xxxiii. 8; Matt. xviii. 10.   [2] Cf. VIII, 64 below; de Orat. XI, 5.
[3] John xiv. 30; I Cor. ii. 6, 8.
[4] See I, 25 and note; V, 45; Celsus in I, 6; VI, 40.   [5] Read with K. tr. πολλοί.
[6] For Christian criticism of pagan gods and images cf. Celsus in VII, 36, 62; VIII, 41.
'They spit at the gods', complains the pagan Caecilius in Minucius Felix, Octavius, VIII, 4.
For the theme, cf. Cicero, de Nat. Deor. III, 35, 84; Arnobius, adv. Nat. VI, 21–2.
[7] Exod. xxii. 28.

speaking evil of any being. For we have heard the command, 'Bless and curse not', and we are taught that 'Revilers shall not inherit the kingdom of God'.[1] Who among us is so foolish as to say this and not to see that this sort of thing can do nothing to destroy the notion held about the supposed gods? Whereas people who are utter atheists and deny providence, and who have brought into being a company of supposed philosophers by their wicked and impious doctrines, do not themselves suffer any evil as the multitude understand it, nor do those who have embraced their doctrines. But they even become rich and enjoy good health of body. But if anyone looks for harm suffered by them, let him notice that in reality they are harmed in their mind.[2] For what greater harm is there than to fail to comprehend the Maker of the world from its order? What misfortune is worse than to have been blinded in mind and not to see the Creator and Father of every mind?

39. After attributing such words to us, and bringing a false charge against Christians who do not say anything of the kind, he thinks that he offers his reply, which is childish mockery rather than an answer. In this he says to us: *Do you not see, my excellent man, that anyone who stands by your daemon not only blasphemes him, but proclaims his banishment from every land and sea, and after binding you who have been dedicated to him like an image takes you away and crucifies you;*[3] *but the daemon or, as you say, the son of God, takes no vengeance on him?* This reply might have been effective if we used such words as he has put into our mouth; and yet not even on his own premisses did he speak correctly, since he said that the Son of God is a daemon. Now in our opinion, since we hold that all daemons are evil, he who converted so many to God was not a daemon but the divine Logos and Son of God. But although Celsus has said nothing about daemons being evil, for some unknown reason he forgot himself and described Jesus as a daemon. Ultimately, however, when the impious have refused all remedies, the threatened punishments will come upon those who are in the grip of, so to speak, incurable evil.

40. Whatever we may say about punishment, we turn many from their sins just by our teaching of punishment. But let us consider what reply is made by *the priest of Apollo or Zeus* quoted by Celsus: ' *The mills of God grind slowly*',[4] he says, even

> *To children's children, and to those who are born after them.*[5]

---

[1] Rom. xii. 14; I Cor. vi. 10.   [2] Read with K. tr. εἰσι νοῦν βεβλαμμένοι.
[3] For persecution, cf. Celsus in VIII, 41, 54, 69. For the failure of God to vindicate His people, v, 41; VIII, 69.
[4] Also quoted by Sextus Empiricus, *adv. Math.* I, 287; Plutarch, *Mor.* 549D.
[5] Homer, *Il.* xx, 308.

See how much better than this is the saying 'The fathers shall not die for the children, nor shall the sons die for their fathers. Each man shall die for his own sin.' And this saying: 'The teeth of him who ate a sour grape are set on edge.' And 'The son shall not receive the iniquity of the father, and the father shall not receive the iniquity of the son; the righteousness of the righteous man shall be upon him, and the wickedness of the wicked shall be upon him.'[1] And if, as equivalent to the verse '*To children's children and to those who are born after them*', anyone quotes 'Rendering the sins of the fathers upon the children unto the third and fourth generation',[2] let him learn that in Ezekiel this is said to be a 'parable'; for he finds fault with people who say: 'The fathers ate a sour grape and the children's teeth are set on edge.' And he goes on to say 'As I live, saith the Lord, each man shall die for his own sin.'[3] However, it is not the right time to explain now what is meant by the parable about the sins being visited unto the third and fourth generation.

41. Then like old women he pours abuse on us saying: *You pour abuse on the images of these gods and ridicule them, although if you did that to Dionysus himself or to Heracles in person, perhaps you would not escape lightly. But the men who tortured and punished your God in person suffered nothing for doing it, not even afterwards as long as they lived.[4] What new thing has happened since then which might lead one to believe[5] that he was not a sorcerer but son of God? And He who sent His son to deliver certain messages overlooked him when he was so cruelly punished so that the messages also were destroyed with him;[6] and though such a long time has passed, He has not paid any attention. What father is so ruthless? But perhaps it was His will, as you say; for this reason he submitted to insult. But these gods whom you blaspheme could say that this too was their will, and that that is why they endure it when they are blasphemed. Where the matters are equal, it is best to compare them fairly on the same level. The latter, however, actually do take severe revenge on anyone who blasphemes them; for either he runs away and hides himself on account of what he has done, or he is caught and destroyed.*

To this I would reply that we do not pour abuse on anyone, since we are persuaded that 'revilers shall not inherit the kingdom of God', and we read the word 'bless them that curse you', and 'bless and curse not'; and we also know the saying 'being reviled we bless'.[7] Even if a man who appears to have been wronged may have some reasonable ground for

---

[1] Deut. xxiv. 18; Jer. xxxviii. 30; Ezek. xviii. 20.
[2] Exod. xx. 5.   [3] Ezek. xviii. 3–4.
[4] Cf. Celsus in II, 34–5.
[5] Read with We., K. tr. γέγονεν ᾧ πιστεύσαι ἄν τις ὡς . . . .
[6] Read with K. tr. συνδιαφείρεσθαι.
[7] Luke vi. 28; Rom. xii. 14; I Cor. iv. 12.

revenging himself of abuse, yet not even this is allowed to us by the word of God. How much more ought we not to revile when the abuse displays utter foolishness? It is equally silly to pour abuse on stone or gold or silver, which are shaped into the customary form of gods by people who are far from God. So also we do not laugh at lifeless statues, but, if at all, only at people who worship them. Moreover, even if there are certain daemons established in certain images, and some particular one is thought to be Dionysus and another Heracles, we would not revile even these. That sort of behaviour is futile, and not at all consistent with the character of a man who is meek and peaceful and gentle in his soul, who has learnt that not even for evil is it right to revile anyone, whether man or daemon.

42. For some unknown reason Celsus unintentionally fell into proving that the daemons and gods, whose praises he was singing a little while ago, are in actual practice very wicked, since they take revenge in a vindictive spirit rather than inflict punishment with the purpose of reforming anyone who reviles them. For he says: *Although if you reviled Dionysus himself or Heracles in person, perhaps you would not escape lightly.* But let anyone who wishes show how the god hears anything when he is absent, and why he is sometimes there *in person* and sometimes absent, and what is the business of the daemons that they depart from one place to another.

After this, thinking that we maintain that the tortured and punished body of Jesus, and not the divine nature in him, was God, and that even while being tortured and punished he is regarded as God, he says: *But the men who tortured and punished your God in person suffered nothing for doing it.* As we have earlier spoken at length about his human sufferings,[1] we now omit the story intentionally lest we should appear to be repeating ourselves. But since he says that those[2] who punished Jesus *suffered nothing even afterwards as long as they lived,* we will point out to him, and to all who are willing to learn, that the city in which the people of the Jews thought Jesus worthy of being crucified, when they said, 'Crucify him, crucify him'[3] (for they preferred that the robber should be set free, who had been thrown into prison for sedition and murder, but that Jesus who had been delivered for envy should be crucified)[4]—this city was attacked not long afterwards and was besieged so fiercely for a long time that it was utterly ruined and deserted, since God judged the people who inhabited that place to be unworthy to share human life. In fact He was sparing them, if I may put it paradoxically, because He saw that they were incurable beyond any change for a better life and were daily becoming

---

[1] Cf. III, 25; VII, 16–17.   [2] Read with We. τούς.
[3] Luke xxiii. 21; for the theme, II, 13; IV, 22.
[4] John xviii. 40; Luke xxiii. 19, 25; Matt. xxvii. 18; Mark xv. 10.

worse in the flood of wickedness, and gave them up to their enemies. This happened on account of the blood of Jesus which because of their plot was poured out upon their land, so that it was no longer able to tolerate people who dared to commit such a great crime against him.

43. This, then, is the *new thing* that has happened since the time when Jesus suffered, I mean the history of the city and of all the nation, and the sudden birth of the race of Christians which was, so to speak, born in an instant. And it was new also that people who were strangers to the covenants of God and alien to the promises,[1] who were far from the truth, accepted it by some divine miracle. These were not the works of a human sorcerer, but of God, who to deliver His messages sent His Logos in Jesus who was so cruelly punished, that the cruelty which he endured most courageously and with all meekness was the ground of accusation against the people who had wrongly punished him. But his punishment did not destroy God's messages but, if I may so say, enabled them to be known. Jesus himself taught this when he said: 'Unless a grain of wheat falls into the ground and dies, it stays alone; but if it dies, it bears much fruit.'[2] Jesus, then, the grain of wheat, died and bore much fruit; and the Father in His providence is always caring for the fruits which have resulted from the death of the grain of wheat, which are still being produced and will continue to be produced. The Father of Jesus, therefore, is a holy Father. For He 'spared not his own Son, but delivered him up for us all' as His lamb, that the lamb of God, who died for every man, might bear away the sin of the world.[3] He was not compelled by his Father, but he willingly endured the sufferings inflicted by those who insulted him.

Then after this Celsus repeats his words to those who blaspheme images, saying: *But these gods whom you blaspheme could say that this too was their will, and that that is why they endure it when they are blasphemed. Where the matters are equal, it is best to compare them fairly on the same level. The latter, however, actually do take severe revenge on anyone who blasphemes them; for either he runs away and hides himself on account of what he has done, or he is caught and destroyed.* The daemons are accustomed to taking vengeance on Christians not because Christians blaspheme them, but because they drive them out of the statues and human bodies and souls. Although Celsus did not realize what he was doing, he did say something true on this point. For it is true that the souls of people who condemn Christians and betray them, and delight in fighting against them, are filled by evil daemons.

44. However, since the souls of those who die for Christianity, who for the sake of religion are gloriously delivered from their body, destroy

---

[1] Eph. ii. 12.   [2] John xii. 24.   [3] Rom. viii. 32; John i. 29.

the power of the daemons and make their designs against men weak, for this reason I believe the daemons have learnt by experience that they are overcome and conquered by the martyrs of the truth, and have been afraid of returning to take vengeance. And so, until they forget the troubles which they have suffered, the world will probably be at peace with the Christians. But when they gather their strength and, being blinded by their wickedness, desire once again to take vengeance on Christians and to persecute them, they will again be vanquished. Then again the souls of the pious, who for their religion have put off their bodies, will destroy the army of the evil one.[1]

It is my opinion that as the daemons perceive that some who conquer and die for their piety destroy their domination, while others who are defeated by the tribulations and deny their religion become subject to them, sometimes they contend eagerly for Christians who have been brought to court, because they suffer pain if the Christians confess their faith, but are relieved if they deny it. Traces of this can be seen in the fact that the judges are distressed by those who endure the outrages and tortures but exult whenever a Christian is overcome. Moreover, they do not do this on account of any feeling for humanity as they think it; for they clearly see that though the tongue of those overcome by pain has sworn, yet 'the mind has not taken the oath'.[2] This is our answer to his words: *The latter, however, actually do take severe revenge on anyone who blasphemes them; for either he runs away and hides himself on account of what he has done, or he is caught and destroyed.* But even if a Christian were to run away, he would not do so for cowardice, but because he was keeping the commandment of his Master[3] and preserving himself free from harm that others[4] might be helped to gain salvation.

45. Let us look at the next passage which runs as follows: *Why need I enumerate all the events which on the ground of oracular responses have been foretold with an inspired utterance both by prophets and prophetesses and by other inspired persons, both men and women, all the wonderful things that have been heard from the shrines themselves, all the truths manifested to those who use victims and sacrifices, and all those indicated by other incredible signs? To some people there have been distinct appearances.[5] The whole of life is full of*

---

[1] For the belief that martyrdom vanquishes the daemons cf. I, 31; *Comm. in Joann.* VI, 54 (36); Eusebius, *H.E.* v, 1, 42 (Lyons and Vienne).

[2] A hackneyed quotation from Euripides (*Hippol.* 612): Plato, *Theaet.* 154D; *Symp.* 199A; Cicero, *de Offic.* III, 29, 108; Justin, *Apol.* I, 39, 4; Max. Tyr. XL, 6 f.

[3] Matt. x. 23. The problem was of recurrent interest in the period of the persecutions and even later. Cf. Tertullian, *de Fuga in Persecutione* (arguing for the opposite view to that held by Origen); Cyprian, *Ep.* 20 (defending his flight in the Decian persecution); Athanasius, *de Fuga.*

[4] Read ⟨ὑπὲρ⟩ ἑτέρων.   [5] Cf. Celsus in VII, 35, and note.

*these experiences. How many cities have been built by oracles, and have got
rid of diseases and famines, and how many that have neglected or forgotten
them have suffered terrible destruction? How many have been sent to form
a colòny and have prospered by attending to their commands?*[1] *How many
rulers and common people have come off better or worse for this reason? How
many that have been distressed at being childless have come to possess that for
which they prayed and escaped the wrath of daemons? How many ailments of
the body have been healed? How many, on the other hand, have insulted the
temples and have at once been caught? For some have been overcome by madness
on the spot; others have declared what they had done; others have made an end
of themselves; and others have become bound by incurable diseases. Some have
even been destroyed by a deep voice from the actual shrines.* I do not know
why Celsus describes these as *distinct* and yet regarded as *myths* the
miracles recorded in our writings, whether those of the Jews or those
which are about Jesus and his disciples.[2] Why should not our writings be
true and the stories which Celsus mentions mythical fictions? Not even
the philosophical sects of the Greeks have believed them, such as the
schools of Democritus, Epicurus, and Aristotle.[3] But on account of the
distinct proof of our miracles they would probably have believed if they
had met with Moses or one of the prophets who performed miracles, or
even with Jesus himself.

46. It is related that the Pythian priestess sometimes proclaimed
oracles after she had been corrupted.[4] But our prophets were admired for
the distinctness of their utterances not only by their contemporaries but
also by posterity. For as a result of what the prophets proclaimed,
cities were set on the right path, men were restored to health, famines
ceased, and furthermore, it is clear that the whole Jewish nation came to
form a colony when they left Egypt and came to Palestine in accordance
with the oracles. When the nation attended to God's commands they
prospered, and when they went wrong they repented. But why need
I mention all the rulers and common people in the Biblical stories who

[1] Cf. Celsus in VII, 2, and note. For the use of oracular utterances as charms against
plague, cf. Lucian, *Alexander* 36; for inscriptions, Latte in P.-W. XVIII, 1 (1939), 864. The
appeal to experience as proof of the truth of divination is commonplace: e.g. the Stoic in
Cicero, *de Nat. Deor.* II, 65, 162–3; *de Divin.* I, 16; Iamblichus, *de Myst.* III, 3.
[2] Cf. Celsus in V, 57.
[3] Cf. I, 43; VII, 66. For Epicurus' view of divination, cf. Usener, *Epicurea*, pp. 261 f.
For Democritus and Aristotle cf. A. S. Pease's commentary on Cicero, *de Divin.* I, 3, 5 (pp.
57–8). Also VII, 3, above.
[4] For bribery of the Pythian priestess, cf. Herodotus, VI, 66. Origen may have in mind
the story of Demosthenes' complaint concerning the anti-Athenian tendency of Delphi—
'the Pythia philippizes'—for which cf. Parke, *History of the Delphic Oracle*, pp. 248 f.
Demosthenes' remark was exploited by Sceptic critics of oracles: cf. Cicero, *de Divin.* II, 57,
118; Minucius Felix, *Octavius*, XXVI, 6.

came off better or worse according as they paid attention to the prophecies
or neglected them?

If we may also speak of childlessness, for which some fathers and
mothers were in distress and sent up their prayers about this to the
Creator of the universe, anyone may read the story of Abraham and
Sarah.[1] For Isaac was born of them after they had already become old,
and he was the father of all the Jewish nation and of others beside them.
Let him read also the story of Hezekiah who not only received deliverance
from sickness according to the prophecies of Isaiah, but also boldly said:
'For from henceforth I shall beget children who shall declare thy righteousness.'[2] And in the fourth book of the Kingdoms the woman who entertained Elisha, who by the grace of God had prophesied about the birth of
a child, became a mother in accordance with Elisha's prayers.[3] Moreover,
countless ailments were healed by Jesus. And many[4] suffered the punishments recorded in the books of the Maccabees because they ventured to
insult the Jewish worship at the temple in Jerusalem.

47. The Greeks, however, would call these stories myths, though
their truth is witnessed by two entire nations. Why should not the stories
of the Greeks be myths rather than these? Suppose that one were to face
up to that question and, lest it appear that one is arbitrarily accepting one's
own histories and disbelieving those of strangers, were to say that the
stories of the Greeks were caused to be written by certain daemons and
those of the Jews by God through the prophets, or by the angels, or by
God through the angels, and those of the Christians by Jesus and his
power in the apostles. Let us compare them all with one another, and
consider the aim which those who caused them to be written had in view,
and the resulting help or harm, or neither, to those who were the recipients
of the supposed benefits. One may see the philosophy of the ancient
Jewish nation before they insulted God, who forsook them on account of
their great wickedness, and that the Christians came to exist as a society
in an amazing way and at the beginning were led more[5] by the miracles
than by the words of exhortation to abandon their traditional ways and to
choose customs foreign to those of their ancestors. Moreover, if I may
give a likely account of the way in which Christians originally came to
form a society, I would say that it is not plausible either that the apostles of
Jesus, unlettered and ignorant men,[6] should have been bold enough to

[1] Gen. xvii. 16–21.   [2] Isa. xxxviii. 1–8, 19.
[3] II Kings (IV Regn.) iv. 8–17.
[4] Read πολλοί with K. tr. Cf. I Macc. ii. 23–5; vii. 47; ix. 54–6; II Macc. iii. 24–30;
iv. 7–17; ix. 5–12.
[5] Read μᾶλλον with Del., K. tr.
[6] Cf. Acts iv. 13; I, 62, III, 39 above.

proclaim Christianity to mankind in reliance upon any strength other
than the power which was granted to them and the grace in the doctrine
which made the facts clear; or furthermore, that the people who heard
them should have been changed from keeping ancestral customs of long
standing, unless some considerable force and miraculous events had moved
them to change to doctrines so strange and foreign to those in which they
had been brought up.

48. Then for some unknown reason Celsus mentions the zeal of those
who struggle to the point of death to avoid abjuring Christianity;[1] and
as though putting our doctrines on a level with the utterances of priests
and initiators in the mysteries, he goes on to say: *Above all, my excellent
fellow, just as you believe in eternal punishments, so also the interpreters of the
mysteries, the priests and initiators, do the same.*[2] *You threaten others with
these punishments while they threaten you. It is possible to consider which of
the two is nearer the truth or more successful. For so far as talk is concerned
both sides make equally strong assertions*[3] *about their own system. But if
proofs are required, they point to a lot of distinct evidence and produce works
done by certain miraculous powers and oracular utterances and in consequence
of oracles of all kinds.*

By this he means that both we and the priests of the mysteries are on the
same level in our belief in eternal punishments, and would inquire which
of the two are nearer the truth. I would affirm that those are right who are
able to make the people who hear what they say live as though these
things were real. Jews and Christians are convinced about what they call
the age to come, and that there are rewards in it for the righteous and
punishments for the sinners. Let Celsus and anyone who likes show us
who have been convinced about eternal punishments by the priests and
initiators of the mysteries. It is probable that the intention of the author
of the punishments alleged to exist was not merely to talk about punishments in a casual way, but to impress those who hear so that they do all in
their power to avoid doing the actions which cause punishments. Moreover, to people who do not give a merely superficial attention to the
foreknowledge in the prophecies, they seem to me to be adequate to
persuade anyone who reads both with intelligence and with an open mind
that there was a divine spirit in those men. Not even the slightest comparison is possible between them and any of the wonderful works to which
we are referred, or the miracles done in consequence of oracular utterances,
or the oracles.

---

[1] Origen does not quote this passage from Celsus.
[2] For the pains of hell as a theme in the mystery religions, cf. Celsus in III, 16; IV, 10.
[3] Read with K. tr. διαβεβαιοῦνται.

49. Let us look at Celsus' next remarks to us, as follows: *Furthermore, are not these notions of yours absurd? For on the one hand you long for the body and hope that it will rise again in the same form as if we possessed nothing better or more precious than that,*[1] *while on the other hand you would cast it into punishments as though it were of no value. However, it is not worth while discussing this with people who believe this, who are absolutely bound to the body; for they are people who in other respects also are boorish and unclean, who are destitute of reason and suffer from the disease of sedition.*[2] *But I will discuss the matter with those who hope that they will possess their soul or mind eternally with God (whether they wish to call this mind spiritual, or a holy and blessed intellectual spirit,*[3] *or a living soul,*[4] *or a super-celestial and indestructible offspring of a divine and incorporeal nature, or whatever name they care to give it). Their opinions are right in this respect at least, that those who have lived good lives will be happy, while people who are totally wicked will be afflicted with eternal evils. And this doctrine may never be abandoned either by them or by any other person.*[5]

He has often reproached us about the resurrection. But we have shown as far as possible what seemed to us the reasonable view of the matter, and we do not intend to give an answer several times over to a particular objection which is often advanced. Celsus, however, misrepresents us when he asserts that we hold that in our constitution there is nothing better or more precious than the body. We maintain that the soul, and especially the rational soul, is more precious than any body, since the soul contains that which is 'after the image of the Creator'[6] whereas this is in no sense true of the body. In our opinion also God is not a material substance. We would not fall into the absurd ideas held by the philosophers who follow the doctrines of Zeno and Chrysippus.[7]

50. Since he reproaches us as if we *long for the body*, let him realize that if longing is a bad thing, we have no desire at all; but if it is morally indifferent, we long for all that God promises to the righteous. It is in this sense that we long and hope for the resurrection of the righteous. But Celsus thinks that our behaviour is inconsistent, when on the one hand we hope for the resurrection of the body as though it were worthy to receive honour from God and, on the other hand, when we cast it to punishments

---

[1] Cf. Celsus in v, 14; vii, 36, 42, 45; Minucius Felix, *Octavius*, 11.

[2] Cf. Celsus in iii, 5; viii, 2.

[3] Celsus is using some dictionary definitions: cf. Diels, *Dox. Gr.* 292, 23 (the Stoics define the essence of God as *pneuma noeron*). The same definition of God is ascribed to Posidonius (*ibid.* 302). Similarly the Stoic definition of the soul (*ibid.* 388).

[4] Cf. Celsus in vi, 34; Origen in vi, 35.

[5] Origen has already quoted this in iii, 16.

[6] Col. iii. 10. Cf. vi, 63.   [7] Cf. i, 21; iii, 75; iv, 14.

as if it were of no value. The body which suffers for its piety and chooses
tribulations for the sake of virtue is certainly not of no value; what is
entirely valueless is the body that has wasted itself in evil pleasures.[1] At
any rate the divine word says: 'What sort of seed is honourable? The seed
of man. What sort of seed is dishonourable? The seed of man.'[2]

Then Celsus thinks that he ought not to discuss this with people who
hope for a reward for their body, as they are absolutely and irrationally
bound to a thing which cannot grant the fulfilment of their hopes. He
calls them boorish and unclean, saying that they are destitute of reason
and come together for sedition. But if he is one who loves his fellow-men
he ought to help even those who are most boorish. There is no limit
prescribed for helping one's fellow-men so that the more boorish men are
excluded just like the irrational animals. No. Our Maker created us to be
equally helpful to all men. Therefore it is worth while discussing these
things both with boorish people, in order to convert them as far as possible
to a more refined life, and with unclean people, to make them cleaner as
far as possible, and with those who hold any view whatever being destitute
of reason and sick in their soul, that they may no longer do anything
without reason and may not be sick in their soul.

51. After this he approves of those who hope for the eternity of the
soul or the mind, or what they call the spiritual element or rational spirit,
intellectual, holy, and blessed, or a living soul, and trust that it will exist
with God. He accepts as the correct opinion the doctrine that people who
have lived good lives will be happy, and that those who are totally wicked
will be afflicted with eternal evils. Indeed, I am amazed at the following
words of Celsus, which he adds to those I have just mentioned, more than
at anything else which he says, where he asserts: *And this doctrine may never
be abandoned either by them or by any other person.* He who writes against
the Christians ought to have seen that, since the whole foundation of their
faith is God and the promises concerning the righteous given by Christ
and the teachings about the punishment of the wicked, a Christian who as
a result of Celsus' arguments against the Christians was led to abandon
his faith would probably together with the Gospel give up also the doctrine
which, he says, ought not to be abandoned either by Christians or by any
other person.

However, I think that in his book, 'On the Cure of the Passions',[3]
Chrysippus acted with more consideration for mankind than Celsus. He
wishes to heal the passions which incite and distress the human soul,
choosing for preference the doctrines he thinks to be right, but allowing
as a second and third possibility even those doctrines that he does not

---

[1] Cf. VIII, 30 above.   [2] Sirach x. 19.   [3] See I, 64 above.

hold. 'For supposing', he says, 'there are three kinds of good,[1] the passions may also be healed on this basis. The man who is troubled by passion should not worry about the doctrine which has gained possession of his mind at the moment when the passions are at their height, lest somehow he should be concerned at the wrong moment with the refutation of the doctrines that have gained possession of his soul, and the possibility of a cure is lost.' And he says that 'even if pleasure were the greatest good,[2] and supposing that the man overcome by passion held this opinion, nevertheless he ought to be helped and shown that even for people who maintain that pleasure is the greatest and ultimate good any passion is inconsistent'.

Accordingly, as Celsus once said that he accepts the doctrine that those who have lived good lives will be happy and that those who have been totally wicked will be afflicted with eternal evils, he ought to have followed up his own assertion. If he was able, he ought to have established what seemed to him the main argument, and also to have given many more proofs that it is true that those who are totally wicked will be afflicted with eternal evils, and that people who have lived good lives will be happy.

52. For our part, because of the many and innumerable facts which have persuaded us to live the Christian life, it is our primary desire to do all in our power to make all men familiar with the whole of the doctrine of Christians. But where we find some who are prejudiced by slander against the Christians so that, under the impression that Christians are godless folk, they pay no attention to those who claim to teach about the divine word, there we do everything possible, in accordance with the principle of love to mankind, to establish the truth of the doctrine that there will be eternal punishment for the impious, and to make even those who are unwilling to become Christians accept the doctrine. So also we want to implant a conviction that those who have lived good lives will be happy,[3] seeing that even people alien to the faith make many affirmations about the upright life which are much the same as ours; for one would find that their teachings have not entirely lost the universal notions of good and bad, righteous and unrighteous.[4]

All men who see the world and the appointed movement of the heaven in it and of the stars in the fixed sphere, and the order of the so-called planets which travel in the opposite direction to the movement of the world, and who also observe the mixture of airs which is for the advantage of animals and especially of men, and the abundance of things created for

---

[1] Peripatetic doctrine: cf. Diog. Laert. v, 30.   [2] Epicurean teaching.
[3] Read with K. tr. ⟨ὡς εὐδαιμονησόντων⟩ πεῖσμα.   [4] Cf. 1, 4.

men,[1] should beware of doing anything displeasing to the Creator of the universe and of their souls and of their mind within their souls. They should be convinced that punishment will be inflicted for their sins, and that He who deals with each individual on his merits will grant rewards corresponding to the deeds he has done successfully or performed rightly.[2] All men should be convinced that if they live good lives they will come to a better end, but, if evil, they will be given over to evil pains and torments for their misdeeds and acts of lasciviousness and licentiousness and, moreover, for their effeminacy and cowardice, and for all their folly.

53. Having said so much on this subject, let us also consider another passage of Celsus, which reads as follows: *Men are born bound to the body, whether because of the administration of the world, or because they are paying the penalty for their sin, or because the soul is weighed down by certain passions until it has been purified through the appointed periods. For according to Empedocles, it must*

> *Wander about for thirty thousand ages away from the blessed,*
> *Becoming every possible shape of mortal being in the time.*[3]

We must believe, then, that they are handed over to certain officers in charge of this prison.

Notice here also how, as befits a mere man, he has some hesitation about such profound matters, and shows some caution by mentioning the doctrines of several people about the cause of our birth; he would not dare to assert that any one of these was false. Would it not be consistent for this man, once he had decided neither to give random assent to, nor boldly to reject, the opinions of the ancients, to be at least in doubt, if he was unwilling to believe, both about the doctrine of the Jews which is apparent in their prophets, and about Jesus, and to have considered that it was probable also that those who serve the supreme God and often face countless dangers and deaths for the sake of worshipping Him and for the laws believed to have been given by Him, should not have been over-looked by God, but that some revelation should have been made to them? For they scorned the product of the human art of image-making, and attempted to ascend by their reason to the supreme God Himself. He ought to have considered that the common Father and Creator of all men, who sees everything and hears everything,[4] and judges the purpose of each individual who seeks Him and desires to be religious, in accordance with his merits, assigns to these people also some fruit of His care in order

---

[1] The argument is Stoic: cf. Cicero, *de Nat. Deor.* II, 19, 49 ff.; III, 7, 16 (Cleanthes).
[2] With K. tr. omit the dittography (267, 26–7) ἀνάλογον to ἀποδοθεῖσιν.
[3] Empedocles, *frag.* 115 Diels. Cf. V, 49, above, for his doctrine of metempsychosis. For the earth as a prison, Plato, *Phaedo*, 114B, C; *Rep.* 517B.
[4] Homer, *Il.* III, 277; *Od.* XI, 109; XII, 323.

that they may further advance in the notion of Him which they have once received. Had this been taken into account by Celsus and by those who hate Moses and the Jewish prophets and Jesus and his true disciples who toil for his word, they would not have poured abuse in this way on Moses and the prophets and on Jesus and his apostles. Nor would they have rejected the Jews alone as inferior to all the nations on earth,[1] declaring that they are even worse than the Egyptians who have done all they can to degrade the worship offered to God to the level of irrational animals, whether through superstition or for some other reason or misconception.

We have made these remarks not with the intention of moving any to have doubts about the doctrine of Christianity, but to show that it is preferable for people who pour unmitigated abuse upon the doctrine of Christians at least to have doubts about it, and not to speak so rashly about Jesus and his disciples, saying things which they do not know for certain, and which they affirm without 'direct apprehension' as the Stoics term it,[2] nor with any other criterion by which each sect of the philosophers has established, as it thought, the reality of a given phenomenon.

54. Then Celsus says: *We must believe, then, that they are handed over to certain officers in charge of this prison.* I should reply to him that a good soul, even in the earthly life of 'the prisoners of the earth',[3] as Jeremiah calls them, would have been set free from the bonds of evil, because of Jesus who said, as Isaiah the prophet foretold long before his coming, 'to the prisoners Come forth, and to those in darkness Show yourselves'.[4] It was this Jesus, as the same Isaiah predicted concerning him, who 'rose up a light to those who sit in the land and shadow of death', so that on this account we may say: 'Let us break their bonds asunder and cast their yoke from us.'[5]

If Celsus and those who, like him, are opposed to us had been able to understand the profundity of the gospels, he would not have advised us to believe in *officers in charge of this prison,* as he calls them. It is written in the Gospel that a certain woman 'was bent double, and could not straighten herself at all; Jesus saw her, and perceiving the reason why she was bent double and incapable of straightening herself at all said, Ought not this woman, being a daughter of Abraham whom Satan has bound, lo, for eighteen years, to have been set free from this bond on the sabbath day?'[6] How many others are there even now who have been bound by Satan and are bent double, not being able to straighten themselves at all

[1] Cf. Celsus in .v, 31; v, 41; vi, 80.   [2] Cf. i, 42 above.
[3] Lam. iii. 34. The text of this sentence is doubtful. Perhaps read λυθείη ἄν for λυθεῖσα with K. tr. Possibly we should read at 270, 6 εἰπόντα for προειπόντα.
[4] Isa. xlix. 9; cf. i, 53 above.   [5] Isa. ix. 2; Ps. ii. 3.
[6] Luke xiii. 11, 16.

because of him who wishes us to look downwards? And no one can make them upright except the Logos who came to dwell in Jesus, and inspired men before that. Jesus came to set free 'all those under the domination of the devil'.[1] And with a profundity appropriate to the subject he said of him 'And the prince of this world is judged.'[2]

Therefore we do not *pour abuse on the daemons on earth*; but we prove that their activities are ruinous to the human race. Under the excuse of oracles and healing of bodies and certain other means they try to separate from God the soul that has fallen into 'the body of humiliation'.[3] Those who have understood this utter the words 'O wretched man that I am, who will deliver me from this body of death?'[4] Furthermore, we do not *offer our bodies to be tortured and crucified to no purpose*. It is not to no purpose that the body is offered to these sufferings by the man who, because he does not call the daemons in the earthly region gods, is subject to attack at their hands and at the hands of their worshippers. It is with good reason that we have regarded it as a matter dear to God if one is crucified for virtue, and is tortured for piety, and dies for holiness. 'Precious before the Lord is the death of his holy ones.'[5] And we affirm that it is good to *have no love for this life*. Celsus compares us to *evildoers who with good reason undergo the punishments which they suffer for robbery*, and is not ashamed to assert that such a noble purpose resembles the attitude of robbers. By these remarks he makes himself a brother of the people who reckoned Jesus with the transgressors, who fulfilled the scripture which says 'He was reckoned with the transgressors.'[6]

55. After this Celsus says: *Reason demands one of two alternatives. If they refuse to worship in the proper way the lords in charge of the following activities,[7] then they ought neither to come to marriageable age, nor to marry a wife, nor to beget children, nor to do anything else in life. But they should depart from this world leaving no descendants at all behind them, so that such a race would entirely cease to exist on earth. But if they are going to marry wives, and beget children, and taste of the fruits, and partake of the joys of this life, and endure the appointed evils (by nature's law all men must have experience of evils; evil is necessary and has nowhere else to exist), then they ought to render the due honours to the beings who have been entrusted with these things. And they ought to offer the due rites of worship in this life until they are set free from their bonds, lest they even appear ungrateful to them. It*

---

[1] Acts x. 38.   [2] John xvi. 11.   [3] Phil. iii. 21.
[4] Rom. vii. 24.   [5] Ps. cxv. 6.   [6] Isa. liii. 12.
[7] For τούτων δέ read with Wifstrand τοὺς τῶνδε. Cf. Epict. II, 8, 12; 20, 27.
[8] Celsus follows Plato, *Theaetetus*, 176A (cf. Origen in IV, 62): 'It is not possible for evil to be abolished...for there must always be something opposed to the good; nor is it established among the gods, but of necessity it wanders about mortal nature and this earth.'

is wrong for people who partake of what is their property to offer them nothing in return.

We say in reply to this that no occasion for taking leave of life seems reasonable to us except that alone which is for the sake of piety or virtue, as when those who are supposed to be judges, or who seem to have power over our lives, offer us the alternative either to live and act contrary to the precepts enjoined by Jesus, or to die and believe his words. Moreover, God has allowed us to marry wives, because not everybody is capable of the superior condition which is to be entirely pure. And when we do marry wives, He certainly requires us to bring up the offspring and not to destroy the children given by providence.[1] These matters do not cause difficulties to us when we refuse to obey the daemons who are allotted the earth. Since we have been armed with the whole armour of God,[2] as athletes of piety, we resist the race of daemons which is hostile to us.

56. Even though by his words Celsus dismisses us utterly from life in order that, as he supposes, this race of ours may entirely cease to exist on earth, yet we who are concerned with the business of our Creator will live according to the laws of God. We have no desire to serve the laws of sin. And if we wish, we will marry wives and accept the children granted to us in our marriages. If necessary, we will also partake of the joys of this life and endure the appointed evils as trials of the soul. For this is the term by which the divine scriptures usually designate the troubles that occur among men.[3] In them the soul of the man who is being tested, like gold in the fire,[4] is either convicted of failure or is manifested as reliable.[5] In fact we are so far prepared for the evils Celsus mentions that we even say: 'Prove me, O Lord, and try me; test my kidneys and my heart by fire.'[6] Moreover, no man is crowned unless he strives lawfully even here upon earth with the body of humiliation.[7]

Besides this we do not render the customary honours to the beings to whom, Celsus says, earthly things have been entrusted. For we worship the Lord our God, and serve Him only, praying that we may become imitators of Christ. For when the devil said to him 'All these things will I give thee if thou wilt fall down and worship me', he said 'Thou shalt worship the Lord thy God and him only shalt thou serve.'[8] That is why we do not render the customary honours to the beings to whom, Celsus says, earthly things have been entrusted, since 'no man can serve two masters';[9] and we cannot at the same time serve God and mammon,

---

[1] For child exposure, cf. E. H. Blakeney's note on *Ep. ad Diognetum* v, 6.
[2] Eph. vi. 11, 13.
[3] Luke xxii. 28; Acts xx. 19; Jas. i. 2; I Pet. i. 6.
[4] Wisd. of Sol. iii. 6.
[5] Read δοκιμαστή with Wif.
[6] Ps. xxv. 2.
[7] II Tim. ii. 5; Phil. iii. 21.
[8] Matt. iv. 9–10.
[9] Matt. vi. 24; cf. VIII, 2 above.

whether that name refers to any one particular thing or to many. Further-more, if anyone dishonours the lawgiver 'by the transgression of the law',[1] it appears obvious to us that, if there are two laws opposed to one another, the law of God and the law of mammon, it is preferable for us to dishonour mammon by the transgression of the law of mammon in order to pay honour to God by keeping God's law, rather than to dishonour God by the transgression of the law of God in order to pay honour to mammon by keeping mammon's law.

57. Celsus thinks it right to offer the due rites of worship in this life until men are set free from their bonds, as when in accordance with the popular customs one renders the sacrifices to each of the supposed gods in every city. He did not comprehend what is truly fitting as understood by those who are exact in their religion. But we say that a man offers worship in this life with the due rites if he remembers who is the Creator, and what things are dear to Him, and if he does everything with regard to what God loves.

Again, Celsus does not want us to be ungrateful to the earthly daemons, thinking that we owe them thank-offerings. But we, who have a clear idea of the meaning of thanksgiving (*eucharistia*), say to the beings who do no good whatever but are on the opposite side, that we behave without any ingratitude when we do not sacrifice to them nor worship them. But we avoid being guilty of ingratitude to God who loads us with His benefits. We are His creatures and are cared for by His providence. Our condition is subject to His judgement, and we entertain hopes of Him beyond this life. Moreover, we have a symbol of our thanksgiving to God in the bread which is called 'eucharist'.[2]

Further, as we also remarked earlier,[3] daemons do not possess the care of the things that have been created for our needs. Therefore we do nothing wrong when we partake of the created things and fail to sacrifice to beings who have no concern with them. But if we see that it is not certain daemons, but angels who have been appointed in charge of the fruits of the earth and the birth of animals, we speak well of them and call them blessed, as they have been entrusted by God with the things benefi-cial to our race. But we certainly do not assign to them the honour we owe to God. This is desired neither by God nor by the beings themselves who have been entrusted with these matters. In fact they approve of us more when we take care not to sacrifice to them than if we were to offer them sacrifices. They are in no need of the exhalations from earth.

[1] Rom. ii. 23.
[2] Cf. Justin, *Apol.* I, 66, I 'This food is called among us eucharist.'
[3] Cf. VIII, 33–5.

58. After this Celsus says: *That in these matters, even including the very least, there is a being to whom authority has been given, one may learn from the teaching of the Egyptians. They say that the body of man has been put under the charge of thirty-six daemons, or ethereal gods of some sort, who divide it between them, that being the number of parts into which it is divided (though some say far more). Each daemon is in charge of a different part. And they know the names of the daemons in the local dialect, such as Chnoumen, Chnachoumen, Knat, Sikat, Biou, Erou, Erebiou, Rhamanoor, and Rheianoor, and all the other names which they use in their language. And by invoking these they heal the sufferings of the various parts.*[1] *What is there to prevent anyone from paying honour both to these and to the others if he wishes, so that we can be in good health rather than be ill, and have good rather than bad luck, and be delivered from tortures and punishments?*

By these remarks Celsus is trying to drag our souls down to the daemons, as though they had obtained charge over our bodies, and declares that each one has authority over a part of our body. He wishes us to believe the daemons he mentions and to worship them that we may be in good health rather than be ill, and have good rather than bad luck, and as far as possible be delivered from tortures. He has such a low opinion of paying an undivided and indivisible honour to the God of the universe that he does not believe[2] that the only God who is worshipped and splen-

---

[1] According to ancient astrology each of the twelve signs of the Zodiac is divided into three sections of ten degrees each. Each section is subordinate to a power called a *dekanos*. Accordingly the total number of these decans is thirty-six. Each is assigned a name; and lists of these names are preserved in several Egyptian documents and monuments. The literature on this subject is considerable. Reference may be made to W. Scott, *Hermetica*, III (1926), pp. 363 ff.; A. E. Housman, *M. Manilii Astronomicon* (1937), IV, pp. vi–x; A. Bouché-Leclerq, *L'Astrologie grecque* (1899), pp. 215–35; and above all, W. Gundel, *Dekane und Dekansternbilder* (1936). Gundel gives a summary in P.-W., Suppl. VII (1940), 118 ff. s.v. 'Dekane'.

For the names of the decans see Gundel's table, giving the lists in parallel columns (*Dekanst.* pp. 77 ff.). German translations of the texts concerning the decans are given by Gundel, pp. 327–425.

Their connexion with the various parts of the body is differently represented in different texts. In some texts, as here in Celsus, the decans are protecting gods who heal the diseased part. Cf. the Hermetic tractate on the decans (text edited by Ruelle in *Revue de Philologie*, XXXII (1908), pp. 250 ff.), where Hermes says to Asclepius: 'I have set down for you below both the outward forms and the inward natures of the 36 decans in the zodiac.... Carry this with you and you will have a mighty phylactery. For all the sufferings which are sent upon men as a result of the emanation from the stars are healed by them.' The tractate goes on to give particulars of each decan, naming that part of the body which each one heals. (For commentary, cf. Gundel, pp. 270 f., and Festugière, *La Révélation d'Hermès Trismégiste*, I (1950), pp. 139 ff.) But in other texts the decans are hostile gods who inflict diseases on particular parts of the body. Cf. Boll-Bezold, *Sternglaube und Stern-deutung* (4th ed. 1931), p. 135. For an example of this, cf. the *Testamentum Salomonis*, 18 (Gundel, pp. 383 f.).

[2] Read πιστεύειν with Bo., K. tr.

didly honoured is sufficient to grant the man who honours Him, in consequence of the actual worship he offers to Him, a power which prevents the attacks of daemons against the righteous person. For he has never seen how, when the formula 'in the name of Jesus' is pronounced by true believers, it has healed not a few people from diseases and demonic possession and other distresses.

59. It is probable that anyone who approves of Celsus' remarks will laugh when we say that 'in the name of Jesus every knee shall bow in heaven and on earth and beneath the earth, and every tongue be led to confess that Jesus Christ is Lord to the glory of God the Father'.[1] But although he may laugh he would get proofs that this is the case, which are clearer evidence[2] than the names of which he relates that, when they are invoked, they heal the sufferings of the bodily parts—Chnoumen, Chnachoumen, Knat, Sikat and the rest of the Egyptian list. Notice also how he discourages us from believing in the God of the universe through Jesus Christ, and invites us to believe, because they heal our bodies, in thirty-six barbarian daemons, whom only the Egyptian magicians invoke, in some unknown way declaring to us profound truths. According to Celsus we might practise magic and sorcery rather than Christianity, and believe in an unlimited number of daemons rather than in the self-evident, living, and manifest supreme God through him who with great power scattered the pure word of religion throughout all the world of mankind. And I would not be wrong if I went on to say that he also did this for the other rational beings which are in need of correction and healing and conversion from evil.

60. At any rate Celsus suspected that those who have learnt this sort of thing easily slip into magic, and somehow felt that harm might come to his hearers. For he says: *We must however be careful about this, lest by association with these beings anyone should become absorbed in the healing with which they are concerned, and by becoming a lover of the body and turning away from higher things should be held down without realizing it. For perhaps we ought not to disbelieve wise men who say that most of the earthly daemons are absorbed with created things, and are riveted to blood and burnt-offering and magical enchantments,[3] and are bound to other things of this sort, and can do nothing better than healing the body and predicting the coming fortune of men and cities, and that all their knowledge and power concerns merely mortal activities.*

---

[1] Phil. ii. 10–11.
[2] Read ἐναργεστέρας with M, Wi., We., Wif.; and, with Wif., λήψεται ⟨τοῦ⟩ ταῦθ' οὕτως.
[3] Cf. III, 28 and note.

Since then there is such danger in this matter, as even the enemy of God's truth testifies, how much better is it to avoid all suggestion of becoming absorbed in these daemons, of loving the body and turning away from higher things, and of being held down by forgetfulness of higher things; and rather to entrust oneself to the supreme God through Jesus Christ who gave us teaching to this effect? We ought to ask him for all the assistance and protection of the holy and righteous angels, that they may deliver us from the earthly daemons. For the latter are absorbed in created things, and are riveted to blood and burnt-offering, and are induced by outlandish magical enchantments, and are bound to other things of this sort. Even Celsus has to admit that they can do nothing better than healing the body. However, I would affirm that it is not clear that these daemons, in whatever way they are worshipped, are even capable of healing bodies. A man ought to use medical means to heal his body if he aims to live in the simple and ordinary way. If he wishes to live in a way superior to that of the multitude, he should do this by devotion to the supreme God and by praying to Him.

61. Consider for yourself what sort of person will be more acceptable to the supreme God who has power possessed by no one else to control all things and to do good to man, whether in the matter of the soul or the body or external things. Does He prefer a man who is in all respects devoted to Him, or a man who interests himself in the names of daemons, powers, practices, charms, plants related to daemons, stones, and the emblems on them which correspond to the traditional shapes of daemons, whether these are symbolical[1] or have some other significance? However, it is obvious to anyone who has even slight ability to understand the question that the person of simple and unaffected character, who because of his character is dedicated to the supreme God, will be acceptable to the supreme God and all those akin to Him. But the man who, for the sake of bodily health and love for his body and good luck in matters of moral indifference, concerns himself with names of daemons and seeks how he may charm the daemons with certain spells, will be abandoned by God to the daemons which he who pronounces such spells has chosen, as a wicked and impious fellow more daemonic than human, that he may be torn asunder by the thoughts put into his mind by each daemon or by other evils as well. For seeing that they are evil and, as Celsus admitted, riveted to blood and burnt-offering and magical enchantments and other things of this sort, they probably do not keep faith and, as it were, their

[1] Read συμβολικῶς with Wif. For the magical use of plants and stones, cf. e.g. Numenius in v, 38; Celsus in vi, 39; *Corp. Herm. Asclepius* 37–8 (Nock-Festugière, II, pp. 347 f.). Discussion in Festugière, *La Révélation d'Hermès Trismégiste*, I, pp. 123 ff.

pledges even with those who offer them these gratifications. If other
people were to invoke them and buy their service at the price of more
blood and sacrifices and the worship that they require, then they would
conspire against one who had worshipped them the previous day and who
used to give them a share of the feast which they love.

62. In his earlier remarks Celsus has said much to send us to oracles
and their prophecies as if they were gods.[1] But now he has improved
matters by admitting that the beings who foretell the coming fortune of
men and cities, and all the earthly daemons who are concerned with mortal
activities, are absorbed in created things, and are riveted to blood and
burnt-offering and magical enchantments, and are bound to other things
of this sort, having no capacity for anything higher than these. It is
probable that, when we oppose Celsus for regarding as divine the oracles
and the worship offered to the supposed gods, some one might suspect us
of being impious, because we maintain that these are the works of daemons
who drag the souls of men down to created things. Now, however,
anyone who harboured that suspicion about us may be convinced that
the declarations of Christians are right[2] when he sees that even a man who
was writing against the Christians wrote this, being at long last overcome
as it were by the spirit of truth.

Therefore, even though Celsus says that *we ought to pay formal
acknowledgement to them, in so far as this is expedient—for reason does not
require us to do this in all cases*, we ought not to pay any acknowledgement
to daemons who are absorbed in burnt-offerings and blood. We ought to
do all in our power to avoid defiling God by dragging Him down to
wicked daemons. If Celsus had possessed an accurate understanding of
the conception of expediency, and had seen that, strictly speaking, what
is expedient is virtue and action in accordance with virtue,[3] he would not
have applied the words *in so far as this is expedient* to daemons of such
a character as he himself had admitted them to be. For our part, if our
health and good luck in the affairs of this life are to come through
worshipping daemons of this sort, we would prefer to be ill and to have
bad luck in life and to know that our devotion to the God of the universe
is pure, rather than to be separated and fall away from God and, at the
last, to be ill and in adversity of soul because we have in this life enjoyed
health of body and better luck. And we ought to approach Him who is
in need of nothing whatever, except of the salvation of men and of every
rational being, rather than those who long for burnt-offering and blood.

---

[1] Cf. Celsus in VIII, 45, 48.   [2] Read with Bo., K. tr. ⟨ὡς⟩ καλῶς.
[3] Stoic teaching. Cf. *S.V.F.* III, 208, 310, etc. This is a dictionary definition (Klostermann in *Z.N.W.* XXXVII (1938), p. 60).

63. After all that Celsus has said about daemons needing burnt-offering and blood, he seems to come, I think, to making a wicked[1] recantation when he says: *We ought rather to think that the daemons do not long for anything and need nothing, but are pleased with people who perform acts of devotion to them.* If he thought this was true, either he ought not to have made his earlier statements or he should have deleted this. However, human nature has not been entirely abandoned by God and His only-begotten truth. That is why Celsus spoke the truth in his words about the burnt-offering and blood for which daemons long. But again by his characteristic wickedness he sank down to falsehood comparing the daemons to men who strictly perform what is right even if no one acknowledges their gratitude to them, while to people who do return thanks they do acts of kindness.

He seems to me to be confused on this subject. Sometimes his mind is distracted by the daemons, and sometimes, when he recovers his senses a little from the irrationality which the daemons produce, he gets a glimpse of the truth. For again he continues: *But we ought never to forsake God at all, neither by day nor by night, neither in public nor in private. In every word and deed, and in fact, both with them and without them,*[2] *let the soul be continually directed towards God.*[3] I understand his words *with them* to mean *in public* and *in every deed* and *in every word*.

Then again, as if wrestling in mind against the distractions caused by the daemons and being for the most part overcome, he goes on to say: *If this is the case, what is dreadful in propitiating the powers on earth, both the others*[4] *and the rulers and emperors among men, since not even they hold their position without the might of the daemons?*[5] Earlier he did all he could to bring our soul down to the level of daemons. But now he wants us to propitiate also the rulers and emperors among men. Of these life and history are full, and I have not thought it necessary to quote any examples now.

64. We ought, then, to propitiate the one supreme God and to pray that He may be gracious, propitiating Him by piety and every virtue. But if Celsus also wants us to propitiate others besides the supreme God, let him realize that, just as a moving body is followed by the movement of its shadow,[6] in the same way if the supreme God is propitiated it follows that all the angels who are dear to Him, and souls, and spirits, are kindly

[1] Read with We., K. tr. μοχθηράν.
[2] I.e. the daemons; but Origen chooses to take Celsus' words in another sense. Read with K. tr. ἀκούω ⟨οὕτω⟩.
[3] For the language, cf. I, 8; Clem. Al. *Strom.* IV, 9, 5.   [4] I.e. daemons.
[5] For the divine right of kings, cf. Celsus in VIII, 67–8.
[6] For this illustration, cf. Philo, *de Virtut.* 118, 181; Clem. Al. *Strom.* VII, 82, 7; Origen, *de Orat.* XVI, 2.

disposed as well. For they perceive who are worthy of God's kindness; and they not only become kindly disposed themselves to those who are worthy, but also work together with people who wish to worship the supreme God; and they are propitiated and pray and intercede together with them. Consequently we dare to say that for men who of set purpose put forward higher things when they pray to God, there are praying with them countless sacred powers who have not been invoked, assisting our mortal race.[1] And, if I may say so, they strive with us because of the daemons whom they see fighting and working against the salvation especially of those who dedicate themselves to God and pay no attention to the hostility of daemons, if they savagely attack the person who avoids worshipping them by burnt-offering and blood and who in every way by words and deeds earnestly attempts to draw close and be united to the supreme God through Jesus. For he overthrew countless daemons when he went about healing and converting those who were under the power of the devil.[2]

65. We ought to despise the kindly disposition of men and of emperors if to propitiate them means not only that we have to commit murders and acts of licentiousness and savagery, but also that we have to blaspheme the God of the universe or make some servile and cringing utterance, alien to men of bravery and nobility who, together with the other virtues, wish to possess courage as the greatest of them. Here we are doing nothing contrary to the law and word of God. We are not *mad*, nor do we *deliberately rush forward to arouse the wrath of an emperor or governor which brings upon us blows and tortures and even death.*[3] For we have read the precept: 'Let every soul be subject to the higher powers; for there is no power except by God's permission; the powers that be are ordained of God; so that those who resist the power resist the ordinance of God.'[4] In our commentary on the epistle to the Romans we have studied these words at length to the best of our ability, and given various interpretations. But now with a view to our present task we have followed the more usual interpretation, and taken them more simply, since Celsus says: *Not even they hold their position without the might of daemons.*

The doctrine concerning the institution of emperors and rulers is profound. Many questions are raised on this subject by the existence of

[1] Read συμπαρέχουσαι ⟨ἑαυτάς⟩ with K. tr. For the idea, cf. v, 57; VIII, 36; de Orat. XI, 5.   [2] Acts x. 38.
[3] Christians who deliberately courted martyrdom were denied the name of martyr: cf. Clem. Al. Strom. IV, 17, 1; Mart. Polyc. I, 4; also canon 60 of the Council of Elvira early in the fourth century. For the belief in the value of violent death, cf. Cumont, Lux perpetua, p. 339.
[4] Rom. xiii. 1–2; cf. Origen, Comm. in Rom. IX, 26 ff. (VII, 327 ff. Lomm.).

those who have ruled savagely and tyrannically,[1] or of those who have
drifted from exercising rule into debauchery and wantonness. On this
account we here omit any discussion of the problem. However, we
certainly do not *swear by the fortune (genius) of the emperor,*[2] in the same
way as we do not swear by any other supposed god. For if, as some have
said, fortune is only a mode of expression like an opinion or a disagreement,
we do not swear by something which does not exist as though it were
a god, or as if it were a certain reality and had the power to do something,[3]
lest we apply the force of an oath to the wrong things. Or if, as some
think who say that people who swear by the genius of the Roman emperor
are swearing by his daemon, the so-called genius of the emperor is
a daemon, in this case also we ought rather to die[4] than to swear by
a wicked and faithless daemon which often commits sin with the man to
whom it has been assigned, or sins even more than he does.

66. Then again, like those who sometimes recover from daemonic
possession and then once more have a relapse, as if he were sober Celsus
says something to this effect: *If you happen[5] to be a worshipper of God and
someone commands you either to act blasphemously or to say some other
disgraceful thing, you ought not to put any confidence in him at all. Rather
than this you must remain firm in face of all tortures and endure any death
rather than say or even think anything profane about God.* Then again
because he is ignorant of our doctrine and, in addition to this, because he
is muddled about all these things, he says: *But if anyone tells you to praise
Helios or with a noble paean to speak in enthusiastic praise of Athena, in so
doing you will appear much more to be worshipping the great God when you
are singing a hymn to them. For the worship of God becomes more perfect by
going through them all.*

Our answer is that we do not wait for anyone to tell us to praise Helios
since we have learnt to speak well not only of those which are subordinate
to God's ordering but even of our enemies.[6] We praise Helios (the sun) as
a noble creation of God, which keeps God's laws and hears the saying,
'Praise the Lord, sun and moon',[7] and with all its power praises[8] the
Father and Creator of the universe. But the traditions of the Greeks have
concocted a legend about Athena, whom he puts with Helios, and, whether
with or without some secret meaning, assert that she was born armed

---

[1] Cf. Origen in I, I, above.

[2] For swearing by the genius of the emperor as a mark of loyalty, cf. Epict. *Diss.* I, 14, 4;
IV, I, 14; *Mart. Polyc.* 9; *Passio sanctorum Scillitanorum* (ed. J. A. Robinson, *Texts and
Studies*, I, 2 (1891), p. 112); Tertullian, *Apol.* XXXII; XXXV, 10; Minucius Felix, *Octavius*, 29.

[3] Cf. Constantine, *Or. ad Sanctos*, VI, I.   [4] Read with K. tr. ἀποθανητέον.

[5] Read with K. tr. τύχοις (also λέγει for λέγων).   [6] Matt. v. 44.

[7] Ps. cxlvii. 3.   [8] Read perhaps with K. tr. ὑμνοῦν.

from the head of Zeus. And they say that she was chased at that time by Hephaestus who desired to ruin her virginity. She escaped from him, but loved and brought up the seed resulting from his lust which fell to the earth, and called the child Erichthonios whom, they say, Athena

The daughter of Zeus brought up, an offspring of the grain-giving earth.[1]

So we see that anyone who addresses worship to Athena, the daughter of Zeus, must accept many myths and fictitious stories which would not be accepted by anyone who avoids myths and seeks the truth.

67. But supposing that Athena is given an allegorical interpretation, and is said to be Intelligence,[2] let anyone show that she has a real and substantial existence and that her nature conforms to this allegorical meaning. But if Athena was some person who lived in ancient times and received honour because those who desired to have her name praised among men as if she were a goddess declared secret rites and mysteries to those who were in their power, how much rather ought we to avoid singing hymns of praise to Athena and glorifying her as a goddess if, in fact, it is not even right for us to worship the mighty sun, though we may speak well of it?

Celsus then says that we appear to worship the great God much more if we sing praise to Helios and Athena. We know that the reverse is the case. We address our hymns of praise to the supreme God alone and to His only-begotten Son, the divine Logos. And we sing praise to God and His only-begotten Son, as also do the sun, moon, and stars, and all the heavenly host.[3] For all these form a divine choir and with just men sing the praise of the supreme God and His only-begotten Son.

We observed earlier[4] that we ought not to swear by the emperor among men, nor by what is called his genius. It is therefore unnecessary for us to reply again to this: *Even if some one tells you to take an oath by an emperor among men, that also is nothing dreadful. For earthly things have been given to him, and whatever you receive in this life you receive from him.*[5] But in our

---

[1] Homer, *Il.* II, 547–8. For the myth, cf. J. G. Frazer's notes on Apollodorus, *Bibl.* I, 3, 6 (20); III, 14, 6 (188–9); A. B. Cook, *Zeus*, III (1940), pp. 656 ff., 218 ff.

[2] This is the usual Stoic interpretation; cf. Philodemus, *de Pietate*, 16 (Diels, *Dox. Gr.* 549); Porphyry, *Antr.* 32; *de Imag.* p. 14 Bidez; ap. Macrobius, *Sat.* I, 17, 70; Libanius, *Or.* XXIV, 37, etc. Also Plato, *Cratylus*, 407B. Discussion in A. B. Cook, op. cit. pp. 726 ff.

[3] Ps. cxlviii. 3; cf. V, 10, above.   [4] VIII, 65.

[5] For the divine right of kings and Roman imperial theology, cf. M. P. Charlesworth, 'Providentia and Aeternitas', in *H.T.R.* XXIX (1936), pp. 107–32; F. J. Dölger, 'Zur antiken und frühchristlichen Auffassung der Herrschergewalt von Gottes Gnaden', in *Antike und Christentum*, III (1932), pp. 117–31; N. H. Baynes, 'Eusebius and the Christian Empire', in *Mélanges Bidez* (1934), pp. 13–18; A. Alföldi, 'Insignien und Tracht der römischen Kaiser', in *Röm. Mitt.* L (1935), at pp. 68 ff. Full discussion in W. Ensslin, 'Gottkaiser und Kaiser von Gottes Gnaden', in *Sitzungsberichte der bayerischen Akademie der Wissenschaften*, phil.-hist. Abt. 1943, Heft 6.

judgment it is certainly not true that all earthly things have been given to him; nor do we receive from him whatever we receive in this life. Whatever we receive that is right and good we have from God and His providence, such as cultivated crops and bread 'that strengthens man's heart', and the pleasant vine and 'wine that gladdens the heart of man'. From the providence of God we also have the fruits of the olive 'to make the face shine with olive-oil'.[1]

68. Then Celsus next says that *we ought not to disbelieve the ancient man who long ago declared*

Let there be one king, him to whom the son of crafty Kronos gave the power.[2]

And he continues: *For, if you overthrow this doctrine, it is probable that the emperor will punish you. If everyone were to do the same as you, there would be nothing to prevent him from being abandoned, alone and deserted, while earthly things would come into the power of the most lawless and savage barbarians, and nothing more would be heard among men either of your worship or of the true wisdom.*

Let there be one ruler, one king,

I agree, yet not

Him to whom the son of crafty Kronos gave the power,

but the one whose power was given by Him who 'appoints and changes kings and from time to time raises up a useful man on the earth'.[3] Kings are not appointed by the son of Kronos who drove his father from his rule and, as the Greek myths say, cast him down to Tartarus,[4] not even if anyone were to interpret the story allegorically; but by God who governs all things and knows what He is doing in the matter of the appointment of kings.

Accordingly we do *overthrow the doctrine* of the words

To whom the son of crafty Kronos gave the power

because we are convinced that a God or the Father of a God would have no crafty or crooked designs. But we do not overthrow the doctrine of providence, and of the things which are produced by it, either as those which are primarily intended or as those which are the product of certain consequences.[5] Moreover, it is not *probable* that an emperor would punish us for asserting that the son of crafty Kronos did not give him the power to reign, but that it was He who 'changes and appoints kings'. Let *all*

---

[1] Ps. ciii. 15.

[2] Homer, *Il.* II, 205, a stock quotation in this context. See E. Peterson, *Monotheismus* (1935).

[3] Dan. ii. 21; Sirach x. 4. [4] Apollodorus, *Bibl.* I, 2, 1 (6–7).

[5] See VI, 53, above.

men do just the same as I. Let them deny the Homeric doctrine, while keeping the doctrine of the divine right of the king and observing the command 'Honour the king.'[1] Yet[2] on such a basis as this neither would the emperor be left alone, nor would he be deserted, nor would earthly things be in the power of the most lawless and savage barbarians. For if, as Celsus has it, every one were to do the same as I, obviously the barbarians would also be converted to the word of God and would be most law-abiding and mild. And all other worship would be done away and only that of the Christians would prevail. One day it will be the only one to prevail, since the word is continually gaining possession of more souls.

69. Then as Celsus did not understand himself, his remarks are inconsistent with his words *For if every one were to do the same as you,* when he says: *You will surely not say that if the Romans were convinced by you and were to neglect their customary honours to both gods and men and were to call upon your Most High, or whatever name you prefer, He would come down and fight on their side, and they would have no need for any other defence. In earlier times also the same God made these promises and some far greater than these, so you say, to those who pay regard to him. But see how much help he has been to both them*[3] *and you. Instead of being masters of the whole world, they have been left no land or home of any kind. While in your case, if anyone does still wander about in secret, yet he is sought out and condemned to death.*[4]

He raises the question of what would happen if the Romans were to become convinced by the doctrine of the Christians, and neglect the honours paid to the supposed gods and the old customs observed among men, and were to worship the *Most High*. Let him hear,[5] then, what our opinion is on these matters. We believe that if two of us agree on earth as touching any thing, if they pray for it, it shall be given to them by the heavenly Father of the righteous.[6] For God rejoices when the rational beings agree and turns away when they disagree. What must we think if it is not only, as now, just a few who agree but all the Roman Empire? For they will be praying to the Logos who *in earlier times* said to the Hebrews when they were being pursued by the Egyptians: 'The Lord will fight for you, and you shall keep silence.'[7] And if they pray with complete agreement they will be able to subdue many more pursuing enemies than those that were destroyed by the prayer of Moses when he cried to God and by the prayer of his companions. If God's promises to those who

---

[1] I Pet. ii. 17.   [2] Read καίτοι ὡς. (K. tr. proposes καὶ διὰ τοῦτο ὡς.)

[3] I.e. the Jews; cf. v, 41, 50. For God's promises, cf. Celsus in vi, 29; vii, 18.

[4] Cf. Celsus in ii, 45; viii, 39; Minucius Felix, *Octavius*, xii, 2; Clem. Al. *Strom.* iv, 78–80. Cicero, *pro Flacco*, 28, 69.

[5] Read with K. tr. ἀκουέτω.   [6] Matt. xviii. 19.

[7] Exod. xiv. 14.

keep the law have not come to pass, this is not because God tells lies, but because the promises are made on condition that the law is kept and that men live in accordance with it. If the Jews, who received the promises upon these conditions, have neither land nor home left, the reason for that is to be found in all their transgressions of the law and especially in their crime against Jesus.

70. However, if as Celsus suggests all the Romans were convinced and prayed, they would be superior to their enemies, or would not even fight wars at all, since they would be protected by divine power which is reported to have preserved five entire cities for the sake of fifty righteous men.[1] For the men of God are the salt of the world, preserving the permanence of things on earth, and earthly things hold together so long as the salt does not turn bad. For if the salt has lost its savour, it is of no further use either for the earth or for the dunghill, but is cast out and trodden under foot by men. Let him who has ears to hear, understand what this means.[2] We, moreover, are only persecuted when God allows the tempter and gives him authority to persecute us. And when it is not God's will that we should suffer this, even in the midst of the world that hates us by a miracle we live at peace, and are encouraged by him who said: 'Be of good cheer, I have overcome the world.'[3] And he really has overcome the world, so that the world prevails only in so far as he who overcame it wills, for he received from his Father the victory over the world. And by his victory we are encouraged.

If it is his will that we should again wrestle and strive for our religion, let antagonists come forward. To them we will say: 'I can do all things by Christ Jesus our Lord who strengthens me.'[4] For, though sparrows are sold, as the Bible has it, at two for a farthing, 'one does not fall into a snare against the will of the Father in heaven'. And to such an extent has divine providence included everything that not even the hairs of our head have escaped being numbered by Him.[5]

71. Then again, as usual with Celsus, he gets muddled, and in his next remarks says things which none of us has written. This is what he says: *It is quite intolerable of you to say that if those who now reign over us were persuaded by you and were taken prisoner, you would persuade those who reign after them, and then others, if they too are taken prisoner, and others after them until, when all who are persuaded by you are taken prisoner, there will be a ruler who, being a sensible man and foreseeing what is happening, will utterly destroy you all before you destroy him first.* Reason does not require us to speak about these remarks; for none of us says of those who now

[1] Gen. xviii. 24-6. [2] Matt. v. 13. [3] John xvi. 33.
[4] Phil. iv. 13. [5] Matt. x. 29-30.

reign that if they are persuaded and taken prisoner, we will then persuade their successors, and if they are taken prisoner we will in turn persuade those who follow them. And how did he come to remark that if the last in the succession are persuaded by us and are taken prisoner because they fail to defend themselves against their enemies, there will be a ruler who, being a sensible man and foreseeing what is happening, will utterly destroy us? In these words he seems to be putting together nonsensical statements and to have shrieked out stuff he invented out of his own head.

72. After this he utters a sort of wish: *Would that it were possible to unite under one law the inhabitants of Asia, Europe, and Libya, both Greeks and barbarians even at the furthest limits.* As if he thought this impossible he continues that *he who thinks this knows nothing.*[1] If I must say something about this subject which needs much study and argument, I will say a little in order to make it clear that his remark about uniting every rational being under one law is not only possible but even true. The Stoics say that when the element which, as they think, is stronger than the others becomes dominant, the conflagration will take place and all things change into fire.[2] But we believe that at some time the Logos will have overcome the entire rational nature, and will have remodelled every soul to his own perfection, when each individual simply by the exercise of his freedom will choose what the Logos wills and will be in that state which he has chosen. And we hold that just as it is unlikely that some of the consequences of physical diseases and wounds would be too hard for any medical art, so also it is unlikely in the case of souls that any of the consequences of evil would be incapable of being cured by the rational and supreme God. For since the Logos and the healing power within him are more powerful than any evils in the soul, he applies this power to each individual according to God's will, and the end of the treatment is the abolition of evil. But to teach whether or not the consequence is that it can under no

---

[1] This is a difficult sentence to interpret. Is it that Celsus makes a pious ejaculation, only to confess wistfully that the ideal is impossible of realization? So Keim, and Bader, comparing Celsus in I, 14. But Völker (*Das Bild*, pp. 29 f.) thinks that Celsus is bringing forward the Christians' idea that one law will dominate the world, only to deny roughly that it is a reasonable ideal at all. 'According to this interpretation the beginning of the section contains the secret desire of the Christians, the world-domination of their religion, and so would fit on to the preceding VIII, 71 where Celsus refutes another fantastic hope of his opponents.' For the ideal of a single polity Völker quotes only the Christian apologist Tatian (28). But the evidence brought together by W. W. Tarn, *Alexander the Great* (1948), II, pp. 399–449, suggests that the ideal had been familiar in the Hellenistic world (cf. especially Plutarch, *Mor.* 330 D, E; Tarn, II, p. 419) long before Christian times.

[2] Read with K. tr. ἐπικρατήσαντος, ὡς οἴονται, τοῦ. . .ἐκπύρωσίν (φασιν). For the idea, cf. my remarks in *J.T.S.* XLVIII (1947), at p. 48 n. 3. Now also, M. Pohlenz, *Die Stoa* (1948), I, p. 79; II, pp. 45 ff. (esp. for discussion of Dio Chrys. *Or.* XXXVI, 39 ff.).

circumstances be allowed any further existence, is not relevant to the present discussion.[1]

The prophecies say much in obscure terms about the total abolition of evils and the correction of every soul. But it is enough now to quote the passage from Zephaniah which reads as follows:

Get ready and wake up early; all their small grapes are destroyed. On this account wait patiently for me, saith the Lord, in the day when I rise up for a witness; for my decision is to assemble the peoples to receive the kings, to pour out upon them all the anger of my wrath. For in the fire of my zeal all the earth shall be consumed. Then I will turn to the peoples a language for its generation, that they may all call upon the name of the Lord and serve him under one yoke. From the furthest rivers of Ethiopia they shall offer sacrifices to me, in that day thou shalt not be ashamed of all thy habits which thou hast impiously practised against me. Then I will take away from thee the contempt of thy pride, and thou shalt no longer continue to boast upon my holy mountain. And I will leave in you a people meek and humble, and the remnants of Israel shall fear the name of the Lord, and they shall not do wickedness nor say foolish things, and a crafty tongue shall not be found in their mouth. Wherefore they themselves shall feed and lie down and there shall be none to make them afraid.[2]

Anyone who has the ability to enter into the meaning of the scripture[3] and has understood all these statements may show the explanation of the prophecy, and, in particular, may study what is the meaning of the words that when all the earth is consumed there will be turned to the people 'a language for its generation', which corresponds to the state of affairs before the Confusion.[4] And let him understand what is the meaning of the words 'That all men may call upon the name of the Lord, and may serve him under one yoke', so that 'the contempt of their pride' is taken away and there is no more wickedness nor foolish words nor crafty tongue.

I have thought it right to quote this passage, with an ordinary interpretation and without a careful discussion, because of the remark of Celsus who thinks that it is impossible for the inhabitants of Asia, Europe, and Libya, both Greeks and barbarians, to be agreed. And it is probably true that such a condition is impossible for those who are still in the body; but it is certainly not impossible after they have been delivered from it.

[1] For the eschatology, cf. IV, 69; VI, 20; VII, 29. For discussion, *J.T.S. loc. cit.*; Bigg, *The Christian Platonists* (1913 ed.), pp. 273–80.
[2] Zeph. iii. 7–13.
[3] Something has fallen out of the MS. text. The translation above follows the emendation of K. tr. which at least has the right sense: ὁ δυνάμενος δ' εἰσ⟨ελθεῖν εἰς τὸν τῆς γραφῆς νοῦν⟩ ταῦτα.
[4] Gen. xi. For the ideal of a single language, cf. Plutarch, *Mor.* 370B (quoted by Tarn, *op. cit.* II, p. 431).

73. Then Celsus next exhorts us to *help the emperor with all our power, and cooperate with him in what is right, and fight for him, and be fellow-soldiers if he presses for this, and fellow-generals with him.*[1] We may reply to this that at appropriate times we render to the emperors divine help, if I may so say, by taking up even the whole armour of God.[2] And this we do in obedience to the apostolic utterance which says: 'I exhort you, therefore, first to make prayers, supplications, intercessions, and thanksgivings for all men, for emperors, and all that are in authority.'[3] Indeed, the more pious a man is, the more effective he is in helping the emperors—more so than the soldiers who go out into the lines and kill all the enemy troops that they can.

We would also say this to those who are alien to our faith and ask us to fight for the community and to kill men: that it is also your opinion that the priests of certain images and wardens of the temples of the gods, as you think them to be, should keep their right hand undefiled for the sake of the sacrifices, that they may offer the customary sacrifices to those who you say are gods with hands unstained by blood and pure from murders. And in fact when war comes you do not enlist the priests.[4] If, then, this is reasonable, how much more reasonable is it that, while others fight, Christians also should be fighting as priests and worshippers of God, keeping their right hands pure and by their prayers to God striving for those who fight in a righteous cause and for the emperor who reigns righteously, in order that everything which is opposed and hostile to those who act rightly may be destroyed? Moreover, we who by our prayers destroy all daemons which stir up wars, violate oaths, and disturb the peace, are of more help to the emperors than those who seem to be doing the fighting. We who offer prayers with righteousness, together with ascetic practices and exercises which teach us to despise pleasures and not to be led by them, are cooperating in the tasks of the community. Even more do we fight on behalf of the emperor. And though we do not become fellow-soldiers with him, even if he presses for this, yet we are fighting for him and composing a special army of piety through our intercessions to God.

74. If Celsus wishes us to be generals for our country, let him realize that we do this; but we do not do so with a view to being seen by men and to being proud about it. Our prayers are made in secret in the mind itself, and are sent up as from priests on behalf of the people in our country. Christians do more good to their countries than the rest of mankind, since

[1] For discussion, see A. v. Harnack, *Militia Christi* (1905); C. J. Cadoux, *The Early Christian Attitude to War* (1919).   [2] Eph. vi. 11.
[3] I Tim. ii. 1-2.   [4] Cf. Plutarch, *Camillus* 41.

they educate the citizens and teach them to be devoted to God, the guardian of their city; and they take those who have lived good lives in the most insignificant cities up to a divine and heavenly city. To them it could be said: You were faithful in a very insignificant city;[1] come also to the great city where 'God stands in the congregation of the gods and judges between gods in the midst', and numbers you even with them, if you no longer 'die like a man' and do not 'fall like one of the princes'.[2]

75. Celsus exhorts us also to *accept public office in our country if it is necessary to do this for the sake of the preservation of the laws and of piety.* But we know of the existence in each city of another sort of country, created by the Logos of God. And we call upon those who are competent to take office, who are sound in doctrine and life, to rule over the churches.[3] We do not accept those who love power. But we put pressure on those who on account of their great humility are reluctant hastily to take upon themselves the common responsibility of the church of God. And those who rule us well are those who have had to be forced to take office, being constrained by the great King who, we are convinced, is the Son of God, the divine Logos. Even if it is power over God's country (I mean the Church) which is exercised by those who *hold office* well in the Church, we say that their rule is in accordance with God's prior authority, and they do not thereby *defile* the appointed *laws*.[4]

If Christians do avoid these responsibilities, it is not with the motive of shirking the public services of life. But they keep themselves for a more divine and necessary service in the church of God for the sake of the salvation of men. Here it is both necessary and right for them to be leaders and to be concerned about all men, both those who are within the Church, that they may live better every day, and those who appear to be outside it, that they may become familiar with the sacred words and acts of worship; and that, offering a true worship to God in this way and instructing as many as possible, they may become absorbed in the word of God and the divine law, and so be united to the supreme God through the Son of God, the Logos, Wisdom, Truth, and Righteousness, who unites to Him every one who has been persuaded to live according to God's will in all things.

76. You have here, holy Ambrose, the end of the task that you set me, according to the ability possessed by and granted to me. We have concluded in eight books·everything which we have thought fit to say in

---

[1] Cf. Luke xvi. 10; xix. 17.   [2] Ps. lxxxi. 1, 7.
[3] Cf. III, 30, above.
[4] Read λέγομεν ὅτι for λεγόμενοι ἥ, otherwise keep A's text intact. Tertullian (*Idol.* 17–18), rejecting appeals to Joseph and Daniel, forbids public office because of idolatrous pollution, punitive duties, and the incompatibility of power with humility.

reply to Celsus' book entitled *The True Doctrine*. It is for the reader of his treatise, and of our reply against him, to judge which of the two breathes more of the spirit of the true God and of the temper of devotion towards Him and of the truth attainable by men, that is, of sound doctrines which lead men to live the best life.

Observe, however, that Celsus promises to compose *another treatise*[1] after this, in which he has promised to *teach those who are willing and able to believe* him *the right way to live*. If he did not write the second book which he promised, we may well be content with the eight books written in reply to his argument. But if he began the second book and finished it, search out and send the treatise that we may make to that also the reply that is given to us by the Father of the truth, and may refute the false opinions in that as well. If in any place he makes some true statement, we shall bear witness that he is right in this respect without seeking occasion for disagreement.

[1] Cf. Introduction, p. xxvi.

APPENDED NOTE ON III, 7-8

The order in which Origen presents his arguments in these chapters is highly peculiar, according to the text of the Vatican MS., and I am indebted to my brother, the Reverend W. O. Chadwick, Fellow of Trinity Hall, for the suggestion that there may well have been some dislocation of the text. The section from 'However, a more profound study...' in chapter 7 (p. 132, last sentence) to the fourth sentence of chapter 8, '...which they also employed to give names to their sons', would more naturally follow on after chapter 6. The preceding section, from the beginning of chapter 7 to the words '...to defend themselves against their persecutors', would naturally follow this and in subject-matter links on to the fifth sentence of chapter 8, 'Concerning the Christians...'.

In the Vatican MS. the words in chapter 7 from ὁμοίως δὲ ψεῦδος to τοὺς διώκοντας (Koetschau's edition, p. 207, l. 30 to p. 208, l. 14) occupy eleven and a half lines. The words from καίτοι γε βαθύτερον to τοῖς υἱοῖς ἐτίθεντο (Koetschau, p. 208, l. 14 to p. 209, l. 3) occupy twelve lines. The number of words coincides sufficiently closely to invite the explanation that a leaf of the archetypal codex was accidentally reversed so that the recto was read as the verso, and the verso as the recto.

This conclusion is considerably fortified by consideration of the sentence beginning περὶ δὲ Χριστιανῶν (K. p. 209, l. 3). Its opening words seem to hang in the air, and in his translation Koetschau seeks to emend the sentence by inserting ⟨λεκτέον ὅτι⟩ after Χριστιανῶν. If this sentence really follows τοὺς διώκοντας (K. p. 208, l. 14) all is explained: περὶ δὲ Χριστιανῶν is an insertion made by a scribe who wished to make sense of the extraordinary order he found in his codex and to give a proper connecting link. After διώκοντας a comma should replace the full stop, so that the Greek sentence runs on still further in its lengthy course. The period ends at νομοθεσίαν (K. p. 209, l. 5). On this simple reconstruction no insertion is necessary.

If this hypothesis is correct, it tells us approximately the number of words to a page in the original archetype.

GENERAL INDEX

[References to the fragments of Celsus are indicated by an asterisk]

Abaris, 148*
Acarnanians, 151*
Achilles, 39
Adonai, 23f.*, 297*, 348–9
Aeacus, 62*
Aegina, cult of Hecate, 335
Aeneas, 39
Agape, 7*
Ailoeaeus, 348–9
Alexander of Pherae, 237
Alexander the Great, 303f.; cf. 96
Alexandria, 147
Allegory
    of Homer, 358*, 400
    of O.T., 21*, 27*, 68f., 197*, 213*, 225f.*,
        286f., 345*, 410f.
Aloadae, 198*
Ambrose, 3, 129, 184, 264, 316, 395, 510
Ammon, 290*, 396*
Amoun, 297*
Amphiaraus, 151*, 422*
Amphilochus, 151*
Amphion, 62*
Anaxagoras, 245, 272, 424
Anaxarchus, 439*
Angel(s), 153, 203f.*, 264ff., 305*, 449, 456,
        474f.
    archontic, 342*, 451*
    checked by circumcision, 302
    guardian, 56, 471, 477ff.
Antinous, 152f.*, 313*, 459
Antiope, 37*
Antiphon, 201
Antisthenes, 400
Ants, 248ff.*
Apelles, artist, 464
Apelles, heretic, 306
Aphrodite, planet, 334*
Apollo, 24
    compared with Jesus, 153*
    father of Plato, 36, 321
    mage of, 479*
    oracles, 64, 143f., 395f.*
    = sun, 223
Apollonius of Tyana, 356
Apostles, 56f.*, 101*
Arabians, 291*
Arcadians, autochthonous, 211*
Archilochus, 87, 143
Ares, 39
    planet, 334*
Aristander, 321
Aristeas, 130*, 144ff.*
Aristobulus, 226

Aristocreon of Cyprus, 441
Aristophanes, 424
Aristotelianism, 13, 79, 178, 181, 230, 396,
        449, 485
Aristotle, 16, 21, 60, 78, 136, 299
Artemis, 24, 223, 284
    cult at Comana, 336
Ascalaphus, 39
Ascalon, wells, 219
Asclepius, 130*, 140f.*, 157*, 265, 439*
Assyrians, 17*
Astaphaeus, 348–9
Athena, 24, 285, 502*
Athenians
    autochthonous, 211*
    hierophant, 436
Athens, 147
Attica, 285f.
Atonement, 39, 50f., 56, 80, 408
Auge, 37*
Augustus, 92
Axe, cult-symbol, 353

Babel, tower, 197f.*
Balaam, magus, 55
Barnabas, Epistle of, 58
Beans, 297*
Bees, 248*
Begging priests, 12*
Behemoth, 340
Bellerophon, 366*
    and Joseph, 222
Bishops, 134, 147f., 161, 510
Boreas's daughters, 359*
Brahmans, 23
Branchidae, 395

Cabeiri, 337*
Cainites, 136
Callimachus, 157
Cappadocians, 336
Carpocrates, 312f.*
Castalian cave, 396
Chaldeans, 55*, 393*
Christology
    of Celsus, 63–4*, 98f.*, 127*, 383*, 460*
    of Origen, 32f., 61, 64, 73f.*, 82f., 88, 99,
        115ff., 137, 144, 146, 156, 193f., 195,
        296, 302, 362, 364f., 382, 387, 390, 405,
        407f., 460, 482
Chrysippus, 38, 59, 78, 223, 235, 308, 489f.;
    see also Stoicism
Church
    and secular *ecclesia*, 147

INDEX OF CLASSICAL AUTHORS

INDEX OF BIBLICAL PASSAGES

OLD TESTAMENT

NEW TESTAMENT

Printed in the United States
77918LV00003B/52-60